TALKIN'
AMERICAN

A Dictionary of
Informal Words
and Expressions

Ronald M. Harmon
California State University, Fullerton

Signal Press

Library of Congress Cataloging-in-Publication Data

Harmon, Ronald M.
  Talkin' American : a dictionary of informal words and expressions
  / Ronald M. Harmon.
    p.   cm.
  ISBN 0-8384-5804-1
  1. English language—Terms and phrases. 2. English language—Textbooks
  for foreign speakers. 2. Figures of speech—Dictionaries. I. Title
  PE1689.H35 1995
  423'.1—dc20   93-42855
                                                                      CIP

Copyright © 1995

Manufactured in the United States of America

ISBN 0-8384-5804-1

10 9 8 7 6 5 4 3 2 1

In memory of Mel and Canela

Acknowledgements

My loving thanks to my wife, Dr. María R. Montaño-Harmon, for her support, encouragement, and many useful suggestions.

I thank Erik Olmsted for suggesting several entries, and the California State University, Fullerton Foundation for its support.

Special thanks go to the nine evaluators who rated the frequency of use of this dictionary's entries. Their efforts have provided a unique and most useful contribution to this work. They are, listed here with the states where they have had extended residence:

Robert J. Childs	(California)
Daniel Bragg Cook, Jr.	(Alabama, Colorado, California)
Darrel F. Crose	(Ohio, California)
Kathleen C. deVries	(New York, Connecticut)
Kathi A. Johnson	(Ohio, Arkansas, California)
Brian P. Kariger	(California)
Faye Folkins Miltenberger	(Arizona, California)
Lisa Morgan	(Michigan, Massachusetts, California)
Sharon Portman	(Texas, California)

Thanks also to the following reviewers for their helpful comments during the development of this manuscript:

Barbara Campbell, State University of New York at Buffalo
Suzanne Koons, Massachusetts Institute of Technology
Guillermo Perez, Miami-Dade Community College
Elizabeth Xiezopolski, Contra Costa Community College

Introduction

Talkin' American—A Dictionary of Informal Words and Expressions is a descriptive compilation of more than 6,200 terms and expressions commonly used in informal American English. It is both a reference and a learning tool. Its entries have definitions or explanations, example sentences, and frequency-of-use markers determined by a team of native speakers of American English.

The United States is the largest community of English speakers in the world, and the terms and expressions listed in this book are the common stock of language used in everyday circumstances in American society, including conversation in almost all situations (among friends, family members, even strangers), much writing (contemporary fiction, much nonfiction, plays, and letters) and the media (television, radio, and movies).

Talkin' American focuses on the informal language of the United States. While it is also largely relevant to Canadian English, the selection of its entries is based solely on U.S. usage. Its entries are not necessarily *exclusively* American. Many of them occur in informal English throughout the world, but their inclusion here affirms their use in the U.S.

This book was designed for users who were not born and raised in the United States, especially those whose first language is not English. But to benefit from it, the user should have at least a basic knowledge of English grammar and vocabulary.

Informal Language

Talkin' American has sought to include all common terms and expression that are generally used only in informal circumstances and avoided in formal speech or writing (in meetings, conferences, reports, etc.). Of course, many terms are informal when they have special *meanings* in informal circumstances, while they are not informal when they have their basic meanings. For example, *buy* is informal when it means "believe" or "accept" but in not informal when it means "purchase." While much language is neutral in style (i.e., it may be used, with the same meaning, in formal or informal circumstances), this dictionary includes only those items with meanings generally limited to informal situations.

Common Usage

Talkin' American includes only terms and expressions that have widespread use in the United States, that is, items that a majority of Americans know and understand. Thus, it does not include strict regionalisms, ethnic speech, jargon, or slang that is restricted to special groups of speakers. It does include items coming from such groups if they are widely understood throughout the country and among the general population. The team of frequency-of-use evaluators has determined that all entries meet this criterion.

Format

This element indicates the frequency of use of the entry: two asterisks mean frequently heard or read, one asterisk means regularly heard or read, and a dash (—) means occasionally heard or read.

Each entry is listed under a key word in bold type and capital letters. Cross-references may lead the user to the entry (this one is cross-referenced under SHIRT).

A usage indicator shows the level of informality or the situation that the entry is appropriate for.

LOSE
* **lose [one's] shirt** (colloq.): suffer a big financial loss, lose all that [one] has >*He lost his shirt on that deal and had to declare bankruptcy.*

Definitions/explanations give the entry's meaning or shades of meaning to convey the scope and tone of the entry's use. They also indicate grammatical function.

The entry is listed in bold type. It may include grammatical indicators such as "[one's]" or "[s/one]," where specific pronouns or nouns appear in actual use.

A "(vt)" indicates a transitive verb or verb phrase (one taking a direct object). A "(vi)" indicates an intransitive verb or verb phrase (one not taking a direct object).

PICK
** **pick up**[1] (vt) (colloq.): learn informally or through experience >*Patty picked up quite a bit of Spanish when she lived in Mexico.*

Two or more entries having the same form but different meanings have superscripts to distinguish them (there are five different "pick up" entries).

An example sentence, in italics and preceded by an arrow, uses the entry in a typical and natural context to help point up its meaning and grammatical usage.

The key word may be a compound written as separate words (BIG DEAL), as one (RUBBERNECK), or hyphenated (KNOCK-DOWN-DRAG-OUT).

BIG DEAL
** **(it's) no big deal** (colloq.): it's not so important, it's not worth being concerned about, it's no problem >*It's no big deal if you get there a little late.*

A pronunciation transcription is given, in parentheses, for entry words not occurring outside informal situations and for word spellings with more than one pronunciation (e.g., lead: lēd and led).

Optional parts of an entry are included in parentheses.

A second example sentence shows the entry used with its additional grammatical function or with a different shade of meaning.

BUMMER
** **bummer** (bum´ər) (sl.): disappointment, upsetting or unpleasant thing or occurrence (also interj.) >*This party's a bummer—let's split.* >*Bummer, man! My surfboard's cracked.*

An additional grammatical function besides that given in the definitions/explanations is shown following them in parentheses.

iii

Additional Format Notes

Frequency-of-use indicators:

Entries with two asterisks (those rated as frequently heard or read) constitute 12% of the total number of entries, those with one asterisk (rated as regularly heard or read) make up 42%, and those with a dash (rated as occasionally heard or read) represent 46%.

Entries:

When more than one entry is listed under a key word, entries that are just that key word are listed first, and nouns come before verbs. After that, multi-word entries are listed alphabetically by their first word, taking into account words in parentheses (optional parts of an expression), but not words in brackets (grammatical indicators).

Some entries contain variants, indicated by a slash that separates them. For example, **"like a million dollars/bucks"** may be used in the form **"like a million dollars"** or in the form **"like a million bucks."**

Entries made of letters pronounced separately are listed as capital letters with periods after them (for example, **"P.C.P."**). This spelling is generally used throughout, although such terms may be seen written elsewhere without periods or, at times, with lowercase letters.

Usage indicators:

The three main usage indicators are *colloq.* (for "colloquial"), *sl.* (for "slang"), and *vulg.* (for "vulgar"):

- **Colloquial** terms and expressions are those that can be used in any informal setting. They are not characteristic of specific groups in society and are widely accepted and used in everyday language. They do not have the "youth-oriented" and "in-group" dimensions that slang items do, they are not taboo in polite social settings as vulgar items are, and they are less informal than items in these other two categories.

- **Slang** terms and expressions are very informal. They tend to be more contemporary, playful, inventive, and youth-oriented than colloquial items and generally serve to enhance group identity.

- **Vulgar** terms and expressions are considered coarse or obscene and are offensive to many people. They are inappropriate in polite society and may even be censured in some social circumstances.

Other usage indicators, which may be added to the three above, are *pej.* (for "pejorative"), *hum.* (for "humorous") and *sarc.* (for "sarcastic"):

- **Pejorative** terms or expressions degrade or belittle a person or group on the basis of gender; race; age; occupation; sexual orientation; physical traits; or national, religious, ethnic, or regional background. They are offensive to most people, and there may be social and even legal sanctions against their use in some situations (for example, in the workplace).

- **Humorous** terms or expressions are generally used in a funny or playful way.
- **Sarcastic** terms or expressions are generally used in an ironic or mocking way.

Definitions/explanations:

Parts in parentheses are more explanatory than definitional and include such phrases as "(used esp. [especially] ...)," "(freq. [frequently] used ...)," and "(intens. [intensifier] to ...)."

Example sentences:

The tone of the example sentences reflects the circumstances of usage indicated for the entry item. Shortened *-ing* forms (for example, *givin'* instead of *giving*) and combined forms (for example, *gonna* instead of *going to*) are used in sentences for slang and vulgar entries to reflect extra informality. Also, nonstandard forms (for example, *Him and me* for *He and I*, *them* for *those*, and double negatives) appear occasionally in example sentences to reflect the informality of the content.

Suggestions for the User

Finding an entry:

The exact boundaries or listed form of an expression that one hears or reads may not be easily determined. So if the expression is not readily found where expected, you should check all entries under the key word, since an optional part of a variant may have it listed in another place. If it is still not found, you should check entries under other possible key words, including compound words (e.g., the expression **"it's no big deal"** is found under **"BIG DEAL,"** not under **"BIG"** or **"DEAL"**). Not all that you hear or read and do not understand is necessarily informal; consulting a conventional dictionary may be in order.

You should note that many compound words do not have a standardized spelling in English. Compounds may be seen written as one word, separate words or hyphenated words. Also, the spelling of informal words is not always standard (for example, words ending in -y, -ey, or -ie). Although *Talkin' American* includes many cross-references with alternate spellings, you should apply some flexibility regarding spelling.

Common derivatives of entries are not generally listed (for example, the -ing gerund or the -er marker for agent [or doer] of verbs); the user should keep derivatives in mind when comparing forms heard or read with entries in this dictionary.

Using the frequency-of-use markers:

The frequency-of-use markers are especially valuable as guides for making this book a learning tool and not just a reference. You may first select items marked for highest frequency of use to learn and incorporate into your active vocabulary, either systematically or as they are encountered and looked up. Later, items marked for lower frequency can be learned.

Using caution with vulgar and pejorative items:

Language is a powerful tool and must be used with caution. Since vulgar and pejorative terms do exist in American English and are widely used in restricted circumstances, it is important that this work list and describe them; you need to have a means with which to recognize them and their meanings. But it is equally important that you realize that using them in inappropriate circumstances may have very negative consequences. Some people are offended by vulgar terms and expressions in any circumstances, and most people use them with moderation. Similarly, most people avoid using pejorative terms and expressions. Inappropriate use of such items may not only offend others and reflect poorly on you, but may also make you subject to social and even legal sanctions.

Suggestions for Teachers

Talkin' American is a useful reference for all adult ESL learners of American English at an intermediate or higher level. As a descriptive work, it documents all the types of informal language that learners will continually hear and read in real, everyday circumstances. For this reason it includes terms that may be offensive because they are vulgar or pejorative. Because of the inclusion of such items, this book may not be appropriate for secondary or younger students, but it will make information on all types of language encountered in American English more accessible to adult learners.

Talkin' American is recommended as a supplemental text in conversation and vocabulary-building classes. You can either treat all terms and expressions in designated categories (e.g., all colloquial entries with two asterisks) or glean specific items for treatment based on some other criterion (e.g., entries derived from sports terminology or verbs with prepositional particles). It is recommended that vulgar and pejorative items not be targeted for active vocabulary acquisition, although they may be studied for recognition.

This work and its usage indicators can be used to tech important basic sociolinguistic principles regarding language register and style, such as the use of nonstandard forms and taboo language and the importance of language appropriateness by situation. Regarding items labeled vulgar and pejorative, you should emphasize 1) the need to recognize them and their meanings, 2) the restricted circumstances in which they are generally used, and 3) the possible negative consequences of using them.

The definitions/explanations can be used for practice and testing of entries, and example sentences can serve as models for students to generate their own sentences using entry items and for creating broader contexts in which the example sentences might occur.

For students who speak nonstandard dialects of English, *Talkin' American* may be used in "reverse" fashion, where students learn more formal ways of expressing informal words and expressions that they already know by studying entry definitions, in the manner of a thesaurus. In this way, it could be a useful tool for vocabulary expansion from a casual register to a more formal standard usage.

Finally, *Talkin' American* serves as a basic instructor resource for exploring informal language use and for the creation of dialogues, specific vocabulary lists and other pedagogical materials.

Pronunciation Key

Symbol:	As in:	Symbol:	As in:
a	apple, hat	n	new, dinner
ā	say, page	ng	thing, singer
â	hair, bare	o	pot, bottle
ä	father, start	ō	open, low
b	book, ribbon	ô	organ, law
ch	chair, reach	oi	point, boy
d	dog, paddle	ou	down, out
ð	that, brother	p	put, rapid
e	bed, second	r	red, marry
ē	tea, party	s	sell, muscle
ə	along, butter	sh	shell, motion
ᵊ	ti()re, sou()r	t	take, better
f	food, tough	th	think, author
g	get, bigger	u	under, bus
h	here, behave	ŭ	look, put
hw	why, everywhere	ū	food, who
i	sit, public	û	urban, turn
ī	light, reply	v	value, movie
j	job, magic	w	way, aware
k	kind, bacon	y	yet, million
l	lot, pillow	z	zip, easy
m	man, hammer		

A

ABS
— **abs** (abz) (colloq.): abdominal muscles >*He's working on his abs to try and get rid of his potbelly.*

ACAPULCO GOLD
— **Acapulco gold** (aˈkə pŭlˈkō/äˈkə pŭlˈkō …) (sl.): high-grade marijuana (cultivated in Mexico) >*He got arrested with a kilo of Acapulco gold.*

ACCIDENT
** **have an accident** (colloq.): urinate or defecate in (one's) clothes, urinate or defecate in an inappropriate place (said esp. of children and pets) >*Uh, oh! The dog had an accident on the rug.*

ACCIDENTALLY-ON-PURPOSE
— **accidentally-on-purpose** (colloq.): maliciously (although apparently unintentionally) >*He said "excuse me," but I think he stepped on my foot accidentally-on-purpose.*

ACCORDING
— **according to Hoyle** (… hoil) (colloq.): following the rules or proper procedures, fairly >*I don't think they made that campaign contribution according to Hoyle.*

A.C./D.C.
— **A.C./D.C.** (sl.): bisexual >*They say he's gay, but actually he's A.C./D.C.*

ACE
* **ace**[1] (colloq.): expert, very talented or able person (in some activity) (also adj.) >*He's an ace at ballroom dancing.* >*Captain Riggins is an ace pilot.*

** **ace**[2] (vt) (sl.): receive a grade of "A" on (a test), complete (a competition) perfectly >*She's so smart that she aces all her exams.* >*He aced the drivin' course.*

— **ace [s/one] out (of [s/thing])** (sl.): better [s/one] (to achieve [s/thing]), trick or outmaneuver [s/one] (to gain [s/thing]) >*Kelly aced him out of the job by flatterin' the manager's wife. >We were both after her, but he aced me out.*

* **ace/card up [one's] sleeve** (colloq.): important hidden resource or advantage ready to use when needed >*Martin's got an ace up his sleeve. His father-in-law owns the land they want to build on. >She doesn't seem worried. She must have a card up her sleeve.*

ACE IN THE HOLE
* **ace in the hole** (colloq.): important hidden resource or advantage ready to use when needed >*My ace in the hole is that the supervisor is a friend of mine.*

ACID
* **acid** (sl.): L.S.D. (lysergic acid diethylamide, a hallucinogenic drug) >*He started out smokin' marijuana, but he's been droppin' acid lately.*

ACIDHEAD
* **acidhead** (sl.): habitual user of the drug L.S.D. >*That guy used to be an acidhead, and I think he fried his brain.*

ACROSS
— **come across** (see **COME**)
— **come across (as)** (see **COME**)
* **get/put [s/thing] across** (colloq.): explain [s/thing] successfully, make [s/thing] understood >*He just couldn't get his plan across to the boss. >You've got to put it across to them that they can't do it.*

ACT
** **act up**[1] (vi) (colloq.): behave badly, be mischievous >*If that kid starts acting up I'll throw him out.*

** **act up**[2] (vi) (colloq.): start functioning poorly, begin causing problems for proper function >*The TV's acting up again. Look how blurry the picture is. >That damn shoulder! My arthritis has been acting up lately.*

— **clean up [one's] act** (see **CLEAN**)
** **get/have [one's] act together** (colloq.): put/have [one's] affairs in order, get/

have control over how [one] lives (his/
her) life, get/have things functioning
well: >*If the staff doesn't get its act
together soon, we're going to have to
close down the office. >He used to be a
mess, but he has his act together now.*

** **get in on/into the act** (colloq.):
participate also, get included in what is
going on >*All Jeff's friends were taking
up golf, so he decided to get in on the
act, too.*

ACTION

** **action** (sl.): exciting activity (esp. a
vice) >*The sailors wanted some action,
so they went to the casino. >The sailors
wanted some action, so they went to the
red light district.*

— **piece of the action** (see PIECE)

— **where the action is** (see WHERE)

ADAM

— **not know [s/one] from Adam** (see
KNOW)

ADD

** **add up** (vi) (colloq.): make sense, seem
reasonable, be consistent (said of
stories, explanations, actions, etc.) (freq.
used in the neg.) >*It just doesn't add up
that he'd leave his wife like that.*

— **add up to** (colloq.): signify, be
equivalent to, indicate >*It adds up to
murder if they keep buying him booze.*

AD-LIB

** **ad-lib** (ad´lib´) (vi, vt) (colloq.): say or
perform (s/thing) without special
preparation, improvise >*You'd better
plan what you're going to say, because
if you ad-lib you're liable to mess it up.
>If they ask me to speak, I'll just ad-lib
it.*

ADORABLE

** **adorable** (colloq.): charming, cute, very
likable >*Her baby is adorable.*

ADORE

* **adore** (vt) (colloq.): like very much,
love >*I adore your new furniture!*

AFTER

** **after [s/one]** (colloq.): pressuring [s/
one], constantly requesting of [s/one]
>*They've been after him for his opinion,
but he's keeping quiet. >My wife was
after me to fix that broken window.*

** **get after** (colloq.): scold or reprimand
>*Dad's going to get after you if you
don't clean this up.*

AGAIN

— **you can say that again!** (see SAY)

AGES

** **ages** (colloq.): a long time >*It's been
ages since I've seen Debbie. >Oh, he
moved there ages ago!*

AGGRAVATE

** **aggravate** (vt) (colloq.): annoy, bother,
irritate >*My children insist on
aggravating me.*

AGGRAVATION

** **aggravation** (colloq.): annoyance,
irritation, bother >*Don't get him
started. Who needs the aggravation?*

AH

— **ooh and ah** (see OOH)

AHEAD

** **ahead of the game** (colloq.): having an
advantage, winning >*He tries to stay
ahead of the game by keeping up with
the new software.*

AHOLD

** **get ahold of**[1] (… ə hōld´ …) (colloq.):
make contact with, communicate with
(esp. by telephone) >*I'll see if I can get
ahold of him at the office.*

* **get ahold of**[2] (colloq.): obtain >*It'll be
hard to get ahold of the right part for
this old car.*

AIN'T

* **ain't** (ānt) (colloq.): am not, is not, are
not, have not, has not >*I'm right about
this, ain't I? >You ain't seen nothin'
yet!*

AIR

** **up in the air** (colloq.): undecided, not certain or settled >*I'm up in the air about how to handle this.* >*Our plans are up in the air until we know when Phil can get time off.*

AIRHEAD

** **airhead** (sl.): stupid or silly person, flighty person >*You're not gonna put an airhead like her in charge, are ya?*

A.K.A.

* **A.K.A.** (colloq.): also known as, alias >*The cops are looking for a Winston Legret, A.K.A. "The Spider."*

ALIVE

* **alive and kicking** (colloq.): well, in good health >*My grandma's alive and kicking at ninety-two.*

— **look alive!** (see LOOK)

— **not (even) know [s/one] is alive** (see KNOW)

— **skin [s/one] alive** (see SKIN)

ALL

* **all kinds (of ...)** (colloq.): much (...), many (...) >*Let Baxter pay. He's got all kinds of money.* >*No more ice cream for me—I still got all kinds left.*

* **all [s/one] needs** (colloq., sarc.): exactly what [s/one] does not need, what is very detrimental or inconvenient for [s/one] >*All I need is for your mother to come for a visit right now!* >*Cream pie? That's all he needs when he's on his diet!*

* **all over [s/one]** (sl.): making sustained physical contact with [s/one], touching or hitting [s/one] aggressively >*As soon as he got her alone in the car, he was all over her.* >*The guy was all over me before I even got through insultin' him.*

* **all sorts (of ...)** (colloq.): much (...), many (...) >*Let's go skiing. They say there's all sorts of snow in the mountains.* >*Not another necktie! I already got all sorts in my closet.*

— **as/like all get-out** (see GET-OUT)

— **be all ears** (see EARS)

— **be all over but the shouting** (colloq.): be virtually finished or won, have an imminent and obvious outcome >*They're leading eight to one with a minute to go—it's all over but the shouting.*

** **be all set** (colloq.): be ready, be prepared >*We're all set, so start any time you like.*

** **[neg.] be all there** (colloq.): be mentally unbalanced, be somewhat crazy, be feebleminded >*That guy's acting real weird. I'd say he's not all there.*

— **be all thumbs** (see THUMBS)

— **be all wet** (see WET)

— **for all [one] is worth** (colloq.): to the greatest degree that [one] can, (doing) [one's] best >*Jules tried for all he was worth, but only came in fifth.*

** **go all out (to)** (colloq.): proceed with complete determination or all resources (to) (do s/thing) >*They went all out to see that we were comfortable.* >*Jimmy's going all out because he really wants to win this game.*

* **go all the way** (sl.): have sexual intercourse (not just kiss and caress) >*They've been datin' for a while, but I don't think they've gone all the way yet.*

— **have it all over** (see HAVE)

— **let it all hang out** (see HANG)

— **not have all day** (see HAVE)

* **that's all she wrote!** (sl.): it's finished! it's all gone! >*It was his last chance. If he blew it, that's all she wrote!* >*That's all she wrote! We just ran outta paint.*

ALLEY

* **(right) up/down [s/one's] alley** (colloq.): (very) pertinent to [one's] interests or abilities >*He was glad they asked him about sports on the quiz show because it was right up his alley.* >*Give it to Will. That's down his alley.*

ALL-FIRED

— **all-fired** (colloq.): extreme, excessive (said esp. of emotions) (also adv.) >*His all-fired enthusiasm won't help if he doesn't have the know-how.* >*You don't have to be so all-fired smug about it.*

ALL-NIGHTER

* **all-nighter** (ôl´nī´tər) (colloq.): activity that lasts all night >*My bachelor party was an all-nighter.*

* **pull an all-nighter** (sl.): remain awake all night (in order to complete a task) >*I had to pull an all-nighter last night to get this presentation ready.*

ALL-OUT

** **all-out** (colloq.): using all resources, with complete determination, total >*We got to make an all-out effort to win this one.*

ALL RIGHT

** **all right!** (colloq.): hurrah! wonderful! >*All right! We're ahead by ten points!*

* **all right already!** (colloq.): that's enough! don't keep going on about it! >*All right already! Shut up for a while, will you?*

— **all right for [s/one]!** (colloq.): I'm finished with [s/one]! I will no longer deal favorably with [s/one]! (due to perceived unfairness or mistreatment on his/her part) >*All right for you, if you want to be that way! Just don't expect me to help you.*

** **be all right** (colloq.): be likable, be good, be reliable >*I like your friends. They're all right.* >*Hey, this party's all right.*

ALL-RIGHT

* **all-right** (colloq.): likable, good, reliable >*I guess it's an all-right school, but it ain't Harvard.* >*His brothers are all-right guys.*

ALL RIGHTY

— **all righty** (… rī´tē) (interj.) (colloq.): all right, yes, very well >*All righty, I'll take care of that right away.*

ALONG

— **along about** (colloq.): approximately (a point in time) >*Along about then, the phone rang.*

** **far along** (colloq.): advanced, having made considerable progress >*Terry's pretty far along in his studies now.* >*How far along are you on your building project?*

— **get along** (colloq.): leave, move on >*My, it's late! I'd better be getting along.*

* **(just) along for the ride** (colloq.): present without participating, having joined in without contributing >*We don't want anybody in this organization who's just along for the ride—everyone's got to help out.*

* **will be along** (colloq.): will arrive, will appear >*Jon said he'd be along about six.*

ALONGSIDE

— **alongside (of)** (colloq.): when compared to, in comparison with >*He's a good player, but alongside the pros he's nothing.*

ALREADY

* **… already!** (colloq.): … without further delay! (used to express impatience or frustration) >*So get to the point already!*

AMBULANCE CHASER

— **ambulance chaser** (colloq.): unscrupulous lawyer (esp. one who urges victims to file suits) >*Some ambulance chaser talked her into letting him take the driver to court.*

AMMO

* **ammo** (am´ō) (colloq.): ammunition >*They surrendered when they ran out of ammo.* >*His opponent used the scandal as ammo against him during the campaign.*

AND

— **and …** (see entry under … word)

4

ANDS
— **no ifs, ands, or buts (about it)** (see
  IFS)

ANGEL DUST
* **angel dust** (sl.): phencyclidine
  (hallucinogenic drug) >*The dude was
  high on angel dust, and it took six cops
  to hold him down.*

ANGLE
* **angle** (sl.): personal or secret motive,
  sly strategy to gain advantage >*What's
  his angle in this business? >I got an
  angle on how to get a few bucks from
  these tourists.*

ANIMAL
* **animal** (colloq.): thing (used esp. when
  questioning or denying its existence)
  >*A seven-piston engine? I don't think
  there is any such animal.*

ANNIHILATE
* **annihilate** (vt) (sl.): defeat decisively
  >*The Rockets got annihilated in last
  night's game.*

ANOTHER
** **have another thing/think coming**
  (colloq.): will experience s/thing other
  (and neg.) than what (one) expects >*If
  he thinks I'm just going to give up and
  not fight back, he's got another thing
  coming.*

ANTE
— **ante** (colloq.): cost of participation,
  share of expenses >*That's a pretty high
  ante for a two-day fishing trip.*

— **ante up** (vi, vt): pay (for the cost of
  participation or one's share of expenses)
  >*OK, everyone ante up so we can rent
  the boat. >I anted up my ten bucks, so I
  get to go, too.*

ANTS
* **have ants in [one's] pants** (sl.): be
  overly eager, be impatient (to begin s/
  thing) >*He's got ants in his pants to get
  to the slopes and start skiin'.*

ANTSY
* **antsy** (ant´sē) (colloq.): nervous,
  fidgety, impatient >*I'm getting antsy
  about the job interview. >We're antsy to
  get started.*

A-NUMBER-ONE
— **A-number-one** (colloq.): excellent,
  first-rate >*He's an A-number-one guy
  for this kind of job.*

ANY
* **any old** (freq. ... ōl) (colloq.): any
  (without regard to quality or type)
  >*Any old pan will do to heat this up.
  >Ask me any old question you want.
  >Do it any old way you can.*

— **give [s/one] [s/thing] any day** (see
  GIVE)

ANYTHING
— **(as) ... as anything** (colloq.): very ...,
  extremely ... >*He was as mean as
  anything to his kids when they were
  little.*

— **like anything** (colloq.): to the utmost
  degree, intensely, wholeheartedly >*We
  tried like anything to get him to see it
  our way, but he wouldn't. >It was
  raining like anything when we left.*

A-O.K.
* **A-O.K.** (colloq.): very good, excellent
  (also adv.) >*This room we rented is A-
  O.K. >I feel A-O.K. now.*

A-ONE
* **A-one** (colloq.): excellent, first-rate
  >*They do A-one work at that garage.*

APART
* **come apart at the seams** (colloq.):
  become overwrought, lose emotional
  control >*He was under so much stress
  that he just came apart at the seams.*

* **coming apart at the seams** (colloq.): in
  a ruinous state, deteriorating badly >*We
  got to move. This apartment's coming
  apart at the seams.*

— **fall apart** (see **FALL**)

* **rip/take/tear apart** (vt) (sl.): criticize severely >*The critics ripped him apart in that film.* >*The poor slob's old lady really tore him apart in front of everyone.*

— **take/tear apart** (vt) (sl.): beat up, thrash >*You try messin' with my kids, and I'll take you apart.*

APE

* **ape** (colloq.): big and clumsy person, coarse person >*She came in with some ape who started busting up the place.*

* **go ape (over)**[1] (sl.): become very enthusiastic (about), show favorable excitement (toward) >*Her fans went ape over her new hit.*

— **go ape (over)**[2] (sl.): lose emotional control (because of), become very excited or furious (about) >*When he got the bill for all their new clothes, he went ape.*

APE SHIT

— **go ape shit (over)**[1] (... āp´shit ...) (vulg.): lose emotional control (because of), become very excited or furious (about) >*They went ape shit over the jukebox breakin' down and started trashin' the place.*

— **go ape shit (over)**[2] (vulg.): become very enthusiastic (about), show favorable excitement (toward) >*When the girls see these new shoes, they're gonna go absolutely ape shit.*

APPLE-POLISH

— **apple-polish** (vi) (colloq.): be servile or obsequious to gain favor, engage in flattery >*He apple-polished his way to the top.* >*I can't stand his apple-polishing around the boss.*

APPLE-POLISHER

— **apple-polisher** (colloq.): person who is servile or obsequious to gain favor, servile flatterer >*He's always got a bunch of yes-men and apple-polishers around him.*

APPLES

— **how do you like *them* apples?** (see **THEM**)

APRON STRINGS

— **tied to [s/one's] apron strings** (see **TIED**)

ARE

— **there you go/are** (see **THERE**)

ARM

** **an arm and a leg** (colloq.): a large amount of money (seen as a sacrifice to pay) >*This place cost me an arm and a leg, but it's worth it.*

— **shot in the arm** (see **SHOT**)

— **twist [s/one's] arm** (see **TWIST**)

— **would give [one's] right arm** (see **GIVE**)

ARMPIT

— **the armpit of** (sl.): the worst place in, the most unpleasant part of >*This lousy town's the armpit of the state.*

AROUND

** **around** (colloq.): near, close to (also adv.) >*We ran out of gas around Fifth Street.* >*I'll be around if you need me.*

** **get around** (vi) (colloq.): become known (said of information) >*When it gets around that he's an ex-convict, he'll have a hard time getting a job.*

** **get around [s/thing]** (colloq.): evade or circumvent (an obstacle) >*He says he knows how to get around that tax law.*

** **get around to** (colloq.): eventually deal with, find the time to take care of >*She finally got around to explaining why she'd come.* >*I'd like to wash the car today, but I don't know if I'll get around to it.*

** **have been around** (colloq.): be experienced in worldly matters, not be naive or innocent >*You won't fool him with that—he's been around.*

* **have been around the block (a few times)** (sl.): be (very) experienced in worldly matters, not be (at all) naive or

innocent >*That woman he goes out with has been around the block a few times.*

ARTILLERY
— artillery (colloq.): small firearms >*You should have seen the artillery the guy was toting—three pistols and a sawed-off shotgun!*

ARTIST
— ... artist (sl.): ... expert, person good at (doing)... (esp. s/thing neg.) >*They say that playboy's a real seduction artist. >Don't trust that ripoff artist.*

ARTSY-FARTSY
— artsy-fartsy (ärt´sē färt´sē) (sl., sarc., freq. vulg.): pretentious, showy, pseudosophisticated (said of artistic efforts) >*She wants to go to some artsy-fartsy exhibit of ceramic plants.*

AS
— as/like all get-out (see GET-OUT)

** as is (colloq.): in its present condition, without improvements made >*I'll sell you the car for eight hundred bucks as is.*

A.S.A.P.
** A.S.A.P. (colloq.): as soon as possible, right away >*Phone me with that info A.S.A.P., all right?*

ASK
** ask for it (colloq.): invite trouble, behave as to risk punishment, court danger >*You'd better shut up. You're asking for it. >He was asking for it by driving drunk.*

* ask out (vt) (colloq.): invite (s/one) out on a date >*He'd like to ask Tricia out, but he's afraid she'll turn him down.*

** if you ask [s/one] (colloq.): in [s/one's] opinion >*If you ask me, it'll never work.*

ASS
** ass¹ (vulg.): buttocks, rump, anus, rectum >*He fell on his ass. >The nurse stuck a thermometer up his ass.*

* ass² (vulg., pej.): woman or women (seen as sex object[s]) >*He said there was a lot of nice ass at the dance.*

* ass³ (vulg.): sexual intercourse (with a woman) (freq. used with *some* or *any*) >*He finally got some ass last night.*

** [one's] ass (vulg.): [one]self, [one] (esp. when seen as troublesome or contemptible) >*Hey, get your ass over here right now! >I'm gonna beat his ass this time.*

— [for one's] ass [to be] in a sling (vulg.): [for one to be] in serious trouble >*He's got his ass in a sling because he didn't declare a bunch of income to the I.R.S.*

— [one's] ass is grass (vulg.): [one] is doomed, [one] is sure to get hurt or be punished >*Your ass is grass if they catch ya.*

* ... [one's] ass off (vulg.): ... with maximum effort or sacrifice, ... to the utmost >*Beth worked her ass off to get where she is today. >I danced my ass off last night.*

* be [s/one's] ass (vulg.): [s/one] is subject to punishment, [s/one] must pay the consequences >*Remember, if anything goes wrong, it's your ass.*

— be no skin off [s/one's] ass (see SKIN)

— blow it out your ass/asshole! (see BLOW)

— bust/break [one's] ass (see BUST)

— cover [one's] ass (see COVER)

— drag [one's] ass (see DRAG)

— fall flat on [one's] ass (see FALL)

* get off [one's] ass (vulg.): stop being lazy, start moving or working >*If he'd just get off his ass he could make something of himself.*

— give a rat's ass (see RAT'S)

— haul ass (see HAUL)

— have [s/one's] ass (vulg.): punish or hurt [s/one] severely, take revenge on [s/

one] >*If he crosses me, I'll have his ass.*

— **(have) ... coming out (of) [one's] ass** (see **COMING**)

— **have ... up the ass** (vulg.): have an abundance of ..., have ... in large supply >*They got four-wheel-drive trucks up the ass at that dealership.*

— **kick [s/one's] ass** (see **KICK**)

— **kick (some) ass** (see **KICK**)

— **kiss ([s/one's]) ass** (see **KISS**)

— **kiss my ass!** (see **KISS**)

— **my ass!** (see **MY**)

— **not know/can't tell [one's] ass from a hole in the ground** (see **KNOW**)

* **off [s/one's] ass** (vulg.): no longer putting pressure on [s/one], no longer being critical of [s/one] (cf. "**on [s/one's] ASS**") >*Let's just pay the bill! I want 'em off my ass about it.*

* **on [s/one's] ass** (vulg.): putting pressure on [s/one], being critical of [s/one] (cf. "**off [s/one's] ASS**") >*The media's sure been on his ass since the scandal broke.*

— **out on [one's] ass** (see **OUT**)

— **pain in the ass** (see **PAIN**)

— **piece of ass** (see **PIECE**)

— **(tell [s/one] to take [his/her s/thing] and) shove/stick it up [his/her] ass** (see **SHOVE**)

* **up to [one's] ass in** (vulg.): having an abundance or excess of, very occupied with >*Poor Eric's up to his ass in irate customers.*

* **up your ass!** (vulg.): (interj. to express great anger or contempt to s/one) >*Up your ass, you idiot!*

— **you (can) bet your ass** (see **BET**)

ASSBACKWARDS

* **assbackwards** (as´bak´wərdz) (sl., freq. vulg.): backwards, in reversed order, confused (cf. "**BASSACKWARDS**") >*No, you got it assbackwards—the washer goes on first, then the nut.*

ASSHOLE

** **asshole**[1] (vulg.): contemptible or reprehensible person, stupid person (also adj., also voc.) >*That asshole just kicked his dog for no reason.* >*I don't wanna have anything to do with you or your asshole friends.* >*You really screwed up this time, asshole.*

— **asshole**[2] (vulg.): anus >*They fixed his asshole and got rid of his hemorrhoids.*

— **blow it out your ass/asshole!** (see **BLOW**)

ASS-KICKING

— **ass-kicking** (vulg.): decisive beating, disciplinary action, punishment >*If anyone screws up, there's gonna be some serious ass-kickin' around here.*

ASS-KISSER

— **ass-kisser** (vulg.): person who is servile or obsequious to gain favor, adulator, servile flatterer >*Everyone in the office hates Kevin. He's such an ass-kisser.*

ASS-KISSING

— **ass-kissing** (vulg.): servility or obsequiousness to gain favor, adulation, flattery to gain favor >*The supervisor wants hard work from the employees, not ass-kissin'.*

AT

— **where it's at** (see **WHERE**)

ATTABOY

* **attaboy!** (at´ə boi´) (colloq.): you're doing very well! keep it up! hurrah for you! congratulations! (said to a male) >*Attaboy! Nice shot you made!*

ATTACHED

— **strings (attached)** (see **STRINGS**)

ATTACK

* **... attack** (colloq.): sudden craving or desire for ... >*I got a pizza attack at midnight and called for one to be delivered.*

ATTAGIRL

— **attagirl!** (at´ə gûrl´) (colloq.): you're doing very well! keep it up! hurrah for

you! congratulations! (said to a female)
>*You got the scholarship? Attagirl!*

ATTITUDE

** **attitude** (sl.): bad attitude, hostility,
uncooperativeness >*Boy, does that
stupid jerk have an attitude!* >*Get rid
of that attitude, or you'll get thrown off
the team.*

AUSSIE

— **Aussie** (ô´sē) (colloq.): Australian
>*Those Aussies sure do like racing.*

AVOID

* **avoid [s/one, s/thing] like the plague**
(sl.): avoid [s/one, s/thing] at all costs,
do everything (one) can to avoid [s/one,
s/thing] >*What did I do to Bucky? He's
been avoidin' me like the plague.*
>*She's a recovering alcoholic who
avoids liquor like the plague.*

AW

* **aw!** (ô) (colloq.): (interj. to express
irritation, disappointment, or sympathy)
>*Aw! Why'd he go and do that?* >*Aw,
that's too bad!*

AWAY

— **get away with** (see **GET**)

— **get away with murder** (see **GET**)

— **put away** (see **PUT**)

AWESOME

** **awesome** (sl.): impressive, excellent
>*That dude's got, like, an awesome
motorcycle.* >*Ya got a ten-dollar raise
at work?! Awesome!*

AWFUL

* **awful** (colloq.): very, extremely
>*Herb's an awful nice guy.*

— **something awful** (colloq.): awfully,
badly >*What's with Billy? He's been
acting something awful lately.*

A-WHISTLING

— **you just ain't (a-)whistlin' Dixie!** (see
WHISTLING)

AX

* **get the ax** (colloq.): be fired, be
abruptly dismissed >*They caught him*

*padding his expense account, and he got
the ax.*

* **give [s/one] the ax** (colloq.): fire [s/
one], abruptly dismiss [s/one] >*If
Swensen doesn't start doing a better job,
we'll have to give him the ax.*

B

BABE

* **babe** (sl., freq. pei,); attractive young person (esp. a woman) >*Who was that babe I saw your brother with yesterday?* >*Greg is such a babe!*

* **([one's]) babe** (sl.): ([one's]) sweetheart, ([one's]) darling (also voc.) >*I'm gonna buy some roses for my babe.* >*He's got a babe that treats him like a king.* >*Hey, babe, let's go dancin'.*

BABOON

— **baboon** (colloq.): coarse or brutish person >*Did you see that baboon picking up all the food and asking what it was?*

BABY

** **baby** (sl.): thing of special interest or concern (to s/one) >*The Eastside project is Conally's baby.* >*Watch how this baby accelerates.*

— **([one's]) baby** (sl.): ([one's]) sweetheart, ([one's]) darling (also voc.) >*My baby's takin' me out to dinner tonight.* >*Hey, baby, come here, will ya?*

BABY-BOOMER

** **baby-boomer** (colloq.): person born between 1946 and 1965 in the U.S. (period of sharp birth-rate increase) >*Who's going to take care of the baby-boomers when they get old?*

BACH

— **bach it** (bach ...) (sl.): live alone, live as a bachelor (said of a male) >*He's bachin' it this week because his wife's outta town visitin' her mother.*

BACK

** **back off** (vi) (colloq.): decrease the pressure or intensity, become less hostile or aggressive >*Why don't you back off on the kid—he's only eight years old!* >*Back off, buddy! You're asking for trouble.*

* **back up** (vi) (colloq.): explain what (one) just said, repeat more clearly what (one) just said >*Hey, back up a minute, what did you say he threatened to do?*

— **be no skin off [s/one's] back** (see **SKIN**)

— **from way back** (see **WAY**)

** **get back at** (colloq.): take revenge on, retaliate against >*You'd better watch your step, because he'll get back at you someday.*

** **get back to** (colloq.): communicate again with (s/one) at a later time >*I'm not sure—I'll have to get back to you about that.*

— **go back to square one** (see **SQUARE ONE**)

— **go way back** (see **WAY**)

* **it's back to the (old) drawing board** (colloq.): it's necessary to do some new planning (because the present attempt has failed) >*Well, that idea didn't work, so I guess it's back to the old drawing board.*

— **monkey on [one's] back** (see **MONKEY**)

** **off [s/one's] back** (sl.): no longer pressuring or criticizing [s/one], having stopped annoying [s/one] (cf. "**on [s/one's] BACK**") >*I want 'em off my back about how I'm doin' the job.* >*Get off my back, will ya?*

** **on [s/one's] back** (sl.): pressuring or criticizing [s/one], annoying [s/one] (cf. "**off [s/one's] BACK**") >*I got the boss on my back to finish this up by five.* >*If ya don't want the government on your back, ya'd better get it right.*

— **pat on the back** (see **PAT**)

— **pat [s/one] on the back** (see **PAT**)

— **scratch [s/one's] back** (see **SCRATCH**)

— **stab in the back** (see **STAB**)

— **stab/knife [s/one] in the back** (see **STAB**)

— **way back when** (see **WAY**)

— **would give [s/one] the shirt off [one's] back** (see **SHIRT**)

BACK BURNER
* **on the back burner** (colloq.): with low priority, temporarily of less importance to deal with (than s/thing else) >*Our vacation plans are on the back burner until we straighten this problem out.*

BACKSEAT
* **take a backseat (to)** (colloq.): allow (s/one) to have preeminence, assume a secondary or subordinate position (to) >*He's ambitious and aggressive. He takes a backseat to no one.*

BACKSEAT DRIVER
* **backseat driver** (colloq.): passenger who gives unwanted advice and criticism to the driver about his/her driving >*I can't stand backseat drivers, so either shut up or get out!*

BACK TALK
* **back talk** (colloq.): impudent talk, disrespectful response (cf. "**TALK back**") >*Don't give me any back talk! Just do it!*

BACKWARD
** **bend/lean over backward(s)** (colloq.): put out a great effort, try harder than is necessary or reasonable >*She bent over backward to help you, and you don't even care.* >*The committee has leaned over backwards to be objective.*

* **know [s/thing] backward(s) and forward(s)** (colloq.): know [s/thing] thoroughly, have [s/thing] mastered >*He'll get the bugs out. He knows computers backwards and forwards.*

BACON
— **bring home the bacon** (see **BRING**)

— **save [s/one's] bacon** (see **SAVE**)

BAD
** **bad[1]** (colloq.): strongly, urgently (said of a desire or urge) >*The addict needs some drugs bad.* >*She wanted a kid real bad.*

— **bad[2]** (sl.): excellent, impressive >*That rap song is bad!*

* **bad off[1]** (colloq.): in poor circumstances, suffering financially >*Lots of folks have been pretty bad off since the factory shut down.*

— **bad off[2]** (colloq.): very ill or seriously injured >*The car wreck killed his friend, and he's bad off in the hospital.*

** **give [s/one] a bad time** (colloq.): annoy or harass [s/one], tease [s/one] relentlessly >*They're always giving him a bad time because he's fat.*

— **in a bad way** (colloq.): in trouble, in poor condition, suffering >*Darren's in a bad way, losing his job and owing all that money.* >*Abe's been in a real bad way since his wife left him.*

— **in bad with** (colloq.): in trouble with, disliked by >*If you're in bad with Mr. Sumner, you won't get anywhere in this company.*

— **not half bad** (see **HALF**)

— **on [s/one's] good/bad side** (see **SIDE**)

— **so much/bad I can taste it** (see **SO**)

BAD APPLE
— **bad apple** (colloq.): troublemaker, dishonest person (in a group) >*Watch out for that kid. He's a bad apple.* >*All it takes is one bad apple to spoil it for everyone.*

BADASS
— **badass** (bad´as´) (vulg.): mean, tough, intimidating (also noun) >*Stay away from them badass gangs!* >*That dude thinks he's a real badass, but I could whip him.*

BADDER
— **badder** (bad´ər) (sl.): better, more impressive (cf. "**BAD[2]**") >*This drummer is bad, badder even than the first one.*

BADDEST
— **baddest** (bad´əst) (sl.): best, most impressive (cf. "BAD[2]") *That's the baddest car I ever seen!*

BADMOUTH
** **badmouth** (vt) (sl.): criticize, defame, insult *>Bert badmouths everyone behind their back. >You badmouth me like that again, and I'll knock your block off.*

BAD NEWS
** **bad news** (sl.): troublesome, dangerous *>That clean-up job's gonna be bad news. >That mean guy's real bad news.*

BAD RAP
* **bad rap** (sl.): unjust criticism or condemnation *>The guy's gotten a bad rap. He's really doin' an all-right job.*

BAD SCENE
— **bad scene** (sl.): awful situation, unpleasant occurrence *>It was a bad scene when Marty and Louie started screamin' at each other. >This party's a bad scene. Let's split.*

BAD TRIP
— **bad trip** (sl.): unpleasant experience, bad situation *>Gettin' arrested by the cops was a bad trip, man.*

BAG
— **bag** (vt) (colloq.): secure, catch, obtain *>I hear Michael's bagged that promotion. >She's got her eye on that guy and is determined to bag him.*

* **[one's] bag** (sl.): [one's] area of special interest or skill *>Campin' out is not my bag. I'd rather stay at a nice hotel.*

* **in the bag** (sl.): assured, virtually achieved or won *>Don't worry about gettin' the job—it's in the bag, man.*

— **leave [s/one] holding the bag** (see HOLDING)

— **let the cat out of the bag** (see LET)

* **old bag** (colloq., pej.): old woman (esp. seen as troublesome or contemptible)

>There's some old bag outside yelling at Don.

BAG OF BONES
— **bag of bones** (colloq.): very skinny or emaciated person *>He's been so sick he's nothing but a bag of bones.*

BAG OF WIND
— **bag of wind** (colloq.): person who talks too much (esp. while saying little of substance), pretentious talker *>Can't somebody shut that bag of wind up for a while?*

BAIL
— **bail out (of)** (sl.): abandon (s/thing), not carry through (on), give up (on) *>After he lied to her, she bailed outta the relationship.*

* **bail [s/one] out (of)** (colloq.): get [s/one] out (of a difficulty), provide critical assistance [to s/one] (in) *>If you won't budget your money, don't expect me to bail you out at the end of the month. >Just who does he think's going to bail him out of this mess?*

— **jump/skip bail** (see JUMP)

BALDIE
— **baldie** (bôl´dē) (colloq., freq. pej.): bald man (also voc.) *>Grayson's already a baldie at thirty-five. >Hey, baldie, did you put any sunblock on your head today?*

BALDY
— **baldy** (see "BALDIE")

BALL
— **ball** (vi, vt) (vulg.): have sexual intercourse (with) *>She looks sweet and innocent, but he says she loves to ball. >He said he balled her last night.*

** **a ball** (colloq.): a very good time, great fun *>Our trip to Boston was a ball. >Stream fishing for trout's a ball.*

— **carry the ball** (see CARRY)

— **drop the ball** (see DROP)

* **get/keep the ball rolling** (colloq.): get/keep things going, start/continue an activity or operation >*Let's get the ball rolling. Who'll volunteer to go first?* >*He kept the ball rolling by telling another joke.*

** **have a ball** (colloq.): have great fun, enjoy (oneself) very much >*You're going to have a ball on your cruise.*

* **have ... on the ball** (colloq.): be alert or sharp (to some degree), be competent (to some degree) >*That kid's going to be a success. He's got a lot on the ball.* >*That joker won't make it. He has nothing on the ball.*

* **on the ball** (colloq.): alert, sharp, competent >*If you're on the ball, you can make big bucks in this business.* >*Get on the ball, or you'll be out of a job!*

* **play ball (with)** (colloq.): cooperate (with), work together (with) >*If you want to get ahead in this business, you got to play ball with the inspectors.*

— **run with the ball** (see RUN)

* **that's the way the ball bounces** (colloq., freq. sarc.): that's how things happen, that's fate >*So the judge fined you, but let the other guy off, huh? Well, that's the way the ball bounces.*

* **the ball is in [s/one's] court** (colloq.): the next action or response is up to [s/one] >*We've given Tony all the information. The ball's in his court now.*

— **the whole ball of wax** (sl.): all of it, the whole set, everything involved >*If my number comes up, I win the whole ball of wax.*

BALL-BREAKER
— **ball-buster/breaker** (see "BALL-BUSTER")

BALL-BUSTER
— **ball-buster/breaker**[1] (vulg.): very difficult task, activity requiring strenuous effort (cf. "BUST/break [one's] balls") >*Unloadin' this huge truck's gonna be a ball-buster.*

— **ball-buster/breaker**[2] (vulg.): woman who emasculates a man, woman who injures a man's sense of maleness (cf. "BUST/break [s/one's] balls") >*The guys stay away from her. They say she's a real ball-breaker.*

BALL GAME
* **ball game** (colloq.): (a particular) competitive situation >*Now that Morgan's been fired, it's a whole new ball game.* >*You got to have a state license if you want to be in the ball game and bid on jobs.*

BALLISTIC
— **go ballistic** (sl.): become furious, lose (one's) temper >*He went ballistic when the dude called him a liar.*

BALL OF FIRE
— **ball of fire** (colloq.): energetic and capable person, dynamo >*That woman's a ball of fire! She's gotten more done in a week than Richards did in a month.*

BALLPARK
** **ballpark figure** (colloq.): approximate quantity or sum, general estimate >*Give us a ballpark figure for the cost of painting the whole house.*

** **in the ballpark** (colloq.): approximately the quantity or price expected >*An offer of $2,000 is in the ballpark.*

BALLS
** **balls**[1] (vulg.): testicles >*The stick hit him right in the balls.*

* **balls**[2] (vulg.): courage, boldness, daring >*Ya got the balls to fight him?*

— **bust/break [one's] balls** (see BUST)

— **bust/break [s/one's] balls** (see BUST)

— **freeze [one's] balls/nuts off** (see FREEZE)

* **have [s/one] by the balls/nuts** (vulg.): have [s/one] at (one's) mercy, control [s/one] by threat, have [s/one] in a helpless situation under (one's) power (esp. a

BALLSY–BARBIE

man) >*I got him by the balls—if he tries anything, he knows I'll turn him in.*

BALLSY
— **ballsy** (bôl´zē) (sl., freq. vulg.): bold, courageous, audacious >*It took a ballsy woman to talk to the mayor like that.*

BALONEY
* **baloney**[1] (colloq.): nonsense, false or exaggerated story, mistaken opinion (also interj.) >*Don't give me that baloney about your sick grandmother! >Him, a good actor?! Baloney!*

— **baloney**[2] (colloq.): annoying or tedious work or demands >*Having to fill out these forms is baloney.*

BAMBOOZLE
— **bamboozle [s/one] (into)** (bam bū´zəl …) (colloq.): deceive or trick [s/one] (into), hoodwink [s/one] (into) >*Those crooks have bamboozled half the town into investing in their worthless business venture.*

BANANA
— **second banana** (see SECOND)

— **top banana** (see TOP)

BANANAS
* **bananas** (sl.): crazy, mentally unbalanced >*That guy must be bananas to argue with a cop. >That kid practicin' his drums is drivin' me bananas.*

* **go bananas (over)** (sl.): become very enthusiastic (about), like (s/thing) very much >*He goes bananas over tall, slim blonds.*

BAND
— **to beat the band** (see BEAT)

BANDIT
* **make out like a bandit** (sl.): make a great deal of profit, earn an inordinate amount of money >*I'm gonna make out like a bandit on this deal. >Corporate lawyers make out like bandits.*

BANDWAGON
— **jump/hop/get on the bandwagon** (colloq.): join a popular movement or activity, follow a popular fad >*All her friends started investing in the stock market, so she jumped on the bandwagon too.*

BANG
— **bang**[1] (vulg.): act of sexual intercourse >*How long's it been since you've had a good bang?*

— **bang**[2] (vt) (vulg.): have sexual intercourse with >*He said he took her to a motel and banged her.*

— **bang for [one's] buck** (sl.): value for the money [one] pays >*Ya get more bang for your buck with this baby than with any other model.*

* **get a (big) bang out of** (colloq.): really enjoy, become thrilled or excited by >*The whole family gets a big bang out of that comedian. >I get a bang out of watching wrestling on Saturday night.*

* **with a bang** (colloq.): with vitality, with a burst of energy, with an impressive success >*Green started out with a bang in his new job, then sort of ran out of gas.*

BANG-UP
— **bang-up** (colloq.): excellent, very well done >*You guys did a bang-up job painting the house.*

BANK
* **bank on** (colloq.): rely on, be assured of, count on >*I'll be here at eleven sharp. You can bank on it. >We're banking on your support.*

BANKROLL
— **bankroll** (vt) (colloq.): finance, back with money >*Who's bankrolling her singing tour?*

BARBIE
— **barbie** (bär´bē) (colloq.): barbecue grill >*Come on over! I'll throw a couple more steaks on the barbie for you.*

14

BARE-ASSED

* **bare-assed** (bâr´ast´) (sl., freq. vulg.): naked >*They caught some crazy guy walkin' down the street bare-assed singin' "Happy Birthday to You."*

BARF

** **barf¹** (bärf) (sl.): vomit >*There was barf all over the floor.*

** **barf²** (vi, vt) (sl.): vomit >*He got carsick and barfed out the window.* >*I bet he barfs that chili he ate.*

BARF BAG

* **barf bag** (bärf…) (sl.): paper bag to be used in case of vomiting due to motion sickness >*I hope I don't have to use a barf bag on this flight.*

BARFLY

— **barfly** (sl.): person who spends a great deal of time in bars or taverns (esp. one who drinks heavily) >*The poor gal doesn't get any help from her old man, a barfly who blows all his money on booze.*

BARGAIN-BASEMENT

— **bargain-basement** (colloq.): low-priced, of inferior quality >*Don't put that bargain-basement oil in your engine.*

BARHOP

* **barhop** (vi) (colloq.): patronize a succession of bars in one outing >*They went barhopping last night and ended up at the Linger Inn, drunk as a skunk.*

BARKING

* **barking up the wrong tree** (colloq.): pursuing the wrong person or resource (to achieve a goal), misdirected in (one's) efforts >*If you've come to ask me for money, you're barking up the wrong tree.*

BARREL

* **barrel** (vi, vt) (sl.): go very fast, move (a vehicle) very fast >*We were barrelin' down the interstate at ninety miles an hour.* >*Barney barreled his truck through the stream.*

— **a barrel of fun** (colloq.): great fun >*We had a barrel of fun at the fair.*

* **a barrel of laughs** (colloq.): a funny or entertaining person or thing, great fun >*That funny brother of yours is a barrel of laughs.* >*He thinks professional wrestling's a barrel of laughs.*

— **more fun than a barrel of monkeys** (see FUN)

— **over a barrel** (colloq.): at the mercy of another, unable to act (due to another's control), in a helpless position >*I'm over a barrel because I have no authority here.* >*We've got them over a barrel and can call the shots.*

BARRELS

— **let [s/one] have it with both barrels** (see LET)

BASE

** **off base** (colloq.): mistaken, using wrong assumptions >*He was way off base when he said that more money would solve all this school's problems.*

— **touch base(s) (with)** (see TOUCH)

BASES

— **touch all bases** (see TOUCH)

BASH

* **bash¹** (bash) (sl.): wild party, exciting celebration >*We're gonna have a big bash to celebrate.*

— **bash²** (colloq.): strong hit or blow, crash >*The bash on his head is what hurt him most.*

— **bash³** (vi, vt) (colloq.): strike or hit forcefully, crash >*A drunk driver bashed into the telephone pole.* >*He bashed me on the shoulder with a heavy book.*

BASHING

** **…-bashing** (… bash´ing) (colloq.): hateful attacking or defaming of … >*He's some ultraconservative who's into liberal-bashing.*

BASKET CASE

** **basket case** (colloq.): useless or incapacitated person (esp. due to emotional trauma) >*Don't put Bickworth in charge! He's a basket case.* >*He was a basket case for months after his mother died.*

BASSACKWARDS

— **bassackwards** (bas´ak´wərdz) (sl., freq. vulg.): backwards, in reversed order, confused (cf. "ASSBACKWARDS") >*No wonder it leaks. Someone put the gasket on bassackwards.*

BASTARD

** **bastard** (sl., freq. vulg.): despicable or mean person >*That bastard just broke his kid's toy on purpose.*

* **poor bastard** (colloq.): very unfortunate or pathetic man >*First they fired the poor bastard, and then they took away his pension.*

BAT

— **(as) blind as a bat** (see **BLIND**)

* **bat a thousand** (sl.): not have even one failure, succeed completely (cf. "BAT five hundred" and "BAT zero") >*Six houses, six sales—I'm battin' a thousand.*

— **bat around** (vt) (colloq.): discuss or debate, consider the merits of (an idea) >*We batted his proposal around at the meeting, but decided against it.*

— **bat five hundred** (sl.): have an equal number of successes and failures (cf. "BAT a thousand" and "BAT zero") >*If you can bat five hundred in phone sales, you're doin' fantastic.*

— **bat 500** (see "BAT five hundred")

— **bat zero** (sl.): not have even one success, fail completely (cf. "BAT a thousand" and "BAT five hundred") >*He tried to pick up at least ten women at the party, but he batted zero.*

* **[neg.] (even) bat an eye** (colloq.): show no surprise or shock (at all) >*He never even batted an eye when they told him how much it would cost.*

* **go to bat for** (colloq.): defend, vouch for, give support to (esp. under adversity) >*You can count on me to go to bat for you if anyone questions you on this.*

* **like a bat out of hell** (colloq.): rapidly, quickly and determinedly >*The bully started after him, and he took off like a bat out of hell.*

* **old bat** (colloq., pej.): contemptible old woman >*That old bat from down the street is back complaining about our service.*

— **right off the bat** (see **RIGHT**)

BATH

— **take a bath** (colloq.): lose a large amount of money (in a deal) >*A lot of investors took a bath in that land-fraud case.*

BATHROOM

** **go to the bathroom** (colloq.): urinate or defecate >*Mommy, I need to go to the bathroom.*

BATS

— **bats** (sl.): crazy >*I'll go bats if I don't get outta here.*

— **have bats in [one's] belfry** (colloq.): be crazy >*If you ask me, that guy talking to himself over there's got bats in his belfry.*

BATTLE-AX

— **battle-ax** (sl.): overbearing and/or belligerent woman >*Watch out for that old battle-ax. She'll yell at ya just for lookin' at her.*

BATTY

* **batty** (bat´ē) (sl.): crazy >*Ya must be batty to go into that bar alone at night, Susie.*

BAWL

* **bawl out** (vt) (colloq.): reprimand loudly, scold severely >*When he got*

home at four in the morning, his mom really bawled him out.

BAZOOMS
— **bazooms** (bə zūmz´) (sl., freq. vulg.): (woman's) breasts (esp. large or shapely ones) >*Her bazooms really look good in that tight sweater.*

BE
** **be [s/one]** (colloq.): be very appropriate for [s/one], be especially suited to [s/one] >*Oh, you should buy that dress. It's you.*

— **be my guest!** (see GUEST)

— **be/feel up to** (see UP)

— **be with** (see WITH)

* **(well,) I'll be (a monkey's uncle)!** (colloq.): I'm surprised! I didn't expect that! >*Well, I'll be! He really did finish the marathon!* >*I'll be a monkey's uncle! I won first prize in the raffle!*

BEAK
— **beak** (colloq.): (person's) nose (esp. a large one) >*Look at the beak on that guy! He's all nose!*

BEAM
— **on/off the beam** (colloq.): correct/incorrect, proceeding well/poorly, on the right/wrong track >*Our productivity is way up. The whole operation is on the beam.* >*You're off the beam if you don't consider the politics of the situation.*

BEAMER
— **Beamer** (see "BEEMER")

BEAN
— **bean¹** (sl.): (person's) head >*Use the old bean and figure it out.*

— **bean²** (vt) (sl.): hit (s/one) hard on the head >*She beaned him with a fryin' pan.*

BEANER
— **beaner** (bē´nər) (sl., pej.): Mexican, Mexican-American >*The stupid jerk called Victor a beaner.* >*He said he didn't like his beaner friends.*

BEANPOLE
* **beanpole** (colloq.): tall and skinny person >*What a pair! He's short and fat, and she's a beanpole.*

BEANS
* **([neg.]) beans** (sl.): nothing >*He don't know beans about fixin' a car.* >*Kyle knows beans about how to act around women—watch him make a fool of himself.* >*Joe never does beans around the house.*

— **full of beans** (see FULL)

— **spill the beans** (see SPILL)

— **worth beans** (see WORTH)

BEAN TOWN
— **Bean Town** (colloq.): Boston, Massachusetts >*He moved from New York City to Bean Town.*

BEAR
* **bear** (sl.): very difficult task, troublesome thing, arduous undertaking >*That zoology exam was a bear.* >*Clearin' this road is gonna be a bear.*

— **grin and bear it** (see GRIN)

BEAST
— **beast** (sl.): powerful vehicle >*Watch me take that steep hill with this beast.*

BEAT
** **beat¹** (vt) (colloq.): be better than, be preferable to >*Flying standby beats paying full fare.* >*This old car ain't much, but it beats walking.*

** **beat²** (vt) (colloq.): baffle, confound, perplex >*It beats me why Rosie said such a dumb thing.*

* **beat³** (vt) (colloq.): escape from, avoid, get around (a problem) >*Karl goes to the beach to beat the heat.* >*He was guilty as hell, but somehow he beat the rap.*

** **beat⁴** (colloq.): very tired, exhausted >*What a day! I'm beat.*

** **beat around the bush** (colloq.): talk about irrelevant things (to avoid dealing with a subject), not come directly to the

BEATING

point >*Stop beating around the bush and talk to me. What's the problem?*

* beat [one's] brains out (colloq.): think hard, exert great mental effort >*I've been beating my brains out trying to figure out how to do it.*

— beat [s/one's] brains out (sl.): beat [s/one] severely, beat [s/one] up >*He tries anything with me and I'll beat his brains out.*

— beat down [s/one's] door (colloq.): seek out [s/one] in great numbers, (for [s/one] to) have great popularity or attraction >*The studios have been beating down her door since she starred in that big hit.* >*They're going to beat down Pratt's door for interviews when he announces his discovery.*

* beat [one's] head against the wall (colloq.): (do s/thing) in vain, put out effort without chance of success >*Lombardi tried to make some changes in the company, but he was just beating his head against the wall.*

* beat it (sl.): leave quickly, escape >*We beat it when the sheriff showed up.* >*Beat it! You're gettin' on my nerves.*

— beat [one's] meat (vulg.): masturbate (said of a male) >*His old lady caught him beatin' his meat.*

— beat off (vi, vt) (vulg.): masturbate (said of a male) >*He said he beat off a lot when he was a kid.* >*She agreed to beat him off.*

* beat [s/one] out (of) (colloq.): prevail over [s/one] (to gain s/thing) >*You'd better do good in the interview if you want to beat John out of the job.*

— beat the heck out of (see HECK)

— beat the hell out of (see HELL)

— beat/kick the heck out of (see HECK)

— beat/kick the hell out of (see HELL)

— beat/knock the (living) daylights out of (see DAYLIGHTS)

— beat/knock/kick the (living) shit out of (see SHIT)

* beat the pants off (of) (colloq.): defeat decisively (esp. in a competition) >*We beat the pants off them in basketball yesterday.*

— beat the rap (see RAP)

— beat the socks off (of) (colloq.): defeat decisively (esp. in a competition) >*We'll get the socks beat off of us if we don't tighten up our defense.*

— beat/knock the stuffing out of (see STUFFING)

— beat/knock the tar out of (see TAR)

* beat [s/one, s/thing] to a pulp (colloq.): beat [s/one, s/thing] severely (esp. a part of the body) >*Don't take him on—he'll beat you to a pulp.* >*He got his face beaten to a pulp in that fight.*

— beat [s/one] to the draw (colloq.): take decisive action before [s/one], gain an advantage over [s/one] by acting sooner >*Go ask her to dance before somebody beats you to the draw.*

— beat [s/one] to the punch (colloq.): take decisive action before [s/one], gain an advantage over [s/one] by acting sooner >*Greg found out about the job before me, so he beat me to the punch.*

** can't be beat (colloq.): is the best, is excellent >*A cold beer on a hot day just can't be beat.*

— ... to beat all ...s (colloq.): extraordinary ..., impressive ..., the ultimate ... >*We saw a show to beat all shows last night. It was great!*

— to beat the band (colloq.): wholeheartedly, enthusiastically >*I saw them in the corner hugging and kissing to beat the band.*

BEATING

** take a beating (colloq.): suffer a severe loss or defeat >*The stock market took a beating last month.* >*Their side really took a beating in court.*

BEAT-UP
* **beat-up** (colloq.): dilapidated, run-down, in poor condition >*My car's real beat-up, but it gets me there.*

BEAUCOUP
— **beaucoup** (bō kū′) (sl.): much, many >*That bad dude means beaucoup trouble.* >*They made beaucoup bucks with that scheme.*

BEAUT
* **a beaut** (… byūt) (colloq.): an impressive or beautiful thing (freq. sarc.) >*His blunder was a beaut—he embarrassed everybody there.* >*His new motorcycle's a beaut.*

BEAUTY
** **a beauty** (colloq.): an impressive or beautiful thing (freq. sarc.) >*The black eye he gave you is a beauty.* >*That last pitch he threw was a beauty.*

* **the beauty** (colloq.): the particularly advantageous aspect (of s/thing) >*The beauty of my new job is that I work my own hours.*

BEAVER
— **beaver** (vulg.): woman's pubic region >*He buys porno magazines to look at beavers.*

— **(as) busy as a beaver** (see BUSY)

BED
— **get up on the wrong side of the bed** (see GET)

** **go to bed (with)** (colloq.): have sexual intercourse (with) >*It seems that all men want to do is go to bed with you.* >*Do you think they've gone to bed yet?*

** **in bed** (colloq.): engaged in sexual activity, having sex >*He says he loves her, but all he really wants is to get her in bed.* >*He looks real shy, but he's a tiger in bed.*

BEE
— **(as) busy as a bee** (see BUSY)

BEEF
— **beef**[1] (sl.): complaint, dispute >*I got no beef about the job, except for the long hours.* >*My beef ain't with you—it's with your brother.*

— **beef**[2] (sl.): criminal charge or accusation >*They had him up on some embezzlement beef.*

— **beef**[3] (vi) (sl.): complain >*Gardner's never happy. He's always got somethin' to beef about.*

* **beef up** (vt) (colloq.): strengthen, reinforce >*If we get that new territory, we'll have to beef up our sales force.* >*You'd better beef chapter two up.*

BEEFCAKE
— **beefcake** (sl.): photograph(s) of (a) sexually attractive man/men (esp. with little clothing and meant to be sensual) (cf. "CHEESECAKE") >*She bought a beefcake calendar just 'cause she liked Mr. September.*

BEEMER
* **Beemer** (bē′mər) (sl.): B.M.W. automobile >*He always says he's broke, but he drives a brand-new Beemer.*

BEER BUST
— **beer bust** (colloq.): lively party where beer is consumed in large quantities >*The frat house had a beer bust Saturday night.*

BEES
— **the birds and the bees** (see BIRDS)

BEESWAX
— **[one's] (own) beeswax** (colloq.): [one's] business, [one's] personal affair or concern (used esp. sarc.) >*Mind your own beeswax!* >*He doesn't need to know. It's none of his beeswax.*

BEET
— **(as) red as a beet** (see RED)

BEHIND
** **behind** (colloq.): buttocks, rump >*She slipped and fell on her behind.*

— **behind the eightball** (sl.): in a difficult or unfavorable situation, in a predicament >*I'm really behind the eightball—two of the company big shots disagree over this, and I got to make the decision.*

— **(still) wet behind the ears** (see **WET**)

BEING

— **being (that/as how)** (colloq.): since, because >*Being it's late, I have to get going.* >*Being as how you're such a nice guy, I'm going to help you out.*

BELFRY

— **have bats in [one's] belfry** (see **BATS**)

BELIEVE

— **believe you me!** (colloq.): I'm telling you the truth! I'm speaking seriously! >*Believe you me, it was the biggest trout I'd ever seen in my life!*

** **so ... I can't believe it** (colloq.): incredibly ..., very ... >*Don't trust him. He's so crooked I can't believe it.*

* **you('d) better believe ...!** (colloq.): ... is the truth! absolutely ...! you can be sure ...! >*You'd better believe he's not going to get away with this!* >*You're asking if Bubba's tough? You better believe it!*

BELL

— **(as) clear as a bell** (see **CLEAR**)

— **ring a bell** (see **RING**)

BELLS

— **be [s/where] with bells on** (colloq.): arrive [s/where] eager to have fun or participate >*Your party? I'll be there with bells on.*

— **bells and whistles** (sl.): added features, special extras >*He got a real fancy C.D. player with all the bells and whistles.*

BELLY

— **belly up to** (sl.): approach, come up next to (esp. to seek gratification or favor) >*Chet bellied up to the bar and ordered a whiskey.* >*I hate it when they belly up to ya all friendly-like, then ask ya for a few bucks.*

* **go belly up** (colloq.): die, come to an end, go bankrupt >*The company started off with a bang, but after two years it went belly up.*

BELLYACHE

— **bellyache** (vi) (colloq.): complain, grumble (esp. unreasonably) >*What's that whiner bellyaching about now?*

BELLYBUTTON

** **bellybutton** (colloq.): navel >*His shirt's so short you can see his bellybutton.*

BELLYFUL

— **a bellyful** (colloq.): as much as (one) can tolerate, more than (one) can endure >*We've had a bellyful of your bitching, so cut it out!*

BELOW

* **(hit) below the belt** (colloq.): (do s/thing) unfair or lacking decency, (be) unsportsmanlike >*Bringing up her jailbird father was hitting below the belt.* >*The alcoholism remark was below the belt.*

BELT

— **belt¹** (sl.): shot or drink (of liquor) >*Gimme a belt of whiskey, will ya?*

— **belt²** (sl.): blow or punch (esp. with the fist) >*He took a belt to the jaw and went down.*

— **belt³** (vt) (sl.): strike or hit (esp. with the fist) >*He started the fight and got belted right in the face.*

— **belt down** (vt) (sl.): gulp down, drink quickly (esp. liquor) >*She belted down four scotches, one right after the other.*

— **belt out** (vt) (colloq.): sing (a song) loudly and forcefully >*Janis could really belt them out!*

— **(hit) below the belt** (see **BELOW**)

— **tighten [one's] belt** (see **TIGHTEN**)

* **under [one's] belt¹** (colloq.): having become useful experience >*With six

years as supervisor under his belt, Kirk's the right man for the job.

— **under [one's] belt²** (colloq.): eaten or drunk, in [one's] stomach >*You'll feel better after you've gotten a nice hot meal under your belt.* >*Stu starts acting weird when he gets a few drinks under his belt.*

BELT-TIGHTENING

— **belt-tightening** (colloq.): economizing, cutting back on expenses (cf. "**TIGHTEN [one's] belt**") >*We're going to have to do some belt-tightening around here since they cut back on Mom's hours at work.*

BENCH

— **warm the bench** (see **WARM**)

BENCHWARMER

* **benchwarmer** (colloq.): player who rarely plays or who serves as a substitute (on a team) (cf. "**WARM the bench**") >*Why's she on the team if she's nothing but a benchwarmer?*

BEND

* **bend [s/one's] ear** (colloq.): bore [s/one] with talk, speak incessantly to [s/one] >*Mack's got Tina in the corner and is bending her ear about his golf game.*

— **bend/lean over backward(s)** (see **BACKWARD**)

BENNY

— **benny¹** (ben´ē) (sl.): Benzedrine or amphetamine tablet >*The trucker took a couple of bennies to stay awake.*

— **benny²** (sl.): benefit (as part of a job situation) >*My new job pays a little less than the old one, but the bennies are a lot better.*

BENT

** **(all) bent out of shape** (sl.): very upset, exasperated, having lost emotional control >*She got all bent out of shape when he told her to get lost.*

BEST

** **best bet** (colloq.): best option >*If you want to learn how to do it, your best bet is to take a class.*

— **[one's] Sunday best** (see **SUNDAY**)

BET

— **best bet** (see **BEST**)

** **you bet** (colloq.): of course, surely >*You bet I can help him.* >*She wants to know if they can sing? You bet.*

* **you (can) bet your ass** (vulg.): you can be sure, you can rest assured >*You bet your ass I ain't gonna let 'em steal my car!*

— **you (can) bet your boots** (colloq.): you can be sure, you can rest assured >*You bet your boots we followed the rules.*

— **you (can) bet your life** (colloq.): you can be sure, you can rest assured >*You can bet your life there's something fishy going on here.*

BETCHA

* **you betcha** (... be´chə) (sl.): of course, surely >*You betcha we can do that—no problem.*

BETTER

— **a damn(ed) sight better** (see **DAMN**)

— **a darn(ed) sight better** (see **DARN**)

— **go [s/one] one better** (see **GO**)

— **have seen better days** (see **SEEN**)

— **you('d) better believe ...!** (see **BELIEVE**)

BETTER HALF

* **[one's] better half** (colloq.): [one's] wife >*Come here, Greg—I want you to meet my better half.*

BETWEEN

* **between a rock and a hard place** (sl.): in a predicament, in a difficult situation >*Ben's between a rock and a hard place. He's gonna catch hell for any move he makes.*

— **between the sheets** (sl.): engaged in sexual activity, having sex >*He's a real* *snob, but they say he's great between the sheets.*

B.F.D.

— **B.F.D.!** (= "big fucking deal") (sl., freq. vulg., sarc.): I don't find that so impressive! >*So you got an A on the quiz. B.F.D.!*

BIBLES

— **swear on a stack of Bibles** (see SWEAR)

BIBLE-THUMPER

— **Bible-thumper** (sl., freq. pej.): Protestant fundamentalist >*He says he hates it when the Bible-thumpers come to his door and start preachin' to him.*

BIDDY

— **old biddy** (... bid´ē) (colloq., pej.): talkative and meddlesome old woman >*Who asked that old biddy for her opinion?*

BIG

** **big**[1] (colloq.): in a successful or impressive way >*He made it big as an actor.* >*His practical joke didn't go over too big with her parents.* >*I want to do this party up big.*

** **big**[2] (colloq.): popular, well-known >*That band's not very well-known here, but it's real big back east.*

* **big**[3] (colloq.): boastful, self-important, exaggerated (also adv.) >*He's full of big talk, but can he do the job?* >*Walt likes to talk big and act big when he's got an audience.*

* **be big on** (colloq.): especially like, be enthusiastic for >*They're really big on basketball in Indiana.*

— **(big) bucks** (see BUCKS)

— **[one's] big (fat) mouth** (see MOUTH)

— **hit it big** (see HIT)

* **in a big way** (colloq.): very much, overwhelmingly, enthusiastically >*Danny loves pro football in a big way.*

— **make a big production out of** (see PRODUCTION)

— **talk big** (see TALK)

* **too big for [one's] britches** (colloq.): asserting [oneself] beyond [one's] authority or position, cocky >*He's getting too big for his britches. Somebody's going to have to put him in his place.*

— **what's the big idea?** (see WHAT'S)

BIG APPLE

** **the Big Apple** (colloq.): New York City >*Her acting's OK, but she won't make it in the Big Apple.*

BIG BOYS

* **the big boys** (sl.): the men in power, the most influential group, the leaders >*We'll have to wait and see what the big boys decide.*

BIG C.

— **the big C.** (sl.): cancer >*He's in the hospital, and I hear it's the big C.*

BIG CHEESE

* **big cheese** (sl.): important or influential person >*He's a big cheese in state government.*

BIG DEAL

* **big deal** (colloq.): important event or issue, important or influential person >*They're having some big deal at school tomorrow night.* >*She thinks her boyfriend's a real big deal.*

** **big deal!** (colloq., sarc.): that's nothing important! what of it? >*So your brother's a lawyer. Big deal!*

** **(it's) no big deal** (colloq.): it's not so important, it's not worth being concerned about, it's no problem >*It's no big deal if you get there a little late.*

BIG EASY

— **the Big Easy** (colloq.): New Orleans, Louisiana >*We heard a lot of Cajun music in the Big Easy.*

BIGGIE

— **biggie** (big´ē) (sl.): important or influential person, large or impressive thing >*Treat him nice. He's a biggie in* the front office. >The two trucking biggies in the area are talking about a merger.

* **(it's) no biggie** (sl.): it's not so important, it's not worth being concerned about, it's no problem >You can't pay me today? No biggie. Just bring it by next week.

BIG GUN

* **big gun** (sl.): powerful or influential person, leader (in an area) >They're bringing in the big guns to try to figure it out.

BIGGY

— **biggy** (see "BIGGIE")

BIG HEAD

* **big head** (colloq.): conceit, excessive sense of self-importance >She's had a big head ever since she started dating that rock star.

BIG HOUSE

— **the big house** (sl.): penitentiary >He ended up doin' ten to twenty years in the big house.

BIG LEAGUE

* **the big league(s)** (colloq.): area of greatest competition, highest professional level >Dave's a pretty good architect for small commercial projects, but he's not ready for the big leagues.

BIG-LEAGUE

— **big-league** (colloq.): in the highest competitive or professional level, important or significant >What's a big-league company like that doing in this dinky town?

BIG MAN

* **big man** (colloq.): man in authority, important person, boss >You got to talk with the big man to get the OK for this. >Jason's a big man on campus.

BIGMOUTH

** **bigmouth** (colloq.): overly talkative or indiscrete person >Who's the bigmouth that blabbed the secret to everyone?

BIGMOUTHED

— **bigmouthed** (colloq.): overly talkative, indiscrete >Tell your bigmouthed friend to shut up, will you?

BIG RIG

* **big rig** (colloq.): large truck (esp. with a tractor-trailer) >I hate it when the highway's full of big rigs.

BIG SHOT

** **big shot** (colloq.): important or influential person (also adj.) >Maggie's a big shot down at city hall. >He thinks he's got all the answers, with his big shot attitude.

BIG TALK

* **big talk** (colloq.): boastful talk, pretentious exaggeration, bragging (cf. "TALK big") >We've heard a lot of big talk, but they haven't shown us any results.

BIG-TICKET

— **big-ticket** (colloq.): high-priced, costing a lot of money >Those salesmen are always trying to push the big-ticket items.

BIG TIME

* **the big time** (colloq.): area of greatest competition, highest professional level >If this song's a hit, he'll make the big time.

BIG-TIME

** **big-time** (colloq.): in the highest competitive or professional level, important or significant (also adv.) >Dobson's a big-time lawyer in Chicago. >I hear he lost big-time in Vegas last week.

BIG WHEEL

* **big wheel** (colloq.): important or influential person >Dolly's a big wheel in this town. Nothing happens without her OK.

BIGWIG
* **bigwig** (colloq.): important or influential person >*Some bigwig from the state capital's coming to inspect the project.*

BIKE
** **bike** (bīk) (colloq.): bicycle or motorcycle >*Jimmy fell off his bike and skinned his knee.* >*He likes Harleys better than the Japanese bikes.*

BIKER
** **biker** (bī´kər) (colloq.): motorcycle gang member >*A bunch of bikers roared through town and scared old Mrs. Tyson half to death.*

BILL
— **bill** (sl.): one hundred dollars >*I gave him three bills for the stereo.*
— **fill the bill** (see **FILL**)
— **foot the bill** (see **FOOT**)

BILL OF GOODS
— **bill of goods** (colloq.): fraudulent article, misrepresented thing >*He sold you a bill of goods if you paid him full price for this discontinued model.*

BIMBO
* **bimbo** (bim´bō) (sl.): dumb or shallow person, silly or inept person (esp. a young woman) >*I can't believe he dumped his classy wife for that bimbo.*

BIND
** **bind** (colloq.): difficult or awkward situation >*I'm really in a bind this month. Could you lend me a hundred bucks?* >*What a bind you got yourself into with the law this time!*

BINGE
** **binge** (binj) (colloq.): period of intense overindulgence >*He went on a binge and drank for three days straight.* >*Their last shopping binge cost them two thousand bucks.*

BINGO
* **bingo!** (bing´gō/bĕng´gō) (sl.): that's it! that's right! it's ready! I've got it! eureka! >*Just zap it in the microwave*

for five minutes, and bingo—hot popcorn! >*Bingo! Here's the answer, on page twelve.*

BIO
— **bio** (bī´ō) (colloq.): biography >*His bio says he was in the Marines.*

BIRD
— **a little bird told me** (colloq.): I learned from a source I do not wish to reveal >*A little bird told me you'd like to go out with Beverly.*
— **... bird** (colloq.): ... person (seen as having some remarkable, usually neg., trait) >*The guy wearing all the earrings is a real weird bird.* >*My neighbor's a mean old bird.*
— **eat like a bird** (see **EAT**)
— **flip [s/one] the/a bird** (see **FLIP**)
— **the bird** (sl.): obscene gesture of contempt (the middle finger raised, with the palm of the hand toward the person making the gesture) >*I gave him the bird when he cut in front of me.*

BIRDBRAIN
* **birdbrain** (sl.): stupid or foolish person >*That birdbrain couldn't begin to figure it out.*

BIRD-DOG
— **bird-dog** (vt) (colloq.): secretly follow, keep under surveillance >*Bird-dog him everywhere he goes!*

BIRDS
* **for the birds** (colloq.): useless, worthless, uninteresting, unappetizing >*I think golf is for the birds.* >*That awful cafeteria food is for the birds.*
* **the birds and the bees** (colloq.): basic sex education (esp. for children) >*Have you told Johnny about the birds and the bees yet?*

BIRTHDAY SUIT
* **in [one's] birthday suit** (colloq.): naked >*He was just standing there in his birthday suit, with his clothes all over the floor.*

BIT

* **bit** (colloq.): pertinent matter, part of a story, particulars >*Tell me the bit about how you outran the cops.* >*The cost overrun bit in the contract has me worried.*

— **every bit** (see **EVERY**)

* **(...) bit** (colloq.): situation or actions (relevant to ...), habitual set of behaviors or attitudes (related to ...) >*Hey, don't try the tough-guy bit on me.* >*She cried, screamed, threatened—the whole bit.* >*Oh, no, not that bit again!*

BITCH

** **bitch**[1] (sl., freq. vulg., pej.): unpleasant woman, malicious or spiteful woman >*Rosalie can really be a bitch when things don't go right for her.*

** **bitch**[2] (sl., freq. vulg.): very difficult task, troublesome thing, arduous undertaking >*Getting that report done right was a bitch.* >*It's a bitch to pull the clutch outta that car.*

— **bitch**[3] (sl., freq. vulg.): complaint (esp. an unreasonable one) >*Bubba's always complainin' about somethin'. What's his bitch this time?*

** **bitch**[4] (vi) (sl., freq. vulg.): complain (esp. unreasonably) >*I'm tired of his bitchin' about every little thing he doesn't like.*

BITCHEN

— **bitchen** (bich´ən) (sl., freq. vulg.): wonderful, beautiful, impressive >*Wow! Did ya see that bitchen wave I caught?*

BITCHIN'

— **bitchin'** (see "BITCHEN")

BITCHY

* **bitchy** (bich´ē) (sl., freq. vulg.): spiteful, malicious, unpleasant (esp. a woman) >*I can't stand his bitchy wife.*

BITE

** **bite** (colloq.): small meal, snack >*Don't fix lunch for me. I'll grab a bite downtown.*

* **(about) bite/snap [s/one's] head off** (colloq.): respond [to s/one] quickly and with unexpected anger or aggression >*Herb about bit my head off when I asked him how his diet was going.* >*Don't mention her tax audit, or she'll snap your head off.*

* **bite the bullet** (colloq.): accept a loss, force (oneself) to endure a painful or damaging experience >*We're going to have to bite the bullet on this one. There's no way out of it.*

* **bite the dust** (colloq.): be defeated, fail, die >*They were the favored team, but they bit the dust in the first round.*

— **put the bite on** (sl.): try to borrow money from (esp. vigorously), borrow money from >*He put the bite on me for a few bucks, but I told him no.* >*He put the bite on her for a fiver, and she'll never get it back.*

— **will bite** (vi) (colloq.): be interested (in a proposition), go along (with s/thing proposed), accept (a deception) >*This is probably a trick, but I'll bite.* >*Go try pulling that on Fred—he'll bite.*

BITING

— **be biting [s/one]** (colloq.): be bothering or annoying [s/one] >*I don't know what's biting him, but he's real grumpy today.*

BITS

— **two/four/six bits** (colloq.): twenty-five/ fifty/seventy-five cents >*The newspaper's two bits.*

BIZ

— **... biz** (... biz) (colloq.): ... business >*How's the furniture biz these days?* >*She's been in show biz since the early days of TV.*

BLAB–BLEEDS

BLAB

* **blab¹** (blab) (vi, vt) (colloq.): speak indiscreetly (about), reveal (a secret) >*He blabbed to the cops.* >*Perkins blabbed the whole story to a reporter for some scandal magazine.*

* **blab²** (vi) (colloq.): speak incessantly, converse endlessly >*Henrietta talked nonstop for over an hour. She really loves to blab.*

BLABBERMOUTH

* **blabbermouth** (blab´ər mouth´) (colloq.): person who speaks indiscreetly or reveals secrets >*Don't say a thing to that blabbermouth unless you want the whole world to know.*

BLABBY

— **blabby¹** (bla´bē) (colloq.): indiscreet >*Be sure you don't tell your blabby sister the secret.*

— **blabby²** (colloq.): overly talkative >*His blabby brother told boring stories all night.*

BLACK

— **little black book** (see **LITTLE**)

BLACK AND WHITE

— **black and white** (colloq.): police patrol car >*Two more black and whites raced down the street.*

BLACK HAT

— **black hat** (colloq.): villain, unvirtuous character (in a story, esp. a Western) (cf. **"WHITE HAT"**) >*Darryl's the black hat in this situation.* >*He always played a black hat in those old Westerns.*

BLAH

* **blah, blah(, blah)** (blä) (sl.): and so on and so forth, and the like >*He said he loved her, couldn't live without her, blah, blah.*

BLAH-BLAH(-BLAH)

— **blah-blah(-blah)** (blä) (sl.): boring talk, chatter >*I can't take any more of that dummy's blah-blah-blah.*

BLAHS

— **the blahs** (… bläz) (sl.): malaise, lethargy, mild depression, discomfort >*I woke up with the blahs and didn't even wanna get outta bed.*

BLANKETY-BLANK

— **blankety-blank** (blăng´ki tē blangk´) (colloq.): contemptible, detestable >*Get your blankety-blank feet off the coffee table!*

BLANKS

— **shoot/fire blanks** (see **SHOOT**)

BLAST

* **blast¹** (vt) (colloq.): criticize, denounce >*The opposition blasted the governor's policy.*

— **blast²** (vi, vt) (colloq.): shoot, use a firearm (against) >*He pulled a gun and started blasting.* >*They blasted him with a shotgun.*

** **a blast** (sl.): a great time, a great deal of fun >*We had a blast at the carnival.* >*His party's gonna be a blast.*

— **blast …!** (colloq.): curse …! I find … contemptible! >*Blast his concerns! He's got nothing to do with it.*

BLASTED

— **blasted¹** (colloq.): cursed, annoying, contemptible >*I can't get this blasted radio to work right.*

— **blasted²** (sl.): very drunk, intoxicated >*They bought a bottle of rum and got blasted.*

BLAZES

— **blazes** (colloq.): hell >*They told him to go to blazes.* >*It's hotter than blazes in here!*

BLEED

— **bleed [s/one] (dry)** (colloq.): force (excessive) payments from [s/one], extort (all) [s/one's] money >*The loan sharks are bleeding the guy dry.*

BLEEDS

— **my heart bleeds for …!** (see **HEART**)

BLESSED

— **blessed** (colloq.): cursed, annoying, contemptible >*Every blessed time I call, the line's busy.* >*Get your blessed hands off my things!*

BLIMP

— **blimp** (sl., pej.): very fat person >*When did your uncle get so fat? He's a blimp!*

BLIND

* **(as) blind as a bat** (colloq.): blind, having poor vision >*You're as blind as a bat if you can't tell what she's wearing.*

— **steal/rob [s/one] blind** (see STEAL)

BLIND DATE

* **blind date**[1] (colloq.): date between people who have not met >*I hate going out on blind dates.*

* **blind date**[2] (colloq.): person that (one) has not met and with whom (one) has a date >*Hey, his blind date turned out to be real good-looking.*

BLINDSIDE

— **blindside** (vt) (colloq.): attack or criticize unexpectedly >*The guy blindsided me at the meeting with some wild accusations.*

BLINK

* **on the blink** (colloq.): not working properly, in need of repair (said of machines) >*Better call the repairman. That damn washer's on the blink again.*

BLISTER

— **blister [s/one's] butt** (sl.): spank [s/one], thrash [s/one] (as punishment) >*He blistered Hal's butt for breakin' the window.*

BLITZED

— **blitzed** (blitst) (sl.): very drunk, intoxicated >*Don't let him drive. He's blitzed.*

BLOCK

— **be a chip off the old block** (see CHIP)

— **have been around the block (a few times)** (see AROUND)

— **knock [s/one's] block off** (see KNOCK)

— **new kid on the block** (see NEW)

BLOCKBUSTER

** **blockbuster** (colloq.): very successful thing or undertaking, big hit (esp. a film) >*The movie was a blockbuster. Its box office take was incredible.*

BLOCKHEAD

— **blockhead** (colloq.): stupid or inept person, fool >*That blockhead'll never get it right.*

BLONDIE

* **blondie** (voc.) (colloq.): blond person >*Hey, blondie, you're getting sunburned.*

BLOOD

— **blood** (sl.): black man (used esp. among blacks) >*Then a blood came up and asked me what was happenin'.*

— **sweat blood** (see SWEAT)

— **too rich for [s/one's] blood** (see RICH)

BLOODY

— **bloody** (colloq.): cursed, annoying, contemptible >*It's a bloody shame he lost.* >*Get your bloody hands off me!*

— **scream bloody murder** (see SCREAM)

BLOOMING

— **blooming** (sl.): cursed, annoying, contemptible >*I can't put up with his bloomin' wisecracks.*

BLOOPER

* **blooper** (blū'pər) (colloq.): embarrassing mistake made in public (esp. a spoken one), faux pas >*The senator made a blooper that's going to get him in a lot of trouble.*

BLOTTO

— **blotto** (blot'ō) (sl.): very drunk, intoxicated >*Of course ya don't remember anything. You were blotto.*

BLOW

BLOW

** **blow**[1] (vt) (sl.): ruin through ineptitude, lose through carelessness or error, fail to take advantage of (an opportunity) >*They blew the game in the ninth inning.* >*Don't blow it with Bess, 'cause you'll never find another like her.*

* **blow**[2] (vt) (sl.): spend (money) (esp. recklessly), squander (money) >*He blew two hundred bucks on that stupid date.*

— **blow**[3] (vi, vt) (sl.): leave (from), take off (from) >*I'm gonna take my money and blow.* >*They blew the joint and headed up the street.*

— **(about) blow a gasket** (sl.): become furious, lose (one's) temper >*He about blew a gasket when they scratched his car.*

— **let/blow/cut a fart** (see **FART**)

— **blow a fuse** (sl.): become furious, lose (one's) temper >*Marty blew a fuse when he saw the dent in his car.*

* **blow away**[1] (vt) (sl.): astonish or overwhelm, greatly impress >*The film's fantastic! It blew me away.*

* **blow away**[2] (vt) (sl.): defeat decisively >*That team was no good. We blew 'em away.*

— **blow away**[3] (vt) (sl.): kill (with a firearm) >*They blew the guy away with a shotgun.*

— **blow/lose [one's] cool** (see **COOL**)

— **pop/blow [one's] cork** (see **CORK**)

— **blow [s/one's, one's] cover** (see **COVER**)

— **blow in/into** (sl.): arrive (at) (esp. unexpectedly) >*Look who just blew in.* >*When did you blow into town?*

— **blow it out your ass/asshole!** (vulg.): (interj. to express great anger or contempt to s/one) >*Same to you, buddy—blow it out your ass!*

— **blow it out your ear!** (sl.): (interj. to express great anger or contempt to s/one) >*If ya don't like it, blow it out your ear!*

* **blow [s/one's] mind** (sl.): astonish or overwhelm [s/one], greatly impress [s/one] >*It blew my mind when he told me he'd been in prison for murder.*

— **let/blow off steam** (see **STEAM**)

— **blow [s/one] out of the water** (sl.): defeat [s/one] decisively >*My lawyer blew their star witness outta the water.*

— **blow/toot [one's] own horn** (colloq.): brag, boast, promote [oneself] >*That jerk's always blowing his own horn. What an ego!*

— **blow smoke** (see **SMOKE**)

— **blow [one's] stack** (sl.): become furious, lose [one's] temper >*My boss is gonna blow his stack when he finds out how I messed up this deal.*

— **blow the lid off (of)** (colloq.): expose publicly, reveal (a scandal or illegal activity) >*This report's going to blow the lid off that influence peddling racket.*

* **blow the whistle (on)** (colloq.): denounce (s/one) to the authorities, expose (s/one's) wrongdoing >*He blew the whistle on his boss when he discovered the embezzlement.* >*The scam's over if anyone blows the whistle.*

* **blow [one's] top** (sl.): become furious, lose [one's] temper >*She called him a jerk, and he blew his top.*

** **blow up (at)** (vi) (colloq.): become furious (with), lose (one's) temper (with) >*Pratt blew up at his kid because she locked the keys in the car.*

* **blow up in [s/one's] face** (colloq.): have unexpected and very negative results for [s/one], backfire on [s/one] (said of a plan or action) >*Your friend's scheme is liable to blow up in his face.*

* **blow [s/thing] wide open** (colloq.): expose [s/thing] publicly, reveal [s/thing] (a scandal or illegal activity) >*A*

reporter found out about the politician's mistress and blew it wide open.

BLOW-HARD

— **blow-hard** (sl.): obnoxious boaster, braggart >*Everyone's sick and tired of hearin' that blow-hard talk about how much money he makes.*

BLOW JOB

** **blow job** (vulg.): act of fellatio >*He said she gave him a blow job.*

BLOWOUT

— **blowout** (sl.): extravagant party, wild celebration >*They had a big blowout at the club to celebrate his graduation.*

BLUE

* **blue** (colloq.): depressed, gloomy, sad >*It helps to talk to someone when you're feeling blue.*

* **until/till [one] is blue in the face** (colloq.): until [one] tires out, until [one] gives up in frustration (esp. while speaking in vain) >*You can complain till you're blue in the face, but it won't do any good.*

BLUES

* **the blues** (colloq.): a state of depression or melancholy >*That song gives me the blues.*

BLUE STREAK

— **talk a blue streak** (colloq.): talk incessantly, be very talkative >*Miles talks a blue streak—you can't get a word in edgewise.*

BLUFF

— **call [s/one's] bluff** (see **CALL**)

B.M.

— **B.M.** (colloq.): bowel movement, act of defecating >*He said he hasn't had a B.M. in three days.*

B.M.O.C.

— **B.M.O.C.** (= "big man on campus") (colloq., freq. sarc.): popular or important male student >*He got on the basketball team, so now he thinks he's a B.M.O.C.*

B.O.

* **B.O.** (colloq.): body odor, (person's) bad smell >*After that workout I had some bad B.O.*

BOARD

— **(as) flat as a board** (see **FLAT**)

BOAT

— **miss the boat** (see **MISS**)

— **rock the boat** (see **ROCK**)

BOD

* **bod** (bod) (sl.): (person's) body (esp. seen in relation to health or beauty) >*Aerobic exercise is good for the bod.* >*She's got a great bod!*

BOGUS

— **bogus** (sl.): bad, unfair, false >*Him lyin' to me like that is really bogus, man.*

BOILING

— **boiling mad** (colloq.): very angry, furious >*The price increases have got him boiling mad.*

BOLONEY

— **boloney** (see "BALONEY")

BOMB

** **bomb**[1] (sl.): complete failure, flop >*The book was a bomb. It didn't sell even a thousand copies.*

— **bomb**[2] (sl.): large and powerful automobile >*That old bomb can really move!*

** **bomb**[3] (vi) (sl.): be a complete failure, flop >*The movie bombed at the box office.*

* **bomb**[4] (vt) (sl.): fail miserably, do very poorly in/on >*Herb said he bombed the algebra exam.* >*I hope I don't bomb this interview.*

* **the bomb** (colloq.): the atomic bomb, the first bomb of nuclear war >*When they drop the bomb, it's all over.*

BOMBED

* **bombed** (sl.): very drunk, intoxicated >*He got bombed at the party yesterday.*

BOMBSHELL
— **bombshell[1]** (sl.): very attractive and sexy woman >*Marilyn Monroe was a bombshell.*

— **bombshell[2]** (colloq.): shocking thing, sensational news >*The news of his indictment was a bombshell.* >*She dropped a bombshell when she told them she was pregnant.*

BONE
— **(as) dry as a bone** (see **DRY**)

— **bone up (on)** (colloq.): study hard (for), review through study >*You'd better bone up before the test.* >*I studied French in high school, but I need to bone up on it before I go to Paris.*

— **have a bone to pick with** (colloq.): have a complaint to register with, have a dispute to settle with >*Come here, you rat! I've got a bone to pick with you.*

BONEHEAD
— **bonehead** (sl.): stupid or inept person, fool (also adj.) >*You don't expect that bonehead to fix it, do ya? >What a bonehead thing to say!*

BONEHEADED
— **boneheaded** (sl.): stupid, foolish >*That was a boneheaded thing to do! >I expected that boneheaded brother of his to screw up.*

BONER
— **boner[1]** (bō´nər) (sl.): blunder, faux pas, mistake >*Him asking her her age in front of everyone was a real boner.*

— **boner[2]** (vulg.): erect penis >*He hoped no one would notice his boner while he was dancin' with her.*

— **pull a boner** (sl.): blunder, make a faux pas, make a mistake >*I pulled a real boner by invitin' her ex-husband to the party, too.*

BONES
— **jump [s/one's] bones** (see **JUMP**)

* **make no bones about** (colloq.): leave no doubts about, keep no secrets regarding, deal openly with >*Porter's a die-hard liberal, and he makes no bones about it.*

BONEYARD
— **boneyard** (colloq.): cemetery >*Bertie won't walk by the boneyard at night.*

BONK
— **bonk[1]** (bongk) (sl.): hit, blow >*I think that bonk on the head made him a little daffy.*

— **bonk[2]** (vt) (sl.): hit, strike >*He bonked his knee on the table leg when he got up.*

BONKERS
* **bonkers[1]** (bong´kərz) (sl.): crazy, mentally unbalanced >*That weird dude is really bonkers.*

— **bonkers[2]** (sl.): wildly enthusiastic, uncontrollably excited >*The fans went bonkers when he scored.*

BOO
* **not say "boo"** (… bū) (colloq.): not say anything at all >*She's so shy she didn't say "boo" all night.*

BOOB
** **boob[1]** (būb) (sl., freq. vulg.): (woman's) breast >*She thinks her boobs are too big.*

— **boob[2]** (sl.): stupid person, fool >*Why didn't that boob just call instead of comin' here to tell us?*

BOO-BOO
* **boo-boo[1]** (bū´bū´) (sl.): silly mistake, small error >*I think I made a boo-boo by mentioning his tax troubles.*

* **boo-boo[2]** (colloq.): minor injury (used esp. with children) >*Daddy, I got a boo-boo on my finger.*

BOOB TUBE
** **boob tube** (būb …) (sl.): television (esp. seen as neg.) >*Doesn't Eva get tired of watchin' the boob tube every night?*

BOOBY
— **booby** (bū´bē) (sl., freq. vulg.): (woman's) breast >*Jeanie's startin' to get boobies.*

BOOBY HATCH

— **booby hatch** (bŭ´bē ...) (sl.): insane asylum, mental institution >*They threw him in the booby hatch after he attacked a bunch of people for no reason.*

BOOGER

* **booger**[1] (bŭ´gər) (sl., freq. vulg.): piece of nose mucus (esp. dried) >*His hanky was full of boogers.*

— **booger**[2] (sl.): person or thing (esp. seen as troublesome or endearing) >*One day I'll catch that little booger and beat him up.* >*See if this booger will fit over the opening.* >*That kid's a cute little booger.*

BOOGIE

— **boogie** (bŭg´ē/bŭg´ē) (vi) (sl.): dance, party, have fun >*Where's the party? I'm ready to boogie!*

BOO-HOO

— **boo-hoo**[1] (bū´hū´) (colloq., freq. sarc.): (representation of the sound of crying) >*Boo-hoo! I really feel for you.*

— **boo-hoo**[2] (bū´hū´) (vi) (colloq.): cry noisily >*You can cut your boo-hooing because nobody cares.*

BOOK

— [neg.] **crack a book** (see CRACK)

** **(go) by the book** (colloq.): (proceed) according to standard procedure, (act) following the rules or established steps >*Go by the book the first few times you do it.* >*He's got no complaint—we did everything by the book.*

* **in [s/one's] book** (colloq.): in [s/one's] opinion, according to [s/one's] values >*In my book, it's wrong to lie.*

— **one for the book(s)** (see ONE)

— **read [s/one] like a book** (see READ)

— **throw the book at** (see THROW)

— **wrote the book on** (see WROTE)

BOOKIE

** **bookie** (bŭk´ē) (colloq.): person who takes and pays off bets (esp. as an illegal business), bookmaker >*His bookie left town after he placed a big bet.*

BOOKS

— **cook the books** (see COOK)

— **hit the books** (see HIT)

BOOM

— **lower the boom (on)** (see LOWER)

BOOM-BOOM(-BOOM)

— **boom-boom(-boom)** (sl.): in fast succession, one right after another >*Business was slow in the morning, but in the afternoon the customers came in boom-boom-boom.*

BOOM BOX

* **boom box** (sl.): large and powerful portable radio or tape player (esp. one carried or used on the street) >*Turn down that damn boom box, will ya?!*

BOONDOCKS

* **the boondocks** (... bŭn´doks´) (colloq.): back country, place far from civilization, remote area >*He lives way out in the boondocks and hardly ever gets into town.*

BOONIES

* **the boonies** (... bŭ´nēz) (sl.): back country, place far from civilization, remote area >*Ike has a cabin out in the boonies.*

BOOT

— **boot (out)** (vt) (sl.): dismiss, fire, oust >*She kept botchin' things up at work, so they booted her out.* >*I hear he got booted yesterday.*

— **get the boot** (sl.): be fired or dismissed, be ousted >*You'll get the boot if the boss finds out what you've been up to.*

— **give [s/one] the boot** (sl.): fire or dismiss [s/one], oust [s/one] >*They gave him the boot after he came in late for the fifth time.*

* **to boot** (colloq.): in addition, as extra >*He paid me the hundred he owed me and twenty bucks to boot as interest.*

BOOTS

— **shake in [one's] boots/shoes** (see SHAKE)

— **you (can) bet your boots** (see BET)

BOOZE

** **booze[1]** (būz) (sl.): alcoholic drink (esp. hard liquor) >*You bring the eats, and I'll bring the booze.*

* **booze[2]** (vi) (sl.): drink heavily >*He's out boozin' with his drinkin' buddies.*

* **booze it up** (sl.): drink heavily, have a drinking spree >*Everyone boozed it up at his bachelor party.*

BOOZED-UP

* **boozed-up** (būzd´up´) (sl.): drunk >*They came in all boozed-up, yellin' and carryin' on.*

BOOZEHOUND

— **boozehound** (būz´hound´) (sl.): drunkard, heavy drinker >*He hangs around the tavern with a bunch of other boozehounds.*

BOOZER

* **boozer** (bū´zər) (sl.): heavy drinker, drunkard >*She used to be quite a boozer, but she's been sober for over two years now.*

BOP

— **bop[1]** (bop) (sl.): hit, blow >*That was a nasty bop ya took on the head.*

— **bop[2]** (vt) (sl.): hit, strike >*Behave or I'll bop ya one.*

— **bop (on) over/down/up to** (sl.): go to, proceed to (esp. impulsively) >*Later, we decided to bop on over to Joey's house to see what he was doin'. >Hey, let's bop down to Willy's for a drink.*

BORN

* **wasn't born yesterday** (colloq.): am/is not naive, can't easily be fooled >*We're going to put this in writing. I wasn't born yesterday, you know.*

BOTHERED

— **(all) hot and bothered** (see HOT)

BOTTLE

— **hit the bottle** (see HIT)

BOTTOM

* **bottom** (colloq.): buttocks, rear >*My bottom is really hurting after that twelve-hour bus ride.*

— **low/bottom man on the totem pole** (see LOW)

* **hit bottom** (colloq.): reach the worst or most desperate point (of a long and unhappy experience) >*When she started stealing to buy drugs, she knew she'd hit bottom and decided to get some help.*

— **scrape the bottom of the barrel** (see SCRAPE)

BOTTOM DOLLAR

— **[one's] bottom dollar** (colloq.): the last of [one's] money >*He just bet his bottom dollar on the game. >I lost my bottom dollar in that scam.*

BOTTOM LINE

** **bottom line** (colloq.): ultimate decision, crucial fact, fundamental truth, decisive conclusion >*We've looked at it from every legal angle, and the bottom line is that you're going to have to move out. >Stop stalling! What's the bottom line?*

BOTTOMS

* **bottoms up!** (colloq.): drink up! let's drink! >*You still on your first beer? Come on, bottoms up!*

BOUNCE

** **bounce[1]** (vi) (colloq.): (for a check to) be sent back by a bank because of insufficient funds >*This check better not bounce, or you're in trouble.*

— **bounce[2]** (vt) (colloq.): eject, dismiss >*They bounced him from the nightclub after he started a fight. >I got bounced from my job today.*

* **bounce [s/thing] off [s/one]** (sl.): consult [s/one] about [s/thing], get [s/one's] reaction or suggestions concerning [s/thing] >*Let me bounce*

your idea off my boss before we go ahead on it.

** **bounce (right) back** (vi) (colloq.): recover (quickly) >*She bounced right back from her operation.* >*When do you think this sluggish economy will bounce back?*

BOUNCER

** **bouncer** (colloq.): person employed to eject disorderly patrons (esp. from a nightclub) >*That huge guy over there is the bouncer.*

BOUNCES

— **that's the way the ball bounces** (see **BALL**)

BOUNCING

— **bouncing off the walls** (sl.): very agitated or nervous, frantic >*The kids were bouncin' off the walls after bein' kept inside all day.*

BOWELS

— **get [one's] bowels in an uproar** (sl.): become very upset or anxious >*Now, don't get your bowels in an uproar. Everything's gonna be OK.*

BOWL

— **bowl over** (vt) (colloq.): greatly surprise, astound, shock >*Hearing him swearing just bowled us over.*

BOWWOW

— **bowwow** (sl.): ugly woman >*He wants me to take his sister out, but I hear she's a real bowwow.*

BOX

— **box** (vulg.): vagina >*He was just starin' at the centerfold's box.*

BOY

** **boy!** (colloq.): (interj. to express surprise or wonder) >*Boy, is it ever hot today!*

— **old boy** (colloq.): man (esp. seen as contemptible or extraordinary) >*That old boy'd as soon shoot you as look at you.*

— **that's my boy!** (see **THAT'S**)

BOYS

* **the boys** (colloq.): group of men (esp. friends) >*He's down at the club having some beers with the boys.*

BOZO

* **bozo** (bō´zō) (sl.): obnoxious or contemptibly stupid person, fool >*Keep that bozo outta my way!*

BRACELETS

— **the bracelets** (sl.): set of handcuffs >*The cops put the bracelets on him and hauled him off to jail.*

BRAIN

** **brain**[1] (colloq.): very intelligent person >*Seymour's a brain—he aces every test.*

— **brain**[2] (vt) (sl.): hit hard on the head >*The pitcher brained the batter with a high, inside fastball.*

— **have [s/thing] on the brain** (colloq.): be obsessed with [s/thing], constantly think about [s/thing] >*What a sports fanatic! He's got sports on the brain.*

— **pick [s/one's] brain** (see **PICK**)

BRAINCHILD

— **[s/one's] brainchild** (colloq.): [s/one's] invention or plan (esp. a creative or impressive one) >*This form for keeping better track of our expenses was my brainchild.*

BRAIN-PICKING

— **brain-picking** (colloq.): act of getting information or ideas from another (esp. from an expert) (cf. "**PICK [s/one's] brain**") >*With a little brain-picking and a little experimenting we should be able to come up with a good plan.*

BRAINS

— **beat [one's] brains out** (see **BEAT**)

— **beat [s/one's] brains out** (see **BEAT**)

— **fuck/screw [s/one's] brains out** (see **FUCK**)

** **the brains** (sl.): intellectual leader, main strategist >*He gets all the publicity, but his wife is the brains of the operation.*

BRAINY

* **brainy** (colloq.): intelligent >*He's afraid to go out with brainy girls.*

BRAND

— **(brand) spanking new** (see SPANKING)

BRASS

— **brass** (colloq.): impudence, audacity, brashness >*He's got a lot of brass asking her for a date in front of her fiancé.*

* **the (top) brass** (colloq.): high officials, leadership >*The company brass is coming tomorrow to look over the project.* >*It's up to the top brass.*

BRASS TACKS

— **get down to brass tacks** (colloq.): discuss the essentials, take up the fundamental concerns >*Those are minor details. Let's get down to brass tacks.*

BRASSY

— **brassy** (colloq.): impudent, audacious, brash >*You got to be pretty brassy to confront the boss like that.*

BREAD

— **bread** (sl.): money >*I hate the job, but I need the bread.*

BREAD AND BUTTER

* **bread and butter** (colloq.): means of support, basic source of income >*When I can play at the club it pays better, but these party gigs are my bread and butter.*

BREADBASKET

— **the breadbasket** (sl.): (one's) stomach, (one's) abdomen >*He got kicked right in the old breadbasket.*

BREAK

** **break**[1] (colloq.): chance, unexpected opportunity, piece of luck >*Janet got her break in show business when she was offered that part.* >*Getting that big contract was a real break.*

** **break**[2] (colloq.): act of leniency or clemency, act of mercy >*The cop gave me a break and let me off with just a warning.*

— **[for] all hell [to] break loose** (see HELL)

— **break a leg!** (colloq.): do well! (in a performance) >*You're on, kid—break a leg!*

— **bust/break [one's] ass** (see BUST)

— **bust/break [one's] balls** (see BUST)

— **bust/break [s/one's] balls** (see BUST)

— **break down and ...** (colloq.): abandon (one's) opposition or reluctance to (doing s/thing), cease resisting (doing s/thing) >*She's been asking me for years to get a new car, so I finally broke down and bought one.*

** **break even** (vi) (colloq.): neither gain nor lose, come out without profit or loss >*I almost broke even gambling when I was in Vegas.*

— **break [s/one's] face** (sl.): hit [s/one] hard in the face, beat [s/one] up >*Try that again, buddy, and I'll break your face!*

* **break [one's] neck** (colloq.): work hard, put out great effort (to reach a goal) >*Gomez has been breaking his neck to finish the job on time.*

* **break the ice** (colloq.): overcome initial reserve, succeed in relaxing a tense or formal atmosphere (esp. in a social setting) >*He broke the ice at the dinner party with a funny story.*

* **break up** (vt) (colloq.): cause to laugh hard >*That guy breaks me up with the faces he makes.*

** **give me a break!** (sl.): stop trying to fool me! stop being unreasonable or ridiculous with me! >*Gimme a break! No way I'm gonna pay ya before the job's done.* >*That jerk for mayor? Gimme a break!*

BREAKS

* **the breaks** (colloq.): fate, how things happen (esp. neg. things) >*That's the breaks, kid. You win some, and you lose some.*

BREATH

— **not hold [one's] breath** (see **HOLD**)

— **save [one's] breath** (see **SAVE**)

BREATHER

** **breather** (colloq.): rest period, break >*Whew! Let's take a breather.*

BREATHING

* **breathing down [s/one's] neck** (colloq.): pursuing [s/one], putting pressure on [s/one] >*He's on the run with the cops breathing down his neck. >Let me work alone! I don't like people breathing down my neck.*

BREECHES

— **too big for [one's] breeches** (see "too **BIG** for [one's] britches")

BREEZE

** **a breeze** (colloq.): a very easy thing or task >*This machine's a breeze to run. >Getting people to help with this will be a breeze.*

— **breeze in** (vi) (sl.): arrive with a carefree attitude >*Todd breezed in about eleven and didn't say a word about comin' so late.*

* **breeze through [s/thing]** (colloq.): finish [s/thing] quickly and with little effort >*Julie breezed through the math test. She really knows that stuff.*

— **shoot the breeze** (see **SHOOT**)

BREW

* **brew** (sl.): (can or bottle of) beer >*How about a cold brew to beat the heat?*

BREWSKY

— **brewsky** (brū´skē) (sl.): (can or bottle of) beer >*A nice cold brewsky would be great right now.*

BRICK

— **(about) shit a brick** (see **SHIT**)

BRICKS

— **hit the bricks** (see **HIT**)

— **like a ton of bricks** (see **TON**)

BRIGHT-EYED

* **bright-eyed and bushy-tailed** (colloq.): alert and eager, energetic and enthusiastic >*They were on the job at eight sharp, all bright-eyed and bushy-tailed.*

BRING

* **bring down the house/the house down** (colloq.): be wildly applauded, greatly please the audience >*He brought down the house with his portrayal of Hamlet. >This act'll bring the house down.*

* **bring home the bacon** (colloq.): provide money to live on, support a family >*Yeah, Stu's not too bright, but he brings home the bacon.*

— **bring home the groceries** (colloq.): provide money to live on, support a family >*She doesn't care if he's romantic or not as long as he brings home the groceries.*

BRIT

— **Brit** (*brit*) (colloq., freq. pej.): British >*The Brits won that battle.*

BRITCHES

— **too big for [one's] britches** (see **BIG**)

BRO

— **bro** (brō) (voc.) (sl.): friend, chum (used with a male) >*Hey, bro, what's happenin'?*

BROAD

* **broad** (sl., pej.): woman >*We don't want no broads around when we're playin' poker.*

BROKE

** **broke** (colloq.): penniless, with no money >*You had fifty bucks yesterday, and now you're broke?*

— **flat broke** (see **FLAT**)

— **go for broke** (colloq.): bet everything, apply all resources (to achieve s/thing)

>*Let's go for broke. If it works out, we'll make a bundle of money.*

BROKEN

— **(like) a broken record** (colloq.): person who harps (on s/thing), person who insists tiresomely (on some theme) >*The guy's like a broken record. Can't he talk about anything except how we need to crack down on crime?*

BRONX

— **Bronx cheer** (brongks ...) (colloq.): (noise expressing contempt or disapproval made by extending the tongue between the lips and blowing) >*What a lousy actor! He got more Bronx cheers than applause.*

BROTHER

* **brother**[1] (colloq.): black man (used esp. among blacks) >*The brothers got to stick together at a time like this.*

— **brother**[2] (voc.) (colloq.): friend, mister (esp. used with a male stranger) >*Can you spare some change, brother?*

* **brother!** (colloq.): (interj. to express surprise, wonder, or contempt) >*Brother! Did you see that shot she made? >Oh, brother! Not that lecture again!*

BROWN-BAG

* **brown-bag it** (colloq.): take (one's) lunch from home (esp. in a brown paper bag, esp. to work) >*I can't afford to eat in the plant cafeteria every day. I'm going to start brown-bagging it.*

BROWNIE POINT

— **Brownie point** (brou´nē ...) (colloq., freq. sarc.): credit obtained or perceived as obtained from s/one whom (one) wants to impress (esp. when obtained through flattery or obsequiousness) >*Burgess is trying to chalk up Brownie points with the boss by volunteering for his community-service project.*

BROWN-NOSE

* **brown-nose** (vi, vt) (sl.): be servile or obsequious (with) to gain favor, adulate,

flatter to gain favor >*Ya won't get ahead here by brown-nosin'. >He told his wife to brown-nose the general's wife.*

BROWN-NOSER

* **brown-noser** (sl.): person who is servile or obsequious to gain favor, adulator, servile flatterer >*What a brown-noser! He's always tellin' the dean what a great job he's doin'.*

BRUISER

* **bruiser** (colloq.): large and powerful man >*The bouncer was a big bruiser that must have weighed 300 pounds.*

BRUISING

— **cruising for a bruising** (see CRUISING)

BRUSH

* **brush up (on)** (colloq.): review (s/thing), regain previous knowledge or skill (of) >*I used to know a lot of math, but I need to brush up. >I'll brush up on my German before I leave for Munich.*

BRUSH-OFF

* **the brush-off** (colloq.): a snubbing, a rebuff, a refusal to listen, an abrupt turndown >*I tried to strike up a conversation, but I got the brush-off. >He gave us the brush-off when we brought up the subject of donations.*

B.S.

** **B.S.**[1] (= "bullshit") (sl., freq. vulg.): lies, false or exaggerated story, nonsense >*If ya believe that B.S., you're crazy.*

* **B.S.**[2] (= "bullshit") (sl., freq. vulg.): bad treatment, unjust dealings >*This intimidation B.S. has got to stop.*

* **B.S.**[3] (= "bullshit") (sl., freq. vulg.): annoying or tedious work or demands >*Who thought up this B.S. of recordin' every telephone message?*

** **B.S.**[4] (= "bullshit") (vi, vt) (sl., freq. vulg.): lie (to), tell false or exaggerated stories (to), speak nonsense (to) >*Don't*

pay him no mind—he just likes to B.S.
>That can't be! You're B.S.in' me.

B.S.ER

* **B.S.er** (= "bullshitter") (sl., freq. vulg.):
person who lies, person who tells false
or exaggerated stories or speaks
nonsense >Don't believe everything
Barry says. He's quite a B.S.er.

BUB

— **bub** (bub) (voc.) (colloq.): friend, mister
(used esp. with a male stranger, freq. in
a contentious way) >Hey, bub, gotta
match? >Just watch your step, bub!

BUBBLEGUMMER

— **bubblegummer** (bub´əl gu´mər) (sl.):
adolescent, young teenager >All the
bubblegummers think that band's the
greatest.

BUBBLY

* **bubbly** (colloq.): champagne >We
drank a little bubbly and had a good
time.

BUBBY

— **bubby** (see "BOOBY")

BUCK

** **buck**[1] (colloq.): dollar >I'm sure it
costs over a hundred bucks.

— **buck**[2] (vi, vt) (colloq.): resist, put up
opposition (to), object (to) >The
taxpayers are going to buck if the
government takes away that deduction.
>You can bet they're going to buck that
new requirement.

— **bang for [one's] buck** (see BANG)

— **buck for** (colloq.): strive for, work hard
toward, vie for >Krause has been
putting in a lot of extra hours lately. I
guess he's bucking for a promotion.

— **buck naked** (colloq.): completely naked
>When the curtain opened, he was
standing there buck naked.

— **pass the buck** (see PASS)

BUCKET

— **kick the bucket** (see KICK)

BUCKET OF BOLTS

— **bucket of bolts** (sl.): dilapidated vehicle
>You think that bucket of bolts will
make it all the way to Vancouver?

BUCKS

** **(big) bucks** (sl.): a large amount of
money >It takes bucks to buy a car like
that. >He makes big bucks as a
corporate lawyer.

— **... dollars/bucks says** (see DOLLARS)

— **like a million dollars/bucks** (see
MILLION)

BUD

— **bud** (voc.) (colloq.): friend, mister (used
esp. with a male stranger) >Say, bud!
Could you tell me how to get to Adams
Street?

BUDDY

* **buddy** (bud´ē) (colloq.): friend, chum
(also voc.; when voc., used esp. with a
male stranger, freq. in a contentious
way) >One of my buddies just got
arrested, and I got to go bail him out of
jail. >Hey, buddy! Watch out for that
wet paint!

— **buddy up to** (colloq.): act friendly
toward (to gain favor) >I see Conrad's
been buddying up to Joan ever since she
was put in charge of scheduling
vacations.

BUDDY-BUDDY

* **buddy-buddy** (bud´ē bud´ē) (sl.): very
close or friendly, intimate (esp. in a
conniving way) >Something fishy's
goin' on. Those two have been actin'
real buddy-buddy lately.

BUFF

** **... buff** (colloq.): ... enthusiast, person
interested in and knowledgeable about
... >Science fiction buffs are waiting
for his new novel to hit the bookstores.

— **in the buff** (colloq.): completely naked
>She posed in the buff for some girlie
magazine.

BUFFALO

— **buffalo¹** (vt) (sl.): puzzle, baffle, bewilder >*This engine's got me buffaloed. I can't find what's makin' it run rough.*

— **buffalo²** (vt) (sl.): intimidate, overawe >*Don't let 'em buffalo ya. You're smarter than any of 'em.*

BUG

** **bug¹** (colloq.): virus or microorganism (that makes one ill) >*She caught a bug somewhere and is staying in bed for a couple of days.*

** **bug²** (colloq.): defect, minor malfunction or problem (esp. in s/thing electronic or mechanical) >*When they get all the bugs out of this model, it'll be a real nice truck.* >*There's a bug somewhere in the software.*

* **bug³** (colloq.): hidden microphone (to record secretly) >*The cops placed a bug in his hotel room to gather info.*

** **bug⁴** (vt) (colloq.): annoy, bother >*It bugs me that I can't find my glasses.* >*Don't bug him! He's trying to study.*

* **bug⁵** (vt) (colloq.): place a hidden microphone in/on (to record secretly) >*Have they finished bugging the suspect's apartment?*

— **... bug¹** (colloq.): ... enthusiast, person interested in ... >*Clint's a sports car bug. He owns six of them.*

— **... bug²** (colloq.): ... fad, ... craze, ... urge >*When the skateboard bug hit school, every kid wanted one.* >*When I see my suitcases in the closet, I get the travel bug.*

* **bug off!** (sl.): go away! >*Who invited you? Bug off!*

— **bug out** (vi) (sl.): escape, flee >*If he shows with his goons, we bug out, got it?* >*When big Larry got mad, I bugged outta there fast.*

— **put a bug in [s/one's] ear** (colloq.): give [s/one] an idea or suggestion (esp.

in hopes of generating action favorable to one) >*I put a bug in her ear about getting a new coffeepot, and the next day it was there.*

BUGGER

— **bugger** (see "BOOGER¹")

BUGGY

— **buggy¹** (sl.): automobile (esp. an old one) >*How much ya want for this buggy?*

— **buggy²** (sl.): extremely nervous or anxious, crazy >*These brats are makin' me buggy!*

BUILD

— **light/build a fire under** (see **LIGHT**)

BUILDUP

* **buildup** (colloq.): publicity, systematic promotion or praise >*They gave the comic a big buildup for weeks before he came, but I didn't think he was so funny.*

BUILT

* **built¹** (sl.): having an attractive or well-developed physique, having a nice body >*Look at those curves! Is she ever built!* >*Look at those muscles! That guy is really built!*

— **built²** (colloq.): of sturdy construction >*These old houses are really built.*

BULL

** **bull¹** (sl.): lie, false or exaggerated story, nonsense (also interj.) >*That's a bunch of bull! There's no way it'll happen.* >*Bull! I did not!*

* **bull²** (sl.): bad treatment, unjust dealings >*Don't put up with any bull from Flagg.*

— **bull³** (sl.): annoying or tedious work or demands >*I hate this bull about filin' everything in triplicate.*

— **shoot the bull** (see **SHOOT**)

BULL DIKE

— **bull dike** (see "BULL DYKE")

BULLDOZE

— **bulldoze** (vt) (colloq.): intimidate, coerce, cow >*He was a mean old* buzzard that would bulldoze anyone that got in his way.

BULL DYKE

— **bull dyke** (... dīk) (sl., pej.): lesbian with masculine traits >She's been hangin' around with some bull dyke she met.

BULLET

— **bite the bullet** (see BITE)

BULL SESSION

* **bull session** (colloq.): informal discussion, lengthy and spontaneous conversation >The four of us had a bull session that lasted till three in the morning.

BULLSHIT

** **bullshit¹** (bŭl´shit´) (vulg.): lie, false or exaggerated story, nonsense (also adj., also interj.) >Get outta here with your right-wing bullshit! >Cut the bullshit excuses! >Bullshit! She didn't either say that!

** **bullshit²** (vulg.): bad treatment, unjust dealings (also adj.) >I can't take the bullshit I have to put up with in dealin' with that crook. >We've had it with their bullshit tax hikes.

* **bullshit³** (vulg.): annoying or tedious work or demands (also adj.) >We gotta go through that reorganizin' bullshit again? >This job's nothin' but bullshit. >More bullshit forms to fill out?

* **bullshit⁴** (vi, vt) (vulg.): lie (to), tell false or exaggerated stories (to) >Don't believe everything the boss says. He likes to bullshit. >Don't bullshit us! You never played pro ball.

BULLSHITTER

** **bullshitter** (bŭl´shit ər) (sl.): person who lies, person who tells false or exaggerated stories or speaks nonsense >What a bullshitter! He didn't finish high school, much less graduate from college.

BUM

* **bum¹** (bum) (colloq.): person without a steady job or residence >I gave my old coat to some bum living under the overpass.

* **bum²** (colloq.): person without prestige or merit, contemptible person >You ought to find some nice friends instead of hanging around with those bums.

* **bum³** (colloq.): defective, crippled, faulty >He can't walk too far because he's got a bum leg. >The informant gave the cops some bum information, and they came up empty-handed.

* **bum⁴** (vt) (sl.): beg, request and take without intending to pay back >I'm gettin' sick and tired of Jeff bummin' cigarettes from me all the time. >Can I bum a ride downtown with ya?

— **... bum** (colloq.): ... enthusiast, (esp. one who devotes an excessive amount of time at ...) >The guy's a tennis bum— he's always on the courts.

* **bum around** (vi) (colloq.): go around without purpose or destination, pass time idly >Kelly and I bummed around together when we were kids. >Let's just bum around downtown till the movie starts.

— **bum out** (vt) (sl.): upset, disappoint, depress >It really bummed us out when they threw us off the beach.

BUMMER

** **bummer** (bum´ər) (sl.): disappointment, upsetting or unpleasant thing or occurrence (also interj.) >This party's a bummer—let's split. >Bummer, man! My surfboard's cracked.

BUMP

** **bump** (vt) (colloq.): displace because of seniority or authority (esp. from an airliner) >We're going to have to bump two passengers because we've got to get a couple of company big shots on this flight to Houston.

** **bump into** (colloq.): meet by chance >*I bumped into Doris at the market this morning.*

* **bump off** (vt) (sl.): murder >*He paid someone to bump off his old lady so he could collect the insurance.*

* **like a bump on a log** (colloq.): idle, without helping, useless >*Polly just sat there like a bump on a log and didn't lift a hand to help.*

BUM RAP

* **bum rap** (bum ...) (sl.): unjust charge or punishment >*He claimed it was a bum rap, but there were two good witnesses.*

BUM'S RUSH

— **the bum's rush** (... bumz ...) (sl.): forced ejection (from a place) >*The bouncer gave that troublemaker the bum's rush.*

BUM STEER

* **bum steer** (bum ...) (sl.): piece of advice or information that is wrong or that leads to failure, misguidance >*His informant gave him a bum steer, and he came up with nothin'.*

BUNCH

* **bunch** (colloq.): group (of people) >*Thelma's family's an odd bunch.*

** **a (whole) bunch (of ...)** (colloq.): much (...), many (...) >*I can't go out. I've got a bunch of studying to do.* >*She has a whole bunch of problems she wants to discuss.* >*She knows kids because she's got a whole bunch herself.*

BUNCO

— **bunco** (see "BUNKO")

BUNDLE

** **bundle** (sl.): large sum of money >*She made a bundle in commissions on those sales.*

BUNDLE OF NERVES

* **bundle of nerves** (colloq.): very nervous or anxious person >*Harry's been a bundle of nerves since he got called for the interview.*

BUNK

— **bunk**[1] (colloq.): lies, false or exaggerated story, nonsense >*That story about him being a race-car driver is a lot of bunk.*

— **bunk**[2] (vi) (colloq.): sleep, spend the night (esp. on a temporary basis) >*You can bunk at my house tonight.*

BUNKO

— **bunko** (bung´kō) (colloq.): swindle, confidence game >*The old lady lost two thousand bucks on some bunko scheme.*

BUNS

** **buns** (sl.): buttocks >*She thought he had cute buns.*

* **... [one's] buns off** (sl.): ... with maximum effort or sacrifice, ... to the utmost >*Scream your buns off if you want. I don't care.*

— **bust [one's] buns** (see **BUST**)

— **freeze [one's] buns off** (see **FREEZE**)

BURGER

** **burger** (bûr´gər) (colloq.): hamburger >*We had burgers and fries for lunch.*

BURN

** **burn**[1] (vt) (sl.): cheat, cause (s/one) a loss, hurt, greatly disillusion (used esp. in passive voice) >*A lot of investors really got burned on that deal.* >*She's been burned by a couple of bad relationships.*

— **burn**[2] (vi) (sl.): die in the electric chair >*You're gonna burn for what ya did!*

** **burn out** (vi) (colloq.): become mentally or physically exhausted (esp. due to an extended period of overwork or stress) >*He taught junior high for six years, then burned out.*

— **lay/burn rubber** (see **RUBBER**)

* **burn (up)** (vt) (colloq.): anger greatly, make furious >*It really burns her when her husband flirts with other women.* >*His bad attitude burns me up.*

— **have money to burn** (see **MONEY**)

BURNED-OUT

* **burned-out** (colloq.): mentally or physically exhausted (esp. due to an extended period of overwork or stress) >*Some burned-out executive just up and quit.*

BURNOUT

** **burnout**[1] (colloq.): mental or physical exhaustion (esp. due to an extended period of overwork or stress) >*Burnout's a big problem among air traffic controllers.*

— **burnout**[2] (colloq.): person who is ineffective or ruined due to overwork or stress, person who is totally exhausted mentally or physically >*You can't put a burnout like him in charge!*

BURP

** **burp**[1] (bûrp) (colloq.): belch >*He drank a beer and let out a big burp.*

** **burp**[2] (vi) (colloq.): belch >*Don't burp at the table!*

BUSH

— **bush** (vulg.): mass of pubic hair (esp. a woman's) >*They rated the movie "X" 'cause it showed the actress's bush.*

— **beat around the bush** (see **BEAT**)

BUSHED

* **bushed** (bŭsht) (colloq.): very tired, exhausted >*After a day of chopping wood, I'm bushed.*

BUSHY-TAILED

— **bright-eyed and bushy-tailed** (see **BRIGHT-EYED**)

BUSINESS

* **be in business** (colloq.): be ready to proceed, have everything set to operate or function >*If I can just get this carburetor adjusted right, I think we'll be in business. >Just plug it in, and you're in business.*

* **do [one's] business** (colloq.): defecate >*I don't want your dog doing its business on my lawn.*

— **give [s/one] the business** (colloq.): scold or reprimand [s/one], berate [s/one] >*His supervisor gave him the business when he screwed up the deal.*

— **like nobody's business** (see **NOBODY'S**)

** **mean business** (colloq.): have a serious intent, be determined >*When she gets that look in her eye, she means business.*

BUSINESS END

— **business end** (colloq.): part that's crucial to the functioning (of a tool or weapon) >*The punk turned around and found himself looking at the business end of a gun.*

BUST

** **bust**[1] (sl.): arrest, detainment >*A street cop made the bust this morning.*

** **bust**[2] (colloq.): police raid >*Twenty cops, who had surrounded the house, were in on the bust.*

— **bust**[3] (colloq.): failure >*The party was a bust. Hardly anyone showed up.*

** **bust**[4] (vt) (sl.): arrest, detain >*He was busted for holdin' ten grams of cocaine.*

** **bust**[5] (vt) (colloq.): raid (by the police) >*The cops busted the joint because there was a gambling operation going on there.*

— **bust**[6] (vt) (colloq.): hit, strike (esp. with the fist) >*Someone's going to bust him in the mouth if he doesn't shut up.*

— **bust**[7] (vt) (colloq.): fracture, break >*He busted his collarbone when he fell. >Don't sit on my glasses! You'll bust them.*

— **bust**[8] (vt) (colloq.): demote >*They busted him back to private. >You'll get busted back to a field office if you don't produce.*

— **(about) bust/split a gut**[1] (colloq.): work hard, put out great effort (to reach a goal) >*We busted a gut to fill the order on time.*

— **(about) bust/split a gut²** (colloq.): laugh very hard >*I about busted a gut when I saw him start flirting with that transvestite.* >*Joey split a gut laughing at Martin's jokes.*

* **bust/break [one's] ass** (vulg.): work hard, put out great effort (to reach a goal) >*We've been breakin' our ass all day diggin' that trench.* >*I busted my ass to get where I am today.*

— **bust/break [one's] balls** (vulg.): work hard, put out great effort (to reach a goal) (cf. "**BALL-BUSTER/breaker¹**") >*We've been breakin' our balls tryin' to get this ready by Monday.*

— **bust/break [s/one's] balls** (vulg.): emasculate [s/one], injure [s/one's] sense of maleness (cf. "**BALL-BUSTER/breaker²**") >*She really busted Pearson's balls when she listed all his screwups in front of everybody.*

* **bust [one's] buns** (sl.): work hard, put out great effort (to reach a goal) >*If ya wanna get ahead, ya gotta bust your buns.*

— **bust [one's] chops** (sl.): work hard, put out great effort (to reach a goal) >*Man, I busted my chops fixin' this damn car's transmission!*

— **bust out (of)** (colloq.): break out (of), escape (from) >*They busted out of jail and headed out of town.*

— **bust up¹** (vi, vt) (colloq.): (cause to) separate or divorce >*The partnership busted up because of a mis-understanding.* >*Him messing around with other women is what busted up their marriage.*

— **bust up²** (vt) (colloq.): destroy, put an end to >*Someone busted up his tree house.* >*Some gate-crashers came in and busted up the party.*

— **bust up³** (vi) (colloq.): laugh hard >*You're going to bust up when he does the hat routine.*

— **go bust** (colloq.): become bankrupt, lose all (one's) money >*His shop went bust after just two months.*

— **... or bust!** (colloq.): (one is) determined to reach ... at any cost! (one will make) an all-out effort to attain ... >*Frisco or bust!* >*A new world's record or bust!*

BUSTED

— **busted** (bus´təd) (colloq.): penniless, with no money >*They're busted, with no place to live.*

BUSTER

— **Buster** (bus´tər) (voc.) (colloq.): mister, you there (used esp. with a male, freq. in a contentious way) >*Listen, Buster! I've had about all I'm going to take from you!*

— **... buster** (colloq.): destroyer or preventer of ... >*That cop thinks he's the city's greatest crime buster.* >*This game's a real boredom buster.*

BUSY

* **(as) busy as a beaver** (colloq.): very busy, very industrious >*She's been busy as a beaver decorating her new house.*

* **(as) busy as a bee** (colloq.): very busy >*I'm as busy as a bee these days with my volunteer work.*

BUT

— **but** (colloq.): very, definitely >*We beat them but good.* >*This car moves but fast!*

BUTCH

— **butch** (bŭch) (sl., pej.): lesbian (esp. with masculine traits), masculine woman (also adj., also adv.) >*This butch has been givin' her the eye.* >*She likes the butch look.* >*She dresses real butch.*

BUTS

— **no ifs, ands, or buts (about it)** (see **IFS**)

BUTT

** **butt[1]** (sl., freq. vulg.): buttocks, rump, anus >*He belted him and knocked him on his butt.* >*The doctor had to take a look up his butt.*

* **butt[2]** (sl.): cigarette >*Give me a butt and those matches there, will ya?*

— **blister [s/one's] butt** (see BLISTER)

** **[one's] butt** (sl., freq. vulg.): [one]self, [one] (esp. when seen as troublesome or contemptible) >*They threw his butt in jail for drunk and disorderly conduct.*

* **butt heads (with)** (colloq.): enter into conflict (with) >*The governor's going to butt heads with the legislature over this.* >*Me and him usually butt heads when the budget's being discussed.*

** **butt in(to)** (colloq.): interfere (in), participate (in) without invitation, meddle (in) >*Mind if I butt in to add something?* >*Don't go butting into what's none of your business!*

* **... [one's] butt off** (sl., freq. vulg.): ... with maximum effort or sacrifice, ... to the utmost >*I argued my butt off, but they just wouldn't agree to it.*

** **butt out** (vi) (sl.): stop meddling or interfering, stop participating (esp. when one was not invited) >*She'd better butt out or they're gonna get mad.* >*Butt out, buddy!*

— **drag [one's] butt** (see DRAG)

** **get off [one's] butt** (sl., freq. vulg.): stop being lazy, start moving or working >*Get off your butts, guys—we got a lot to do.*

— **kick [s/one's] butt** (see KICK)

— **kick (some) butt** (see KICK)

* **off [s/one's] butt** (sl., freq. vulg.): no longer putting pressure on [s/one], no longer being critical of [s/one] (cf. "on [s/one's] BUTT") >*You'll get the press off your butt if you just explain the whole situation.*

* **on [s/one's] butt** (sl., freq. vulg.): putting pressure on [s/one], being critical of [s/one] (cf. "off [s/one's] BUTT") >*She's been on my butt all week, ever since I came home late and drunk.*

— **out on [one's] butt** (see OUT)

— **pain in the butt** (see PAIN)

BUTTER

* **butter up** (vt) (colloq.): flatter or adulate (to gain favor) >*Am I really that great, or are you just buttering me up so I'll help you?*

BUTTERBALL

— **butterball** (colloq.): chubby or fat person >*Have you see how much weight he's gained? He's a real butterball!*

BUTTERFINGERS

— **butterfingers** (colloq.): person who drops things (also voc.) >*If you pass it to that butterfingers, she'll drop it for sure.* >*Hold on to it tight this time, butterfingers!*

BUTTERFLIES

** **butterflies (in [one's] stomach)** (colloq.): nervousness, feeling of uneasiness (due to apprehension), fearful anticipation >*I still get butterflies in my stomach before going on stage.*

BUTTFUCK

— **buttfuck** (but´fuk´) (vi, vt) (vulg.): have anal intercourse (with) (as penetrator) >*They say he's kinky—likes to buttfuck.* >*They say he got buttfucked in prison.*

BUTTHEAD

— **butthead** (vulg.): contemptible or reprehensible person, stupid person (also voc.) >*I hope that butthead doesn't start arguin' with me again.* >*Get lost, butthead!*

BUTTINSKY

— **buttinsky** (but in´skē) (sl.): meddlesome person, uninvited participant, person who interrupts (also voc.) >*Tell that buttinsky it's none of his business.* >*Who asked you, buttinsky?*

BUTTON

— **(as) cute as a button** (see **CUTE**)

— **button up** (vi) (sl.): keep quiet, shut up >*I want ya to button up—they ain't supposed to know.*

* **button (up) [one's] lip** (sl.): keep quiet, shut up >*If Brad doesn't button his lip, he's gonna get into trouble.*

* **on the button** (colloq.): exactly as expected, precisely as required >*Right! Nine hundred and twenty-three on the button.* >*He predicted the outcome right on the button.*

BUTTONS

— **push [s/one's] buttons** (see **PUSH**)

BUY

** **buy¹** (colloq.): bargain >*This shirt was a real buy at just ten dollars.*

** **buy²** (vt) (colloq.): believe, accept, approve >*I don't buy that. It just won't work.* >*Do you think the boss will buy his plan?*

* **buy³** (vt) (sl.): bribe >*If ya ask me, they bought the judge so he'd dismiss the case.*

** **buy into** (colloq.): accept as truth, embrace >*He used to be a free spirit, but now he's bought into the system.*

— **buy it** (sl.): die, get killed >*He stepped in front of a bus and bought it.*

— **buy the farm** (sl.): die, get killed >*The dude took a slug in the head and bought the farm.*

* **buy time** (colloq.): use delaying tactics to gain time, stall >*She's trying to buy time so her crooked husband can escape.*

BUZZ

* **buzz¹** (sl.): feeling of exhilaration, excitement, slight intoxication >*Skydivin' gives ya a real buzz.* >*I got a buzz on after just one drink.*

— **buzz²** (vt) (colloq.): telephone >*I'll buzz you tomorrow and see how you're doing.*

— **buzz³** (vt) (colloq.): fly very low over >*They took away his license after he buzzed the tower in a small plane.*

** **buzz off!** (sl.): go away! >*No one invited you, so buzz off!*

** **give [s/one] a buzz** (colloq.): telephone [s/one] >*If I hear anything new, I'll give you a buzz.*

BUZZARD

— **old buzzard** (sl., freq. pej.): old man (esp. seen as troublesome or contemptible) >*The boss says he doesn't want that old buzzard around the shop.*

BUZZED

— **buzzed** (sl.): excited, exhilarated, slightly intoxicated >*He's really buzzed about his first road trip.* >*That wine's got me a little buzzed.*

BY

— **by (a/the) ...** (see entry under ... word[s])

BYE-BYE

** **bye-bye!** (colloq.): goodbye! >*Bye-bye! Drive safely.*

* **go bye-bye** (colloq.): go somewhere, leave (used with small children) >*Come on, Jimmy! Want to go bye-bye?*

B.Y.O.B.

* **B.Y.O.B.** (colloq.): on a bring-your-own-booze/bottle basis >*The party's B.Y.O.B. because I can't afford to buy all that liquor.*

C

CABBIE
— **cabby** (see **CABBY**)

CABBY
* **cabby** (ka´bē) (colloq.): taxicab driver >*He works as a cabby at night.*

CABOODLE
— **the (whole) kit and caboodle** (see **KIT**)

CADDY
* **Caddy** (ka´dē) (sl.): Cadillac automobile >*He drove up in a brand-new Caddy.*

CADILLAC
— **the Cadillac of ...** (... ka´də lak ...) (colloq.): the best ..., the top of the ... line >*This model's the Cadillac of blenders.*

CAGE
— **rattle [s/one's] cage** (see **RATTLE**)

CAHOOTS
* **in cahoots** (... kə hūts´) (colloq.): conspiring together, in partnership, collaborating (esp. for s/thing questionable) >*They say that labor leader's in cahoots with the mafia.* >*I know the lobbyist and the consultant are in cahoots.*

CAIN
— **raise Cain** (sl.): cause trouble, create a disturbance, be raucous and rowdy >*Them drunk cowboys are raisin' Cain over at Millie's again.*

— **raise Cain (with)** (sl.): complain strenuously (to), severely reprimand (s/one) >*The foreman raised Cain with Ziggy for drinkin' on the job.*

CAKE
— **icing/frosting on the cake** (see **ICING**)

— **piece of cake** (see **PIECE**)

* **take the cake** (colloq.): be unsurpassable (esp. in a negative quality), be highly unusual >*I've seen a lot of pompous people before, but that jerk takes the cake.* >*If that dancing elephants act don't take the cake!*

CAKEWALK
— **cakewalk** (colloq.): easy thing to do, assured success >*Beating that lousy team will be a cakewalk.*

CALL
* **call [s/one's] bluff** (colloq.): ask [s/one] to prove a claim or carry out a threat (when that claim or threat is considered false) >*He wanted us to believe he was an inspector, but I called his bluff and asked for I.D.* >*Go ahead, call Mindy's bluff—she won't really quit.*

** **call it a day/night** (colloq.): stop (an activity) for the day/night >*I'm dead tired—let's call it a day.*

— **call it quits** (see **QUITS**)

— **call of nature** (colloq.): need to defecate and/or urinate >*Excuse me. I got to answer the call of nature.*

* **call [s/one] on [s/thing]** (colloq.): ask [s/one] to prove (a claim) (when that claim is considered false) >*The old man claimed he could speak German, but I called him on it and he couldn't even say "Ich spreche Deutsch."*

— **call [s/one] on the carpet** (colloq.): bring [s/one] before an authority for a reprimand >*He was called on the carpet for screwing up the deal.*

* **call the shots** (colloq.): be in charge, have the authority to make decisions >*Gabe is the manager, but he lets Judy call the shots.*

CALL GIRL
* **call girl** (colloq.): prostitute (esp. one contracted by telephone) >*He's got an expensive call girl he contacts every time he's in town.*

CALLING CARD
— **[one's] calling card** (colloq.): [one's] particular or typical sign, trace or characteristic by which [one] can be identified >*The pattern on these footprints is the killer's calling card.*

>*Damn dog left his calling card on my front lawn again.*

CAMPER

— **happy/unhappy camper** (colloq., freq. hum.): satisfied/dissatisfied participant >*We're going to have a bunch of unhappy campers if there are any more delays.*

CAN

* **can¹** (sl.): buttocks, rump >*The jolt knocked him on his can.*

** **can²** (vt) (sl.): fire, dismiss >*He got canned last week, and he's lookin' for work.*

* **can³** (vt) (sl.): put a stop to (esp. talking or noise) (used esp. as a command) >*Hey, can the B.S.! We all know better. >Can it! I'm tryin' to sleep.*

— **no can do** (see **NO**)

* **the can¹** (sl.): toilet, bathroom >*He was sittin' on the can readin' a magazine. >I went to the can to take a leak.*

— **the can²** (sl.): jail >*He took a punch at a cop and ended up in the can.*

CANCER STICK

— **cancer stick** (sl.): cigarette (esp. seen as injurious) >*Ya still smokin' those damn cancer sticks?*

CAN-DO

— **can-do** (colloq.): efficient, purposeful, enthusiastic to accomplish things >*What this firm needs is more can-do execs like him.*

CANDY ASS

— **candy ass** (vulg.): overly timid person, sissy, coward (also voc.) >*That candy ass won't even try jumpin' off the high dive. >Come on, candy ass—what're ya afraid of?*

CANDY-ASS

— **candy-ass(ed)** (vulg.): cowardly, overly timid, sissy >*I don't want no candy-assed college boy goin' huntin' with us.*

CANNED

* **canned** (colloq.): prerecorded, prepared previously >*I hate the canned laughter on these sitcoms. >The candidate gave a canned answer on the need to balance the budget.*

CAN OF WORMS

* **can of worms** (colloq.): problematic matter, troublesome situation >*Don't open up a can of worms by questioning his qualifications.*

CAPER

— **caper** (kā´pər) (colloq.): criminal act >*He got indicted for an insider stock trading caper.*

CARB

— **carb** (kärb) (colloq.): carburetor >*Sounds like you need to adjust the carb.*

CARBOS

— **carbos** (kär´bōz) (colloq.): carbohydrates (in food) >*I think she needs more carbos in her diet.*

CARBS

— **carbs** (kärbz) (colloq.): carbohydrates (in food) >*He eats a lot of carbs the day before a race.*

CARCASS

— **[one's] carcass** (sl.): [one's] body, [one]self (esp. seen as contemptible or troublesome) >*Get your carcass outta bed and get to work!*

CARD

— **card¹** (colloq.): funny person, odd or eccentric person >*Milton's a real card. He always has us cracking up.*

* **card²** (vt) (sl.): check the identification of (to ascertain required age) >*I'm over thirty, and I still get carded in bars.*

— **ace/card up [one's] sleeve** (see **ACE**)

CARD-CARRYING

— **card-carrying ...** (colloq.): dedicated or absolute ... >*Every card-carrying conservative's going to love that scheme.*

CARDS
— **hold all the cards** (see **HOLD**)

* **in the cards** (colloq.): likely to happen (esp. soon) >*Be patient—your promotion's in the cards.*

* **lay [one's] cards on the table** (colloq.): be open about [one's] interests, deal straightforwardly, not keep anything secret >*Let's stop fooling around and lay our cards on the table.*

— **play [one's] cards right** (see **PLAY**)

— **stack the deck/cards** (see **STACK**)

CARE
** **could care less** (colloq.): could not be less concerned or interested >*I could care less what that clown thinks.*

** **take care of** (colloq.): make suffer, take revenge on, murder >*I'll take care of that idiot.* >*They had a hit man take care of the informer.*

CARPET
— **call [s/one] on the carpet** (see **CALL**)

CARROT-TOP
— **carrot-top** (sl.): red-headed person >*Are these carrot-tops your kids?*

CARRY
* **carry (a lot of) weight** (colloq.): be (very) influential, be (very) important >*What she says carries a lot of weight at meetings.* >*Let him talk—he doesn't carry any weight around here.*

— **carry a torch for** (colloq.): be in love with (s/one who does not love one in return) >*Owen carries a torch for her, but she doesn't care if he's dead or alive.*

* **carry off** (vt) (colloq.): complete successfully, accomplish without suffering neg. consequences (esp. s/thing tricky or objectionable) >*If they carry off that deal, they'll make a fortune.* >*It's a neat scheme if you can carry it off.*

* **carry on** (vi) (colloq.): act childishly or excitedly, behave objectionably >*What's that lady carrying on about?*

What's her problem? >*I saw them carrying on together in a parked car.*

— **carry the ball** (colloq.): take on the main responsibility, take charge >*You're going to have to carry the ball on this one, Betsy, because the rest of us are already busy.*

CARRYING
— **carrying** (sl.): armed, carrying a gun >*Be careful with that dude—I think he's carryin'.*

CART
— **cart off/away** (vt) (colloq.): take (s/one) away roughly or unceremoniously >*The sheriff carted two drunks off to jail to sober up.*

CASE
— **case¹** (colloq.): funny person, odd or eccentric person >*The lady in the fireman's hat is a real case.*

* **case²** (vt) (sl.): examine or check out (a place) (esp. in preparation for a robbery) >*They cased the bank on Thursday and hit it on Friday.* >*Go case the party and let us know if it's OK to come in.*

** **off [s/one's] case** (sl.): no longer pressuring or criticizing [s/one], no longer bothering [s/one] (cf. "**on [s/one's] CASE**") >*Hey, get off his case and let him do his job, will ya?*

** **on [s/one's] case** (sl.): pressuring or criticizing [s/one], bothering [s/one] (cf. "**off [s/one's] CASE**") >*I'm sick and tired of havin' ya on my case about how I'm raisin' the kids!*

CASH
— **cash in ([one's] chips)** (sl.): die >*When I cash in my chips, I don't want no fancy funeral.* >*He was old and sick. It was time for him to cash in.*

* **cash in on** (colloq.): profit from (an opportunity), take advantage of (s/thing) for profit >*You got to act fast to cash in on fads.*

CAST-IRON
— **have a cast-iron stomach** (colloq.): be able to eat strong or very spicy food, be able to digest almost anything >*Bob smothers everything he eats with jalapeño peppers. He's got a cast-iron stomach.*

CAT
— **cat** (sl.): man, fellow (esp. a stylish one) >*Who was that cat playin' bass guitar last night?*

— **let the cat out of the bag** (see LET)

— **something/what the cat dragged in** (sl.): very messy or disreputable thing or person (in appearance) >*Well, look what the cat dragged in! What the hell happened to you?* >*That slob she's with looks like something the cat dragged in.*

— **[for] the cat [to] have [s/one's] tongue** (colloq.): [for s/one to] be speechless, [for s/one to] have difficulty saying (s/thing) >*Seemed like the cat had his tongue when his wife asked him where he'd been all night.* >*What's the matter—the cat got your tongue?*

CATCH
** **catch¹** (colloq.): drawback, unexpected flaw >*The job pays OK, and it would be a good promotion. The catch is that the hours are lousy.* >*That's too good to be true—what's the catch?*

* **catch²** (colloq.): desirable mate, good marriage prospect >*Her mother thinks Seymour is quite a catch.*

** **catch³** (vt) (colloq.): make contact with, meet >*He wasn't in the office when I phoned, but I caught him at home.* >*I'll catch you at Lew's party tomorrow night.*

** **catch⁴** (vt) (colloq.): attend, see (a show, etc.) >*Did you catch that play when it was in town?* >*Let's catch a movie after dinner.*

— **catch/get [s/one's] drift** (see DRIFT)

— **catch/get hell** (see HELL)

* **catch it** (colloq.): be scolded or punished >*You're going to catch it when Mom finds out where you've been.*

** **catch on¹** (vi) (colloq.): finally understand >*Christie found the routine hard to follow at first, but she caught on after a couple of days.*

** **catch on²** (vi) (colloq.): become popular, turn into a fad >*I doubt that dance will ever really catch on.*

— **catch shit (from)** (see SHIT)

— **catch some rays** (see RAYS)

— **get/catch some Zs** (see ZS)

* **catch [s/one] with [his/her] pants down** (colloq.): surprise [s/one] in a compromising or embarrassing act or position, catch [s/one] red-handed >*He was caught with his pants down when his wife saw him coming out of a motel room with another woman.*

CATCH-22
* **catch-22** (colloq.): impossible situation or requirement (due to self-contradiction or illogic) >*It's a catch-22. You can't get in without a pass, and they only give out the passes inside.*

CATCH-UP
* **play catch-up** (colloq.): make an effort to reach the level of a competitor that has taken the lead, work to recover a loss >*If they get that new product on the market by next year, we're going to have to play catch-up.* >*The team fell behind ten points and had to play catch-up to finally win.*

CATHOUSE
— **cathouse** (sl.): house of prostitution, brothel >*Earl got arrested at some cathouse across town.*

CATS
— **rain cats and dogs** (see RAIN)

CAT'S MEOW
— **the cat's meow** (sl.): person or thing that is excellent or very special >*Mom*

thinks Judy's boyfriend is the cat's meow.

CAT'S PAJAMAS
— **the cat's pajamas** (sl.): person or thing that is excellent or very special >*Hot chocolate on a cold night is the cat's pajamas.*

CAUGHT
— **wouldn't be caught dead** (see **DEAD**)

'CAUSE
** **'cause** (kuz) (colloq.): because >*Do it 'cause I said to!*

CAVE
* **cave in (to)** (vi) (colloq.): desist, yield (to), no longer oppose (esp. under pressure) >*Management held out for a long time but finally caved in to the union's demands.*

CAVE MAN
— **cave man** (colloq.): brutish or violent man (esp. toward women), male sexist >*I can't believe that Grace, who calls herself a feminist, is actually falling for that cave man.*

C.B.ER
— **C.B.er** (colloq.): citizen's band radio user or enthusiast >*A C.B.er told me about the detour.*

CEILING
— **hit the ceiling** (see **HIT**)

CELEB
— **celeb** (sə leb´) (colloq.): celebrity (person) >*She says a lot of celebs will be at the benefit show.*

CERTIFIABLE
— **certifiable** (colloq.): insane, undoubtedly crazy >*The guy went berserk for no reason at all—he's certifiable.*

CHAIN
— **pull [s/one's] chain** (see **PULL**)
— **yank [s/one's] chain** (see **YANK**)

CHAIR
* **the chair** (sl.): the electric chair, death by electrocution in the electric chair >*The District Attorney's askin' that the defendant get the chair in this case.*

CHALK
* **chalk up** (vt) (colloq.): earn or score, add on (to one's record) >*The new prof has really been chalking up the publications.* >*George chalked a big sale up yesterday.*

CHAMP
** **champ** (champ) (colloq.): champion >*He was the heavyweight champ for years.*

CHANCE
— **fat chance** (see **FAT**)

CHANGE
* **and change** (colloq.): plus an unspecified smaller amount of money more >*That job'll run you two thousand and change.*

* **change [one's] tune** (colloq.): change [one's] attitude or opinion, modify [one's] view (esp. from one seen as erroneous) >*When the governor saw how much opposition there was to his plan, he changed his tune real quick.*

— **piece of change** (see **PIECE**)

CHARACTER
** **character**[1] (colloq.): odd or eccentric person >*Your uncle Ned's quite a character—does he always act like that?*

* **character**[2] (colloq.): person, man (esp. seen as troublesome or contemptible) >*Who's the character with the big mouth?* >*What a rough character he is!*

CHARGE
* **get a charge out of** (colloq.): be thrilled by, very much enjoy >*I get a charge out of hiking in the mountains.* >*Everyone got a charge out of her act.*

CHARLEY HORSE
* **charley horse** (chär´lē ...) (colloq.): muscle cramp (esp. in the arm or leg)

>*Ow! I've got a charley horse in my calf from running too much.*

CHARM
— **work like a charm** (see **WORK**)

CHARTS
* **the (...) charts** (colloq.): the ranking of popularity of (...) songs (esp. by week) >*He's had a hit on the pop charts just about every week for the last two years.* >*Think that song'll make the charts?*

CHASE
* **chase** (vi) (colloq.): rush, go hurriedly (esp. without a clear destination) >*I chased all over town looking for the right part.*

— **chase skirts** (sl.): be a womanizer (cf. "SKIRT-CHASER") >*Billings should never marry. He gambles, drinks, and chases skirts.*

— **cut to the chase** (see **CUT**)

CHASER
* **chaser** (colloq.): drink taken after a stronger one >*Give me a whiskey with a beer chaser.*

CHEAP
* **cheap** (colloq.): morally loose (said of a woman) >*He spends his time running around with cheap women.*

CHEAPIE
* **cheapie** (chē´pē) (colloq.): inexpensive or inferior item (also adj.) >*Show me the best suit you got—I don't want any cheapies.* >*I bought this cheapie shirt, and it fell apart after one washing.*

CHEAPO
— **cheapo** (chē´pō) (sl.): cheap, inferior (cf. "EL CHEAPO") >*Don't ya know those cheapo pens are gonna leak all over the place?*

CHEAP SHOT
* **cheap shot** (colloq.): unfair or mean remark or action (esp. one directed at s/one vulnerable) >*Reminding her of her past in front of her new friends was a cheap shot.*

CHEAPSKATE
* **cheapskate** (colloq.): miser, stingy person >*What a cheapskate! He didn't even offer to pay his part.*

CHEAT
** **cheat (on)** (colloq.): be sexually unfaithful (to) >*She threw him out when she found out he'd been cheating on her.*

CHECK
— **check!** (colloq.): all right! >*Check! I'll be there at ten if that's when you want me.*

** **check out**[1] (vt) (colloq.): look over, inspect, evaluate >*I want to check out the new models.* >*What a babe! Check her out.*

* **check out**[2] (vi) (colloq.): prove to be accurate or valid >*If his story checks out, we'll hire him.*

— **check out**[3] (vi) (sl.): die >*He got pneumonia and checked out last month.*

— **cut ([s/one]) a check** (see **CUT**)

CHEEK
* **cheek** (sl.): buttock >*The nurse told me to drop my pants, and then she gave the shot in my right cheek.*

CHEESE
— **cut the cheese** (see **CUT**)

CHEESECAKE
— **cheesecake** (sl.): photograph(s) of (a) sexually attractive woman/women (esp. with little clothing and meant to be sensual) (cf. "BEEFCAKE") >*Timmy buys all the girlie magazines. He really goes for cheesecake.*

CHEESY
— **cheesy** (sl.): tasteless, low-quality, cheap >*Where does he get those cheesy polyester jackets he wears?*

CHEMISTRY
* **chemistry** (colloq.): interpersonal feelings, rapport >*I knew they wouldn't get along—the chemistry between them*

was all wrong. >If the chemistry's right, you'll hit it off with him.

CHERRY
— **cherry[1]** (vulg.): hymen, virginity *>He lost his cherry at fifteen. >She still has her cherry.*

— **cherry[2]** (sl.): in perfect condition, like new *>The car is cherry—completely restored.*

— **pop [s/one's] cherry** (see **POP**)

CHEST
** **get [s/thing] off [one's] chest** (colloq.): relieve [oneself] of [s/thing worrisome] by talking about it, talk over [s/thing worrisome] (with another) *>If there's something you want to get off your chest, I'm a good listener.*

— **will put hair on [s/one's] chest** (see **HAIR**)

CHEVY
** **Chevy** (she´vē) (colloq.): Chevrolet automobile *>He drives an old Chevy station wagon.*

CHEW
* **chew out** (vt) (sl.): reprimand, scold severely *>Let's do it right 'cause I don't want to get chewed out by the boss.*

— **chew the fat** (colloq.): talk idly, chat, converse *>We spent the afternoon drinking beer and chewing the fat.*

— **chew the rag** (colloq.): talk idly, chat, converse *>We were chewing the rag, and he told me all about when he was growing up.*

CHICK
* **chick** (sl., freq. pej.): young woman (esp. an attractive one) *>Howie thinks every chick in town is hot for him.*

* **[one's] chick** (sl.): [one's] girlfriend or sweetheart *>What was your chick doin' with Malcolm at the game last Friday?*

CHICKEN
** **chicken** (sl.): coward, fearful person (also adj.) *>He won't fight 'cause he's a*

chicken. >Their chicken brother didn't even try to help 'em.

** **chicken out** (vi) (sl.): desist or withdraw due to fear *>Russ was gonna ask her to dance, but he chickened out.*

— **play chicken (with)** (sl.): run a risk (along with) until one side desists, have a decisive confrontation (with) until one side withdraws *>They were playin' chicken in their cars to see who would swerve outta the way first. >I played chicken with him, and he finally backed off.*

— **run around like a chicken with its head cut off** (see **RUN**)

CHICKEN FEED
— **chicken feed** (sl.): an insignificant amount of money *>Paul's lookin' for a better job. They're payin' him chicken feed where he's at now.*

CHICKEN-LIVERED
— **chicken-livered** (colloq.): cowardly, fearful *>That chicken-livered bastard turned and ran.*

CHICKENSHIT
* **chickenshit[1]** (vulg.): coward, fearful person (also adj.) *>Why didn't that chickenshit go inside with us? >Your chickenshit friend's afraid to do it.*

— **chickenshit[2]** (vulg.): petty action or attitude, excessive upholding of rules, overemphasis on detail (also adj.) *>Makin' him redo his whole paper is chickenshit. >Are they really gonna enforce that chickenshit registration deadline?*

CHICKIE
— **chickie** (chi´kē) (sl., freq. pej.): young woman (esp. an attractive one) *>He's over fifty, but he's always got some chickie on his arm.*

CHIEF
— **chief** (colloq.): leader, boss (also voc.) *>I don't know if the chief wants us to start on this yet. >Anything you say, chief.*

CHILL

* **chill out** (vi) (sl.): calm down, relax, let (one's) anger or anxiousness subside >*Chill out, man—no need to get all worked up about it!*

CHIME

— **chime in** (vi) (colloq.): interrupt (a conversation) to participate without invitation >*Her brother-in-law kept chiming in with his dumb opinions.*

CHIMNEY

— **smoke like a chimney** (see **SMOKE**)

CHIMP

** **chimp** (chimp) (colloq.): chimpanzee >*The chimps we saw at the zoo were funny.*

CHIN

— **take it on the chin** (colloq.): suffer a great loss or defeat >*Thompson's firm really took it on the chin when that deal went bad.*

CHINK

— **Chink** (chēngk) (sl., pej.): Chinese >*The stupid jerk says he thinks the Chinks are to blame.* >*He says he doesn't like Chink food.*

CHINTZY

* **chintzy** (chin´sē) (colloq.): cheap, miserly >*What a chintzy screwdriver! The tip bent the first time I used it.* >*Her chintzy uncle never offers to buy the drinks.*

CHIP

* **be a chip off the old block** (colloq.): be just like (one's) father or mother, behave or look like one of (one's) parents (said esp. of a son with respect to his father) >*He's a chip off the old block—he loves sports as much as his dad.* >*Your boy looks just like you. He's a chip off the old block, all right.*

** **chip in** (vi, vt) (colloq.): contribute (money or help) >*If each one chips in five bucks, we can buy him a real neat present.* >*Everyone chipped in, and we finished in an hour.*

* **chip on [one's] shoulder** (colloq.): belligerent nature, quickness to anger, disposition for quarreling >*Boy, does he ever have a chip on his shoulder! You say anything to him and he jumps all over you.*

CHIPS

— **cash in ([one's] chips)** (see **CASH**)

— **in the chips** (sl.): wealthy, having gotten a great deal of money >*Dwayne's in the chips now—his uncle died and left him a bundle.*

— **when the chips are down** (colloq.): in bad times, in a discouraging situation >*You can count on McGregor to come through when the chips are down.*

CHISEL

— **chisel [s/one, s/thing] (out of [s/one, s/thing])** (sl.): cheat or swindle [s/one] (out of [s/thing]), get ([s/thing]) from [s/one] through deception >*Bret got chiseled outta twenty bucks by some con man.* >*He tried to chisel five dollars outta me.* >*Ya got chiseled on that deal.*

CHISELER

— **chiseler** (sl.): cheater, swindler >*Some chiseler got a hundred bucks outta the old man.*

CHITCHAT

— **chitchat[1]** (chit´chat´) (colloq.): light conversation, idle talk >*I hate all the chitchat you hear at cocktail parties.*

— **chitchat[2]** (vi) (colloq.): engage in light conversation, talk idly >*I ran into Delores at the market, and we chitchatted for a while.*

CHOKE

** **choke up[1]** (vi, vt) (colloq.): become/make unable to speak due to a strong emotion, become/cause to be overcome with emotion >*She choked up during the eulogy and couldn't finish.* >*That sad movie really choked me up.*

* **choke up[2]** (vi) (colloq.): become unable to perform well due to nervousness or stress >*The trainee choked up on the*

approach, and the instructor had to land the plane.

CHOMPING

* **chomping at the bit** (chom´ping ...) (colloq.): showing impatience or eagerness (to begin s/thing) >*Hurry up! The kids are chomping at the bit to get to the beach.*

CHOO-CHOO

* **choo-choo** (colloq.): train (used esp. with small children) >*Look at the big choo-choo coming down the tracks, Cindy.*

CHOP-CHOP

— **chop-chop** (sl.): immediately, in a hurry >*The chief wants that report chop-chop. >Do it now! Chop-chop!*

CHOPPER

** **chopper**[1] (colloq.): helicopter >*They were evacuated by chopper.*

* **chopper**[2] (sl.): motorcycle (esp. a customized one belonging to a motorcycle gang member) >*He roared down the highway on his chopper.*

CHOPPERS

— **choppers** (sl.): teeth (esp. a set of false ones) >*I'm gonna have to get me some new choppers made 'cause these just don't fit right.*

CHOPS

— **bust [one's] chops** (see **BUST**)
— **lick [one's] chops** (see **LICK**)
— **the chops** (sl.): (one's) jaw, (one's) mouth area >*He hit me right in the chops.*

CHOP SHOP

— **chop shop** (sl.): shop where stolen automobiles are dismantled so that the parts can be sold >*Somebody stole his Mercedes this morning, and it's probably in a chop shop by now.*

CHOW

— **chow** (chou) (sl.): food >*How's the chow in this joint?*

* **chow down** (vi) (sl.): eat (esp. heartily) >*The players really chowed down after the game.*

CHRISTMAS TREE

— **lit up like a Christmas tree** (see **LIT**)

CHROME DOME

— **chrome dome** (sl., freq. hum.): man with a shiny bald head (also voc.) >*He's over there talkin' to that chrome dome. >Hey, chrome dome, why don't ya buy yourself a rug?*

CHUCK

— **chuck** (vt) (colloq.): give up, relinquish, throw away >*I'm going to chuck this lousy job. >If you're not going to use it, chuck it.*

— **chuck up** (vi, vt) (sl.): vomit >*She chucked up right on the car seat. >He ate too much and later chucked it all up.*

CHUG

* **chug** (chug) (vt) (sl.): drink in large gulps >*He chugged two beers before sayin' a word.*

CHUG-A-LUG

* **chug-a-lug** (chug´ə lug´) (vt) (sl.): drink all at once (without stopping to breathe) (esp. a container of beer) >*I saw him chug-a-lug a sixteen-ounce mug of beer.*

CHUMMY

* **chummy** (chu´mē) (colloq.): friendly, intimate (esp. when seen as insincere) >*He's been real chummy with me lately, and I wonder what he wants.*

CHUMP

* **chump** (chump) (colloq.): fool, dumb person, dupe (also voc.) >*Don't be a chump—she's just using you. >You lose, chump.*

CHUTE

* **chute** (shūt) (colloq.): parachute >*His main chute didn't open, but his backup did.*

CHUTZPA

— **chutzpa** (hŭt´spə) (sl.): brazenness, audacity, gall >*I can't believe her* *chutzpa—she confronted the governor in front of everyone.*

CHUTZPAH
— chutzpah (see "CHUTZPA")

CIG
* **cig** (sig) (sl.): cigarette >*Got an extra cig on ya?*

CIGAR
— **(close, but) no cigar** (klōs ...) (colloq.): (almost, but) (one's) effort or guess is not successful >*Nine hundred points? Close, but no cigar—you need a thousand to win.* >*No cigar, buddy. Better luck next time.*

— **give [s/one] a cigar!** (colloq., freq. sarc.): [s/one] is correct! [s/one] guessed right! [s/one] wins! >*Yes, indeed, I did break my arm. Give that man a cigar!*

CIGGY
— **ciggy** (si´gē) (sl.): cigarette >*Someone left their ciggies and lighter on the backseat.*

CINCH
* **cinch**[1] (sl.): easy thing to accomplish, assured thing >*Replacin' the fan belt' ll be a cinch.* >*That quiz was a cinch.* >*It's a cinch he' ll lose his shirt in that harebrained scheme.*

* **cinch**[2] (sl.): easy winner, person or thing that is sure to accomplish (s/thing) >*That team's a cinch for the championship this year.* >*You're a cinch for the promotion.*

— **cinch**[3] (vt) (sl.): ensure achievement of or success with >*She cinched the sale by extendin' the warranty a year.*

CIRCLES
* **... circles around [s/one]** (colloq.): easily outdo [s/one] in ...ing (used with actions of movement) >*Bet on Billings—he can run circles around the others.* >*He thought he was a good swimmer, but I swam circles around him.*

CIRCULAR FILE
* **circular file** (sl., hum.): wastebasket >*I put most of my mail right into the circular file.*

CIRCULATION
* **in/out of circulation** (colloq.): currently active/inactive (esp. socially) >*Pierson's out of circulation for a while with a broken hip.* >*She's back in circulation since she broke up with Vic.*

CIRCUS
* **circus** (colloq.): disorderly or noisy place or event >*It was a circus at the department store during the sale.*

CITY
— **... city** (sl.): a place or thing of great ..., an experience involving much ... >*His messy apartment is filth city.* >*It was tension city. They almost came to blows.*

CITY HALL
* **city hall** (colloq.): bureaucracy, rules and regulations (esp. on the city level) >*We'll have to fight city hall, but something's got to be done about it.*

CITY SLICKER
* **city slicker** (colloq.): shrewd or stylish city resident (as seen by rural or small-town people) >*We don't like city slickers coming into our town and looking down their noses at us.* >*The city slickers are buying up all the good farmland.*

CIV
* **civ** (siv) (colloq.): civilization (esp. as a course of study) >*I got to take Western Civ next semester.*

CIVIES
— civies (see "CIVVIES")

CIVVIES
— **civvies** (si´vēz) (colloq.): civilian clothes >*The sergeant usually wore his civvies into town.*

CLAM
— **clam** (sl.): dollar >*That' ll cost ya twenty clams.*

* **clam up** (vi) (sl.): refuse to talk, refrain from giving information >*Everyone clammed up when the cops got there.*

CLAMBAKE

— **clambake** (sl.): party, celebration, social gathering >*Freddy's plannin' some big clambake at his place for all his old college buddies.*

CLAMP

** **clamp down (on)** (colloq.): become stricter (with), impose greater discipline (on) >*The police are clamping down on drunk drivers.* >*The kids are getting too rowdy—we'd better clamp down.*

CLAP

— **the clap** (sl., freq. vulg.): gonorrhea >*He got the clap from some girl he met.*

CLASS

* **class** (colloq.): elegance, dignity, integrity, status (also adj.) >*Let's rent a limousine and arrive with class.* >*Her answer to the irate customer was a class way to handle the situation.*

CLASS ACT

* **class act**[1] (sl.): high-quality performance, praiseworthy or dignified action >*That singer puts on a class act.* >*Your helpin' out that old man was a class act.*

* **class act**[2] (sl.): person of great quality, person of great integrity or style >*That lady is sharp and charming—a real class act.*

CLASSY

** **classy** (kla´sē) (colloq.): elegant, dignified, high-quality >*We're going to celebrate by going to a real classy restaurant.*

CLEAN

* **clean**[1] (sl.): free from drug addiction >*Why were ya tryin' to buy heroin, Harry? You've been clean for three months.*

* **clean**[2] (sl.): not possessing illegal items >*We searched him and found no weapons or drugs. He's clean.*

* **clean**[3] (sl.): innocent (of a crime), with no criminal record >*The guy's clean on this robbery. He was outta town.* >*How can Penfield be a suspect? He's completely clean.*

— **clean**[4] (colloq.): completely >*We're clean out of that size, ma'am.* >*I cut my finger clean to the bone.*

* **(as) clean as a whistle** (colloq.): very clean >*They worked all day, but the house's clean as a whistle now.*

— **clean [s/one's] clock** (sl.): beat [s/one] up, defeat [s/one] decisively >*If ya keep mouthin' off, Buster, I'm gonna clean your clock!*

* **clean out** (vt) (sl.): take all or almost all of (s/one's) money or possessions >*The casino cleaned out every last one of us.* >*Burglars hit their house Saturday night and cleaned 'em out.*

* **clean up** (vi) (colloq.): make a great deal of money (esp. in a short period of time) >*We're going to clean up when this gets on the market.*

** **clean up [one's] act** (colloq.): start behaving better, start following the rules, reform [oneself] >*If you don't clean up your act, you're off the team.*

* **come clean** (sl.): confess, admit the truth >*Come clean, Perry, and it'll go easier for ya in court.*

— **keep [one's] nose clean** (see **NOSE**)

CLEANERS

* **take [s/one] to the cleaners**[1] (sl.): take all or almost all of [s/one's] money or possessions >*She took him to the cleaners in the divorce settlement.*

— **take [s/one] to the cleaners**[2] (sl.): defeat [s/one] decisively >*In last night's game the Pistons took 'em to the cleaners, 119 to 83.*

CLEAR

* **clear** (colloq.): completely >*Go clear to the end of the block, and then turn right.*

* **(as) clear as a bell** (colloq.): very clear >*The sky's as clear as a bell tonight.* >*His explanation was clear as a bell.*

— **(as) clear as mud** (sl., hum., sarc.): not at all clear, quite confusing >*He thought he explained it all right, but what he said was as clear as mud.*

* **clear out (of)** (colloq.): leave, get out (of) (esp. hurriedly) >*They decided to clear out before the cops got there.* >*Those deadbeats cleared out of the apartment before the manager could get the rent they owed.*

— **loud and clear** (see LOUD)

CLICK

* **click¹** (vi) (sl.): work together well, relate well, be compatible >*We clicked when we first met, and we've been good friends ever since.*

* **click²** (vi) (sl.): finally be perceived, become understood or clear >*I knew I'd seen him somewhere before, and then it clicked—he's Betsy's ex-husband.*

— **click³** (vi) (sl.): succeed, gain popularity, be a hit >*If this movie clicks, it'll start a trend.*

CLIFF-HANGER

* **cliff-hanger** (colloq.): story with moments of great suspense, contest or situation with an uncertain outcome >*That spy movie was a real cliff-hanger.* >*The game was cliff-hanger. The Lakers won with a basket in the last two seconds.*

CLIMB

** **climb the walls** (sl.): be very tense or anxious, be desperately bored >*She's climbin' the walls after bein' with that two-year-old all day.* >*Let's go to town and do somethin'. I'm climbin' the walls here.*

CLINCHER

* **clincher** (klin´chǝr) (colloq.): conclusive remark, decisive fact, deciding factor >*Then she found out he was married. But the clincher was that*

he had two wives! >*I was just about decided on the pickup. The clincher was the $500 rebate they offered me.*

CLINGING VINE

— **clinging vine** (colloq.): overly emotionally dependent person >*I want a girl with a mind of her own, not some clinging vine.*

CLINK

— **the clink** (sl.): jail >*They threw him in the clink until he sobered up.*

CLIP

* **clip¹** (colloq.): fast pace >*I was moving at a pretty good clip when I hit the pothole.*

— **clip²** (colloq.): sharp and quick blow >*Clint took a clip on the ear but didn't go down.*

— **clip³** (vt) (colloq.): hit sharply and quickly >*The stick clipped him on the chin.*

— **clip⁴** (vt) (sl.): cheat, swindle, overcharge >*I think they clipped us for about ten bucks in that bar.*

— **clip along** (vi) (colloq.): move fast, speed >*We were clipping along about eighty when the cop stopped us.*

CLIP JOINT

— **clip joint** (sl.): establishment that cheats or overcharges customers >*Don't go into that clip joint unless ya got money to waste.*

CLIT

— **clit** (klit) (vulg.): clitoris >*The movie showed her clit.*

CLOBBER

* **clobber¹** (klo´bǝr) (vt) (sl.): strike heavily, beat severely >*He clobbered the guy with a wrench.*

* **clobber²** (vt) (sl.): defeat decisively >*The Tigers clobbered 'em last night.*

CLOCK

— **clean [s/one's] clock** (see CLEAN)

CLOD

* **clod** (colloq.): stupid or contemptibly insensitive person >*That clod couldn't begin to understand how she feels.*

CLOSE

— **(close, but) no cigar** (see **CIGAR**)

** **close call** (klōs ...) (colloq.): narrow escape, near miss >*That was a close call. A foot further and that car would have smashed into us.*

* **close down** (klōz ...) (vt) (colloq.): stay at (an establishment) until it closes for the night >*We closed down the joint and got home at dawn.*

* **close shave** (klōs ...) (colloq.): narrow escape, near miss >*I hear you had a close shave with someone who was trying to rob you.*

CLOSET

** **come out of the closet** (colloq.): reveal a secret identity (esp. as a homosexual) >*When he came out of the closet, a lot of people were surprised to find out he was gay.*

CLOTHESHORSE

* **clotheshorse** (colloq.): person concerned with dressing fashionably >*Gunther's quite a clotheshorse—he spends half his time in men's stores.*

CLOUD NINE

* **on cloud nine** (colloq.): elated, very happy >*Jerry's been on cloud nine ever since he got the good news.*

CLOUT

** **clout** (klout) (colloq.): influence, political power >*We need someone with clout in the capital to help us with this.*

CLOWN

* **clown** (sl.): obnoxious or contemptible man, foolish person >*Who's the clown flirtin' with Jessica? >Don't count on those clowns gettin' it right.*

CLUB

— **join the club!** (see **JOIN**)

— **welcome to the club!** (see **WELCOME**)

CLUELESS

— **clueless** (sl.): ignorant, unaware, stupid >*The poor guy's clueless as to why people avoid him.*

CLUNKER

* **clunker¹** (klung´kər) (colloq.): dilapidated vehicle >*I'm surprised he can still get around in that clunker.*

— **clunker²** (colloq.): ineffectual thing, failure >*His second movie was a clunker.*

CLUNKY

— **clunky** (klung´kē) (colloq.): awkward, big and heavy >*Are you really going to dance in those clunky boots?*

CLUTCH

— **in the clutch** (colloq.): in a critical or tense situation >*We need someone who can stay calm in the clutch.*

— **pop the clutch** (see **POP**)

C-NOTE

— **C-note** (sl.): one-hundred-dollar bill >*They gave him a C-note for his info.*

COALS

— **rake [s/one] over the coals** (see **RAKE**)

COAST

* **the Coast** (colloq.): the Pacific Coast (of the U.S.) >*She's from Texas but has lived on the Coast for seven years.*

COCK

* **cock¹** (vulg.): penis >*He felt his cock gettin' hard.*

— **cock²** (vulg.): sexual intercourse (with a man) (freq. used with *some* or *any*) >*He said she was always ready for some cock.*

COCKAMAMIE

— **cockamamie** (kok´ə mā´mē) (sl.): nonsensical, ridiculous, absurd >*The guy gave me some cockamamie story about why he had to wear his shirt inside out.*

COCKEYED

* **cockeyed** (koʹkīd) (colloq.): absurd, foolish >*The hitchhiker had some cockeyed idea of going to New Jersey to prospect for gold.*

COCKSUCKER

— **cocksucker**[1] (vulg.): contemptible or malicious person >*I don't like that cocksucker at all.*

— **cocksucker**[2] (vulg.): person who performs fellatio >*He was known in prison as a cocksucker.*

— **cocksucker**[3] (vulg.): person or thing (esp. seen as troublesome) >*I was able to fit every part back in except this little cocksucker. >There's some cocksucker on the phone who says he's got to talk to ya.*

COCKSUCKING

— **cocksucking** (adj.) (vulg.): (intens. to express anger, aggression, or contempt) >*Keep your cocksuckin' hands off my car!*

COCKTEASER

* **cockteaser** (vulg.): woman who flirts with or arouses a man but who will not have sexual intercourse with him >*That cockteaser's givin' ya the come-on, but don't expect to get her into bed.*

CODGER

— **old codger** (… kodʹjər) (colloq., freq. pej.): old man (esp. seen as troublesome or contemptible) >*What's that old codger up to now?*

COED

— **coed**[1] (kōʹed) (colloq.): woman college student >*Do many of the coeds here belong to sororities?*

** **coed**[2] (colloq.): coeducational, involving both male and female students >*They've just finished a new coed dorm.*

COIN

— **coin** (sl.): money >*It'd take a lot of coin to buy a stereo like that.*

COKE

** **coke**[1] (kōk) (colloq.): Coca-Cola, soft drink >*Want a beer or a coke or something?*

** **coke**[2] (sl.): cocaine >*He spent everything he had on his coke habit.*

COLD

* **cold** (colloq.): without advanced preparation >*I went into the test cold. >He got there late and had to play cold.*

— **go cold** (sl.): become ineffective (esp. in a competition) >*They really scored in the first half but went cold in the second.*

* **have [s/thing] down cold** (colloq.): have learned or mastered [s/thing] thoroughly >*I studied the equations all night, and I have them down cold.*

— **hot and cold** (see **HOT**)

— **know [s/thing] cold** (colloq.): know [s/thing] thoroughly, have [s/thing] mastered >*Stravinsky knows the federal regulations cold.*

* **(out) cold** (colloq.): unconscious >*The blow knocked him cold. >He was out cold for eight hours after drinking half a bottle of scotch.*

COLDER

— **colder than a witch's tit** (… tit) (sl., freq. vulg.): extremely cold (weather) >*Turn on the heater. It's colder than a witch's tit this morning.*

COLD FEET

* **cold feet** (colloq.): loss of courage, attack of uncertainty, fear >*She got cold feet and called off the wedding.*

COLD FISH

— **cold fish** (colloq.): person who lacks warmth, overly reserved or unfeeling person >*What a cold fish! Doesn't he ever show any emotion?*

COLD ONE

— **a cold one** (sl.): a cold beer >*Boy, is it hot! How does a cold one sound to ya?*

COLD SHOULDER
* **the cold shoulder** (colloq.): a show of disregard, a snub >*What did he do to Bernice? She's been giving him the cold shoulder.*

COLD TURKEY
* **cold turkey** (colloq.): complete and abrupt withdrawal (from an addictive substance) (also adv.) >*Going through cold turkey is hell for heroin addicts.* >*I quit smoking cold turkey.*

COLLAR
— **collar**[1] (sl.): arrest, person arrested >*The detective made the collar usin' information from an informant.* >*He put the collar in the backseat of the squad car.*

— **collar**[2] (vt) (sl.): arrest >*The cops collared him when he ran from the store.*

— **hot under the collar** (see **HOT**)

COLLEGE TRY
— **the old college try** (colloq.): a sincere effort (esp. when success is doubtful, esp. for a group objective) >*It'll be tough to get it all done today, but we'll give it the old college try.*

COMBO
** **combo**[1] (colloq.): (kom´bō) combination >*I'll have the steak and lobster combo.*

* **combo**[2] (colloq.): small musical group (esp. for jazz or dance music) >*The combo played mostly slow pieces at the reception.*

COME
* **come**[1] (vulg.): semen >*He got come on the sheets.*

* **come**[2] (vi) (vulg.): have an orgasm >*She came before he did.*

* **come**[3] (vi) (vulg.): ejaculate semen >*He came on the sheets.*

* **come across** (vi) (sl.): fulfill a promise, do what is expected (esp. payment of money) >*Lennie came across with fifty bucks when I needed it.*

* **come across (as)** (colloq.): give the impression (of being), seem, be seen (as) >*Your boyfriend comes across as a real nice guy.*

— **come again?** (colloq.): what? please repeat what you said! >*Come again? I didn't hear you.*

— **come apart at the seams** (see **APART**)

— **come clean** (see **CLEAN**)

— **come down** (vi) (sl.): lose the effects of a drug, lose a feeling of exhilaration >*He's gonna feel real bad when he comes down from that high.* >*Let her enjoy her victory—when she comes down, we'll talk business.*

* **come down (hard) on** (colloq.): reprimand or criticize (severely), punish (severely) >*The coach came down hard on Jones when he messed up the play.* >*The cops have really been coming down on addicts lately.*

— **come down the pike** (colloq.): appear, come forth, come into being >*Ned gets caught up in every fad to come down the pike.*

— **come hell or high water** (colloq.): whatever may happen, no matter what >*I'm determined to succeed, come hell or high water.*

** **come in handy** (colloq.): prove to be useful or beneficial >*That overtime pay will sure come in handy this month.*

— **come off**[1] (vi) (colloq.): occur, take place, be realized >*If this deal comes off, we'll make a fortune.* >*The play came off without a hitch.*

— **come off**[2] (vi) (colloq.): result, turn out, be viewed (in conclusion) >*How did your party come off?* >*He tried to keep his cool, but he came off like an ass.*

* **come off it!** (colloq.): stop insisting on or trying to promote (s/thing ridiculous or untrue)! >*Come off it! We all know that's a lie.* >*She ain't going to fall for a clown like you, so just come off it!*

* **come on** (vi) (colloq.): present (oneself) (in a certain way), make a (certain) impression >*The speaker came on as a regular kind of guy.* >*He came on real sweet and soon had them agreeing with everything he said.*

** **come on!**[1] (colloq.): hurry up! >*Come on! We don't have all day.*

** **come on!**[2] (colloq.): please! don't resist! >*Come on! Let me have a taste.*

* **come on!**[3] (colloq.): stop that! (esp. objectionable behavior) >*Come on! We can't have you two fighting.*

* **come on strong** (colloq.): present (oneself) in a very assertive or showy way, behave overly aggressively >*Use a little finesse, because if you come on too strong you'll scare her off.*

* **come on to** (sl.): flirt with, make sexual advances toward >*She can't stand it when guys in bars come on to her.*

— **come out of the closet** (see **CLOSET**)

* **come/crawl out of the woodwork** (colloq.): appear quickly and unexpectedly (said esp. of a large number of persons seen as troublesome or contemptible) >*When they announced she'd won the lottery, con men, people with investment schemes, and long-lost friends came out of the woodwork.*

— **come out on top** (see **TOP**)

** **come over** (vi) (colloq.): pay (s/one) an informal visit >*Mildred came over yesterday, and we had a nice chat.*

* **come through** (vi) (colloq.): fulfill expectations, perform well >*Don't forget you promised to help. You'll come through, won't you?* >*Kraft came through at the meeting, and we made the sale.*

— **come unglued** (see **UNGLUED**)

— **come up roses** (colloq.): turn out well, have a successful result >*We were worried about that deal, but everything's coming up roses.*

** **come up with** (colloq.): supply, produce, elaborate (esp. a solution or proposal) >*We got to come up with a way to deal with this.*

— **come/go with the territory** (see **TERRITORY**)

— **where [s/one] comes in** (see **WHERE**)

COMEDOWN
— **comedown** (colloq.): disappointment, humiliation >*Losing out to the younger man was a real comedown for him.*

COME-ON
** **come-on** (sl.): enticement, lure, inducement >*That special is just a come-on—everything else is overpriced.* >*Did ya see her smile at me? What a come-on!*

— **give [s/one] the come-on** (sl.): flirt with [s/one], convey a romantic or sexual invitation to [s/one] >*Peggy's been givin' ya the come-on. Why don't ya ask her for a date?*

COMER
— **comer** (kuˊmər) (colloq.): person with promise, person progressing toward success >*Wilson's got what it takes— he's a comer in this organization.*

COMEUPPANCE
— **comeuppance** (kumˊupˊəns) (colloq.): deserved punishment, just desserts >*Moe finally got his comeuppance for acting like a jerk.*

COMFY
* **comfy** (kumˊfē) (colloq.): comfortable >*You comfy in your nice, warm bed?*

COMING
— **coming apart at the seams** (see **APART**)

* **get what's coming to [one]** (colloq.): receive the punishment that [one] deserves >*If I get my hands on her she'll get what's coming to her.*

— have another thing/think coming (see ANOTHER)

* (have) ... coming out (of) [one's] ass (vulg.): (have) an abundance of ..., (have) ... in large supply >*Whatcha mean they can't afford it? They got money comin' out their ass.* >*He's had offers comin' outta his ass since he quit his job.*

* (have) ... coming out (of) [one's] ears (colloq.): (have) an abundance of ..., (have) ... in large supply >*We need extra help—we have customers coming out of our ears.*

** have it coming (colloq.): deserve (a punishment) >*He got beat up bad, but he had it coming.*

— where [s/one] is coming from (see WHERE)

COMMIE
* commie (ko´mē) (colloq., pej.): communist >*The commies were behind it.* >*He used to think everything was a commie plot.*

COMP
— comp (komp) (colloq.): comprehensive exam >*She's passed all her comps but one.*

COMPANY
— the Company (colloq.): the U.S. Central Intelligence Agency >*He got tired of the espionage game and quit the Company.*

COMPUTER
— (computer) hacker (see HACKER)

CON
* con[1] (kon) (sl.): convict, ex-convict >*The guy's a con. Are ya gonna trust him?*

* con[2] (sl.): swindle, confidence game, theft through deception >*He lost a lot of money in the con.*

** con[3] (vt) (sl.): swindle, trick, deceive (using persuasion) >*Before I knew it,*

the guy had conned me outta ten bucks. >*Don't get conned into helpin' clean up.*

CON ARTIST
— con artist (kon ...) (sl.): confidence man, swindler, trickster >*Don't let that con artist sweet-talk ya into anything.*

CONDITION
** condition (colloq.): chronic malady, disease, or impairment >*I can't because of my heart condition.* >*She has this condition and can't eat fatty foods.*

CONDO
** condo (kon´dō) (colloq.): condominium (residence) >*They just sold their house and bought a new condo.*

CONFAB
— confab (kon´fab) (colloq.): confabulation, discussion, conversation >*The club had a confab to plan its next event.*

CON GAME
* con game (kon ...) (sl.): confidence game, swindle >*I can't believe he fell for that old con game.*

CONGRATS
* congrats! (kən grats´) (colloq.): congratulations! >*Congrats on your win!* >*I hear you got the scholarship. Congrats!*

CON JOB
* con job (kon ...) (sl.): confidence game, trick, deception (using persuasion) >*That con job landed him in jail.* >*They did a real con job on him to get him to take responsibility for the whole mess.*

CONK
— conk[1] (kongk/kôngk) (sl.): hit, blow (esp. to the head) >*The conk on his head left a big bump.*

— conk[2] (vt) (sl.): hit (esp. on the head) >*She conked him good with a broom handle.*

— **conk out**[1] (vi) (sl.): fall asleep, lose consciousness >*Gretchen was so tired she conked out durin' the movie.*

— **conk out**[2] (vi) (sl.): fail, come to a stop (esp. an engine) >*My car conked out halfway up the hill.*

CON MAN

* **con man** (kon …) (sl.): confidence man, swindler, trickster >*The judge gave the con man a ten-year sentence.*

CONNECT

* **connect**[1] (vi) (colloq.): discover compatibility, relate well >*When they met, they connected, and they got married two weeks later.* >*Don't make them work together—they just don't connect.*

— **connect**[2] (vi) (colloq.): hit (s/thing) squarely >*Fritz connected with a right jab and the dude went right down.*

CONNECTED

— **connected** (colloq.): having influential friends or associates >*He never has any problems getting permits because he's connected downtown.*

CONNECTION

* **connection** (sl.): drug dealer or provider (for s/one) >*His connection deals dope in the projects.*

CONNIPTION FIT

— **conniption fit** (kə nip´shən …) (colloq.): fit of anger, tantrum >*The boss is going to have a conniption fit when she finds out we lost the account.*

CONTRACT

* **put a contract out on** (sl.): give an order to kill, hire a killer to murder >*The mafia put a contract out on him 'cause he informed on 'em.*

CONTRAPTION

* **contraption** (kən trap´shən) (colloq.): machine, device (seen unenthusias- tically) >*You expect me to sit on that contraption?*

COOK

* **cook** (vi) (sl.): perform enthusiastically and well, work energetically, be full of activity >*That saxophone player is really cookin'!* >*This nightclub really cooks on Saturdays.*

— **cook [s/one's] goose** (see **GOOSE**)

— **cook the books** (sl.): manipulate financial records (for illegal purposes) >*He's been cookin' the books for years, but the auditors have never caught it.*

* **cook up** (vt) (colloq.): plan, contrive, invent (esp. s/thing questionable) >*Joey and his brother are cooking up a scheme to cheat tourists.* >*Who cooked up that lame excuse?*

COOKIE

* **… cookie** (sl.): … person (seen as having some impressive quality) >*Ya won't beat him easily—he's a tough cookie.* >*It's gonna take a real smart cookie to figure this one out.*

— **that's the way the cookie crumbles** (colloq., freq. sarc.): that's how things happen, that's fate >*Too bad she dumped you for me, but that's the way the cookie crumbles.*

COOKIES

— **toss [one's] cookies** (see **TOSS**)

COOKING

* **cooking** (sl.): happening, going on >*What's cookin', buddy?* >*There's a hot party cookin' tonight at Chris's.*

— **cooking with gas** (sl.): working effectively, performing well >*Ya get the right tools, and you'll be cookin' with gas.*

COOKY

— **… cooky** (see **COOKIE**)

COOL

** **cool**[1] (sl.): fine, terrific, excellent >*That's a real cool truck he drives.*

** **cool**[2] (sl.): socially valued, behaviorally desirable, stylish, sophisticated >*Those* *punks think it's cool to smoke.* >*It's not cool to ask for free drinks, man.*

** **cool³** (vt) (sl.): curtail, halt, restrict (an undesirable activity) >*Hey, will ya cool the talkin'? We can't hear the movie.* >*I'd cool the name-callin' if I was you. The dude's got a short fuse.*

— **a cool ...** (colloq.): a full ... or at least ... (a sum of money), ... (a sum of money) without exaggeration >*He lost a cool two grand at the races.* >*They'll get a cool twenty million for the hotel.*

— **(as) cool as a cucumber** (colloq.): completely maintaining (one's) composure, in complete control of (one's) emotions >*Wes stayed cool as a cucumber during the robbery.*

* **blow/lose [one's] cool** (sl.): lose [one's] composure, lose control of [one's] emotions, get angry >*I hope I don't blow my cool in the interview.* >*He lost his cool at the meeting and started yellin' at everybody.*

— **cool [one's] heels** (colloq.): be kept waiting >*I cooled my heels in the mayor's office for over an hour before she'd see me.*

** **cool it** (sl.): calm down, stop (one's undesirable behavior) >*Cool it! Yellin' won't help.* >*I told Danny to cool it when he started tellin' a dirty joke.*

* **cool it with** (sl.): stop doing or saying >*I told him to cool it with the animal imitations.* >*Cool it with your dumb remarks about my sister!*

* **cool off** (vi) (colloq.): calm down, let (one's) anger subside >*You'd better cool off before you go accusing anyone.*

— **cool out** (vi) (sl.): calm down, let (one's) anger or anxiousness subside >*I told him to cool out before he talked to the judge.*

** **keep [one's] cool** (sl.): keep [one's] composure, remain calm >*If we all keep our cool, we'll work this out without a major hassle.*

— **play it cool** (see **PLAY**)

COOLER
— **the cooler** (sl.): jail >*A couple of days in the cooler will straighten him up.*

COON
— **coon** (kŭn) (sl., pej.): black person >*Did ya hear that jerk call that black guy a coon?*

COON'S
— **a coon's age** (... kŭnz ...) (sl.): a long time (esp. that s/thing has not recurred) >*How is old Jake? I ain't seen him in a coon's age.*

COOP
— **fly the coop** (see **FLY**)

COOT
— **old coot** (... kŭt) (colloq., freq. pej.): old man (esp. seen as troublesome or contemptible) >*What's that old coot griping about now?*

COOTIE
— **cootie** (kū′tē) (colloq.): louse, germ (used esp. by children) >*He touched my sandwich and got his cooties all over it.*

COP
** **cop¹** (kop) (colloq.): police officer >*Some cop stopped him for speeding.* >*Thief! Call the cops!*

— **cop²** (vt) (sl.): steal >*The shoplifter copped a radio from the department store.*

— **cop a feel** (sl., freq. vulg.): feel or fondle (s/one) sexually (esp. furtively) >*He tried to cop a feel, but she slapped him.*

* **cop a plea** (sl.): plead guilty to a lesser charge to avoid being prosecuted on a more serious charge >*He was charged with first-degree murder, but he copped a plea for voluntary manslaughter.*

** **cop out** (vi) (sl.): back out (of a commitment), avoid (one's) responsibility, renege >*I'm countin' on ya, so don't cop out on me.* >*He got cold feet and copped out.*

— **cop some rays** (see **RAYS**)

— **cop some Zs** (see **ZS**)

COP-OUT

** **cop-out** (kop´out´) (sl.): evasion of responsibility, reneging >*Sayin' you're too busy to help is a cop-out.*

COPPER

— **copper** (sl., freq. pej.): police officer (also voc.) >*He says he hates the copper that arrested him.* >*Ya won't take me alive, copper!*

COPTER

* **copter**[1] (kop´tər) (colloq.): helicopter >*We took a copter ride over the site.*

— **copter**[2] (vi, vt) (colloq.): travel/take by helicopter >*They coptered from the airport to their headquarters.* >*They coptered him to the hospital.*

COPYCAT

* **copycat** (colloq.): imitator, person who copies another >*Why does that copycat have to do everything the same way as me?*

CORK

— **pop/blow [one's] cork** (sl.): become furious, lose [one's] temper >*Richards popped his cork when they accused him of stealin'.*

— **put a cork in it** (sl.): stop talking, shut up >*I wish that loudmouth would just put a cork in it.*

CORKER

— **corker** (kôr´kər) (colloq.): astounding or remarkable person or thing >*Now I've heard everything—that was sure a corker of a story.* >*Her old man's a corker. You should just hear him.*

CORN

— **corn** (colloq.): s/thing trite or overly sentimental, s/thing tastelessly unsophisticated >*Don't see that sappy movie. It's nothing but corn.*

CORNBALL

— **cornball** (colloq.): trite or overly sentimental person, tastelessly unsophisticated person (also adj.) >*What a cornball! He made her a heart-shaped cake with their initials on it.* >*Her and her cornball ideas about love conquering all!*

CORNERS

— **cut corners** (see **CUT**)

CORNHOLE

— **cornhole** (vt) (vulg.): have anal intercourse with (as penetrator) >*They say he got cornholed in prison.*

CORNY

* **corny** (colloq.): trite or overly sentimental, tastelessly unsophisticated >*Those small-town parades are so corny.*

CORRAL

— **corral** (vt) (colloq.): gather, capture, obtain >*Where did you corral these helpers?*

COTTON

— **cotton to** (colloq.): become fond of, approve of, agree with (freq. used in the neg.) >*I don't cotton to having folks borrow my things without asking.*

COTTONPICKING

— **cottonpicking** (sl.): contemptible, cursed, annoying >*Keep your cottonpickin' feet off the couch!*

COUCH POTATO

** **couch potato**[1] (sl.): person who spends an excessive amount of time watching television (esp. while on a couch) >*Dave's becomin' a real couch potato. He watches the tube at least eight hours a day.*

— **couch potato**[2] (vi) (sl.): spend an excessive amount of time watching television (esp. while on a couch) >*I don't feel like goin' out. Let's just couch potato this weekend.*

COUGH

* **cough up** (vi, vt) (sl.): give or contribute reluctantly or with sacrifice (esp. money) >*I had to cough up fifty*

bucks to get my car back. >Come on! You can cough up like everyone else for Ruby's present.

COULD
— **could care less** (see **CARE**)
— **could eat a horse** (see **EAT**)

COUNT
— **count noses** (colloq.): count the number of people present >*Let's count noses to be sure no one's missing.*

COUNTRY MILE
— **a country mile** (colloq.): a long distance >*He can throw a football a country mile.*

COURSE
— **be par for the course** (see **PAR**)
— **the ball is in [s/one's] court** (see **BALL**)

COVER
* **blow [s/one's, one's] cover** (colloq.): accidentally allow [s/one's, one's] true identity to be discovered, ruin [s/one's, one's] assumed identity >*Pretend you don't know me, or you'll blow my cover. >The detective blew his cover when he let his gun be spotted.*

** **cover [one's] ass** (vulg.): take steps to avoid suffering blame or harm >*You'd better cover your ass by writin' a memo tellin' just what happened.*

** **cover for** (colloq.): substitute for (s/one) during (his/her) absence, take care of (s/one's) responsibilities while (he/she) is away >*Can you cover for me this afternoon? I got to take my car to get fixed.*

COW
— **cow** (sl., pej.): large and slovenly woman >*Why doesn't that cow take better care of herself?*

* **have a cow** (sl.): become furious, lose emotional control >*The boss had a cow when he saw how they'd screwed everything up.*

COWBOY
— **cowboy** (sl.): reckless person, dangerous show-off, person who confronts dangerous situations without due caution (esp. a driver) (also adj.) >*That damn cowboy's gonna cause a bad wreck. >We can't have anyone with a cowboy mentality in charge of these weapons.*

COW PIE
— **cow pie** (colloq.): piece of cow dung >*Don't step in that cow pie!*

COYOTE
— **coyote** (sl.): smuggler of undocumented immigrants across the border from Mexico to the U.S. >*The coyotes charge at least 500 bucks a head to bring 'em across the river.*

COZY
— **cozy up (to)**[1] (colloq.): become friendly (toward) (esp. to gain favor) >*I don't like the way Redfield's been cozying up to the new supervisor.*

— **cozy up (to)**[2] (colloq.): move nearer to (s/thing, s/one) for comfort or affection >*Come and cozy up to the stove. >My girl and me like to cozy up on cold nights.*

CRAB
— **crab**[1] (colloq.): crab louse >*She got crabs from some guy she slept with.*

— **crab**[2] (colloq.): bad-tempered or grouchy person >*I'm sick and tired of trying to please that crab.*

— **crab**[3] (vi) (colloq.): complain, find fault >*That grouchy old lady's always crabbing about something that doesn't suit her.*

CRABBY
* **crabby** (krab´ē) (colloq.): bad-tempered, grouchy, complaining >*A bunch of crabby old men are driving the social director crazy.*

CRACK
** **crack**[1] (sl.): rock cocaine >*Smokin' crack'll kill ya.*

* **crack²** (colloq.): sarcastic or humorous comment, snide remark >*What did you mean by that crack?*

* **crack³** (colloq.): chance, opportunity to try, attempt >*I get first crack at the new video game.* >*Do you want a crack at the job?*

— **crack⁴** (vulg.): vagina >*He peeked up her dress tryin' to get a look at her crack.*

* **crack⁵** (vt) (colloq.): tell (jokes) >*The guy's a real card—he kept cracking jokes all night.*

* **crack⁶** (vi) (colloq.): lose mental or emotional control (esp. due to stress or pressure), break down >*If he doesn't take a vacation soon, he's going to crack.* >*Pressure her a little and she'll crack.*

* **[neg.] crack a book** (colloq.): [neg.] study at all >*He passed the test without even cracking a book.*

* **crack a smile** (colloq.): let (even a small) smile show, start to smile >*He thought he was being funny, but she didn't even crack a smile.*

** **crack up¹** (vi, vt) (colloq.): laugh/make laugh hard >*Joanna cracked up when she heard the story.* >*That comedian cracks me up.*

* **crack up²** (vi) (colloq.): go crazy, have a mental breakdown >*He used to be an air traffic controller, but he cracked up under the pressure.*

— **crack up³** (vi, vt) (colloq.): crash, wreck (a vehicle) >*They cracked up on the freeway.* >*Barlow cracked up his plane when he tried to land in a wheat field.*

— **hard/tough nut to crack** (see **NUT**)

* **take/have a crack at** (colloq.): make an attempt at, give (s/thing) a try >*Here, you take a crack at setting the timer, because I can't.* >*Lew had a crack at the job, but they took a guy with more experience.*

CRACKED
* **cracked** (colloq.): mentally unbalanced, very eccentric >*If you ask me, the guy is really cracked. He's just too weird.*

* **cracked up to be** (colloq.): with the reputation of being (freq. used after a neg.) >*The film wasn't as good as it was cracked up to be.* >*Mason's cracked up to be quite a lawyer.*

CRACKER
— **cracker** (sl., pej.): poor white person from the U.S. South, white person (used esp. among blacks) >*The brothers don't want no crackers tellin' 'em what to do.*

CRACKERJACK
— **crackerjack** (sl.): skilled or talented person (in some activity), expert (also adj.) >*Watch him make this jump shot— he's a crackerjack at 'em.* >*We need a crackerjack analyst for this project.*

CRACKING
* **get cracking** (colloq.): begin moving quickly, begin working hard >*Come on, guys! Let's get cracking on this so we can finish by noon.*

CRACKPOT
* **crackpot** (colloq.): fanatical or very eccentric person, mentally unbalanced person (also adj.) >*He interviewed some crackpot who thinks the world is cube-shaped.* >*Get out of here with your crackpot ideas!*

CRACKS
— **fall/slip through/between the cracks** (see **FALL**)

CRACKUP
* **crackup¹** (colloq.): extremely funny person or thing >*The comic is a real crackup.* >*His fly-in-the-soup act is a crackup.*

— **crackup²** (colloq.): mental or nervous breakdown >*Her crackup was right after her divorce.*

— **crackup³** (colloq.): crash, wreck (of a vehicle) >*There was a big crackup on the highway that jammed up traffic for hours.

CRACKY
— **by cracky!**[1] (… krak´ē) (colloq.): (interj. to express determination or resolve) >*I'll find out who did it, by cracky!*

— **by cracky!**[2] (colloq.): (interj. to express surprise, wonder, or admiration) >*By cracky, it looks like it's finally going to rain!*

CRADLE
— **rob the cradle** (see **ROB**)

CRAM
** **cram** (vi) (colloq.): study hard at the last moment (for an examination) >*I haven't been studying much, so I'm going to have to cram for my tests.*

CRAMP
* **cramp [s/one's] style** (colloq.): interfere with [s/one's] usual skilled performance, hamper [s/one] >*Don't look over my shoulder, man! You're cramping my style.*

CRANK
— **crank**[1] (colloq.): bad-tempered or grouchy person >*That crank can't get along with anyone.*

— **crank**[2] (colloq.): fanatical or overly zealous person, rancorous zealot (also adj.) >*All the cranks showed up when the issue was discussed by the city council.* >*The talk show gets a lot of crank calls.*

* **crank out** (vt) (colloq.): produce in large quantities or with ease >*He cranks out four or five speeches a week for the party bosses.*

* **crank up** (vt) (colloq.): start up, put into operation >*Go crank up the generator, will you?*

CRANKY
** **cranky** (krang´kē) (colloq.): bad-tempered, grouchy >*She's always*

cranky before her first cup of coffee in the morning.

CRAP
** **crap**[1] (krap) (vulg.): excrement, dung >*He stepped in some dog crap.*

** **crap**[2] (sl., freq. vulg.): lie, false or exaggerated story, nonsense (also interj.) >*That talk about him knowin' the mayor is a bunch of crap.* >*I don't wanna hear none of his political crap.* >*Him, a movie star?! Crap!*

** **crap**[3] (sl., freq. vulg.): bad treatment, unjust dealings >*I wouldn't take that crap from anyone.*

** **crap**[4] (sl., freq. vulg.): junk, litter, worthless things >*We need to clean up all the crap in the yard.*

* **crap**[5] (sl., freq. vulg.): annoying or tedious work or demands >*I got a bunch of crap to take care of before I leave work today.*

— **crap**[6] (sl., freq. vulg.): (one's) belongings, things in general (that belong to s/one) >*Let's help her load her crap in the car.*

* **crap**[7] (vi) (vulg.): defecate >*Some bird crapped on my car.*

— **crap!** (sl., freq. vulg.): (interj. to express anger, surprise, or irritation) >*Ya forgot to lock the door? Crap!*

— **crap around** (vi) (sl., freq. vulg.): pass time idly, work halfheartedly or unproductively >*We're losin' money because too many of our employees are crappin' around.*

* **crap out** (vi) (sl.): give up, back out, withdraw (esp. due to fear or lost enthusiasm) >*Don't crap out on me now—an hour more and we'll have the job done.* >*We were all havin' a good time, but Ernie crapped out after two beers and went home.*

— **full of crap** (see **FULL**)

* **give a crap** (sl., freq. vulg.): be concerned, care, take interest (freq. used

in the neg.) >*He's gettin' lousy grades 'cause he doesn't give a crap about school.*

* **like crap** (sl., freq. vulg.): bad, awful (also adv.) >*Your car looks like crap. Why don't ya wash it?* >*Can ya type this for me? I type like crap.*

— **piece of crap** (see **PIECE**)

* **take a crap** (vulg.): defecate >*Some dog took a crap on the sidewalk.*

— **... the crap out of [s/one, s/thing]** (sl., freq. vulg.): ... [s/one, s/thing] to the utmost degree, ... [s/one, s/thing] extraordinarily (esp. in a neg. way) >*His racin' motorcycles worries the crap outta his wife.*

CRAPOLA
— **crapola** (kra pō'lə) (sl., freq. vulg.): lie, false or exaggerated story, nonsense >*Who's gonna fall for that crapola?*

CRAPPER
— **crapper** (krap'ər) (vulg.): toilet, bathroom >*He's in the crapper, but he'll be out in a minute.*

CRAPPY
* **crappy**[1] (krap'ē) (sl., freq. vulg.): offensive, contemptible >*What a crappy attitude some of those kids have!*

* **crappy**[2] (sl., freq. vulg.): inferior, worthless >*These crappy scissors don't work at all.*

CRASH
* **crash**[1] (vt) (colloq.): enter (a social event) without permission or invitation (cf. "GATE-CRASHER") >*Some of your brother's jerky friends crashed our party.*

* **crash**[2] (vi) (sl.): spend the night, sleep (s/where) (esp. on an impromptu, non-payment basis) >*Can we crash at your place tonight?*

* **crash**[3] (vi) (sl.): fall asleep >*He drove all night, got home, and crashed.*

— **crash**[4] (vi) (sl.): lose the effects of a drug, lose a feeling of exhilaration >*This guy's really feeling high, but when he crashes he's gonna be in bad shape.*

— **crash**[5] (vi) (sl.): (for a computer or software program to) fail >*Crap! My program just crashed, and I didn't save my data!*

* **crash**[6] (colloq.): intensive (endeavor) (esp. when under a time constraint) >*They're going to need a crash course in Spanish before they move to Guatemala.* >*I'm going on a crash diet to lose ten pounds before my birthday.*

— **crash the gate** (colloq.): enter (a social event) without permission or invitation >*Some rowdy guys tried to crash the gate last night at the dance, but we threw them out.*

CRASH PAD
— **crash pad** (sl.): temporary and free lodging >*His apartment's the crash pad for all the musicians that come through town.*

CRATE
— **crate** (colloq.): dilapidated or rickety old vehicle >*When are you going to trade in this old crate on a new car?* >*Is this crate safe to fly?*

CRAWL
— **come/crawl out of the woodwork** (see **COME**)

CRAWLING
* **crawling with** (colloq.): having a large number of (living things) >*The awards banquet was crawling with reporters.* >*Call the exterminator—the kitchen's crawling with ants!*

CRAZY
* **crazy**[1] (sl.): weird person, oddball, extreme nonconformist >*A bunch of crazies that eat only brown rice rent that house.* >*Watch out for the crazies if ya go out at night.*

** **crazy**[2] (colloq.): impractical, not sensible >*That's a crazy idea—it's too complicated.*

** **crazy**[3] (colloq.): unusual, strange >*Have you seen the crazy books he's been reading?*

* **crazy**[4] (colloq.): wildly enthusiastic, very fond, enamored >*He's crazy about Brenda.* >*I'm just crazy about skiing.*

— **crazy**[5] (sl.): wonderful, terrific >*That was a crazy ride, man—let's do it again.*

* **...-crazy** (colloq.): wildly enthusiastic or very fond of ... >*Their fifteen-year-old is boy-crazy.* >*Al's been car-crazy since he was sixteen.*

* **like crazy** (sl.): wholeheartedly, to the utmost degree >*Everyone was workin' like crazy to finish on time.* >*There were people like crazy out shoppin' today.*

CRAZY BONE

— **crazy bone** (colloq.): olecranon, ulnar nerve in elbow (which gives a sharp, tingling pain when hit) >*Ow! I hit my crazy bone on the corner of the table!*

CRAZY HOUSE

— **crazy house** (sl.): insane asylum, mental institution >*The judge ruled he was insane, and he ended up in the state crazy house.*

CREAM

— **cream**[1] (vt) (sl.): defeat decisively >*We creamed them, seventeen to three!*

— **cream**[2] (vt) (sl.): strike heavily, beat severely >*If he calls me that again, I'll cream him.*

— **cream**[3] (vi) (vulg.): ejaculate (semen) >*He said he creamed in his pants.*

— **(about) cream [one's] jeans** (vulg.): be overcome with delight, be enraptured >*She about creamed her jeans when she saw the movie star.*

CREAM PUFF

— **cream puff** (colloq.): weak and timid person, sissy >*The other team's a bunch of cream puffs—we'll massacre them!*

CREATE

* **create a monster** (colloq.): give impetus to s/one who becomes excessively involved in s/thing, give a start to s/one who becomes a fanatic >*You created a monster when you took Billy to that first hockey game. That's all he thinks and talks about now.*

CREEK

— **up shit creek** (see SHIT)

* **up the creek (without a paddle)** (... krēk ...) (sl.): in (serious) trouble, in a (bad) predicament >*We'll be up the creek if they don't OK the loan.*

CREEP

** **creep** (colloq.): very weird or repugnant person >*I don't want that creep coming around here any more.*

CREEPS

* **the creeps** (colloq.): goose bumps or sensation on the skin caused by fear or revulsion, feeling of horror or disgust >*This old house gives me the creeps.* >*I got the creeps when I saw all those maggots.*

CREEPY

* **creepy** (krē´pē) (colloq.): repugnant, uncomfortably weird, scary >*Keep your creepy hands off me!* >*Let's get out of this creepy place.*

CRIB

— **crib** (colloq.): list of answers used to cheat on a test >*The teacher caught them using a crib during the test.*

CRIMINY

— **criminy!** (krī´mə nē) (colloq.): (interj. to express anger, surprise, or irritation) >*Criminy! Can't you fix it before Friday?*

CRIP

— **crip** (krip) (sl., pej.): crippled person (also voc.) >*Hey, the crip's crutches are over here.* >*Outta my way, crip!*

CRIPES
— **cripes!** (krīps) (colloq.): (interj. to express anger, surprise, or irritation) >*Cripes! I almost hit that pedestrian.*

CROAK
* **croak[1]** (vi) (sl.): die >*The old man caught pneumonia and croaked.*

— **croak[2]** (vt) (sl.): murder, kill >*They said they'd croak him if he went to the cops.*

CROC
— **croc** (krok) (colloq.): crocodile >*They had a Nile croc on display at the zoo.*

CROCK
* **crock** (sl.): lie, false or exaggerated story, nonsense >*What he told ya was a crock—I know better.*

* **crock of shit** (… shit) (vulg.): lie, false or exaggerated story, nonsense >*Ya wouldn't have believed the crock of shit he tried to give us!*

CROCKED
— **crocked** (krokt) (sl.): drunk >*They picked up a bottle of vodka and got crocked.*

CROOK
** **crook** (colloq.): thief, swindler, criminal, dishonest person >*They should put that crook in prison and throw away the key.*

CROOKED
** **crooked** (colloq.): dishonest, fraudulent, criminal >*I bet there were some kickbacks or other crooked dealings involved.*

CROSS
* **cross** (vt) (sl.): betray or cheat (an associate) >*If Davy crosses me, he's had it.*

— **(I) cross my heart (and hope to die)!** (colloq.): I swear that it is true! >*I did too pay him back, cross my heart!*

CROSSED
— **get [one's] wires crossed** (see WIRES)

— **have/keep [one's] fingers crossed** (see FINGERS)

CROSS-EYED
— **look at [s/one] cross-eyed** (see LOOK)

CROW
— **eat crow** (see EAT)

CROWD
— **crowd** (vt) (colloq.): pressure unfairly, threaten, encroach upon >*That new guy at work better stop crowding me, or I'm going to have to talk to the supervisor.*

CROWN
— **crown** (vt) (colloq.): hit (s/one) on the head >*The cop crowned him with her baton.*

CRUD
* **crud[1]** (krud) (sl.): filth, layer of dirt or grime >*I gotta wash this crud off my hands before I eat.*

— **crud[2]** (sl.): offensive or filthy person, contemptible person >*There are a couple of real cruds in my class, but I stay away from 'em.*

— **crud[3]** (sl.): (one's) belongings, things in general (that belong to s/one) >*I don't want ya leavin' your crud in my room.*

— **crud!** (sl.): (interj. to express anger, surprise, or irritation) >*Crud! My pencil just broke.*

— **piece of crud** (see PIECE)

CRUDDY
* **cruddy[1]** (krud´ē) (sl.): filthy, dirty >*Why don't ya wash these cruddy windows?*

* **cruddy[2]** (sl.): inferior, worthless >*I don't wanna see that cruddy movie.*

— **cruddy[3]** (sl.): offensive, contemptible >*Some cruddy guy tried to sell us some pornography.*

CRUISE
* **cruise[1]** (vi, vt) (colloq.): travel (along/ throughout) for fun (esp. in an automobile, esp. to make contact with possible sex partners) >*Let's cruise*

Central Avenue and see if we can pick up some chicks. >*Meg and me went cruising last Saturday.*

* **cruise**[2] (vi) (sl.): go (s/where) (esp. without hurry or strong purpose) >*Let's cruise by Eddie's and see what he's doin'.* >*I think I'll cruise over to the mall and check it out.*

CRUISING

— **cruising for a bruising** (sl., freq. hum.): looking for trouble, risking being beaten up >*You're cruisin' for a bruisin' if ya mess with that rough character.*

CRUMB

— **crumb** (sl.): contemptible or worthless person >*I hate how that crumb treats her.*

CRUMBLES

— **that's the way the cookie crumbles** (see COOKIE)

CRUMBY

— **crumby** (see "CRUMMY")

CRUMMY

** **crummy** (krum´ē) (sl.): inferior, worthless, contemptible >*I don't watch that crummy show.* >*You expect me to do the job for a crummy fifty bucks?*

CRUNCH

* **crunch** (colloq.): crisis situation (esp. due to a shortage) >*A crunch is going to come because a lot of teachers are retiring while enrollments are going up.* >*Business is worried about the credit crunch.*

— **crunch numbers** (colloq.): do numerical calculations, process numerical data (esp. in large quantities) (cf. "NUMBER CRUNCHER") >*He crunches numbers for some accounting firm.* >*We need more powerful software to crunch all these numbers.*

CRUSH

** **crush (on)** (colloq.): romantic infatuation (for) (esp. a short one, esp. of an adolescent) >*Dolly had a crush on her math teacher.*

CRY

* **cry [one's] eyes out** (colloq.): cry continually or inconsolably >*He cried his eyes out but finally got over her.*

— **cry [one's] heart out** (colloq.): cry continually or inconsolably >*She's been crying her heart out over that bum that left her.*

— **say/cry uncle** (see UNCLE)

CRYING

* **for crying out loud!** (colloq.): (interj. to express anger, surprise, or irritation) >*Why didn't you tell me she'd called, for crying out loud?!*

CUCKOO

— **cuckoo** (sl.): crazy, foolish >*The guy's cuckoo if he thinks I'm gonna agree to that.*

CUCUMBER

— **(as) cool as a cucumber** (see COOL)

CUE

— **cue in** (vt) (colloq.): give pertinent information to, bring (s/one) up-to-date >*I'll cue you in later on the plans for next month.*

CUFF

* **cuff** (vt) (colloq.): handcuff >*Be sure to cuff him before you put him in the patrol car.*

— **off the cuff** (colloq.): extemporaneously, without preparation, unofficially (regarding things said) >*Morgan spoke off the cuff about what he thought might happen.*

CUFFS

* **cuffs** (colloq.): handcuffs >*The cuffs were cutting into his wrists.*

CUM

— **cum** (see "COME")

CUNT

* **cunt**[1] (kunt) (vulg., pej.): woman >*He called her a cunt just 'cause she wouldn't sleep with him.*

— **cunt**[2] (vulg.): vagina >*The dancer had a G-string covering her cunt.*

— **cunt**[3] (vulg., pej.): woman or women (seen as sex object[s]) >*He said he saw a lot of nice cunt wearin' bikinis at the beach.*

— **cunt**[4] (vulg.): sexual intercourse (with a woman) (freq. used with *some* or *any*) >*He asked me if I got any cunt when I took her home.*

CURL

— **curl [s/one's] hair** (colloq.): shock or frighten [s/one], horrify [s/one] >*Some of Gunther's war stories would curl your hair.*

CURTAINS

— **curtains** (sl.): end, death, ruin (esp. by violent means) >*It's curtains for 'em if they don't come out and give up.*

CURVE

— **throw [s/one] a curve** (see **THROW**)

CUSHY

* **cushy** (kŭsh´ē) (sl.): easy, soft, undemanding (esp. a job) >*Grant got hisself a real cushy job in his uncle's furniture store.*

CUSS

— **cuss**[1] (kus) (colloq.): man, person (seen as troublesome or contemptible), rascal >*Now where did that cuss take off to with my tools?*

* **cuss**[2] (vi) (colloq.): curse, swear >*I don't want to hear anyone cussing around here.*

* **cuss out** (vt) (colloq.): swear at, reprimand by using vulgarity >*The boss cussed him out for not putting the tools back.*

CUSSWORD

* **cussword** (kus´wûrd´) (colloq.): curse word, obscene or vulgar term >*His mom got mad because she heard him use a cussword.*

CUSTOMER

* **… customer** (colloq.): … person (seen as having some impressive quality) >*A shrewd customer like Barnes will never*

fall for that. >*Good luck—she's a tough customer.*

CUT

** **cut**[1] (colloq.): share of earnings or profit >*Your cut is ten percent if you make the sale.*

** **cut**[2] (vt) (colloq.): intentionally not attend (a class) >*Jason's been cutting math a lot, and he's probably going to flunk.*

— **cut ([s/one]) a check** (sl.): write out a check (to [s/one]) >*I'll cut him a check for fifty bucks just to get rid of him.* >*If ya ain't got the cash, just cut a check.*

— **cut a deal** (colloq.): make a deal, reach an agreement >*I don't want them cutting a deal unless we're in on it.*

— **let/blow/cut a fart** (see **FART**)

* **cut corners** (colloq.): reduce costs, not take due care (in doing s/thing) >*It's not worth it to cut corners on the wiring.*

— **knock/cut [s/one] down to size** (see **KNOCK**)

— **cut in** (vi) (colloq.): interrupt a dancing couple to dance with one of them >*I didn't like Boris cutting in on me when I was dancing with Peggy.*

* **cut it** (colloq.): meet a standard of performance, demonstrate at least a minimum required ability (freq. used in the neg.) >*Old Bernie just can't cut it anymore in this job.* >*This sloppy work just doesn't cut it in our firm.*

— **cut loose (with)**[1] (sl.): send forth aggressively, hurl, shoot, unleash >*She cut loose a punch that doubled him over.* >*They all cut loose with rocks at the same time.*

— **cut loose (with)**[2] (sl.): blurt out, yell, say aggressively >*He cut loose a string of cusswords that would embarrass a sailor.* >*If you cut loose with another belch like that, I'm leavin'.*

— **cut no ice (with)** (colloq.): fail to impress (s/one), not be important (to)

>*Your fame as a football star cuts no ice with anyone in this company.* >*That award cuts no ice here.*

— **cut [s/one] off at the knees** (colloq.): severely incapacitate [s/one] (from accomplishing s/thing) (esp. by undermining or humiliating him/her) >*Spread that rumor around enough, and we'll cut him off at the knees.*

— **cut one** (sl., freq. vulg.): break wind, expel intestinal gas >*Phew! Who cut one?*

** **cut (out)** (vt) (colloq.): stop (doing s/thing) (esp. s/thing bothersome) >*Hey, cut the clowning around, will you?* >*I asked him to cut out the loud talking in the library.* >*Cut it out, dang it!*

— **cut out** (vi) (sl.): depart, leave quickly >*They were here for a few minutes; then they cut out.*

* **cut out for** (colloq.): capable of, having the aptitude or talent for >*I just wasn't cut out for police work, so I quit the force.*

* **cut [one's] own throat** (colloq.): bring harm to [oneself], cause [one's] own ruin or defeat (esp. when trying to bring harm or defeat to another) >*He's cutting his own throat by bringing up the morality business, because he's no saint himself.*

— **cut [s/one] some slack** (sl.): be flexible or lenient with [s/one], reduce the pressure on [s/one] >*Hey, cut me some slack, man. I can't pay it all back right now.*

— **cut the cheese** (sl., freq. vulg.): break wind, expel intestinal gas >*All right, who cut the cheese?*

* **cut the mustard** (sl.): meet a standard of performance, demonstrate at least a minimum required ability >*We'll try ya for a week, and if ya can cut the mustard, you're hired.*

— **cut to the chase** (sl.): come to the point, stop talking about irrelevant or unimportant things (used esp. as a command) >*Stop stallin' and cut to the chase.*

* **cut up** (vi) (colloq.): clown around, play pranks, be mischievous >*Tommy, if you keep cutting up in class, I'm going to have to call your parents.*

— **have [one's] work/job cut out for [one]** (see WORK)

* **(how) you cut/slice it** (colloq.): (how) (a situation) is viewed or analyzed >*No matter how you cut it, someone's going to get hurt.* >*No one can blame me, any way you slice it.*

CUTE

* **cute** (colloq., sarc.): clever, witty (esp. when seen as obnoxious or insolent), impudent >*That jerk thinks he's real cute, doesn't he?* >*Don't try and be cute with them, or they'll slap you around.*

— **(as) cute as a button** (colloq.): very cute >*Her baby's as cute as a button.*

CUTEY

— **cutey** (see "CUTIE")

CUTESY

— **cutesy** (kyūt´sē) (colloq., freq. sarc.): forcedly cute, presumptuously clever >*Cut it out, will you? We're tired of your cutesy remarks.*

CUTIE

* **cutie** (kyūt´ē) (colloq.): cute or attractive person, endearing person (also voc.) >*Sandra thinks Will is a real cutie.* >*Come and sit by me, cutie!*

CUTIE-PIE

— **cutie-pie** (kyūt´ē pī´) (colloq.): cute or attractive person, endearing person (also voc.) >*Who's the cutie-pie that all the boys have been eyeing?* >*How you doing, cutie-pie?*

CUTOFFS

* **cutoffs** (kut´ofs´) (colloq.): shorts made from pants (esp. jeans) cut above the knees >*She hung around the house all summer in T-shirts and cutoffs.*

CUTUP

* **cutup** (colloq.): prankster, mischievous person, clown >*I remember him. He was a cutup in class and was always getting into trouble.*

D

DAD
** **dad** (dad) (colloq.): father (also voc.) >*Glenda's dad bought her a new bike.* >*Hey, Dad, look at this!*

DAD-BLAMED
— **dad-blamed** (dad´blãmd´) (colloq.): contemptible, detestable >*I don't want to go to any dad-blamed tea party.*

DAD-BLASTED
— **dad-blasted** (dad´blas´tid) (colloq.): contemptible, detestable >*Will you turn down that dad-blasted radio?*

DAD-BURNED
— **dad-burned** (dad´bûrnd´) (colloq.): contemptible, detestable >*Where'd I put my dad-burned glasses?*

DADDY
** **daddy** (dad´ē) (colloq.): father (esp. among children) (also voc.) >*Did your daddy bring you to school today?* >*I hurt my finger, Daddy!*

DAFFY
— **daffy** (daf´ē) (colloq.): crazy, silly, foolish >*Does your daffy friend still call himself Tarzan?*

DAGO
— **dago** (dā´gō) (sl., pej.): Italian-American, Italian >*He's gonna get it if he calls me a dago again!* >*He calls it dago wine.*

DAISIES
— **pushing up daisies** (see PUSHING)

DAMAGE
* **the damage(s)** (colloq.): cost, payment due >*A fine meal, waitress! Now, what's the damage?*

DAME
— **dame** (dām) (sl., pej.): woman >*Sorry, honey—no dames allowed in the men's section.*

DAMMIT
— **dammit!** (see "DAMN (it)!")

DAMN
— **a damn(ed) sight better** (colloq.): considerably better >*The new gal's a damned sight better than that last clerk.* >*He sings a damn sight better than his sister.*

** **damn(ed)**[1] (colloq.): very, extremely >*That was a damned good speech.* >*Don't drive so damn fast!*

** **damn(ed)**[2] (colloq., freq. vulg.): contemptible, detestable >*We don't want any damn drugs in our school.*

* **damn(ed)**[3] (colloq.): extraordinary, impressive >*That damn guy can lift over 500!* >*That's the damnedest dog— he must know a hundred tricks!*

* **damn(ed) well** (colloq., freq. vulg.): most certainly (must do s/thing) >*They damn well better pay for the damage.* >*He damned well ought to know—he's the expert.*

** **damn (it)!** (colloq., freq. vulg.): (interj. to express anger, surprise, irritation or disappointment) >*Damn! I cut my finger.* >*Can't you understand, damn it?*

* **damn near** (colloq., freq. vulg.): almost, nearly >*I damn near fell of the roof yesterday when I tripped over my hammer.*

** **give a damn** (colloq., freq. vulg.): be concerned, care, take interest (freq. used in the neg.) >*Don't say I don't give a damn about your feelings—I do too give a damn!*

— **worth a damn** (see WORTH)

— **(you're) damn(ed) straight ...!** (see STRAIGHT)

DAMNED (also see DAMN)
* **(well,) I'll be damned!** (colloq., freq. vulg.): what a surprise! how interesting! >*You mean that bum has a house in Beverly Hills? Well, I'll be damned!*

DAMNEDEST
* **[one's] damnedest** (... dam´dist) (colloq.): [one's] utmost, [one's] best

effort >*She tried her damnedest but just couldn't make it.*

DANDER

— **get [one's] dander up** (... dan´dǝɪ ...) (colloq.): become angry or irritated >*Mable gets her dander up every time another woman flirts with her husband.*

— **get [s/one's] dander up** (colloq.): anger or irritate [s/one] >*It really got the judge's dander up when the defendant called him "buddy."*

DANDY

— **dandy** (colloq.): excellent, fine (also noun) >*I've got a dandy idea for our vacation.* >*Isn't their new car a dandy?*

— **fine and dandy** (see **FINE**)

DANG

— **dang(ed)**[1] (dang[d]) (colloq.): contemptible, detestable >*I don't want any of your dang excuses.*

— **dang(ed)**[2] (colloq.): very, extremely >*It's too dang hot for jogging.*

— **dang(ed)**[3] (colloq.): extraordinary, impressive >*That danged comedian's the best!*

— **dang(ed) well** (colloq.): most certainly (must do s/thing) >*You're danged well going to pay me every cent you owe.*

* **dang (it)!** (colloq.): (interj. to express anger, surprise, irritation, or disappointment) >*Turn down the TV, dang it!* >*Dang, she's pretty!*

— **dang near** (colloq.): almost, nearly >*That fall dang near killed him.*

— **give a dang** (colloq.): be concerned, care, take interest (freq. used in the neg.) >*You just don't give a dang about me, do you?*

— **worth a dang** (wee **WORTH**)

DANGED (also see DANG)

— **(well,) I'll be danged!** (... dangd) (colloq.): what a surprise! how interesting! >*I'll be danged! He made it after all.*

DANGEDEST

— **[one's] dangedest** (... dang´dist) (colloq.): [one's] utmost, [one's] best effort >*We've done our dangedest, but we just can't fix it.*

DARK

— **shot in the dark** (see **SHOT**)

DARK MEAT

— **dark meat** (vulg., pej.): black person/ people (seen as sex object[s]) (cf. **"WHITE MEAT"**) >*He said he cruised the boulevard lookin' for dark meat.*

DARKY

— **darky** (där´kē) (sl., pej.): black person >*That bigoted jerk said the darkies were takin' over his neighborhood.*

DARLING

* **darling** (colloq.): charming, nice >*What a darling party, dear!*

DARN

— **a darn(ed) sight better** (... därn[d] ...) (colloq.): considerably better >*Joel's a darn sight better player than him.* >*She's doing a darned sight better than last week.*

* **darn(ed)**[1] (colloq.): contemptible, detestable >*I just can't get rid of those darned ants.*

* **darn(ed)**[2] (colloq.): very, extremely >*You did a darned nice thing by staying to help.*

* **darn(ed)**[3] (colloq.): extraordinary, impressive >*That darn kid of mine won first prize.*

* **darn(ed) well** (colloq.): most certainly (must do s/thing) >*You darn well better save your money if you want to take that trip.*

** **darn (it)!** (colloq.): (interj. to express anger, surprise, irritation, or disappointment) >*Darn it! I missed my bus by two minutes.*

* **darn near** (colloq.): almost, nearly >*That stupid driver darn near hit us.*

* **give a darn** (colloq.): be concerned, care, take interest (freq. used in the neg.) >*I guess nobody gives a darn about what happens to him.*

— **worth a darn** (see **WORTH**)

— **(you're) darn(ed) straight ...!** (see **STRAIGHT**)

— **you're darn tooting ...!** (see **TOOTING**)

DARNED (see also DARN)

* **(well,) I'll be darned!** (... därnd) (colloq.): what a surprise! how interesting! >*Well, I'll be darned! There's a hole in my shirt!*

DARNEDEST

* **[one's] darnedest** (... därn´dist) (colloq.): [one's] utmost, [one's] best effort >*Do your darnedest, and you just might win.*

DAY

— **call it a day/night** (see **CALL**)

* **from day one** (colloq.): from the very beginning, from the first day >*I didn't like that clown from day one.*

— **(go ahead,) make my day!** (see **MAKE**)

— **that'll be the day!** (see **THAT'LL**)

DAYLIGHT

— **(can) see daylight** (colloq.): be near the end, have finished the largest part (of a task) >*I thought I'd never finish summarizing all these reports, but now I can see daylight.*

DAYLIGHTS

* **beat/knock the (living) daylights out of** (colloq.): beat unconscious, beat severely >*The girl's boyfriend beat the living daylights out of Frank when he tried to kiss her.*

* **scare the (living) daylights out of** (colloq.): scare very much, terrify >*It scared the daylights out of me when I heard that growl behind me.*

D-DAY

— **D-day** (colloq.): day of special meaning, day of a significant occurrence >*Tomorrow's D-day—my comprehensive exams.*

DEAD

** **dead¹** (colloq.): extremely tired, exhausted >*I've been on my feet all day—I'm dead!*

** **dead²** (sl.): doomed, assured of being killed or hurt >*If ya touch my car, you're dead!*

— **(as) dead as a doornail** (colloq.): unequivocally dead >*The lightning bolt knocked him dead as a doornail.*

— **(dead) giveaway** (see **GIVEAWAY**)

— **dead in the water** (colloq.): no longer workable, failed, no longer under consideration >*The senator's proposal is dead in the water this session.*

— **dead to rights** (colloq.): red-handed, unable to escape culpability >*We've got him dead to rights on this charge.*

* **dead to the world** (colloq.): sound asleep, unconscious >*Nothing can wake him up—he's dead to the world.*

— **drop dead!** (see **DROP**)

— **knock [s/one] dead** (see **KNOCK**)

* **over my dead body!** (sl.): under no circumstances (will I allow s/thing)! >*She'll marry you over my dead body!*

** **wouldn't be caught dead** (sl.): would under no circumstances (be in a situation), would be very embarrassed or humiliated (to be in a situation) >*I wouldn't be caught dead drivin' that piece of junk.* >*That snob wouldn't be caught dead in a discount store.*

DEADBEAT

* **deadbeat¹** (colloq.): person who does not pay his/her debts >*I want those deadbeats evicted!*

* **deadbeat²** (colloq.): loafer, lazy person >*Why doesn't that deadbeat get a job?*

DEAD DUCK
— **dead duck** (colloq.): person who is doomed, person who cannot escape death or failure >*If they try an escape, they're dead ducks.*

DEAD-EYE
— **dead-eye** (colloq.): expert marksman >*Larry's a dead-eye—he never misses.*

DEADLY
— **deadly** (colloq.): extremely boring >*That instructor's deadly in the classroom.*

DEAD MEAT
* **dead meat** (sl.): doomed, assured of being killed or hurt >*Ya tell anyone about it, and you're dead meat.*

DEAD-ON
— **dead-on** (colloq.): exactly right, perfectly accurate >*You're dead-on— that's exactly why it happened.*

DEAD RINGER
— **dead ringer for** (sl.): person who resembles (another) almost exactly >*My supervisor's a dead ringer for Frank Sinatra.*

DEAL
** **deal¹** (colloq.): situation >*The deal is I just can't afford those payments.* >*What's the deal? Why the crowd?*

* **deal²** (colloq.): treatment, disposition (toward s/one) >*You got a lousy deal from that teacher. Why'd he flunk you?*

** **deal³** (vi, vt) (sl.): sell (illicit drugs) >*That dude's dirty. He deals and uses.* >*She deals crack mostly.*

— **big deal** (see "BIG DEAL")

— **cut a deal** (see CUT)

— **deal [s/one] in** (sl.): include [s/one] as participant >*Hey, deal me in if you're gonna go camping.*

** **it's a deal** (colloq.): I agree to that, that's all right with me >*Meet you at Victor's at nine? It's a deal.*

* **no deal** (colloq.): (it is/was) unsuccessful or futile, (s/one) refused (it) >*I asked him to give me a chance, but no deal.*

— **wheel and deal** (see **WHEEL**)

DEALER
** **dealer** (sl.): illicit drug dealer >*See that fancy car? It belongs to this big-time dealer.*

DEAR JOHN LETTER
* **Dear John letter** (colloq.): letter in which a woman breaks off a relationship with a man >*Pete got a Dear John letter from her when he was overseas.*

DEATH
— **be death on** (colloq.): be extremely strict with >*That coach is death on rookie players.*

** **... [s/one] to death** (colloq.): ... [s/one] greatly, ... [s/one] to the utmost >*His present tickled her to death.* >*I was scared to death he'd got caught in the storm.* >*I think I bored the poor woman to death.*

DEBUG
* **debug¹** (dē'bug´) (vt) (colloq.): detect and correct defects or minor problems (esp. in s/thing electronic or mechanical) >*I got to debug the program before it will run right.*

— **debug²** (vt) (colloq.): detect and remove hidden microphones from >*They checked the room over and debugged it before leaving.*

DECAF
** **decaf** (dē'kaf´) (colloq.): decaffeinated coffee >*You want regular coffee or decaf?*

DECENT
** **decent¹** (colloq.): sufficiently dressed (to be seen) >*Are you decent? Can I come in?*

** **decent²** (sl.): good, of fair quality >*It was a pretty decent movie, but not great.*

DECK

* **deck** (vt) (colloq.): knock to the floor (esp. with a fist) >*The trucker decked him with one punch.*

— **hit the deck** (see HIT)

— **not be playing with a full deck** (see PLAYING)

— **on deck** (colloq.): having (one's) turn next, next scheduled, ready to take (one's) turn >*You're on deck, Ross—as soon as Mark finishes, you're on.* >*We got a guy on deck who can take over at any time.*

— **stack the deck/cards** (see STACK)

DEEJAY

— **deejay** (see "D.J.")

DEEP

— **go off the deep end** (colloq.): go crazy, start behaving very irrationally >*Billings is in the boss's office threatening him with an umbrella. He's really gone off the deep end this time.*

— **in deep**[1] (colloq.): greatly in debt >*He's really in deep with some loan shark.*

— **in deep**[2] (sl.): seriously involved >*It's gonna be hard for him to get outta the gang, 'cause he's in deep.* >*I think he's in deep—he's seen her every night for the last three weeks.*

* **in deep shit** (... shit) (vulg.): in serious trouble, in a very dangerous situation >*Drake's gonna be in deep shit if they catch him stealin' from the company.*

DEEP-SIX

— **deep-six** (vt) (sl.): get rid of, reject, throw away >*I hear they're gonna deep-six the subway project.*

DELI

** **deli** (del´ē) (colloq.): delicatessen >*Don't fix dinner—I'll pick up something at the deli on the way home.*

DELISH

— **delish** (di lish´) (colloq.): delicious >*This casserole is delish!*

DELIVER

* **deliver (the goods)** (colloq.): do or provide what was promised or expected, perform well >*You can count on Chuck, because he always delivers the goods.* >*Just tell me what you want done—I'll deliver.*

DEMO

** **demo** (dem´ō) (colloq.): demonstration, demonstrator, sample used for demonstration >*It's real easy to do. I saw a demo.* >*This car's a demo, so it's discounted.*

DENT

* **make a dent (in)** (colloq.): reduce in the least notable amount or number, make some progress (in completing a task) (freq. used in the neg.) >*I've been working on that stack of papers all day, and I haven't even made a dent in it.*

DESK JOCKEY

— **desk jockey** (colloq.): office worker, petty bureaucrat >*Some desk jockey in the tax department probably lost the paperwork.*

DETOX

* **detox** (dē´toks) (colloq.): detoxification, treatment to rid (s/one) of alcohol or drug dependence >*Bryan's been sober ever since he went through that detox program.*

DEVIL

— **a devil of a ...** (colloq.): a very troublesome ..., a very problematic ... >*We're going to have a devil of a time cleaning up this mess.*

— **speak of the devil!** (see SPEAK)

* **what/who/[etc.] (in) the devil ...?** (colloq.): (intens. to express impatience, anger, or surprise) >*What in the devil do you think you're doing with my briefcase?* >*When the devil are they going to get here?*

DIARRHEA

— **diarrhea of the mouth** (vulg.): annoying tendency to talk too much

>*You try to shut Jerry up! He's got diarrhea of the mouth.*

DIBS

* **(have) dibs on** (... dibz ...) (sl.): (I) claim, (I) have a right to >*Our team has dibs on this basket.* >*Dibs on the aisle seat!*

DICE

— **no dice** (sl.): (it is/was) unsuccessful or futile, (s/one) refused (it) >*We tried to convince him to come with us, but no dice.* >*I already asked the boss about it, and he said no dice.*

DICEY

— **dicey** (dī´sē) (colloq.): risky, uncertain >*Sending in troops is a pretty dicey proposition.*

DICK

** **dick**[1] (dik) (vulg.): penis >*He said he had a sore spot on his dick.*

* **dick**[2] (vulg.): contemptible or obnoxious man >*What a dick he is! He doesn't give a crap about anyone but himself.*

— **dick**[3] (sl.): detective >*Some private dick's been snoopin' around here askin' questions.*

— **dick**[4] (vt) (vulg.): have sex with (a woman) >*He claims he dicked her last night.*

— **dick around** (vi) (vulg.): pass time idly, work halfheartedly or unproductively >*I'm tired of ya dickin' around—go out and find a job!*

— **dick (around) with** (vulg.): treat without due respect or seriousness, handle capriciously, toy with >*Bill was dickin' around with the engine and now it doesn't work right.* >*Stop dickin' with that guy or he'll knock your teeth out.*

DICKENS

— **like the dickens** (... dik´inz) (colloq.): wholeheartedly, to the utmost degree >*He ran like the dickens when he saw the snake.* >*That sprain hurt like the dickens.*

— **...er than the dickens** (colloq.): extraordinarily ..., very ... >*That prof's exams are tougher than the dickens.*

— **... the dickens out of [s/one, s/thing]** (colloq.): ... [s/one, s/thing] to the utmost degree, ... [s/one, s/thing] extraordinarily >*Heights scare the dickens out of me.* >*I love the dickens out of that kid.*

— **what/who/[etc.] (in) the dickens ...?** (colloq.): (intens. to express impatience, anger, or surprise) >*Who the dickens are you, and what in the dickens are you doing in my yard?*

DICKHEAD

— **dickhead** (dik´hed´) (vulg.): contemptible or reprehensible person, stupid person (also voc.) >*Tell that dickhead to stop wastin' time.* >*Cut it out, dickhead!*

DIDDLE

— **diddle around** (did´l ...) (vi) (colloq.): pass time idly, work halfheartedly or unproductively >*Why don't you boys find a nice hobby instead of diddling around all day?*

— **diddle (around) with** (colloq.): treat without due respect or seriousness, handle capriciously, toy with >*You'd better not diddle around with me.* >*Don't diddle with those gauges!*

DIDDLY

— **diddly** (did´lē) (sl.): insignificant, worthless, contemptible >*I ain't gonna work for no diddly five bucks an hour.*

* **([neg.]) diddly** (sl.): nothing at all >*He don't know diddly about cars.* >*That lazy bum did diddly to help.*

DIDDLYSHIT

— **([neg.]) diddlyshit** (... did´lē shit´) (vulg.): nothing at all >*She never says diddlyshit about her job.* >*You can believe diddlyshit of what that clown says.*

DIE

** **(about) die** (colloq.): have a strong
emotional reaction (fear, shame,
amusement, vexation, etc.) >*I about
died when my husband yelled at the
host.* >*The film was so funny we died.*
>*She's going to die when she sees this
picture of herself.*

— **die (off)/drop like flies** (colloq.): die in
large numbers (esp. over a short period
of time) >*During the typhoid outbreak,
people were dying off like flies.* >*They
dropped like flies in that battle.*

— **eat shit (and die)!** (see **EAT**)

DIFF

— **diff** (*dif*) (colloq.): difference >*A
twenty or two tens—what's the diff?*

DIFFERENCE

— **the same difference** (see **SAME**)

DIFFERENT

* **different strokes for different folks**
(sl.): there is a great variety of people
and their preferences >*So he's got a pet
snake. Different strokes for different
folks, isn't that so?*

DIG

— **dig**[1] (colloq.): critical or sarcastic
remark, barb >*Did you hear that dig?
Fred just badmouthed your girlfriend's
clothes.*

— **dig**[2] (vi, vt) (sl.): understand,
comprehend >*Yeah, I dig—I know the
feeling, man.* >*Do ya dig what I'm
sayin'?*

— **dig**[3] (vt) (sl.): like, enjoy, be fond of
>*She digs modern jazz.* >*I could really
dig that beautiful chick.*

— **dig**[4] (vt) (sl.): notice, take a look at (esp.
in amusement) >*Hey, dig that crazy hat
he's wearin'!*

— **dig down (deep)** (colloq.): make
sacrifices (to pay for s/thing) >*They
have to dig down deep to send their kid
to that exclusive school.*

* **dig in(to)** (colloq.): attack with
enthusiasm, consume vigorously >*The
defense lawyer can hardly wait to dig
into the case.* >*OK, everyone, dig in
while it's hot.*

* **dig up** (vt) (colloq.): locate, find, obtain
>*Where'd you dig up these records?*
>*I'll see if I can dig up something on
the suspect.*

DIGGETY

— **hot (diggety) dog!** (see **HOT DOG**)

DIGS

— **digs** (sl.): residence, dwelling >*Let's go
to your place—my digs are on the other
side of town.* >*Nice digs ya got here!*

DIKE

— **dike** (see "**DYKE**")

DILDO

— **dildo** (dil´dō) (vulg.): artificial erect
penis (used for sexual stimulation)
>*They were sellin' all kinds of dildos at
the porn shop.*

DILLY

— **dilly** (dil´ē) (colloq.): extraordinary or
remarkable thing or person >*That was
a dilly of a game.* >*Their new cook's a
dilly.*

DIME

* **a dime a dozen** (colloq.): cheap,
abundant, readily available >*Applicants
with college degrees are a dime a dozen
these days.*

— **one/a thin dime** (colloq.): the least
amount of money >*The best thing is
that it won't cost me one thin dime.*

— **stop/turn on a dime** (colloq.): (can)
stop/turn quickly, stop/turn (a vehicle) in
a short distance >*With disc brakes all
around and the wide tires, this car can
stop on a dime.* >*Great handling! It
turns on a dime.*

DIMWIT

— **dimwit** (dim´wit´) (sl.): stupid or dense
person (also voc.) >*That dimwit just*

DIN-DIN–DIRT-CHEAP

don't get what I'm sayin'. >Don't ya see how it works, dimwit?

DIN-DIN
— **din-din** (din´din´) (colloq.): dinner, a meal (used esp. with small children) >*Come on, Bobby—let's have din-din.*

DINERO
— **dinero** (di nâr´ō) (sl.): money >*I'd like to buy it, but I ain't got the dinero.*

DING
* **ding**[1] (ding) (colloq.): small dent, nick (esp. on an automobile) >*The car's in pretty good shape, even if it's got a few dings on it.*

— **ding**[2] (sl.): critical remark >*I don't mind those other jerks badmouthin' me, but that ding from Martha really hurt.*

* **ding**[3] (vt) (colloq.): make a small dent or nick in (esp. an automobile) >*Someone dinged my car door with their door.*

— **ding**[4] (vt) (sl.): criticize >*He got dinged for missin' the deadline. >The boss's always dingin' her for her typin' errors.*

DING-A-LING
* **ding-a-ling** (ding´ə ling´) (sl.): stupid or silly person, eccentric person >*Do we have to listen to that ding-a-ling? >That ding-a-ling's got some real strange ideas.*

DINGBAT
— **dingbat** (ding´bat´) (sl.): stupid or silly person >*Don't expect Casper to be of any help. The guy's a total dingbat.*

DING-DONG
— **ding-dong** (ding´dong´/dông´) (vulg.): penis >*Zip up your fly, or your ding-dong's liable to flop out.*

DINKY
* **dinky** (ding´kē) (colloq.): small, insignificant, of poor quality >*He sleeps in this dinky room that's hardly big enough for his bed. >I don't want one of those dinky portables—I want a big-screen TV.*

DIP
* **dip**[1] (colloq.): brief swim >*Let's go for a dip in the ocean before eating.*

— **dip**[2] (sl.): annoyingly foolish or inane person >*I don't want that dip with us if we're gonna try to meet some girls.*

DIPPY
— **dippy** (dip´ē) (sl.): annoyingly foolish or inane, silly >*Ya know that dippy kid that always gets on everybody's nerves?*

DIPSHIT
* **dipshit** (dip´shit´) (vulg.): obnoxious fool, annoyingly inane person (also adj., also voc.) >*Did he really say that? What a dipshit! >I don't want your dipshit brother hangin' around here anymore. >Scram, dipshit!*

DIRT
* **dirt on [s/one]** (colloq.): embarrassing or scandalous information about [s/one], compromising information about [s/one] >*That busybody has dirt on everyone in the front office. >What's the dirt on Peabody that's making him so nervous?*

— **hit the dirt** (see **HIT**)

— **treat [s/one] like dirt** (see **TREAT**)

DIRTBAG
— **dirtbag** (sl.): contemptible or reprehensible person (also voc.) >*I'm gonna beat that dirtbag up some day. >Stay away from my sister, dirtbag!*

DIRT BIKE
** **dirt bike** (colloq.): trail bike, motorcycle designed for rough terrain >*They tore up the desert with their dirt bikes.*

DIRT-CHEAP
* **dirt-cheap** (colloq.): very inexpensive (also adv.) >*They're dirt-cheap, but they don't last. >Old man Boggs'll clear out that dead brush for you dirt-cheap.*

DIRTY

** **dirty**[1] (colloq.): obscene or vulgar (also adv.) >*He loves telling dirty jokes.* >*She said he talked dirty to her.*

* **dirty**[2] (colloq.): mean or unfair (also adv.) >*That dirty guy cheated me!* >*Watch out for number nine. He plays dirty.*

— **dirty**[3] (sl.): guilty, involved in illegal activities >*If ya ask me, that sleazy politician's dirty as anything.*

— **dirty**[4] (colloq.): obtained illegally, stolen >*I don't want none of that dirty drug money.* >*Is this stuff so cheap because it's dirty?*

— **dirty**[5] (sl.): in possession of or using illegal drugs >*The parolee was dirty when they stopped him for speedin', so they sent him back to the joint.*

— **do [s/one] dirty** (sl.): do a reprehensible thing [to s/one], cheat or slander [s/one] >*He really did ya dirty by tellin' your girlfriend that you're still married.*

DIRTY BIRD

— **dirty bird** (sl.): contemptible person, person who has treated (s/one) reprehensibly >*That dirty bird's gonna pay for what he did.*

DIRTY LOOK

** **dirty look** (colloq.): look (on s/one's face) that shows dislike or contempt >*Everyone gave him a dirty look when he burped at the table.*

DIRTY OLD MAN

* **dirty old man** (colloq.): lecherous or obscene middle-aged or older man >*Some dirty old man on the bus tried to touch me.*

DIRTY POOL

— **dirty pool** (colloq.): unfair or unethical behavior or action >*Hey, giving her hints is dirty pool.*

DIRTY TRICKS

* **dirty tricks** (colloq.): espionage activities, unethical behavior (esp. in politics) >*All his dirty tricks helped get him elected.*

DIRTY WORK

** **dirty work** (colloq.): unpleasant or menial task or work >*Anne just sits there giving orders while we do all the dirty work.*

DISASTER AREA

* **disaster area** (colloq.): very messy or disorderly place >*This room is a disaster area! And I just cleaned it three days ago.*

DISC JOCKEY

** **disc jockey** (colloq.): host of a music program using recordings (esp. on the radio) (cf. "**D.J.**") >*That disc jockey plays nothing but oldies.*

DISH

— **dish** (sl.): attractive woman >*Wow! His cousin's really a dish.*

* **dish out** (vt) (colloq.): inflict, say or do (s/thing rigorous or harmful) (to s/one) >*That obnoxious sister of hers can sure dish out the insults.* >*You can dish it out, but you can't take it.*

DISK JOCKEY

— **disk jockey** (see "DISC JOCKEY")

DISSING

— **dissing [s/one]** (dis´ing …) (sl.): speaking disrespectfully to/about [s/one], insulting [s/one], belittling [s/one] >*Don't go dissin' me, ya hear?*

DISTANCE

* **go the distance** (colloq.): complete (a difficult or challenging task) >*He lost the fight, but he went the distance—all fifteen rounds.* >*No backing out! We're going the distance on this project.*

DITCH

* **ditch**[1] (vi, vt) (sl.): stay away (from school or a class) without permission, be truant (from) >*He ditches whenever there's gonna be a math test.* >*They ditched school and played video games.*

DITTO–DO

* **ditch²** (vt) (sl.): get rid of (esp. where s/
thing cannot be traced to the person who
does the ditching) >*He ditched the gun
in a trash can.*

* **ditch³** (vt) (sl.): escape from, abandon
>*She thought he loved her, but he
ditched her in Tulsa.*

DITTO

** **ditto (for)** (dit´ō ...) (colloq.): the same
(for), (s/one) wants or thinks the same
>*Beth wants chocolate fudge—ditto for
me.* >*Bob's against the idea. Greg,
ditto.*

DIVE

— **dive** (sl.): cheap bar or café, low-class
nightclub >*Sid met her in some dive
down by the harbor.*

— **take a dive¹** (colloq.): decrease rapidly
in value >*That company's stock took a
dive when they announced their big
third-quarter losses.*

— **take a dive²** (sl.): pretend to be knocked
out (by illicit prearrangement, in
boxing) >*The challenger took a dive in
the third round for two grand.*

DIVINE

— **divine** (colloq.): wonderful, excellent,
beautiful >*This cheesecake is divine!*
>*Doesn't the bride look divine?*

DIVVY

* **divvy up** (div´ē ...) (vi, vt) (sl.): divide,
distribute portions (of) >*Mom says ya
gotta divvy up with the rest of us.* >*The
crooks divvied up the money after the
robbery.*

DIXIE

— **you just ain't (a-)whistlin' Dixie!** (see
WHISTLING)

DIZZY

— **dizzy** (colloq.): foolish, scatterbrained
>*He's fallen for some dizzy blond whose
goal in life is to be on a game show.*

D.J.

** **D.J.** (colloq.): host of a music program
using recordings (esp. on the radio) (cf.

"DISC JOCKEY") >*Wolfman Jack
was the best D.J. ever.*

DO

— **do¹** (sl.): hairdo, hairstyle >*I like your
new do. It makes ya look sexier.*

** **do²** (vt) (colloq.): travel at (a certain
speed) >*I was doing eighty, but he
passed me flying.*

** **do³** (vt) (colloq.): decorate, furnish
>*We're going to do Sally's room in
yellow.* >*She did her whole house in
Early American.*

** **do⁴** (vt) (colloq.): spend (time in prison),
serve a prison term (of a certain amount
of time) >*She's doing time in the state
pen.* >*He did eight years for armed
robbery.*

* **do⁵** (vt) (sl.): use or take (an illicit drug)
>*I ain't into heroin, man—I just do
crack.*

* **do⁶** (vt) (colloq.): have (a meal) (with s/
one, esp. as an informal meeting)
>*Want to do lunch next week? We can
talk over your idea.*

— **do⁷** (vt) (colloq.): tour or visit (a place)
>*Last year we did Spain, but this
summer we're going to do Western
Canada.*

— **do (a/the) ...** (see entry under ... noun)

— **do [s/one] dirty** (see DIRTY)

— **do [one's] homework** (see
HOMEWORK)

* **do in¹** (vt) (colloq.): kill >*All that
drinking finally did him in.* >*She did in
her husband for the insurance money.*

* **do in²** (vt) (colloq.): exhaust, tire out
>*All that yard work today has done me
in.*

** **do it** (sl.): have sex >*Have you and
your new boyfriend done it yet?*

** **do nothing/not do anything for**
(colloq.): have no appeal to, be of no
interest to >*She says my little jokes do
nothing for her.* >*Most people like his

84

singing, but it doesn't do anything for me.

* **do or die** (colloq.): (the situation calls for one's) best effort, (the situation allows only) complete success or complete failure (cf. **"DO-OR-DIE"**) >*This is your only chance, Nancy—it's do or die.*

* **do [s/one] out of** (colloq.): swindle or cheat [s/one] out of >*That crooked lawyer did them out of twelve hundred bucks.*

— **do [one's] thing** (see **THING**)

D.O.A.

* **D.O.A.** (colloq.): dead on arrival (at a hospital) >*The guy that overdosed was D.O.A. at the E.R.*

DOC

* **doc** (dok) (colloq.): doctor, physician (also voc.) >*What's the doc say about your rash?* >*Hi, doc, how's the pill-pushing business?*

DOCTOR

— **be the doctor** (colloq.): be the authority, be the one whose orders must be followed >*OK, you're the doctor—we do it your way.*

* **(just) what the doctor ordered** (colloq.): exactly what is/was needed, the perfect solution >*Our new secretary is great—just what the doctor ordered.*

— **play doctor** (colloq.): explore (one another's) naked bodies, experiment with nudity (said of people of opposite sexes, esp. children) >*The kids were out behind the garage playing doctor.*

DODO

— **dodo** (dō′dō) (colloq.): simpleton, dull-witted or stupid person >*That guy's such a dodo—he'll fall for any trick.*

DOG

* **dog**[1] (sl., pej.): ugly woman >*He's said his sister set him up for a date with a real dog.*

— **dog**[2] (colloq.): contemptible or reprehensible man >*I wouldn't trust that dog going out with my sister.*

— **dog**[3] (sl.): very inferior product or creation >*This drill is a dog—it doesn't work worth a damn.* >*His last movie was a dog and lost a lot of money.*

— **(as) sick as a dog** (see **SICK**)

* **... dog** (colloq.): ... person (esp. a man, esp. seen enviously) >*So she's going to go out with you, huh, you lucky dog?*

— **dog style/fashion** (vulg.): (in the) sexual position of the man entering the woman from behind >*He said they had sex dog style.*

— **everybody/everyone and his dog** (see **EVERYBODY**)

— **put on the dog** (colloq.): dress ostentatiously, assume an air of wealth or importance >*Wow, look at you! You're really putting on the dog tonight.* >*Who's she trying to impress, putting on the dog like that?*

DOG AND PONY SHOW

— **dog and pony show** (colloq.): elaborate publicity presentation, elaborate show designed to impress >*Does the candidate really expect to get votes with that dog and pony show he brought to town?*

DOGGONE

— **doggone(d)**[1] (dog′gon[d]′/dôg′gôn[d]′) (colloq.): contemptible, detestable >*I don't want those doggone cats of yours on my property.*

— **doggone(d)**[2] (colloq.): extraordinary, impressive >*That doggoned skier jumped a hundred yards.*

— **doggone(d)**[3] (colloq.): very, extremely >*You're doggone right I want a refund.*

* **doggone (it)!** (colloq.): (interj. to express anger, surprise, or irritation) >*Doggone it! Now you've gone and broken it.*

— (well,) I'll be doggone(d)! (colloq.): what a surprise! how interesting! >*I'll be doggoned! It's my old buddy Tim.*

DOGGY

— doggy style/fashion (dog´ē/dôg´ē ...) (vulg.): (in the) sexual position of the man entering the woman from behind >*He said they tried it doggy style last night.*

DOGGY BAG

** doggy bag (dog´ē/dôg´ē ...) (colloq.): bag to take leftovers home in (from a restaurant) >*Oh, I can't finish this now. I'll ask for a doggy bag and eat the rest tomorrow.*

DOGHOUSE

* in the doghouse (with) (sl.): in disfavor (with), having (s/one) mad at (one) >*Marvin's in the doghouse with his wife because he forgot their anniversary.*

DO-GOODER

* do-gooder (dū´gŭd´ər) (colloq.): idealistic but naive reformer, sincere but self-righteous helper of the less fortunate >*We get do-gooders wanting to help out sometimes, but they get scared off pretty quick by some of the rough characters that come in.*

DOGS

— dogs (sl.): feet >*My dogs are killin' me after walkin' around town all day.*

— go to the dogs (colloq.): deteriorate, go to ruin >*This used to be a classy place, but it's gone to the dogs.*

DOG'S

— a dog's age (colloq.): a long time (esp. that s/thing has not recurred) >*We haven't visited old Jeb in a dog's age.*

DOING

— be doing (sl.): be happening >*There's nothin' doin' at the pool hall tonight. >What's doin', bro?*

— nothing doing! (see NOTHING)

* take some doing (colloq.): require special effort or planning >*It'll take some doing, but we'll get it approved by Friday.*

DOLL

— doll[1] (sl.): attractive person (esp. a woman) (also voc.) >*That was quite a doll I saw ya with at the dance. >Can I buy ya a drink, doll?*

— doll[2] (colloq.): charming or generous person >*You're a doll to help me with my history paper.*

DOLLARS

* ... dollars/bucks says (colloq.): I bet ... dollars that >*Twenty dollars says you can't do it again. >Five bucks says he strikes out.*

— like a million dollars/bucks (see MILLION)

DOLLED

— get (all) dolled up (... dold ...) (sl.): get dressed and made up (esp. a woman, esp. elegantly or ostentatiously) >*Gettin' all dolled up for your boyfriend, sis?*

DON

— don (don) (colloq.): head of an organized crime family or syndicate >*The don don't let nobody in the family question his authority.*

DONE

* done for (colloq.): doomed, unable to escape death or ruin >*If he loses the case, he's done for.*

* done in (colloq.): exhausted, tired out >*After the 10-K race, she was done in.*

DONE DEAL

— done deal (sl.): completed arrangement, agreed-upon deal >*Once we get the go-ahead from Alvarez, it'll be a done deal.*

DONG

— dong (dong/dông) (vulg.): penis >*He pulled out his dong right there and took a piss.*

DONKEY
— **donkey** (colloq.): stupid person >*How'd that donkey make it to supervisor?*

DON'TS
— **dos and don'ts** (see **DOS**)

DOO
— **doo** (dū) (colloq.): excrement, dung >*I got dog doo on my shoe.*

DOODAD
— **doodad** (dū´dad´) (colloq.): gadget, object (for which one does not know the name) >*His new car has all kinds of neat doodads.* >*Now, I think this doodad fits in this slot.*

DOODLE
* **doodle**[1] (dūd´l) (colloq.): scribbled or drawn figure (esp. made idly) >*He made doodles on the notepad while he talked to his girl on the phone.*
** **doodle**[2] (vi) (colloq.): scribble or draw figures (esp. idly) >*Don't doodle on my papers!*

DOO-DOO
— **doo-doo**[1] (dū´dū´) (colloq.): excrement, dung (used esp. with small children) >*Don't walk in the doo-doo, Tommy!*
— **doo-doo**[2] (vi) (colloq.): defecate (used esp. with small children) >*Daddy, that bird doo-dooed on our car!*

DOOHICKEY
* **doohickey** (dū´hik´ē) (colloq.): gadget, object (for which one does not know the name) >*I need one of those doohickeys that help you get tight lids off jars.*

DOOR
— **beat down [s/one's] door** (see **BEAT**)
— **get [one's] foot in the door** (see **FOOT**)

DO-OR-DIE
* **do-or-die** (colloq.): calling for (one's) best effort, allowing only complete success or complete failure (cf. "**DO or die**") >*It's a do-or-die situation, so let's win it!*

DOORMAT
— **doormat** (colloq.): person who is habitually mistreated (esp. without protest) >*How does she put up with it? She's nothing but a doormat for that lousy husband of hers.*

DOORNAIL
— **(as) dead as a doornail** (see **DEAD**)

DOO-WOP
— **doo-wop** (dū´wop´) (colloq.): music style of the 1950s emphasizing vocal harmony >*They played some great doo-wop records at the party.*

DOOZIE
— **doozie** (dū´zē) (sl.): extraordinary or impressive thing >*That show was a doozie!* >*That was a doozie of a fight we saw!*

DOOZY
— **doozy** (see "**DOOZIE**")

DOPE
** **dope**[1] (sl.): illicit drugs >*They busted him for sellin' dope to kids.*
* **dope**[2] (colloq.): stupid or foolish person, gullible person >*What a dope! He believed that B.S. about George being from Antarctica.*
— **dope**[3] (sl.): pertinent information, news (esp. when confidential or little known) >*Hey, ya got any dope on that new section head?* >*I got the latest dope on the contract talks.*

DOPED
* **doped up** (sl.): under the influence of drugs >*They say the guy that pulled the robbery was all doped up.* >*The doctors have her so doped up she can hardly speak.*

DOPEHEAD
— **dopehead** (sl.): drug addict or abuser >*You're gonna get into trouble hangin' around with that dopehead.*

DOPER
— **doper** (dō'pər) (sl.): drug addict or abuser >*They arrested a lot of dopers out on the street last night.*

DOPEY
— **dopey** (dō'pē) (sl.): silly, scatterbrained, dull-witted >*What does she see in that dopey jerk?*

DOPY
— **dopy** (see "DOPEY")

DORK
* **dork** (dôrk) (sl.): ridiculous person, irritating or unfashionable oddball >*She's cool, but her brother's a real dork.*

DORKY
* **dorky** (dôr'kē) (sl.): ridiculous, foolish, unfashionable >*Why do ya wear those dorky checkered shirts?*

DORM
** **dorm** (dôrm) (colloq.): dormitory (esp. at a school or university) >*Next year I'm moving out of the dorm and finding my own apartment.*

DOS
** **dos and don'ts** (dūz' ... dōnts') (colloq.): rules, regulations, recommendations >*Now here are a few dos and don'ts while you're here at camp.*

DOT
* **on the dot** (colloq.): precisely (with hours and minutes) >*He got here at eight-thirty on the dot.*

DOUBLE
— **double/triple whammy** (see WHAMMY)

* **on the double** (colloq.): quickly, immediately >*Call an ambulance on the double!*

DOUBLE CROSS
* **double cross** (colloq.): betrayal or cheating of an associate >*What a double cross when Bubba left town with all the dough!*

DOUBLE-CROSS
* **double-cross** (vt) (colloq.): betray or cheat (an associate) >*He'll never forget how his so-called buddies double-crossed him.*

DOUBLE-CROSSING
* **double-crossing** (colloq.): treacherous, capable of betraying or cheating an associate >*Wait till I get my hands on that double-crossing bastard!*

DOUBLE DATE
* **double date** (colloq.): date that includes two couples >*Me and Marge went on a double date with Paul and his girl.*

DOUBLE-DATE
* **double-date** (vi) (colloq.): go on a date that includes two couples >*My wife and I used to double-date with them a lot when we were in high school.*

DOUBLE TROUBLE
— **double trouble** (colloq.): very troublesome or dangerous person or thing >*That mean dude's double trouble when he's mad.* >*We're going to have double trouble if those circuits get wet.*

DOUCHE BAG
— **douche bag** (dūsh ...) (sl., freq. vulg.): contemptible or reprehensible person (also voc.) >*If that douche bag, gets in my way I'll deck him.* >*Stay away from her, douche bag!*

DOUGH
* **dough** (sl.): money >*Myron was makin' lots of dough sellin' real estate.*

DOWN
— **down**[1] (vt) (colloq.): defeat (in sports) >*We downed them six to two.*

** **down**[2] (colloq.): out of order >*The express elevator is down today.* >*We have a computer down in the main office.*

— **(down) in the dumps** (see DUMPS)

— **down in the mouth** (colloq.): depressed, dejected, discouraged >*He's* *really been down in the mouth since he broke up with his girl.*

* **down on** (colloq.): critical of or averse to >*Why are you so down on Cary? What's he ever done to you?*

— **down the hatch!** (colloq.): drink up! let's drink! >*Here's to my buddies— down the hatch!*

* **down the line¹** (colloq.): in the future >*I figure this house will be worth a lot a few years down the line.*

— **down the line²** (colloq.): further ahead (along the same road) >*You'll see the turnoff about four miles down the line.*

* **down to the wire** (colloq.): right to the last minute, very near the deadline >*I went down to the wire, but I met the deadline.* >*This thing's coming down to the wire. If we don't book the place by tonight, we'll have to call the party off.*

— **get down** (vi) (sl.): start dancing, start having a great time, enjoy (oneself) without inhibition >*Me and my chick really got down at the party.*

— **get down to brass tacks** (see BRASS TACKS)

— **go down on** (vulg.): perform cunnilingus or fellatio on >*He said he went down on her.* >*She said she went down on him.*

— **(go) down the drain** (see DRAIN)

— **(go) in(to)/down the toilet** (see TOILET)

— **(go) down the tube(s)** (see TUBE)

— **have [s/thing] down cold** (see COLD)

— **have [s/thing] down pat** (see PAT)

— **hold it down** (see HOLD)

— **put down** (see PUT)

— **(right) up/down [s/one's] alley** (see ALLEY)

— **sell [s/one] down the river** (see SELL)

— **take/knock [s/one] down a peg (or two)** (see TAKE)

DOWNER

* **downer¹** (dou´nər) (sl.): depressant drug (esp. a barbiturate in pill form) >*He was actin' real hyper, so they gave him a downer.*

* **downer²** (sl.): depressing person or experience >*Seein' that old man die was a real downer.*

DOWNSIDE

* **downside** (colloq.): negative side, drawback, cons (of a situation or matter) (cf. "UPSIDE") >*You might make a bundle of money on this deal, but the downside is that it's real risky.*

DOWN UNDER

— **down under** (colloq.): in/to Australia or New Zealand >*I hear you raise a lot of sheep down under.* >*They went down under to see the Great Barrier Reef.*

DOZEN

— **a dime a dozen** (see DIME)

DOZER

— **dozer** (dō´zər) (colloq.): bulldozer >*The dozers knocked the old place down in no time.*

DRAG

* **drag¹** (sl.): unpleasant or bothersome person or thing, irritating or boring situation >*That boring jerk's a real drag.* >*Ya gotta work on Sunday? What a drag!*

* **drag²** (colloq.): puff, inhalation (of smoke from a smoking material) >*He tried to get me to take a drag on his cigar.*

* **drag³** (sl.): women's clothing (worn by a man) >*He showed up at the party in drag.*

— **drag [one's] ass** (vulg.): proceed very slowly (due to exhaustion), show fatigue >*By the end of the three-week tour, everyone was draggin' their ass.*

— **drag [one's] butt** (sl., freq. vulg.): proceed very slowly (due to exhaustion), show fatigue >*Don't start draggin' your butt. We gotta finish.*

* drag [one's] feet (colloq.): proceed slowly, be slow or uncooperative (in some venture) >*I would have had this settled months ago, but my lawyer's been dragging his feet.*

* drag [s/thing] out of (colloq.): extract (information) from (s/one who is reluctant or uncooperative) >*It took me an hour to drag the whole story out of Rose.* >*The cops'll drag it out of you.*

DRAGGED
— something/what the cat dragged in (see CAT)

DRAIN
* (go) down the drain (colloq.): (become) wasted or ruined, (be) lost or squandered >*The poor guy's business is going down the drain.* >*The shirt fell apart the first time I wore it—that's twenty bucks down the drain.*

DRAW
— beat [s/one] to the draw (see BEAT)

* draw [s/one] a picture (colloq.): explain (s/thing) to [s/one] in extremely simple terms >*Do I have to draw you a picture? You push in the clutch before you shift gears!*

— quick on the draw/trigger (see QUICK)

— slow on the draw (see SLOW)

DRAWING BOARD
— it's back to the (old) drawing board (see BACK)

DREAMBOAT
— dreamboat (sl.): very attractive or desirable person (for a romantic relationship) (esp. a man) >*The guy ya introduced me to is a real dreamboat!*

DREAMS
— in your dreams! (sl.): under no circumstance (will what you wish come true)! >*Her, go out with a loser like you? In your dreams!*

DREAMY
— dreamy (colloq.): wonderful, very attractive >*Sherry thinks he has such dreamy eyes.*

DRESS
* dress to kill (sl.): dress exceedingly elegantly, dress so as to be irresistible >*He dresses to kill and really catches the women's eyes.* >*Laura must spend a fortune on clothes—she's always dressed to kill.*

DRIFT
* catch/get [s/one's] drift (colloq.): perceive what [s/one] means, understand what [s/one] is alluding to (esp. when he/she does not wish to say it directly) >*She's a very affectionate girl, if you catch my drift.*

DRINK
* drink like a fish (colloq.): drink alcohol excessively >*Her old man drinks like a fish, but she won't touch a drop.*

— drink [s/one] under the table (sl.): hold (one's) liquor better than [s/one], not get drunk as readily as [s/one] >*She can drink most men I know under the table.*

— in(to) the drink (colloq.): in(to) the water (of a body of water) >*He fell out of the boat and right into the drink.*

— long drink of water (see LONG)

DRIP
— drip (sl.): irritating or socially unattractive person, annoying bore >*Do we have to invite Jack to the party? He's such a drip.*

DRIVE
* drive [s/one] up the/a wall (sl.): make [s/one] frantic, exhaust [s/one's] patience, make [s/one] lose [his/her] composure, drive [s/one] crazy >*That dog barkin' next door is drivin' me up a wall.* >*The insensitive jerk finally drove her up the wall.*

DRIVER'S SEAT

— **in the driver's seat** (colloq.): in control or authority, in charge >*They fired the manager, so Murray's in the driver's seat now.*

DROOL

* **drool (over)** (colloq.): show great desire (for), covet (s/thing) >*She drooled over those expensive Italian shoes.* >*That beautiful model's got all the guys drooling.*

DROP

— **drop¹** (vt) (colloq.): knock to the ground (with a blow or weapon) >*She dropped him with a punch right in the eye.*

— **drop²** (vt) (sl.): take (L.S.D.) (orally) >*He said he dropped a little acid when he was young.*

— **drop³** (vt) (sl.): spend (esp. an exorbitant amount of money) >*We dropped over three hundred bucks in that place for dinner and drinks last night.*

— **(about) drop [one's] teeth** (colloq.): be very surprised, be astonished >*He about dropped his teeth when she lit up a cigar.*

* **at the drop of a hat** (colloq.): with the slightest motivation, (reacting) without hesitation >*He loves to fish—he'll go fishing at the drop of a hat.*

* **drop [s/one] a line** (colloq.): write and send [s/one] a note or short letter >*Drop me a line every now and then and let me know how you're doing.*

* **drop dead!** (colloq.): (interj. to express great anger or contempt to s/one) >*You want me to go out with that stupid brother of yours? Drop dead! >Drop dead, dummy!*

— **(drop [s/thing]) in [s/one's] lap** (see LAP)

— **die (off)/drop like flies** (see DIE)

— **drop out** (vi) (colloq.): leave a conventional life-style, remove (oneself) from conventional pursuits >*He quit his job, left his wife, and joined a commune—completely dropped out.*

— **drop the ball** (colloq.): fail in (one's) responsibility, perform poorly >*This deal's up to you, Thomas—don't drop the ball or we'll lose big bucks.*

— **get the drop on** (colloq.): get (s/one) at a disadvantage (esp. due to timing) >*Another firm's researching this, too, but we got the drop on them and are marketing ours next month.*

DROP-DEAD

— **drop-dead** (colloq.): awe-inspiring, astonishing, very impressive (esp. in beauty) (also adv.) >*She was wearing a drop-dead, strapless black evening gown, and she was drop-dead beautiful.*

DRUGGIE

* **druggie** (drug´ē) (sl.): habitual drug user (esp. illicit drugs) >*That's where all the druggies go to smoke pot.*

DRUNK

— **(as) drunk as a skunk** (sl.): very drunk >*Old Bowers came in drunk as a skunk and passed out right on the floor.*

DRUNK TANK

— **drunk tank** (colloq.): large jail cell used to hold persons arrested for drunkenness >*They threw him in the drunk tank to sober up.*

DRUTHERS

— **if [one] had [his/her] druthers** (... druð´ərz) (colloq.): if [one] could have [his/her] preference, if [one] could choose >*If Mathers had his druthers, he'd be living back in Texas.*

DRY

* **dry¹** (colloq.): having abstained from alcohol (for a certain period) >*Old Claude used to be quite a boozer, but he's been dry now for over two years.*

* **dry²** (colloq.): prohibiting the sale or consumption of alcohol >*This here's a dry town—not a drop to be bought anywhere.*

* **(as) dry as a bone** (colloq.): very dry >*I hope it rains soon—things are as dry as a bone around here.*

* **dry out** (vi) (colloq.): become detoxified from alcohol used abusively >*She'd been drinking pretty heavy, so they sent her to some clinic to dry out.*

— **dry up** (vi) (sl.): stop (one's) annoying talking >*He kept goin' on and on until we finally told him to dry up.*

— **hang/string [s/one] out to dry** (see **HANG**)

DUD

* **dud¹** (dud) (colloq.): person or thing that is ineffective or unsuccessful >*Sidney's been a dud at every job he's tried.* >*Let's take off—this party's a dud.*

— **dud²** (colloq.): explosive that does not detonate >*All the firecrackers went off except for a couple of duds.*

DUDE

* **dude** (dūd) (sl.): guy, man (also voc.) >*Who's the new dude at work?* >*Like, that's totally awesome, dudes!*

DUDED

— **duded up** (dū'dəd ...) (sl.): dressed elegantly >*Why'd ya get all duded up? Got a hot date?*

DUDS

— **duds** (dudz) (colloq.): clothes >*Look at these rags! I got to get me some new duds.*

DUES

— **pay [one's] dues** (see **PAY**)

DUFF

— **duff** (duf) (sl.): rump, buttocks >*Why doesn't he get off his duff and look for a job?*

DUKE

— **duke** (vt) (sl.): hit with the fist >*He badmouthed me, so I duked him.*

— **duke it out** (sl.): fight with the fists >*They pushed each other a couple of times, then started dukin' it out.*

DUKES

— **dukes** (sl.): fists (when used for fighting) >*Put up your dukes and fight!*

DULLSVILLE

— **dullsville** (dulz'vil´) (sl.): boring person(s) or thing(s) >*The slides of their vacation were dullsville.*

DUMB

** **dumb¹** (colloq.): stupid >*That's the dumbest reason for quitting a job that I ever heard.*

** **dumb²** (colloq.): contemptible, detestable >*Get your dumb books off my bed!* >*I don't want to go to his dumb party.*

* **play dumb** (colloq.): pretend not to know, pretend to be stupid >*Ben knows about this, but he's playing dumb.* >*She plays dumb, and the guys love it.*

DUMB-ASS

* **dumb-ass** (vulg.): stupid person (also adj.) >*That dumb-ass couldn't answer the easiest questions.* >*I don't want your dumb-ass brother messin' things up.*

DUMBBELL

— **dumbbell** (colloq.): stupid person (also voc.) >*What do you expect from a dumbbell like her?* >*That's my seat, dumbbell!*

DUMB BUNNY

— **dumb bunny** (colloq.): stupid person, fool >*Some dumb bunny got this all mixed up.*

DUMB CLUCK

— **dumb cluck** (sl.): stupid person, fool >*Can ya explain it so this dumb cluck will get it?* >*You were a dumb cluck to trust him.*

DUMB-DUMB

— **dumb-dumb** (see "DUM-DUM")

DUMBHEAD

— **dumbhead** (sl.): stupid or inept person, fool (also voc.) >*Show that dumbhead* *how to do it.* >*You fell for it, dumbhead!*

DUMBO
— **dumbo** (dum´bō) (sl.): stupid person >*Only a dumbo like him couldn't figure it out.*

DUMB-SHIT
* **dumb-shit** (dum´shit´) (vulg.): stupid person (also adj.) >*Can ya believe what that dumb-shit just said?* >*Get outta here with your dumb-shit schemes.*

DUM-DUM
— **dum-dum** (dum´dum´) (colloq.): stupid person (also adj.) >*Why does that dum-dum insist on repeating his dum-dum ideas?*

DUMMY
* **dummy** (dum´ē) (colloq.): stupid person (also voc.) >*How did a dummy like him get on the planning committee?* >*Get it right, dummy!*

DUMP
* **dump**[1] (colloq.): dilapidated or messy place, disreputable establishment >*Who would want to live in this dump?* >*What's a nice girl like you doing in a dump like this?*

* **dump**[2] (vt) (colloq.): reject, get rid of, fire >*She got dumped by her boyfriend.* >*If Bernstein can't get the job done, we'll dump him and get someone else.*

* **dump on**[1] (sl.): tell all (one's) problems to (esp. inconsiderately) *Why does Myra always dump on me when she's depressed?*

— **dump on**[2] (sl.): criticize severely, verbally abuse >*He dumps on his poor secretary every time something goes wrong.*

— **take a dump** (vulg.): defecate >*Where's the head? I gotta take a dump.*

DUMPS
* **(down) in the dumps** (colloq.): depressed >*He's really been down in the dumps since he lost his job.*

DURN
— **durn (it)!** (dûrn …) (see "DARN [it]!")
— **durn(ed)** (see "DARN[ed]")
— **durn(ed) well** (see "DARN[ed] well")
— **give a durn** (see "give a DARN")
— **worth a durn** (see "WORTH a darn")
— **you're durn tooting …!** (see "you're darn TOOTING …!")

DURNED
— **(well,) I'll be durned!** (… dûrnd) (see "[well,] I'll be DARNED!")

DURNEDEST
— **[one's] durnedest** (… dûrn´dist) (see "[one's] DARNEDEST")

DUST
— **dust** (vt) (sl.): kill, murder >*He just dusted the dude with a thirty-eight.*
— **bite the dust** (see BITE)

DUTCH
* **go Dutch (treat)** (colloq.): each pay (one's) own way (for food or entertainment) >*He doesn't have a lot of money, so I said we could go Dutch to the movies.*
— **in Dutch with** (colloq.): in trouble or disfavor with >*He's running because he's in Dutch with the law.*

DUTY
— **do [one's] duty** (colloq., freq. vulg.): defecate >*The cat just did its duty in the planter.*

DWEEB
— **dweeb** (dwēb) (sl.): socially contemptible or unattractive person, weird and dislikable person >*Who invited that dweeb along?*

DYING
** **dying** (colloq.): having great desire (to/ for) >*Rhonda's dying to tell us about her trip.* >*I'm dying for a cold beer.*

DYKE
* **dyke** (dīk) (sl., pej.): lesbian >*The called her a dyke just 'cause she wouldn't go to bed with him.*

DYNAMITE

DYNAMITE

* **dynamite** (freq. dī´nō´mīt´) (colloq.):
  spectacular or wonderful thing or person
  (also adj., also interj.) >*Their new
  album is dynamite!* >*This guy's got a
  dynamite idea.* >*You got the job?
  Dynamite*

E

EACH
— at each other's throat(s) (see THROAT)

EAGER BEAVER
* **eager beaver** (colloq.): overly motivated or zealous person (also adj.) >*Clint's a real eager beaver. I guess he's trying to impress the boss.* >*His eager beaver attitude's getting on my nerves.*

EAR
— bend [s/one's] ear (see BEND)

— blow it out your ear! (see BLOW)

** **go in one ear and out the other** (colloq.): be unheeded or ignored (by s/one), not be comprehended (by s/one) >*I tried to warn Eddie about those punks, but it went in one ear and out the other.*

— play it by ear (see PLAY)

— put a bug in [s/one's] ear (see BUG)

— stick it in your ear! (see STICK)

— talk [s/one's] ear off (see TALK)

EARFUL
* **earful** (ēr´fŭl´) (colloq.): uninvited harangue or discourse that (one) must listen to (esp. a reprimand or criticism) >*Lance gave the manager an earful about the store's lousy service.*

EARS
* **be all ears** (colloq.): be attentive, want to listen >*Go ahead with your story—we're all ears.*

— (have) ... coming out (of) [one's] ears (see COMING)

— pin [s/one's] ears back (see PIN)

— (still) wet behind the ears (see WET)

— up to [one's] ears in (colloq.): having an abundance or excess of, very occupied with >*The poor guy's been up to his ears in debt since he lost his job.*

EASY
* **(as) easy as pie** (colloq.): very easy (also adv.) >*Changing air filters is as easy as pie.* >*I fixed it easy as pie.*

* **... easy** (colloq.): at least ..., unquestionably ... >*He'll make five thousand easy on a deal like that.* >*That guy must weigh three hundred pounds easy.*

** **easy come, easy go** (colloq.): what is easily obtained may be easily lost >*He gambled away all the lottery money he won. Oh well, easy come, easy go.*

* **easy does it!**[1] (colloq.): proceed carefully! take care (in handling s/thing)! >*Set the piano down there. That's it, easy does it!*

* **easy does it!**[2] (colloq.): stay calm! don't get excited! >*Easy does it! He didn't mean to insult you!*

* **get off easy** (colloq.): be spared harsh punishment, escape serious consequences or heavy payments >*He got off easy with a fine and no jail time.* >*Hey, you're getting off easy. These repairs would normally cost you almost twice as much.*

* **go easy (on)** (colloq.): not treat (s/one) harshly, be lenient (with) >*Go easy on the kid—it wasn't really his fault.*

* **take it easy** (colloq.): proceed slowly or cautiously >*Take it easy driving down the mountain.* >*Take it easy when you work with these chemicals.*

** **take it easy!** (colloq.): relax! calm down! work less! >*Take it easy! No need to get upset.* >*You've been working too hard lately. Why don't you take it easy for a while?*

* **take things easy** (colloq.): live calmly, live a relaxed life >*We're going to retire in the mountains and take things easy.*

EASY STREET
— **on easy street** (sl.): financially secure, in luxury >*We're gonna make a lot on this deal. We'll be livin' on easy street.*

EAT
* **eat** (vt) (vulg.): perform cunnilingus or fellatio on >*He said he was gonna eat her.* >*She said she was gonna eat him.*

— **could eat a horse** (colloq.): be very hungry >*Bring on the chow! I could eat a horse!*

— **eat crow** (colloq.): be forced to admit that (one) was wrong, be humiliated because (one) was in error >*The critics will all eat crow when she wins the Oscar for best actress.*

* **eat [one's] heart out** (colloq.): be overwhelmed with envy or grief, long for greatly >*Eat your heart out! You can't afford a car like this.* >*Why's he eating his heart out over her? She's not worth it.*

* **eat like a bird** (colloq.): eat very little >*How're you going to keep your strength up if you keep eating like a bird?*

* **eat like a horse** (colloq.): eat voraciously, eat a great deal >*That teenager eats like a horse at every meal.*

— **eat my shorts!** (sl., freq. vulg.): (interj. to express great anger or contempt to s/one) >*Eat my shorts if ya feel that way about it!*

— **eat out** (vt) (vulg.): perform cunnilingus on >*He said he ate her out last night.*

* **eat [s/one] out of house and home** (colloq.): eat a great amount in [s/one's] household, cause [s/one] financial hardship by eating very much >*My teenage sons are eating me out of house and home.*

— **eat shit (and die)!** (... shit ...) (vulg.): (interj. to express great anger or contempt to s/one) >*If ya don't like it, eat shit!*

* **eat up** (vt) (colloq.): enjoy very much, be very enthusiastic about, readily accept >*The press is really covering the scandal and the public's eating it up.* >*He eats it up when you flatter him.*

— **I'll eat my hat** (colloq.): I will be very surprised, I'll admit I was wrong >*If your stupid brother-in-law gets that job, I'll eat my hat.*

EATERY
— **eatery** (ē′tə rē) (colloq.): restaurant, café >*I'm going to take you to some fancy eatery tonight to celebrate.*

EATING
* **eating [s/one]** (colloq.): bothering or annoying [s/one] >*What's eating Shirley? She's snapping at everybody.*

* **have [s/one] eating out of [one's] hand** (colloq.): have great persuasive power over [s/one], control or dominate [s/one] (esp. through charm or guile) >*That flirty girl's got the old guy eating out of her hand.*

EATS
— **eats** (sl.): food >*They're gonna have some good eats at the reception.*

ED
— **ed** (ed) (colloq.): education (esp. in combination with another word) >*He's majoring in Special Ed.* >*She got a B in her ed class.*

EDGE
* **live (life) on the edge** (sl.): live dangerously, engage in reckless or perilous activities >*He likes to live on the edge, racin' cars, scuba divin'—that kinda stuff.*

— **on the edge** (sl.): close to a mental breakdown, close to going crazy >*Keep your eye on Brown—I think he's on the edge.*

EDGEWISE
— **cannot get a word in (edgewise)** (see **WORD**)

EENCY-WEENSY
— **eency-weensy** (ēn´sē wēn´sē) (colloq.): very small, tiny >*This eency-weensy bug bit me and made this big welt.*

EF-WORD
— **the ef-word** (see "the F-WORD")

EGG
— **egg on [one's] face** (colloq.): embarrassment, humiliation (after it is shown that [one] was wrong or foolish) >*A lot of people are going to end up with egg on their face after we prove them wrong.*

EGGHEAD
— **egghead** (sl., freq. pej.): intellectual (also adj.) >*There's some egghead on TV talkin' about deconstructionist morality, whatever the hell that is.* >*Is she borin' everyone with her egghead ideas again?*

EGO TRIP
* **ego trip** (sl.): egotistic activity or behavior, action done for vanity or selfish reasons >*He says he's an intellectual, but I think he's just on an ego trip.* >*His ego trip is goin' out with good-lookin' women.*

EIGHTBALL
— **behind the eightball** (see BEHIND)

EINSTEIN
— **Einstein** (īn´stīn) (colloq.): very intelligent person >*The guy's an Einstein! How did he figure that out?*

EITHER
— **[neg.] ... either!** (stressed) (colloq.): [neg.] ... indeed! (used to assertively deny s/one's affirmation) (cf. "... TOO!") >*We didn't either steal your stupid lunch money!* >*Don't tell them she was arrested! She wasn't either!*

ELBOW GREASE
* **elbow grease** (colloq.): strenuous physical effort or work (esp. manual work) >*Put a little elbow grease into it, or you'll never get it clean.*

ELBOWS
— **rub elbows** (see RUB)

EL CHEAPO
— **el cheapo** (el´chē´pō) (sl.): inexpensive or inferior item (cf. "CHEAPO") (also adj.) >*If ya wanna bike that will last ya, don't buy that el cheapo.* >*I never buy el cheapo tires.*

ELSE
— **be something (else)** (see SOMETHING)

* **... or else!** (colloq.): (do s/thing) or be punished, (do s/thing) or suffer the consequences >*Barry, you clean up your room or else!*

— **(so) what else is new?** (see WHAT)

'EM
** **'em** (əm) (colloq.): them (when unstressed) >*I brought the chairs—where should I put 'em?* >*They'll help if we ask 'em to.*

EMCEE
** **emcee**[1] (em´sē´) (= "M.C.") (colloq.): master of ceremonies >*Elton was the emcee at last year's presentations.*

* **emcee**[2] (= "M.C.") (vi, vt) (colloq.): serve as master of ceremonies (for) >*I'll emcee if you make all the arrangements.* >*Who's going to emcee the show?*

ENCHILADA
— **the whole enchilada** (... en´chə lä´də) (sl.): all of it, the whole set, everything involved >*She wants the upscale condo, the fancy car, the expensive clothes, the exotic travel—the whole enchilada.*

END
* **at the end of [one's] rope** (colloq.): at the end of [one's] endurance or tolerance, no longer able to cope >*She's at the end of her rope after being cooped up in the house all day with the kids.*

— **go off the deep end** (see DEEP)

ENOUGH–EVERYTHING

— **no end** (colloq.): very much >*We enjoyed that show no end.*

— **not know which end/way is up** (see **KNOW**)

— **the short end of the stick** (see **SHORT**)

— **... to end all ...s** (colloq.): extraordinary ..., impressive ..., the ultimate ... >*Did you hear that? That was a scream to end all screams!*

ENOUGH
— **sure enough** (see **SURE**)

ENVY
— **green with envy** (see **GREEN**)

E.R.
— **E.R.** (colloq.): emergency room (of a hospital) >*He was bleeding bad, so they took him right to the E.R.*

EVEN
— **break even** (see **BREAK**)

— **even the score (with)** (colloq.): take revenge (on), retaliate (against) >*I'll even the score with that rat some day.*

** **get even (with)** (colloq.): take revenge (on), retaliate (against) >*She'll get even with him for cheating on her.* >*I don't get mad—I get even.*

EVEN-STEVEN
— **even-steven** (ē´vən stē´vən) (sl.): exactly even, fairly divided, neither owing nor owed (also adv.) >*The score was even-steven with two minutes left to play.* >*Give me ten bucks, and we'll be even-steven.* >*We'll divide this up even-steven.*

EVERLOVING
— **everloving** (sl.): contemptible, cursed, annoying >*Get your everlovin' feet off the dinner table!*

EVERY
* **every bit** (colloq.): equally, in every way >*Your son's every bit the man you are.* >*I think this cheaper model's every bit as good as that one.*

* **every time [s/one] turns around** (colloq.): with great or annoying frequency ([s/one] notices an occurrence) >*Every time I turn around, Ben's wanting to borrow money from me.* >*Seems there's a new scandal in that town every time you turn around.*

— **every Tom, Dick, and Harry** (colloq.): virtually everyone >*Seems like every Tom, Dick, and Harry has a car phone these days.*

— **every trick in the book** (colloq.): every strategy, every possible method or attempt >*Jim tried every trick in the book to get their support, but they wouldn't go along.*

* **every which way** (colloq.): in every direction, all over, in disorder >*People ran every which way when the fire alarm went off.* >*He had books stacked every which way in the room.*

EVERYBODY
— **everybody/everyone and his dog** (sl.): almost everyone imaginable, an impressive number of people >*Ya should have been at the party. Everybody and his dog was there.*

EVERYONE
— **everybody/everyone and his dog** (see **EVERYBODY**)

EVERYTHING
* **and everything** (colloq.): and undoubtedly everything else that is pertinent or required (used esp. as an affirmation of faith that s/thing is true) >*Sure he's an expert. He's got a Ph.D. and everything.* >*They say that guy's a gangster—he carries a gun and everything.*

— **everything but the kitchen sink** (colloq.): virtually everything, almost everything imaginable >*They had everything but the kitchen sink for sale at the swap meet.*

EX

** **[one's] ex** (... eks) (colloq.): [one's] former spouse or sweetheart >*Both him and his new wife get along pretty good with his ex.* >*Here comes my ex—pretend you don't see him.*

EXAMINED

— **ought/need to have [one's] head examined** (see **HEAD**)

EXCESS BAGGAGE

— **excess baggage** (colloq.): thing or person not needed or wanted, unnecessary burden >*Do we have to take your little brother along? He's excess baggage.* >*Get rid of that guilt—it's just excess baggage.*

EXCUSE

— **pardon/excuse my French** (see **FRENCH**)

— **poor excuse (for/of a)** (see **POOR**)

* **well, excuse me!** (*-cuse* lengthened and *me* stressed) (sl., sarc.): you're too easily offended! you're overly critical of me! >*Well, excuse me for touchin' your precious coffee cup!* >*Oh, I didn't laugh at your so-called joke? Well, excuse me!*

EXEC

* **exec** (ig zek´) (colloq.): executive (in business) (also adj.) >*This hotel caters to top execs.* >*We'll travel exec class.*

EXPECT

* **expect** (vt) (colloq.): suppose, guess >*I expect you'll want to freshen up after your trip.*

EXPLODE

* **explode** (vi) (colloq.): become furious, lose (one's) temper >*He's going to explode when he sees this mess.*

EXTRA

* **go the extra mile** (colloq.): do more than is expected, make a special effort >*The prof went the extra mile for him by tutoring him individually.*

EYE

— **[neg.] (even) bat an eye** (see **BAT**)

— **give [s/one] the eye** (colloq.): look enticingly or admiringly at [s/one], flirt with [s/one] >*That new woman's been giving all the married men the eye.*

** **have/keep an/[one's] eye out (for)** (colloq.): be watchful (for), stay attentive to notice (esp. to obtain s/thing) >*We're expecting them anytime now, so keep an eye out, will you?* >*Roger's had his eye out for a used flatbed truck.*

** **have [one's] eye on** (colloq.): have a special interest in obtaining, be romantically interested in >*I've had my eye on that gold ring for a while.* >*You seem to have your eye on that cute redhead.*

— **here's mud in your eye!** (see **MUD**)

** **keep an/[one's] eye on** (colloq.): watch over, be vigilant of, take care of >*Keep an eye on Johnny at school, will you?* >*I'll keep my eye on your house for you while you're on vacation.*

— **my eye!** (see **MY**)

EYEBALL

— **eyeball** (vt) (sl.): look fixedly at, scrutinize, check over >*I want ya to eyeball this plan and tell me what ya think.*

EYEBALLS

— **up to [one's] eyeballs in** (colloq.): having an abundance or excess of, very occupied with >*I ain't got time—I'm up to my eyeballs in paperwork.*

EYEFUL

— **eyeful** (ī´fŭl´) (colloq.): very attractive sight (esp. a woman) >*Wow, that woman is an eyeful!*

EYES

— **cry [one's] eyes out** (see **CRY**)

— **keep [one's] eyes peeled** (colloq.): maintain careful watch, stay vigilant, remain alert >*Keep your eyes peeled*

EYES

for cops. I don't want to get a ticket for speeding.

— **lay eyes on** (colloq.): catch sight of, first see >*When I laid eyes on her, I knew she was the girl for me.*

— **make eyes at** (colloq.): look flirtingly or enticingly at >*Didn't you see her making eyes at you? She likes you.*

* **only have eyes for** (colloq.): desire no one but, love only >*Don't be jealous— Roger only has eyes for you.*

— **pull the wool over [s/one's] eyes** (see **WOOL**)

F

FABULOUS

* **fabulous** (colloq.): excellent, wonderful, superb >*We had a fabulous time at your party, dear.*

FACE

— **break [s/one's] face** (see **BREAK**)

— **egg on [one's] face** (see **EGG**)

— **face the music** (colloq.): take the punishment (that one deserves) >*If you get caught, you're going to have to face the music.*

— **feed [one's] face** (see **FEED**)

— **in [s/one's] face** (sl.): pressuring or criticizing [s/one], bothering [s/one] (cf. "out of [s/one's] **FACE**") >*I don't want no inspector in my face while I'm tryin' to work.*

— **in your face!** (sl.): (interj. to taunt an adversary, expressing defiance or contempt, esp. when prevailing) (cf. "**IN-YOUR-FACE**") >*In your face, man! My score puts us ahead!*

— **out of [s/one's] face** (sl.): having stopped pressuring or criticizing [s/one], no longer bothering [s/one] (cf. "in [s/one's] **FACE**") >*You'd better get outta his face, or he's gonna sock ya.*

— **shut [one's] face** (see **SHUT**)

— **slap in the face** (see **SLAP**)

— **staring [s/one] (right) in the face** (see **STARING**)

— **stuff [one's] face** (see **STUFF**)

— **suck face** (see **SUCK**)

— **what's his/her face** (see **WHAT'S**)

FAG

* **fag** (fag) (sl., pej.): male homosexual (also adj.) >*He calls gays fags and says they're perverts. >He said it was a fag bar.*

FAGGOT

— **faggot** (fag´ət) (sl., pej.): male homosexual (also adj.) >*She called the gay guy a faggot. >He asked Brian why he'd bought a faggot magazine.*

FAGGY

— **faggy** (fag´ē) (sl., pej.): homosexual-like, overly effeminate >*Joe said he thought my clothes looked faggy.*

FAIR

* **fair and square** (colloq.): honest, equitable, straightforward (also adv.) >*The evaluation procedure was fair and square. >We'll divide this up fair and square.*

— **fair to middling** (... mid´ling) (colloq.): fair, so-so, acceptable >*It wasn't a great concert—I'd say it was fair to middling.*

FAIR SHAKE

— **fair shake** (colloq.): fair treatment or deal, equitable chance >*I don't play favorites—everyone gets a fair shake from me.*

FAIRY

— **fairy** (sl., pej.): male homosexual, very effeminate man (also adj.) >*He said he left 'cause there were a bunch of fairies there. >They said they didn't like his fairy friends.*

FAKE

** **fake** (vt) (colloq.): get through (s/thing) by improvising or simulating, give the appearance of doing (s/thing) adequately >*If you don't know all the words, just fake it. Nobody will notice. >I don't think he's trained for this. He's just faking the job.*

* **fake out** (vt) (sl.): deceive, trick, bluff >*I got faked out by that bastard—he managed to take credit for my idea. >You faked him out. He believed your story all the way.*

FALL

— **fall** (sl.): blame or punishment for a misdeed (esp. when one is innocent) >*They pulled the robbery, then set him up for the fall.*

* **fall (all) over [oneself]** (colloq.): put out a great effort, try harder than is necessary or reasonable (esp. to please s/one) >*It's pathetic the way Barry's falling all over himself to impress her.*

* **fall all over** (colloq.): be overly affectionate or servile with, fawn over >*Everyone was falling all over Rob after he won the big jackpot.*

* **fall apart** (colloq.): lose emotional control, become overwrought, begin sobbing >*When she saw him with another woman, she fell apart.*

— **fall down** (vi) (colloq.): perform poorly, lag in performance, fail >*He did fine on the written exam but fell down on the orals.*

* **fall flat on [one's] ass** (vulg.): fail utterly >*He thought he could make a go of it in that business, but he fell flat on his ass the first year.*

* **fall flat on [one's] face** (colloq.): fail utterly >*He tried selling real estate but fell flat on his face, so he's back to teaching.*

* **fall for**[1] (colloq.): be deceived by, be tricked by >*Did the teacher fall for the "my dog ate my homework" excuse?*

* **fall for**[2] (colloq.): fall in love with >*She's fabulous! I think I'm falling for her.*

* **fall/slip through/between the cracks** (colloq.): go through a process without receiving due care or treatment, be overlooked or neglected >*On this contract, we can't afford to let anything fall through the cracks. >Too many kids are slipping between the cracks in public education today.*

— **go/fall to pieces** (see **PIECES**)

— **take the fall (for)** (sl.): assume the responsibility (for s/thing illicit), accept the punishment (for) (esp. when one is innocent) >*Ya expect me to take the fall for what you did? >He'll take the fall for ya if ya pay him enough.*

FALL GUY
— **fall guy** (… gī) (sl.): scapegoat, dupe >*They made him the fall guy for the robbery 'cause they thought he was gonna cross 'em.*

FALSIES
— **falsies** (fôl′sēz) (sl.): pads (placed in a brassiere to make the breasts appear fuller) >*Is she wearin' falsies, or are those all hers?*

FAMILY
— **family** (sl.): local organized crime unit >*The city's family is mostly into prostitution and gamblin'.*

FAMILY JEWELS
— **family jewels** (vulg., freq. hum.): testicles >*The ball bounced up and hit him right in the family jewels.*

FAN
— **fan [s/one's] fanny** (… fan′ē) (colloq.): spank [s/one] on the buttocks >*Your father's going to fan your fanny when he sees this mess!*

— **hit the fan** (see **HIT**)

— **[for] the shit [to] hit the fan** (see **HIT**)

FANCY-DANCY
— **fancy-dancy** (fan′sē dan′sē) (sl., sarc.): pretentiously fancy, overly ornate or sophisticated >*I suppose ya'd rather be with your fancy-dancy college friends than go bowlin' with the guys.*

FANCY PANTS
— **fancy pants** (sl.): effeminate or showy male, sissy (also voc.) >*Who's the fancy pants with all the gold jewelry? >What's the matter, fancy pants, are ya scared?*

FANNY
* **fanny** (fan′ē) (colloq.): buttocks, rump >*She's been working out because she thinks her fanny's too big.*

— **fan [s/one's] fanny** (see **FAN**)

FANTASTIC

** **fantastic** (colloq.): wonderful, excellent, superb >*You did a fantastic job on this report, Pete.*

FAR

— **far along** (see ALONG)

— **so far, so good** (see SO)

— **trust [s/one] (about) as far as [one] can throw [him/her]** (see TRUST)

FAR-GONE

— **far-gone** (sl.): drunk, intoxicated >*Ted's too far-gone to drive.*

FARM

— **buy the farm** (see BUY)

FAR-OUT

* **far-out[1]** (sl.): very unconventional, avant-garde, radical >*I saw this really far-out movie about mental telepathy between two reincarnated Roman soldiers.*

— **far-out[2]** (sl.): wonderful, excellent, beautiful >*Hey, man, that chick you're datin' is really far-out.*

FART

** **fart[1]** (*färt*) (vulg.): burst of intestinal gas expelled through the anus, expelled flatus >*Someone's fart disgusted everybody at the wedding.*

* **fart[2]** (sl., freq. vulg.): person (esp. seen as troublesome or contemptible) >*What did the old fart want this time? >That little fart took off with my hammer.*

** **fart[3]** (vi) (vulg.): break wind, expel intestinal gas >*If anyone farts inside this tent, they get thrown out!*

* **fart around** (vi) (sl., freq. vulg.): pass time idly, work halfheartedly or unproductively >*Ray farted around for a couple of years before goin' back to school.*

— **fart (around) with** (sl., freq. vulg.): treat without due respect or seriousness, handle capriciously, toy with >*Ya can't be fartin' around with guns! >Just don't fart with the controls, OK?*

* **let/blow/cut a fart** (vulg.): break wind, expel intestinal gas >*He was lettin' farts all night. >What's that smell? Did somebody blow a fart?*

FAST

** **fast[1]** (colloq.): quickly earned (esp. questionably) >*Want to make a fast hundred bucks? Just deliver this package to big Eddie.*

* **fast[2]** (colloq.): morally loose (esp. a woman) >*He likes hard liquor and fast women.*

* **fast worker/operator** (colloq.): person who gains personal advantage quickly and shrewdly >*That student's a fast worker—he's already got the instructor eating out of his hand. >Watch out for Al, because he's a fast operator with the ladies.*

— **play fast and loose** (see PLAY)

— **(so fast that) it will make [s/one's] head spin** (see HEAD)

FAST LANE

* **live (life) in the fast lane** (colloq.): live at a fast and reckless pace, engage in exciting and competitive activities >*Rick's been living in the fast lane—too much boozing, racing, and gambling.*

FAST ONE

* **pull a fast one** (sl.): execute a trick or instance of deceit, deal dishonestly >*He tried to pull a fast one by leavin' what he agreed to outta the contract.*

FAST-TALK

* **fast-talk** (vt) (colloq.): persuade with glib talk (esp. by misleading or deceiving) >*Don't let him fast-talk you into bed, honey.*

* **fast-talk [one's] way** (colloq.): achieve (a goal) with persuasively glib talk (esp. by misleading or deceiving) >*Josh fast-talked his way into the chairman's office, saying he was his lawyer. >Let's see you fast-talk your way out of this mess.*

FAST TRACK
— **on the fast track** (colloq.): advancing or being promoted esp. fast (esp. in an organization) >*Get in good with Hawkins—he's on the fast track in this company.*

FAST-TRACK
— **fast-track** (colloq.): advancing or being promoted esp. fast (esp. in an organization) >*I know a young, fast-track exec who will just love this assignment.*

FAT
— **chew the fat** (see **CHEW**)

* **fat chance** (sl., sarc.): (there is) very little chance, (there is) almost no possibility >*A fat chance you'll have marryin' into that rich family! >Fat chance that bum'll pay ya back! >That jerk, cooperate? Fat chance!*

FAT-ASS
* **fat-ass** (vulg., pej.): fat person (also adj.) >*That fat-ass's gonna break the chair. >His fat-ass brother couldn't keep up with us.*

FAT CAT
— **fat cat** (sl.): rich and privileged person (esp. an influential one) >*They say some important fat cats are backin' this candidate.*

FAT FARM
* **fat farm** (colloq.): resort designed to help guests lose weight >*If this diet doesn't work, I'm going to a fat farm on my next vacation.*

FATHEAD
— **fathead** (sl.): stupid person (also adj., also voc.) >*That fathead just can't figure it out. >Some fathead clerk got it all screwed up. >Get it right, fathead!*

FATSO
— **fatso** (fat´sō) (sl., pej.): fat person (also voc.) >*She's thin, but her brother's a fatso. >Get outta the way, fatso!*

FATTY
— **fatty** (voc.) (sl., pej.): fat person >*Don't break the scales, fatty!*

FED
** **fed up (to here) (with)** (colloq.) (*to here* accompanied by a gesture of the fingers against the throat or head): disgusted or bored (with), no longer able to tolerate (s/thing) >*We're all fed up to here with your whining and complaining. >I'm fed up—I'm quitting this lousy job.*

FEDERAL CASE
* **make a federal case out of** (colloq.): exaggerate the seriousness or importance of (s/thing improper) >*All right, so I was speeding—you don't have to make a federal case out of it.*

FEDS
* **feds** (fedz) (sl.): federal authorities >*When the feds hear about this they'll come down hard on ya.*

FEED
— **feed**[1] (colloq.): meal (esp. a large or sumptuous one) >*My uncle puts on quite a feed on Christmas Eve.*

* **feed**[2] (vt) (colloq.): tell (s/one s/thing) (esp. s/thing false or exaggerated) >*Don't feed me that "I'm too tired" bit.*

* **feed [one's] face** (sl.): eat (esp. intently or voraciously) >*What a glutton! All he thinks about is feedin' his face.*

FEEDBAG
— **put on the feedbag** (sl.): eat, eat a meal >*My stomach's growlin'—let's go put on the feedbag.*

FEEL
* **feel** (sl., freq. vulg.): act of feeling or fondling (s/one) sexually (esp. furtively) >*Him, get laid? He didn't even get a good feel.*

— **be/feel up to** (see **UP**)

— **cop a feel** (see **COP**)

** **feel like** (colloq.): want, have a desire or urge to/for >*I feel like a pepperoni* pizza. >*Do you feel like going shopping with me?*

— **feel rotten** (see ROTTEN)

— **feel up** (vt) (sl., freq. vulg.): feel or fondle sexually >*He said he felt her up on their first date.*

FEELIE

— **feelie** (fē´lē) (sl.): instance of sexual fondling, sexual caress >*She let me have a few feelies, but nothin' more.*

FEELING

— **feeling [one's] oats** (colloq.): feeling lively or high-spirited, feeling playful >*That frisky dog is really feeling his oats this morning.*

* **feeling good** (colloq.): tipsy, somewhat intoxicated (on alcohol or drugs) >*Three beers and I'm feeling good.*

* **feeling no pain** (colloq.): drunk, intoxicated (on alcohol or drugs) >*After six scotches he was feeling no pain.*

FEET

— **drag [one's] feet** (see DRAG)

* **get [one's] feet wet** (colloq.): become initiated (in an activity), gain some preliminary experience >*After you've gotten your feet wet, we'll give you more responsibility.*

— **have two left feet** (see LEFT)

— **six feet under** (see SIX)

— **stand on [one's] (own) two feet** (see STAND)

— **sweep [s/one] off [his/her] feet** (see SWEEP)

FELLA

* **fella** (fel´ə) (colloq.): fellow (also voc.) >*He's a fella I know.* >*Hey, watch it, fella!*

FELLER

— **feller** (fel´ər) (colloq.): fellow >*Some feller at the bank explained it to me.*

FELLOW

— **fellow** (colloq.): boyfriend, sweetheart (male) >*I hear Marie's got a new fellow.*

FENCE

— **fence[1]** (colloq.): buyer of stolen goods for resale >*His fence buys all the gold jewelry he can steal.*

— **fence[2]** (vt) (colloq.): sell (stolen goods) to a buyer who will resell them, buy (stolen goods) for resale >*How are you going to fence those earrings you swiped?* >*Sammy will fence everything you steal.*

FENDER BENDER

** **fender bender** (colloq.): automobile accident causing minor damage >*A couple of fender benders really slowed things down on the freeway this morning.*

FESS

— **fess up** (fes ...) (vi) (sl.): confess, admit (to s/thing) >*Whoever did it better fess up.*

FEST

— **...fest** (... ´fest) (colloq.): situation of great ..., occasion dedicated to ... >*The two groups started trading insults and ended up in a slugfest.* >*The employees were all mad as hell, so they got together for a general gripefest.*

FIDDLE

* **fiddle** (vi) (colloq.): play the violin or fiddle >*That old boy fiddles, and his brother plays the banjo.*

— **(as) fit as a fiddle** (see FIT)

* **fiddle around** (vi) (colloq.): pass time idly, work halfheartedly or unproductively >*They'll dock your pay if they think you're fiddling around on the job.*

* **fiddle (around) with** (colloq.): treat without due respect or seriousness, handle capriciously, toy with >*If I catch anyone fiddling with my tools, they're*

going to get it. >He fiddled around with it and got it to work somehow.

FIELD
— **play the field** (see PLAY)

FIELD DAY
* **field day** (colloq.): opportunity for unrestricted amusement or advantage >*The press is going to have a field day with this scandal.*

FIEND
* **... fiend** (sl.): ... enthusiast, ... fanatic, person excessively or obsessively interested in ... >*The guy's a sports fiend—that's all he watches on TV. >Watch out for Mort—he's a sex fiend.*

FIERCE
— **something fierce** (sl.): strongly, violently >*He wanted a drink something fierce. >She told him off something fierce.*

FIFTH
* **take the Fifth** (colloq.): decline to answer in a legal proceeding so as not to incriminate (oneself) (based on the Fifth Amendment to the U.S. Constitution), decline to answer (to avoid embarrassing or compromising oneself) >*The D.A. couldn't get anything out of her because she kept taking the Fifth. >You're asking me if I bet at the races? I take the Fifth.*

FIFTH WHEEL
— **fifth wheel** (colloq.): extra or unwanted person (esp. in relation to a couple) >*Don't invite your roommate, honey. She'd just be a fifth wheel.*

FIFTY-FIFTY
** **fifty-fifty** (colloq.): equal, equally likely or unlikely, even (also adv.) >*I think I got a fifty-fifty chance of getting the job. >We'll divide whatever we make fifty-fifty.*

** **go fifty-fifty (on)** (colloq.): divide (s/thing) evenly >*Stop arguing about the bill and just go fifty-fifty on it.*

FIGHT
— **spoiling for a fight** (see SPOILING)

FIGURE
** **figure[1]** (vt) (colloq.): deduce, conclude, reason >*I may be wrong, but that's how I figure it. >My wife figures that I ought to help out more around the house.*

* **figure[2]** (vt): come to understand, reach a logical conclusion about >*I just can't figure that weird guy.*

* **figure[3]** (vi) (colloq.): seem logical, be expected, not be surprising >*It figures that the judge wouldn't let him off again. >This game figures to be real exciting.*

— **ballpark figure** (see BALLPARK)

* **figure on** (colloq.): take into account, plan on, count on >*You'd better figure on Colton being against your plan. >We didn't figure on it raining the day of the picnic.*

** **figure out** (vt) (colloq.): solve, decipher, come to understand >*We got to figure out how to fix it. >I can't figure out these assembly instructions. >I just can't figure a guy like that out.*

— **figure up** (vt) (colloq.): total, calculate >*Let me figure up how much the whole package will cost you.*

FIGURES
— **five/six/etc. figures** (colloq.): a sum of money of five/six/etc. figures, at least ten thousand/one hundred thousand/etc. dollars >*I hear he made six figures on that deal.*

FILL
** **fill in** (vt) (colloq.): provide with pertinent information, brief >*Hey, fill me in on what's happened so far.*

** **fill in (for)** (colloq.): temporarily substitute (for) >*Can you fill in for Phil while he's out sick?*

— **fill the bill** (colloq.): be just what is needed, serve a purpose well >*Mary's got the right training and experience—she'll fill the bill.*

FILL-IN

* **fill-in** (colloq.): temporary substitute (for s/one) >*We got to get a fill-in for Mandy while she's on vacation.*

FILLY

— **filly** (colloq.): girl or young woman >*Who's going to marry a headstrong filly like her?*

FILTHY

* **filthy rich** (colloq.): extremely rich, very wealthy >*He can have any car he wants because his folks are filthy rich.*

FINAGLE

— **finagle** (finã´gəl) (vi, vt) (colloq.): obtain through shrewdness or trickery, gain through manipulation >*How did you finagle a raise out of the boss?* >*Hank'll get us some tickets somehow because he really knows how to finagle.*

FINDERS

* **finders keepers(, losers weepers)!** (colloq.): (a situation where) whoever finds s/thing can keep it (and whoever has lost it has no claim to it) >*Look, a five-dollar bill! Finders keepers! >No, you can't have the marble you lost back. It's finders keepers, losers weepers!*

FINE

— **fine**[1] (sl.): good-looking (esp. a woman) >*She's not so pretty, but her sister is really fine.*

** **fine**[2] (colloq.): very well, in a positive way >*He's doing fine on his new job. >I like your present just fine. >The kids are behaving fine.*

— **a fine how-do-you-do** (see HOW-DO-YOU-DO)

— **fine and dandy** (colloq., freq. sarc.): very good, all right (also adv.) >*If you want to throw your dough away betting on racehorses, it's fine and dandy with me. >Oh yeah, her new job's working out fine and dandy.*

FINGER

— **finger** (vt) (sl.): identify as culpable, inform on (to the authorities) >*His ex-partner fingered him for the burglary.*

* **give [s/one] the finger** (sl.): make an obscene gesture (cf. "**the BIRD**") at [s/one] >*He just kept yellin' at her, so she gave him the finger.*

— **lay a hand/finger on** (see LAY)

— **lift a hand/finger** (see LIFT)

* **put [one's] finger on** (colloq.): recall exactly, identify by remembering (used esp. in the neg.) >*That name is familiar, but I can't put my finger on where I've heard it.*

— **wrap/twist [s/one] around [one's] little finger** (see WRAP)

FINGERFUCK

— **fingerfuck** (fing´gər fuk´) (vt) (vulg.): stimulate with the finger(s) the vagina of >*He said he fingerfucked her while they were parked.*

FINGERS

* **have/keep [one's] fingers crossed** (colloq.): be/continue hoping (for a positive outcome) >*Keep your fingers crossed for me—they announce the award winners tomorrow.*

FINK

— **fink**[1] (*fingk*) (sl.): scoundrel, contemptible person (esp. s/one untrustworthy) >*I don't want nothin' to do with that double-crossin' fink.*

— **fink**[2] (sl.): treacherous person, traitor, informer >*I know that fink told the cops what we were plannin'.*

— **fink (on)** (sl.): inform (on), denounce (s/one) >*If he gets caught, he'll fink. >If you fink on Big Al, you're dead!*

— **fink out** (vi) (sl.): desert (s/one), fail to come through, retreat >*Don't fink out now—we need ya!*

FIRE

* **fire away** (vi) (colloq.): ask questions (esp. continuously and aggressively) >*The reporters fired away at the news conference.*

— **shoot/fire blanks** (see SHOOT)

* **fire up**[1] (vt) (colloq.): enthuse, inspire, agitate, stir up >*Some union organizer's got the workers down at the plant all fired up about going out on strike.*

* **fire up**[2] (vt) (sl.): start (an engine or motor) >*Fire it up, and I'll adjust the carburetor.*

— **light/build a fire under** (see **LIGHT**)

— **where's the fire?** (see **WHERE'S**)

FIREBALL
— **fireball** (colloq.): energetic and capable person, dynamo >*We need a real fireball in charge of this tough project.*

FIREBUG
— **firebug** (colloq.): arsonist, pyromaniac >*They think a firebug's responsible for the brush fire.*

FIREWATER
— **firewater** (colloq.): liquor >*Give me a shot of that there firewater.*

FIREWORKS
— **fireworks** (colloq.): heated argument, fighting, open contention >*At the meeting I'm going to tell what they've been saying about each other, then sit back and watch the fireworks.*

FIRST
* **first off** (colloq.): before anything else, immediately >*I'd like to tell you first off how glad I am you're here.*

FIRST BASE
— **not (even) get to first base** (sl.): not have (even) an initial success (in achieving s/thing), not succeed in taking (even) the first step (toward a goal) (esp. a sexual conquest) >*Skinny Harry ain't even gonna get to first base with that babe.*

FISH
— **drink like a fish** (see **DRINK**)

FISHY
* **(smell) fishy** (colloq.): (seem) implausible or suspect, (appear) ungenuine >*You don't believe that fishy story, do you? >There's something fishy*

about that guy who claims to be the dead man's brother. >*This whole scheme smells fishy to me.*

FIST
— **hand over fist** (see **HAND**)

FIT
— **fit** (vi) (colloq.): make sense, seem plausible or logical >*Why is he taking a vacation at the busiest time of the year? It doesn't fit.*

— **(as) fit as a fiddle** (colloq.): very fit, in excellent health, in good physical condition >*The doc checked me over and said I'm fit as a fiddle.*

— **fit to be tied** (colloq.): very angry, furious >*Warren was fit to be tied when the new guy was promoted over him.*

** **throw/have a fit** (colloq.): become furious, lose (one's) temper >*When Lou saw the dent in the fender, he threw a fit. >I had a fit when I heard what they'd done.*

FITS
— **give [s/one] fits** (colloq.): make [s/one] very upset or angry, make [s/one] very anxious >*Those rowdy high schoolers have been giving the principal fits.*

FIVE
— **bat five hundred** (see **BAT**)

** **give [s/one] five** (sl.): slap [s/one's] open palm (as a gesture of greeting or congratulations) >*Nice shot, man! Give me five.*

* **take five** (colloq.): rest five minutes, rest a short while >*The men are getting tired—let's take five.*

FIVE-FINGER DISCOUNT
— **with a/[one's] five-finger discount** (sl.): by shoplifting or stealing >*That punk gets parts for his motorcycle with his five-finger discount.*

FIVE O'CLOCK SHADOW
— **five o'clock shadow** (colloq.): dark stubble of beard (seen on a man several hours after shaving, esp. in the late

afternoon) >*Aren't you going to shave? You can't go to the party with that five o'clock shadow.* >*His beard grows so fast he gets a five o'clock shadow by noon.*

FIVER
— **fiver** (fī´vər) (sl.): five-dollar bill >*Here's a fiver. Go buy something to eat.*

FIVE-SPOT
— **five-spot** (sl.): five-dollar bill >*I bet ya a five-spot he doesn't finish the race.*

FIX
** **fix¹** (colloq.): predicament, difficult situation >*Jim's really in a fix. He's got to come up with four hundred bucks by tomorrow or they'll repossess his car.* >*How'd you get yourself into this fix?*

* **fix²** (sl.): dose or injection of a drug (esp. an illicit one), dose of a habitual product or experience >*The junkie needed a fix real bad.* >*I need my coffee fix to get goin' in the morning.*

— **fix³** (colloq.): dishonest prearrangement (of the outcome of a game or contest), game or contest whose outcome is dishonestly prearranged >*Of course you kept losing—the game was a fix.*

* **fix⁴** (vt) (colloq.): dishonestly prearrange the outcome of (a game or contest) >*One of the promoters tried to fix the fight, but the challenger wouldn't take a dive.* >*This poker game is fixed!*

* **fix⁵** (vt) (colloq.): neuter (an animal) >*Ginger can't have puppies—she's been fixed.*

* **fix⁶** (vt) (colloq.): take revenge on, retaliate against >*I'll fix you for screwing up my chances for that job!*

* **fix [s/one] up (with)¹** (colloq.): arrange a date for [s/one] (with) >*If you need a date for Friday, I can fix you up with my sister.*

— **fix [s/one] up (with)²** (colloq.): furnish [s/one] (with), provide [s/one] (with) >*If this new model's too expensive, I can fix you up with a nice clean used car.*

— **fix [s/one's] wagon** (sl.): take revenge on [s/one], get retribution from [s/one], punish [s/one] >*Caruthers thinks he's really fooled me, but I'll fix his wagon real soon.*

FIXED
* **fixed for life** (colloq.): wealthy enough to be assured of a comfortable living for the rest of (one's) life >*If I pull off this deal I'll be fixed for life.*

FIXER-UPPER
* **fixer-upper** (fik´sər up´ər) (colloq.): low-priced and dilapidated dwelling >*We started with a fixer-upper and moved to a better house after a few years.*

FIXING
— **fixing to** (colloq.): planning to, intending to, preparing to >*I'm fixing to retire in a couple of years.*

FIXINGS
— **fixings** (colloq.): necessary ingredients or side dishes, trimmings >*We have the fixings for a nice green salad.* >*I want pot roast with all the fixings.*

FIZZLE
* **fizzle (out)** (fiz´əl ...) (vi) (colloq.): fail (esp. after a promising start) >*He started off strong, but the campaign fizzled out after the first two primary elections.*

FLAK
* **flak** (colloq.): criticism, hostile reaction >*His proposal drew a lot of flak from the opposition.*

FLAKE
* **flake** (sl.): very eccentric person, person with very odd ideas >*What flake came up with that weird plan?* >*Don't pay any attention to that flake.*

— **flake off!** (sl.): go away! >*Flake off! You're buggin' me.*

— **flake out** (vi) (sl.): fall asleep, lose consciousness >*Everyone just flaked out after the long drive home.*

FLAKY

* **flaky** (flā´kē) (sl.): very eccentric or odd >*Jean goes to some flaky therapist who has her chant her name backwards.*

FLAME

— **flame** (colloq.): object of (one's) passion, sweetheart >*She's been getting dressed up a lot lately because she's got a new flame.* >*His wife thinks he's been seeing some old flame of his.*

FLAMING FAG

— **flaming fag** (… fag) (sl., pej.): very effeminate male homosexual >*He thinks everyone who's gay is a flamin' fag.*

FLAP

— **flap** (sl.): commotion, scandal, uproar >*It caused quite a flap when Higgins blew the whistle on his own company.*

FLASH

* **flash** (vi, vt) (sl.): suddenly expose (one's) genitals in public (to s/one) (in order to shock) >*The cops picked him up for flashing at some women's club meeting.* >*He flashed a couple of old ladies, but they just laughed at him.*

— **flash in the pan** (colloq.): short-lived success, promising but short-lived effort >*The kid's a flash in the pan—he'll be back in the minor leagues before you know it.* >*Those three articles he published last year were just a flash in the pan.*

FLASHER

* **flasher** (sl.): person who suddenly exposes his/her genitals in public (in order to shock) >*Some flasher in the park about scared her to death.*

FLAT

** **flat**[1] (colloq.): flat tire >*We got a flat on our way over here.*

* **flat**[2] (colloq.): having very small or no breasts >*She uses falsies because she's flat.*

— **(as) flat as a board** (colloq.): having no breasts >*She's got nice legs, but she's flat as a board.*

* **(as) flat as a pancake** (colloq.): very flat, very flattened >*The truck squashed Billy's tricycle as flat as a pancake.*

— **fall flat on [one's] ass** (see **FALL**)

— **fall flat on [one's] face** (see **FALL**)

** **… flat** (colloq.): precisely (an amount of time), merely (an amount of time) >*He ran the mile in four minutes flat.* >*I can go from zero to sixty in seven seconds flat in this baby.*

* **flat broke** (colloq.): absolutely penniless, without any money at all >*Can you help me out this month? I'm flat broke.*

— **in no time (flat)** (see **TIME**)

— **in nothing flat** (see **NOTHING**)

— **leave [s/one] flat** (see **LEAVE**)

FLAT-ASS

— **flat-ass** (vulg.): absolute, unequivocal, downright (esp. about s/thing neg.) (also adv.) >*I gave him a flat-ass no on his proposal.* >*He flat-ass refuses to help.*

FLATFOOT

— **flatfoot** (sl.): policeman >*Some flatfoot came around askin' questions about ya.*

FLAT-OUT

* **flat-out**[1] (sl.): absolute, unequivocal, downright (esp. about s/thing neg.) (also adv.) >*He told me a flat-out lie.* >*He flat-out lied to me.*

— **flat-out**[2] (sl.): at top speed >*He was going flat-out when he hit the tree.*

FLEA

— **wouldn't hurt a fly/flea** (see **HURT**)

FLEABAG

— **fleabag** (sl.): dilapidated or dirty public establishment (esp. a hotel or other lodging) >*I ain't gonna sleep in that rundown fleabag again.*

FLESH
— **press the flesh** (see PRESS)

FLICK
* **flick** (sl.): movie, film >*Did ya see that new spy flick?*

FLIES
— **die (off)/drop like flies** (see DIE)

FLIMFLAM
— **flimflam**[1] (flim´flam´) (colloq.): trick, swindle, trickery >*The old lady lost all her savings on the flimflam that con man tricked her with.*

— **flimflam**[2] (vt) (colloq.): trick, swindle, deceive >*Don't let them flimflam you with their sweet talk.*

FLIP
* **flip ([s/one]) for** (colloq.): flip a coin (with [s/one]) to determine who is entitled to >*I'll flip you for the last piece of pie.* >*Stop arguing about who goes first! Just flip for it.*

— **flip [one's] lid**[1] (sl.): become very agitated or angry, lose [one's] control or temper >*Mom's gonna flip her lid when she sees how I ruined my pants.*

— **flip [one's] lid**[2] (sl.): become insane, go crazy >*The poor guy was under too much pressure—he flipped his lid and they had to take him away.*

* **flip off** (vt) (sl.): make an obscene gesture (cf. "the BIRD") toward >*The old lady yelled at me, so I flipped her off.*

* **flip (out)**[1] (vi) (sl.): become very agitated or angry, lose (one's) control or temper >*He flipped out and started yellin' at everybody when they criticized him.* >*The boss is gonna flip when he sees these rotten sales figures.*

* **flip (out)**[2] (vi) (sl.): become insane, go crazy >*Von always was kinda weird, and now he's completely flipped out.*

* **flip (out) (over)** (sl.): become very excited or enthused, become impassioned >*You're gonna flip over my new motorcycle.* >*He's flipped out over some girl he met at work.* >*They loved it! They absolutely flipped!*

— **flip [s/one] the/a bird** (sl.): make an obscene gesture (cf. "the BIRD") toward [s/one] >*All I did was say "Watch out!" and he flipped me the bird.*

— **flip [one's] wig**[1] (sl.): become very agitated or angry, lose [one's] control or temper >*Leona flipped her wig when she saw that someone had broken the vase.*

— **flip [one's] wig**[2] (sl.): become insane, go crazy >*The poor guy flipped his wig after he got fired.*

FLIP-FLOP
* **flip-flop**[1] (colloq.): unexpected reversal (in a belief or policy) >*For some reason the company did a complete flip-flop on the smoking regulations.*

— **flip-flop**[2] (vi) (colloq.): reverse (oneself) unexpectedly (in a belief or policy) >*His opponent accused him of flip-flopping on the issues.*

FLOOR
* **floor**[1] (vt) (colloq.): overwhelm, greatly surprise, stun >*Everyone was floored when they heard he was arrested for dealing drugs.*

— **floor**[2] (vt) (colloq.): knock to the ground >*Horace floored him with a punch straight to the chin.*

* **floor it** (colloq.): accelerate (a vehicle) to the maximum, depress the accelerator to the floorboard >*When Steve saw the cops, he floored it and tried to outrun them.*

— **mop (up) the floor with** (see MOP)

FLOOZY
— **floozy** (flū´zē) (sl.): woman of loose morals (esp. one of sexually suggestive dress or behavior) >*Why doesn't he get rid of that floozy and find him a nice girl?*

FLOP

** **flop**[1] (colloq.): complete failure >*The movie was a flop at the box office. >He's a flop as an accountant.*

** **flop**[2] (vi) (colloq.): fail completely >*He had two hits, but his last play flopped.*

FLOPHOUSE

— **flophouse** (colloq.): cheap or run-down hotel or other lodging >*Can't you afford to stay somewhere besides this flophouse?*

FLOW

* **go with the flow** (sl.): relax and adjust to circumstances, accept the way things happen >*Ya worry too much about everything workin' out just right. Just go with the flow, will ya?*

FLUB

— **flub** (flub) (colloq.): blunder, mistake >*Now, how are we going to fix a flub like that?*

— **flub (up)** (vi, vt) (colloq.): blunder, botch, make a mistake (on) >*No excuses—I flubbed up. >Don't flub it, because you won't get another chance.*

FLUB-UP

— **flub-up** (flub´up´) (colloq.): blunder, mistake >*A little flub-up in accounting can cause a lot of headaches.*

FLUNK

** **flunk** (flungk) (vi, vt) (colloq.): fail (an exam/class or s/one in an exam/class) >*I flunked the geometry test. >I passed chemistry, but Hannah flunked. >Mr. Peters flunked him on the writing exam.*

** **flunk out** (vi) (colloq.): be expelled (from school/a class) because of poor academic performance >*Sherry couldn't hack college and flunked out.*

FLY

— **(fly) by the seat of [one's] pants** (see SEAT)

— **fly off the handle** (colloq.): lose (one's) control or temper (esp. without good reason) >*Jennings must be under a lot of pressure to go flying off the handle like that.*

— **fly right** (colloq.): behave honestly, perform well, act ethically >*You'd better straighten up and fly right, or you're going to get fired.*

— **fly the coop** (sl.): leave quickly, escape >*By the time the cops got there, the suspect had flown the coop.*

— **fly (with)** (sl.): be convincing or acceptable (to), work right (for) (freq. used in the neg.) >*His explanation of why he was late didn't fly with the boss. >This plan just ain't gonna fly.*

— **go fly a kite!** (sl.): get out of here! stop annoying me! >*Go fly a kite! I'm not in the mood for any of your B.S.*

— **have to fly** (colloq.): have to leave right away >*It's late! I got to fly.*

— **on the fly**[1] (colloq.): in a hurry, rushing about >*He's been on the fly all week trying to put the deal together.*

— **on the fly**[2] (colloq.): while moving or doing other things >*I caught a bite to eat on the fly between meetings.*

— **[for] (the) fur [to] fly** (see FUR)

— **wouldn't hurt a fly/flea** (see HURT)

FLYBOY

— **flyboy** (sl.): aircraft pilot (esp. in the military), member of the U.S. Air Force >*The flyboys are out searchin' the area now.*

FLYING

* **flying high** (colloq.): euphoric, elated, feeling joy (esp. due to a success) >*Ellen's been flying high since she got word that she won the scholarship.*

— **(go) take a flying leap!** (sl.): get out of here! stop annoying me! >*You're full of crap! Go take a flyin' leap!*

FOAM

— **foam at the mouth** (colloq.): be extremely angry >*The governor's foaming at the mouth because they didn't pass his legislation.*

FOGGIEST

* **not have the foggiest** (colloq.): have no idea, not know at all >*I don't have the foggiest why she left without saying good-bye.*

FOLD

* **fold** (vi) (colloq.): fail financially >*The restaurant folded after just three months.* >*The play folded after the critics gave it bad reveiws.*

— **fold (up)** (vt) (colloq.): close up (a business) (esp. due to financial troubles) >*We were losing money, so we had to fold up the business.*

— **fold up shop** (colloq.): go out of business, cease a financial activity >*They were getting too old to run things, so they decided to fold up shop.*

FOLKS

** **[one's] folks[1]** (colloq.): [one's] parents >*I want to go to camp, but my folks can't afford it.*

* **[one's] folks[2]** (colloq.): [one's] family members >*Most of his folks live in Texas.*

FOOL

— **fool** (colloq.): silly, foolish, contemptible >*Let him talk his fool head off. Nobody will listen.* >*Help me up on this fool horse, will you?*

— **be a fool for** (colloq.): be very fond of, be very enthusiastic about >*He's a fool for good Japanese food.*

** **fool around** (vi) (colloq.): pass time idly, work halfheartedly or unproductively >*If you want to fool around, do it on your own time.*

** **fool around (with)** (colloq.): be sexually involved (with) (esp. illicitly), be sexually promiscuous (with) >*He got fired for fooling around with his students.* >*She can't trust her husband because he likes to fool around.*

** **fool (around) with** (colloq.): treat without due respect or seriousness, handle capriciously, toy with >*Don't fool around with that pistol!* >*He was fooling with the dial and broke it.*

— **...ing fool** (colloq.): ...ing enthusiast, ...ing fanatic, expert at ...ing >*My brother's climbed in the Alps, the Andes, and the Himalayas. He's a mountain climbing fool.*

— **play [s/one] for a fool/sucker** (see **PLAY**)

FOOT (also see FEET)

* **get [one's] foot in the door** (colloq.): have an initial success (in an area where full participation is difficult) >*It's not easy marketing screenplays, but if you can get your foot in the door at a major studio it's a lot easier.*

* **foot the bill** (colloq.): bear the expense, pay (for s/thing) >*Cathy's aunt's footing the bill for her to go to college.*

— **my foot!** (see **MY**)

* **put [one's] foot down** (colloq.): be decisive or insistent, take a firm stand >*Dad was going to let us go, but Mom put her foot down and we had to stay home.*

— **put [one's] foot in it** (colloq.): make a blunder, create an impropriety (esp. by saying s/thing indiscreet or embarrassing) >*They were getting along fine until Oscar put his foot in it by mentioning her ex-husband's girlfriend.*

* **put [one's] foot in [one's] mouth** (colloq.): make a blunder, create an impropriety (esp. by saying s/thing indiscreet or embarrassing) >*Gus really put his foot in his mouth when he mentioned her face-lift.*

— **shoot [oneself] in the foot** (see **SHOOT**)

FOOT-IN-MOUTH DISEASE

— **foot-in-mouth disease** (colloq., hum.): tendency to say insensitive or indiscreet things at inappropriate times >*Bart's got foot-in-mouth disease, so try to get him to keep quiet at our party.*

FOOTSIE

— **play footsie(s) (with)**[1] (… fŭt´sē[z] …) (colloq.): flirt (with) (esp. by touching s/one's feet under a table) >*I can't believe his wife started playing footsie with me right there in the restaurant.*

— **play footsie(s) (with)**[2] (colloq.): try to gain advantage (from) (esp. discreetly or clandestinely) >*Lorena's been playing footsies with the county supervisors lately. She must be trying to swing some important deal.*

FOR

— **for real** (see REAL)

FORGET

** **forget …!** (colloq.): I don't care at all about …! I find … contemptible! >*Well, if that's the way he's going to be about it, forget him!*

** **forget it!**[1] (colloq.): (interj. to reject a request or idea) >*Me, sing a solo? Forget it!* >*If you think she's going to go along with that, forget it!*

** **forget it!**[2] (colloq.): you're welcome! it was nothing! >*Forget it! You can return the favor some day.*

FORK

— **fork over** (vt) (colloq.): hand over, give (s/thing valuable, esp. begrudgingly) >*I had to fork over my watch to pay him off.* >*You lost the bet, so fork over ten bucks.*

* **fork up/out** (vt) (colloq.): pay (an amount) (esp. with sacrifice) >*We had to fork up two grand as a down payment.* >*How much did you have to fork out for that?*

FORT

— **hold down the fort** (see HOLD)

FORTY WINKS

— **forty winks** (colloq.): a short nap >*I'm going to grab forty winks now so I won't be tired tonight.*

FOUL

* **foul up** (vi, vt) (colloq.): bungle, spoil >*We're depending on you, so don't foul up.* >*Grace fouled up the party by putting the wrong address on the invitations.*

FOUL-UP

* **foul-up** (colloq.): careless mistake, confusion or disorder caused by (s/one's) error or incompetence >*There was some foul-up in the delivery instructions, and we didn't get the plans on time.*

FOUR-BANGER

— **four-banger** (sl.): four-cylinder engine, automobile with a four-cylinder engine >*This car's got quite a bit of power for a four-banger.*

FOUR-BY-FOUR

— **four-by-four** (colloq.): four-wheel-drive vehicle >*He takes his four-by-four all over the mountains.*

4 X 4

— **4 X 4** (see "FOUR-BY-FOUR")

FOUR-EYES

— **four-eyes** (voc.) (sl., pej.): person who wears glasses >*You tryin' to pick a fight, four-eyes?*

FOUR-LETTER WORD

** **four-letter word**[1] (colloq.): vulgar or obscene word or expression >*That foul-mouthed jerk can't say a sentence without two or three four-letter words in it.* >*Mommy, Jamie just said a four-letter word!*

* **four-letter word**[2] (colloq.): word for s/thing repugnant or offensive (to s/one) >*Work is a four-letter word to that bum.* >*Smoking is a four-letter word in this health club.*

FOX

* **fox** (sl.): attractive woman (esp. sexually) >*My girl's a fox—she really turns men's heads.*

FOXY
— **foxy** (sl.): attractive, sexy (woman) >*Who was that foxy chick I saw ya with last night?*

FRACTURE
— **fracture** (vt) (sl.): cause to laugh hard >*What a joker! The guy fractured us.*

FRAIDY-CAT
— **fraidy-cat** (frā´dē kat´) (colloq.): coward, easily frightened person (used esp. by children) (also voc.) >*Go on and jump, or are you a fraidy-cat? >I dare you to do it, fraidy-cat!*

FRAME
* **frame** (vt) (sl.): falsely incriminate, rig or contrive evidence to blame unjustly >*Whoever forged your signature was tryin' to frame ya. >I didn't do it! I've been framed!*

* **frame(-up)** (sl.): false incrimination (of s/one), rigging or contriving of evidence to blame (s/one) unjustly >*I don't believe the witness—I think this is a frame. >He claims he's innocent, that it was a frame-up.*

FRANK
* **frank** (colloq.): frankfurter, wiener, hot dog >*We're having franks and beans at the picnic.*

FRAT
* **frat** (frat) (colloq.): fraternity (of a college or university) >*You going to join a frat when you go to college? >He took her to a frat party.*

FRAT RAT
— **frat rat** (frat ...) (sl.): member of a fraternity (of a college or university) (esp. when seen as neg.) >*The frat rats think they're better than us independents.*

FRAZZLE
— **frazzle**[1] (fraz´əl) (colloq.): state of exhaustion (esp. nervous exhaustion) >*I was worn to a frazzle by the kid's party.*

— **frazzle**[2] (vt) (colloq.): wear out, exhaust (esp. with nervous exhaustion) >*I was frazzled by the end of exam week.*

FREAK
* **... freak** (sl.): ... enthusiast, ... fanatic, ... addict >*Joe's a Dodger freak. He never misses one of their games. >I don't want ya hangin' out with those drug freaks at school.*

** **freak (out)** (vi, vt) (sl.): lose/cause to lose emotional control (due to fear, anger, shock, effect of drugs, etc.), become/cause to become astonished >*It really freaked her out when she ran over the cat. >I was freaked out when the old lady cussed at me. >He took some L.S.D. and just freaked.*

FREAKING
— **freaking** (adj., adv.) (sl.): (intens. to express anger, contempt, or wonder) >*Get your freakin' hands off me! >The guy's freakin' nuts! >It's a freakin' miracle!*

FREAKY
* **freaky** (sl.): very odd, astonishing, weird >*The way they came screamin' at us was really freaky, man.*

FREE
** **for free** (colloq.): without charge, gratis >*I bought the radio, and the saleswoman threw in the batteries for free.*

FREEBASE
* **freebase**[1] (sl.): smokable cocaine extract >*Messin' with that freebase is dangerous.*

* **freebase**[2] (vi) (sl.): smoke a cocaine extract >*She was freebasin' when the cops raided her apartment.*

FREEBEE
— **freebee** (see "FREEBIE")

FREEBIE
** **freebie** (frē´bē) (sl.): s/thing given gratis, item or activity free of charge >*They're givin' out T-shirts, decals, and*

other freebies at the store's grand opening.

FREELOAD

* **freeload** (vi) (colloq.): take unfair advantage of others' generosity or hospitality, sponge >*I don't want your brother here freeloading off us again this summer.*

FREELOADER

* **freeloader** (colloq.): person who takes unfair advantage of others' generosity or hospitality, sponger >*Let's try to keep the freeloaders away from the buffet table.*

FREE LUNCH

* **free lunch** (colloq.): s/thing given without repayment or responsibility expected (used esp. in the neg.) >*You'd better think about how you're going to make it when you leave home—there's no free lunch out in the real world.*

FREE RIDE

* **free ride** (colloq.): s/thing obtained without cost or effort >*Walter got a free ride up the promotion ladder because his brother owns most of the company.*

FREEWHEELING

— **freewheeling** (colloq.): unrestrained, carefree, reckless (in behavior or attitude) >*Carl and his freewheeling buddies really like to drink.*

FREEZE

** **freeze** (vi) (colloq.): stop moving completely, become motionless >*I yelled for her to freeze when I saw the snake next to her.* >*Freeze! You're under arrest!*

— **freeze [one's] balls/nuts off** (vulg.): feel very cold (used for men) (cf. "FREEZE [one's] tits off") >*Damn, it's cold—I'm freezin' my balls off!*

* **freeze [one's] buns off** (sl.): feel very cold >*Light a fire. we're freezin' our buns off.*

— **freeze [s/one] out (of)** (colloq.): exclude [s/one] (from membership or

participation) (esp. by snubbing) >*After the scandal they froze her out of all their social activities.* >*They're giving all the good promotions to men and freezing the women out.*

— **freeze [one's] tits off** (... tits ...) (vulg.): feel very cold (used for women) (cf. "FREEZE [one's] balls/nuts off") >*Let's go inside, girls—we're gonna freeze our tits off out here.*

* **freeze (up)** (vi) (colloq.): become paralyzed with fear or anxiety >*The kid just froze up the first time he took the controls.*

FREEZES

— **until/till hell freezes over** (see HELL)
— **when hell freezes over** (see HELL)

FRENCH

* **pardon/excuse my French** (colloq.): pardon me for using vulgar language >*I don't give a shit! Oops, pardon my French!* >*He's a real (excuse my French) asshole.*

FRESH

* **fresh** (colloq.): overly forward, impudent, presumptuous >*I don't like that kid—he's too fresh.* >*She slapped him when he got fresh with her.*

* **fresh out (of)** (colloq.): recently depleted (of), having just run out (of) >*I don't know what else to try—I'm fresh out of ideas.* >*No more cabbage, lady; we're fresh out.*

FRIDGE

** **fridge** (frij) (colloq.): refrigerator >*Check the fridge and see if we need milk.*

FRIES

** **fries** (frīz) (colloq.): french-fried potatoes >*Give me a cheeseburger and fries.*

FRIGGING

— **frigging** (frig´ing) (adj., adv.) (sl., freq. vulg.): (intens. to express anger, contempt, or wonder) >*Give me the* *friggin' newspaper already!* >*You get it friggin' right, or you'll be out on your friggin' butt!*

FRISCO
* **Frisco** (fris´kō) (colloq.): San Francisco, California >*You flying into Frisco, Oakland, or San Jose?*

FRITZ
— **on the fritz** (... frits) (colloq.): inoperative, not in working order, working poorly >*We got to get a new TV. This one's on the fritz again.*

FROG
— **frog** (sl., pej.): French person, French >*He said the frogs were snotty to him when he was in Paris.* >*I don't want none of that frog food! Give me steak and potatoes any day.*

FROM
— **from (the)** ... (see entry under ... word)
— **(straight/right) from the horse's mouth** (see HORSE'S MOUTH)

FRONT
— **out front** (see OUT)
— **up front** (see UP)

FRONT OFFICE
* **the front office** (colloq.): the decision-making executives or administrators (of a business) >*The front office just put out some new safety regulations.*

FROSH
— **frosh** (frosh) (colloq.): freshman, freshmen (in high school or college) (also adj.) >*The frosh are still learning their way around campus.* >*I met her at a frosh dance.*

FROST
— **frost** (vt) (sl.): make angry, irritate >*It really frosts me when he tries to blame me for his own screwups.*

FROSTING
— **icing/frosting on the cake** (see ICING)

FRUIT
— **fruit** (sl., pej.): male homosexual, very effeminate male >*She thinks my friend Steve is a fruit just 'cause he's a dancer.*

FRUITCAKE
— **fruitcake** (sl.): crazy person, very eccentric person >*That fruitcake doesn't make any sense at all.*
— **(as) nutty as a fruitcake** (see NUTTY)
— **nuttier than a fruitcake** (see NUTTIER)

FRUITY
— **fruity** (sl., pej.): homosexual, very effeminate >*He said he saw a lot of fruity guys at the concert.* >*Where'd ya get those fruity pink shoes?*

FRY
— **fry** (vi, vt) (sl.): die/be executed in the electric chair >*He'll fry for those murders.* >*They'll fry her for that.*

FUCK
** **fuck**[1] (fuk) (vulg.): copulation, episode of sexual intercourse >*He said that he had a good fuck with her.*
* **fuck**[2] (vulg.): sex partner >*She said he's always a good fuck.*
* **fuck**[3] (vulg.): contemptible or reprehensible person >*I don't want that fuck comin' around here.*
** **fuck**[4] (vt) (vulg.): harm through deceit or malice, badly mistreat, victimize >*He really fucked his partner when he took off with their dough.*
* **fuck**[5] (vi, vt) (vulg.): have sex (with) >*He wants to know if she fucks.* >*He fucked her and then left her.*
** **fuck!** (vulg.): (interj. to express anger, surprise, or irritation) >*Fuck! I cut my finger.*
** **fuck ...!** (vulg.): I don't care about ...! I want nothing to do with ...! I find ... contemptible! >*I don't give a damn about your brother—fuck him!* >*Aw, fuck it all! I give up.*

* **fuck around**[1] (vi) (vulg.): be sexually promiscuous >*It's a wonder she hasn't gotten V.D., the way she fucks around.*

* **fuck around**[2] (vi) (vulg.): pass time idly, work halfheartedly or unproductively >*Do ya come to school to learn or just to fuck around?*

* **fuck (around) with** (vulg.): treat without due respect or seriousness, handle capriciously, toy with >*I'm not gonna fuck with a court order.* >*Hey, you guys, don't fuck around with that equipment!*

* **fuck/screw [s/one's] brains out** (vulg.): have sustained or repeated sex with [s/one], have vigorous sex with [s/one] >*She said she'd fuck his brains out.*

* **fuck off** (vi) (vulg.): pass time idly, work halfheartedly or unproductively >*If you guys spent more time workin' and less time fuckin' off, we'd get something done around here.*

* **fuck off!** (vulg.): get out of here! stop annoying me! >*Fuck off! I'm sick of hearin' ya.*

— **fuck over** (vt) (vulg.): harm through deceit or malice, badly mistreat, victimize >*We can't let management keep fuckin' us over with these extra payroll deductions.* >*They really got fucked over by some shyster lawyer.*

** **fuck up**[1] (vi) (vulg.): make a mistake, botch things up >*I don't want anybody fuckin' up, 'cause we gotta get this done right.*

** **fuck up**[2] (vt) (vulg.): botch, ruin, spoil >*If ya fuck things up, you'll get fired.* >*The rain fucked up our plans.*

* **fuck up**[3] (vt) (vulg.): injure, hurt severely >*He got his hand caught in the gears and really fucked it up.*

* **fuck up**[4] (vt) (vulg.): traumatize, create anxiety in, make neurotic >*Seein' her old man get killed when she was a kid really fucked her up.*

— **fuck you very much!** (vulg., sarc.): (interj. to express contempt for or anger at s/one for his/her mistreatment or inconsiderateness) >*Well, fuck you very much! Your big mouth just got me into all kinds of trouble.*

** **give a fuck** (vulg.): be concerned, care, take interest (freq. used in the neg.) >*That jerk doesn't give a fuck about anyone but himself.* >*Do ya really give a fuck what she says?*

** **the fuck** (vulg.): (intens. to express impatience, anger, or wonder, used in intransitive verb phrases between the verb and its prepositional particle) >*Hey, shut the fuck up!* >*That's when I decided to get the fuck out of there.*

— **the fuck …!** (vulg.): certainly not …! not really …! in no way …! >*He says he's a movie producer? The fuck he is!*

— **what the fuck!** (see **WHAT**)

* **what/who/[etc.] (in) the fuck …?** (vulg.): (intens. to express impatience, anger, or surprise) >*Who the fuck told ya you could do it?* >*Where in the fuck's that report?*

— **worth a fuck** (see **WORTH**)

FUCKED

— **fucked** (fukt) (vulg.): crazy, irrational, unworkable >*If he told ya that story, he's fucked.* >*This whole plan is fucked.*

— **(go) get fucked!** (vulg.): (interj. to express great anger or contempt to s/one) >*If ya don't like the way I did it, ya can go get fucked!*

FUCKER

* **fucker**[1] (fuk´ər) (vulg.): contemptible or reprehensible person (esp. a man) (also voc.) >*Tell that fucker to stay away from me!* >*Watch your step, fucker!*

— **fucker**[2] (vulg.): thing (esp. seen as troublesome) >*I think this fucker came off a '65 Chevy.*

FUCKFACE

— **fuckface** (fuk´fās´) (voc.) (vulg.): contemptible or reprehensible person >*Get outta my way, fuckface!*

FUCK FILM

— **fuck film** (fuk …) (vulg.): pornographic film >*He got a couple of fuck films for the bachelor party.*

FUCKHEAD

— **fuckhead** (fuk´hed´) (vulg.): contemptible or reprehensible person, stupid person (also voc.) >*What fuckhead told him to come to us for help? >Get outta here, fuckhead!*

FUCKING

** **fucking** (fuk´ing) (adj., adv.) (vulg.): (intens. to express anger, contempt, or wonder) >*What's your fuckin' brother want this time? >Keep your fuckin' nose outta this or I'll fuckin' break it for ya.*

— **…-fucking-…** (vulg.): (intens. used between syllables in a word to express anger, contempt, or wonder) >*What that guy did was in-fucking-credible! >This party's gonna be fan-fucking-tastic!*

— **fucking A!** (vulg.): that's absolutely right! yes indeed! >*Fuckin' A! You said it, buddy!*

FUCKOFF

— **fuckoff** (fuk´of´/fuk´ôf´) (vulg.): person who passes time idly, person who works halfheartedly or unproductively >*I won't have no fuckoffs workin' for me.*

FUCKUP

* **fuckup**[1] (fuk´up´) (vulg.): mistake, blunder, botch >*There was some fuckup in accounting, and they billed the customer twice.*

* **fuckup**[2] (vulg.): person who habitually makes mistakes or blunders, botcher >*Don't have Hanson do it—he's a complete fuckup.*

FUDGE

* **fudge**[1] (fuj) (vi) (colloq.): cheat slightly (esp. by manipulating an amount or measurement) >*Stop fudging and get back behind the line. >He says everybody fudges a little on their income tax forms.*

* **fudge**[2] (vt) (colloq.): cheat slightly by manipulating (an amount or measurement) >*He fudged a few points in his grade point average when he filled out his application.*

— **(oh,) fudge!** (colloq.): (interj. to express irritation or disappointment) >*Oh, fudge! I got spaghetti sauce on my new dress.*

FULL

— **full of beans** (colloq.): lying, very mistaken, not knowing anything >*Bert's full of beans if he says you can drive to Hawaii.*

* **full of crap** (… krap) (sl., freq. vulg.): lying, very mistaken, not knowing anything >*You're full of crap! There's no such thing.*

** **full of it** (sl.): lying, very mistaken, not knowing anything >*Brian's full of it if he says they're gonna win the championship.*

— **full of pee/piss and vinegar** (… pē/pis …) (colloq., freq. vulg.): energetic, high-spirited, lively >*Mort's full of pee and vinegar this morning. He was up at six and ready to go.*

* **full of shit** (… shit) (vulg.): lying, very mistaken, not knowing anything >*Don't believe anything he tells ya—he's full of shit.*

— **not be playing with a full deck** (see PLAYING)

FULL-BLAST

** **full-blast** (colloq.): at top speed, at full power, at maximum volume >*He was going full-blast when he hit the bump. >My darned neighbor had his stereo turned up full-blast.*

FULL-UP

— **full-up** (colloq.): completely full >*All the flights leaving tomorrow are already full-up.*

FUMBLEBUM

— **fumblebum** (fum´bəl bum´) (colloq.): clumsy person, person who habitually drops things >*Don't let that fumblebum set the table—he'll break something.*

FUN

** **fun** (colloq.): entertaining, full of fun >*Pam's a real fun gal.* >*We had a fun time at the party.*

— **a barrel of fun** (see BARREL)

— **fun (with)** (colloq.): tease (s/one), joke (with) >*Don't get mad—I'm just funning.* >*That grouch doesn't like anyone funning with him.*

— **like fun …!** (colloq.): certainly not …! not really …! in no way …! >*Borrow my new car? Like fun you will!*

— **more fun than a barrel of monkeys** (colloq.): a funny or entertaining person or thing, great fun >*Watching him learning to bowl was more fun than a barrel of monkeys.*

FUN AND GAMES

* **fun and games** (colloq., freq. sarc.): frivolous fun, diversion >*We're here to do a job, not for fun and games.* >*Yeah, going to traffic school's going to be fun and games.*

FUNERAL

— **it's [s/one's] funeral!** (sl.): [s/one] will have to pay the consequences (of [his/her] action or decision) >*Go ahead and pick a fight with him if ya wanna. It's your funeral!*

— **will be late to/for [one's] own funeral** (see LATE)

FUNKY

* **funky** (fung´kē) (sl.): unconventionally stylish, pleasantly odd >*Did ya see his funky hat with all the feathers?*

FUNNIES

** **funnies** (fun´ēz) (colloq.): newspaper comics page or section >*The first part of the Sunday paper I read is the funnies.*

FUNNY

* **funny**[1] (colloq.): impertinent, overly forward >*Don't try and get funny with him, or he'll get you fired.*

* **funny**[2] (colloq., freq. sarc.): witty or humorous remark, joke >*Laugh everybody! Roger made a funny.*

FUNNY BONE

* **funny bone** (colloq.): olecranon, ulnar nerve in elbow (which gives a sharp, tingling pain when hit) >*Tim's yelling because he hit his funny bone on the edge of the table.*

FUNNY BUSINESS

* **funny business** (colloq.): deceitful or improper conduct, illicit activity, trickery >*There was some funny business going on in the mayor's office, so the city council called for an investigation.*

FUNNY FARM

— **funny farm** (sl.): insane asylum, psychiatric hospital >*He flipped out and was sent to the funny farm.*

FUNNY MONEY

— **funny money** (sl.): counterfeit money >*He's doin' five to eight years in prison for makin' funny money.*

FUNNY PAPER

* **funny paper(s)** (colloq.): newspaper comics page or section >*What's your favorite strip in the funny paper?*

FUR

— **[for] (the) fur [to] fly** (colloq.): [for] there [to] be a fight or commotion >*The fur's going to fly when she finds out what her husband's been up to.* >*Sounds like fur's flying next door. Guess they're fighting again.*

FUSE
— **blow a fuse** (see BLOW)

FUZZ
— **fuzz** (sl., freq. pej.): police, police officer >*Watch out! Here comes the fuzz!* >*This fuzz came up and started hasslin' me for no reason, man.*

F-WORD
** **the F-word** (colloq.): "fuck" (or one of its derivatives) (a euphemism) >*Mommy, Davey just said the F-word!*

G

G.
— **G.** (= "grand") (sl.): thousand dollars >*He makes over five G.s a month.*

GAB
* **gab** (gab) (vi) (colloq.): talk idly, converse, chat >*We gabbed on the phone for over an hour.*

GABBY
— **gabby** (gab´ē) (colloq.): overly talkative >*Some gabby woman spent almost an hour telling us about her grandchildren.*

GAG
* **gag** (colloq.): comic routine, practical joke >*The comic always gets a lot of laughs from his hat gags.*

GAGA
— **gaga**[1] (gä´gä´) (sl.): wildly enthusiastic, infatuated >*The guys are all gaga over the foxy new girl in school.*

— **gaga**[2] (sl.): crazy, demented >*I'm goin' gaga listenin' to him beatin' on those drums all day.*

GAL
* **gal** (gal) (colloq.): woman, girl (also voc.) >*This side's for the guys. The gals dress on the other side.* >*Say, gal, want to dance?*

GALS
* **the gals** (… galz) (colloq.): group of women (esp. friends) >*What're you and the gals doing tonight?*

GAME
* **game** (colloq.): business, profession >*Hi, I'm Don. Real estate's my game.* >*I hear you're in the business consultant game now.*

— **ahead of the game** (see **AHEAD**)

* **game (for)** (colloq.): willing (to), interested (in) >*Howie and me want to go fishing. Are you game?* >*I'm game for a little poker.*

— **play the game** (see **PLAY**)

— **the name of the game** (see **NAME**)

GANDER
— **take a gander (at)** (… gan´dər …) (sl.): observe, take notice (of) (esp. s/thing extraordinary) (used esp. as a command) >*Take a gander at the diamond she's wearing.*

GANG
** **gang up on** (colloq.): attack as a group >*The bigger kids ganged up on Melvin and beat him up.*

GANGBANG
— **gangbang**[1] (vulg.): successive sexual intercourse between a woman and several men, multiple rape of a woman >*They paid some hooker to come over for a gangbang.*

— **gangbang**[2] (vt) (vulg.): (for several men to) have successive sex with (a woman), commit multiple rape (on a woman) >*She says they gangbanged her.*

— **gangbang**[3] (vi) (sl.): engage in the activities of a youth gang >*Jimmy used to gangbang with the home boys, but he got outta that.*

GANGBANGER
— **gangbanger** (sl.): member of a youth gang >*There's always a bunch of gangbangers hangin' out on this corner.*

GANGBUSTERS
— **like gangbusters** (colloq.): with great speed or intensity, with great success >*The new coach came on like gangbusters and got the players into shape in less than two weeks.* >*They're making money like gangbusters with that operation.*

GARBAGE
* **garbage** (colloq.): utterly contemptible or reprehensible person(s) >*You can't believe the garbage that comes into this sleazy place.* >*Why don't you divorce that garbage and get on with your life?*

GARDEN-VARIETY
— **garden-variety** (colloq.): ordinary, unremarkable, common >*He's no big-*

*time criminal, just your garden-variety
pickpocket.*

GAS
— **a gas** (sl.): a good time, a very enjoyable
or funny experience or person >*We had
a gas at the Halloween party.* >*Your
sister's a gas—she can really tell jokes.*

— **cooking with gas** (see **COOKING**)

— **run out of gas** (see **RUN**)

— **step on the gas** (see **STEP**)

GAS-GUZZLER
* **gas-guzzler** (gas´guz´lər) (colloq.):
automobile that consumes much
gasoline >*I can't afford to take this gas-
guzzler on a long trip.*

GAS HOG
— **gas hog** (colloq.): automobile that
consumes much gasoline >*Why don't
you trade that gas hog in on something
more economical?*

GASKET
— **(about) blow a gasket** (see **BLOW**)

GATE
— **crash the gate** (see **CRASH**)

GATE-CRASHER
— **gate-crasher** (colloq.): person who
enters a social event without permission
or invitation (cf. "**CRASH the gate**")
>*We got to control who gets into the
reception—I don't want any gate-
crashers.*

GATOR
— **gator** (gā´tər) (colloq.): alligator >*We
visited a gator farm in Florida.*

GAZONGAS
— **gazongas** (gə zong´gəz) (sl., freq.
vulg.): (woman's) breasts (esp. large or
shapely ones) >*He said the first thing
he noticed about her was her nice
gazongas.*

GEAR
* **get [oneself] in gear** (colloq.): become
active, stop being idle or unproductive,
start moving >*I better get myself in
gear and finish this job.*

GEE
— **gee** (see "**G.**")

** **gee!** (jē) (colloq.): (interj. to express
surprise, wonder, or disappointment)
>*Gee, she's pretty!* >*Gee! Why can't I
go, too?*

GEEK
* **geek** (gēk) (sl.): unattractive and
socially contemptible person, weird and
dislikable person >*Hey, man, only
geeks and losers are in that stupid club.*

GEE WHILLIKERS
— **gee whillikers!** (jē´hwil´i kərz/wil´i
kərz) (colloq.): (interj. to express
surprise, wonder, or disappointment)
>*Gee whillikers! Did you see the size of
that trout?* >*Gee whillikers! I got soup
all over my favorite tie.*

GEE WHIZ
— **gee whiz!** (jē´hwiz´/wiz´) (colloq.):
(interj. to express surprise, wonder, or
disappointment) >*Gee whiz! Can he
ever swim!* >*Gee whiz! Why won't you
help me?*

GEEZ
— **geez!** (see "**JEEZ!**")

GEEZER
— **geezer** (gē´zər) (sl., pej.): eccentric or
contemptible old man >*There's some
old geezer out there complainin' about
somethin'.*

GENT
— **gent** (jent) (colloq.): gentleman, man
>*The ladies sit here and the gents over
there, please.*

GERONIMO
— **Geronimo!** (jə ron´ ə mō´) (colloq.):
(interj. to indicate that one is starting to
jump from a height) >*Watch the splash
I'm going to make. Geronimo!*

GET
** **get**[1] (vt) (colloq.): understand,
comprehend >*Ah! Now I get what you
mean.* >*You just don't get it, do you?*
>*I didn't get the joke.*

GET

** **get²** (vt) (colloq.): puzzle, stump >*What gets me is how he could get away with it for so long without anyone finding out.* >*I've got you there. You can't figure that one out.*

* **get³** (vt) (colloq.): take revenge on, retaliate against >*They're going to get him for insulting their sister.*

* **get⁴** (vt) (colloq.): annoy, anger >*His stupid remarks really get us.* >*It gets me how she just ignores us.*

— **get⁵** (vi) (colloq.): leave, run away >*I've had enough of you kids—now, get!* >*When he pulled a knife, I decided to get.*

— **get⁶** (vt) (sl.): observe, take notice of (esp. s/thing extraordinary or contemptible) (used esp. as a command) >*Hey, get Larry in his new hat!* >*Get her, actin' like she owns the place.*

— **get⁷** (vt) (colloq.): kill, murder >*The mafia got him before the cops could offer him protection.*

— **get⁸** (vt) (colloq.): cause (s/one) sorrow, pain, distress >*It gets her real bad to see her son in jail.*

— **cannot get a word in (edgewise)** (see WORD)

** **cannot get over** (colloq.): find difficult to believe, be very surprised about >*I just can't get over how much weight you've lost!*

* **get [one's]** (sl.): receive the punishment or retaliation that [one] deserves >*That dirty rat's gonna get his one of these days.*

* **get [one] [s/thing]** (colloq.): obtain [s/thing] [for oneself] >*I'm going to get me a new stereo—this one's had it.* >*He got him a new shotgun for hunting.*

— **get (a/the/[one's]) ...** (see entry under ... noun)

— **get a little/some** (sl., freq. vulg.): have sexual intercourse (with a woman) >*He's gonna take her to his place and try to get a little tonight.* >*It's been a long time since he's gotten some.*

— **get a little/some on the side** (sl., freq. vulg.): be sexually unfaithful >*He said he'd been gettin' a little on the side when his wife was outta town.*

— **get/put [s/thing] across** (see ACROSS)

— **get after** (see AFTER)

— **get ahold of** (see AHOLD)

— **get along** (see ALONG)

— **get around** (see AROUND)

— **get around [s/thing]** (see AROUND)

— **get around to** (see AROUND)

** **get away with** (colloq.): successfully carry out (s/thing illicit or improper) without being caught or punished >*How did he get away with yelling at the boss in front of everybody?* >*You won't get away with this!*

* **get away with murder** (sl.): successfully carry out s/thing illicit or very improper without being caught or punished >*No one's catchin' him on these false insurance claims. They're lettin' him get away with murder.*

— **get back at** (see BACK)

— **get back to** (see BACK)

— **get cracking** (see CRACKING)

— **get down** (see DOWN)

— **get down to brass tacks** (see BRASS TACKS)

— **get even (with)** (see EVEN)

— **get going (on)** (see GOING)

— **get hitched** (see HITCHED)

— **get [oneself] in gear** (see GEAR)

— **get in on/into the act** (see ACT)

— **get in on the ground floor** (see GROUND FLOOR)

— **get into it** (sl.): begin fighting, start throwing punches >*They're really mad at each other. I think they're gonna get into it right here.*

— **get in(to) [s/one's] pants** (see PANTS)

** **get it** (colloq.): be punished >*Look what you did! You're going to get it when Mom and Dad get home.*

— **get it into [one's] head (that)** (colloq.): come to believe (that), become convinced (that) (esp. mistakenly) >*Somehow Ernie got it into his head that they were laughing at him, but it had nothing to do with him.*

— **get it on (with)** (sl., freq. vulg.): have sex (with) >*He said he'd like to get it on with her.* >*She said they got it on last night.*

— **get/have it together** (see TOGETHER)

* **get it up** (vulg.): achieve an erection of the penis >*He's all worried 'cause he couldn't get it up last night.*

— **get lost!** (see LOST)

— **get lost in the shuffle** (see LOST)

— **get nowhere fast** (see NOWHERE)

— **get off** (vt) (vulg.): cause to experience an orgasm or sexual excitement >*He says watchin' her undress really gets him off.*

— **get off [one's] ass** (see ASS)

— **get off [one's] butt** (see BUTT)

— **get [s/thing] off [one's] chest** (see CHEST)

— **get off easy** (see EASY)

* **get off (on)**[1] (sl., freq. vulg.): experience an orgasm or sexual excitement (due to) >*He's so horny he'll get off if she just touches him.* >*She says Darren gets off on watchin' porno films.*

— **get off (on)**[2] (sl., freq. vulg.): enthusiastically enjoy, be very excited (by) >*Do ya get off on beatin' up little kids?* >*Singin' in front of a lot of people is how she says she gets off.*

— **get off [one's] rear** (see REAR)

— **get off [one's] tail** (see TAIL)

— **get off the ground** (see GROUND)

* **get on** (colloq.): scold, reprimand >*She got on her kids for being so noisy.*

— **jump/hop/get on the bandwagon** (see BANDWAGON)

— **get on the stick** (see STICK)

* **get out of here!** (colloq.): stop your teasing! don't expect me to believe that! >*That jerk's a judge?! Aw, get out of here!*

— **get real!** (see REAL)

— **get/catch some Zs** (see ZS)

* **get somewhere** (colloq.): make progress, gain some advantage >*I hope I get somewhere with the boss when I talk to her about a raise.* >*I tried to find out more, but I didn't get anywhere.*

— **get [s/thing] straight** (see STRAIGHT)

— **get the/this show on the road** (see SHOW)

* **get [s/thing] through [one's] (thick) head** (colloq.): come to understand or realize [s/thing] (freq. used in the neg.) >*Josh just couldn't get it through his thick head that he wasn't really qualified for the job.*

** **get to**[1] (colloq.): begin (doing s/thing) (esp. spontaneously) >*One day I got to thinking about starting up my own business.* >*I don't know how the subject came up—we just got to talking about it.*

** **get to**[2] (colloq.): be permitted to (do s/thing), have the right to (do s/thing) >*I get to see any movie I want this Saturday.* >*I paid, so I get to go in.*

* **get to**[3] (colloq.): cause sorrow or regret in, pain, distress >*The program on those starving children really got to us.* >*His high-pressure job's starting to get to him.*

— **get under [s/one's] skin** (see SKIN)

* **get up on the wrong side of the bed** (colloq.): start the day in a bad mood >*What a bad mood you're in! I'd say*

you got up on the wrong side of the bed this morning.

— get what's coming to [one] (see COMING)

— get while the getting's good (sl.): get out or escape while it is still safe or convenient >*Things are gonna start gettin' kinda scary here pretty soon, so you'd better get while the gettin's good.*

* get with it (sl.): become active or involved, react to what is needed >*Hoyt had better get with it, or he's gonna get cut from the program.*

— get with the program (see PROGRAM)

— (go) get fucked! (see FUCKED)

— (go) get screwed! (see SCREWED)

— (go) get stuffed! (see STUFFED)

— not (even) get to first base (see FIRST BASE)

— out to get [s/one] (see OUT)

— tell [s/one] where to get off (see WHERE)

— where does [s/one] get off [doing s/ thing]? (see WHERE)

GET-GO
— from the get-go (see "from the GIT-GO")

GET-OUT
— as/like all get-out (sl.): wholeheartedly, vehemently, to the utmost degree >*They were punchin' each other like all get-out. >That guy's funny as all get-out.*

GETTING
* what [s/one] is getting at (colloq.): what [s/one] means or is trying to say, what [s/one] is implying >*Get to the point! Just what are you getting at?*

GETTING'S
— get while the getting's good (see GET)

GET-TOGETHER
** get-together (colloq.): informal social gathering >*Can you come to a little get-together at our place Friday night?*

GET-UP
— get-up (colloq.): costume, outfit, clothing ensemble >*Where you going in that get-up, to a Halloween party?*

GET-UP-AND-GO
* get-up-and-go (colloq.): energy, motivation, drive >*We need someone with a lot of get-up-and-go to keep this project on schedule.*

GHETTO BLASTER
* ghetto blaster (sl.): large and powerful portable radio, tape player, or compact disk player (esp. one carried or used on the street) >*The dude came boppin' down the sidewalk with a huge ghetto blaster on his shoulder turned up full-blast.*

GIFT OF GAB
— the gift of gab (… gab) (colloq.): a natural talent for speaking persuasively or artfully, glibness >*Murray's such a good salesman because he's got the gift of gab.*

GIG
* gig (gig) (sl.): short-term job, work engagement (esp. in the entertainment business) >*We had a gig playin' at a wedding reception yesterday. >How long is this magician's helper gig gonna last?*

GILLS
— green around the gills (see GREEN)

— stewed (to the gills) (see STEWED)

GIMME
** gimme (gim´ē) (colloq.): give me (used esp. as a command) >*Gimme another beer, will ya?*

GIMP
— gimp[1] (gimp) (sl., pej.): person who walks with a limp >*He said some gimp was run over in the street.*

— **gimp**[2] (sl.): limp (in one's walk) >*Ya know that guy with the gimp that works next door?*

GIMPY

— **gimpy** (gimp´ē) (sl.): having a limp, lame >*He can't go hikin' with that gimpy leg of his.*

GIRL

** **girl** (colloq., freq. pej.): woman >*Why don't you girls chat in the kitchen while us men watch the game?*

— **that's my girl!** (see **THAT'S**)

* **the girl next door** (colloq.): wholesome young woman from (one's) neighborhood (seen as an ideal wife) >*He dated a lot of women while he was away at college, but he eventually married the girl next door.*

GIRLIE

— **girlie**[1] (gûr´lē) (colloq.): featuring women who are nude or scantily clothed >*Want to go downtown and catch a girlie show?*

— **girlie**[2] (voc.) (colloq., pej.): girl, woman >*So, who asked you, girlie?*

GIRLS

** **the girls** (colloq.): group of women (esp. friends) >*All the girls are getting together at Sally's Monday night.*

GIRLY

— **girly** (see "GIRLIE")

GISMO

— **gismo** (see "GIZMO")

GIT-GO

— **from the git-go** (… git´gō´) (sl.): from the outset, since the very beginning >*He's backed this deal from the git-go.* >*I told ya from the git-go that it just wouldn't work.*

GIVE

— **give** ([s/one, s/thing]) (a/the) … (see entry under … noun)

* **give [s/one] [s/thing] any day** (colloq.): [s/one] much prefers [s/thing] >*He likes fancy wines, but give me a cold beer any day.*

— **give 'em hell!** (see **HELL**)

— **give good …** (sl.): be proficient in the use of (a) …, be talented with (a) … >*He wants her in the front office 'cause she gives good phone.*

— **give it to** (colloq.): punish, make suffer >*I'm going to give it to you if you're lying to me.*

** **give or take …** (colloq.): … more or less, plus or minus … >*I'd say she weighs a hundred and fifty, give or take five pounds.*

— **(just) say/give the word** (see **WORD**)

— **won't (even) give [s/one] the time of day** (see **TIME**)

— **would give [one's] left/right nut** (vulg.): would pay any price, be willing to make a great sacrifice (said esp. of a man) >*I'd give my left nut to be able to sing like that guy.*

* **would give [one's] right arm** (colloq.): would pay any price, be willing to make a great sacrifice >*Crandall would give his right arm for that job.*

— **would give [s/one] the shirt off [one's] back** (see **SHIRT**)

GIVEAWAY

* **giveaway** (colloq.): free gift (esp. to promote a business) >*They'll have free T-shirts and other giveaways at the store's grand opening.*

* **(dead) giveaway** (colloq.): thing that unintentionally reveals a secret >*The lipstick on Dave's collar was a dead giveaway as to what he'd been doing.*

GIVER-UPPER

— **giver-upper** (giv´ər up´ər) (colloq.): person who gives up easily >*I'm no giver-upper, so don't worry about me quitting.*

GIVES

* **what gives?** (sl.): what's happening? explain what's happening! >*What*

gives? Why's everyone screamin' at each other?

GIZMO

— **gizmo** (giz´mō) (sl.): device, gadget, instrument (for which one does not know the name) >*What's this gizmo on the dashboard for?* >*I need a spring for that gizmo next to the carburetor.*

GLAD HAND

— **glad hand** (colloq.): overly friendly or insincerely enthusiastic handshake or greeting >*That politician's giving everyone the glad hand to get votes.*

GLAD-HAND

— **glad-hand** (vt) (colloq.): give (s/one) an overly friendly or insincerely enthusiastic handshake or greeting >*I hate salesmen who glad-hand you.*

GLAD RAGS

— **glad rags** (sl.): party clothes, dressy clothes >*Put on your glad rags—we're gonna party.*

GLITCH

* **glitch** (glich) (sl.): minor malfunction or technical problem >*The copier has a glitch in it somewhere. The pages ain't comin' out clear.*

GLITZ

— **glitz** (glits) (sl.): tasteless showiness, flashiness, ostentatious decoration >*I prefer simple, low-key decor to all this glitz.*

GLITZY

— **glitzy** (glit´sē) (sl.): tastelessly showy, flashy, ostentatious >*Who decorated this glitzy joint?*

GLOW

— **have a glow on** (colloq.): be slightly intoxicated, be tipsy >*I've got a glow on after that stiff drink.*

GLUED

** **glued to** (colloq.): spending a great deal of time looking at, paying fixed attention to (esp. the television) >*How's that kid going to make any friends if he's glued to the tube all day?* >*The nation was glued to the TV during the crisis.*

GO

* **go**^{1} (colloq.): approval or authorization to proceed >*Once Harry gives us the go, we can start.*

** **go**^{2} (vt) (colloq.): say, do (a gesture or expression) (used in present tense to indicate dialogue or gestures in a narration) >*First, I tell him he's lazy, then he goes, "Why are ya raggin' on me?" Then I go, "'Cause ya never lift a finger to help around the house," and then he goes, like this, with his eyes.*

** **go**^{3} (vi) (colloq.): urinate or defecate >*Where's the bathroom? I got to go.*

* **go**^{4} (vi) (colloq.): fail, break down, become inoperative >*First I heard a whining noise, then the whole transmission went.* >*Doc says my heart's going on me and I need to take it real easy.*

— **go**^{5} (vt) (colloq.): bid, be willing to pay >*I'll go three hundred bucks for your motorcycle.*

* **go**^{6} (colloq.): ready for action, having all arrangements made, operative >*Everything's go for the game tomorrow.*

— **be a go** (colloq.): be approved or authorized (to be done) >*The dean's given his OK, so the course you proposed is a go.* >*If it's a go, we start tomorrow.*

— **be (a) no go** (see "be (a) NO-GO")

* **from the word "go"** (colloq.): from the outset, since the very beginning >*He's supported us on this from the word "go."*

* **give [s/thing] a go** (colloq.): give [s/thing] a try, make an attempt at [s/thing] >*I've never skied before, but I'll give it a go.*

— **(go ahead,) make my day!** (see MAKE)

— go all out (to) (see ALL)

— go all the way (see ALL)

* go and ... (colloq.): (do s/thing) unexpectedly or foolishly >*Our dog went and died on us last week.* >*What did you go and say that for?*

— go ape (over) (see APE)

— go ape shit (over) (see APE SHIT)

* go at it (colloq.): fight (esp. violently) >*They were really going at it, so we called the cops.*

— go back to square one (see SQUARE ONE)

— go ballistic (see BALLISTIC)

— go bananas (over) (see BANANAS)

— go belly up (see BELLY)

— go bust (see BUST)

— (go) by the book (see BOOK)

— (go) by the numbers (see NUMBERS)

— go down[1] (vi) (sl.): occur, take place >*What's goin' down over there where the crowd is?* >*I didn't even notice when the robbery went down.*

— go down[2] (vi) (vulg.): readily have sex, grant sexual favors (said of a woman) >*They say she'll go down for almost any guy.*

— go down on (see DOWN)

— (go) down the drain (see DRAIN)

— go down the list (see LIST)

— (go) down the tube(s) (see TUBE)

— go Dutch (treat) (see DUTCH)

— go easy (on) (see EASY)

— go fifty-fifty (on) (see FIFTY-FIFTY)

— go fly a kite! (see FLY)

** go for[1] (colloq.): be attracted to, have a special interest in or liking for >*Tony really goes for tall redheads.* >*I could go for a nice cold beer about now.*

** go for[2] (colloq.): attempt to attain, aim for >*I hear Reid's going for the vice*

presidency that just opened up. >*If you want first prize, then go for it!*

— go for/take a spin (see SPIN)

— go for broke (see BROKE)

— (go) get fucked! (see FUCKED)

— (go) get screwed! (see SCREWED)

— (go) get stuffed! (see STUFFED)

— go great guns (see GREAT GUNS)

— go halfsies (on) (see HALFSIES)

— (go) haywire (see HAYWIRE)

— (go) hog-wild (see HOG-WILD)

— go in one ear and out the other (see EAR)

— (go) in(to)/down the toilet (see TOILET)

— go jump in the lake (see JUMP)

— sell/go like hot cakes (see HOT CAKES)

— go native (see NATIVE)

— do/go number one (see NUMBER ONE)

— do/go number two (see NUMBER TWO)

— (go off) half-cocked (see HALF-COCKED)

— go off the deep end (see DEEP)

— go [s/one] one better (colloq.): outdo or surpass [s/one] (esp. with one extra action or effort) >*I'll go you one better and make the same shot from ten feet farther out.*

* go out like a light (colloq.): lose consciousness suddenly >*Shaun got slugged on the jaw and went out like a light.*

* go out of [one's] way (colloq.): make a special effort, inconvenience [oneself] >*I went out of my way to help Max, and he didn't even thank me.* >*Please make Susie feel welcome, but don't go out of your way for her.*

** go out (on) (colloq.): fail to function (for), quit working (to the detriment of)

>*I had to stop playing because my knee went out on me.* >*Sounds like your clutch is going out.*

** **go (out) with** (colloq.): date regularly, be the sweetheart of >*Cynthia's going out with some guy she met at work.* >*Is he going with anyone now?*

— **go over [s/one's] head** (see **OVER**)

— **go over like a lead balloon** (see **LEAD**)

— **go overboard** (see **OVERBOARD**)

— **go places** (see **PLACES**)

— **go potty** (see **POTTY**)

— **go round and round** (see **ROUND**)

— **go sour** (see **SOUR**)

— **go steady (with)** (see **STEADY**)

— **go straight** (see **STRAIGHT**)

— **(go) take a flying leap!** (see **FLYING**)

— **go the distance** (see **DISTANCE**)

— **go the extra mile** (see **EXTRA**)

* **go through the roof**[1] (colloq.): become furious, lose (one's) temper >*Mom'll go through the roof if she finds out about this.*

— **go through the roof**[2] (colloq.): (for prices to) increase alarmingly >*Medical costs have gone through the roof the last few years.*

— **go to bat for** (see **BAT**)

— **go to bed (with)** (see **BED**)

— **go to hell** (see **HELL**)

— **go to hell!** (see **HELL**)

* **go to it** (colloq.): start (doing s/thing) enthusiastically or vigorously >*When we told them they could start eating, they really went to it.*

— **go/fall to pieces** (see **PIECES**)

— **go to pot** (see **POT**)

— **go to the bathroom** (see **BATHROOM**)

— **go to the dogs** (see **DOGS**)

— **go to town (on)** (see **TOWN**)

— **go together** (see **TOGETHER**)

— **go way back** (see **WAY**)

— **go whole hog** (see **WHOLE HOG**)

— **go with the flow** (see **FLOW**)

— **come/go with the territory** (see **TERRITORY**)

* **have a go (at)** (colloq.): give (s/thing) a try, make an attempt (at) >*You want to have a go at tennis with me?* >*If you can't figure the directions out, let me have a go.*

— **let ([oneself]) go** (see **LET**)

— **let go (with)** (see **LET**)

* **make a go of** (colloq.): be successful at >*Think they'll be able to make a go of their consulting business?*

* **no go** (sl.): (it is/was) unsuccessful or futile, (s/one) refused (it) >*I asked Henry to play the role, but no go.*

** **on the go** (colloq.): active, busy, constantly going (s/where) >*People on the go don't have time to cook fancy meals.* >*She's over eighty years old, but keeps on the go.*

— **there you go** (see **THERE**)

— **there you go/are** (see **THERE**)

** **to go** (colloq.): (food/drink) ordered to be taken elsewhere to be consumed >*Give me two burgers and a medium coke to go.*

— **way to go!** (see **WAY**)

GO-AHEAD

* **go-ahead** (colloq.): approval or authorization to proceed >*We just got the go-ahead from the front office, so let's get started!*

GOAT

* **get [s/one's] goat** (colloq.): annoy [s/one], anger or vex [s/one] >*It really gets his goat when the girl he trained outperforms him.*

— **old goat** (colloq., freq. pej.): old man (esp. seen as troublesome or contemptible) >*Tell that old goat to keep his nose out of my business!*

GOB
— **a gob (of …)** (… gob …) (colloq.): much (…), many (…) >*Murray must have spent a gob of dough for that bike.* >*You like washing dirty dishes? There's a gob to do.*

GOBS
* **gobs (of …)** (gobz …) (colloq.): much (…), many (…) >*We got gobs of work to do before we're through.* >*Don't buy any more towels—we have gobs at home.*

GOD-AWFUL
* **god-awful** (colloq.): awful, very bad, shocking >*Where'd you get that god-awful painting?*

GODDAMMIT
— **goddammit!** (see "GODDAMN (it)!")

GODDAMN
— **give a goddamn** (colloq., freq. vulg.): be concerned, care, take interest (freq. used in the neg.) >*He's so tired up he just doesn't give a goddamn any more.*

* **goddamn(ed)[1]** (colloq., freq. vulg.): contemptible, detestable >*Keep your goddamn feet off the table!*

— **goddamn(ed)[2]** (colloq., freq. vulg.): very, extremely >*Goddamn smart kid you got there.* >*You're working too goddamned hard, Lonnie.*

* **goddamn (it)!** (colloq., freq. vulg.): (interj. to express anger, surprise, irritation, or disappointment) >*Watch where you're going, goddamn it!* >*Goddamn! It broke.*

— **worth a goddamn** (see WORTH)

GODDAMNED (also see GODDAMN)
— **(well,) I'll be goddamned!** (colloq., freq. vulg.): what a surprise! how interesting! >*Two flat tires the same week? I'll be goddamned!*

GODDAMNEDEST
— **[one's] goddamnedest** (… god'dam'dist) (colloq., freq. vulg.): [one's] utmost, [one's] best effort >*All I could do was just give my goddamnedest to win.*

GOD'S GIFT
* **think [one] is God's gift to** (colloq., sarc.): conceitedly believe [one] is critically important or irresistibly attractive to >*That hack actually think's she's God's gift to literature.* >*Romeo there thinks he's God's gift to women.*

GOES
— **here goes!** (see HERE)
— **here goes nothing!** (see HERE)
— **how goes it?** (see HOW)
— **it (just) goes to show you (that)** (see SHOW)

GOFER
* **gofer** (gō'fər) (sl.): errand-running employee >*We need to hire a gofer to take care of some of these errands.*

GO-GETTER
* **go-getter** (gō'get'ər) (colloq.): enterprising or aggressively ambitious person >*She's a real go-getter who's making her mark in county government.*

GO-GO DANCER
— **go-go dancer/girl** (colloq.): woman who dances as a performer in a discotheque or nightclub (esp. solo) >*Can you believe she worked her way through grad school as a go-go dancer?*

GO-GO GIRL
— **go-go girl** (see "GO-GO DANCER/girl")

GOING
* **get going (on)** (colloq.): become excitedly interested (in), start talking excitedly (about) >*The genetic engineering issue has really got the biologists going.* >*Don't start talking politics, or you'll get him going on deficit spending.*

— **have a good thing going** (see **GOOD**)

* **have [s/one] going** (colloq.): be fooling or baffling [s/one] >*That card trick you showed Francine really had her going.*

* **have [s/thing] going for [one]** (colloq.): have [s/thing] as [one's] special quality or advantage (to gain success) >*She ain't too bright, but she's got her good looks going for her.* >*The poor slob has nothing going for him.*

* **have/get something going** (colloq.): have/start a romantic or sexual relationship >*If you ask me, the way they look at each other, they have something going.* >*I'd sure like to get something going with him.*

* **like it's going out of style** (sl.): wildly, extravagantly, without moderation >*People were buyin' up property like it was goin' outta style.* >*That bunch of students has been partyin' like it's goin' outta style.*

GOING-OVER

* **going-over**[1] (colloq.): close review, inspection, examination >*The police gave the murder scene a complete going-over.*

— **going-over**[2] (colloq.): thorough beating >*The thugs took his wallet and gave him a going-over before taking off.*

GOINGS-ON

— **goings-on** (gō'ingz on'/ôn') (colloq.): activities, behavior (esp. when seen with disfavor) >*Somebody better look into the goings-on at the club parties.*

GOLD

* **gold** (sl.): (a record) having sold at least one million copies as a single or one-half million as an album (cf. "PLATINUM") >*That artist already has nine gold records to her credit.*

GOLDARN

— **goldarn(ed)** (gol'därn[d]') (colloq.): contemptible, detestable >*Tell them goldarned kids to quiet down!*

— **goldarn (it)!** (colloq.): (interj. to express anger, surprise, irritation, or disappointment) >*Goldarn! I brought the wrong pair of glasses.*

GOLDARNEDEST

— **[one's] goldarnedest** (... gol'därn'dist) (colloq.): [one's] utmost, [one's] best effort >*I did my goldarnedest, but I just couldn't finish.*

GOLDBRICK

— **goldbrick** (vi) (sl.): avoid (one's) duties or responsibilities, work halfheartedly >*Why should I work my butt off while that clown is goldbrickin'?*

GOLDBRICKER

— **goldbricker** (gōld'brik'ər) (sl.): person who avoids his/her duties or responsibilities, person who works halfheartedly >*I ain't gonna do any of that goldbricker's work.*

GOLD DIGGER

— **gold digger** (colloq.): woman who dates or marries chiefly for material gain >*She says she loves the boss, but I think she's just a gold digger.*

GOLDEN OLDIE

— **golden oldie** (... ōl'dē) (colloq.): popular song from the past (esp. one that is still popular) >*They played a golden oldie from the sixties on the radio.*

GOLD MINE

* **gold mine** (colloq.): source of wealth or something valuable >*This book is a gold mine of information on aviation.* >*That shop is a gold mine because of its location.*

— **sitting on a gold mine** (see **SITTING**)

GOLD STAR

— **gold star** (colloq., freq. sarc.): symbol of approval, recognition of success >*Do you expect a gold star for meeting your sales quota?*

GOLLY

— **by golly!**[1] (… gol´ē) (colloq.): (interj. to express determination or resolve) >*I'll get even with that son of a gun, by golly!*

— **by golly!**[2] (colloq.): (interj. to express surprise, wonder, or admiration) >*By golly, he got a perfect score!*

— **golly!** (colloq.): (interj. to express surprise, wonder, or disappointment) >*Golly, is she pretty!* >*Golly! Why can't I play, too?*

GONE

— **be gone on** (colloq.): be utterly in love (with), be infatuated (with) >*Look at his face when he's with her. Boy, is he gone!* >*Angie's really gone on that guy she met last month.*

GONER

* **goner** (gon´ər/gô´nər) (colloq.): person who is doomed, person unable to avoid death or ruin >*When the doc listened to her heart, he knew she was a goner.* >*If that deal falls through, we're goners in this business.*

GONNA

** **gonna** (gə nə) (colloq.): going to >*We're gonna wait and see what happens.*

GOO

— **goo** (gū) (colloq.): thick and sticky substance >*What's that goo in the bottom of the can?*

GOOCHIE-GOO

— **goochie(-goochie)-goo!** (gū´chē [gū´chē] gū´) (colloq.): (interj. said by a person as he/she tickles another) >*Are you ticklish? Goochie-goo!*

GOOD

** **good** (colloq.): well >*He did real good in that race.*

— **… [s/one] a good one** (sl.): … [s/one] forcefully, … [s/one] accurately or effectively >*Marie slapped him a good one when he tried to get fresh with her.* >*He touched the bare wire and got shocked a good one.*

* **(as) good as** (colloq.): in effect, tantamount to, virtually >*If he crosses Bad Eddie, he's good as dead.* >*Don't worry—his credit is good. The bill is as good as paid.*

— **feeling good** (see FEELING)

— **give good …** (see GIVE)

** **good and** (colloq.): very, completely >*After putting two six-packs away, he's good and drunk.* >*I'll do it when I'm good and ready.*

* **good deal!** (colloq.): that's fine! I'm glad about that! >*Burt said he'd do it? Good deal!* >*Good deal! Seven o'clock it is, then.*

* **good old** (freq. … ōl) (colloq.): valuable, trustworthy, likable (esp. s/one or s/thing of long-time proven worth) >*I never go camping without my good old hunting knife.* >*You can count on good old Derek to help us out on this.*

* **have a good thing going** (colloq.): enjoy a very favorable situation, have a lucrative business >*He has a good thing going, working at home without his boss looking over his shoulder all the time.*

* **in good with** (colloq.): in favor with, liked by >*Simmons is nothing but an ass-kisser who's trying to get in good with the boss.*

* **it's no good …** (colloq.): (doing s/thing) is futile >*It's no good trying to reason with anyone as stubborn as him.*

— **make (good) time** (see TIME)

— **on [s/one's] good/bad side** (see SIDE)

— **what's the good word?** (see WHAT'S)

GOOD-BYE

* **good-bye …** (colloq.): that's the end of (the) …, (the) … is over >*You come in late once more and good-bye job.*

— **kiss [s/thing] good-bye** (see KISS)

GOOD EGG
— **good egg** (colloq.): good person, nice or affable person >*Don't worry about Stacy—she's a good egg.*

GOODIE
— **goodie** (see "GOODY")
— **goodie!** (see "GOODY!")

GOOD-LOOKER
— **good-looker** (colloq.): attractive person >*Every girl he dates is a good-looker.*

GOOD OLD BOY
* **good old boy** (colloq.): member of a group of men who cooperate to maintain control (esp. white men, esp. at a local government level, esp. while excluding others) >*Let's vote the good old boys out of county government and make some changes!*

GOODS
— **deliver (the goods)** (see **DELIVER**)
— **have the goods on** (sl.): have incriminating evidence against >*They got the goods on ya, so ya better make a plea bargain with the District Attorney.*

GOODY
— **goody** (gŭd´ē) (colloq.): attractive or pleasing thing, s/thing delicious >*The first joke wasn't so hot, but that last one was a goody.* >*She brought cookies, brownies, and other goodies.*

— **goody!** (colloq.): good! hurrah! wonderful! (used esp. among children) >*Goody! Dad's taking us to the beach today.*

GOODY-GOODY
* **goody-goody** (gŭd´ē gŭd´ē) (colloq., sarc.): self-righteous, affectedly moral, naively idealistic (also noun) >*His goody-goody sister thinks she's better than us.* >*That goody-goody won't last five minutes counseling drug addicts.*

GOOEY
— **gooey** (gū´ē) (colloq.): thick and sticky >*The oatmeal's all gooey now—I don't want it.*

GOOF
** **goof**[1] (gūf) (vi) (sl.): make a silly error or mistake, blunder >*It's my fault. I goofed.*

* **goof**[2] (sl.): silly error, blunder, mistake >*That goof is gonna cost us two days' work.*

— **goof**[3] (sl.): foolish or eccentric person >*What a goof! How can anybody take him seriously?*

** **goof around** (vi) (sl.): pass time idly, work halfheartedly or unproductively >*While you've been goofin' around, Burt's gone out and found hisself a good job.*

— **goof around with** (sl.): treat without due respect or seriousness, handle capriciously, toy with >*If ya goof around with drugs, you're gonna get into deep trouble.*

** **goof off** (vi) (sl.): pass time idly, work halfheartedly or unproductively >*You kids stop goofin' off and finish your homework!*

* **goof up** (vi, vt) (sl.): botch, ruin, spoil >*We can't have anyone goofin' up on this project.* >*Mayer goofed up the shipment by usin' the wrong labels.*

GOOFBALL
— **goofball** (gūf´bôl´) (sl.): foolish or eccentric person >*Some goofball tried to tell me the Martians were gonna invade Earth.*

GOOF-OFF
* **goof-off** (gūf´of´/ôf´) (sl.): person who passes time idly, person who works halfheartedly or unproductively >*That goof-off will never make anything of himself.*

GOOF-UP
* **goof-up** (gūf´up´) (sl.): silly error, blunder, mistake >*That one little goof-up ruined the whole report.*

GOOFY

* **goofy** (gū′fē) (sl.): ridiculous, foolish, silly, odd >*The teacher's tired of your goofy answers.* >*Some goofy guy with thick glasses was askin' for ya.*

GOO-GOO EYES

— **make goo-goo eyes at** (… gū′gū′ …) (sl.): look at with a foolish look of love >*He's really fallen for Jane. See him makin' goo-goo eyes at her?*

GOOK

— **gook**[1] (gūk/gŭk) (sl.): thick and sticky substance >*She slapped some green gook on her face and said it would help her skin.*

— **gook**[2] (gūk) (sl., pej.): Asian, Oriental >*Some idiot just called Joon a gook.*

GOON

— **goon**[1] (gūn) (colloq.): foolish or stupid person >*Don't say that to her, you goon!*

— **goon**[2] (colloq.): hired thug, large and mean man >*He had his goons rough up the store owner.*

GOONY

— **goony** (gū′nē) (sl.): foolish, awkward or unattractive (also noun) >*What does she seen in that goony dork?* >*All the goonies hang out at that video arcade.*

GOOP

— **goop** (gūp) (sl.): thick and sticky substance >*Put some of this goop on the gasket first.*

GOOSE

— **goose**[1] (sl.): poke between the buttocks (in order to startle, as a prank) >*A good goose in the behind will wake him up.*

— **goose**[2] (vt) (sl.): poke between the buttocks (in order to startle, as a prank) >*Goose him with the broomstick and see what he does.*

— **cook [s/one's] goose** (colloq.): ruin [s/one's] chances, spoil [s/one's] plans, get [s/one] in trouble >*We can cook their goose by telling the cops what they're doing.* >*After they spread those rumors about him, his goose was cooked.*

— **(silly) goose** (colloq.): silly or foolish person >*What did that silly goose say that for?*

GOOSE BUMPS

** **goose bumps** (colloq.): small bumps on the skin due to cold or strong emotion, goose flesh >*I need a sweater—I've got goose bumps on my arms.* >*That horror movie gave me goose bumps.*

GOPHER

— **gopher** (see "GOFER")

GORILLA

— **gorilla**[1] (colloq.): big and clumsy or coarse person >*Can you believe that gorilla has taken up knitting?*

— **gorilla**[2] (sl.): hired thug, large and mean man >*Call off your gorillas and we'll work something out.*

GO-ROUND

— **go-round** (colloq.): quarrel, fight >*They had a big go-round about whose turn it was to wash the dishes.*

GOSH

* **gosh!** (gosh) (colloq.): (interj. to express surprise, wonder, or disappointment) >*Gosh, how you've grown!* >*Really? Gosh, that's too bad!*

GOT

* **you got it** (sl.): I'll give you or do (what you request) >*If ya want me to write it down for ya, you got it.* >*Another beer? You got it.*

* **you got it!** (sl.): that's exactly right! I completely agree with you! >*You got it! Throw every last one of them bums in jail.*

GOTCHA

** **gotcha** (goch′ə) (colloq.): got you >*There's no gettin' away. I gotcha now.*

GOTTA

** **gotta** (got′ə) (colloq.): got to >*I gotta go to work now.*

GOURD–GRASS

GOURD

— **out of [one's] gourd** (sl.): crazy, very irrational >*She's outta her gourd if she thinks she'll get away with this!*

GOY

— **goy** (goi) (colloq., pej.): non-Jew, gentile (used esp. among Jews) >*Mel said the goys didn't understand him.*

GRAB

— **grab** (vt) (sl.): cause an emotional reaction in, affect, interest, get the attention of >*That sad movie really grabbed me.* >*How does his plan grab ya?* >*His new book just didn't grab me.*

GRABS

* **up for grabs** (colloq.): available to be competed for, obtainable >*There's a new city council seat up for grabs.* >*You don't have pay for college—there are lots of scholarships up for grabs.*

GRAD

** **grad** (grad) (colloq.): graduate (also adj.) >*A lot of recent grads are trying to find jobs.* >*Are you going to grad school?*

GRAMPS

— **Gramps** (gramps) (voc.) (colloq.): grandfather, old man (freq. pej. when used with a stranger) >*Can you help me fix my toy, Gramps? >Hey, Gramps, hurry it up!*

GRAND

* **grand** (sl.): thousand dollars >*That car'll run ya almost fifty grand.*

GRAND CENTRAL STATION

* **like Grand Central Station** (colloq.): full of people and activity, very busy >*With our big family, Grandma's house at Christmas time is like Grand Central Station.*

GRANDDAD

* **granddad** (gran´dad´) (colloq.): grandfather (also voc.) >*Her granddad's in great shape for his age.* >*How're you feeling today, Granddad?*

GRANDDADDY

— **granddaddy** (gran´dad´ē) (colloq.): grandfather >*My granddaddy came out here forty years ago.*

— **the granddaddy (of …)** (colloq.): the oldest or largest (…), the most impressive (…) >*Look at that one! That's got to be the granddaddy of all lobsters!*

GRANDMA

** **grandma** (gran´mä´/gram´mä´) (colloq.): grandmother, old lady (also voc.; freq. pej. when used with a stranger) >*My grandma made my dress for me.* >*Thanks for my nice present, Grandma.* >*Hey, what you doing out alone this time of night, Grandma?*

GRANDPA

** **grandpa** (gran´pä´/gram´pä´) (colloq.): grandfather, old man (also voc.; freq. pej. when used with a stranger) >*I was named after my grandpa.* >*I love you, Grandpa.* >*Step up, Grandpa, you're next.*

GRANDSTAND

— **grandstand** (vi) (colloq.): perform ostentatiously to impress spectators >*The other players don't like him because he grandstands too much.*

GRANNY

* **granny** (gran´ē) (colloq.): grandmother, old lady (also voc.; freq. pej. when used with a stranger) >*How's your granny feeling today?* >*Tell me a story, Granny.* >*Go on, Granny! You're blocking the aisle.*

GRAPEVINE

* **the grapevine** (colloq.): source of rumors, system for information spread by mouth >*The grapevine has it that he's going to resign soon.* >*I heard it through the grapevine.*

GRASS

* **grass** (sl.): marijuana >*He's been smokin' grass for years.*

— **[one's] ass is grass** (see ASS)

GRAVE
— **turn (over)/spin in [one's] grave** (see TURN)

GRAVEYARD
** **graveyard (shift)** (colloq.): early morning work shift (gen. starting at midnight) >*I was working afternoons, but now I'm on graveyard.*

GRAVY
— **gravy** (sl.): money or benefits obtained easily or unexpectedly >*We've covered our costs, so from now on everything is gravy.*

GRAVY TRAIN
— **gravy train** (sl.): situation in which excessive pay or benefits are received for little or no effort >*This "consultation commission" is nothin' but a gravy train for the brokers.* >*His so-called job is a real gravy train.*

GRAY MATTER
— **gray matter** (colloq.): brains, intelligence >*He's got the gray matter to do the job right.*

GREASE
— **grease [s/one's] palm** (sl.): bribe [s/one] >*He greased the inspector's palm, and the inspection went off without a problem.*

GREASED LIGHTNING
— **like greased lightning** (colloq.): very fast >*That kid runs like greased lightning.*

GREASE MONKEY
— **grease monkey** (sl.): mechanic (esp. for automobiles) >*Billy's a grease monkey at Roy's Garage.*

GREASER
— **greaser** (sl., pej.): Mexican, Mexican-American >*Ralph called Tony a greaser and got belted for it.*

GREASY SPOON
— **greasy spoon** (sl.): cheap or dirty restaurant or café >*The chili I had in that greasy spoon gave me a stomachache.*

GREAT
** **great**[1] (colloq.): excellent, outstanding >*This is great ice cream.* >*My trip was great.*

** **great**[2] (colloq.): very well, excellently >*I think she sings great.*

— **be no great shakes** (see SHAKES)

** **great!** (colloq., sarc.): how annoying! how disappointing! >*Great! You've messed up the door I just painted.*

** **great at** (colloq.): skilled at, expert at >*Martha's great at bird imitations.*

** **great big** (colloq.): very large >*This great big dog jumped out at us and scared us to death.*

GREAT GUNS
— **go great guns** (colloq.): do very well, have great success (esp. in a dynamic or active way) >*His business has been going great guns since he started advertising.*

— **great guns!** (colloq.): (interj. to express surprise or wonder) >*Great guns! What're the firemen doing here?*

GREEK
* **Greek to** (colloq.): unintelligible to >*His talk on atavistic parapsychology was Greek to me.*

GREEN
— **green around the gills** (colloq.): pale, sickly, nauseated >*Troy looks a little green around the gills after his roller coaster ride.*

* **green with envy** (colloq.): very envious >*Jason was green with envy when he saw my new Porsche.*

GREEN LIGHT
* **the green light** (colloq.): approval or permission to proceed, authorization >*We're waiting for the green light to go ahead with the project.*

GREEN STUFF–GROPE

GREEN STUFF

— **green stuff** (sl.): money (esp. in the form of bills) >*He wants to see some green stuff before he hands over the goods.*

GREEN THUMB

* **a green thumb** (colloq.): talent for cultivating plants, excellent gardening skills >*Oh, you should see her beautiful garden! She really has a green thumb.*

GRIEF

— **give [s/one] grief** (sl.): annoy or harass [s/one], make trouble for [s/one] >*The old lady's been givin' me grief about finishin' school.* >*She's got enough problems already without you givin' her any grief.*

GRILL

* **grill** (vt) (colloq.): question or cross-examine relentlessly >*Are you ready to be grilled by their lawyer?*

GRIN

* **grin and bear it** (colloq.): resign (oneself) to (a neg. situation), deal with (a neg. situation) as best one can >*I don't like the judge's ruling, either, but we're going to have to grin and bear it.*

GRIND

* **grind** (colloq.): difficult and tiring routine or task >*How can he take that same old grind day after day?* >*Addressing all these envelopes is going to be a real grind.*

GRINGO

* **gringo** (gring´gō) (colloq., freq. pej.): foreigner (esp. an American) (from the perspective of Latin Americans) (also adj.) >*The Mexicans don't like gringos raising hell in their towns.* >*The gringo tourists spend a lot of money in town.*

GRIPE

* **gripe**[1] (grīp) (colloq.): complaint >*If you got any gripes, come and talk them over with me.*

* **gripe**[2] (vi) (colloq.): complain (esp. constantly) >*Everyone's been griping about the lousy food.*

* **gripe**[3] (vt) (colloq.): annoy, irritate, frustrate >*His arrogant attitude really gripes me.*

GRIT

— **grit** (colloq.): strength of character or spirit, strong determination or resoluteness >*She's got a lot of grit to carry on after those setbacks.*

GROCERIES

— **bring home the groceries** (see **BRING**)

GRODY

— **grody** (grō´dē) (sl.): filthy, dirty, disgusting >*I can't stand to look at the grody feet of people that go around barefoot.*

GROOVE

— **groove** (sl.): pleasurable experience, good time >*The party was a groove, man.*

— **groove (on)** (sl.): enjoy (s/thing) very much, experience great pleasure (with) >*My friends really groove on modern jazz.* >*He really grooves rock-'n'-roll music.* >*They were just sittin' there at the party groovin'.*

— **in the groove** (sl.): in good form, in style >*When Arnie's in the groove, nobody can shoot baskets like him.* >*If ya wanna be in the groove, ya gotta get the right clothes.*

GROOVY

— **groovy** (grū´vē) (sl.): pleasing, attractive, excellent >*What a groovy chick! I think I'm in love.* >*It's a groovy song from the sixties.*

GROPE

— **grope** (vt) (sl.): grab (s/one's) genitals (or a woman's breasts) >*My girlfriend just walked right up and groped me! I couldn't believe it!*

GROSS

** **gross** (sl.): disgusting, despicable, very ugly >*I'd never go out with him. He's gross.* >*Where'd ya find those gross boots?*

* **gross out** (vt) (sl.): disgust, shock, or offend (with s/thing repugnant) >*It really grossed me out when he started blowin' his nose.*

GROSS-OUT

— **gross-out** (sl.): disgusting or very offensive thing or person >*We saw a cheap porno flick that was a gross-out.* >*Like, this geek's a total gross-out.*

GROTTY

— **grotty** (see "GRODY")

GROUND

** **ground** (vt) (colloq.): restrict to (one's) home and deny social privileges to as punishment (esp. parents to children) >*Dad grounded me for two weeks for lying to him.*

* **get off the ground** (colloq.): have an initial success, get firmly under way (esp. an enterprise) >*If their business ever gets off the ground, they just might make some bucks.*

— **run [s/thing] into the ground** (see RUN)

GROUND FLOOR

* **get in on the ground floor** (colloq.): join an enterprise at its beginning (esp. to gain future advantage) >*He got in on the ground floor and now takes ten percent of the profits.*

GROUND ZERO

— **ground zero** (colloq.): most elementary level, very beginning (of a process) >*I didn't know the first thing about computers, so I had to learn from ground zero.*

GROUPIE

* **groupie** (grü´pē) (sl.): fan or admirer (esp. female) who is infatuated with a famous person or group or with members of a certain profession and who follows him/her/them in hopes of gaining intimacy >*The rock star was always havin' to dodge groupies.* >*Kay's a cop groupie—she's always hangin' around the police station.*

GROW

* **grow like a weed** (colloq.): (for a child to) grow very fast >*Mark started growing like a weed when he turned thirteen.*

GRUB

— **grub** (sl.): food >*They serve real good grub at camp.*

GRUBBIES

— **grubbies** (grub´ēz) (sl.): clothing that is old or worn-out but comfortable >*Can I go in my grubbies, or do I have to change into something nicer?*

GRUNGE

— **grunge** (grunj) (sl.): filth, dirt >*I'm gonna scrub all the grunge outta the shower before I use it.*

GRUNGY

— **grungy** (grun´jē) (sl.): dirty, unkempt, run-down >*Get your grungy socks off the floor!* >*He rents this grungy old apartment for $400 a month.*

GRUNT

— **grunt**[1] (sl.): soldier (esp. an infantryman) >*He was a grunt in Vietnam and saw a lot of action.*

— **grunt**[2] (sl.): laborer, unskilled worker >*Don't worry about it. We'll hire a couple of grunts to clean it up.*

GRUNT WORK

— **grunt work** (sl.): tedious or hard work >*We'll pay a bunch of kids six bucks an hour to do all the grunt work.*

GUCK

— **guck** (guk) (sl.): messy and sticky substance >*Clean out that guck in the corners, will ya?*

GUESSTIMATE

— **guesstimate** (ges´tə mit) (colloq.): impromptu and approximate estimate

>*I know you can't say exactly, but give me a guesstimate of how much it'll cost.*

GUEST

* **be my guest!** (colloq., freq. sarc.): I won't object if you really want (s/thing, to do s/thing)! go ahead! >*If you think you can do this better than me, be my guest!*

GUFF

— **guff** (guf) (sl.): nonsense, insolence, impudence >*Don't give me none of your guff—just shut up and do it!*

GUILT TRIP

* **guilt trip** (sl.): attack of guilt, feeling of self-reproach >*He's on a guilt trip because he told his mother off.* >*Hey, don't lay a guilt trip on me—it wasn't my fault.*

GUM

— **gum up** (vt) (sl.): ruin, botch, spoil >*Terri gummed everything up by invitin' her in-laws along.* >*He's gonna gum up the deal if he doesn't come through with the money.*

GUMPTION

— **gumption** (gump´shən) (colloq.): courage, initiative, resoluteness, pluck >*It took a lot of gumption for her to file a complaint against her boss.*

GUMSHOE

— **gumshoe** (sl.): detective >*He was a gumshoe with the New York police for ten years.*

GUN

— **give [s/thing] the gun** (sl.): give full power or speed to [s/thing] >*The engine sounds OK idlin'. Give it the gun and we'll have a listen.*

— **jump the gun** (see **JUMP**)

* **under the gun** (colloq.): under pressure (esp. to meet a deadline) >*Stan's under the gun to finish the report by Monday.*

GUNBOATS

— **gunboats** (sl.): pair of very large shoes >*Did ya see the gunboats that basketball player wears?*

GUNG-HO

* **gung-ho** (gung´hō´) (colloq.): very enthusiastic and loyal, overly eager, zealous >*They're proposing some gung-ho young executive for top management.* >*They're really gung-ho on the idea.*

GUNK

* **gunk** (gungk) (colloq.): thick and greasy substance >*What's that gunk he uses on his hair?*

GUNNING

— **gunning for** (colloq.): seeking (s/one) with the intention of harming or defeating (him/her) >*The contender has come gunning for the champ here in the finals.*

GUNS

— **stick to [one's] guns** (see **STICK**)

GUSSY

— **gussy up**[1] (gus´ē …) (vi) (colloq.): dress (oneself) up, make (oneself) elegant >*I see she's gussying up for the big party.*

— **gussy up**[2] (vt) (colloq.): decorate, adorn, make pretty >*I see she's gussied up your place some.*

GUT

** **gut**[1] (colloq.): large belly, potbelly >*Look at the gut on that guy! They say he drinks two six-packs of beer a day.*

* **gut**[2] (colloq.): instinct, intuition (also adj.) >*His gut told him something just wasn't right.* >*My gut reaction was to get the hell out of there.*

— **(about) bust/split a gut** (see **BUST**)

GUTLESS

— **gutless** (colloq.): cowardly, fearful >*The gutless bastard dropped his gun and ran.*

GUTS

** **guts** (colloq.): courage, fortitude, nerve >*It took guts to testify against that mafioso.*

— **hate [s/one's] guts** (see **HATE**)

— **spill [one's] guts** (see **SPILL**)

GUTSY

* **gutsy** (gut´sē) (colloq.): courageous, plucky >*Some gutsy woman walked right up to the jerk and punched him out.*

GUTTER

— **[one's] mind in the gutter** (see **MIND**)

GUY

** **guy** (gī) (colloq.): man, boy (also voc.) >*A guy I know has a car like that.* >*Say, guy, where'd you get that application form?*

— **this guy** (colloq.): this thing or device >*With this guy you can use your drill as a screwdriver.*

GUYS

** **the guys** (... gīz) (colloq.): group of men (esp. friends) >*I'm going camping with the guys.*

— **you guys** (see **YOU**)

GYM

** **gym** (jim) (= "gymnasium") (colloq.): physical education class >*What did you do in gym today?*

GYP

* **gyp**[1] (jip) (colloq.): swindle, unfair transaction (where what one buys is not worth the money spent) >*Nine bucks for two hot dogs, onion rings, and a coke? What a gyp!*

* **gyp**[2] (vt) (colloq.): swindle, cheat (in a transaction) >*Are you trying to gyp me? The change you gave me is two dollars short.*

GYP JOINT

— **gyp joint** (jip ...) (colloq.): establishment that overcharges or provides inferior goods or services >*Lousy food and high prices—what a gyp joint!*

H

HACK

* **can hack** (vt) (sl.): can tolerate, can withstand, can cope with (freq. used in the neg.) >*He just couldn't hack all the crap at work.* >*I don't like this job, but I guess I can hack it another couple of weeks.*

HACKER

* **(computer) hacker** (sl.): computer expert, computer fanatic >*Some hacker broke into the system and screwed up half our files.*

HAD

* **be had** (colloq.): be swindled or tricked, be defeated >*We were had by a con man.* >*Anna put Rod in his place but good! He's really been had.*

— **have had it** (see HAVE)

— **have had it (with)** (see HAVE)

HAIR

— **curl [s/one's] hair** (see CURL)

— **hair of the dog** (colloq.): drink of liquor (esp. one to cure a hangover) >*How about a little hair of the dog to get rid of your headache?*

— **[neg.] hide nor hair of** (see HIDE)

* **in/out of [s/one's] hair** (colloq.): bothering/not bothering [s/one], in/out of [s/one's] way >*I don't want those kids in my hair while I'm trying to work.* >*Keep the newspaper people out of our hair, will you?*

— **let [one's] hair down** (see LET)

— **will put hair on [s/one's] chest** (colloq.): is very strong, is appropriate for a manly person (said of liquor or spicy food) >*Have a shot of this tequila—it'll put hair on your chest.*

HAIRY

* **hairy** (sl.): very difficult, frightening, dangerous >*That boat ride over the rapids was hairy.* >*This is gonna be a hairy negotiatin' session.*

HALF

— **... and a half** (sl.): very ..., extraordinarily ... >*He had to be stupid and a half not to see that comin'.*

— **have half a mind to** (colloq.): be tempted to, seriously consider >*I have half a mind to take next week off, but I doubt my boss would OK it.*

* **not half bad** (colloq.): fairly good, satisfactory (also adv.) >*Hey, this casserole's not half bad.* >*He don't play half bad.*

HALF-ASSED

** **half-assed** (haf´ast´) (vulg.): inadequate, incompetent, poorly planned, disorganized >*He did a half-assed job, then expected to be paid right away.*

HALF-BAKED

— **half-baked** (colloq.): poorly thought out, ill-conceived >*You don't really expect his half-baked scheme to work, do you?*

HALF-COCKED

* **(go off) half-cocked** (colloq.): (act) without sufficient preparation, (proceed) without proper knowledge or planning >*Don't you go off half-cocked, or you'll ruin everything.* >*Him and his half-cocked ideas about making a fortune are too much!*

HALF-DOZEN

— **it's six of one, (and) half-(a-)dozen of the other** (see SIX)

HALF PINT

— **half pint** (sl., pej.): very short or small person (also adj.) >*Does that half pint really wanna play basketball with us?* >*Looks like his half pint buddy can't reach it.*

HALFSIES

— **go halfsies (on)** (... haf´sēz/hav´zēz ...) (colloq.): divide (s/thing) equally >*Mom said we've got to go halfsies on the rest of the ice cream.*

HAM

* **ham**[1] (colloq.): performer who exaggerates in his/her performance (esp. an actor) >*Why did they cast that ham in the leading role?*

— **ham**[2] (colloq.): amateur radio operator >*He contacted another ham in Brazil, and then they put a call through to Salvador.*

* **ham it up** (colloq.): overact, behave in an exaggerated way (esp. for attention) >*Their two-year-old really likes to ham it up when people are watching.*

HAMMER

* **hammer away at** (colloq.): make persistent and repeated efforts or attempts at >*I hammered away at him till he agreed to let me do it.* >*Dale's been hammering away at that report he's got to turn in Friday.*

HAMMY

— **hammy** (ham´ē) (colloq.): displaying overacting, exaggerated (in performance) >*Couldn't they find someone better than that hammy actor?*

HAND

* **hand** (vt) (colloq.): tell (nonsense or a lie) (to s/one) >*Don't hand me that crap about you hearing voices.* >*He handed her some story about having a big yacht.*

— **hand over fist** (colloq.): (make money) fast and in large amounts >*Robbie and his brother are making money hand over fist leasing luxury cars in Beverly Hills.*

— **have [s/one] eating out of [one's] hand** (see EATING)

* **have to hand it to** (colloq.): recognize (s/one's) talent or achievement, give credit to (esp. begrudgingly) >*I have to hand it to you—you handled the situation a lot better than I thought you would.*

— **lay a hand/finger on** (see LAY)

— **lift a hand/finger** (see LIFT)

— **tip [one's] hand** (see TIP)

* **with one hand tied behind [one]/ [one's] back** (colloq.): (prevail) with ease, with effortless confidence >*She could beat you at tennis with one hand tied behind her.* >*Blair could have won with one hand tied behind his back.*

HANDFUL

* **handful** (colloq.): person(s) or thing(s) not easily handled >*Any two-year-old's a handful.* >*These final reports are going to be a handful.*

HAND JOB

— **hand job** (vulg.): act of masturbation (esp. done by one person to another) >*He said she gave him a hand job.*

HANDLE

— **handle** (colloq.): nickname, code name (esp. among C.B. radio users) >*His C.B. handle is Big Red.*

— **fly off the handle** (see FLY)

* **get/have a handle on** (colloq.): achieve/ have a basic understanding or competency regarding >*I think Brad finally has a handle on his geometry theorems.* >*I got to get a handle on how this software program works.*

HANDS

* **get [one's] hands on** (colloq.): seize, capture (esp. to punish) >*Wait till I get my hands on that bum!*

* **hands down** (colloq.): effortlessly, very easily >*They won the championship hands down.*

* **lay/get [one's] hands on** (colloq.): obtain >*You know where I can lay my hands on a water pump for a '57 Chevy?* >*I need to get my hands on a good set of metric wrenches.*

— **sit on [one's] hands** (see SIT)

HANDY

— **come in handy** (see COME)

HANG

— **give a hang** (colloq.): be concerned, care, take interest (freq. used in the neg.)

HANGING

>*Old Buddy don't seem to give a hang what others think of him.*

* **hang a left/right** (sl.): turn left/right (in a vehicle) >*Do I hang a right here or at the next corner?*

** **hang around** (vi) (colloq.): linger, loiter, remain (in a place) solely to pass time >*Tell your friends they can't hang around while you're working.*

** **hang around with** (colloq.): spend a great deal of time with, socialize much with >*She's worried because she thinks her son's hanging around with the wrong people.*

** **hang in there** (sl.): remain steadfast, not give up, persevere >*I know ya feel like quittin', but hang in there 'cause it'll get better.*

* **hang it up** (colloq.): quit, give up, resign >*After thirty-five years on the job, he decided to hang it up.*

— **hang/stay loose** (see **LOOSE**)

** **hang on** (vi) (colloq.): wait, stop, not become impatient (freq. used as a command) >*Hang on till we get there. >Now, hang on! Hear me out.*

— **hold/hang on to your hat!** (see **HOLD**)

— **hang one on** (sl.): get drunk >*Morrison heads to the tavern every Friday afternoon to hang one on.*

** **hang out**[1] (vi) (colloq.): spend a great deal of time (in a place) (esp. to socialize) >*A lot of the girls hang out at the mall in the summer.*

** **hang out**[2] (vi) (colloq.): do nothing special, spend time idly >*Me and my friends usually just hang out on Saturdays.*

— **hang out/up [one's] shingle** (colloq.): establish [one's] (doctor's or lawyer's) office >*Sid hung out his shingle as soon as he passed the bar exam.*

— **hang/string [s/one] out to dry** (sl.): severely punish or harm [s/one], make [s/one] suffer grave consequences >*You mess with the boss and you'll be hung out to dry. >If they catch the judge taking bribes, they'll string him out to dry.*

** **hang out with** (colloq.): spend a great deal of time with, socialize much with >*They're a couple of guys I hang out with.*

— **hang together** (vi) (colloq.): be coherent or cohesive, form a logical whole >*The novel wasn't half bad, though the plot didn't really hang together.*

* **hang tough** (sl.): persevere (with strength of will), remain resolved, withstand (difficulties) >*I know you're under a lot of pressure, but ya gotta hang tough, buddy. >We're going to hang tough on the salary demand—no compromises!*

* **hang up** (vt) (colloq.): delay, be an impediment to >*Sorry I'm late—I got hung up in traffic. >The teamsters' strike is going to hang this project up for weeks.*

— **hang with** (sl.): spend a great deal of time with, socialize much with >*I don't like the guys Wanda hangs with.*

* **have/get the hang of** (colloq.): have/get the knack or talent to use or do, have acquired/acquire the ability to use or do >*I couldn't run this tractor at first, but now I think I have the hang of it. >You'll feel more comfortable when you get the hang of the job.*

* **let it all hang out** (sl.): become completely uninhibited, be completely open >*Don't be so up-tight at parties, man—ya gotta let it all hang out. >My shrink told me to let it all hang out when I talk about what's botherin' me.*

HANGING

— **how (are) they hanging?** (sl., freq. vulg.): how are you doing? how are things going? >*Hey, buddy, whatcha say? How they hangin'?*

HANG-OUT

* **hang-out** (colloq.): place where (s/one) spends a great deal of time (esp. to socialize) >*You can probably find Jerry at the basketball court—that's his hang-out.*

HANG-UP

** **hang-up¹** (colloq.): psychological block or complex, strong inhibition >*If you don't like having a woman for a boss, it's your hang-up.* >*She's got some hang-up about going to the bathroom anywhere but in her own house.*

* **hang-up²** (colloq.): snag, impediment to progress >*The hang-up on getting the building permit is a soil report they need.*

HANKIE

— **hankie** (see "HANKY")

HANKY

— **hanky** (hang´kē) (colloq.): handkerchief >*Take a hanky to that movie—it's a real tearjerker.*

HANKY-PANKY

* **hanky-panky** (hang´kē pang´kē) (colloq.): illicit sexual activity, unethical behavior, deceit >*I think there's some hanky-panky going on between Morgan and his secretary.* >*They suspect some hanky-panky between the councilman and the land developers.*

HAPPENING

— **what's happening?** (see WHAT'S)

HAPPY

— **happy/unhappy camper** (see CAMPER)

HAPPY HOUR

** **happy hour** (colloq.): period of time when drinks are served at a reduced price >*I'll meet you at the Oxbow Lounge for their happy hour on Friday.*

HARD

— **between a rock and a hard place** (see BETWEEN)

— **give [s/one] a hard time** (see HARD TIME)

— **hard/tough nut to crack** (see NUT)

* **hard up (for)** (colloq.): in great need (of), anxious for >*He lost his job six months ago and is real hard up for work.* >*Carolyn must really be hard up if she's going out with that loser.*

HARD-ASS

— **hard-ass** (vulg.): strict enforcer of rules, unlenient disciplinarian, unmerciful taskmaster (also adj.) >*Are you such a hard-ass that ya'd fire him for bein' late just once?* >*My hard-ass supervisor works our tails off.*

HARDBALL

— **hardball** (colloq.): highly competitive, tough, ruthless >*I don't think Del's ready for hardball investment finance.*

* **play hardball** (colloq.): compete aggressively and ruthlessly >*He's too innocent to be a legislator—they play hardball in state politics.*

HARD-HAT

— **hard-hat** (colloq.): working-class conservative person >*The hard-hats are going to complain about it being another government giveaway.*

HARD KNOCKS

— **hard knocks** (colloq.): hardships, adversity, misfortune >*Linda's turned out OK despite all the hard knocks she's had.*

HARD-NOSED

— **hard-nosed** (colloq.): tough, strict, willful >*Don't think you can talk that hard-nosed character into anything.*

HARD-ON

** **hard-on** (vulg.): erection of the penis >*He said he got a hard-on watchin' the porno video.*

HARD SELL

* **hard sell** (colloq.): aggressive promotion, high-pressure selling (cf. "SOFT SELL") >*I hope that salesman*

doesn't give me the old hard sell, because I'm just looking today.

HARD STUFF

* **hard stuff**[1] (sl.): hard liquor >*I like wine sometimes, but I stay away from the hard stuff.*

* **hard stuff**[2] (sl.): very addictive drug(s) >*He started out smokin' grass, but now he's on the hard stuff.*

HARD TIME

— **hard time** (sl.): time actually served in prison >*Smith was sentenced to ten to fifteen, but he only did six years hard time before he got paroled.*

** **give [s/one] a hard time** (colloq.): annoy or harass [s/one], tease [s/one] relentlessly >*If you give Marie a hard time, she just might file a grievance.* >*The guys were giving me a hard time about my pink shirt.*

HARD-TO-GET

* **play hard-to-get** (colloq.): pretend not to be interested, act coy >*Liz likes the guy, but her mother told her to play hard-to-get.*

HARDWARE

— **hardware** (sl.): firearm(s) (carried by s/one) >*See the bulge under his coat? The guy's packin' hardware.*

HARDY-HAR-HAR

— **hardy-har-har!** (här´dē här´här´) (colloq., sarc.): (interj. imitating laughter to express contempt for another's attempt at humor) >*Hardy-har-har! Putting a "kick me" sign on my back is just so funny!*

HAS-BEEN

* **has-been** (colloq.): person who is no longer popular or successful >*No one buys his records anymore—he's a has-been.*

HASH

— **hash** (hash) (sl.): hashish >*They caught him with almost a kilo of hash.*

— **hash out** (vt) (colloq.): come to an agreement regarding (through discussion or argument) >*We still have a few details to hash out before the deal's final.*

— **hash over** (vt) (colloq.): thoroughly review or discuss >*They hashed it over again but couldn't reach an agreement.*

HASSLE

** **hassle**[1] (has´əl) (colloq.): disagreement, dispute, fight >*I got into a big hassle with the manager when I tried to return the broken stereo.*

** **hassle**[2] (colloq.): trouble, inconvenience, bother >*Driving in heavy traffic is always a hassle.* >*What a hassle it is to fill out all these forms!*

** **hassle**[3] (vt) (colloq.): bother, inconvenience, cause trouble for, engage in a dispute with >*My dad's hassling me because I got some bad grades.*

* **hassle**[4] (vi) (colloq.): argue, quarrel, fight >*I can't believe you two are hassling over a couple of dollars!*

— **hassle with** (colloq.): trouble or bother (oneself) with, be inconvenienced by, spend time and effort dealing with >*We've been hassling with this copier, which breaks down just about every day.* >*I just can't hassle with your stupid brother-in-law today.*

HAT

— **at the drop of a hat** (see DROP)

— **be old hat** (see OLD HAT)

* **[for one's] hat [to] be off to [s/one]** (colloq.): [for one to] recognize [s/one's] achievement, [for one to] compliment [s/one] >*My hat's off to my opponent for running a clean campaign.*

— **hold/hang on to your hat!** (see HOLD)

— **I'll eat my hat** (see EAT)

— **keep [s/thing] under [one's] hat** (see KEEP)

— **pass the hat** (see PASS)

— **talk through [one's] hat** (see TALK)

HATCH
— **down the hatch!** (see DOWN)

HATCHET MAN
— **hatchet man** (colloq.): person hired to do unpleasant or unscrupulous things to others >*They got a hatchet man to evict the tenants.*

HATE
** **hate** (vt) (colloq.): be sorry to have to (do s/thing) >*I hate to tell you this, but you flunked the test.* >*He hated firing her, but she just wasn't working out.*

* **hate [s/one's] guts** (sl.): hate [s/one] intensely >*Don't put 'em together 'cause they hate each other's guts.*

HAUL
— **haul** (colloq.): money or valuables collected or taken, proceeds from an endeavor >*Their haul from the robbery was ten grand in cash and another twenty in jewels.* >*What was your haul from the garage sale?*

— **haul ass** (vulg.): depart quickly, move very fast >*When he pulled out a gun, I hauled ass outta there.* >*This truck can really haul ass!*

— **haul (in)** (vt) (colloq.): arrest and transport (for processing in the legal system) >*He got hauled in for dealing dope.* >*They hauled Jim before the judge, who gave him ninety days in the county jail.*

— **haul off and** (sl.): draw back an arm and (strike s/one) >*When the sailor told me to get screwed I hauled off and slugged him.*

— **long haul** (see LONG)
— **over the long haul** (see LONG)

HAVE
— **(already) have two strikes against [one]** (see TWO)

* **have [one] [s/thing]** (colloq.): enjoy [s/thing] (consumed or experienced) >*I'm going to have me a big, juicy steak.* >*We had us a good time at your party.*

— **have (a/the/[s/one's]/[one's]) ...** (see entry under ... noun)

— **have a good thing going** (see GOOD)

— **[neg.] have all [one's] marbles** (see MARBLES)

— **have at it** (colloq.): begin (doing s/thing) vigorously or enthusiastically >*If he wants to race motorcycles so bad, let him have at it.*

— **have been there** (see THERE)

— **have [s/one] by the balls/nuts** (see BALLS)

— **have [s/one] by the short hairs** (see SHORT HAIRS)

— **have [s/thing] down cold** (see COLD)

— **have [s/thing] down pat** (see PAT)

— **have [s/one] eating out of [one's] hand** (see EATING)

— **have [s/one] going** (see GOING)

— **have [s/thing] going for [one]** (see GOING)

** **have had it**[1] (colloq.): be worn out, no longer function or be useful >*I need to get a new watch—this one's had it.*

* **have had it**[2] (colloq.): be doomed, be assured of ruin or defeat, be assured of punishment >*By the end of the third quarter, our team knew we'd had it.* >*You've had it if the manager finds out about this.*

* **have had it (with)** (colloq.): be disgusted or bored (with), can no longer tolerate (s/one, s/thing) >*No more summer reruns, please! I've had it.* >*I've had it with you! Now clear out!*

* **have it** (colloq.): have the required ability or talent >*Some people have it to make it in show business, and some don't.* >*Sorry, but you just ain't got it to drive a big truck like this.*

— **have it all over** (colloq.): be superior to, be more talented or desirable than >*Stick with Jane—she's got it all over*

Trixie. >*My car has it all over that piece of junk.*

— **have it coming** (see COMING)

— **have it in for** (see IN)

— **have it made** (see MADE)

— **have it made in the shade** (see MADE)

* **have it out (with)** (colloq.): fight or quarrel (with) (to finally resolve a conflict) >*I'm going to have it out with that jerk about his snide remarks.* >*It sounded like Marsha and her boyfriend really had it out last night.*

— **get/have it together** (see TOGETHER)

— **have [s/thing] knocked** (see KNOCKED)

— **have [s/thing] licked** (see LICKED)

— **have [s/one's] name on it/them** (see NAME)

* **have [s/thing] on** (colloq.): know or possess evidence of [s/thing] detrimental to or incriminating for >*He's got something on Sophie he can use against her at the meeting.* >*Do you have anything on him that'll hold up in court?*

— **have ... on the ball** (see BALL)

— **have [s/thing] on the brain** (see BRAIN)

— **have one too many** (see ONE)

— **have ... plus** (see PLUS)

— **have/get something going** (see GOING)

— **have to fly** (see FLY)

— **have to hand it to** (see HAND)

— **have two left feet** (see LEFT)

— **have [s/thing] wired** (see WIRED)

— **let [s/one] have it** (see LET)

— **let [s/one] have it with both barrels** (see LET)

** **not have all day** (colloq., sarc.): cannot keep waiting, be becoming impatient >*Hurry up with that lunch order, will you? I don't have all day.*

— **not have both oars in the water** (see OARS)

— **not have the foggiest** (see FOGGIEST)

HAY

— **ain't hay** (ānt ...) (colloq.): is a substantial amount of money >*Eight hundred dollars for that job ain't hay.* >*He's making eighty grand a year, and that ain't hay.*

— **hit the hay** (see HIT)

— **in the hay** (colloq.): in bed >*He's already in the hay? It's only eight-thirty.*

— **roll in the hay** (see ROLL)

HAYSEED

— **hayseed** (sl., pej.): unsophisticated person from a rural area, yokel >*Everyone knew he was a hayseed by his clothes and the way he talked.*

HAYWIRE

* **(go) haywire** (colloq.): (begin) working wrong, (go) out of control, (go) out of order >*Everything went haywire when lightning hit the power lines.* >*There's something haywire with this machine.* >*The poor guy's been kind of haywire since his son died.*

HEAD

— **head**[1] (colloq.): bathroom, toilet >*You can't talk to him. He's in the head.* >*You got a head I can use?*

— **head**[2] (sl.): headache (esp. due to a hangover) >*Boy, did I ever have a head the morning after the party!*

— **(about) bite/snap [s/one's] head off** (see BITE)

— **beat [one's] head against the wall** (see BEAT)

— **can [do s/thing] standing on [one's] head** (see STANDING)

* **cannot make head(s) or tail(s) (out) of** (colloq.): not understand at all, be

unable to find meaning in >*We can't make heads or tails out of this so-called report.*

— **get/have [one's] head together** (colloq.): get/have control over [oneself], find/have emotional stability, resolve/have resolved [one's] personal problems >*Margie went on a long trip after her divorce to try and get her head together.*

— **get it into [one's] head (that)** (see GET)

— **get [s/thing] through [one's] (thick) head** (see GET)

* **give head** (vulg.): perform fellatio >*He says she gives good head.*

— **go over [s/one's] head** (see OVER)

— **have [one's] head (screwed) on straight** (colloq.): be a rational person, be mentally healthy >*Anyone with his head screwed on straight wouldn't have done something so dumb.* >*Don't worry about Scott getting in trouble—he has his head on straight.*

— **have rocks in [one's] head** (see ROCKS)

— **head for the hills** (colloq.): flee, escape >*Ollie headed for the hills when they started asking for volunteers.*

* **... [one's] head off** (colloq.): ... with maximum effort, ... to the utmost (esp. talking or yelling) >*I had to talk my head off to convince him.* >*Andy was just standing there screaming his head off.*

* **head out** (vi) (colloq.): start off (on a trip), depart >*We're going to be heading out about six in the morning.*

— **[for] [s/one's] head/heads [to] roll** (colloq.): [for] [s/one]/people to be punished severely >*Your head's going to roll if they find out you've been taking bribes.* >*Heads rolled after the auditors investigated.*

— **off the top of [one's] head** (see TOP)

* **ought/need to have [one's] head examined** (colloq.): have very irrational behavior, appear to be crazy >*You ought to have your head examined for loaning money to that deadbeat.*

— **out of [one's] head** (colloq.): crazy, very irrational >*You were out of your head to sign the contract without having a lawyer look at it first.*

* **(so fast that) it will make [s/one's] head spin** (colloq.): (so fast that) it will surprise or confuse [s/one], very fast >*You try it and I'll sue you so fast it'll make your head spin.*

— **where [s/one's] head is at** (see WHERE)

HEADACHE

* **headache** (colloq.): source of problems or trouble, annoyance >*This damn car's been nothing but a headache ever since I bought it.*

HEADHUNTER

— **headhunter** (colloq.): professional personnel recruiter or job finder >*She paid a headhunter $1500 to line her up that job.*

HEADS

— **butt heads (with)** (see BUTT)

HEAD SHRINKER

— **head shrinker** (sl.): psychiatrist or psychoanalyst >*Molly's been seein' this head shrinker to help her with her problems.*

HEADS-UP

— **heads-up** (colloq.): sharp, attentive, alert >*That was a real heads-up move you made to get us some of that grant money.* >*We got to play heads-up ball if we want to win this one.*

HEAD TRIP

— **head trip** (sl.): egotistic activity or behavior, action done for vanity or selfish reasons >*I think her enterin' that beauty contest is nothin' but a head trip.*

HEALTH

* **not ... for [one's] health** (colloq., sarc.): not ... because [one] likes it, be obligated to ... >*I didn't take this crappy job for my health, you know—I need the money.*

HEAP

— **heap** (sl.): automobile (esp. one that is old or in poor condition) >*When are you gonna get rid of that heap and buy a new car?*

— **a heap (of ...)** (colloq.): much (...), many (...) >*Poor devil's got a heap of troubles.* >*How many old tires you want? I got a heap you can have.*

— **top of the heap** (see TOP)

HEAPS

— **heaps (of ...)** (colloq.): much (...), many (...) >*Tyler ain't hurting for dough—he made heaps in the stock market.* >*There were heaps of problems with his plan.*

HEAR

* **hear** (vt) (colloq.): completely understand what (s/one) is saying >*I hear you—you've made a good point.*

* **(it's so quiet) you can hear a pin drop** (colloq.): there's complete silence >*When her ex-husband walked in, you could hear a pin drop.*

— **see/hear things** (see THINGS)

HEART

— **cry [one's] heart out** (see CRY)

— **eat [one's] heart out** (see EAT)

— **have a heart!** (colloq.): be compassionate! show mercy! >*Aw, come on—have a heart and give me another chance!*

— **(I) cross my heart (and hope to die)!** (see CROSS)

— **my heart bleeds for ...!** (colloq., sarc.): I don't sympathize at all with ...! >*Those rich guys are complaining about the tax increase? My heart bleeds for them!*

HEART-ON

— **heart-on** (see "HARD-ON")

HEAT

* **heat¹** (colloq.): pressure, stress, demands >*They're putting the heat on us at work because we have a deadline coming up.* >*He just can't take the heat in that job.*

* **heat²** (colloq.): criticism, recriminations, expression of opposition >*He's taken a lot of heat for his tough policies.*

— **heat³** (sl.): firearm(s) (carried by s/one) >*Watch out for that dude—he's packin' heat.*

— **the heat** (sl.): the police >*Ned's runnin' with the heat on his trail.*

HEAVE

— **heave** (hēv) (vi, vt) (colloq.): vomit >*She got carsick and heaved out the window.* >*He just heaved his dinner.*

HEAVE-HO

— **the heave-ho** (... hēv´hō´) (colloq.): act of forcible ejection or dismissal >*If the bartender doesn't like the way you act, he'll give you the heave-ho.*

HEAVY

* **heavy¹** (colloq.): villain, culpable person >*Don't try to make me the heavy just because I'm watching out for my own interests.*

— **heavy²** (sl.): influential or important person >*I take it the guy with the fancy office is one of the heavies around here.*

— **heavy³** (sl.): impressive, important, serious >*That's gonna be one heavy scene when the two big bosses meet to work out the problem.* >*I'd say you and Sal got somethin' heavy going on between ya.*

— **heavy into** (colloq.): seriously involved in >*His sister used to be so straight, but now she's heavy into drugs.* >*He's really gotten heavy into collecting baseball cards.*

— **hot and heavy** (see HOT)

HEAVY-DUTY

* **heavy-duty** (sl.): impressive, important, serious >*Gene's all dressed up 'cause he's got a heavy-duty date tonight.* >*That sounded like a pretty heavy-duty fight you two had.*

HEAVY HITTER

— **heavy hitter** (sl.): very influential or effective person, top person (in his/her field) >*That university's been recruitin' lots of heavy hitters to boost its reputation as a research institution.*

HEAVY METAL

** **heavy metal** (colloq.): very loud and aggressive or bizarre rock music >*It's not going to work out—I like Bach and she's into heavy metal.*

HEAVYWEIGHT

— **heavyweight** (colloq.): important, influential, powerful (also noun) >*The president met with some heavyweight economists for advice.* >*Only the heavyweights in the industry deal on this level.*

HECK

* **a heck of a**[1] (... hek ...) (colloq.): an extraordinarily, a very >*Your friend's a heck of a nice guy.*

* **a heck of a**[2] (colloq.): an extraordinary, an impressive, a surprising >*He's a heck of a golfer.* >*That's a heck of a thing to say to a friend.*

— **... (all) to heck** (colloq.): ... to a state of ruin, ... to a terrible degree >*The truck smashed her bike all to heck.*

— **(as) ... as heck** (colloq.): extraordinarily ..., very >*Everyone's as mad as heck about the layoffs.*

— **beat the heck out of**[1] (sl.): be much better than, be greatly preferable to >*Fishin' beats the heck outta workin' any day.*

— **beat the heck out of**[2] (sl.): baffle or confound very much, greatly perplex >*Why he quit beats the heck outta me.*

— **beat/kick the heck out of** (sl.): beat severely, defeat decisively >*They cornered him and beat the heck outta him.* >*She kicked the heck outta him in the election.*

— **heck!** (colloq.): (interj. to express anger, surprise, or irritation) >*Heck! My screwdriver broke.*

* **(just) for the heck of it** (colloq.): for amusement, out of curiosity, for no special reason or purpose >*We decided to dam up the creek for the heck of it.*

— **like heck**[1] (colloq.): bad (also adv.) >*I feel like heck after eating all that pizza.* >*This car runs like heck—it needs a tune-up.*

— **like heck**[2] (colloq.): wholeheartedly, to the utmost degree >*I've been trying like heck to get ahold of him, but no luck.*

— **like heck ...!** (colloq.): certainly not ...! not really ...! in no way ...! >*He thinks they won't find out? Like heck they won't!*

* **one heck of a**[1] (colloq.): an extraordinary, an impressive, a surprising >*That was one heck of a speech she gave.*

* **one heck of a**[2] (colloq.): an extraordinarily, a very >*We had one heck of a rough time convincing him not to leave.*

— **raise heck** (colloq.): celebrate wildly or noisily, be loud and rowdy >*I can't have those kids raising heck in my restaurant.*

— **raise heck (with)** (colloq.): severely reprimand (s/one), complain strenuously (to) >*This old guy was raising heck at the grocery store because they wouldn't take his expired coupons.*

— **...er than heck** (colloq.): extraordinarily ..., very ... >*They're happier than heck together.* >*I'm* madder than heck at Pete for what he did.

— **the heck** (colloq.): (intens. to express impatience, anger, or wonder, used in intransitive verb phrases between the verb and its prepositional particle) >*It's late—I'd better take the heck off.* >*It's time you grew the heck up!*

— **the heck ...!** (colloq.): certainly not ...! not really ...! in no way ...! >*You say he's going to borrow my car? The heck he is!*

— **the heck of it** (colloq.): the worst or most problematic part (of s/thing) >*The heck of it is that repairing the old stereo cost me more than buying a brand-new one would have.*

— **... the heck out of [s/one, s/thing]** (colloq.): ... [s/one, s/thing] to the utmost degree, ... [s/one, s/thing] extraordinarily >*It bent the heck out of the bumper when he hit it.*

* **to/the heck with ...!** (colloq.): I don't care about ...! I want nothing to do with ...! I find ... contemptible! >*If McClean's going to act like an ass, to heck with him!* >*The heck with it! It's not that important.*

— **what the heck!** (see **WHAT**)

* **what/who/[etc.] (in) the heck ...?** (colloq.): (intens. to express impatience, anger, or surprise) >*Where in the heck are you going at this time of night?* >*What the heck did he just call us?*

HECKUVA
— **a heckuva** (see "**a HECK of a**")

— **one heckuva** (see "**one HECK of a**")

HEEL
— **heel** (colloq.): contemptible person, person who has done s/thing shameful >*Everyone thought Don was a heel for embarrassing his wife in public.*

HEELS
— **cool [one's] heels** (see **COOL**)

— **kick up [one's] heels** (see **KICK**)

HEINIE
— **heinie** (hī´nē) (sl.): buttocks >*He slipped on the ice and fell right on his heinie.*

HEINZ
— **Heinz 57 (variety)** (hīnz ...) (sl.): mixed-breed dog, mongrel >*Misty's a purebred golden retriever, but Sparky's a Heinz 57.*

HEIST
— **heist**[1] (hīst) (sl.): robbery, holdup >*They caught the guy that pulled that bank heist.*

— **heist**[2] (vt) (sl.): rob, steal, hold up >*Someone heisted her diamond necklace, but it's insured.* >*They heisted a convenience store using a fake gun.*

HELL
** **a hell of a**[1] (colloq., freq. vulg.): an extraordinary, an impressive, a surprising >*I've got a hell of a hangover this morning.* >*That's a hell of a car you bought.*

** **a hell of a**[2] (colloq., freq. vulg.): an extraordinarily, a very >*He's a hell of a smooth talker.*

* **[for] all hell [to] break loose** (colloq.): [for] chaos [to] begin, [for] confusion or violence [to] take over >*All hell broke loose when the lion got out of its cage.* >*If they don't control that crowd, all hell's going to break loose.*

* **... (all) to hell** (colloq., freq. vulg.): ... to a state of ruin, ... to a terrible degree >*This board ain't worth a damn—it's warped all to hell.*

** **(as) ... as hell** (colloq., freq. vulg.): extraordinarily ..., very ... >*It's cold as hell out today.*

* **beat the hell out of**[1] (sl., freq. vulg.): be much better than, be greatly preferable to >*His work beats the hell outta the other guy's.*

* **beat the hell out of**[2] (sl., freq. vulg.): baffle or confound very much, greatly

perplex >*It beats the hell outta us why she left.*

* **beat/kick the hell out of** (sl., freq. vulg.): beat severely, defeat decisively >*Keep mouthin' off and you'll get the hell kicked outta ya.* >*We beat the hell out of 'em in overtime.*

* **catch/get hell** (sl.): suffer a severe scolding or reprimand, be severely punished >*He caught hell from his girlfriend for starin' at that cute blond.* >*They're gonna get hell for tellin' his secret.*

— **come hell or high water** (see **COME**)

* **give 'em hell!** (... əm ...) (sl.): perform well! best wishes for success in your endeavor! >*Give 'em hell on opening night!* >*When ya get to college, give 'em hell!*

* **give [s/one] hell** (colloq.): severely scold or reprimand [s/one] >*She gave her daughter hell for coming home so late.*

* **go to hell** (colloq., freq. vulg.): become ruined >*The whole project went to hell after the labor dispute.*

** **go to hell!** (vulg.): (interj. to express great anger or contempt to s/one) >*If ya won't do it my way, then go to hell!*

— **hell!** (colloq., freq. vulg.): (interj. to express anger, surprise, or irritation) >*Hell! The car's overheating!*

— **hell on** (sl.): rough on, painful to, harmful to >*The sergeant's hell on rookie cops.* >*This drought's been hell on the corn crop.*

— **hell on wheels** (sl.): very quick and aggressive, dynamically effective >*That little kid is hell on wheels.* >*Watch this short-order cook—he's hell on wheels in the kitchen.*

— **hell to pay** (colloq.): severe punishment to be suffered, serious consequences to pay >*There'll be hell to pay if you get caught running this plant without a permit.*

** **(just) for the hell of it** (colloq., freq. vulg.): for amusement, out of curiosity, for no special reason or purpose >*Let's go to the other side of the lake just for the hell of it.*

— **like a bat out of hell** (see **BAT**)

** **like hell**[1] (colloq., freq. vulg.): bad (also adv.) >*You look like hell this morning— are you hung over?* >*Who hired her? She sings like hell.*

* **like hell**[2] (colloq., freq. vulg.): wholeheartedly, to the utmost degree >*They've been partyin' like hell since yesterday afternoon.*

** **like hell ...!** (colloq., freq. vulg.): certainly not ...! not really ...! in no way ...! >*You expect me to help? Like hell I will!* >*Ya say that crummy team's gonna win? Like hell!*

** **one hell of a**[1] (colloq., freq. vulg.): an extraordinary, an impressive, a surprising >*We had one hell of a time partyin' at Monty's last night.*

** **one hell of a**[2] (colloq., freq. vulg.): an extraordinarily, a very >*He's one hell of a good-lookin' man!*

* **raise hell** (colloq.): celebrate wildly or noisily, be loud and rowdy >*On Saturday nights they have a few beers and go raise hell in town.*

* **raise hell (with)** (colloq.): severely reprimand (s/one), complain strenuously (to) >*Calvin's old man raised hell with him when he wrecked the car.* >*The customers are gonna raise hell about this extra charge.*

* **...er than hell** (colloq., freq. vulg.): extraordinarily ..., very ... >*That football player's uglier than hell, but don't tell him I said so.*

— **the hell** (colloq., freq. vulg.): (intens. to express impatience, anger, or wonder, used in intransitive verb phrases between the verb and its prepositional particle) >*Shoot! I give the hell up.*

>*Why don't ya find a job instead of hangin' the hell around here?*

* **the hell ...!** (colloq., freq. vulg.): certainly not ...! not really ...! in no way ...! >*What do ya mean you're gonna learn to fly? The hell ya are!*

— **the hell of it** (colloq., freq. vulg.): the worst or most problematic part (of s/thing) >*Haley thought he'd come out with a better job after the company reorganized, but the hell of it is he got demoted.*

* **... the hell out of [s/one, s/thing]** (colloq., freq. vulg.): ... [s/one, s/thing] to the utmost degree, ... [s/one, s/thing] extraordinarily >*Her singin' impressed the hell out of everyone.*

* **to/the hell with ...!** (colloq., freq. vulg.): I don't care about ...! I want nothing to do with ...! I find ... contemptible! >*Aw, the hell with the picnic! It's just too much trouble.* >*Who cares what that slob thinks? I say to hell with him!*

* **until/till hell freezes over** (colloq.): forever, always (in the future) >*I'll love her till hell freezes over.*

— **what the hell!** (see WHAT)

** **what/who/[etc.] (in) the hell ...?** (colloq., freq. vulg.): (intens. to express impatience, anger, or surprise) >*Who the hell does he think he is talking to me that way?* >*Where in the hell are my keys?*

* **when hell freezes over** (colloq.): never (in the future) >*I'll vote for that bum when hell freezes over.*

HELL-RAISER
— **hell-raiser** (colloq.): person who celebrates wildly or noisily, person who behaves in a rowdy way >*The cops had to quiet down a few hell-raisers after Saturday night's game.*

HELL'S BELLS
— **hell's bells!** (colloq., freq. vulg.): (interj. to express anger, surprise, or irritation)

>*Hell's bells! What are you two doing here?*

HELLUVA
— **a helluva** (see "a HELL of a")
— **one helluva** (see "one HELL of a")

HE-MAN
— **he-man** (colloq.): strong and virile man >*She dreamed of marrying a real he-man.*

HEN
— **hen** (colloq., pej.): meddlesome or gossipy woman >*Dan called Priscilla an old hen and told her to stop snooping around.*

HEN PARTY
— **hen party** (colloq., freq. pej.): gathering of women, party for women only >*They went bowling while their wives were at a hen party.*

HERD
— **ride herd on** (see RIDE)

HERE
— **be out of here** (see OUT)
— **fed up (to here) (with)** (see FED)

** **here goes!** (colloq.): let me/us begin! let's see what happens! (esp. when eventual success is unsure) >*You got the rewired lamp plugged in? OK, here goes!*

* **here goes nothing!** (colloq.): let me/us begin! let's see what happens! (esp. when eventual success is doubtful) >*This ski slope looks real steep! Oh, well, here goes nothing!*

— **(the) same here** (see SAME)

* **up to here with** (colloq.) (usually accompanied by a gesture of the fingers against the throat or head): disgusted or bored with, no longer able to tolerate >*I tell you, I'm up to here with his snide remarks!*

HERE'S
— **here's looking at you!** (see LOOKING)

— **here's mud in your eye!** (see MUD)

HEY

— **what the hey!** (see WHAT)

HI

— **hi ya!** (see "HIYA!")

HICK

— **hick** (hik) (colloq., pej.): unsophisticated and gullible person from a rural area, rustic, yokel (also adj.) >*He makes a lot of money showing hicks around the city.* >*His hick cousin doesn't know what an elevator is.*

HICKEY

* **hickey** (hik´ē) (colloq.): reddish mark on the skin caused by suction (esp. from a passionate kiss) >*Myra was really embarrassed when I asked her how she got the hickey on her neck.*

HICK TOWN

— **hick town** (hik …) (colloq.): small and unsophisticated town in a rural area >*He's from some hick town in the Midwest.*

HIDE

— **[neg.] hide nor hair of** (colloq.): not the least sign or trace of (s/one) >*I ain't seen hide nor hair of that kid all day.*

— **risk [one's] hide** (see RISK)

— **save [one's, s/one's] hide** (see SAVE)

— **tan [s/one's] hide** (see TAN)

HIGH

** **high**[1] (sl.): intoxication, euphoria, exhilaration (due to alcohol, drugs, or an experience) >*He's on a cocaine high.* >*Gettin' that award was a real high.*

** **high**[2] (sl.): intoxicated, euphoric (esp. from alcohol or drugs) >*The way he was drivin', I'd say he was high on somethin'.*

— **(as) high as a kite** (sl.): very drunk or intoxicated >*The fella staggered outta the tavern high as a kite.*

— **flying high** (see FLYING)

* **high off/on the hog** (colloq.): lavishly, with great luxury or prosperity >*They've been living high on the hog since the old man won the lottery.*

— **stink to high heaven** (see STINK)

HIGHBALL

— **highball** (vi, vt) (sl.): go at full speed (in), move (a vehicle) at full speed >*The truck went highballin' through town.* >*He highballed his tractor-trailer down the turnpike.* >*Let's highball it outta here!*

HIGHBROW

— **highbrow** (colloq.): person who believes him/herself to be of superior culture or taste, intellectual snob (also adj.) >*I can't stand them opera highbrows.* >*He don't care for that highbrow music.*

HIGHER

— **higher than a kite** (sl.): very drunk or intoxicated >*He was higher than a kite 'cause he'd been boozin' and takin' pills!*

HIGHER-UP

— **higher-up** (colloq.): person of higher rank or position, superior >*Mack's got to discuss it with the higher-ups to get their OK.*

HIGHFALUTIN

— **highfalutin** (hī´fə lūt´n) (colloq.): pompous, ostentatious, pretentious >*Her highfalutin friends won't give me the time of day.*

HIGH-FIVE

* **high-five**[1] (sl.): slap on (s/one's) raised and open palm (as a gesture of congratulations or greeting) >*He gave me a high-five after I made the shot.*

— **high-five**[2] (vt) (sl.): slap (s/one's) raised and open palm (as a gesture of congratulations or greeting) >*His teammates high-fived him after he scored.*

HIGH HORSE

— **on [one's] high horse** (colloq.): assuming a haughty or superior attitude >*If you try and criticize David, he gets on his high horse and reminds you that he's got a Ph.D.*

HIGH JINKS

— **high jinks** (… jingks) (colloq.): loud or uninhibited fun, pranks, capers >*The principal is getting tired of those kids' high jinks.*

HIGH-RENT

— **high-rent** (sl.): expensive, elegant, chic >*Phil took Wanda to a high-rent party uptown.*

HIGH ROLLER

* **high roller** (colloq.): big spender, person who lives extravagantly >*That fancy nightclub's where the high rollers go to be seen.*

HIGHTAIL

— **hightail it** (sl.): move fast, flee, escape >*Carl was hightailin' it down the road goin' about seventy. >We hightailed it outta there when the fight broke out.*

HIGH WATER

— **come hell or high water** (see COME)

HIGHWAY ROBBERY

* **highway robbery** (colloq.): charging of excessive prices, exorbitant price >*Forty bucks for this lousy lunch? That's highway robbery!*

HIJINKS

— **hijinks** (see "HIGH JINKS")

HIKE

* **take a hike!** (sl.): go away! don't bother me! >*Who asked you? Take a hike!*

HILL

* **over the hill** (colloq.): in decline, having passed (one's) prime, no longer effective, getting old >*Blake just can't produce like he used to—he's over the hill. >I'd say by the time you're forty in this business you're over the hill.*

HILLBILLY

— **hillbilly** (hil´bil´ē) (colloq., freq. pej.): unsophisticated person from a rural area (esp. a mountainous one) (also adj.) >*She heard that tale from some hillbilly she met in West Virginia. >Do you really like that hillbilly music?*

HILL OF BEANS

— **[neg.] a hill of beans** (colloq.): very little money, an insignificant amount >*That offer doesn't amount to a hill of beans. >What he earns recycling aluminum cans ain't worth a hill of beans.*

HILLS

— **(as) old as the hills** (see OLD)

— **head for the hills** (see HEAD)

HIP

— **hip** (sl.): up-to-date with the latest styles, socially valued, avant-garde >*It ain't hip to take a date bowlin'. >All the hip kids are wearin' these.*

— **be hip** (sl.): be willing or interested (in doing s/thing) >*We were thinkin' of cruisin' the boulevard. Are ya hip?*

— **hip (to)** (sl.): aware or informed (of) >*Are ya hip to what's goin' on? >Ya don't got to explain it to me—I'm hip.*

— **shoot from the hip** (see SHOOT)

HIPPO

** **hippo** (hip´ō) (colloq.): hippopotamus >*We saw a baby hippo in the water at the zoo.*

HIRE

* **hire** (colloq.): person hired >*Jackson's our new hire in sales.*

HIRED GUN

— **hired gun** (colloq.): hired assassin, contract killer >*They got some hired gun to get rid of him.*

HISSELF

— **hisself** (hi self´/hiz self´) (colloq.): himself >*He told me so hisself. >He helped hisself to more pie.*

HISTORY

— **history** (colloq.): past shared emotional experience or relationship (between or among people) >*The way they were acting, I'd say there's some history between them.*

* **be history** (sl.): be finished, be passé, be doomed >*Patricia and me? Na, that's history.* >*You screw up once more and you're history around here.*

HIT

— **hit[1]** (sl.): assassination, contract murder >*He did the hit, ditched the gun, and left town.*

— **hit[2]** (sl.): puff of a marijuana cigarette >*Good grass! Wanna hit?*

** **hit[3]** (vt) (colloq.): occur to, dawn on >*Then it hit me that she was flirting with me.*

* **hit[4]** (vt) (colloq.): arrive at, reach >*We hit the state line before midnight.* >*Let's hit Lester's party and see what's happening there.* >*I bet I can hit a hundred in this car.*

— **hit[5]** (vt) (sl.): rob, hold up >*Two gunmen hit the bank this morning.*

— **hit[6]** (vt) (sl.): assassinate, attack in order to murder (esp. by contract) >*The gangster ordered three members of their family hit.*

— **can't hit the (broad) side of a barn** (colloq.): have very poor aim, be very inaccurate (in shooting or throwing) >*I'm a real bad shot—can't hit the side of a barn at twenty yards.*

— **hit/strike a (raw) nerve (with)** (see **NERVE**)

— **(hit) below the belt** (see **BELOW**)

— **hit bottom** (see **BOTTOM**)

* **hit it** (sl.): begin (s/thing), put (s/thing) into action or motion (esp. suddenly or forcefully) >*All right, maestro, hit it!* >*I put the truck in low gear and hit it.*

* **hit it big** (colloq.): win or earn a great deal, have great success (esp. fortuitously) >*Morgan really hit it big with that gadget he invented.*

* **hit it off** (colloq.): gain a liking (for one another), be compatible, get along well >*Ted's a nice guy—me and him hit it off right away.*

* **hit on[1]** (colloq.): discover (esp. through experimentation) >*One of the accountants hit on a way to process the billings a lot faster.*

— **hit on[2]** (sl.): make sexual advances toward >*How can Mandy stand the singles bars with all the guys hittin' on her all the time?*

— **hit/strike pay dirt** (see **PAY DIRT**)

— **hit the ...** (sl.): drink (an alcoholic beverage) (esp. secretly or uncontrollably) >*He was sober for quite a while, but he's hit the booze again.* >*Who's been hittin' the cherry brandy?*

* **hit the books** (colloq.): study hard >*We partied on Saturday and hit the books on Sunday.*

* **hit the bottle** (sl.): drink heavily >*Look at Earl's nose—I'd say he's been hittin' the bottle again.*

— **hit the bricks** (colloq.): walk the streets, go out in public on foot (esp. when working or searching) >*I'm going to hit the bricks until I come up with a job.*

* **hit the ceiling** (colloq.): become furious, lose (one's) temper >*Dad hit the ceiling when he saw my awful report card.*

— **hit the deck[1]** (sl.): fall facedown on the ground (to avoid danger) >*When I saw the shed explode, I hit the deck.*

— **hit the deck[2]** (sl.): get up out of bed (esp. early, esp. to begin work) >*Hit the deck, boys! We got work to do.*

— **hit the dirt** (sl.): fall facedown on the ground (to avoid danger) >*I hit the dirt when he pulled a gun.*

* **hit the fan** (sl.): (for the neg. consequences to) occur, (for the inevitable scandal to) begin >*We can't keep this quiet for long, and when it hits the fan, people are gonna get fired.*

— **hit the hay** (colloq.): go to bed >*I'm bushed. I'm going to hit the hay.*

* **hit the jackpot** (colloq.): have a great stroke of luck, gain s/thing valuable (esp. by luck) >*That land's worth twice what Emily paid for it—she really hit the jackpot there.* >*You hit the jackpot when you married that great gal.*

— **hit/push the panic button** (see **PANIC BUTTON**)

* **hit the road** (colloq.): start off (esp. on a trip), leave >*Let's get up early. I want to hit the road by six.* >*Hit the road, Jack! You're givin' me a headache.*

— **hit the roof** (colloq.): become furious, lose (one's) temper >*Dad will hit the roof when he sees that bill.*

— **hit the sack** (sl.): go to bed >*I didn't hit the sack till three in the morning.*

— **hit the skids** (sl.): start the process of ruin or failure, start becoming poor or deteriorated >*After Hank lost his job, he started drinkin' heavy and really hit the skids.* >*That part of town has hit the skids.*

* **hit the spot** (colloq.): (for a drink or food to) satisfy a thirst or hunger >*Iced tea sure hits the spot on a hot afternoon.*

— **hit the trail** (colloq.): start off (esp. on a trip), leave >*It's getting late—let's hit the trail.*

* **hit [s/one] up (for [s/thing])** (sl.): ask [s/one] to lend or give (one [s/thing]) >*Some bum on the street just hit me up for a couple of bucks.* >*I'm never gonna get that raise. I hit the boss up today, and he gave me a bunch of excuses.*

— **hit [s/one] with [s/thing]¹** (sl.): serve [s/thing] to [s/one] >*When the dealer hit me with the third queen, I knew the pot was mine.* >*Hey, barkeep, hit me with another beer.*

— **hit [s/one] with [s/thing]²** (sl.): present [s/thing] to [s/one] (esp. an idea, proposal or information) >*When I hit the boss with my plan, he's gonna love it.* >*Wait till I hit 'em with this news!*

* **[for] the shit [to] hit the fan** (vulg.): [for] the negative consequences [to] occur, [for] the inevitable scandal [to] begin >*The shit's really gonna hit the fan when the boss finds out about this!* >*The press doesn't know yet about the bribes the candidate took, but when the shit hits the fan he'll have to withdraw from the race.*

HITCH

— **hitch¹** (colloq.): period of military service, military enlistment >*He did a hitch in the Army before going to college.*

* **hitch²** (vt) (colloq.): hitchhike (a ride or distance) >*We hitched a ride with a trucker.* >*I hitched my way home.*

HITCHED

— **get hitched** (sl.): get married >*They ran off to Las Vegas to get hitched.*

HIT MAN

* **hit man** (sl.): hired murderer >*They brought in a hit man from Cleveland to do the job.*

HIT LIST

* **hit list** (sl.): list of persons or things to be attacked or eliminated, targets for disposal >*They've got a hit list of every prominent liberal in the state.* >*Her wildlife study program is on the governor's hit list for the next fiscal year.*

HIYA

* **hiya!** (hī´yə) (colloq.): hello there! how are you? >*Hiya! How're things at work?*

HOCK

— **hock** (hok) (vt) (colloq.): pawn >*He hocked his gold watch to pay off a gambling debt.*

— **in/out of hock** (colloq.): in/out of debt >*They really got in hock by overusing their credit cards.* >*Once we pay this off, we'll be out of hock.*

HOG

— **high off/on the hog** (see **HIGH**)

HOG HEAVEN

— **hog heaven** (sl.): state or situation of great happiness, paradise >*Betty'll be in hog heaven if she wins the contest.* >*Pullin' trout outta the lake is hog heaven to Roger.*

HOG-WILD

— **(go) hog-wild** (colloq.): (become) overly excited or extremely enthusiastic >*The crowd went hog-wild when he started playing his big hit.* >*How are we going to control a bunch of hog-wild kids?*

HO-HUM

— **ho-hum** (hō´hum´) (colloq.): boring, uninspiring, routine >*It was a ho-hum presentation full of clichés and generalizations.*

HOKEY

— **hokey**[1] (hō´kē) (sl.): overly sentimental, trite >*Why do ya watch those hokey soap operas?*

— **hokey**[2] (sl.): contrived, artificial, false >*Do ya really believe that hokey story about her mother bein' a spy?*

HOLD

— **hold all the cards** (colloq.): be in control (of a situation), have the critical advantage >*The landowners are holding all the cards in this deal.*

* **hold down the fort** (colloq.): take care of things (at home or a business) temporarily, govern or administer things temporarily >*You hold down the fort till I get back, OK?*

— **hold [one's] horses** (colloq.): not be so impatient, not begin yet (freq. used as a command) >*Hold your horses! I'll be with you in a minute.* >*Tell him to hold his horses—the others aren't ready yet.*

* **hold it down** (colloq.): quiet down, stop making so much noise >*The cops showed up and told us to hold it down.*

** **hold on** (vi) (colloq.): wait, stop, not become impatient (freq. used as a command) >*Now, hold on a minute— that's not the way it happened.* >*Hold on there! What do you think you're doing?* >*Hold on. We'll get this straightened out.*

— **hold/hang on to your hat!** (colloq.): prepare yourself! (for s/thing exciting or surprising) >*OK, here we go. Hold on to your hat!* >*Hang on to your hat! Wait till you hear this!*

* **hold out (on)** (colloq.): refrain from giving (s/one) what is expected or due, keep (s/thing) (from) >*That's all the money you've got? If you're holding out on me, you're going to be in trouble.* >*I'm sure there's more to it than that—I think they're holding out.*

** **hold the** (colloq.): not include (a certain part of a food order) >*Give me a cheeseburger and hold the onions.*

— **hold the phone!** (colloq.): wait! don't proceed! not so fast! (used to express objections or reservations) >*Hold the phone! Don't say I'm going to pay for it, because I'm not.*

— **hold water** (colloq.): be logical, stand up under examination, be provable (used esp. in the neg.) >*His alibi just doesn't hold water.* >*If the theory holds water, he'll be famous.*

* **not hold [one's] breath** (colloq.): not wait having unrealistic expectations (for s/thing to happen) >*He might ask you out again, but don't hold your breath.*

HOLDING–HOME BOY

HOLDING
— **holding** (vi) (sl.): in possession of illegal drugs >*He was holdin' when they stopped him, so now he's back in the slammer.*

* **leave [s/one] holding the bag** (colloq.): leave [s/one] to suffer all the consequences or blame (while escaping one's own responsibility) >*When they discovered the theft, Gabe took off and left his partner holding the bag.*

HOLE
— **have a hole in [one's] head** (colloq.): be very foolish, be irrational >*You've got a hole in your head if you think I'm going to get involved in that fiasco.*

— **hole up** (vi) (colloq.): hide out, take refuge >*He holed up in a cabin in the mountains for three months while he finished his book.*

* **in/out of the hole** (colloq.): in/out of debt, below/above the break-even amount >*We're really in the hole this month.* >*I came out twenty bucks in the hole at last night's poker game.* >*Two more paychecks and I'll be out of the hole.*

* **need [s/thing] like ([one] needs) a hole in the head** (colloq.): definitely not need [s/thing] >*Brenda needs that bum like she needs a hole in the head.* >*I need your stupid advice like a hole in the head.*

— **not know/can't tell [one's] ass from a hole in the ground** (see **KNOW**)

— **not know/can't tell [s/thing] from a hole in the ground** (see **KNOW**)

HOLE IN THE WALL
— **hole in the wall** (colloq.): small and modest shop or dwelling >*I don't see how you can live in this dinky hole in the wall.*

HOLLER
— **holler** (vi) (colloq.): complain loudly >*The students are hollering about the fee increase.*

— **give [s/one] a holler** (colloq.): call or contact [s/one] >*Give me a holler if you need any help.*

HOLY
— **holy cow!** (sl.): (interj. to express surprise or wonder) >*Holy cow! Did ya see how fast he was goin'?*

— **holy mackerel!** (sl.): (interj. to express surprise, wonder, or irritation) >*Holy mackerel! That lightning hit real close.* >*Holy mackerel! Can't we change the subject?*

— **holy moley!** (see "**HOLY moly!**")

— **holy moly!** (... mō´lē) (sl.): (interj. to express surprise or wonder) >*Holy moly! My horse won!*

* **holy shit!** (... shit) (vulg.): (interj. to express surprise, wonder, or irritation) >*Holy shit! That jerk went through a red light and almost creamed us!*

— **holy smoke(s)!** (sl.): (interj. to express surprise or wonder) >*Holy smoke! Did ya see how tall that gal was?*

— **(holy) terror** (see **TERROR**)

HOLY ROLLER
— **Holy Roller** (colloq., pej.): member of a Christian sect whose services are marked by shouting and frenetic movement >*He said the Holy Rollers have set up a big tent outside of town.*

HOMBRE
— **hombre** (om´brā) (sl.): man (esp. seen as extraordinary) >*Boris is a real weird hombre.* >*We need a tough hombre for this job.*

HOME
— **nobody's home** (see **NOBODY'S**)

HOME BOY
* **home boy** (sl.): young man from (one's) neighborhood (esp. a gang member from a poor neighborhood) (also voc.) >*I recognized him—he's a home boy I know.* >*Hey, home boy, what's happenin'?*

HOME EC

* **home ec** (… ek) (colloq.): home economics (esp. as a course of study) >*This semester he's taking math, psych, English, and home ec, just for fun.*

HOMEWORK

* **do [one's] homework** (colloq.): prepare [oneself] through investigation, obtain pertinent information beforehand >*If you'd done your homework, you would have known this guy was likely to skip town without paying.*

HOMO

* **homo** (hō´mō) (sl., pej.): homosexual (also adj.) >*That dummy says only homos do that kinda work. >He calls it a homo bar.*

HON

* **hon** (hun) (voc.) (colloq.): sweetheart, dear >*Say, hon, where did you put the car keys?*

HONCHO

— **honcho** (hon´chō) (sl.): boss, chief, important person >*Some honcho from the main office is comin' to this branch next week. >He's the head honcho around here.*

HONEST

— **honest Injun!** (… in´jən) (colloq., freq. pej.): honestly! I'm telling the truth! >*I tell you he was carrying a gun. Honest Injun!*

* **honest to God!** (colloq.): honestly! I'm telling the truth! >*I didn't do it, honest to God!*

HONESTLY

* **honestly!** (colloq.): (interj. to express mild annoyance or disbelief) >*Honestly! Do you have to use such language?*

HONEST-TO-GOD

— **honest-to-God** (colloq.): genuine, authentic, real >*I've never met an honest-to-God movie star.*

HONEY

** **honey¹** (colloq.): sweetheart, loved one (also voc.) >*I got to find me a new honey to love. >What's for dinner, honey?*

* **honey²** (voc.) (colloq., freq. pej.): (affectionate term of address, esp. by men toward women or older women toward younger people) >*Type this letter right away, will you, honey? >I'll get your order in a minute, honey.*

— **a honey (of a)** (colloq.): an excellent or beautiful (example of s/thing) >*That's a honey of a street bike you got there. >I'm glad I bought this old desk—it's a honey.*

HONEYBUNCH

— **honeybunch** (colloq.): sweetheart, loved one (also voc.) >*How's my honeybunch this morning? >Good morning, honeybunch.*

HONKER

— **honker** (sl.): (person's) large nose >*Did you see the honker on that guy she's with?*

HONKY

— **honky** (hong´kē/hông´kē) (sl., pej.): white person (used esp. among blacks) (also adj.) >*He said he didn't like honkies in his part of town. >The jerk said I was givin' him honky jive.*

HONKY-TONK

— **honky-tonk** (hong´kē tongk´/hông´kē tôngk´) (colloq.): cheap and rowdy night club or dance hall >*The cowboys spend most of their evenings at that honky-tonk.*

HONOR

— **scout's honor!** (see SCOUT'S)

HOOCH

— **hooch** (hūch) (sl.): liquor >*Hey, where do ya keep the hooch? I need a drink.*

HOOD

— **hood** (sl.): hoodlum, thug, criminal, ruffian >*We wanna have our streets safe from the hoods.*

— **the hood** (sl.): (one's) neighborhood (esp. in a poor, urban setting) >*Some dude from the hood got me the job.*

HOOEY

— **hooey** (hū´ē) (sl.): nonsense, lie, false or exaggerated story (also interj.) >*That sounds like a lot of hooey to me. >Hooey! I don't believe a word of it.*

HOOF

— **hoof it** (sl.): walk (s/where) >*My car's broke down—guess I'll have to hoof it to work.*

HOOK

* **hook**[1] (vi) (sl.): engage in prostitution >*She's been hookin' around the convention hotels.*

— **hook**[2] (vt) (colloq.): obtain, capture (esp. through contrivance or cleverness) >*I don't know how she did it, but she hooked a great job with the city. >She says she's out to hook a rich man.*

— **hook up with** (colloq.): form an association with, join forces with >*Joey's been getting in trouble ever since he hooked up with that hood. >I want to hook up with a good firm where I can advance fast.*

* **off the hook** (colloq.): freed of responsibility, no longer in trouble >*Martin confessed, so you're off the hook. >He wants me to get him off the hook by paying his tax bill.*

— **ring off the hook** (see **RING**)

— **swallow [s/thing] hook, line, and sinker** (see **SWALLOW**)

HOOKED

* **hooked (on)** (colloq.): addicted to, obsessed with, very enthusiastic about >*He's hooked on cigarettes. >She's gotten hooked on some daytime soap opera. >The first time I ate Thai food I was hooked.*

HOOKER

** **hooker** (sl.): prostitute >*She was a hooker in Vegas for a couple of years.*

HOOKS

— **get [one's] hooks into** (sl.): gain control over, come to dominate >*Once he gets his hooks into her, she ain't got a chance. >They can't wait to get their hooks into his business.*

HOOKY

— **play hooky** (… hŭk´ē) (colloq.): be absent without permission, be truant >*Billy was playing hooky while his classmates were taking a test. >We missed you at work yesterday. Were you playing hooky?*

HOOPLA

* **hoopla**[1] (hūp´lä´) (colloq.): misleading or confusing talk or writing >*It's hard to understand the issues with all the hoopla surrounding them.*

— **hoopla**[2] (colloq.): commotion, noisy excitement >*What was all the hoopla about in front of your house last night?*

HOOPS

— **jump through hoops** (see **JUMP**)

HOOSEGOW

— **the hoosegow** (… hūs´gou) (sl.): jail >*The sheriff threw him into the hoosegow till he sobered up.*

HOOT

— **a hoot** (… hūt) (sl.): a great time, a great deal of fun >*Ridin' that roller coaster was a hoot.*

— **give a hoot** (colloq.): be concerned, care, take interest (freq. used in the neg.) >*Don't ask him which color he wants because he doesn't give a hoot.*

HOOTCH

— **hootch** (see "**HOOCH**")

HOOTERS

— **hooters** (hū'tərz) (sl., freq. vulg.): large (woman's) breasts >*Look at her hooters!*

HOP

— **hop[1]** (colloq.): dance, dance party >*They used to like to dance at the hops they held in the gym.*

* **hop[2]** (vi, vt) (colloq.): board (a vehicle) >*We hopped on a bus downtown.* >*I hopped a plane to Denver last Monday.*

— **hop[3]** (vi) (colloq.): move or travel frequently (from place to place) >*I quit that job because I got tired of hopping all over the country making sales presentations.*

— **hop[4]** (vi) (sl.): be full of noisy or exciting activity, have a festive atmosphere >*Things'll start hoppin' once people have a few drinks.*

* **a hop, skip, and a jump** (colloq.): a short distance >*Come on over—we live just a hop, skip, and a jump from there.*

— **jump/hop/get on the bandwagon** (see BANDWAGON)

* **hop to it** (colloq.): start moving or working immediately >*We'd better hop to it if we're going to finish this today.*

— **hop up** (vt) (sl.): modify (an engine) to make (it) more powerful >*It's a stock engine now, but he'll hop it up for racin'.*

HOPE

— **I hope to tell you!** (colloq.): I agree completely! it's certainly true! >*I hope to tell you she's beautiful! She's a knockout!*

HOPPED-UP

— **hopped-up[1]** (sl.): with an engine modified for more power >*He runs around town in his hopped-up pickup.*

— **hopped-up[2]** (sl.): intoxicated, highly stimulated (esp. by an illicit drug) >*I don't know what he was hopped-up on, but he was high as a kite.*

HOPPER

— **in the hopper** (colloq.): being prepared or planned, being developed or processed >*They got some new ad campaign in the hopper that they're going to launch in September.*

HOPPING

— **hopping mad** (colloq.): very angry >*Gracie was hopping mad after her argument with that rude clerk.*

HORN

— **blow/toot [one's] own horn** (see BLOW)

— **horn in** (vi) (sl.): intrude, participate without invitation, push (s/one) aside to take (his/her) place >*Every time I try to talk to her, that jerk horns in and ruins it.* >*I don't want 'em hornin' in on my territory.*

— **on the horn** (sl.): on the telephone >*Get on the horn to Memphis and tell 'em to hold that shipment.*

HORNET

— **(as) mad as a hornet** (see MAD)

HORNS

— **lock horns** (see LOCK)

HORNSWOGGLE

— **hornswoggle** (hôrn'swog'əl) (vt) (sl.): trick, deceive, swindle >*Nobody tries to hornswoggle me and gets away with it!*

HORNY

** **horny** (sl., freq. vulg.): lustful, feeling the need for sexual release >*The sailors came back from three weeks at sea horny as hell.*

HORROR STORY

* **horror story** (colloq.): recounting of a distressing experience >*She had horror stories about the cost of traveling in Europe that year.*

HORSE

— **horse** (sl.): heroin >*The cops busted him for dealin' horse.*

— **could eat a horse** (see EAT)

— **eat like a horse** (see EAT)

* **horse around** (vi) (colloq.): spend time playfully, engage in horseplay, play innocent pranks >*I don't want you kids horsing around in the living room.* >*We're just horsing around with Sammy. We wouldn't hurt him.*

HORSEFEATHERS

— **horsefeathers!** (colloq.): nonsense! that's a lie! I don't believe it! >*Horsefeathers! He doesn't know a word of Chinese, much less speak it fluently.*

HORSES

— **horses** (colloq.): horsepower >*How many horses you got under the hood there?*

— **(a team of) wild horses couldn't** (see **WILD**)

— **hold [one's] horses** (see **HOLD**)

HORSE'S ASS

— **horse's ass** (vulg.): foolish or stupid person, person who behaves obnoxiously >*Her husband's a real horse's ass, flirtin' with other women right in front of her.*

HORSE SENSE

— **horse sense** (colloq.): common sense >*Anyone with a little horse sense ought to be able to figure this out.*

HORSESHIT

— **horseshit¹** (hôrs´shit´/hôrsh´it´) (vulg.): nonsense, lie, false or exaggerated story (also adj., also interj.) >*Him bein' an English earl is horseshit.* >*Ya didn't believe that horseshit story, did ya?* >*That clown, a psychiatrist? Horseshit!*

— **horseshit²** (vulg.): annoying or tedious work or demands (also adj.) >*The horseshit ya gotta go through to get licensed is unbelievable.* >*Why do I have to take some horseshit aptitude test?*

HORSE'S MOUTH

* **(straight/right) from the horse's mouth** (colloq.): from the original or most authoritative source (said of information) >*I got it straight from the horse's mouth that the company's going to be sold.* >*Believe it! It comes from the horse's mouth.*

HORSE-TRADE

— **horse-trade** (vi) (colloq.): negotiate or barter shrewdly, bargain hard >*Old man Harkins loves to horse-trade at swap meets.*

HORSE TRADING

— **horse trading** (colloq.): shrewd negotiating or bartering, hard bargaining >*We did some horse trading and finally came away with a deal.*

HOT

** **hot¹** (colloq.): very popular or successful, much sought after >*Everyone's talking about this hot new star.* >*This style's really hot this year.*

* **hot²** (sl.): having luck, on a winning streak, playing successfully >*Deal the cards! I'm hot tonight.* >*Kyle's not one of their best players, but he was sure hot last night.*

* **hot³** (sl.): stolen >*He's tryin' to sell that car real cheap—I think it's hot.*

* **hot⁴** (sl.): sexually aroused >*She got him all hot, then left with another guy.*

* **hot⁵** (colloq.): fast and powerful (said of a vehicle) >*He hopped up his old Ford and now it's really hot.*

* **hot⁶** (colloq.): exciting, sensational, scandalous >*Who's that hot chick I saw you with?* >*I've heard the hottest rumor about Reverend Billings!*

* **hot⁷** (colloq.): very eager or anxious, desirous >*He's really hot to try out his new motorboat.* >*Johnny's hot for a camping trip this summer.* >*I'm not so hot on that idea.*

— **hot⁸** (colloq.): dangerous, risky >*It got a little hot for him covering the war, so he came back to the States.*

— **hot**[9] (colloq.): very angry >*Everett found out they lied to him, and is he ever hot!*

* **(all) hot and bothered**[1] (colloq.): very angry or upset >*Now, don't go getting hot and bothered—I'll fix it good as new.*

— **(all) hot and bothered**[2] (sl.): very excited or aroused >*The girls are all hot and bothered over that hunk of an actor.*

— **hot and cold** (colloq.): inconsistent, at times good and at times bad (also adv.) >*He gave a hot and cold performance.* >*We played hot and cold but finally won by two points.*

* **hot and heavy** (colloq.): passionate, intense, vehement (also adv.) >*He's got some hot and heavy thing going with his dentist.* >*They've been going at it pretty hot and heavy, but they haven't come to blows yet.*

— **hot damn!** (sl., freq. vulg.): wonderful! hurrah! >*Hot damn! I won five hundred bucks in the lottery!*

— **hot to trot** (sl., freq. vulg.): eager to have sex, very aroused sexually >*The way he's actin', I'd say he's hot to trot.*

* **hot under the collar** (colloq.): very angry, furious >*Boy, was Jim hot under the collar when he found out what they'd been doing behind his back.*

— **make it hot for** (colloq.): cause trouble or create difficulties for >*They're going to make it hot for him when they find out he's organizing a union.*

— **piping hot** (see **PIPING**)

** **[neg.] so hot** (colloq.): bad, poor, inferior (also adv.) >*She liked the movie, but I didn't think it was so hot.* >*After all that pizza I ate I don't feel so hot.*

HOT AIR

* **hot air** (colloq.): empty or pretentious talk, boasting >*That business about him going all over the country to speak is a bunch of hot air.*

HOT CAKES

* **sell/go like hot cakes** (colloq.): be bought at a fast rate, be doing very well on the market >*Condos are selling like hot cakes in the suburbs.*

HOT DOG

— **hot dog** (sl.): person who shows off with difficult stunts (requiring athletic ability) >*We don't need no hot dogs on the court—we need team players.*

— **hot (diggety) dog!** (… dig´ə tē …) (colloq.): wonderful! hurrah! >*Hot diggety dog! She loves me!* >*I got the job! Hot dog!*

HOT-DOG

— **hot-dog** (vi) (sl.): perform difficult stunts, show off (in athletic ability) >*He went hot-doggin' down the slopes doin' every trick he knew.*

HOTFOOT

— **hotfoot it** (colloq.): go quickly, run >*I want you to hotfoot it to Chris's and tell her that her mom needs her right now.*

HOT NUMBER

— **hot number** (sl.): very sexy or attractive person >*He's been goin' out with a hot number—a former Miss Idaho!*

HOT PANTS

— **have hot pants (for)** (sl., freq. vulg.): be eager to have sex (with), be very aroused sexually (by) >*He's got hot pants for some bimbo that works in his office.*

HOT POTATO

— **hot potato** (colloq.): difficult issue, unpleasant matter or thorny problem to deal with >*Sex education's a hot potato that neither candidate wants to deal with.*

HOT PROPERTY

— **hot property** (colloq.): very popular or valuable person >*She's been a real hot property around Hollywood ever since she starred in that big hit.*

HOT ROD

— **hot rod** (sl.): automobile modified to be fast and powerful >*Ya know that kid that zooms around town in his hot rod?*

HOT-ROD

* **hot-rod** (vi, vt) (sl.): drive (an automobile) very fast >*The cops don't like us hot-roddin' in the residential neighborhoods.* >*He hot-rodded his Chevy all over town.*

HOTS

* **have the hots (for)** (... hots ...) (sl., freq. vulg.): be eager to have sex (with), be very aroused sexually (by) >*He's got the hots for some babe at work, but she ain't interested.*

HOT SEAT

— **the hot seat[1]** (colloq.): an uncomfortable situation, a distressing position (esp. where one has to make a hard decision) >*The new board member's in the hot seat on this one because she has to cast the deciding vote.*

— **the hot seat[2]** (sl.): the electric chair, death by electrocution in the electric chair >*If he's convicted of murder one, he'll probably get the hot seat.*

HOT SHIT

* **think [one] is hot shit** (... shit) (vulg.): mistakenly believe that [one] is extraordinary or superior, be arrogant and conceited >*She thinks she's hot shit just 'cause she aced the test.* >*Look at Lee strut—he really thinks he's hot shit.*

* **think [s/one] is hot shit** (vulg.): mistakenly believe that [s/one] is extraordinary or superior >*Pauline thinks her boyfriend's hot shit, but if ya ask me, he's an idiot.*

HOTSHOT

* **hotshot** (sl.): person who is skilled or talented (at s/thing) (esp. one who is conceited or ostentatious) (also adj.) >*Ya ever see him play tennis? He's a hotshot, all right, and he knows it.*

>*The thug's got him some hotshot lawyer who'll probably get the charges dropped.*

HOT SPOT

— **hot spot** (colloq.): area where there is danger, place of ongoing contention >*Gang activity has made that part of town a real hot spot.*

HOT STUFF

* **hot stuff** (sl.): person or thing that causes great interest or excitement >*She's hot stuff in country music.* >*That new movie about the Civil War is really hot stuff now.*

HOT WATER

* **in hot water** (colloq.): in trouble, in a difficult situation >*You'll be in hot water if you don't pay them back on time.*

HOT-WIRE

* **hot-wire** (vt) (sl.): start (an automobile) by short-circuiting the ignition >*The thief hot-wired a new Buick and took off in it.*

HOUND

* **hound** (vt) (colloq.): nag or constantly urge (s/one to do s/thing) >*The bill collectors have been hounding them.* >*She's been hounding me to see a doctor, so I made an appointment.*

— **... hound** (colloq.): ... devotee, lover of ... >*All the rock hounds gathered at the gem show.* >*He's a real jazz hound. You should see his record collection.*

HOUSE

— **bring down the house/the house down** (see **BRING**)

— **eat [s/one] out of house and home** (see **EAT**)

— **like a house afire** (colloq.): intensely, wholeheartedly >*They worked like a house afire to get the patio ready in time for the party.*

** **on the house** (colloq.): provided free of charge by the establishment >*You pay for the first two, and the third's on the house.

HOW

* **and how!** (colloq.): most certainly! extremely so! >*Sure I want to see that play, and how!*

* **how about …!** (colloq.): (interj. to express surprise, wonder, or admiration regarding …) >*How about that! I have the winning ticket.* >*How about those Bears! Ain't they something this season?*

— **how (are) they hanging?** (see HANGING)

** **how come?** (colloq.): why? for what reason? how is it that? >*How come you didn't call me last night like you said you would?*

— **how do you like *them* apples?** (see THEM)

* **how goes it?** (colloq.): how is it going? how are things? >*What do you say, Warner? How goes it?*

— **(how) you cut/slice it** (see CUT)

HOW-DO-YOU-DO

— **a fine how-do-you-do** (colloq., sarc.): (another's) unexpectedly disappointing or unpleasant behavior, an unjustly unpleasant situation >*He wouldn't lend me the book. That's a fine how-do-you-do after all I've done for him.*

HOWDY

— **howdy!** (hou´dē) (colloq.): hello! hi! >*Howdy! How y'all doing?*

HOWL

— **howl** (vi) (sl.): laugh hard >*That movie was so funny! It had everyone howlin'.*

HOWLING

— **howling success** (colloq.): absolute success >*Their exhibit was a howling success.*

HOW'S

* **how's that?** (intonation rising on *that*) (colloq.): what? pardon me? please repeat that! >*How's that? I didn't hear you.*

— **how's tricks?** (sl.): how are things going? how are you doing? >*Hey, Stan, how's tricks?*

HOYLE

— **according to Hoyle** (see ACCORDING)

HUBBA-HUBBA

— **hubba-hubba!** (hub´ə hub´ə) (sl.): (interj. to express approval or delight; esp. used in a sexist way by a man regarding an attractive woman) >*Hubba-hubba! What a doll!*

HUBBY

* **hubby** (hub´ē) (colloq.): husband >*Ladies, be sure to bring your hubbies to the awards banquet.*

HUCKSTER

— **huckster** (huk´stər) (sl.): aggressively persuasive person (esp. a salesperson), person able to talk people into things >*He let some huckster talk him into an extended warranty that's gonna cost him nearly a thousand bucks.*

HUH

* **huh!** (hu/hū) (colloq.): (interj. to express disbelief or contempt) >*Huh! I just bet he was sorry.* >*Huh! I don't give a damn.*

** **huh?** (colloq.): what? would you repeat that? are you joking? >*Huh? What did you say?* >*Huh? She actually slapped the judge?*

HUH-UH

** **huh-uh** (hu´u/hū´ū) (colloq.): no >*Huh-uh—I haven't seen him.*

HUMDINGER

— **humdinger** (hum´ding´ər) (colloq.): excellent or remarkable example (of s/thing), extraordinary person or thing >*That was a humdinger of a party last night, Joe.* >*That new salesman's a humdinger. He sold eight houses his first month.*

HUMONGOUS

— **humongous** (hyū mung´gəs) (sl.): extremely large >*There was a humongous traffic jam on the freeway this morning.*

HUMP

— **hump** (vi, vt) (vulg.): have sex (with) >*He said they humped all night. >Jerry said he humped her on the couch.*

HUMUNGOUS

— **humungous** (see "HUMONGOUS")

HUNG

— **hung** (vulg.): having a large penis >*He thinks he's really hung.*

** **hung over** (colloq.): suffering from a hangover >*Was I ever hung over the morning after the party!*

** **hung up (on)** (sl.): obsessed (with), having a psychological block or complex (regarding) >*The poor slob's really hung up on that woman. >Do ya really wanna get involved with a hung up jerk like him?*

HUNGRY

* **hungry (for)** (colloq.): feeling a strong need (for), aggressively seeking a chance (at) >*The company's hungry for a new contract. >The guy'll probably take a low offer because he's hungry.*

HUNK

* **hunk** (sl.): handsome man (esp. a well-built one) >*You should see the hunk she's goin' out with!*

— **hunk/pile/piece of junk** (see JUNK)

HUNKER

— **hunker (down)** (hung´kər ...) (vi) (colloq.): hunch down, be squatting >*They were hunkered under a low overhang during the storm. >See if you can hunker down in those bushes and stay out of sight.*

— **hunker down** (vi) (colloq.): become resolute, take a firm attitude (esp. when encountering opposition or when needing to become productive) >*They*

tried to convince him, but he hunkered down and wouldn't budge. >*We got to hunker down and finish this, no matter what.*

HUNKY-DORY

— **hunky-dory** (hung´kē dôr´ē/dōr´ē) (sl., freq. hum.): fine, very satisfactory, going well >*Trudy says everything's just hunky-dory at home.*

HURT

— **wouldn't hurt a fly/flea** (colloq.): is harmless, is completely nonviolent >*He talks tough, but he's really an old softy that wouldn't hurt a fly.*

HURTING

* **hurting (for)** (colloq.): in great need (of), desperate (for) >*Contractors are hurting for work in this town. >I need a loan bad—I'm really hurting.*

HUSH-HUSH

* **hush-hush** (colloq.): very confidential, secret >*This weapons test is a real hush-hush operation.*

HUSH MONEY

— **hush money** (colloq.): bribe (to keep s/one from divulging s/thing illicit) >*There was a crooked cop getting hush money from the drug dealers.*

HUSTLE

— **hustle**[1] (hus´əl) (colloq.): hurriedness, quick or energetic pace >*You got to put a little more hustle in your step to keep up.*

— **hustle**[2] (colloq.): aggressive work routine, competitive struggle >*I'm getting tired of the constant hustle at the office.*

— **hustle**[3] (sl.): swindle, deception, trick >*He tried the old five-dollar-bill hustle on ya, huh?*

* **hustle**[4] (vi) (colloq.): work alertly and aggressively, be continually competitive >*You really got to hustle to get ahead in this business. >The good salesmen know how to hustle.*

* **hustle[5]** (vi) (colloq.): move quickly or energetically >*We'd better hustle if we're going to catch the early show.* >*She was hustling around the kitchen all day.*

* **hustle[6]** (vt) (sl.): sell aggressively (to) >*He got a job hustlin' magazines door-to-door.* >*Don't let 'em hustle ya into buyin' a car ya don't really want.*

— **hustle[7]** (vi) (sl.): engage in prostitution >*She hustles to support her drug habit.*

— **hustle[8]** (vt) (sl.): make sexual advances toward, make a sexual conquest of >*There's horny Greg tryin' to hustle that cute redhead.*

— **hustle[9]** (vt) (sl.): swindle, cheat, deceive >*Ya got hustled by that guy—these tickets were for last week.* >*They hustled him outta ten bucks.*

— **hustle[10]** (vt) (sl.): steal, obtain illicitly >*Where'd ya hustle this expensive watch?*

HUSTLER

* **hustler[1]** (hus´lər) (colloq.): aggressive and ambitious worker >*You won't make much in commissions unless you're a hustler.*

— **hustler[2]** (sl.): swindler, trickster >*He was a big-time hustler in the precious metals racket.* >*A pool hustler took him for fifty bucks.*

HUTZPA

— **hutzpa** (see "CHUTZPA")

HYMIE

— **Hymie** (hī´mē) (sl., pej.): Jew >*She caught hell for callin' Maury a Hymie.*

HYPE

* **hype[1]** (hīp) (colloq.): exaggerated or false advertising, deception >*Don't fall for some public relations hype!*

* **hype[2]** (vt) (colloq.): promote or advertise with exaggeration, promote with false claims or fanfare >*I'm sick of hearing those campaign workers hyping their candidates.*

* **hype up** (vt) (colloq.): excite, enthuse >*What a speaker! He got the audience all hyped up over his programs.*

HYPER

** **hyper** (hī´pər) (colloq.): high-strung, overexcitable or overexcited, obsessed >*That kid's hyper. How does his mother control him?* >*Marv is hyper about his new ball club.*

HYSTERICAL

* **hysterical** (colloq.): very funny >*You should see this comedian—she's hysterical.*

I

ICE

— ice[1] (sl.): diamond(s) >*They got some nice ice in that jewelry store.*

— ice[2] (sl.): smokable rock methamphetamine >*He was really high on some ice he took.*

— ice[3] (vt) (colloq.): have assured of obtaining or winning >*The team will ice the championship with this win.*

— ice[4] (vt) (sl.): murder, kill >*The mob had him iced 'cause he knew too much.*

— break the ice (see **BREAK**)

— cut no ice (with) (see **CUT**)

— on ice (colloq.): assured, sure to be obtained or won >*I talked to the manager today, and we got the contract on ice.*

ICEBERG

— iceberg (colloq.): cold or insensitive person >*Talk about being unfeeling! He's a regular iceberg.*

ICING

* icing/frosting on the cake (colloq.): unexpected and desirable extra >*My new job's a whole lot better than the old one, and the icing on the cake is that I can earn more overtime.*

ICKY

— icky (ik´ē) (colloq.): repulsive, offensive, distasteful >*I told him to get his icky hands off me.* >*I'm not going to eat this icky junk.*

I.D.

** I.D.[1] (colloq.): identification, identification card or tag >*Do you have any I.D. with you?* >*I hate my picture on my I.D.*

— I.D.[2] (vt) (colloq.): identify >*They I.D.ed the robber right away.*

IDEA

— what's the big idea? (see **WHAT'S**)

IDIOT

— like an idiot (colloq.): vigorously, to the utmost degree >*I sweat like an idiot on muggy days.* >*We worked like idiots planning the banquet.*

IDIOT BOX

— idiot box (sl.): television set (esp. when seen as contemptible) >*The kid sits glued to that damn idiot box all evening!*

IDIOT LIGHT

— idiot light (sl.): automobile dashboard indicator light (in contrast to more precise gauges) >*Damn idiot light! I know the car isn't overheatin'.*

IFFY

* iffy (if´ē) (colloq.): doubtful, having unresolved aspects >*The forecast for rain makes tomorrow's picnic pretty iffy.*

IFS

* no ifs, ands, or buts (about it) (… ifs andz … buts …) (colloq.): no excuses or exceptions will be accepted >*I want this finished by tomorrow—no ifs, ands, or buts about it!*

ILLEGAL

** illegal (colloq., freq. pej.): undocumented immigrant, illegal alien >*They tell me a lot of illegals live in that neighborhood.*

IMAGE

— spit and image (see "**SPITTING IMAGE**")

IN

** in (colloq.): fashionable, in vogue, currently popular >*Short skirts were in that year.* >*It's the in place to have lunch.*

* have an in (with) (colloq.): have an advantageous relationship or connection (with), have influence (with) >*She's got an in with the governor because a friend of hers is on his staff.* >*Forget about joining that club unless you have an in.*

* **have it in for** (colloq.): wish to harm, seek revenge on >*He's had it in for me ever since I told on him.*

— **in (a/the/[s/one's]) ...** (see entry under ... noun)

— **in deep** (see **DEEP**)

— **in deep shit** (see **DEEP**)

— **in for it** (colloq.): bound to receive punishment, going to suffer bad consequences >*Huey's in for it when Dad gets home, because he broke his new drill.*

— **in no time (flat)** (see **TIME**)

— **in nothing flat** (see **NOTHING**)

— **in one piece** (see **PIECE**)

* **in with** (colloq.): having an advantageous relationship or connection with, having influence with >*Lloyd's a good man to know—he's in with all the big shots in county government.*

INDIAN GIVER
— **Indian giver** (colloq., freq. pej.): person who takes back (s/thing) after giving (it) >*Hey, you said I could keep those sunglasses, so don't be an Indian giver.*

INFO
** **info** (in´fō) (colloq.): information >*I'll send you all the info on the conference in the mail.*

IN-GROUP
* **in-group** (colloq.): small and exclusive group, clique, most socially desirable group to belong to (also adj.) >*She wants to be part of the in-group, but they ignore her.* >*I didn't get it—must be some kind of in-group humor.*

INJUN
— **Injun** (in´jən) (colloq., pej.): Native American, American Indian (also adj.) >*He said his grandpa fought the Injuns.* >*He calls it Injun jewelry.*

— **honest Injun!** (see **HONEST**)

INNARDS
— **innards** (in´ərdz) (colloq.): internal body parts, inner parts (esp. of a machine) >*The doc checked all his innards during the operation.* >*Let's oil the clock's innards and see if it runs better.*

INNIE
— **innie** (in´ē) (colloq.): nonprotruding or concave navel (cf. "**OUTIE**") >*Let's see your bellybutton. Is it an innie or an outie?*

INS
* **ins and outs** (inz ... outs) (colloq.): intracacies, pertinent details, relevant particulars >*Let's ask Quincy. He knows the ins and outs of the current regulations.*

INSIDE
— **inside of** (colloq.): within (a period of time) >*I bet Grayson gives up inside of ten minutes.*

** **know [s/thing] inside out** (colloq.): know [s/thing] thoroughly, have [s/thing] mastered >*He knows mainframe computers inside out.*

INSIDE JOB
* **inside job** (colloq.): crime committed by or with the help of s/one working for the victim >*It had to be an inside job because they knew right where to look for the jewels.*

INSIDES
* **insides** (in´sīdz´) (colloq.): internal body parts (esp. the stomach), inner parts (esp. of a machine) >*This soup warms my insides.* >*You ever seen the insides of a tape recorder?*

INSIDE TRACK
— **the inside track** (colloq.): the most advantageous position, the favored situation (in a competition) >*Gail's got the inside track for the job because they already know her and like her work.*

INTERFERENCE
— **run interference (for)** (colloq.): deal with troublesome matters (for) (to facilitate s/one's work or progress) >*We need someone to run interference for us in Washington so we can get this deal approved fast.*

INTO
** **into** (colloq.): very interested in or involved with >*Ray's been into computers ever since his brother bought one.* >*I feel sorry for you jerks who are into drugs.*

— **into [s/one] for** (sl.): in debt to [s/one] for (an amount of money) >*He's into me for over a hundred bucks and he'd better pay up by next week.*

INTRO
* **intro** (in'trō) (colloq.): introduction >*How was the intro to philosophy class?* >*They gave the speaker a nice intro.*

INVITE
— **invite** (in'vīt) (colloq.): invitation >*Hey, we got an invite to a dinner party.*

IN-YOUR-FACE
— **in-your-face** (sl.): defiantly self-assured, insolently provocative (cf. **"in your FACE!"**) >*His in-your-face, confrontational style turns a lot of people off.*

I.O.U.
** **I.O.U.** (= "I owe you") (colloq.): written promise to pay a debt >*Grady owes me twenty bucks—here's his I.O.U.*

IRON
* **iron out** (vt) (colloq.): resolve or reach agreement on (problems or differences) (esp. through discussion or compromise) >*We ought to be able to sit down and iron out these details in no time.*

— **pump iron** (see **PUMP**)

IT
— **out of it** (see **OUT**)

ITCHING
— **itching for/to** (colloq.): restlessly desirous of/to, badly wanting (to) >*After the argument with his wife, Les came into the bar itching for a fight.* >*What a workaholic! He's itching to get back to his desk.*

ITCHY
— **itchy** (colloq.): restless, eager (to begin s/thing) >*I'm itchy to get started on that job.*

ITEM
* **be an item** (sl.): be romantically or sexually involved (with one another) (esp. when worthy of gossip) >*Ever since Jane and Alex met at my party, they've been a real item.*

ITSY-BITSY
— **itsy-bitsy** (it'sē bit'sē) (colloq.): very small, tiny >*Give me just an itsy-bitsy serving—I'm on a diet.*

ITTY-BITTY
— **itty-bitty** (it'ē bit'ē) (colloq.): very small, tiny >*The guy was holding this itty-bitty Chihuahua dog in his hand.*

IVORIES
— **ivories** (sl.): piano keyboard >*Man, can he ever play those ivories!*

J

JACK

— **Jack** (voc.) (colloq.): fellow, mister (used esp. with a male stranger in a contentious way) >*Watch it, Jack, or you'll be sorry! Beat it, Jack!*

— **([neg.]) jack** (sl.): nothing at all >*We didn't do jack at work today.* >*He knows jack about radios.*

— **jack around** (vt) (sl.): mislead, deceive (esp. to delay s/one) >*Stop jackin' me around and give me the info I need.*

* **jack off** (vi, vt) (vulg.): masturbate (said of a male) >*He said he jacked off a lot when he was a kid.* >*He said he asked her to jack him off.*

* **jack up** (vt) (colloq.): increase, raise (esp. a price) >*Every time someone even mentions inflation, that store jacks up its prices.*

JACKOFF

— **jackoff** (vulg.): person who passes time idly, person who works halfheartedly or unproductively >*You don't expect that jackoff to get ahead in life, do ya?*

JACKPOT

— **hit the jackpot** (see **HIT**)

JACK SHIT

— **([neg.]) jack shit** (… shit) (vulg.): nothing at all >*I want jack shit from you!* >*We didn't understand jack shit of what he said.*

JAG

* **Jag** (jag) (colloq.): Jaguar automobile >*That new Jag must have cost you a fortune.*

— **… jag** (colloq.): period of intense …, period of overindulgence in …, … binge >*His last drinking jag lasted three days.* >*Let her have her crying jag, and she'll feel better.*

JAILBAIT

— **jailbait** (sl.): girl under the age of legal consent for sex (usually eighteen) (seen as off-limits as a sexual partner due to the sanctions against statutory rape) >*Forget about his younger sister—she's jailbait.*

JAILBIRD

— **jailbird** (colloq.): prisoner, ex-convict >*You better watch your step, or you're going to end up a jailbird.* >*They don't care what he served time for—they don't want any jailbirds working for them.*

JALOPY

— **jalopy** (jə lop´ē) (colloq.): old or dilapidated automobile >*This old jalopy doesn't look like much, but it gets me to work.*

JAM

* **jam** (colloq.): awkward or difficult situation, predicament >*I want to see how Quinn gets himself out of the jam he's in with the tax people.*

JAMMIES

* **jammies** (jam´ēz) (colloq.): pajamas (used esp. with small children) >*Bedtime, Mikey—let's put on your jammies.*

JAM-PACKED

* **jam-packed** (colloq.): completely full, crowded >*The cart was jam-packed with food.* >*You can hardly move around in that jam-packed mall.*

JAP

— **Jap** (jap) (sl., pej.): Japanese >*Don't call the Japanese Japs, stupid!* >*Don't call it Jap food, dummy!*

— **JAP** (= "Jewish-American Princess") (sl., pej.): Jewish girl (stereotyped as materialistic and self-centered) >*Sheila really hates all those awful JAP jokes.*

JAVA

— **java** (jav´ə/jä´və) (sl.): brewed coffee >*Bring us a couple of cups of java, will ya?*

JAYBIRD

— **(as) naked as a jaybird** (see **NAKED**)

JAZZ

— **jazz**[1] (sl.): nonsense, false or exaggerated story, lie >*Don't give me that jazz about your car breakin' down on your way here.*

— **jazz**[2] (sl.): liveliness, enthusiasm, spirit >*Put a little jazz in your life—try water skiin'.*

— **jazz**[3] (sl.): similar things, related items >*They sell tents, backpacks, camp stoves—all that jazz.* >*He studies radio, electronics, jazz like that.*

* **jazz**[4] (vt) (sl.): excite, enthuse >*He got everyone jazzed about the tour.*

* **jazz up** (vt) (sl.): enliven, make exciting, embellish >*We got to jazz his speech up a little.* >*I see they've jazzed up the place since I was last here.*

JAZZY

— **jazzy** (jaz´ē) (sl.): lively, flashy, showy >*He drove by in a real jazzy Cadillac convertible.*

JEEPERS

— **jeepers (creepers)!** (jē´pərz …) (colloq.): (interj. to express surprise, wonder, or concern) >*Jeepers! Where did that big dog come from?* >*Jeepers creepers! I'm going to get home real late.*

JEEZ

** **jeez!** (jēz) (colloq.): (interj. to express surprise, wonder, or disappointment) >*Jeez! I wish I could run like that.*

JELLYFISH

— **jellyfish** (colloq.): person of weak character or resolve >*That jellyfish won't stand up to him.*

JERK

** **jerk** (sl.): foolish and contemptible person, socially obnoxious or insensitive person (also voc.) >*Who invited that jerk, anyway?* >*Did ya hear him ask her if she was wearin' a wig? What a jerk!* >*Buzz off, jerk!*

— **jerk around**[1] (vi) (sl.): pass time idly, work halfheartedly or unproductively >*He got fired for jerkin' around on the job too much.*

— **jerk around**[2] (vt) (sl.): mislead, deceive, (esp. to delay s/one) >*If the cops find out you've been jerkin' 'em around with false information, you're gonna be in deep trouble.*

* **jerk off** (vi, vt) (vulg.): masturbate (said of a male) >*He said he jerks off when he's horny.* >*He paid the hooker to jerk him off.*

JERKWATER

— **jerkwater town** (colloq.): remote and insignificant town >*She grew up in some jerkwater town, but made it big as an actress in New York.*

JERKY

— **jerky** (sl.): foolish and contemptible, socially obnoxious or insensitive >*That jerky kid down the street just rode his bike through Mom's flower bed.*

JESUS FREAK

— **Jesus freak** (colloq., freq. pej.): fundamentalist Christian (esp. a zealous, young one) >*The Jesus freaks were holding a prayer meeting at the park.*

JEW

* **Jew** (colloq., pej.): Jewish >*The jerk said he didn't want to eat any Jew food.*

** **jew down** (vt) (sl., pej.): bargain with (s/one) until (he/she) reduces a price >*He said they were askin' five hundred dollars, but he jewed 'em down to four.*

JIBE

— **jibe** (jīb) (vi) (colloq.): be in accord, fit logically >*His story doesn't jibe with what the other kid told us.*

JIFF

— **in a jiff** (… jif) (colloq.): in an instant, in a very short time >*I'll have this ready for you in a jiff.*

JIFFY
— **in a jiffy** (... jif´ē) (colloq.): in an instant, in a very short time >*Wait here—I'll be back in a jiffy.*

JIG'S
— **the jig's up** (sl.): the game or scheme is over, it's futile to continue (a deceit or wrongdoing), there's no chance left >*The jig's up—they found out that he's been embezzlin' funds.*

JILLION
— **jillion** (jil´yən) (colloq.): very many, a huge number (of) >*There were a jillion people at the concert.*

JIM-DANDY
— **jim-dandy** (jim´dan´dē) (colloq.): excellent, top-quality >*They've bought theirselves a jim-dandy new house.*

JIMINY
— **jiminy!** (jim´ə nē) (colloq.): (interj. to express surprise or wonder) >*Jiminy! Did you see that falling star?*

JINGLE
— **give [s/one] a jingle** (colloq.): telephone [s/one] >*I'll give you a jingle tomorrow to let you know what's happening.*

JINX
* **jinx**¹ (jingks) (colloq.): thing or person seen as bringing bad luck >*You're a jinx. Every time you're with me in Las Vegas, I lose.*

* **jinx**² (vt) (colloq.): bring bad luck to >*Don't celebrate till we've won, or you'll jinx us.*

JITTERS
— **the jitters** (... jit´ərz) (colloq.): nervousness, nervous shaking or agitation >*I get the jitters just thinking about speaking in front of all those people.*

JIVE
— **jive**¹ (jīv) (sl.): nonsense, false or exaggerated story, lie >*Don't go believin' that jive about some big business deal he's workin' on.*

* **jive**² (vi, vt) (sl.): speak nonsense (to), exaggerate (a story) (to), tease >*He's just jivin' when he says he'll take ya to Houston with him. >Did she really, or are ya just jivin' me?*

— **jive**³ (sl.): deceitful, pretentious >*Don't trust that jive dude. >Get outta here with your jive bullshit!*

JOB
* **job** (sl.): criminal act (esp. a theft or robbery) >*They pulled a convenience store job and then got outta town.*

— **do a job on**¹ (sl.): defeat or beat severely >*Those guys really did a job on Casey after he picked a fight with 'em.*

— **do a job on**² (sl.): deceive, mistreat, hurt >*He did a job on his wife when he dumped her for that teenage bimbo. >Dugan did a real job on his thumb with the power saw.*

— **have [one's] work/job cut out for [one]** (see **WORK**)

— **... job** (sl.): distinctive type of ..., example of ... >*Whose little Italian job is that parked out front? >How much is that chrome job with the pearl handle?*

— **lay/lie down on the job** (see **LAY**)

— **on the job** (colloq.): alert, observant >*The supervisor was really on the job to catch that little defect.*

JOCK
** **jock** (jok) (sl., freq. pej.): athlete (esp. one obsessed by athletics) (also adj.) >*Do those jocks ever study? >He's a great athlete, but he doesn't have a jock mentality.*

JOCKEY
— **jockey** (vi, vt) (colloq.): drive, maneuver, manipulate (s/thing) >*See if you can jockey the truck in back of the store. >He's jockeying for the chairmanship of the committee. >Let me jockey these figures around and see if I can get them to come out right.*

JOE–JUG

— ... **jockey** (colloq.): driver or operator of a ..., ... controller >*We need some good bulldozer jockeys for the highway project.* >*All the tank jockeys were out on maneuvers.*

JOE

* **Joe ...** (colloq.): the typical ... (type or group of men) >*Joe Taxpayer is tired of government waste.* >*When Joe Union Member hears about this, he's going to go out on strike.*

* **... Joe** (colloq.): ... man, ... fellow >*The average Joe doesn't give a damn about local politics.* >*Kyle's a good Joe. He'll help us out.*

JOE BLOW

— **Joe Blow** (sl.): the average man >*Joe Blow doesn't care about the details, just about how it's gonna affect him.*

JOHN

* **john¹** (sl.): toilet, bathroom >*If ya gotta use the john, it's down the hall.*

— **john²** (sl.): prostitute's customer >*They arrested a hooker and her john in the motel room.*

JOHN HANCOCK

* **[one's] John Hancock** (jon´han´kok) (colloq.): [one's] signature >*Just put your John Hancock on the dotted line, and it's all legal.*

JOHN HENRY

— **[one's] John Henry** (jon´hen´rē) (colloq.): [one's] signature >*That's his John Henry on the contract, all right.*

JOHN Q. PUBLIC

— **John Q. Public** (colloq.): the average or typical citizen >*Do you think John Q. Public really knows why they passed that legislation?*

JOIN

* **join the club!** (sl.): I'm/we're in that situation too! you're not the only one to suffer or experience that! >*You flunked the psych exam? Join the club! Most of us did.*

JOINT

* **joint¹** (sl.): marijuana cigarette >*He was just sittin' there smokin' a joint and llstenin' to music.*

* **joint²** (sl.): public establishment or accommodation (esp. a cheap, dilapidated, or disreputable one) >*I ain't gonna eat in this joint.* >*When are ya gonna move outta this crummy joint?* >*He eats at that hamburger joint.*

— **have [one's] nose (all) out of joint** (see NOSE)

— **put [s/one's] nose (all) out of joint** (see NOSE)

— **the joint** (sl.): prison >*He spent a couple of years in the joint for auto theft.*

JOKER

* **joker** (sl.): man, guy (esp. seen as obnoxious or contemptible) >*Some joker in a pickup truck slammed into my rear fender.*

JOLLIES

— **get [one's] jollies** (... jol´ēz) (sl.): have capricious or mischievous fun, get [one's] thrills or excitement >*They get their jollies by overturnin' trash cans late at night.*

JONESES

— **keep up with the Joneses** (see KEEP)

JOSH

— **josh** (josh) (vi, vt) (colloq.): jest or joke (with), tease >*Take it easy, man! I'm just joshing.* >*Are you joshing me? That can't be right.*

JOYSTICK

— **joystick** (colloq.): control lever of a vehicle or machine >*This joystick controls the whole video game.*

JUG

— **the jug** (sl.): jail >*I gotta go bail old Rufus outta the jug.*

JUGS

— **jugs** (sl., freq. vulg.): (woman's) large breasts >*He said the dancer had some jugs on her!*

JUICE

— **juice**[1] (colloq.): electrical energy >*This air conditioner uses a lot of juice.*

— **juice**[2] (sl.): liquor >*Pete's been hittin' the juice pretty hard lately—he needs to dry out.*

— **juice up** (vt) (colloq.): enliven, make exciting >*They should have juiced up the movie with a little sex and violence.*

JUICED

— **juiced (up)** (sl.): drunk >*Meryl was pretty juiced by the time the party ended.*

JUICY

* **juicy** (colloq.): exciting, scandalous >*I've got a juicy bit of gossip about Dora's sister.* >*Tell me about it, and give me all the juicy details!*

JUMBO

** **jumbo** (jum´bō) (colloq.): very large (size) (also noun) >*Buy the jumbo size—you know how those boys eat.* >*Give the kid a regular popcorn, and I'll take a jumbo.*

JUMP

* **jump**[1] (vt) (colloq.): assault or attack without warning (esp. from ambush) >*They jumped him on the corner and stole his watch.*

* **jump**[2] (vi) (sl.): be full of noisy or exciting activity, have a festive atmosphere >*That joint was really jumpin' Saturday night.*

— **a hop, skip, and a jump** (see HOP)

— **(about) jump out of [one's] skin** (colloq.): be very startled, become very frightened >*She about jumped out of her skin when she heard the shot.*

* **get the jump on** (colloq.): get a head start on, gain an initial advantage over >*They got the jump on us, so we're going to have to work real hard to catch up.*

— **go jump in the lake!** (sl.): get out of here! stop annoying me! >*Ah, you and your conspiracy crap! Go jump in the lake!*

** **jump all over** (colloq.): severely scold or rebuke, verbally attack >*The boss jumped all over me just because I forgot to lock the storeroom.*

— **jump at** (colloq.): eagerly take (an opportunity) >*I'd jump at the chance to act on Broadway.*

— **jump/skip bail** (colloq.): flee while free on bail >*He jumped bail and left town.*

— **jump [s/one's] bones** (sl., freq. vulg.): have sex with [s/one], get physical with [s/one] (in order to have sex) >*Man, would I like to jump her bones!*

* **jump down [s/one's] throat** (colloq.): respond to [s/one] quickly and angrily, rebuke or criticize [s/one] immediately and violently (for what he/she has said) >*Susan jumped down Rich's throat before he even finished his crack about women.*

— **jump on** (colloq.): scold or rebuke, verbally attack >*Don't go jumping on me! It wasn't my fault.*

— **jump/hop/get on the bandwagon** (see BANDWAGON)

— **jump ship** (colloq.): abandon (a group or cause), withdraw (one's) support (for an enterprise) >*If they don't show results soon, their investors are going to jump ship.*

* **jump the gun** (colloq.): begin before (one) should, act too hastily >*Let's not jump the gun—we'll wait a day or two and see what develops.*

— **jump through hoops** (colloq.): do anything (that s/one orders or requests) unquestioningly >*She's got him eating out of her hand and jumping through hoops.* >*He'd jump through hoops for his boss.*

* **one jump ahead (of)** (colloq.): having already foreseen or acted on (s/thing) (before), one step ahead (of) >*I'm one jump ahead of you—I already took care of it.* >*You got to stay one jump ahead, or you can lose control of the situation quick.*

JUMPY

** **jumpy** (jum´pē) (colloq.): nervous, easily startled >*You're acting real jumpy. How much coffee have you had today?*

JUNGLE BUNNY

— **jungle bunny** (sl., pej.): black person >*He called Leroy a jungle bunny, so Leroy call him a jive honkey.*

JUNK

** **junk**[1] (colloq.): (one's) belongings, things in general >*Tell him not to leave his junk on my bed!* >*Get your junk and let's go.* >*What do you want me to do with all the junk on the porch?*

— **junk**[2] (sl.): heroin >*He robs people for money to buy junk.*

** **junk**[3] (colloq.): worthless, low-quality, cheap >*I hate getting all this junk mail.* >*You should fix you some good meals instead of eating all that junk food.*

— **hunk/pile/piece of junk** (colloq.): dilapidated or useless machine (esp. an automobile) >*Why don't you trade in that hunk of junk on a new car?* >*This pile of junk's beyond repair.*

JUNKER

— **junker** (jung´kər) (sl.): dilapidated or useless automobile (esp. one not worth repairing) >*We can't give ya much for this junker.*

JUNK HEAP

— **junk heap** (colloq.): dilapidated or useless automobile >*How does he get to work and back in that junk heap?*

JUNKIE

** **junkie** (jung´kē) (sl.): heroin addict >*Mostly junkies and hookers live there.*

— **... junkie** (colloq.): ... enthusiast or devotee, person with an excessive desire for ... >*The guy's a tennis junkie—plays twice a day, every day.* >*You bought seven different flavors?! You're a real ice cream junkie.*

JUST

— **you just ain't (a-)whistlin' Dixie!** (see WHISTLING)

K

K.

— **K.** (sl.): thousand >*He makes a hundred K. a year, easy.*

KAPUT

* **kaput** (kə pŭt′/kə pūt′) (sl.): ruined, finished, unsuccessful, broken >*If Doyle pulls out, the whole operation's kaput.* >*Nothing's happenin'—the TV's kaput.*

— **go kaput** (sl.): become ruined, fail, break down >*All of a sudden the washing machine went kaput—it just stopped.*

KEEN

— **keen** (sl.): excellent, wonderful >*That was a really keen ride! Can we go on it again?*

KEEP

— **keep (a/the/[one's]) ...** (see entry under ... noun)

— **keep on trucking** (see **TRUCKING**)

— **keep [s/thing] under [one's] hat** (colloq.): keep [s/thing] secret or confidential >*I heard some real juicy gossip about Gibson, but you've got to keep it under your hat.*

— **keep up with the Joneses** (... jōn′zəz) (colloq.): not be outdone materially or socially by (one's) neighbors or colleagues >*They went broke trying to keep up with the Joneses.*

KEEPER

— **keeper** (sl.): thing or person worth keeping, thing or person not to be discarded or lost >*The book is OK, but it's not a keeper.* >*Don't ruin it with that neat girl—she's a keeper.*

KEEPERS

— **finders keepers(, losers weepers)!** (see **FINDERS**)

KEEPING

— **where (have) you been keeping yourself?** (see **WHERE**)

KEEPS

* **for keeps[1]** (colloq.): permanently, for always >*You can have my ring for keeps.* >*They're together now for keeps.*

— **for keeps[2]** (colloq.): with serious intent, seriously and definitively (also adj.) >*Don't mess with that thug—he plays for keeps.* >*This isn't a game. This trial is for keeps.*

KEESTER

— **keester** (see "KEISTER")

KEISTER

— **keister** (kē′stər) (sl.): buttocks, rump >*Get off your keister and help us out!*

KETTLE OF FISH

— **kettle of fish** (colloq.): troublesome situation, predicament, mess >*That's a fine kettle of fish he's gotten himself into by lying.*

KEY

— **key** (sl.): kilogram (of an illicit drug) >*The cops found five keys of marijuana on the boat.*

KIBITZ

— **kibitz** (kib′its) (vi) (colloq.): look on and offer uninvited advice or comments >*Morley loves to kibitz while we're trying to concentrate.*

KICK

* **kick[1]** (colloq.): enjoyable or exciting experience or person, thrill >*Taking the rapids in a raft is a real kick.* >*Your funny brother-in-law's a kick.*

— **kick[2]** (colloq.): ability to intoxicate >*This vodka's a hundred proof. It's really got a kick.*

** **kick[3]** (vt) (sl.): free (oneself) of or give up (s/thing addictive) >*He's been snortin' cocaine so long I don't think he can kick the habit.* >*I got to kick these damn cigarettes.*

— **kick[4]** (vi) (colloq.): complain, voice objections >*The farmers are kicking because the government lowered some*

KICK

price subsidies. *>You ain't got nothing to kick about in this easy job.*

kick⁵ (vt) (sl.): release from custody *>The cops didn't have any real evidence, so they kicked him.*

* **could kick [oneself]** (colloq.): regret (one's action), be angry with [oneself] *>I could kick myself for not investing with them three years ago. >Stu kicked himself when he found out what he'd missed.*

** **get a kick out of** (colloq.): very much enjoy, become thrilled or excited by *>I really get a kick out of watching my dogs play.*

— **... kick** (colloq.): intense but short-lived interest in ..., ... fad *>The pet rock kick didn't last long.*

* **kick around¹** (vt) (colloq.): mistreat, treat unjustly *>I'm tired of being kicked around by my supervisor.*

* **kick around²** (vt) (colloq.): discuss, consider the merits of (an idea or proposal) *>Management kicked his idea around for a while, but finally decided against it.*

— **kick around³** (vi) (colloq.): move from place to place or job to job (for a certain period), be on the move (instead of settling down) *>He kicked around for a few years on the East Coast before finally buying a house in Seattle.*

** **kick [s/one's] ass** (vulg.): defeat [s/one] decisively, beat [s/one] up *>The team got their ass kicked on Friday. >Dwayne picked the fight, but the dude kicked his ass.*

* **kick back¹** (vi) (colloq.): relax, take it easy *>I need a couple of days to kick back before I take on another project.*

* **kick back²** (vt) (colloq.): pay (an amount or percentage to a person whose influential intervention makes an income possible) (esp. when unethical or illicit) *>They kick back ten percent to the supervisor who arranges the contracts.*

* **kick [s/one's] butt** (sl., freq. vulg.): defeat [s/one] decisively, beat [s/one] up *>We're gonna kick their butts in the playoffs. >Don't mouth off, or I'll kick your butt!*

* **kick in¹** (vt) (colloq.): contribute, pay (one's share) *>If everyone kicks in five bucks we can buy a keg of beer.*

* **kick in²** (vi) (colloq.): become mechanically engaged, take effect, start up *>It was so hot the air conditioning kicked in by ten in the morning. >I hope that aspirin kicks in pretty soon, because this headache's pretty bad.*

— **kick in the teeth** (sl.): unexpected shock, undeserved and surprising mistreatment *>It was a real kick in the teeth when he found out she'd been goin' out with other guys behind his back.*

** **kick off¹** (vt) (colloq.): inaugurate, initiate (s/thing planned) *>He's going to kick off his campaign next week.*

— **kick off²** (vi) (sl.): die (esp. of old age) *>The old man got pneumonia and kicked off a week later.*

** **kick out** (vt) (colloq.): eject, dismiss, oust *>They kicked him out of school for missing too many classes. >If you don't pay your dues, you're going to get kicked out of the club.*

* **kick (some) ass** (vulg.): discipline or punish (s/one), control (a group) with strictness or power tactics *>The coach is really gonna kick ass after the lousy way the team played last night. >We need a new manager to come in here and kick some ass.*

— **kick (some) butt** (sl., freq. vulg.): discipline or punish (s/one), control (a group) with strictness or power tactics *>Dad's gonna kick butt when he sees this mess. >If they get outta line he'll start kickin' some butt.*

— **kick the bucket** (sl.): die >*He came into a lot of dough when his old man kicked the bucket.*

— **beat/kick the heck out of** (see HECK)

— **beat/kick the hell out of** (see HELL)

— **beat/knock/kick the (living) shit out of** (see SHIT)

— **kick up [one's] heels** (colloq.): celebrate, behave uninhibitedly >*The cowboys really like to kick up their heels in the local bars when they come into town.*

* **on a ... kick** (colloq.): having an intense but short-lived interest in ..., following a ... fad >*Jan's been on a science fiction kick the last few weeks.*

KICKBACK

* **kickback** (colloq.): an amount or percentage given to a person whose influential intervention makes an income possible (esp. when unethical or illicit) >*That crooked city manager's made a bundle of money from contractor kickbacks over the years.*

KICKER

— **kicker** (colloq.): drawback, unexpected disadvantage, unexpected outcome >*He's gorgeous and sweet as can be, but the kicker is that he's gay.* >*The kicker was that when they got to his house, they found out he had left to go see them.*

KICKING

— **alive and kicking** (see ALIVE)

— **still kicking** (colloq.): still alive >*She's real old and a little senile, but still kicking.*

KICKOFF

* **kickoff** (colloq.): inauguration, beginning (of s/thing planned) >*The mayor's going to speak at the kickoff for the festival.*

KICKS

* **kicks** (colloq.): capricious or mischievous fun, thrills or amusement >*They were driving around breaking windows just for kicks.* >*He gets his kicks racing motorcycles.*

KID

** **kid**[1] (kid) (colloq.): child or young person, son or daughter >*He's in charge? Why, he's just a kid.* >*She's only twenty-two, and she's already got four kids.*

** **kid**[2] (vi, vt) (colloq.): jest or joke (with), tease >*No, not really, I'm just kidding.* >*Don't let Davis kid you. It's not as easy as he says.*

— **kid**[3] (voc.) (colloq.): friend, sweetheart (used esp. with s/one younger or to show intimacy) >*Hey, don't worry, kid—you'll learn the ropes.* >*You're looking good today, kid.*

— **I kid you not** (colloq.): I'm serious, I'm not joking >*He was too wearing pantyhose! I kid you not.*

** **kid around (with)** (colloq.): jest or joke (with), tease >*Stop kidding around! Tell me exactly what happened.* >*Don't get mad! I just like to kid around with you.*

— **kid brother/sister** (colloq.): younger brother/sister >*It was my kid sister's idea.*

— **new kid on the block** (see NEW)

— **the kid** (sl.): I, me >*Don't mess with the kid, or I'll knock your block off.*

KIDDING

** **no kidding** (... kid´ing) (colloq.): honestly, truthfully, really >*No kidding? You really got the job?* >*Your smoking bothers me a lot—no kidding.*

KIDDO

— **kiddo** (kid´ō) (voc.) (colloq.): friend, sweetheart (used esp. with s/one younger or to show intimacy) >*Give me a kiss, kiddo.*

KIDDY

* **kiddy** (kid´ē) (colloq.): child (esp. a young one) (also adj.) >*We have a special show for the kiddies.* >*Julie,* *you have to stay in the kiddy end of the pool.*

KID STUFF

* **kid stuff** (kid …) (colloq.): s/thing that is very easy or infantile >*Making those shelves will be kid stuff, Andrea.* >*Do we have to do these exercises? They're kid stuff.*

KIKE

— **kike** (kīk) (sl., pej.): Jew (also adj.) >*You'd better not call anyone a kike in this part of town.* >*I hate it when he calls it the kike neighborhood.*

KILL

* **kill**[1] (vt) (colloq.): overwhelm, astonish, perturb >*It kills me how he completely ignores his wife.*

* **kill**[2] (vt) (colloq.): delight, make laugh >*That guy kills me with his impersonations of actors.*

* **kill**[3] (vt) (colloq.): completely consume, finish off (esp. a quantity of liquor) >*Debbie and Pat killed that bottle of sherry last night.*

* **(about) kill** (vt) (colloq.): be a great sacrifice or painful experience for >*It about killed her when she found out her son was using drugs.* >*It killed me to pay that much, but I had no choice.*

— **dress to kill** (see **DRESS**)

* **would kill** (colloq.): would pay any price, be willing to make a great sacrifice >*I'd kill for a hot cup of coffee right about now.* >*Most people would kill to have the kind of job you have.*

KILLER

* **killer**[1] (colloq.): very painful or demanding activity or experience (also adj.) >*That job was a killer.* >*The real killer was having to march twenty miles with full packs.* >*They say that prof gives killer exams.*

* **killer**[2] (sl.): sensational or very impressive performance or experience (also adj.) >*His latest concert's a real*

killer. >*She gave a killer performance in that movie.* >*He's got a killer smile.*

— **killer**[3] (colloq., sarc.): presumably tough or fearsome person (also voc.) >*Oh, yeah, Ralphie's a real killer—I'm shaking in my boots, I'm so afraid.* >*Hey, killer, does your mommy know you're out this late?*

KILLING

* **make a killing** (colloq.): make an unusually large profit, earn a lot of money >*He made a killing in real estate last year.*

KILTER

— **out of kilter** (… kil´tər) (colloq.): not working well, not adjusted properly >*Feels like the front-wheel alignment's a little out of kilter.*

KIND

** **kind of**[1] (colloq.): somewhat, rather, fairly >*She's no beauty queen, but she's kind of pretty.* >*I kind of wanted to see the other movie.* >*I thought this would go fast, but it's going kind of slow.*

** **kind of**[2] (colloq.): amount of (money) (esp. seen as a large amount) >*For the kind of dough Crenshaw makes, he can take a little criticism.* >*What kind of money are we talking about on this deal?*

— **some kind of (a)** (see **SOME**)

KINDA

** **kinda** (kīn´də) (colloq.): kind of >*What kinda ice cream ya got?* >*He's kinda short for pro basketball.*

KINDS

— **all kinds (of …)** (see **ALL**)

KINGDOM

— **kingdom come** (colloq.): very remote place or future time >*The bomb blew the house to kingdom come.* >*I thought that boring guy was going to keep talking till kingdom come.*

KINGPIN

— **kingpin** (colloq.): leader, person of critical importance (esp. in a criminal organization) >*They're trying to nail the kingpin of drug distribution in this area.*

KINKY

* **kinky** (sl.): sexually bizarre >*What they do with those leather straps is pretty kinky.* >*Do they go in for kinky sex?*

KISS

* **kiss ([s/one's]) ass** (vulg.): be servile or obsequious (to [s/one]) to gain favor (with) or adulate ([him/her]), flatter ([s/one]) to gain favor >*You think kissin' my ass is gonna get ya anywhere?* >*He got the promotion by kissin' ass.*

* **kiss [s/thing] good-bye** (sl.): give [s/thing] up, accept [s/thing] as lost >*You can kiss your inheritance good-bye if ya get the old lady mad at ya.*

— **kiss off** (vt) (sl.): give up, accept as lost, see (oneself) rid of >*I kissed off my promotion when I disagreed with the boss.* >*Honey, you'd better kiss that jerk off.*

— **kiss off!** (sl.): go away! stop annoying me! >*Kiss off! I ain't interested.* >*He told the door-to-door salesman to kiss off.*

* **kiss my ass!** (vulg.): (interj. to express great anger or contempt to s/one) >*Me, apologize to you? Kiss my ass!*

* **kiss up to** (sl.): be servile or obsequious to in order to gain favor, adulate, flatter to gain favor >*He thinks he'll get to direct 'cause he kisses up to the producer.*

KISS-ASS

* **kiss-ass** (vulg.): person who is servile or obsequious to gain favor, adulator, servile flatterer >*Some kiss-ass was tellin' the boss how good he looked in his new suit.*

KISSER

— **kisser** (sl.): mouth area, face >*He got slugged right in the kisser.*

KISS-OFF

— **the kiss-off** (sl.): a dismissal, an act of firing or rejection >*The store gave Drew the kiss-off four months ago, and he hasn't worked since.*

KIT

— **the (whole) kit and caboodle** (... kə bū̄d´l) (colloq.): the whole lot, the complete package, everything involved >*I want the big hard drive, the enhanced keyboard, the CD-ROM reader, the modem—the whole kit and caboodle.*

KITCHEN SINK

— **everything but the kitchen sink** (see **EVERYTHING**)

KITE

— **(as) high as a kite** (see **HIGH**)

— **go fly a kite!** (see **FLY**)

— **higher than a kite** (see **HIGHER**)

KITTENS

— **have kittens** (sl.): become furious, lose emotional control >*Mom will have kittens if she finds out what I did.*

KITTY

** **kitty** (kit´ē) (colloq.): kitten, cat (also voc.) >*Look at the pretty kitty!* >*Here kitty, kitty!*

KLEENEX

** **Kleenex** (klē´neks) (colloq.): disposable paper tissue, paper handkerchief >*Marge used up two boxes of Kleenex when she had her cold.*

KLEPTO

— **klepto** (klep´tō) (sl.): kleptomaniac >*That clown's a damn klepto—he'll swipe anything he can get his hands on.*

KLUTZ

* **klutz** (kluts) (sl.): clumsy or awkward person, bungler >*Don't let that klutz handle the dishes!*

KLUTZY

* **klutzy** (klut´sē) (sl.): clumsy, awkward, inept >*We're gonna have to fire that klutzy secretary. He manages to screw up everything.*

KNEE-JERK

— **knee-jerk** (colloq.): reacting automatically or unthinkingly (according to an ingrained attitude or philosophy) >*The knee-jerk reactionaries are going to holler as soon as they hear this proposal.* >*Cut out the knee-jerk reactions and think things through.*

KNEES

— **cut [s/one] off at the knees** (see **CUT**)

KNIFE

— **stab/knife [s/one] in the back** (see **STAB**)

— **under the knife** (colloq.): in surgery, having an operation >*She goes under the knife tomorrow to have her gallbladder taken out.*

KNOCK

— **knock**[1] (sl.): critical remark, instance of criticism >*If ya go into politics, ya gotta be able to take the knocks.*

* **knock**[2] (vt) (sl.): criticize, find fault with >*Don't knock it—it's better than nothin'.* >*Mom's always knockin' the guys I hang around with.*

— **knock around**[1] (vt) (colloq.): beat, physically abuse >*He started knocking her around, so she moved out.*

— **knock around**[2] (vi) (colloq.): pass time idly, wander aimlessly >*Me and Grover knocked around together when we were kids.* >*We knocked around downtown for a couple of hours, then came home.*

— **knock back** (vt) (sl.): drink quickly, gulp down (esp. an alcoholic drink) >*He knocked back three shots of whiskey in a row.*

— **knock [s/one's] block off** (sl.): beat [s/one] up, thrash [s/one] >*Shut up, or I'll knock your block off!*

— **knock [s/one] dead** (sl.): greatly surprise or impress [s/one], delight [s/one] >*You're gonna knock 'em dead with those tricks, kid.*

— **knock down** (vt) (sl.): receive as salary or income >*He knocks down about five grand a month.*

— **take/knock [s/one] down a peg (or two)** (see **TAKE**)

— **knock/cut [s/one] down to size** (colloq.): destroy [s/one's] arrogance or presumptuousness, deflate [s/one] >*She really knocked that pompous ass down to size by correcting him every time he said something wrong.*

— **knock [s/one] for a loop** (colloq.): hit [s/one] very hard >*The bull charged and knocked him for a loop.*

— **throw/knock [s/one] for a loop** (see **THROW**)

** **knock off**[1] (vt) (sl.): stop (an undesirable activity) (used esp. as a command) >*Knock off the yellin'! I can't hear a thing on TV.* >*Ya know I don't like ya badmouthin' my mother, so knock it off!*

* **knock off**[2] (vt) (colloq.): reduce (a certain amount from the price of s/thing) >*I'll knock four bucks off the price if you buy them both.*

— **knock off**[3] (vi) (colloq.): stop working, cease work for a while >*We've put in ten hours on this—let's knock off for today.*

— **knock off**[4] (vt) (sl.): kill, murder >*The mafia had him knocked off 'cause he informed on 'em.*

— **knock off**[5] (vt) (sl.): rob (an establishment) (esp. when armed) >*The robbers knocked off five banks in three days.*

— **knock off**[6] (vt) (sl.): eat or drink quickly, devour, guzzle >*He was hungry! He knocked off two big steaks and two baked potatoes in no time.*

* **knock out**[1] (vt) (colloq.): destroy, eliminate, make inoperable >*The missile knocked the tank out.* >*The scandal knocked him out of the race.* >*The power got knocked out in the storm.*

— **knock out**[2] (vt) (colloq.): produce quickly or easily >*That author knocks out at least three books a year.*

* **knock [oneself] out** (colloq.): work hard, put out great effort (to reach a goal) >*She knocked herself out getting the party together.*

— **knock over** (vt) (sl.): rob (an establishment) (esp. when armed) >*The junkie knocked over a liquor store to get money for drugs.*

— **knock [s/one's] socks off** (sl.): greatly surprise or impress [s/one], delight [s/one] >*Her singin's gonna knock their socks off.*

— **beat/knock the (living) daylights out of** (see DAYLIGHTS)

— **beat/knock/kick the (living) shit out of** (see SHIT)

— **beat/knock the stuffing out of** (see STUFFING)

— **beat/knock the tar out of** (see TAR)

* **knock up** (vt) (sl., freq. vulg.): make pregnant >*Her old man wanted to know who knocked her up.*

KNOCK-DOWN-DRAG-OUT

* **knock-down-drag-out** (colloq.): hard-hitting or violent (fight), action-filled (fight) (also noun) >*It was a knock-down-drag-out fight that almost destroyed the place.* >*The neighbors were having a knock-down-drag-out last night.*

KNOCKED

— **have [s/thing] knocked** (sl.): be assured of success with [s/thing], have [s/thing] virtually achieved >*If we can get Barney's support we got this project knocked.* >*They have it knocked with the grant they're gettin'.*

* **knocked up** (sl., freq. vulg.): pregnant >*When she found out she was knocked up, she ran away from home.*

KNOCKERS

— **knockers** (sl., freq. vulg.): (woman's) breasts (esp. large or shapely ones) >*He says she has nice knockers on her.*

KNOCKOUT

* **knockout** (colloq.): extremely attractive person (esp. a woman) >*Patsy's really pretty, and her sister's a knockout, too.*

KNOT

— **tie the knot** (see TIE)

KNOTHEAD

— **knothead** (colloq.): stupid or inept person, fool >*That knothead's confusing everyone.*

KNOW

* **in the know** (colloq.): having special or secret knowledge or information, well-informed >*Those in the know are buying up that stock.*

— **know [s/thing] backward(s) and forward(s)** (see BACKWARD)

— **know [s/thing] cold** (see COLD)

— **know [s/thing] inside out** (see INSIDE)

— **know [one's] stuff** (see STUFF)

— **know the score** (see SCORE)

— **know [one's] way around ([s/thing, s/where])** (see WAY)

* **not (even) know [s/one] is alive** (colloq.): not notice [s/one] at all, not give [s/one] any attention >*He's so dreamy, but he doesn't even know I'm alive.*

** **not know about** (colloq.): have doubts or suspicions about >*I don't know about that guy—there's something weird about him.*

* **not know/can't tell [one's] ass from a hole in the ground** (vulg.): not know what [one] is doing or saying, be incompetent, be stupid or ignorant >*Don't take Lew's word on it. He don't know his ass from a hole in the ground.* >*You can't tell your ass from a hole in the ground, so shut up!*

— **not know/can't tell [s/thing] from a hole in the ground** (sl.): be completely ignorant about [s/thing], know nothing about [s/thing] >*Jimmy, do a tune-up? He doesn't know a spark plug from a hole in the ground.*

* **not know [s/one] from Adam** (... ad´əm) (colloq.): be completely unacquainted with [s/one], not recognize [s/one] at all >*He greeted me like a long-lost friend, but I didn't know him from Adam.*

— **not know shit from shinola** (... shit ... shī´nō´lə) (vulg.): not know what (one) is doing or saying, be incompetent, be stupid or ignorant >*I know he'll screw it up—he doesn't know shit from shinola.*

* **not know which end/way is up** (colloq.): not know what is happening, be totally confused, be stupid >*You can't put Waldo in charge of this operation—he doesn't know which end is up.*

* **you know ...** (freq. ya ...) (colloq.): uh ... (crutch phrase to fill a pause or introduce s/thing hard to express) >*I want to, you know, try out for the part of, you know, the hero's buddy.*

* **wouldn't you know it!** (colloq.): (interj. to express dismay or fatalism over an ironic complication or unfortunate surprise) >*Wouldn't you know it! Right after I got into the bathtub, the damn phone rang.*

KNOW-HOW

* **know-how** (colloq.): expertise, knowledge and ability (to accomplish s/thing) >*If you need a manual written, Pablo's got the know-how.*

KNOW-IT-ALL

* **know-it-all** (colloq.): person who acts as though he/she knew everything (esp. in an obnoxious way), presumed expert (also adj.) >*I hate having that know-it-all always interrupt.* >*Her know-it-all attitude is getting on everyone's nerves.*

KNUCKLEHEAD

— **knucklehead** (colloq.): stupid or inept person, fool >*Did you really expect that knucklehead to do it right?*

KNUCKLE SANDWICH

— **knuckle sandwich** (sl., hum.): blow with the fist to (s/one's) mouth >*You'd better shut up if ya don't wanna knuckle sandwich.*

K.O.

— **K.O.** (= "knock out") (vt) (sl.): knock out, knock unconscious >*Hector K.O.ed the guy with a piece of lumber.*

KOOK

— **kook** (kūk) (sl.): very strange or eccentric person, crazy person >*Some kook came to my door tryin' to sell me a ticket to Mars.* >*Who's the kook with the orange hat?*

KOOKY

— **kooky** (kū´kē) (sl.): eccentric, very strange, crazy >*I don't like the kooky ideas my son's learnin' at that school.*

KOSHER

* **kosher** (colloq.): proper, fair, legitimate >*It's just not kosher to give confidential information to help your friend's business.*

K.P.

— **K.P.** (= "kitchen police/patrol") (colloq.): cleaning up of the kitchen, washing of the dishes >*I cooked, so you do K.P.*

KRAUT

— **kraut** (krout) (sl., pej.): German >*He said they called 'em krauts during the war.* >*It's German food, not kraut food, ya jerk!*

L

L.A.

** **L.A.** (colloq.): Los Angeles, California
>*He moved to L.A. because he got tired of the cold winters in the Midwest.*

LADY

— **[one's] lady** (colloq.): [one's] wife, [one's] sweetheart or steady companion (a woman) >*Your lady's a fine woman, Doug.*

* **[one's] old lady**[1] (sl., freq. pej.): [one's] mother >*Trent's old lady won't let him go to the movies.*

— **[one's] old lady**[2] (sl., freq. pej.): [one's] wife or girlfriend >*Your old lady's gonna yell at ya if ya come home drunk.*

LADY-KILLER

— **lady-killer** (colloq.): man whom women find sexually or romantically irresistible (esp. a promiscuous man) >*That lady-killer has broken more hearts than you can imagine.*

LAID

— **get laid (by)** (vulg.): have sex (with) >*He says he hopes to get laid tonight.* >*Monica said she got laid by him last night.*

LAID-BACK

* **laid-back** (sl.): relaxed, unworried, carefree, easygoing >*Josh's real laid-back. Nothin' ever bugs him.* >*It was a laid-back kinda party.*

LAKE

— **go jump in the lake!** (see **JUMP**)

LAM

— **on the lam** (... lam) (sl.): escaping, hiding (esp. from the police) >*He's been on the lam ever since he robbed that bank in Lubbock.*

LAMBAST

— **lambast** (lam bast´) (see "LAMBASTE")

LAMBASTE

— **lambaste** (lam bāst´) (vt) (colloq.): reprimand, severely criticize, berate >*He got lambasted in the newspapers for using ethnic slurs.*

LAME

* **lame** (sl.): bad, uninteresting, inadequate >*His so-called party was really lame.*

LAMEBRAIN

— **lamebrain** (colloq.): stupid or inept person, fool >*Keep an eye on that lamebrain so he doesn't mess us up.*

LAMEBRAINED

— **lamebrained** (lām´brānd´) (colloq.): stupid, foolish >*Whose lamebrained idea was it to start the stove with gasoline?*

LAND

* **land** (vt) (colloq.): win, secure, obtain, capture >*He landed a big clean-up contract with the city.* >*I envy whoever lands that gorgeous guy.*

LANGUAGE

— **speak [s/one's] language** (see **SPEAK**)

— **speak the same language** (see **SPEAK**)

LAP

— **(drop [s/thing]) in [s/one's] lap** (colloq.): (make [s/thing]) [s/one's] responsibility or obligation >*She dropped the problem in her husband's lap.* >*I don't want this project in my lap.*

— **lap up** (vt) (colloq.): accept eagerly, receive enthusiastically >*He was sweet-talking them, and they were lapping it up.*

LAPTOP

* **laptop** (colloq.): small and portable personal computer >*I'll work on it on my laptop while I'm on the plane.*

LARD

— **tub of lard** (see **TUB**)

LARDASS
— **lardass** (lärd´as´) (vulg., pej.): very fat person (esp. one with fat buttocks) (also voc.) >*That lardass's gonna break the chair.* >*Hurry up and get on the bus, lardass!*

LATCH
* **latch onto** (colloq.): join or accompany with persistence, cling to, grab, obtain >*Some boring guy latched onto me at the party, and I couldn't get rid of him.* >*Where'd you latch onto that old six-gun?*

LATE
— **will be late to/for [one's] own funeral** (colloq., hum.): is habitually late >*Let's not wait for Frank—he'll be late to his own funeral.*

LATER
* **later!** (sl.): so long! see you later! >*Later, guy! I gotta run.*

LATHER
— **(all) in a lather** (... laŏ´ər) (colloq.): very troubled or agitated, very nervous or excited >*Eloise's all in a lather about her court appearance.*

LATS
— **lats** (lats) (colloq.): latissimus dorsi muscles >*This exercise is good for your lats.*

LAUGH
* **laugh**[1] (colloq.): person or thing worthy of contempt or ridicule, laughable person or thing >*The mayor's so-called Corruption Task Force is a laugh because half its members are taking bribes.* >*Him, a policeman? That's a laugh.*

— **laugh**[2] (colloq.): amusing or funny person or thing >*Invite Virgil to the party—the guy's a laugh.*

— **laugh it up** (colloq.): laugh and joke (esp. continuously) >*The guys were off in one corner laughing it up all night.*

* **laugh [s/one] out of** (colloq.): drive [s/one] out of, destroy [s/one's] credibility in (through ridicule or scorn) >*They'll laugh you out of court if you file that stupid lawsuit.* >*He was laughed out of the university because of his flying saucer theories.*

LAUGHS
* **laughs** (colloq.): capricious or mischievous fun, thrills or amusement >*We used to knock over garbage cans for laughs.* >*Watching him trying to explain it to the cops was good for a few laughs.*

— **a barrel of laughs** (see BARREL)

LAUNDER
* **launder** (vt) (colloq.): conceal the source of (money) by transferring or converting it through an intermediary >*He said some foreign bank was laundering drug money for a ten percent cut.*

LAUNDRY LIST
— **laundry list** (colloq.): list of things desired or matters to be dealt with (esp. a long and varied one) >*The union representative brought a laundry list of demands to the negotiating session.*

LAW
— **lay down the law** (see LAY)

— **the law** (colloq.): the police >*Then the law showed up and started hauling people away.*

LAY
* **lay**[1] (vulg.): copulation, episode of sexual intercourse >*That sailor needs a good lay after bein' at sea for two months.*

— **lay**[2] (vulg.): sex partner >*Was she a good lay?*

* **lay**[3] (vt) (vulg.): have sex with >*He said he laid her last night.*

* **lay a hand/finger on** (colloq.): just touch, hurt in the slightest (used esp. in the neg.) >*Don't worry—we didn't lay a hand on him.* >*Don't you dare lay a finger on my kid!*

* **lay back** (vi) (sl.): relax, get rid of stress >*I'd like to go to Cancún and just lay back for a couple of weeks.*

— **lay [one's] cards on the table** (see **CARDS**)

— **lay/lie down on the job** (colloq.): work halfheartedly, work without due alertness >*The quality control people were laying down on the job when these shoddy pieces got through.*

* **lay down the law** (colloq.): impose (one's) authority, demand obedience to strict measures >*We need someone to lay down the law and get this organization back on track.*

— **lay eyes on** (see **EYES**)

— **lay/get [one's] hands on** (see **HANDS**)

— **lay into** (colloq.): attack vigorously (physically or verbally) >*The kid laid into him with both fists.* >*They laid into the project manager for screwing up the plans.*

* **lay it on the line** (colloq.): speak frankly, deal in a straightforward way (with a sensitive issue) >*Look, I'll lay it on the line—give me a twenty percent raise or I quit.*

* **lay it on (thick)** (colloq.): be overly flattering, exaggerate or lie creatively >*He laid it on thick and pretty soon had her believing it all.* >*He really laid it on, but the cops didn't believe him.*

* **lay/lie low** (colloq.): remain inconspicuous, wait patiently and quietly, not attract attention >*Just lie low until this whole mess is over.* >*He laid low until he saw his chance, and then he made his move.*

* **lay off¹** (colloq.): stop mistreating or annoying (s/one) >*The poor guy's not feeling well, so lay off.* >*Lay off her, will you?*

* **lay off²** (colloq.): stop or quit (s/thing annoying or harmful) >*Lay off the sarcastic remarks, OK?* >*He'd better lay off the liquor and sober up.*

— **lay [s/thing] on** (sl.): tell or give [s/thing] to, force or impose [s/thing] on >*Wait till I lay this juicy piece of gossip on ya!* >*This dude I don't even know just laid a six-pack of beer on me.* >*My mom's always tryin' to lay a guilt trip on my brother for not visitin' her.*

— **lay out¹** (vt) (colloq.): spend (money) (esp. a large amount) >*I bet they laid out over $5000 for this reception.*

— **lay out²** (vt) (sl.): knock down (esp. with a punch) >*He laid the bully out with a right jab to the chin.*

— **lay [s/thing] out for** (colloq.): explain [s/thing] in detail to >*Come over for dinner tomorrow and I'll lay the whole plan out for you.*

— **lay/burn rubber** (see **RUBBER**)

* **lay up** (vt) (colloq.): disable, keep bedridden or unable to work >*That flu laid me up for over a week.* >*He's been laid up with a bad back.*

LAYING

— **laying for** (colloq.): lying in wait for, preparing to attack >*He's been laying for you ever since you badmouthed him.*

LAYOUT

* **layout** (colloq.): establishment or residence and all its features >*You should see his penthouse, with a water bed, built-in stereo, wet bar—it's quite a layout.*

LAZYBONES

— **lazybones** (colloq.): lazy person, person who oversleeps (also voc.) >*Tell that lazybones to get out of bed or he'll be late for work.* >*Wake up, lazybones!*

LEAD

* **get the lead out** (... led ...) (sl.): hurry up, work faster, go faster >*I told 'em to get the lead out 'cause we didn't have all day.*

— **go over like a lead balloon** (... led ...) (sl., sarc.): gain no acceptance or enthusiasm, be received with disapproval, fail >*His idea to hire* convicted sex offenders went over like a lead balloon.

— **lead [s/one] (around) by the nose** (lēd …) (colloq.): dominate or control [s/one] completely >*The poor guy's wife leads him around by the nose.*

LEAD FOOT

— **lead foot** (led …) (colloq.): tendency to drive an automobile very fast >*Tell Victor to keep his eye on the speedometer—he's got a lead foot.*

LEAGUE

* **out of [one's] league** (colloq.): in a situation that [one] cannot properly deal with (due to a lack of talent or experience) >*He's used to selling houses, but he's out of his league tryin' to handle that commercial building.*

LEAK

* **take a leak** (sl., freq. vulg.): urinate >*I'll be right back—I gotta take a leak.*

LEAN

— **lean on** (colloq.): put pressure on (esp. with coercion) >*The boss has been leaning on him to increase production.*

— **bend/lean over backward(s)** (see **BACKWARD**)

LEAP

— **(go) take a flying leap!** (see **FLYING**)

LEAVE

— **can take [s/thing] or leave [it]** (see **TAKE**)

— **leave [s/one] flat** (colloq.): abandon or desert [s/one], leave [s/one] in need >*He promised her the world but left her flat after two weeks.*

— **leave [s/one] holding the bag** (see **HOLDING**)

— **pick up and leave** (see **PICK**)

LECH

— **lech** (see "**LETCH**")

LEFT

* **have two left feet** (colloq.): be awkward at dancing or moving, dance poorly

>*Jimmy's never going to learn to rumba—he's got two left feet.*

— **would give [one's] left/right nut** (see **GIVE**)

LEFT FIELD

* **out in left field** (sl.): not knowing what's happening, having strange or mistaken ideas, very wrong >*Don't ask my sister-in-law about it—she's out in left field.*

— **out of left field** (colloq.): sudden and unexpected, incongruous or strange (also adv.) >*His comments on reincarnation at the Chamber of Commerce meeting were really out of left field. >Johnson's coming out of left field. I don't know what he's trying to say.*

LEFTY

* **lefty** (lef´tē) (colloq.): left-handed person (also voc.) >*Let Barbara sit at this end of the table—she's a lefty. >Hey, lefty, how you doing?*

LEG

— **an arm and a leg** (see **ARM**)

— **break a leg!** (see **BREAK**)

— **have a leg up on** (colloq.): have an advantage over >*We'll have a leg up on the competition if we can get a domestic supplier.*

— **pull [s/one's] leg** (see **PULL**)

— **shake a leg** (see **SHAKE**)

LEGAL EAGLE

— **legal eagle** (colloq.): lawyer (esp. a clever one) >*He got some legal eagle to find a loophole in the contract.*

LEGIT

* **legit** (lə jit´) (sl.): legitimate, authentic (also adv.) >*Stop worryin'! This deal's perfectly legit. >This stuff is legit—fourteen karat gold. >We won it legit.*

— **stretch [one's] legs** (see **STRETCH**)

LEGWORK

* **legwork** (colloq.): physical or routine work involved in a project (esp. the

gathering of information) >*His grad students did all the legwork on the research, but he took all the credit.*

LEMON
** **lemon** (colloq.): defective product (esp. an automobile) >*He's spent a fortune trying to get that lemon to run right.*

LESBO
— **lesbo** (lez´bō) (sl., pej.): lesbian, female homosexual >*He called Audry a lesbo just 'cause she knows how to stand up for herself.*

LESS
— **in less than no time** (colloq.): in a very short time, very quickly >*I'll have this ready for you in less than no time.*

LET
— **let/blow/cut a fart** (see **FART**)

— **let 'er rip!** (… ər …) (colloq.): proceed! (with full speed or power) go ahead! (without restraint or inhibition) >*If you feel like yelling, Mack, just let 'er rip!*

* **let ([oneself]) go** (colloq.): begin behaving without inhibition or restraint >*Quiet old Lenowitz really let himself go last night and was the life of the party.* >*Hey, let go and have some fun!*

— **let go (with)**[1] (colloq.): send forth aggressively, hurl, shoot, unleash >*She let go a snowball that got him right in the face.* >*They let go with all their firepower.*

— **let go (with)**[2] (colloq.): blurt out, yell, say aggressively >*Then the guy let go with a loud yell.* >*Scotty let go a string of insults they'll never forget.*

* **let [one's] hair down** (colloq.): relax, behave uninhibitedly >*Let's go to the party—you can have a few drinks and let your hair down.*

** **let [s/one] have it** (colloq.): vigorously attack or strike out against [s/one] (physically or verbally) >*When Jerry walked through the door, his wife let him have it with a big wooden spoon.* >*Her boss let her have it for screwing up the meeting plans.*

— **let [s/one] have it with both barrels** (sl.): vigorously attack [s/one] verbally, severely reprimand [s/one] >*If Ev says one word about my weight, I'm gonna let him have it with both barrels.*

— **let it all hang out** (see **HANG**)

— **let loose** (colloq.): begin behaving without inhibition or restraint >*Have a couple of drinks and let loose, man.*

— **let loose (with)**[1] (colloq.): send forth aggressively, hurl, shoot, unleash >*Al let loose a punch that knocked the guy right on his butt.* >*If they give you any trouble, let loose with everything you got.*

— **let loose (with)**[2] (colloq.): blurt out, yell, say aggressively >*He let loose with a yell you could hear in the next county.* >*Angie was so mad she let loose a tongue-lashing that really put him in his place.*

— **let/blow off steam** (see **STEAM**)

* **let on (that)** (colloq.): outwardly show (what one supposedly thinks or feels), pretend (that) >*If he's worried, he's sure not letting on.* >*When the salesman came up, Hubie let on that he really wasn't interested.*

* **let [s/thing] ride** (colloq.): let [s/thing] continue without change, not take action on [s/thing] >*Just let things ride and see what happens.*

* **let [s/thing] slide** (colloq.): let [s/thing] continue without remedy, not interfere in or react to [s/thing] >*I don't think the bank examiners are going to let this slide, because they're sticklers for regulations.* >*I can't let it slide when he insults me in public.*

— **let the cat out of the bag** (colloq.): disclose a secret (esp. unintentionally) >*That moron Rudy let the cat out of the bag, and now everybody knows.*

LETCH

— **letch** (lech) (sl.): lecher, lascivious or lustful man >*That letch can't keep his hands off women.*

LEVEL

— **level** (vt) (colloq.): knock down >*She leveled the guy with a punch to the neck.*

** **level with** (colloq.): speak truthfully to, be straightforward with, avoid deceiving >*I'm going to level with you—you don't have a future in this line of work.*

* **on the level** (colloq.): honest, legitimate, without deceit (also adv.) >*Is this massage parlor on the level?* >*You won't have any problems with this car, on the level.*

LEVIS

** **Levis** (lē´vīz) (colloq.): blue jeans >*I want to buy some new Levis before school starts.*

LEZBO

— **lezbo** (see LESBO)

LIB

* **... lib** (lib) (colloq.): ... liberation >*Henry says he's all for women's lib.*

LIBBER

— **... libber** (lib´ər) (colloq.): ... liberation advocate >*He's not gay, but he's a gay libber.*

LIBERATE

— **liberate** (vt) (sl.): steal, take without authorization >*Sneak into the storeroom and see if ya can liberate a new stapler for me, will ya?*

LICK

— **lick¹** (sl.): blow, hit, punch >*He won the fight, but I got in a few good licks.* >*Give it a lick with the sledgehammer.*

— **lick²** (colloq.): single period of activity or effort >*We can load up the truck in one lick.* >*The teacher grades ten exams at a lick.*

* **lick³** (vt) (sl.): defeat, beat, outdo >*He got licked good in that fight.* >*They're a good team, but we can lick 'em.*

— **lick [one's] chops** (colloq.): anticipate (s/thing) with relish or pleasure, wait with anticipation >*They're smelling the roast and licking their chops.* >*I licked my chops thinking about all the dough I was going to make.*

— **whip/lick [s/thing, s/one] into shape** (see WHIP)

LICKED

— **have [s/thing] licked** (colloq.): have finally completed or solved [s/thing] >*Painting the house hasn't been so bad—one more wall and we'll have it licked.* >*I think I've got the problem licked now that I've cleaned off the corrosion.*

LICKETY-SPLIT

— **lickety-split** (lik´i tē split´) (colloq.): very quickly, at great speed >*Get over there lickety-split and find out what the problem is.* >*We were going lickety-split down the highway.*

LICKING

— **licking** (sl.): beating, defeat >*They gave him a good lickin' for mouthin' off.* >*We took a lickin' with that mining company stock.*

LID

* **lid¹** (colloq.): maintenance of silence, veil of secrecy >*We got to keep the lid on our plans for a while.*

— **lid²** (sl.): ounce of marijuana >*He got busied with three lids in his car.*

— **blow the lid off (of)** (see BLOW)

— **flip [one's] lid** (see FLIP)

* **put a lid on** (sl.): stop saying or speaking >*Put a lid on it, mister! We're sick of your complainin'.* >*I told Jake to put a lid on the vulgar language.*

LIE

— **lay/lie down on the job** (see LAY)

— **lay/lie low** (see LAY)

* **lie through [one's] teeth** (colloq.): lie openly or without shame >*He's lying through his teeth if that's what he says.*

* **no lie!** (sl.): that's the truth! that's for sure! >*No lie! It's gonna be dangerous as hell!*

LIFE

** **life** (colloq.): prison sentence extending until death >*The judge could give him twenty-five years to life for the murder.*

* **get a life!** (sl.): stop acting so ridiculously! stop bothering me with your petty concerns! >*Don't ya have anything better to do than squawk about how they're plannin' their wedding? Man, get a life!*

— **fixed for life** (see **FIXED**)

* **for the life of me ... I [neg.]** (colloq.): no matter how hard I try ... I [neg.] >*I met her just last week, but for the life of me I can't remember her name.*

— **live (life) in the fast lane** (see **FAST LANE**)

— **live (life) on the edge** (see **EDGE**)

* **not on your life!** (colloq.): under no circumstances! not for anything in the world! >*Me, try sky-diving? Not on your life!*

* **the life of the party** (colloq.): a very fun or amusing person, the most entertaining or lively person (at a social gathering) >*Belinda had a couple of whiskey sours and became the life of the party.*

— **the time of [one's] life** (see **TIME**)

— **you (can) bet your life** (see **BET**)

LIFE OF RILEY

— **the life of Riley** (... rī´lē) (colloq.): a comfortable and easy life, a pleasant way of living >*He's been leading the life of Riley ever since he came into all that money.*

LIFER

* **lifer** (lī´fər) (sl.): prisoner sentenced to prison until death >*Careful with that dude—he's a lifer and he's as bad as they come.*

LIFT

** **lift¹** (colloq.): ride (esp. in an automobile) >*Can you give me a lift downtown?*

— **lift²** (vt) (sl.): steal, shoplift >*The kid lifted a cassette tape from the record store.*

— **lift³** (vt) (colloq.): plagiarize, take (what another has written) as (one's) own >*The senator got in trouble for lifting material from other people's speeches.*

* **lift a hand/finger** (colloq.): put out the slightest effort (used esp. in the neg.) >*None of those bums would lift a finger to help clean up.* >*He never lifts a hand around the house.*

LIGHT

— **light** (colloq.): below the expected or required amount or number, short >*Hey, this is twenty bucks light. Where's the rest?*

— **go out like a light** (see **GO**)

— **light/build a fire under** (colloq.): stimulate to take action or work faster >*We're going to have to light a fire under the manager if we're going to get this taken care of before Christmas.*

* **light into** (colloq.): attack vigorously (physically or verbally) >*He really lit into his staff for not having the report ready.*

— **light out** (vi) (colloq.): start traveling, depart (esp. quickly) >*We'll light out for the mountains first thing in the morning.* >*They lit out when they saw the police car.*

— **out like a light** (see **OUT**)

* **see the light** (colloq.): finally accept or understand (what one rejected or ignored previously), accept the truth >*She'd tried for years to get him to stop smoking, but when his brother died of lung cancer he saw the light and quit.*

LIGHTEN
** **lighten up** (vi) (sl.): not take (s/thing) so seriously, become less intense, relax >*Lighten up! He didn't mean anything by what he said.*

LIGHTS
— **punch/put [s/one's] lights out** (sl.): beat [s/one] unconscious, beat [s/one] up >*Don't argue with that bruiser or he'll punch your lights out.*

LIGHTWEIGHT
— **lightweight** (colloq.): person of little importance or influence (also adj.) >*Forget what that joker said—he's a lightweight.* >*Do they think they can win this case using that lightweight lawyer?*

LIKE
* **like** (vt) (colloq.): predict as winner, believe (s/one) will prevail, favor >*Who do you like in the Smith-Jones fight tomorrow?*

— **how do you like them apples?** (see THEM)

— **it's like this:** (see THIS)

** **like ...** (colloq.): uh ... (crutch word to fill a pause or introduce s/thing hard to express) >*The movie was, like, really awesome!* >*Like, what do you want to do tonight?*

— **...-like** (colloq.): somewhat ... (also adv.) >*Watching him lose control was weird-like.* >*She was just staring at me sexy-like.*

— **like (a/the) ...** (see entry under ... word[s])

— **like it or lump it** (sl.): take it or leave it, you have no other choice >*I told her old man I was gonna marry his daughter and that he could like it or lump it.*

— **like(d) to** (colloq.): nearly, almost (react strongly) >*He like to had a heart attack when he found out.* >*I liked to split a gut laughing when he told me the story.*

— **tell it like it is** (see TELL)

— **that's more like it** (see THAT'S)

LIKELY
* **a likely story** (colloq., sarc.): a very improbable account or excuse, a probable lie or exaggeration >*He said he was late because he had a flat tire—a likely story!*

LIKES
— **the likes of** (colloq.): anyone/anything like >*I don't want you hanging around with the likes of that punk.* >*Have you ever seen the likes of it?*

LILY-WHITE
— **lily-white** (colloq.): having only white people, excluding people of color >*That company is lily-white because its owner is a racist.*

LIMB
* **out on a limb** (colloq.): in a difficult or vulnerable situation >*I'm not going to go out on a limb and cosign on a loan for that deadbeat brother of yours.*

LIMEY
— **limey** (lī´mē) (sl., freq. pej.): Britisher, Englishman (also adj.) >*He says he met a lot of limeys during the war.* >*He says he don't like limey cookin'.*

LIMIT
— **the limit** (colloq.): outrageous person or thing, utmost person or thing (of a certain quality, esp. an annoying one) >*Man, that jerk's the limit! I can't work with him.*

LIMO
** **limo** (lim´ō) (colloq.): limousine >*He rented a limo to take her to the prom.*

LIMP-WRISTED
— **limp-wristed** (sl.): effeminate, homosexual >*Him and his limp-wristed friends went to some gay bar.*

LINE
* **line¹** (colloq.): glib talk, calculated or exaggerated talk (esp. to impress or persuade) >*He's got a standard line for*

LINGO–LITTLE

picking up women. >Don't give me that
line about how hard things are for you.

* **line²** (colloq.): occupation, profession
>I'm in retail sales. What's your line?

— **down the line** (see DOWN)

— **drop [s/one] a line** (see DROP)

— **lay it on the line** (see LAY)

— **line [one's] (own) pockets** (colloq.):
make money for [oneself] (by illicit or
questionable means) >The
commissioner has been lining his
pockets with bribes and kickbacks.

* **on the line** (colloq.): at risk, in jeopardy
>You'd better get that contract, because
your job's on the line. >He put his
reputation on the line by backing that
risky project.

* **out of line** (colloq.): impertinent,
disregarding rules or protocol >Dixon
was way out of line when he tried to tell
June how to run her department.

— **toe the line** (see TOE)

LINGO

— **lingo** (ling´gō) (colloq.): type or style of
language, jargon, strange or foreign
language >I don't understand much of
that pilot lingo. >You speak Guillermo's
lingo, don't you?

LIP

— **button (up) [one's] lip** (see BUTTON)

— **give [s/one] (some) lip** (sl.): speak
insolently or impudently to [s/one],
answer [s/one] disrespectfully >He
started givin' me some lip, so I punched
him. >Don't' give me no lip or you'll be
outta here.

— **zip [one's] lip** (see ZIP)

LIPS

— **read my lips!** (see READ)

LIQUORED

— **liquored up** (lik´ərd ...) (colloq.):
drunk (esp. from hard liquor) >He went
home all liquored up and picked a fight
with his wife.

LIST

— **go down the list** (colloq.): enumerate,
specify (a number of things) >Why I
don't like that clown? I'll go down the
list for you.

LISTEN

— **give [s/thing]/have a listen** (colloq.):
listen (to), hear, pay attention (to) >The
doc gave my heart a listen and said it
sounded OK. >You say your car's
running rough? Let me have a listen.

* **listen up** (vi) (colloq.): pay close
attention (to what is being said), listen
carefully (used esp. as a command) >I
want you all to listen up—this is
important.

LIT

* **lit** (colloq.): literature (esp. as a course
of study) >What grade did you get in
English lit last semester?

— **lit up like a Christmas tree** (sl.): very
drunk >He stumbled in at two in the
morning lit up like a Christmas tree.

LITTERBUG

* **litterbug** (colloq.): person who litters
public areas with trash >Why can't
those damn litterbugs use the trash
cans?

LITTLE

— **a little bird told me** (see BIRD)

— **get a little/some** (see GET)

— **get a little/some on the side** (see GET)

— **little black book** (colloq.): small
notebook with names and phone
numbers of available or desirable
women (kept by a single man) >I'll just
check my little black book to see who I
can ask to the show.

— **little shaver** (colloq.): small boy
>What's a little shaver like him doing
out on the street at this hour?

— **the little woman** (colloq., freq. pej.):
(one's) wife >Bring the little woman in
to see if she likes it, because I can give
you a good price on it.

— **wrap/twist [s/one] around [one's] little finger** (see **WRAP**)

LITTLE-BITSY
— **little-bitsy** (lit′l bit′sē) (colloq.): very small, tiny >*I was hoping for more than this little-bitsy diamond.*

LITTLE-BITTY
— **little-bitty** (lit′l bit′ē) (colloq.): very small, tiny >*All they served were these little-bitty sandwiches and olives.*

LIVE
* **can live with** (colloq.): find acceptable or satisfactory >*The car we want's not available in blue—just in silver—but we can live with that.*

* **live it up** (colloq.): enjoy (oneself) thoroughly, live in a wild and pleasureful way >*We only got two days of vacation left, so let's live it up.*

— **live (life) in the fast lane** (see **FAST LANE**)

— **live (life) on the edge** (see **EDGE**)

LIVE ONE
— **live one** (līv ...) (sl.): person who is easily tricked or used >*Hey, get the cards and poker chips—we got a live one over at Murray's place.*

LIVE WIRE
— **live wire** (līv ...) (colloq.): vivacious or vibrant person >*Gwen's husband's a real live wire—he entertained us all night.*

LIVING
— **beat/knock the (living) daylights out of** (see **DAYLIGHTS**)

— **beat/knock/kick the (living) shit out of** (see **SHIT**)

— **scare the (living) daylights out of** (see **DAYLIGHTS**)

— **scare the (living) shit out of** (see **SHIT**)

LIVING END
— **the living end** (sl.): the most desirable or beautiful person or thing, the best >*I think Raymond is the living end!*

LOAD
— **a load (of ...)** (colloq.): much (...), many (...) >*That clown's going to be a load of trouble for us.* >*Poor guy's got a load of problems.*

* **get a load of** (sl.): observe, take notice of (esp. s/thing extraordinary or contemptible) (used esp. as a command) >*Hey, get a load of that foxy girl he's with!* >*You should get a load of the lies he's layin' on 'em about how famous he is.*

* **load up (on)** (colloq.): take (for [one's] use) a great deal (of), eat or drink a great deal (of) >*Lillian loads up on cold remedies every November.* >*I don't want the kids loading up on junk food before dinner.*

* **take a load off ([one's] feet)** (sl.): sit down, rest a while >*Take a load off— you've been on your feet all day.*

LOADED
** **loaded**[1] (sl.): very wealthy, having a great deal of money >*You should see the fancy cars Amos drives—the guy's loaded.*

* **loaded**[2] (sl.): fully equipped, having all the accessories or special equipment (esp. an automobile) >*This baby's loaded—air conditioning, power windows and locks, cruise control, you name it.*

* **loaded**[3] (sl.): drunk, intoxicated (on alcohol or drugs) >*The bum was already loaded when he stumbled into the bar and ordered a bottle.*

LOADS
* **loads (of ...)** (colloq.): much (...), many (...) >*We got loads of notebooks at the office.* >*Thanks loads for your help.*

LOAN SHARK

— **loan shark** (colloq.): person who lends money at extremely high rates (esp. illegally) >*He owes some loan shark over $8000.*

LOCAL

— **local yokel** (colloq., pej.): local resident of a small town or rural area >*All the local yokels are against having the dump site near them.*

LOCK

— **have a lock on** (colloq.): be assured of success in or possession of >*We win this one and we got a lock on the championship.* >*They say she has a lock on the senate seat.*

— **lock horns** (colloq.): be in a dispute (with one another), fight or contend (with one another) >*The governor and the legislature have locked horns on this issue before.*

— **lock up** (vt) (colloq.): gain assured success in or possession of >*I want to lock up the award by really working hard this last month.* >*If you ask me, Tornelli's got the vice president's spot locked up.*

LOCO

— **loco** (lōʹkō) (sl.): crazy, mentally unbalanced >*Ya gotta be loco to think ya can get away with cheatin' 'em.*

LOG

— **like a bump on a log** (see BUMP)
— **sleep like a log** (see SLEEP)

LOGS

— **saw logs** (see SAW)

LONESOME

— **(all) by [one's] lonesome** (colloq.): by [one]self, alone >*He couldn't find anyone to help, so he did it all by his lonesome.*

LONG

— **long drink of water** (colloq.): tall and thin person >*Hey, your friend—that long drink of water—does he play basketball?*

* **long haul**[1] (colloq.): long distance, long trip (esp. when traveled with difficulty or sacrifice) >*L.A. to Las Cruces is a long haul for one day's driving.*

* **long haul**[2] (colloq.): long period of time (esp. if endured with difficulty or sacrifice) >*It'll be a long haul, but I'm determined to get my degree.*

* **long time no see** (sl.): I haven't seen you for a long time >*Hey, Fred, long time no see! Where ya been keepin' yourself?*

* **over the long haul** (colloq.): in the long run, over a long period of time >*This is the most stable kind of investment over the long haul.*

— **so long** (see SO)

LONGHAIR

— **longhair** (colloq., freq. pej.): person devoted to intellectual or artistic pursuits (esp. classical music) (also adj.) >*You can bet all the longhairs are going to that concert.* >*He really likes that longhair music.*

LONG JOHNS

* **long johns** (… jonz) (colloq.): long and warm underwear >*I got to get some new long johns for the cold weather.*

LONG SHOT

** **long shot** (colloq.): competitor with little chance to win, venture or attempt with little chance to succeed >*That horse is a long shot, but I got a hunch he'll win.* >*Finding the right combination was a long shot, but we did it.*

* **by a long shot** (colloq.): by far, by a large degree >*Bert's the best bowler here by a long shot.* >*He didn't convince me, not by a long shot.*

LOOK

* **look alive!** (colloq.): be alert! pay attention! speed it up! >*Look alive, people! The big boss will be here any* second. >*Look alive! We ain't got all day for this.*

— **look at [s/one] cross-eyed** (colloq.): offend [s/one] in the slightest way, do anything at which [s/one] may take offense >*You can't look at Louie cross-eyed without him getting mad at you.*

— **look down [one's] nose at** (colloq.): view with contempt, scorn, disapprove of >*The Granvilles look down their noses at anyone living on the other side of the avenue.* >*He looks down his nose at men with earrings.*

* **look who's talking!** (colloq.): (one) could be accused of what (one) is criticizing (another) for! (one) is as guilty as (another) that (one) is blaming! >*Look who's talking! You flunked out of college, same as him!*

LOOKER
— **looker** (sl.): very attractive person >*Why didn't ya tell me your sister was such a looker?*

LOOKIE-LOO
— **lookie-loo** (lŭk´ē lū´) (sl.): curious spectator or onlooker, person who watches or inspects without participating >*There were a few lookie-loos at the open house, but no serious buyers.* >*All the lookie-loos are slowin' down traffic.*

LOOKING
— **here's looking at you!** (colloq.): here's to you! cheers! (said as a toast) >*Well, here's looking at you! Drink up!*

* **looking up** (vi) (colloq.): improving, showing better prospects >*Business has been looking up since we started the advertising campaign.*

LOOK-SEE
— **look-see** (colloq.): quick look, quick inspection >*Your engine's running rough—let me have a look-see.*

LOOKY
— **looky!** (lŭk´ē) (colloq.): look! behold! >*Looky! There's one of those cars you've been talking about.*

LOONY
— **loony** (lū´nē) (colloq.): crazy, mentally unbalanced >*I'd have to be loony to pay them before I checked their work over.*

LOONY BIN
— **loony bin** (lū´nē …) (colloq.): insane asylum, psychiatric hospital >*Wilbur's been acting real weird—I think he's ready for the loony bin.*

LOONY-TOON
— **loony-toon** (see "LOONY-TUNE")

LOONY-TUNE
— **loony-tune** (lū´nē tūn´) (sl.): crazy person >*That poor guy's a real loony-tune—he hears voices and everything.*

LOOP
— **in/out of the loop** (colloq.): involved/ not involved in the decision-making process >*He claims he was out of the loop and doesn't know who gave the OK.*

— **knock [s/one] for a loop** (see **KNOCK**)

— **throw/knock [s/one] for a loop** (see **THROW**)

LOOPED
— **looped** (colloq.): drunk, intoxicated >*Edwin was pretty looped, so I drove him home.*

LOOSE
— **cut loose (with)** (see **CUT**)

* **hang/stay loose** (sl.): stay calm, not let (s/thing) annoy (one), relax >*I'll hang 'loose. What happens, happens.* >*Stay loose, man—don't let it get ya down.*

— **have a screw loose** (see **SCREW**)

— **let loose** (see **LET**)

— **let loose (with)** (see **LET**)

LOOSE CANNON–LOUDMOUTHED

LOOSE CANNON
— **loose cannon** (colloq.): person who is dangerously out of control or irresponsible (esp. within an organization) >*Kearney's a loose cannon—someone's going to have to get him under control.*

LOOT
— **loot** (sl.): money (esp. a substantial amount) >*How's the sales job? Ya makin' a lot of loot?*

LORDY
— **lordy!** (lôr´dē) (colloq.): (interj. to express surprise, wonder, or disappointment) >*Lordy! Just look at those expensive prices! >Canned peas again? Lordy!*

LOSE
* **lose** (vt) (sl.): evade, get rid of >*He tried followin' me, but I lost him. >Hey, lose that clown ya came in with, and let's go somewhere quiet.*

— **lose (all) [one's] marbles** (sl.): go crazy, begin to behave or think irrationally >*Bingham can't be serious! Has he lost all his marbles?*

— **win/lose by a nose** (see **NOSE**)

— **blow/lose [one's] cool** (see **COOL**)

* **lose it** (sl.): lose control or dominance (esp. of one's emotional state) >*Herb's stressed out—give him a vacation or he's gonna lose it.*

* **lose [one's] shirt** (colloq.): suffer a big financial loss, lose all that [one] has >*He lost his shirt on that deal and had to declare bankruptcy.*

LOSER
** **loser** (sl.): misfit, failed person, person unworthy of respect (cf. **"WINNER"**) >*Why do ya hang around with that loser?*

— **...-time loser** (sl.): person sentenced to prison ... times >*He's a three-time loser, once for burglary and twice for armed robbery.*

LOST
** **get lost!** (sl.): go away! stop annoying me! >*He tried to borrow a few bucks from me, but I told him to get lost.*

* **get lost in the shuffle** (colloq.): become lost or ignored (among many), get misplaced (during some process) >*She was the ninth of eleven kids and kind of got lost in the shuffle. >I don't know what happened. I guess your job application got lost in the shuffle.*

LOT
** **a lot (of ...)** (colloq.): much (...), many (...) >*We have a lot to do today. >She likes him a lot. >He's a big shot with a lot of influential friends.*

** **(a) lot of [s/thing] (...)!** (colloq., sarc.): no [s/thing] at all (...)! >*That dummy was sure a lot of help! >Lot of good it did to study! I failed the test anyway.*

LOTS
** **lots (of ...)** (colloq.): much (...), many (...) >*No hurry—we got lots of time. >I'll give you a spider plant. I got lots.*

LOUD
* **loud and clear** (colloq.): with absolute clarity, with no chance of misunderstanding, with emphasis (also adj.) >*Yes, sir! I read you loud and clear. >Tell him loud and clear to get the hell out of there! >His warning was loud and clear.*

LOUDMOUTH
* **loudmouth** (colloq.): overly talkative or indiscreet person, person who comments on everything as if he/she were an authority (also voc.) >*We're sick and tired of listening to that loudmouth. >Shut up, loudmouth!*

LOUDMOUTHED
* **loudmouthed** (colloq.): overly talkative, indiscreet, obnoxiously loud or boastful >*No one can stand that loudmouthed jerk.*

LOUNGE LIZARD

— **lounge lizard** (sl.): flashy man who frequents bars in search of women >*Is she really gonna go out with that slimy lounge lizard?*

LOUSE

— **louse** (sl.): reprehensible or untrustworthy person, contemptible person >*That louse left his wife for a younger woman.*

* **louse up** (vi, vt) (sl.): ruin or spoil (s/thing), botch (s/thing) >*If anyone louses up, the whole deal will go down the drain.* >*If Bruce forgets his lines, he'll louse up the whole show.*

LOUSY

** **lousy** (lou´zē) (colloq.): bad, inferior, incompetent, unpleasant, contemptible >*Turn off that lousy music, will you?* >*That lousy doctor you recommended made me worse.* >*Her lousy cousin put her up to it.*

— **lousy with** (sl.): having an abundance of, well supplied with >*We don't need another lawyer here—this town's already lousy with 'em.*

LOVE HANDLES

* **love handles** (colloq.): bulges of flesh above the hips >*Look at those love handles! You'd better go on a diet.*

LOVER-BOY

— **lover-boy** (sl., freq. sarc.): male lover, boyfriend (also voc.) >*I saw her with her lover-boy last night.* >*Hey, lover-boy, who're the flowers for?*

LOVEY-DOVEY

— **lovey-dovey** (luv´ē duv´ē) (colloq., freq. sarc.): amorous, affectionate (esp. in an overly sentimental way) >*They always act real lovey-dovey after they make up.*

LOW

— **lay/lie low** (see **LAY**)

— **low/bottom man on the totem pole** (colloq.): person with least seniority or rank (in a hierarchy) >*What can I do about it? I'm low man on the totem pole around here.*

LOW BLOW

* **low blow** (colloq.): unfair attack or action (against s/one) >*He didn't have to bring up her alcoholic father—that was a low blow.*

LOW-CAL

** **low-cal** (lō´kal´/lō´kal´) (colloq.): low-calorie, having a reduced number of calories >*I don't use sugar, just low-cal sweetener.*

LOWDOWN

* **lowdown** (colloq.): contemptible, mean, despicable >*Of all the dirty, lowdown tricks!* >*I'll get that lowdown bastard some day.*

* **the lowdown** (sl.): the pertinent information, the news (esp. when confidential or little known) >*What's the lowdown on the guy the cops arrested?*

LOWER

— **lower the boom (on)** (colloq.): take punitive measures (against), become very strict (with) >*If the loggers keep ignoring the regulations, the Forest Service is going to lower the boom.* >*Wanda's dad lowered the boom on her after he saw her lousy report card.*

LOWLIFE

* **lowlife** (colloq.): person of low morals or contemptible habits (also adj.) >*Nothing but a bunch of lowlifes hang around that pool hall.* >*I hate him and his lowlife buddies.*

LOWRIDER

— **lowrider** (colloq.): person who drives or rides in a customized automobile that rides close to the ground (esp. a young Mexican-American) >*The lowriders always cruise the boulevard on Saturday nights.*

LUBE

* **lube** (lūb) (vt) (colloq.): lubricate (esp. a vehicle's suspension system) >*Why* *don't you lube it while you're changing the oil?*

** **lube (job)** (colloq.): lubrication (esp. of a vehicle's suspension system) >*This car needs a lube job.* >*What do you charge for a lube and oil change?*

LUBRICATED

— **lubricated** (sl.): drunk, intoxicated >*They came home from the party pretty lubricated.*

LUCK

— **luck into** (colloq.): acquire or gain by good luck >*He really lucked into a neat job by meeting the right person at the right time.*

** **luck out** (vi) (colloq.): have an instance of very good luck >*He lucked out and wasn't caught.*

— **push [one's] luck** (see **PUSH**)

— **shit out of luck** (see **SHIT**)

LUCKY

— **thank [one's] lucky stars** (see **THANK**)

LUDE

— **lude** (lūd) (sl.): Quaalude, methaqualone (sedative) pill >*He took a couple of ludes and hit the sack.*

LUG

— **lug** (sl.): awkward or dull man, unsophisticated man >*Who's that big lug who's starin' at everything?*

LULU

— **lulu** (lū´lū) (sl.): extraordinary or outstanding thing or person >*Go on that ride—it's a lulu!*

LUMMOX

— **lummox** (lum´əks) (colloq.): awkward and stupid man >*That lummox is getting in everybody's way.*

LUMP

— **lump** (vt) (colloq.): endure, become resigned to, accept (when forced to) >*You expect me to just lump his snide remarks?* >*Dave can't do anything about it—he'll just have to lump it.*

— **like it or lump it** (see **LIKE**)

LUMPS

— **take [one's] lumps** (colloq.): endure inevitable criticism, accept punishment or setbacks >*You got to learn to take your lumps in this job.* >*Herb can take his lumps for what he said.*

LUNCH

— **out to lunch** (see **OUT**)

— **toss [one's] lunch** (see **TOSS**)

LUNY

— **luny** (see "LOONY")

LUNY BIN

— **luny bin** (see "LOONY BIN")

LUNY-TUNE

— **luny-tune** (see "LOONY-TUNE")

LUSH

* **lush** (lush) (sl.): drunkard, alcoholic >*Watch how much the old lady drinks—she's a lush.*

LYING

* **take [s/thing] lying down** (colloq.): suffer [s/thing] without reacting, accept [s/thing] without defending (oneself) (freq. used in the neg.) >*We can't take management's abuse lying down. Let's strike!*

M

MA

** **ma** (mä) (colloq.): mother (also voc.) >*I'll ask my ma if it's OK.* >*Let me give you a hand there, Ma.*

MAC

— **Mac** (mak) (voc.) (colloq.): friend, mister (used esp. with a male stranger) >*Say, Mac, you got a cigarette?*

MAD

— **(as) mad as a hornet** (colloq.): very angry >*Zelda's dad was as mad as a hornet when he found out she'd been seeing that rock musician.*

— **(as) mad as a wet hen** (colloq.): very angry >*She was mad as a wet hen when she saw the dent in her car.*

— **hopping mad** (see HOPPING)

* **like mad** (colloq.): wholeheartedly, to the utmost degree, intensely >*When I drove by they were yelling like mad to get someone's attention.* >*It's been snowing like mad in the mountains.*

— **mad about** (colloq.): wildly enthusiastic about, very fond of >*I'm mad about her, but she doesn't love me.*

MADAM

— **madam** (colloq.): woman who manages a house of prostitution >*She was the madam of some high-class whorehouse in Nevada.*

MADE

** **have it made** (colloq.): be assured of success, be in a thoroughly positive situation >*If he gets that job, he's got it made.*

* **have it made in the shade** (sl.): be assured of success, be in a thoroughly positive situation >*I'll have it made in the shade if I get in good with the boss.*

MADHOUSE

* **madhouse** (colloq.): disorderly or noisy place or event >*The shopping center is a madhouse right before Christmas.*

MAD MONEY

— **mad money** (colloq.): sum of discretional funds for unexpected expenses or impulse purchases >*I'm going to use my mad money and buy that coat.*

MAG

— **mag** (mag) (sl.): magnesium-alloy automobile wheel >*He took off the stock wheels and put on some expensive mags.*

MAIN

— **main** (sl.): favorite, most loved or admired >*Roland's my main man in this here group.*

— **[one's] (main) squeeze** (see SQUEEZE)

MAIN DRAG

* **main drag** (sl.): main street (of a city or town) >*We stopped at a motel on the main drag.*

MAINLINE

— **mainline** (vt) (sl.): inject (a drug, esp. heroin) directly into a vein >*He used to just snort a little cocaine, but now he's into mainlinin' heroin.*

MAJOR

* **major** (sl.): substantive, significant, of consequence >*This isn't a small-time deal—we're talkin' about major bucks here.*

MAKE

* **make^1** (sl.): identification, act of recognizing >*The cops got a make on one of the holdup men.*

* **make^2** (vt) (colloq.): gain the position of, gain a position on >*He made full professor by the time he was thirty-seven.* >*Did you make the team?*

— **make^3** (vt) (sl., freq. vulg.): have sex with, seduce into sex >*He says he made her last night.*

— **make^4** (vt) (sl.): recognize, identify (esp. to the detriment of the person recognized) >*The captain had him* *workin' undercover till some drug dealer made him.*

* **(go ahead,) make my day!** (sl., sarc.): do that and I will punish you! I will take pleasure in hurting you if you try what you threaten! >*Ya wanna fight me? Go ahead, make my day!*

— **make (a/the/[one's]) ...** (see entry under ... noun)

— **make for** (colloq.): escape toward, head for >*I made for the exit when I smelled smoke.*

** **make it[1]** (colloq.): arrive, appear, reach (a place) >*Try to make it to our party Saturday.* >*Think we can make it to Phoenix before dark?*

** **make it[2]** (colloq.): succeed, attain (one's) goal, arrive (at a position) >*I hope their new business makes it.* >*He wanted to win the trophy, and he made it.* >*I think she'll make it to president of the company.*

— **make it hot for** (see HOT)

— **make it snappy** (see SNAPPY)

— **make it (with)** (sl., freq. vulg.): have sex (with) >*I'd like to make it with that cute chick.* >*Hey, honey, let's make it!*

— **make like** (sl.): imitate, pretend (that) >*Make like a movie star and pose for the camera.* >*I made like I was a real expert on the law, and he believed it.*

— **make no bones about** (see BONES)

— **[neg.] make no never mind** (see NEVER)

* **make out[1]** (vi) (colloq.): fare, do fairly well, succeed >*How did you make out at the interview?* >*We'll make out all right if we can keep expenses down a little.*

* **make out[2]** (vi) (colloq.): kiss, caress (one another) (esp. sexually) >*They were making out in the backseat when her old man caught them.*

— **make out like a bandit** (see BANDIT)

— **make [oneself] scarce** (see SCARCE)

* **make something (out) of** (colloq.): start a fight or argument over, use as a motive for fighting >*You heard what I said. You want to make something out of it?*

* **on the make[1]** (sl.): trying to make romantic or sexual conquests, trying to make a seduction >*That singles bar's full of guys on the make.*

— **on the make[2]** (colloq.): trying to improve (one's) social or financial position (esp. in a selfish way) >*Watch out for young executives on the make.*

— **put the make on** (sl.): attempt to make a romantic or sexual conquest of, try to seduce >*Look at Bret puttin' the make on that babe.*

MAKES

— **what makes [s/one] tick** (see TICK)

MALARKEY

— **malarkey** (mə lär´kē) (colloq.): misleading or untrue statements or information, exaggeration, nonsense >*That business about him being a professional golfer is a bunch of malarkey.*

MALE CHAUVINIST PIG

* **male chauvinist pig** (sl., pej.): male chauvinist, man who disparages women because he believes them to be inferior >*You wouldn't believe how that male chauvinist pig puts women down!*

MAMA

* **mama[1]** (mä´mə) (colloq.): mother (also voc.) >*Your mama's a nice lady.* >*Don't let them push you around, Mama!*

— **mama[2]** (sl., freq. pej.): woman (esp. a good-looking or sexually attractive one) (also voc.) >*Man, look at that sweet mama at the next table!* >*Hey, mama, let's dance!*

MAMA'S BOY

* **mama's boy** (mä´məz ...) (colloq.): man or boy who is overly dependent on his mother, sissy >*He's a mama's boy who can't make a decision on his own.*

MAMMA
— **mamma** (see "MAMA")

MAN
** **man** (voc.) (colloq.): mister, friend >*Hey, man, watch where you're going, will you?*

* **[one's] old man**[1] (sl., freq. pej.): [one's] father >*My old man got laid off at work, so I gotta find a job to help the family out.*

* **[one's] old man**[2] (sl., freq. pej.): [one's] husband or boyfriend >*Her old man won't give her enough money to pay all the bills.*

** **man!** (colloq.): (interj. to express surprise, wonder, or disappointment) >*Man! What a play!* >*Man! I just got this suit cleaned and now look at it!*

* **... man** (colloq.): man esp. attracted to (a part of a woman's body) >*Wes is a leg man, but I'm more of an ass man.*

— **[one's] man** (sl.): [one's] friend, [one's] chum >*Meet Johnny—he's my man.*

— **the man** (sl.): the authorities, person or people in control, police (esp. when seen as oppressive) >*The man raised the rent on us again last month.* >*When the man tells ya to halt, you better do it.*

— **the Man upstairs** (colloq.): God >*I was real sick, but I guess the Man upstairs decided it wasn't my time to die.*

— **the old man** (colloq.): the commanding officer, the boss, the man in authority >*We got to get the old man to approve this first.*

MAN-SIZE
— **man-size(d)** (colloq.): large, substantive >*He needs a man-sized steak for his man-sized hunger.*

MARBLES
— **marbles** (sl.): assets put into play, goods or valuables at risk >*When Hilliard saw the deal was about to go bad he pulled all his marbles out.* >*If they get the upper hand, they win all the marbles.*

— **[neg.] have all [one's] marbles** (sl.): be somewhat crazy, think irrationally >*When I see the way Cal's been actin', I don't think he's got all his marbles.*

— **lose (all) [one's] marbles** (see **LOSE**)

MARK
— **mark** (sl.): intended victim of a swindle or theft >*The pickpocket spotted his mark and started toward him.*

MARY JANE
— **Mary Jane** (mâ´rē jān´) (sl.): marijuana >*He scored a little Mary Jane from a dealer he knows.*

MASHER
— **masher** (sl.): man who makes unwanted sexual advances toward a woman >*Mildred had to slap that masher in the face to make him stop.*

MASSACRE
— **massacre**[1] (sl.): decisive defeat (esp. in sports) >*The game was a massacre, forty-nine to nothin'.*

* **massacre**[2] (vt) (sl.): defeat decisively (esp. in sports) >*The home team got massacred last night.*

MAX
** **max** (maks) (sl.): maximum, at the most (also adv.) >*The max I'll pay is two hundred bucks.* >*He can lift three hundred pounds max.*

* **max out** (vi, vt) (sl.): reach the maximum limit (on), be able to do or endure no more (with) >*She's already maxed out all her credit cards.* >*I maxed out after studyin' six hours straight.*

— **... to the max** (sl.): totally ..., ... in the extreme >*That horror movie was gross to the max.*

MAYO
* **mayo** (mā´ō) (colloq.): mayonnaise >*You want that sandwich with mustard or mayo?*

M.C.
— **M.C.** (see "EMCEE")

MCCOY

— **the real McCoy** (... mə koi´) (colloq.): the genuine thing, the authentic article >*It sure looks like a diamond, but it's not the real McCoy.*

MEAL TICKET

— **meal ticket** (colloq.): means of support or financial security >*Leona doesn't love him—she just married him as her meal ticket.* >*He doesn't field so good. His hitting's his meal ticket.*

MEAN

* **a mean ...** (sl.): an excellent ..., (a) ... (done) skillfully or impressively >*That Texan makes a mean chili.* >*He plays a mean saxophone.*

— **mean business** (see BUSINESS)

MEANIE

— **meanie** (see "MEANY")

MEANY

— **meany** (mē´nē) (colloq.): mean or unkind person (used esp. with children) >*Don't let that meany hit you!*

MEASLY

* **measly** (mē´zlē) (colloq.): contemptibly small or inferior >*You expect me to work for a measly five bucks an hour? >That measly little kid isn't going to make it as a lumberjack.*

MEAT

— **meat** (vulg., pej.): woman or women (seen as sex object[s]) >*He said he was tired of her and wanted some fresh meat.*

— **beat [one's] meat** (see BEAT)

— **[one's] meat** (vulg.): [one's] penis >*He pulled out his meat and took a leak.*

MEATHEAD

— **meathead** (sl.): stupid or inept person, fool >*That meathead flunked another test.*

MEAT HOOK

— **meat hook** (sl.): hand (esp. when seen as neg.), fist >*Keep your meat hooks off her! >You get hit by one of them meat hooks and you're out.*

MEAT MARKET

— **meat market** (sl.): place where (one) seeks sex partners (esp. a bar or nightclub) >*I got tired of goin' to singles bars—they're nothin' but meat markets.*

MEGABUCKS

* **megabucks** (meg´ə buks´) (sl.): a very large amount of money >*That development project's gonna cost megabucks.*

MEGASTAR

— **megastar** (meg´ə stär´) (sl.): very popular or successful entertainer >*He dreamed of bein' a megastar even when he was actin' in school plays.*

MELLOW

* **mellow out** (vi, vt) (sl.): relax (s/one), get rid of (one's, s/one's) tension or worry, become/make less contentious >*He needs to take a vacation and mellow out a little. >She's mellowed him out a lot since they've been married.*

MELONS

— **melons** (sl., freq. vulg.): (woman's) large breasts >*He says she's really got a pair of melons.*

MENTAL

— **mental** (colloq.): mentally unstable, crazy >*The way that guy stares at people I'd say he's mental.*

MENTION

** **don't mention it** (colloq.): you're welcome >*Don't mention it—I was glad to help.*

MESS

* **mess** (colloq.): traumatized or neurotic person, anxiety-ridden person >*She's been a real mess since her husband left her.*

* **a mess (of ...)** (colloq.): much (...), many (...) >*I got a mess of bills to pay. >The boss says we have a mess of work to finish by tonight. >I don't want any* *more forms—I got a mess to fill out already.*

** **mess around** (vi) (colloq.): pass time idly, work halfheartedly or unproductively >*Hey, we're not paying you guys to mess around, so get to work!*

* **mess around (with)** (colloq.): be sexually involved (with) (esp. illicitly), be sexually promiscuous (with) >*I hear she's messing around with her husband's partner.* >*She divorced him because he was messing around on her.*

* **mess (around) with** (colloq.): treat without due respect or seriousness, handle capriciously, toy with >*You mess around with that bad dude and you'll be sorry.* >*I don't want anybody messing with my things.*

** **mess up**[1] (vi) (colloq.): make a mistake, botch things up >*They'll fire anyone that messes up.*

* **mess up**[2] (vt) (colloq.): botch, ruin, spoil >*Brad messed up our surprise by telling all his friends.*

* **mess up**[3] (vt) (colloq.): injure, severely beat, hurt >*He messed up his knees playing football.* >*They grabbed him and really messed him up.* >*This delay is going to mess us up.*

* **mess up**[4] (vt) (colloq.): traumatize, create anxiety in, make neurotic >*He's been real messed up ever since his divorce.* >*That rape messed her up bad.*

MESSAGE

* **get the message** (colloq.): understand, catch the meaning (esp. through inference, esp. when the message is neg.) >*Don't return Leon's calls and he'll get the message that you're not interested.*

MESS-UP

* **mess-up** (colloq.): mistake, blunder, botch >*One more mess-up and you're out of this company!* >*There was a schedule mess-up, so they'll be late.*

MEXICAN

— **Mexican standoff** (colloq., freq. pej.): confrontation that cannot be won by either side, standoff, impasse >*It was a Mexican standoff, so they both just backed away.*

MICKEY MOUSE

* **mickey mouse** (mik´ē …) (colloq.): overly simple, trivial, inferior, worthless >*He's been taking a lot of mickey mouse courses just to improve his grade point average.* >*I don't want this mickey mouse saw! Give me your best heavy-duty one.*

MIDDLE

* **the middle of nowhere** (colloq.): a remote or isolated place >*What do you guys do for fun living out there in the middle of nowhere?*

MIDDLE LEG

— **middle leg** (vulg.): penis >*He got his middle leg caught in the zipper.*

MIDDLE NAME

* **… is [s/one's] middle name** (colloq.): [s/one] is very talented in or knowledgeable about … >*Ask Morris about that exemption—tax law is his middle name.*

MIDDLING

— **fair to middling** (see **FAIR**)

MIDTERM

** **midterm** (colloq.): examination given in the middle of a school term >*Lonny didn't do so good on his midterms, so he's hitting the books for his finals.*

MIGHTY

* **mighty** (colloq.): very, extremely >*That plan sounds mighty dangerous to me!*

MIKE

** **mike** (mīk) (colloq.): microphone >*Speak right into the mike, please.*

MIL

— **mil** (mil) (sl.): million dollars >*His new movie took in over twelve mil the first week it played.*

MILE

— **a mile a minute** (colloq.): very fast (esp. in speaking) >*She was so excited she was talking a mile a minute.*

— **go the extra mile** (see EXTRA)

— **stick out a mile** (see STICK)

MILEAGE

* **get mileage out of** (colloq.): get use or advantage from, profit from >*The speaker's gotten a lot of mileage out of that story over the years.* >*I think I've got about all the mileage I'm going to get out of this coat.*

MILK RUN

— **milk run** (sl.): routine trip (esp. on an uneventful, regularly scheduled transport) >*I'll hop on the afternoon milk run and be there this evening.*

MILL

* **through the mill** (colloq.): undergoing a difficult or painful situation >*Claire's really been through the mill with her divorce.* >*The sergeant is putting the recruits through the mill.*

MILLION

* **like a million dollars/bucks** (colloq.): excellent, beautiful, superb (also adv.) >*Honey, you look like a million dollars tonight.* >*This car drives like a million bucks.*

— **one in a million** (see ONE)

* **thanks a million!** (colloq., freq. sarc.): thank you very much! >*Thanks a million! You just sat on my glasses.* >*Thanks a million for all your help!*

MINCEMEAT

— **make mincemeat (out) of** (... mins´mēt´ ...) (colloq.): defeat decisively, beat thoroughly >*You start a fight and he'll make mincemeat out of you.*

MIND

— **blow [s/one's] mind** (see BLOW)

— **give [s/one] a piece of [one's] mind** (see PIECE)

— **have half a mind to** (see HALF)

* **(I) don't mind if I do** (colloq.): I happily accept (an offer) >*Some chocolate chip ice cream? Don't mind if I do.*

— **[neg.] make no never mind** (see NEVER)

* **[one's] mind in the gutter** (colloq.): thinking of obscene or lewd things, having vulgar thoughts >*How can you think that about her? Your mind's in the gutter.*

— **mind the store** (colloq.): attend to business, watch over things (while s/one is away) >*Just go and enjoy your vacation—I'll mind the store.*

MIND-BLOWING

— **mind-blowing** (sl.): astonishing, awesome, very impressive >*Watchin' that huge rocket go up was mind-blowin'!*

MIND-BOGGLING

* **mind-boggling** (mīnd´bog´ling) (colloq.): astounding, awesome, overwhelming >*It's mind-boggling to think how many stars there are in the universe.*

MINT

* **a mint** (colloq.): a very large amount of money >*He's made a mint selling souvenirs to tourists.*

MINUTE

— **a mile a minute** (see MILE)

— **would ... in a minute** (colloq.): would readily ..., would enthusiastically or unhesitantly ... >*If they offered Don the job, he'd take it in a minute.*

MIRRORS

— **smoke and mirrors** (see SMOKE)

MISS

* **miss the boat** (colloq.): lose an opportunity, not take advantage of an opportunity >*You missed the boat by not applying for that grant.*

— **Mrs./Miss ...** (see MRS.)

* **not miss a trick** (colloq.): be aware of everything that happens, be astute, take advantage of every opportunity >*Put Gardner in charge of overseeing the project—he doesn't miss a trick.*

MISSIS
— **the missis** (see "**the MISSUS**")

MISSUS
* **the missus** (... mis´əz/mis´əs) (colloq.): (one's) wife, the housewife >*Let me talk it over with the missus.* >*Is the missus home, please?*

MISTER
* **mister** (voc.) (colloq.): sir, man >*Hey, mister, you got some loose change you can spare?*

— **Mister ...** (see "**MR. ...**")

— **Mister Right** (see "**MR. Right**")

— **no more Mister Nice Guy!** (see "**no more MR. Nice Guy!**")

MITT
— **mitt** (sl.): hand (esp. when seen as neg.) >*Keep your mitts off my things!*

MIX
— **mix it up** (sl.): start fighting, brawl >*They mixed it up after one of 'em called the other a dummy.*

MIXED
** **mixed up** (colloq.): confused, emotionally troubled >*The kid's been real mixed up since his parents divorced.*

* **mixed up in/with** (colloq.): involved in/with (objectionable activity or persons) >*He was mixed up in some insurance fraud case out west.* >*Don't get mixed up with those hoods.*

MOB
** **the Mob** (colloq.): the Mafia, an organized crime syndicate >*They say the Mob had him killed.*

MOBILE
— **...mobile** (... ´mō bēl´) (sl.): automobile used by ...s, automobile of ... quality >*Here comes the nerdmobile with a bunch of geeks inside.* >*Get that junkmobile off the road!*

MOBSTER
* **mobster** (mob´stər) (colloq.): gangster, mafioso, member of an organized crime syndicate >*They finally convicted the mobster for income tax evasion.*

MOD
— **mod** (mod) (colloq.): fashionably modern, in the vanguard of style >*She goes for funky, mod clothes.*

MOI
— **moi?!** (mwä) (sl., sarc.): I?! me?! (used facetiously to deny an accusation) >*You think I'm happy that jerk lost his job? Moi?!*

MOLE
— **mole** (sl.): infiltrator and informer, spy >*The old man's got a mole in the front office of his competitor's firm.* >*He was a C.I.A. mole in Eastern Europe for years.*

MOM
** **mom** (mom) (colloq.): mother (also voc.) >*I think your mom's nice.* >*What's for dinner, Mom?*

MOM-AND-POP
— **mom-and-pop** (mom´ən pop´) (colloq.): owned by a family, small retail (said of a business) >*The mom-and-pop stores just can't compete with the big outfits.*

MOMISM
— **momism** (mom´iz əm) (colloq.): typical expression of advice or concern (spoken by a mother to her children) >*"Put on your coat or you'll catch your death of cold!" is a momism I heard a lot when I was growing up.*

MOMMA
— **momma** (see "**MAMA**")

MOMMY
** **mommy** (mom´ē) (colloq.): mother (used esp. among children) (also voc.)

>*My mommy says that isn't nice.*
>*Read me a story, Mommy!*

MONEY

— **for [one's] money** (colloq.): in [one's] opinion, according to [one's] preference >*For my money, they'd be better off forgetting about the lawsuit.*

— **give [s/one] a run for [his/her] money** (see **RUN**)

* **have money to burn** (colloq.): have a great deal of money >*They can afford that vacation—they've got money to burn.*

— **in the money** (colloq.): having gotten a great deal of money, wealthy >*He'll really be in the money if he swings that deal.*

* **put [one's] money where [one's] mouth is** (colloq.): take action to prove [one] is sincere in what [one] says >*You say you trust him, so put your money where your mouth is and put him in charge.*

* **(right) on the money** (colloq.): precise, at the exact spot, on the dot, accurate (also adv.) >*I called for the correct time, and my watch is right on the money.* >*The bomb hit right on the money.* >*Art said he'd get here at noon, and he arrived on the money.*

— **throw money at** (see **THROW**)

MONEYGRUBBER

— **moneygrubber** (mun´ē grub´ər) (colloq.): overly greedy person, person obsessed with gaining money >*That moneygrubber's always scheming to make a buck.*

MONEYGRUBBING

— **moneygrubbing** (mun´ē grub´ing) (colloq.): overly greedy, obsessed with gaining money >*Don't let those moneygrubbing lawyers talk you into anything.*

MONIKER

— **moniker** (mon´i kər) (sl.): (person's) name or nickname >*His moniker's*

Lucky 'cause he always wins at poker.

MONKEY

* **monkey around** (vi) (colloq.): pass time idly or playfully, work halfheartedly or unproductively >*If you guys would stop your monkeying around we could get some work done around here.*

— **monkey around (with)** (colloq.): be sexually involved (with) (esp. illicitly), be sexually promiscuous (with) >*If Hugh finds out you've been monkeying around with his sister, you're in trouble.* >*Don't marry him—he likes to monkey around.*

* **monkey (around) with** (colloq.): treat without due respect or seriousness, handle capriciously, toy with >*Don't monkey with your computer if it's working OK.* >*I wouldn't monkey around with the cops if I was you.*

— **monkey on [one's] back** (sl.): addiction to drugs, severe and persistent personal vice or problem >*Cigarettes are a real monkey on his back.* >*Joel's got a monkey on his back with that gamblin' habit of his.*

MONKEY BUSINESS

* **monkey business** (colloq.): deceitful or improper conduct, illicit activity, trickery >*Don't try any monkey business when you're out with my daughter!* >*There's some monkey business going on around here because he always get the best commissions.*

MONKEYS

— **more fun than a barrel of monkeys** (see **FUN**)

MONKEY SUIT

— **monkey suit** (sl.): tuxedo, fancy suit, formal uniform >*I hate puttin' on this monkey suit for some dumb banquet.*

MONKEY'S UNCLE

— **(well,) I'll be (a monkey's uncle)!** (see **BE**)

MONKEY WRENCH
— **throw a monkey wrench into** (see THROW)

MONO
* **mono** (mon´ō) (colloq.): infectious mononucleosis >*She says she got mono from kissing her boyfriend.*

MONSTER
— **monster** (sl.): very large, gigantic >*How can I go to the dance with this monster pimple on my nose?*

— **create a monster** (see CREATE)

MONTEZUMA'S REVENGE
* **Montezuma's revenge** (mon´tə zū´məz …) (sl.): diarrhea affecting travelers (esp. foreigners in Mexico) >*She got a bad case of Montezuma's revenge in Guadalajara last summer.*

MONTH
— **a month of Sundays** (colloq.): a long time (esp. that s/thing has not recurred) >*Why, I haven't seen Martha in a month of Sundays.*

MOOCH
— **mooch**[1] (mūch) (sl.): person who habitually begs or borrows without repaying (esp. small things or amounts) >*Don't let that mooch come along unless she's got her own money.*

* **mooch**[2] (vi, vt) (sl.): obtain free of charge, beg or borrow without repaying (esp. small things or amounts) >*People are gettin' tired of your moochin'.* >*He always shows up around dinnertime and mooches a meal.*

MOOCHER
— **moocher** (mū´chər) (sl.): person who habitually begs or borrows without repaying (esp. small things or amounts) >*You'd better chip in, too, 'cause we don't like moochers.*

MOOLA
— **moola** (mū´lə) (sl.): money >*What do ya mean, "ideals"? He's in it for the moola!*

MOOLAH
— **moolah** (see "MOOLA")

MOON
* **moon** (vt) (sl.): bend over and expose the bare buttocks to (as a prank or to show contempt) >*He mooned the whole TV audience from a distance while Maclovio was talkin' in the foreground.*

— **shoot for the moon** (see SHOOT)

MOONLIGHT
** **moonlight** (vi) (colloq.): work at a second job (esp. at night) >*That cop moonlights as a bouncer at a nightclub.*

MOONSHINE
— **moonshine** (sl.): illegally distilled whiskey, homemade liquor >*Have a shot of my cousin's moonshine—it'll curl your toenails.*

MOP
— **mop (up) the floor with** (colloq.): defeat decisively, beat up >*Don't mess with him—he'll mop the floor with you.*

MORE
— **more (…) than you can shake a stick at** (colloq.): an abundance (of …), much (…), many (…) >*There are going to be more people than you can shake a stick at lined up to buy tickets for that show.* >*Sure he's got money—he's got more than you can shake a stick at.*

— **that's more like it** (see THAT'S)

MOSEY
— **mosey (on) (over/down/up to)** (mō´zē …) (colloq.): walk in a slow and leisurely manner (to), stroll (to), go on (to) >*Let's mosey over to Red's and see what's going on.* >*Now, you kids mosey on and stop hanging out around here.* >*I'm going to mosey on down to Pete's for a while.*

MOST
— **the most** (sl.): wonderful, the best >*I want his autograph—he's the most!*

MOTHER

* **mother**[1] (sl., freq. vulg.): person or thing (esp. seen as large or impressive) >*No one on the field can stop that mother today.* >*How we gonna get this mother loaded on the truck?*

* **mother**[2] (sl., freq. vulg.): mean or contemptible person >*I'll make that mother pay for what he did.*

— **the mother of all ...** (colloq.): the largest or most important ... of all >*We're going to have the mother of all beer parties when school's over.*

MOTHERFUCKER

* **motherfucker**[1] (muð´ər fuk´ər) (vulg.): mean or contemptible person (also voc.) >*We can't let that motherfucker get away with stealin' our stuff.* >*Watch your mouth, motherfucker!*

* **motherfucker**[2] (vulg.): person or thing (esp. seen as troublesome or contemptible) >*There's some motherfucker out there bitchin' about the food.* >*Can't find my wrench. Where'd I put the motherfucker?*

MOTHERFUCKING

— **motherfucking** (muð´ər fuk´ing) (vulg.): (intens. to express anger, contempt, or wonder) >*I don't want none of your motherfuckin' sympathy!* >*Where ya think you're motherfuckin' goin'?* >*Biggest motherfuckin' tires I ever saw!*

MOTOR-MOUTH

— **motor-mouth** (sl.): person who constantly talks, compulsive talker >*Will ya tell that motor-mouth to shut up for a while?*

MOTOWN

— **Motown** (mō´toun´) (colloq.): Detroit, Michigan >*He's originally from Motown.*

MOUNTAIN DEW

— **mountain dew** (colloq.): illegally distilled corn liquor, homemade liquor >*He bought a jug of mountain dew from some old guy back in the hills.*

MOUTH

* **mouth** (colloq.): indiscreet or annoying talk, impudence >*Watch your mouth or you're going to get in trouble.* >*Just do what I say and don't give me no mouth!*

— **[one's] big (fat) mouth** (colloq.): [one's] mouth (as the cause of overtalkativeness or indiscretion) >*My big fat mouth always gets me in trouble.* >*Don't open your big mouth or you'll ruin it for us.*

— **diarrhea of the mouth** (see DIARRHEA)

— **down in the mouth** (see DOWN)

— **foam at the mouth** (see FOAM)

** **keep [one's] mouth shut** (colloq.): stay quiet, not reveal a secret >*Keep your mouth shut or we'll all get fired.*

* **mouth off** (vi) (sl.): speak forcefully or imposingly, speak impudently or indiscreetly >*He's always gotta mouth off just to get attention.* >*We don't wanna hear ya mouthin' off about our sister.*

— **put [one's] foot in [one's] mouth** (see FOOT)

— **put [one's] money where [one's] mouth is** (see MONEY)

— **run off at the mouth** (see RUN)

— **shoot [one's] mouth off** (see SHOOT)

MOUTHFUL

* **mouthful**[1] (colloq.): long word or phrase, difficult word or phrase to pronounce >*"Perspicacious periphrasis" is quite a mouthful.*

— **mouthful**[2] (colloq.): very perceptive or relevant remark >*What he said about Vic's really working against himself was a mouthful.*

MOUTHPIECE

— **[one's] mouthpiece** (sl.): [one's] lawyer or spokesperson >*They'll just send *their mouthpiece to court and get a postponement.*

MOVE

* **move¹** (vi) (colloq.): sell well, be commercially popular >*This new model's been moving pretty good.*

* **move²** (vt) (colloq.): sell (esp. quickly or completely) >*We got to move our stock before we take inventory.*

* **get a move on** (colloq.): get underway, begin, hurry (used esp. as a command) >*It's late—let's get a move on.* >*Get a move on! We don't have all day.*

* **make [one's] move** (colloq.): assert [oneself], take determined action (esp. at an opportune time) >*Now's the time to make your move if you want to get some good property cheap.*

* **move in on** (colloq.): make advances toward controlling (s/thing belonging to another), usurp >*The imports were moving in on the computer market.*

** **move it** (sl.): hurry up, begin going fast (used esp. as a command) >*Come on, slowpoke, move it!* >*We'd better move it if we wanna get there on time.*

— **put a move on** (sl.): make a sexual advance toward, make an attempt to seduce >*Trent's thinkin' about puttin' a move on that babe over there.*

MOVER

— **mover** (colloq.): important or influential person >*He's a mover in the organization.*

MOVERS

* **movers and shakers** (colloq.): important or influential people >*The movers and shakers want the program, so they'll get it.*

MOVES

— **put the moves on** (sl.): make sexual advances toward, try to seduce >*I can't believe that nerdy guy's puttin' the moves on that beautiful chick.*

MOXIE

— **moxie** (mok´sē) (sl.): nerve, vigor, assertiveness, pluck >*If you've got the moxie, go right to your boss and complain.*

MR.

* **Mr. ...** (colloq., freq. sarc.): a very ... man or boy >*What an ego! He thinks he's Mr. Perfect.* >*Boswell is Mr. Clean. No one's going to come up with anything against him.*

* **Mr. Right** (colloq.): an ideal (male) romantic partner or potential husband >*She's just waiting for Mr. Right to come along.*

* **no more Mr. Nice Guy!** (colloq.): I am going to stop being so agreeable or lenient! I am no longer going to permit myself to be taken advantage of or mistreated! >*OK, if they want to play rough with me, then no more Mr. Nice Guy!*

MRS.

— **Mrs./Miss ...** (colloq., freq. sarc.): a very ... woman/girl >*He can get away with anything—his wife is Mrs. Understanding.* >*I'm sure little Miss Know-it-all will explain it to us.*

MUCH

— **much obliged** (see OBLIGED)

— **so much for ...** (see SO)

— **so much/bad I can taste it** (see SO)

MUCHO

— **mucho** (mū´chō) (sl.): much, many, very >*He's got mucho power in this town.* >*Hazel made mucho bucks on that deal.* >*The boss is mucho grumpy today.*

MUCK

— **muck up** (muk ...) (vt) (colloq.): botch, ruin, spoil >*Somehow that idiot managed to muck up the whole operation in just two weeks.*

MUCK-A-MUCK

— **muck-a-muck** (muk´ə muk´) (sl.): important or influential person >*Some* *muck-a-mucks from headquarters are comin' down tomorrow to look things over.*

MUD

— **mud** (colloq.): scandalous charges, malicious or defamatory remarks >*They threw a lot of mud at each other during the campaign.*

— **(as) clear as mud** (see CLEAR)

— **here's mud in your eye!** (sl.): here's to you! cheers! (said as a toast) >*Here's mud in your eye! Drink up!*

— **[for s/one's] name [to] be mud** (see NAME)

MUFF

— **muff** (muf) (vt) (colloq.): botch, bungle, ruin >*He muffed the job—we'll have to do it over.*

MUG

— **mug**[1] (colloq.): face >*I don't want to see your mug around here anymore.*

** **mug**[2] (vt) (colloq.): assault and rob >*The old woman was mugged in the park.*

— **mug**[3] (vi) (colloq.): exaggerate facial expressions, clown (esp. for an audience or camera) >*Settle down and stop mugging for the camera!*

MUG SHOT

* **mug shot** (sl.): police photograph of a criminal's or arrestee's face >*The victim identified the robber from mug shots.*

MUGGER

* **mugger** (mug´ər) (colloq.): person who assaults and robs others >*A mugger attacked him just as he turned the corner.*

MULE

— **mule** (sl.): person who transports illegal substances (esp. drugs) >*She's one of his mules bringin' heroin into the country.*

— **(as) stubborn as a mule** (see STUBBORN)

MUNCHIES

* **munchies** (mun´chēz) (colloq.): snack foods, snacks >*I can't watch TV without having some munchies like popcorn or pretzels.*

* **the munchies** (sl.): craving for snack foods >*Jimmy always gets the munchies about an hour before dinner.*

MURDER

* **murder**[1] (sl.): extremely demanding or severe person or thing, arduous or dangerous experience >*They say Professor Benson is murder in English lit.* >*The last three miles of the hike are uphill, and they're murder.* >*Joggin' on concrete is murder on the knees.*

* **murder**[2] (vt) (sl.): defeat decisively >*Their team ain't nothin'—we'll murder 'em.*

— **get away with murder** (see GET)

— **scream bloody murder** (see SCREAM)

MURDER ONE

* **murder one** (colloq.): (criminal charge of) first-degree murder >*She's facing a murder one rap because the killing was premeditated.*

MUSCLE

— **muscle** (sl.): person(s) used to intimidate by force or threat of violence, thug(s), bodyguard(s) >*Those big dudes are his muscle—they do his dirty work for him.* >*If ya need some muscle to deal with that jerk, just let me know.*

— **muscle ([one's] way) in(to)** (colloq.): enter or participate by forceful or aggressive means >*Somehow Kyle muscled his way into the meeting and took it over.* >*That gang's trying to muscle in on the rock cocaine market here.*

MUSCLEMAN

— **muscleman** (sl.): person used to intimidate by force or threat of violence, thug, bodyguard >*That gorilla is the* *mafioso's muscleman—he goes everywhere with him.*

MUSH
— **mush** (colloq.): exaggerated sentimentality, foolish amorousness >*Aw, gee, he's going to kiss her now! Do we have to watch this mush?*

MUSHY
— **mushy** (mush´ē/mŭsh´ē) (colloq.): overly sentimental, foolishly amorous >*I hate these mushy good-byes.*

MUSIC
— **face the music** (see FACE)

MUSTARD
— **cut the mustard** (see CUT)

MUST-SEE
* **must-see** (colloq.): something that should be seen or attended (because it is good) >*His new movie is a must-see.* >*This house is a must-see in your price range.*

MUTT
* **mutt** (mut) (colloq.): dog (esp. a mongrel, esp. a contemptible one) >*Stop that mutt's barking, will you?*

MY
* **my ass!** (vulg.): not so! in no way! not at all! >*A doctor, my ass! He's a bricklayer.*

— **my eye!** (colloq.): not so! in no way! not at all! >*I'll pay you, my eye! You owe me money!*

— **my foot!** (colloq.): not so! in no way! not at all! >*A college graduate, my foot! He dropped out his junior year.*

MYSELF
— **myself** (colloq.): I, me >*My boss and myself took care of the shipment.* >*As for myself, I don't care for opera.*

N

NA

* **na** (nä/na) (colloq.): no >*Neal? Na, don't ask him.*

NAB

— **nab** (nab) (vt) (colloq.): apprehend, arrest, capture >*The cops nabbed him just before he was going to cross into Illinois.*

NADA

— **nada** (nä´dä/nä´də) (sl.): nothing >*Ya know what I got outta that crummy deal? Nada, that's what.*

NAG

— **nag** (colloq.): racehorse (esp. seen as contemptible) >*I can't believe you bet fifty bucks on that nag.*

NAIL

* **nail**[1] (vt) (colloq.): arrest, catch, expose (esp. with proof of culpability) >*The police have been trying to nail that drug dealer for years.* >*With what we know about Green's dirty dealings, we can nail him whenever we want.*

* **nail**[2] (vt) (colloq.): strike, hit (esp. with quickness or accuracy) >*She nailed him with a left jab.* >*He nailed the deer at two hundred yards.*

— **nail [s/one] to the wall** (sl.): punish [s/one] severely, make [s/one] pay dearly (for a mistake or betrayal) >*They'll nail Stubby to the wall if they find out he's been stealin' from 'em.*

NAKED

— **(as) naked as a jaybird** (colloq.): completely naked >*He came to the door naked as a jaybird.*

NAM

* **Nam** (näm/nam) (colloq.): Vietnam (esp. in the context of the Vietnam War) >*In 1966 he was drafted and sent to Nam.*

NAME

— **have [s/one's] name on it/them** (sl.): be destined for or especially appropriate for [s/one], be especially appealing to [s/one] >*Watch out for that hoodlum— he's got a bullet with your name on it.* >*Those boots have my name on 'em— they'd look great on me.*

— **[for s/one's] name [to] be mud** (colloq.): [for s/one to] be despised or held in contempt, [for] people [to] be very angry with [s/one], [for s/one to] be in trouble >*My name will be mud around here if I screw this up.*

— **name names** (colloq.): identify (the guilty) by name, accuse specific persons >*Are you just making vague accusations, or are you going to name names?*

* **the name of the game** (colloq.): the essence, the important thing, the basic purpose, the hard reality >*The name of the game in politics is keeping the important people happy.*

* **... you name it** (colloq.): ... and every other similar thing you can think of, ... et cetera >*I can rent you a pick-up, a van, a station wagon, you name it.*

— **what's his/her name** (see **WHAT'S**)

NARC

* **narc** (närk) (sl.): police officer or agent who enforces drug laws, narcotics detective >*The narcs shut down a crack cocaine lab up in the mountains.*

NARK

— **nark** (see "NARC")

NATCH

— **natch** (sl.): naturally, of course >*You'll get your commission on the sale, natch.*

NATIVE

— **go native** (colloq.): adopt the behavior of a place (one) has moved to or is visiting and identify with it (esp. a less economically developed place) >*I hear Pratt went native over in Samoa and is going to marry a local girl.*

NAW

* **naw** (nä) (colloq.): no, of course not
>*Naw, I wouldn't do that.*

NEANDERTHAL

— **Neanderthal** (nē an´dər thôl´) (colloq.): unenlightened or reactionary person (also adj.) >*You'll never get those Neanderthals to go along with any new idea. >What's that Neanderthal political group those ultraconservatives belong to?*

NEAR

— **damn near** (see DAMN)

— **dang near** (see DANG)

— **darn near** (see DARN)

NEAT

* **neat** (sl.): wonderful, excellent >*That was a neat idea—it saved us a lot of work. >What a neat skateboard!*

NEATO

— **neato** (nē´tō) (sl.): wonderful, excellent (also interj.) >*She got a real neato video game for her birthday. >Neato! We get outta school early today.*

NECK

* **neck** (vi) (sl.): kiss and caress >*Jimmy necked with his girlfriend behind the house.*

— **break [one's] neck** (see BREAK)

— **breathing down [s/one's] neck** (see BREATHING)

— **neck of the woods** (colloq.): area, vicinity >*I've never been in that neck of the woods.*

— **pain in the neck** (see PAIN)

— **risk [one's] neck** (see RISK)

— **save [one's, s/one's] neck** (see SAVE)

— **stick [one's] neck out** (see STICK)

* **up to [one's] neck in** (colloq.): having an abundance or excess of, very occupied with >*Don't give me any more paperwork because I'm up to my neck in it already. >How does Mort do it? He's up to his neck in beautiful women!*

NEED

— **all [s/one] needs** (see ALL)

— **need [s/thing] like ([one] needs) a hole in the head** (see HOLE)

— **ought/need to have [one's] head examined** (see HEAD)

NEEDLE

* **needle** (vt) (colloq.): persistently nag, continually goad or tease >*She finally needled him into fixing the window. >Will you stop needling me about my fat stomach?*

NEIGHBORHOOD

* **in the neighborhood of** (colloq.): approximately, about (an amount) >*That car would run you in the neighborhood of $25,000. >Its population is in the neighborhood of six million.*

NERD

** **nerd** (nûrd) (sl.): socially contemptible or unattractive person, weird and dislikable person (esp. an intelligent person of unconventional behavior) >*Can ya believe that nerd wants to join our fraternity?*

NERDY

* **nerdy** (nûr´dē) (sl.): socially contemptible or unattractive, weird and dislikable >*You can come to the party, but don't bring that nerdy friend of yours.*

NERVE

** **nerve** (colloq.): audacity, impertinence, brashness >*He's got a lot of nerve asking Paula out after insulting her like that.*

* **hit/strike a (raw) nerve (with)** (colloq.): say or do (s/thing) of uncomfortable sensitivity (for) >*Jerome changed the subject when you brought up alcoholism—you must have hit a nerve with him. >She struck a raw nerve when she mentioned Terry's ex-wife.*

NERVY

— **nervy** (nûr´vē) (colloq.): audacious, impertinent, brash >*That was a pretty nervy thing to say to the judge.*

NETWORK

* **network** (vi) (colloq.): cultivate associations with people who may be helpful professionally >*A lot of people went to the conference just to network.*

NEVER

— **[neg.] make no never mind** (colloq.): does not matter, makes no difference >*For this job, it don't make no never mind if you got a college degree or not.*

NEW

— **a new one (on)** (colloq.): a novelty (for), something unheard of or amazing (for) >*A car with three-wheel drive? That's a new one on me.*

— **(brand) spanking new** (see SPANKING)

* **new kid on the block** (colloq.): person who is new to an organization or situation >*You're the new kid on the block, so take it easy till you learn your way around.*

— **(so) what else is new?** (see WHAT)

NICE

* **nice** (sl.): sexually attractive (esp. a woman) >*Oh, is she ever nice!*

** **nice and** (colloq.): quite, very (esp. regarding s/thing positive) >*I like my steak nice and juicy. >The ice on the rink's nice and hard.*

— **no more Mr. Nice Guy!** (see MR.)

NICKEL-AND-DIME

* **nickel-and-dime**[1] (colloq.): of little importance or value, insignificant >*He started out with some nickel-and-dime T-shirt business, and now he owns six department stores.*

* **nickel-and-dime**[2] (vt) (colloq.): drain with continual small expenses, wear down with persistent trivialities or petty criticisms >*We're being nickeled-and-*

dimed out of business by all these extra expenses. >They're nickeling-and-diming him with everything they can to try to get him to retire.

NIFTY

— **nifty** (nif´tē) (colloq.): stylish, attractive, good, clever >*He drives a nifty car. >That was a nifty idea you had.*

NIGGER

— **nigger** (nig´ər) (colloq., pej.): black person (also adj.) >*The racist jerk still calls blacks niggers and says that he hates nigger music.*

NIGHT

— **call it a day/night** (see CALL)

NIGHTCAP

— **nightcap** (colloq.): alcoholic drink taken late at night (as a last drink) >*How about a nightcap before we hit the hay?*

NIGHTIE

* **nightie** (nī´tē) (colloq.): nightgown >*I bought her a pretty pink nightie for her birthday.*

NIGHT OWL

* **night owl** (colloq.): person who habitually stays active late at night >*June's a real night owl—she never goes to bed before three in the morning.*

NIGHTY

— **nighty** (see "NIGHTIE")

NIGHTY-NIGHT

— **nighty-night!** (nī´tē nīt´) (colloq.): good night! >*It's my bedtime. Nighty-night, all!*

NINE

* **the whole nine yards** (colloq.): all the way, to as complete an extent as possible or appropriate (esp. regarding a commitment) >*Tim's a real pal. He'll go the whole nine yards for you.*

NINE-TO-FIVE

** **nine-to-five** (colloq.): of regular workday hours, of a routine office job (esp. a dull one) >*I'm getting sick of* *this nine-to-five stuff. >Gail wants more than just a nine-to-five job.*

NIT-PICK

* **nit-pick** (nit´pik´) (vi, vt) (colloq.): focus on insignificant details (concerning), criticize or argue about trivial things (concerning) >*Stop nit-picking and just give me your general impression of the essay. >I shouldn't have asked him to look the proposal over because he nit-picked it to death.*

NITTY-GRITTY

* **the nitty-gritty** (... nit´ē grit´ē) (sl.): the essence, the important details, the basics (also adj.) >*Let's get down to the nitty-gritty and talk about what's really botherin' ya. >This last part gives ya the nitty-gritty details of the whole proposal.*

NITWIT

— **nitwit** (nit´wit´) (colloq.): foolish or stupid person >*Don't count on that nitwit doing it right.*

NIX

— **nix¹** (niks) (sl.): no, that's not acceptable >*Borrow my car? Nix! >I asked her out to a movie, but she said nix.*

— **nix²** (vt) (sl.): veto, prohibit >*I asked the boss to let me make the presentation, but he nixed it.*

NO

— **(be) no ...** (see entry under ... noun)

— **in less than no time** (see LESS)

— **in no time (flat)** (see TIME)

— **it's no good ...** (see GOOD)

— **no can do** (sl.): it cannot be done, I cannot allow it, it is impossible or prohibited >*I know ya want it fixed by Thursday, but no can do. >Smoke by the gas pump? No can do!*

— **no sirree!** (... sə rē´) (colloq.): in no way! absolutely not! >*I ain't going back to that lousy place again! No sirree!*

NO-ACCOUNT

— **no-account** (colloq.): good-for-nothing person, undependable or irresponsible person (also adj.) >*She married some no-account who left her after two months. >I don't want any of your no-account friends around here.*

NOBODY

* **nobody** (colloq.): unknown or insignificant person, person not given worth or dignity (cf. "SOMEBODY") >*I can't believe they sent that nobody to deal with us. >Forget that clown! He's a nobody.*

NOBODY'S

— **like nobody's business** (sl.): wholeheartedly, to the utmost degree, intensely >*Our team was runnin' the ball like nobody's business!*

* **nobody's home** (sl.): (s/one) is crazy or mentally unbalanced >*That guy's just too weird. If ya ask me, nobody's home there.*

NOD

— **the nod** (colloq.): approval, indication of being selected >*When the supervisor gives us the nod, we'll get going on this. >Four people were being considered, but Jake finally got the nod.*

NOGGIN

— **noggin** (nog´ən) (colloq.): (person's) head >*The ball hit him right on the noggin.*

NO-GO

* **be (a) no-go** (sl.): be canceled, not be approved >*The trip is a no-go because the airport is fogged in. >We just heard the project is no-go—they say it costs too much.*

NO-GOOD

* **no-good** (colloq.): worthless, contemptible >*That no-good brother of yours has been arrested again.*

NOHOW

— **[neg.] nohow** (... nō´hou´) (sl.): under no circumstances, [neg.] anyway >*I* *can't get this stupid toaster to work nohow. >Why buy it? Ya ain't gonna use it nohow.*

NOISE
— **noise** (sl.): empty talk, meaningless complaining, bluster >*Don't give me none of your noise, 'cause I ain't gonna change my mind.*

NO-NO
** **no-no** (colloq.): prohibited thing, ill-advised or forbidden action >*Firearms are a no-no on airplanes.* >*Swimming right after eating is a no-no.*

NOODLE
— **noodle** (sl.): (person's) head, mind >*You can figure it out if you'll just use the old noodle.*

NOOKIE
— **nookie** (see "NOOKY")

NOOKY
— **nooky**[1] (nŭk´ē) (vulg.): sexual intercourse (with a woman) (freq. used with *some* or *any*) >*He says he hasn't gotten any nooky for over a month.*
— **nooky**[2] (vulg., pej.): woman or women (seen as sex object[s]) >*He says a lot of nice nooky showed up at the party.*

NOPE
** **nope** (nōp) (sl.): no >*Nope, I didn't see a thing.*

NOSE
— **be no skin off [s/one's] nose** (see SKIN)
— **have [one's] nose (all) out of joint** (colloq.): be irritated or envious, feel offended or slighted >*Don't get your nose all out of joint—it's nothing personal.*
* **keep [one's] nose clean** (colloq.): behave [oneself], stay out of trouble >*He'd better keep his nose clean or he'll end up back in prison.*
— **look down [one's] nose at** (see LOOK)
* **nose around** (vi) (colloq.): pry, investigate (without invitation) >*Some*

private detective has been nosing around our warehouse.
— **nose out** (vt) (colloq.): defeat or prevail over by a narrow margin >*He was pretty well qualified, but with her experience she nosed him out for the job.*
* **on the nose** (colloq.): precisely, exactly >*He guessed the number of books on the nose.* >*We got there at four on the nose.*
— **pay through the nose** (see PAY)
— **powder [one's] nose** (see POWDER)
— **put [s/one's] nose (all) out of joint** (colloq.): irritate [s/one], make [s/one] envious or jealous, offend or slight [s/one] >*It really put Charlie's nose out of joint when they chose a new employee over him.*
* **(right) under [s/one's] (very) nose** (colloq.): in plain view of [s/one], where [s/one] should easily notice >*The info he needs is right there under his nose.* >*I can't believe Sanders flirted with the boss's wife under his very nose.*
— **rub [s/one's] nose in [s/thing]** (see RUB)
— **stick/poke [one's] nose in(to)** (see STICK)
— **win/lose by a nose** (colloq.): win/lose by a narrow margin >*We lost the game by a nose, twenty to nineteen.* >*He just won by a nose, but at least he won.*

NOSE JOB
* **nose job** (colloq.): plastic surgery to improve the appearance of the nose, rhinoplasty >*Heather got a nose job last summer and looks a lot better.*

NOSES
— **count noses** (see COUNT)

NOSEY
— **nosey** (see "NOSY")

NO-SHOW
* **no-show** (colloq.): person who does not appear for an appointment or reservation

(and who has not canceled it) >*There are three no-shows, so we'll have some empty seats.*

NOSY

** **nosy** (nō´zē) (colloq.): prying, intrusive, overly curious >*What's it to you? Don't be so nosy!*

NOT

— ... **not!** (stressed, after pause) (sl., sarc.): (emphatic negation of a statement in order to tease or express contempt) >*Sure, I'll take your sister to the dance ... not! >Yeah, he sings as good as Elvis ... not!*

— **not on your life!** (see **LIFE**)

NOTCH

— **a notch above/below** (colloq.): a degree or level better/worse than, a grade superior/inferior to >*This movie is a notch above the last one we saw.*

NOTES

— **swap notes** (see **SWAP**)

'NOTHER

— **a whole 'nother** (see **WHOLE**)

NOTHING

— **nothing** (colloq.): worthless, insignificant, unpromising >*I don't want to stay in this nothing town all my life.*

— **here goes nothing!** (see **HERE**)

* **in nothing flat** (colloq.): in a very short time, very quickly >*I could eat that whole pie in nothing flat.*

* **nothing doing!** (colloq.): absolutely not! (it) will not be permitted! >*Me, get on that roller coaster? Nothing doing! >You want me to let you in without a ticket? Nothing doing!*

— **nothing to sneeze at** (see **SNEEZE**)

* **nothing to write home about** (colloq.): something of little significance, nothing of special importance >*I've been dating this guy, but he's nothing to write home about.*

NOTHINGS

— **sweet nothings** (see **SWEET**)

NOW

— **now** (colloq.): up-to-date, in style >*These clothes are the now look.*

* **now you're talking!** (colloq.): finally you're saying or doing s/thing preferable! that's better! >*Steak instead of wieners? Now you're talking!*

NOWHERE

— **nowhere** (sl.): futile, boring, inferior, useless >*They transferred him to some nowhere town in South Dakota. >Why do ya hang around with those nowhere bums?*

* **get nowhere fast** (sl.): make no progress at all >*I gotta get a new tutor—I'm getting nowhere fast with this one.*

— **the middle of nowhere** (see **MIDDLE**)

NO-WIN

* **no-win** (colloq.): incapable of rendering benefit or success, hopeless >*Just get out of there—it's a no-win situation for you.*

NUDIE

— **nudie** (nū´dē/nyū´dē) (colloq.): featuring nudes >*He sure buys a lot of nudie magazines.*

NUKE

* **nuke**[1] (nūk/nyūk) (colloq.): nuclear weapon >*They don't want nukes stored near their town.*

— **nuke**[2] (colloq.): nuclear reactor or power plant >*What if one of those nukes has a meltdown?*

* **nuke**[3] (vt) (colloq.): destroy with nuclear weapons >*Some idiot was yelling, "Nuke the bastards!"*

— **nuke**[4] (vt) (sl.): cook (in a microwave oven) >*Just take it outta the freezer, nuke it ten minutes, and presto! Instant dinner.*

NUMBER

— **number**[1] (colloq.): attractive or sexy woman >*Who was that cute number I saw you with last night?*

— **number**[2] (sl.): calculated act or story (to achieve a goal, esp. using deceit) >*He gave me some number about his mother bein' sick, but I didn't believe it.*

— **A-number-one** (see "A-NUMBER-ONE")

* **do a number on** (sl.): deceive, mistreat, hurt >*They really did a number on that old woman when they sold her that worthless land.* >*I did a number on my ankle playin' football yesterday.*

* **have [s/one's] number** (colloq.): know [s/one's] real intentions, know the hard truth about [s/one] >*Tony thinks he's fooling me, but I've got his number.*

— **… number** (colloq.): … article, … product, … thing >*How much is that red number in the window?* >*They've come out with a real snazzy number this year.*

— **[for s/one's] number [to] be up** (sl.): [for it to] be time [for s/one] to die or suffer ruin >*When my number's up, I wanna go fast.*

NUMBER CRUNCHER

— **number cruncher** (colloq.): person or thing that does numerical calculations or processes numerical data (esp. in large quantities) (cf. "CRUNCH numbers") >*The new computer program he developed is a powerful number cruncher.*

NUMBER ONE

* **number one** (colloq.): (one)self, (one's) own interest or advantage >*I always look out for number one, because who's going to look out for me if I don't?*

* **do/go number one** (colloq.): urinate (used esp. with children) (cf. "do/go NUMBER TWO") >*Mom, Billy did number one in his pants!*

NUMBERS

— **(go) by the numbers** (colloq.): (proceed) according to standard procedure, (act) following the rules or established steps >*He's in trouble because he wouldn't go by the numbers.* >*We're going to investigate this case by the numbers.*

* **the numbers** (colloq.): the actual figures (esp. of money) >*Give me the numbers for travel expenses last month.*

NUMBER TWO

* **do/go number two** (colloq.): defecate (used esp. with children) (cf. "do/go NUMBER ONE") >*Daddy, find a toilet! I got to go number two real bad!*

NUMERO UNO

* **numero uno** (nū′mə rō′ ū′nō) (sl.): (one)self, (one's) own interest or advantage >*Call me selfish, but I always take care of numero uno first.*

NUMB-NUTS

— **numb-nuts** (num′nuts′) (vulg.): foolish or contemptible person (also voc.) >*Who's the numb-nuts that just spilled mustard all over his shirt?* >*Watch where you're wavin' that cigar, numb-nuts!*

NURD

— **nurd** (see "NERD")

NUT

** **nut**[1] (sl.): silly or eccentric person, crazy person >*The guy must be a nut to paint his house hot pink.*

* **nut**[2] (sl.): enthusiast, fanatic >*He's a nut about boat racin'.* >*My girl's a movie nut—she sees everything that comes out.*

— **off [one's] nut** (sl.): crazy or very eccentric >*He's off his nut if he thinks that dumb idea will work.*

— **hard/tough nut to crack** (colloq.): hard problem to solve, tough endeavor >*Finding a way to get all this equipment up there by Friday is a tough nut to crack.*

* **tough nut** (colloq.): stubborn person, person hard to deal with >*I couldn't get anywhere with old Wilkens—he's a tough nut, all right.*

— **would give [one's] left/right nut** (see GIVE)

NUT CASE

— **nut case** (sl.): crazy person >*Watch out for that weirdo. He's a real nut case.*

NUT HOUSE

* **nut house** (sl.): mental institution, psychiatric hospital >*She went off the deep end and landed in the nut house.*

NUTS

* **nuts**[1] (vulg.): testicles >*This cup protects your nuts durin' a game.*

** **nuts**[2] (colloq.): crazy, eccentric >*Caldwell's nuts if he thinks I'll go along with that weird scheme of his.*

— **freeze [one's] balls/nuts off** (see FREEZE)

— **have [s/one] by the balls/nuts** (see BALLS)

— **nuts!** (sl.): (interj. to express irritation, defiance, or disappointment) >*Nuts! I lost again.* >*If they want me to pay more, I'll tell 'em "nuts"!*

* **nuts about/over** (colloq.): liking very much, enthusiastic about, in love with >*I'm nuts about jazz.* >*What a cute couple—they're nuts over each other.*

NUTS AND BOLTS

* **nuts and bolts** (colloq.): basic elements, practical aspects, fundamentals >*The manager's got to know the nuts and bolts of the entire operation.*

NUTTIER

— **nuttier than a fruitcake** (colloq.): very crazy, very eccentric >*They ought to commit O'Brian—he's nuttier than a fruitcake.*

NUTTY

* **nutty** (sl.): crazy, eccentric, silly >*Talbert's kinda nutty, but he's basically a good guy.*

— **(as) nutty as a fruitcake** (colloq.): very crazy, very eccentric >*The old gal's as nutty as a fruitcake, but she's harmless.*

NYMPHO

* **nympho** (nim´fō) (sl.): nymphomaniac >*They say that woman with all the guys around her is a nympho.*

O

OARS

— **not have both oars in the water** (sl.): be mentally unbalanced, be crazy >*That poor old bag lady doesn't have both oars in the water.*

OATS

— **feeling [one's] oats** (see FEELING)

OBIT

— **obit** (ō bit´) (colloq.): obituary >*I read in the obits where old Mr. Drake died last week.*

OBLIGED

— **much obliged** (colloq.): thank you >*Much obliged for all your help.*

O.D.

* **O.D.**[1] (sl.): overdose (of a drug) >*He was shootin' heroin and died from an O.D.*

* **O.D.**[2] (vi) (sl.): overdose (on a drug), consume or experience (s/thing) in excess >*She O.D.ed on cocaine and ended up in the hospital.* >*I think that kid is O.D.in' TV.*

ODDBALL

* **oddball** (colloq.): strange or eccentric person (also adj.) >*Some oddball lives there with forty cats.* >*You don't really think his oddball plan will work, do you?*

ODDS-ON

— **odds-on** (colloq.): most likely to win or succeed, best-bet, almost sure >*Willy-Nilly is the odds-on favorite in the third race.*

OFF

— **off**[1] (vt) (sl.): murder, kill >*They offed the dude 'cause he tried to double-cross 'em.*

* **off**[2] (colloq.): somewhat crazy, rather eccentric >*If you ask me, that strange guy's a little bit off.*

— **off (the) ...** (see entry under ... noun)

OFF-AGAIN

— **on-again, off-again** (see ON-AGAIN)

OFFBEAT

* **offbeat** (colloq.): unconventional, nonconformist, odd >*Timmy joined some offbeat commune up in the Northwest.* >*He hangs around with those offbeat characters in the park.*

OFF-THE-CUFF

* **off-the-cuff** (colloq.): extemporaneous, unrehearsed, impromptu >*You shouldn't take those off-the-cuff remarks too seriously.*

OFF-THE-WALL

* **off-the-wall** (sl.): very nonsensical or incongruent, very unconventional or eccentric >*In the middle of the business meeting Hopkins made some off-the-wall comment about the asteroid belt.* >*That weird guy's totally off-the-wall.*

OH

— **oh, yeah?** (see YEAH)

O.J.

* **O.J.** (colloq.): orange juice >*Want a glass of O.J. with breakfast?*

OK

** **OK**[1] (colloq.): approval, agreement >*All we need is an OK from the supervisor to get started.*

** **OK**[2] (vt) (colloq.): approve, authorize, agree to >*The president OKed the plan yesterday.*

** **OK**[3] (colloq.): correct, right >*Yeah, these figures add up—they're OK.* >*Is this spelling OK?*

** **OK**[4] (colloq.): all right, that's fine, go ahead, good, yes >*OK, I'll go with you if you want.* >*OK—you're next.* >*I'm going to borrow your pencil, OK?* >*Ten dollars an hour? OK!*

** **OK**[5] (colloq.): acceptable, satisfactory (also adv.) >*He's not real fast, but his work is OK.* >*She was sick, but she's OK now.* >*The business is doing OK.*

* **OK**[6] (colloq.): likable, of good character >*Your buddy's an OK guy.*

** **OK?** (colloq.): (interj. to reinforce [one's] complaint in a contentious situation) >*Hey, loudmouth, I'm trying to study here, OK? >I'm sick of your badmouthing me, OK?*

* **OK, ...** (colloq.): (crutch word to introduce s/thing new) >*OK, let's say you're at the movies and, OK, there's a lady with a hat on in front of you, OK, and she's with this really big guy, OK, and ...*

OKAY
— **okay** (see "OK")

OKEY-DOKE
— **okey-doke** (ō′kē dōk′) (colloq.): all right, that's fine, go ahead, good, yes >*Okey-doke—that should do it. >Pick you up at seven? Okey-doke.*

OKEY-DOKEY
— **okey-dokey** (ō′kē dō′kē) (colloq.): all right, that's fine, go ahead, good, yes >*Okey-dokey—looks fine to me.*

OLD
* **old**[1] (freq. ōl) (colloq.): familiar and cherished >*Old Jill's a good worker. >This little old pipe's my favorite.*

— **old**[2] (freq. ōl) (colloq.): contemptible, worthless >*She says she doesn't want to go to some old wedding shower.*

— **any old** (see ANY)

— **(as) old as the hills** (colloq.): very old >*Don't you know any new jokes? That one's as old as the hills.*

— **be a chip off the old block** (see CHIP)

— **old ...** (see entry under ... noun)

OLDEST
* **the oldest trick in the book** (colloq.): a well-known deception or strategy >*He claimed he ran out of gas? That's the oldest trick in the book!*

OLD HAT
* **be old hat** (colloq.): be old-fashioned or trite, no longer be new or exciting >*Making tigers disappear is old hat for magicians now. >Trips to the moon will be old hat by the middle of the next century.*

OLDIE
* **oldie** (ōl′dē) (colloq.): s/thing popular in the past (but still of current interest) >*Casablanca is an oldie, but people still love it. >They're playing an oldie that we used to dance to when we were teenagers.*

OLD-TIMER
— **old-timer**[1] (colloq.): person with long experience (in a place or activity) >*Henry's an old-timer around here— he's been with the company almost thirty years. >The old-timers in the business know better than to try that.*

— **old-timer**[2] (colloq., freq. pej.): old person (esp. a man) (also voc.) >*Some old-timer was telling me this used to be a mining town. >Say, old-timer, you got a match?*

OLE
— **ole** (ōl) (see "OLD")

ON
* **be on**[1] (colloq.): have (one's) proposal or challenge accepted >*Tennis tomorrow? You're on. >If he wants to bet five bucks to see which one of us finishes first, he's on.*

— **be on**[2] (colloq.): behave in a theatrical or artificial way, act in an affected or attention-getting way >*I wonder what Martha's really like—she's always on when she's out in public.*

— **have [s/thing] on** (see HAVE)

** **on [s/one]**[1] (colloq.): being [s/one's] treat, being paid for by [s/one] >*Ed says dinner's on him tonight. >The drinks are on me.*

* **on [s/one]**[2] (colloq.): in [s/one's] immediate possession, being carried by [s/one] >*I don't have a pencil on me. >You got twenty dollars on you?*

ON-AGAIN–ONE-UPMANSHIP

* **on** [s/one][3] (colloq.): to the detriment of [s/one], affecting [s/one] adversely >*My stupid car quit on me!* >*Our dog up and died on us.*

— **on (a/the)** ... (see entry under ... noun)

* **on (for)** (colloq.): having (a time or date) confirmed or scheduled >*I reserved a tennis court. We're on for five o'clock tomorrow afternoon.* >*How about our regular Friday night movie? Are we on this week or not?*

ON-AGAIN

* **on-again, off-again** (colloq.): undecided, uncertain (as to whether or not s/thing will proceed) >*The celebration they're supposed to be planning has been on-again, off-again all year because the city's had trouble getting the money together for it.* >*They've had an on-again, off-again romance for years.*

ONCE-OVER

* **once-over** (colloq.): quick look, quick examination or evaluation >*Would you give this letter a once-over and see if it sounds OK?* >*She gave me the once-over when I walked in.*

ONE

* **one**[1] (stressed) (colloq.): an extraordinarily, a very >*Donny's* one *smart kid!* >*That was* one *fine meal!*

* **one**[2] (stressed) (colloq.): an extraordinary, an impressive, a surprising >*I tell you, that was* one *good-looking woman he went out with last night!*

— **go [s/one] one better** (see GO)

* **have one too many** (colloq.): drink a little too much, become drunk >*Bart's slurring his words—I'd say he's had one too many.*

— **in one piece** (see PIECE)

— **[neg.]** ... **one** (sl.): [neg.] even the first ..., [neg.] the least ... >*He doesn't have idea one about what to do.* >*I don't know thing one about plumbing.*

— **[one's] one and only** (colloq.): [one's] sweetheart, [one's] true love >*Josh is Patty's one and only. She hasn't dated anyone else since she met him.*

— **one for the book(s)** (colloq.): a noteworthy thing or occurrence >*That deadbeat actually paid you back? That's one for the books!*

— **one for the road** (colloq.): one last drink, a final drink before leaving >*Hey, let's have one for the road before you take off.*

— **one heck of a** (see HECK)

— **one hell of a** (see HELL)

* **one in a million** (colloq.): a very good or impressive person or thing, a very valuable person or thing >*My girlfriend's one in a million.* >*I want that job—it's one in a million.*

— **one jump ahead (of)** (see JUMP)

— **[neg.] one/a red cent** (see RED CENT)

ONE-ARMED BANDIT

— **one-armed bandit** (colloq.): slot machine >*That dang one-armed bandit got fifty dollars in quarters from me.*

ONE-NIGHT STAND

* **one-night stand**[1] (colloq.): single sexual encounter (esp. overnight) >*It was just a one-night stand last summer—we never saw each other again.*

— **one-night stand**[2] (colloq.): person with whom (one) has a single sexual encounter (esp. overnight) >*He's a one-night stand she had a couple of months ago.*

ONE-SHOT

* **one-shot** (colloq.): occurring only once, having only one incidence or chance >*This is a one-shot deal—we'll never get another chance at it.*

ONE-UPMANSHIP

— **one-up(s)manship** (wun′up(s)′mən ship′) (colloq.): practice or art of gaining an advantage or showing superiority over another (esp. by way of status symbols or privilege) >*Gerry and Hank spent the evening playing one-upmanship by bragging about their salaries and benefits at work.* >*He's a master at one-upsmanship among the young executives.*

ONLY
— **only have eyes for** (see **EYES**)

ONTO
* **be onto** (colloq.): be aware or informed of (esp. s/thing illicit or supposedly secret) >*He recognized us—he's onto us.* >*The cops are onto your scheme.*

OODLES
— **oodles (of …)** (ūd´lz …) (colloq.): much (…), many (…) >*That songwriter has oodles of talent.* >*Have one of my pencils—I've got oodles at home.*

OOH
— **ooh and ah** (ū´ … ä´) (vi) (colloq.): express praise, express admiration or wonder >*Everyone oohed and ahed over her wedding dress.*

OOMPH
— **oomph** (ūmf) (sl.): energy, vigor, enthusiasm >*Ya gotta put some oomph into your bowling to do it right.* >*I like that boy—he's got oomph.*

OOPS
** **oops!** (ŭps/ūps) (colloq.): (interj. to express dismay or regret for having made a mistake or social blunder or caused an accident) >*Oops! I'm sorry— I didn't know your husband had died.* >*Oops! I dropped Mom's favorite teapot.*

OPEN
* **open up**[1] (vi) (colloq.): speak frankly and without restraint (esp. about a personal problem) >*She finally opened up to her sister and told her everything.*

— **open up**[2] (vt) (sl.): give full acceleration or power to, attain the top speed of >*I'm gonna open this truck up when we hit the highway.*

— **wide open** (see **WIDE**)

OPENERS
* **for openers** (colloq.): to begin with, in the first place >*You want to know why Johnny shouldn't drink? For openers, he's not legally old enough.* >*I'll have your soup of the day for openers.*

OPERATE
— **operate** (vi) (colloq.): be manipulative to attain (one's) ends (esp. by devious means) >*Owens really knows how to operate to get people to invest in his schemes.*

OPERATOR
— **operator** (colloq.): person who attains his/her ends through manipulation (esp. in a devious way) >*The guy's a real operator when it comes to getting his way with women.*

— **fast worker/operator** (see **FAST**)

— **smooth operator** (see **SMOOTH**)

OR
— **… or else!** (see **ELSE**)

— **…, or what?** (see **WHAT**)

ORAL
* **oral** (colloq.): oral examination >*Cecilia passed the written exam, so if she does OK on the oral she'll be admitted.*

ORDER
— **tall order** (see **TALL**)

ORNERY
— **ornery** (ôr´nə rē/on´rē) (colloq.): mean-spirited, mischievous, grouchily stubborn >*That ornery old man just kicked my dog.* >*You'll never change that ornery fool's mind.*

OUGHT
— **ought/need to have [one's] head examined** (see **HEAD**)

OURSELVES
— **ourselves** (colloq.): we, us >*Our friends and ourselves threw the party.* >*Their announcement surprised no one more than ourselves.*

OUT

— **out**[1] (colloq.): excuse, way to escape (s/thing unpleasant) >*My out is that I wasn't there when it was stolen.* >*His lawyer's trying to find an out for him.*

* **out**[2] (colloq.): not in style, not fashionable, not currently popular >*That style is out this year.*

* **out**[3] (colloq.): unconscious, sleeping deeply >*Five martinis and he was out.* >*I went to bed so tired I was out as soon as my head hit the pillow.*

* **out**[4] (colloq.): having suffered a loss or expense of (an amount of money) >*I was out two grand when that stock fell.* >*It's going to put us out six hundred bucks to get the motor fixed.*

— **out**[5] (vt) (sl.): reveal the identity of (s/one) as a homosexual (esp. against his/her will) >*They threatened to out him unless he came outta the closet on his own.*

** **be out of here** (sl.): be leaving, be fired or evicted >*It's five o'clock—I'm outta here.* >*You screw up once more and you're outta here.*

— **come out of the closet** (see **CLOSET**)

— **go out of [one's] way** (see **GO**)

— **go out (on)** (see **GO**)

— **have it out (with)** (see **HAVE**)

— **...ed-out** (colloq.): having had an excess of ..., tired of ... >*Not another cup for me—I'm coffeed-out.* >*All we've seen on this trip is old castles. I'm castled-out by now.*

— **(out) cold** (see **COLD**)

* **out from under** (colloq.): free of (esp. a debt or responsibility) >*I'm glad to be out from under that loan. I finally paid it off.* >*How are you going to get out from under chairing the new committee?*

— **out front** (colloq.): straightforwardly, candidly >*She told me out front that she was after my job.*

— **out in left field** (see **LEFT FIELD**)

* **out like a light** (sl.): unconscious, sleeping deeply >*I don't know what Boomer took, but he was out like a light when I got here.*

— **out of (the/[one's]/[s/one's]) ...** (see entry under ... noun)

* **out of it**[1] (sl.): not fully conscious or aware, unconscious, not alert (esp. due to drugs or alcohol) >*After three drinks she's out of it.* >*I'm usually out of it until I have a cup of coffee in the morning.*

* **out of it**[2] (sl.): not conforming to fashion or popular values, socially deficient >*What does she see in some nerd that's totally out of it?*

— **out of this world** (see **WORLD**)

— **out on a limb** (see **LIMB**)

— **out on [one's] ass** (vulg.): fired, evicted, ejected >*Don't pay the rent and you'll be out on your ass.* >*Crowley was out on his ass when they caught him takin' company property.*

— **out on [one's] butt** (sl., freq. vulg.): fired, evicted, ejected >*Start behavin' yourself around here or you'll find yourself out on your butt.*

* **out to get [s/one]** (colloq.): wanting to hurt [s/one], searching for a way to cause [s/one] harm >*Why is Adams out to get me? What have I ever done to him?*

* **out to lunch** (sl.): not knowing what's happening, eccentric, unfashionable or socially inept >*Don't invite Arnold to the party—that guy's totally out to lunch.*

OUT-A-SIGHT

— **out-a-sight** (see "out of SIGHT[1]")

OUTFIT

* **outfit** (colloq.): association of persons, company >*Clem worked for some oil drilling outfit in Oklahoma for a while.*

OUT-FRONT
— **out-front** (colloq.): straightforward, honest, candid >*Just be out-front with the boss—he'll understand.*

OUTIE
— **outie** (ou´tē) (colloq.): protruding navel (cf. "INNIE") >*Hey, look! Agnes has an outie.*

OUT-OF-SIGHT
— **out-of-sight** (see "out of SIGHT")

OUTS
— **on the outs (with)** (... outs ...) (colloq.): on unfriendly terms (with) (esp. s/one with whom one has had a previously friendly relationship) >*They used to hang around together a lot, but now they're on the outs.* >*She's on the outs with her mother.*

OUTTA
** **outta** (ou´tə) (colloq.): out of >*It's five o'clock—I'm outta here!*

OVEN
— **in the oven** (sl.): (a fetus) in the womb, constituting pregnancy >*He's already got seven kids, and his wife's got another one in the oven.*

OVER
— **all over [s/one]** (see ALL)
— **be all over but the shouting** (see ALL)
— **cannot get over** (see GET)
** **go over [s/one's] head** (colloq.): appeal to a higher authority than [s/one] (without regard for conventional hierarchical procedure) >*I'm going over the manager's head with this problem—straight to the president of the company.*
— **have it all over** (see HAVE)
— **over (a/the) ...** (see entry under ... noun)

OVERBOARD
* **go overboard** (colloq.): go to extremes, be overly enthusiastic, become excessively involved >*Giving to charity is great, but selling your house*

and giving away the money is going overboard.

OWE
* **owe [s/one]**[1] (colloq.): be indebted to [s/one] (for a favor), feel obligated to repay [s/one] (for his/her help) >*Boy, you really came through for me today—I owe you.*
— **owe [s/one]**[2] (sl.): have to pay [s/one] (for a wrong one has done to him/her), be subject to [s/one's] revenge >*He owes me for what he did on Friday, and I'm gonna get him.*

OWN
* **own up (to)** (colloq.): confess (to), admit responsibility (for) >*Why don't you own up to taking the money? You did it, and everyone knows it.*

OX
— **ox** (colloq.): large and strong man (esp. one who is not intelligent) >*He has this big ox who doesn't ask questions to do his dirty work for him.*
— **(as) strong as an ox** (see STRONG)

P

PA

— **pa** (pä) (colloq.)· father (also voc.)
>*Where does your pa work?* >*Can you lend me ten bucks, Pa?*

PACK

— **pack** (vt) (colloq.): carry on (one's) person (esp. when readily available for use) >*He packs a thirty-eight revolver when he carries a lot of cash.* >*Why does she pack that book everywhere she goes?*

— **pack a punch/wallop** (... wol´əp) (colloq.): be able to deliver a powerful blow, be very potent >*He's a skinny little guy, but he really packs a punch in a fight.* >*This rum packs quite a wallop!*

* **pack 'em in** (... əm ...) (colloq.): attract a large audience, be very popular (said of a show, entertainer, etc.) >*They've been packing 'em in down at Larry's Lounge ever since that sexy blonde started singing there.* >*That old comedian still packs 'em in.*

PACK RAT

* **pack rat** (colloq.): person who saves or collects useless things (esp. obsessively) >*Millie's such a pack rat! She's got junk stored all over the place.*

PAD

— **pad** (sl.): home, living quarters >*You can stay at my pad tonight if ya want.* >*Nice pad ya got here.*

PADDY WAGON

— **paddy wagon** (pad´ē ...) (colloq.): police wagon or van >*They rounded up the drunks and hauled them away in the paddy wagon.*

PAIN

** **pain** (colloq.): nuisance, irritating or troublesome person or thing >*That obnoxious jerk is such a pain!* >*This plumbing job's going to be a real pain.*

— **feeling no pain** (see FEELING)

** **pain in the ass** (vulg.): nuisance, irritating or troublesome person or thing >*I'm gonna fire that pain in the ass one of these days.* >*All those forms they make yu fill out are a real pain in the ass.*

* **pain in the butt** (sl., freq. vulg.): nuisance, irritating or troublesome person or thing >*Shut up and stop bein' such a pain in the butt!* >*What a pain in the butt it is to wait in line!*

** **pain in the neck** (colloq.): nuisance, irritating or troublesome person or thing >*Don't bring your brother! He's a pain in the neck.* >*Painting the trim is always a pain in the neck.*

PAINT

— **paint the town (red)** (colloq.): go on a wild spree, celebrate wildly (esp. at several drinking establishments) >*The team painted the town red after winning the championship.* >*He took his winnings and painted the town.*

PAIR

— **pair** (sl., freq. vulg.): (woman's) breasts (esp. large or shapely ones) >*He noticed she had quite a pair on her.*

PAL

* **pal** (pal) (colloq.): friend, chum (also voc.) >*Slim's never home—he's always out with his pals.* >*Watch where you're going, will you, pal?*

* **pal around** (vi) (colloq.): spend time together (as friends) >*His kid and mine pal around together.* >*Les pals around with some of the guys at work.*

PALEFACE

— **paleface** (sl., freq. pej.): white person (from the perspective of Native Americans, historically) >*The Indians really got screwed by the palefaces in that deal.*

PALIMONY

— **palimony** (pal´ə mō´nē) (colloq.): money or property awarded to one partner after a nonmatrimonial romantic relationship breaks up >*She lived with him for four years and is asking for $100,000 a year as palimony.*

PALM
— **grease [s/one's] palm** (see **GREASE**)
— **palm off (on)** (vt) (colloq.): sell or give (to) through deception or fraud, present (to) (as s/thing more valuable than it is) >*Who do you think you're going to be able to palm that cheap perfume off on?* >*He tried to palm off some rhinestones as diamonds.*

PALSY-WALSY
— **palsy-walsy** (pal´zē wal´zē) (sl., freq. sarc.): very friendly, chummy >*He'll get the contract because he's real palsy-walsy with a couple of the supervisors.*

PAN
— **pan** (vt) (colloq.): strongly criticize (esp. in an entertainment review) >*I liked the movie, but the critics panned it.*
— **flash in the pan** (see **FLASH**)
* **pan out** (vi) (colloq.): turn out to be successful, have favorable results >*If Luke's job pans out, we'll be in good shape financially.* >*Their research just didn't pan out.*

PANCAKE
— **(as) flat as a pancake** (see **FLAT**)

PANHANDLE
* **panhandle** (vi, vt) (colloq.): approach (people) in public and beg for money >*Have you seen all the winos who panhandle down on Fifth Street?* >*I don't like bums panhandling me.*

PANHANDLER
* **panhandler** (colloq.): person who approaches people in public and begs for money >*The number of panhandlers in that part of town has grown a lot lately.*

PANIC
— **panic** (sl.): extremely funny person or thing >*The guy's a panic—he kept us laughin' the whole time.*

PANIC BUTTON
— **hit/push the panic button** (colloq.): become panicked, be overcome with alarm, declare an emergency (esp. overly hastily) >*They hit the panic button when they found out their daughter had smoked some marijuana.*

PANSY
— **pansy**[1] (pan´zē) (sl., pej.): male homosexual >*He says nobody but pansies go into that bar.*
— **pansy**[2] (sl.): cowardly or effeminate male >*Don't be a pansy! Jump like the rest of us did!*

PANTS
— **pants** (vt) (sl.): forcibly remove the pants from (to embarrass s/one as a prank or punishment) >*He was actin' real obnoxious, so they pantsed him in front of a bunch of girls.*
— **(about) pee in [one's] pants** (see **PEE**)
— **(about) shit (in) [one's] pants** (see **SHIT**)
— **beat the pants off (of)** (see **BEAT**)
— **catch [s/one] with [his/her] pants down** (see **CATCH**)
— **(fly) by the seat of [one's] pants** (see **SEAT**)
* **get in(to) [s/one's] pants** (sl., freq. vulg.): conquer [s/one] sexually, achieve having sex with [s/one] >*He says he loves her, but he's just tryin' to get in her pants.*
— **have ants in [one's] pants** (see **ANTS**)
— **keep [one's] pants on** (colloq.): not become impatient, calm down (used esp. as a command) >*I told Rich to keep his pants on, because he was getting real nervous.*
* **... the pants off (of) [s/one]** (colloq.): ... [s/one] to an extreme degree >*What a smooth talker—he charmed the pants off everyone at the party.* >*His lecture bored the pants off of us.*
— **wear the pants** (see **WEAR**)

PANTYWAIST

— **pantywaist** (pan´tē wāst´) (sl.): cowardly or effeminate man >*I tell ya I don't want no kid of mine hangin' around with them pantywaists!*

PAPA

— **papa** (pä´pə) (colloq.): father (also voc.) >*Her papa's against her marrying so young.* >*How are you feeling, Papa?*

PAPER

— **push paper** (see **PUSH**)

PAPER-PUSHER

— **paper-pusher** (colloq.): low-ranking bureaucrat, person with an insignificant desk job (cf. "**PUSH paper**") >*Some paper-pusher in the main office probably lost the form.*

PAR

* **be par for the course** (colloq., freq. sarc.): be typical, be what one would expect >*Griffin forgot to get a signature on the contract, but that's par for the course for him.*

PARADE

— **rain on [s/one's] parade** (see **RAIN**)

PARDNER

— **pardner** (pärd´nər) (colloq.): friend, chum (also voc.) >*Me and my pardner built this shed.* >*Hey, pardner, what do you say?*

PARDON

— **pardon/excuse my French** (see **FRENCH**)

PARK

* **park**[1] (vt) (colloq.): place, set, leave >*Park yourself on that bench for a minute—I'll be right back.* >*Where do you want us to park this trunk?*

— **park**[2] (vi) (colloq.): engage in kissing and caressing while in a parked car >*He took her to park down by the lake.*

PARLAY

— **parlay [s/thing] into** (pär´lā ...) (colloq.): transform (a small initial resource) into (s/thing greater or more valuable) >*He parlayed a five hundred dollar investment eight years ago into a huge yearly income today.* >*She parlayed a few key contacts into a successful consulting business.*

PARTY

** **party** (vi) (colloq.): enjoy oneself festively, celebrate >*Exams are over— let's party!*

— **the life of the party** (see **LIFE**)

PARTY ANIMAL

* **party animal** (sl.): person who loves to celebrate wildly, enthusiastic party goer >*Count on Victor showin' up at that bash. He's a real party animal.*

PARTY-POOPER

* **party-pooper** (pär´tē pū´pər) (sl.): person who spoils a happy occasion, person incapable of having fun, pessimistic or ill-humored person, killjoy >*Everyone was havin' a good time till that party-pooper started complainin' about everything.*

PASS

* **pass** (vi) (colloq.): decline (to do or take s/thing) >*Thanks for offering, but I think I'll pass.*

* **make a pass at** (colloq.): make a sexual or romantic advance toward, do or say s/thing to express a sexual or romantic interest in >*Trumbull got drunk and made a pass at Stanton's wife.*

** **pass out** (vi) (colloq.): lose consciousness >*He finally passed out right there on the barstool.*

* **pass the buck** (colloq.): transfer responsibility or blame to another, refer a problem to another >*Everyone keeps passing the buck—so who's going to take care of this?*

— **pass the hat** (colloq.): take up a collection of money >*We passed the hat and people gave what they could to help out.*

PASSION
— **with a purple passion** (see PURPLE)

PAST
— **wouldn't put it past [s/one] (to [do s/thing])** (see PUT)

PASTE
— **paste** (vt) (sl.): hit hard (esp. in the face) >*He kept mouthin' off, so I pasted him.*

PASTURE
— **put [s/one] out to pasture** (see PUT)

PAT
* **have [s/thing] down pat** (colloq.): have mastered or learned [s/thing] thoroughly >*It took Billy a while to learn the system, but now he's got it down pat.*

* **pat on the back** (colloq.): expression of praise or congratulations >*The award she received was a nice pat on the back for her good work.*

* **pat [s/one] on the back** (colloq.): praise or congratulate [s/one] >*Pat Henry on the back every now and then to let him know he's appreciated.* >*I had to pat myself on the back for the way I handled that problem.*

PATSY
— **patsy¹** (pat´sē) (sl.): person who takes the blame for others, scapegoat >*They got some patsy to take the rap for 'em.*

— **patsy²** (sl.): person who is easily deceived or victimized, dupe >*A good con man can spot a patsy right away.*

PAVEMENT
— **pound the pavement** (see POUND)

PAW
— **paw¹** (colloq.): hand (esp. when seen as neg.) >*If Andy puts his paws on my sister, I'll break his face!*

— **paw²** (vt) (colloq.): handle roughly or with excessive familiarity >*He started pawing her and she jumped out of the car.*

PAWN
* **pawn off (on)** (vt) (colloq.): manipulate (s/one) to buy or accept, get rid of (by

having s/one take), push off (on) >*She's trying to pawn her bratty kid off on her sister for a few days while she takes a little vacation.* >*If I talk to my neighbors, I should be able to pawn my old lawn mower off for a few dollars.*

PAY
** **pay** (vi) (colloq.): be worthwhile, be beneficial, bring good results >*It pays to be nice to people.* >*Crime doesn't pay.*

— **hell to pay** (see HELL)

* **pay [one's] dues** (colloq.): merit s/thing because of [one's] efforts or sacrifices, work or suffer so much that [one] deserves s/thing >*I'm glad Rick got promoted, because he's paid his dues.* >*I hope Karen doesn't have any more problems with her son—she's already paid her dues.*

** **pay off¹** (vi) (colloq.): be profitable, be rewarding, result in success or advantage >*All your studying will pay off later.*

* **pay off²** (vt) (colloq.): bribe, pay (s/one) for influential intervention, pay (s/one) not to reveal s/thing incriminating >*He's paying off some politicians to make sure there are no snags on his project.* >*You'd better pay Sammy off if you want him to keep his mouth shut.*

— **pay through the nose** (colloq.): pay an excessive amount >*You really pay through the nose in that tourist trap!*

PAY DIRT
— **hit/strike pay dirt** (colloq.): make a valuable discovery, find a source of wealth or success >*The researcher hit pay dirt when he found those old manuscripts.* >*They struck pay dirt when they marketed that video game.*

PAYOFF
* **payoff** (colloq.): bribe money, money paid for influential intervention or to ensure that s/thing incriminating will not

be revealed >*Some crooked cops have been taking payoffs.*

PAYOLA
— **payola** (pā ō′lə) (sl.): money paid for illicit influential intervention, graft money >*Payola's what keeps things runnin' in this business.*

P.C.P.
* **P.C.P.** (sl.): phencyclidine (a hallucinogenic drug) >*He did some P.C.P., then just went wild.*

P.D.Q.
— **P.D.Q.** (= "pretty darn/damn quick") (colloq.): very quickly, immediately >*The boss wants this taken care of P.D.Q.*

P.E.
** **P.E.** (colloq.): physical education (esp. as a course of study) >*I have history at ten and P.E. at eleven.*

PEACH
— **peach** (colloq.): very likable or charming person >*Marvin's a real peach of a guy.* >*Thanks, hon, you're a peach.*

PEACH FUZZ
— **peach fuzz** (colloq.): immature or downy hair (esp. on an adolescent boy's face) >*Why'd Tommy start shaving? All he's got is peach fuzz.*

PEACHY
— **peachy** (pē′chē) (colloq.): wonderful, excellent, fine >*Everything's been just peachy around here since that old grouch left.*

PEANUT GALLERY
— **peanut gallery** (colloq.): cheapest seats in a theater, seats farthest removed from the performance >*You can't see anything from here in the peanut gallery.*

PEANUTS
* **peanuts** (sl.): insignificant or trivial amount of money >*You're workin' your butt off and they're payin' ya peanuts.*

PEARLY WHITES
— **pearly whites** (colloq.): teeth (esp. bright and handsome ones) >*All he's got to do is keep flashing them pearly whites and he's sure to get elected.*

PEA SOUP
— **pea soup** (colloq.): thick fog >*You're crazy to try and drive in this pea soup.*

PECK
— **peck** (colloq.): quick or perfunctory kiss >*He gave his wife a peck on the cheek and then left for work.*

PECKER
— **pecker** (vulg.): penis >*He thinks his pecker's too small.*

PECS
* **pecs** (peks) (colloq.): pectoral muscles >*Bench presses are good for building up your pecs.*

PEE
** **pee¹** (pē) (sl., freq. vulg.): urine >*I think you just sat in some dog pee.*

** **pee²** (vi) (sl., freq. vulg.): urinate >*Where's the toilet? I got to pee bad.*

* **(about) pee in [one's] pants** (colloq., freq. vulg.): laugh very hard >*We about peed in our pants when Julie sat down on a plate of spaghetti someone had left there.*

— **full of pee/piss and vinegar** (see FULL)

* **take a pee** (sl., freq. vulg.): urinate >*The bum was takin' a pee right there on my lawn!*

PEEL
— **peel out** (vi) (sl.): accelerate a vehicle quickly from a stop (esp. while making the tires squeal on the pavement), leave quickly >*We peeled outta the parkin' lot when some crazy came at us swingin' a baseball bat.*

PEELED
— **keep [one's] eyes peeled** (see EYES)

PEE-PEE
— **pee-pee**[1] (pē´pē´) (colloq.): urine (used esp. with small children) >*Did the diaper soak up all the pee-pee?*

* **pee-pee**[2] (vi) (colloq.): urinate (used esp. with small children) >*Donny says he's got to pee-pee.*

PEEPERS
— **peepers** (pē´pərz) (sl.): eyes >*I'm gonna need glasses—my peepers are goin' bad on me.*

PEEWEE
— **peewee**[1] (pē´wē´) (colloq.): unusually small or short person (also voc.) >*We need a big man for this job, not some peewee like him.* >*Hey, peewee, you'd better not mess with that guy!*

— **peewee**[2] (colloq.): unusually small >*You expect me to get any work done with this peewee hammer?*

PEG
— **peg** (vt) (colloq.): identify, guess the classification or nature of >*Joey pegged him for an undercover cop right away.* >*I had no trouble pegging their act as a fraud.*

— **take/knock [s/one] down a peg (or two)** (see **TAKE**)

PEN
* **the pen** (sl.): a penitentiary, a prison >*He did seven years in the pen for armed robbery.*

PENCIL
— **push a pencil** (see **PUSH**)

PENCIL-PUSHER
— **pencil-pusher** (colloq.): low-ranking bureaucrat, person with an insignificant desk job (cf. "PUSH a pencil") >*I want to talk to the section head, not some pencil-pusher.*

PENNIES
— **pinch pennies** (see **PINCH**)

PENNY
— **a pretty penny** (see **PRETTY**)

PENNY-ANTE
— **penny-ante** (colloq.): of little worth, insignificant in value >*I can't believe he left the firm for some penny-ante sales job.*

PENNY PINCHER
* **penny pincher** (colloq.): very stingy person, miser (cf. "PINCH pennies") >*That penny pincher wouldn't help pay for the party.*

PENNY-PINCHING
* **penny-pinching** (colloq.): very stingy, miserly >*Her penny-pinching husband won't let her buy any decent clothes.*

PEORIA
— **play in Peoria** (see **PLAY**)

PEP
* **pep** (pep) (colloq.): energy, vigor, vitality >*Come on, people! Put some pep in your singing!*

* **pep up** (vt) (colloq.): invigorate, animate, energize >*Maybe a few drinks will pep this party up.* >*That car really goes since he pepped up the engine.*

PEPPER-UPPER
— **pepper-upper** (pep´ər up´ər) (sl.): thing that renews energy or vitality, stimulant >*I need a pepper-upper—maybe a cup of strong coffee—to keep me goin' tonight.*

PEP PILL
— **pep pill** (pep ...) (colloq.): pill containing a stimulant (esp. an amphetamine) >*Michelle planned to drive all night, so she took a couple of pep pills before heading out.*

PEPPY
* **peppy** (pep´ē) (colloq.): energetic, lively, vigorous >*Why are you feeling so peppy this morning?*

PEP TALK
* **pep talk** (pep ...) (colloq.): speech given to motivate or enthuse to succeed >*The coach gave the players a good pep*

talk, and they played better the second half. >*The boss's pep talk fired them up.*

PERK

* **perk**[1] (colloq.): extra benefit of employment or position, perquisite >*Country club membership's one of the perks that come with the job.*

* **perk**[2] (vi, vt): percolate >*Has the coffee finished perking yet?* >*I'll go perk some coffee.*

PERM

** **perm**[1] (pûrm) (colloq.): hair permanent >*Her new perm looks terrible.*

** **perm**[2] (vt) (colloq.): apply a permanent to (hair) >*Should I perm my hair or let it grow straight?*

PERP

— **perp** (pûrp) (sl.): perpetrator (of a crime) >*The cops grabbed the perp in some motel.*

PESKY

* **pesky** (pes´kē) (colloq.): annoying, bothersome, troublesome >*I wish these pesky mosquitoes would leave me alone.*

PET

— **pet** (vi) (colloq.): engage in fondling and caressing >*He jumped in the backseat with her and they petted for over an hour.*

PETER

— **peter** (pē´tər) (vulg.): penis >*He thought the guy at the next urinal was lookin' at his peter.*

* **peter out** (vi) (colloq.): diminish in strength or amount, dwindle, become exhausted >*He petered out after only twenty minutes of tennis.* >*I hear they're going to close the mine because the copper's petering out.*

PET PEEVE

* **pet peeve** (colloq.): special source of annoyance (for s/one) >*My pet peeve is when people talk during a movie.*

P.G.

— **P.G.** (colloq.): pregnant >*Married only two months and she's already P.G.?*

PHILLY

* **Philly** (fil´ē) (colloq.): Philadelphia, Pennsylvania >*He lives in Eastern Pennsylvania, somewhere near Philly.*

PHONE

— **hold the phone!** (see HOLD)

PHONEY

— **phoney** (see "PHONY")

PHONY

** **phony**[1] (fō´nē) (colloq.): ungenuine or false thing or person, insincere person, fake >*This twenty-dollar bill looks like a phony to me.* >*How can you stand that hypocrite? He's such a damn phony.*

** **phony**[2] (colloq.): fake, unauthentic, false, insincere >*This so-called diamond is phony.* >*I hate his phony smile.*

PHOOEY

— **phooey (on …)!** (fū´ē …) (colloq.): (interj. to express disappointment, disgust, or contempt [regarding …]) >*Phooey! The Clippers lost again!* >*Phooey on you and your stupid ideas!*

PHYS ED

* **phys ed** (fiz´ed´) (colloq.): physical education (esp. as a course of study) >*Most of the athletes major in phys ed.*

P.I.

— **P.I.** (colloq.): private investigator, private detective >*Johnson used to be a police sergeant, but he quit and became a P.I.*

PICK

— **pick** (sl.): comb with long and widely spaced teeth (used for curly or kinky hair) >*He don't go nowhere without his pick in his pocket.*

— **have a bone to pick with** (see BONE)

— **pick at** (colloq.): nag at, find fault with (esp. unreasonably) >*They're always*

picking at their poor boy about
everything he does.

* **pick [s/one's] brain** (colloq.): get
information or ideas from [s/one] (esp.
from an expert) >*If you want to pick
someone's brain, hire a consultant.*

— **pick it up** (colloq.): move or work faster
>*Hey, guys, let's pick it up! We need to
finish fast.*

** **pick on** (colloq.): tease or harass,
subject to criticism or scorn >*The kids
pick on him because he's short.* >*Why's
that newspaper been picking on the
president so much lately?*

** **pick up**[1] (vt) (colloq.): learn informally
or through experience >*Patty picked up
quite a bit of Spanish when she lived in
Mexico.*

** **pick up**[2] (vt) (colloq.): meet and gain
the company of (esp. when sexually
motivated) >*We picked up a couple of
gals in a bar and had a good time.*

* **pick up**[3] (vt) (colloq.): take into custody
>*They picked up the suspect in Reno.*
>*Pick him up for questioning.*

* **pick up**[4] (vt) (colloq.): acquire,
purchase >*Where'd you pick up that
great briefcase?* >*I'll pick up some
things at the store on my way home.*

* **pick up**[5] (vt) (colloq.): pay (a bill)
>*Order whatever you want—the boss is
picking up the bill.*

— **pick up and leave** (colloq.): gather
(one's) belongings and leave (esp.
unexpectedly or quickly) >*After twenty
years of marriage she just picked up and
left one day.*

* **pick up on** (colloq.): perceive, become
aware of, notice >*Sure he was high on
something! Didn't you pick up on it?*
>*She picked up on his fear of
commitment right away.*

PICKER-UPPER

— **picker-upper** (pik´ər up´ər) (colloq.):
thing that renews energy or vitality,

stimulant >*I need a picker-upper this
time of the afternoon.*

PICKINGS

— **slim pickings** (see **SLIM**)

PICKLE

— **pickle** (colloq.): awkward or difficult
situation, predicament >*He's got
himself in a real pickle with those loan
sharks.*

PICKLED

— **pickled** (sl.): drunk >*Old Jim got pretty
pickled after a night of hard drinkin'.*

PICK-ME-UP

— **pick-me-up** (colloq.): thing that renews
energy or vitality, stimulant >*Let's go
to the bar for a quick pick-me-up before
dinner.*

PICKUP

— **pickup**[1] (colloq.): person whom (one)
meets and whose company (one) gains
(esp. when sexually motivated) >*She
was just some pickup he met at a bar.*

— **pickup**[2] (colloq.): composed of persons
available at the moment, impromptu
>*He hangs around the basketball court
and plays in pickup games.*

PICKY

** **picky** (pik´ē) (colloq.): overly
meticulous, fussy, choosy >*Don't be so
picky! His performance was fine.*

PICNIC

— **be no picnic** (colloq.): be a difficult
experience, be an ordeal >*It's no picnic
babysitting that two-year-old.* >*That
exam was no picnic.*

PICS

— **pics** (piks) (sl.): pictures, photographs
>*Wanna see the pics of the wedding?*

PICTURE

— **(as) pretty as a picture** (see **PRETTY**)

— **draw [s/one] a picture** (see **DRAW**)

* **get the picture** (colloq.): understand the
situation, become fully aware of the
circumstances >*Now I get the picture—
he's maneuvering for a better position.*

PICTURE-PERFECT

* **picture-perfect** (colloq.): having perfect conditions, executed perfectly >*The weather was picture-perfect for fishing.* >*Teresa's dive was picture-perfect—she won the gold medal.*

PIDDLE

— **piddle**[1] (pid´l) (colloq.): urine (used esp. with children and pets) >*There's doggy piddle on the kitchen floor.*

— **piddle**[2] (vi) (colloq.): urinate (used esp. with children and pets) >*Stop the car! Jimmy's got to piddle.*

* **piddle around** (vi) (colloq.): pass time idly, work halfheartedly or unproductively >*He spends more time piddling around on the job than actually working.*

PIE

— **(as) easy as pie** (see **EASY**)

— **pie in the sky** (colloq.): wishful thinking, illusory reward or benefit, unrealistic hope >*Him thinking his kid's going to get into medical school is pie in the sky.*

PIECE

— **piece**[1] (sl.): pistol >*Watch out for him—he's packin' a piece.*

— **piece**[2] (vulg.): episode of sexual intercourse (with a woman) >*The poor guy says he ain't had a piece in weeks.*

— **piece**[3] (vulg., pej.): woman (seen as a sex object) >*He says he picked up a real nice piece at a party last night.*

* **give [s/one] a piece of [one's] mind** (colloq.): reprimand [s/one] severely, criticize [s/one] angrily, complain strenuously to [s/one] >*I'm going to give that jerk a piece of my mind.*

* **in one piece** (colloq.): unharmed or undamaged >*I can't believe he came out of that wreck in one piece.* >*My camera made it through the whole trip in one piece.*

* **piece of ass**[1] (vulg., pej.): woman (seen as a sex object) >*He said there was a nice piece of ass sittin' at the corner table.*

* **piece of ass**[2] (vulg.): episode of sexual intercourse (with a woman) >*He said he finally got a piece of ass last night.*

** **piece of cake** (colloq.): easy thing to do, assured success >*I know this stuff real well—that test will be a piece of cake.*

— **piece of change** (sl.): substantial amount of money >*A big car like that is gonna cost ya a nice piece of change.*

— **piece of crap** (… krap) (sl., freq. vulg.): worthless or contemptible thing or person >*She liked the movie, but I thought it was a piece of crap.*

— **piece of crud** (… krud) (sl.): worthless or contemptible thing or person >*Couldn't you afford to buy a better stereo than this piece of crud?*

— **hunk/pile/piece of junk** (see **JUNK**)

* **piece of shit** (… shit) (vulg.): worthless or contemptible thing or person >*Who wrote this piece of shit?* >*That bum's a piece of shit—don't even think of marryin' him.*

— **piece of tail**[1] (vulg., pej.): woman (seen as a sex object) >*That was some piece of tail you were with last night!*

— **piece of tail**[2] (vulg.): episode of sexual intercourse (with a woman) >*He went out lookin' for a piece of tail.*

* **piece of the action** (colloq.): some participation in the game or activity, a portion of the profits >*If you're making bets on the fight, I want a piece of the action.* >*My piece of the action is twenty percent off the top.*

— **piece of work** (sl., sarc.): contemptible or reprehensible person >*You're a real piece of work, the way ya tricked that poor slob.*

PIECES

* **go/fall to pieces** (colloq.): lose emotional control, become overwrought, begin crying hard >*Whenever Jay thinks about losing her, he goes to pieces.* >*The poor guy just fell to pieces at the funeral.*

PIE-EYED

— **pie-eyed** (sl.): drunk >*We got pretty pie-eyed on rum and cokes.*

PIG

** **pig**[1] (colloq.): dirty or messy person, obnoxious or ill-mannered person >*Why doesn't that pig clean up his desk?* >*What a pig, burping out loud like that at the dinner table!*

** **pig**[2] (colloq.): glutton, overeater >*That pig ate half the lasagna all by himself!*

— **pig**[3] (sl., pej.): police officer >*Don't tell the pigs nothin'!*

** **pig out (on)** (sl.): eat an excessive amount (of), be gluttonous (with) >*I always pig out at potluck dinners.* >*Burt really pigged out on spare ribs at the picnic.*

— **sweat like a pig** (see SWEAT)

PIG'S

— **in a pig's eye …!** (sl.): not so …! in no way …! never …! >*Me, apologize to that jerk? In a pig's eye, I will!*

PIG-OUT

* **pig-out** (sl.): occasion of gluttony, episode of overeating >*The buffet dinner was one big pig-out.* >*I'd better diet for a week after last night's pig-out.*

PIKE

— **come down the pike** (see COME)

PIKER

— **piker** (pīʹkər) (colloq.): stingy or petty person, person who is overly cautious with money >*Do you really think you're going to get that piker to pay a month in advance?* >*The piker gave only a buck.*

PILE

* **a pile** (colloq.): a large amount of money >*His uncle made a pile in the commodities market.*

— **a pile (of …)** (colloq.): much (…), many (…) >*I got a pile of work to do around the house.* >*Gary's got a pile of racing trophies.*

— **hunk/pile/piece of junk** (see JUNK)

— **pile on/off** (vi, vt) (colloq.): get on/off as a group (esp. quickly or in a disorderly manner) >*The sailors piled off the bus and headed toward the bar.* >*Pile on, everyone! We got to get going.*

PILL

— **pill** (sl.): unpleasant or boring person >*The guy's a pill—keep him away from me, will ya?*

** **the pill** (colloq.): the birth-control pill >*She's on the pill because they don't want kids yet.*

PILL POPPER

— **pill popper** (colloq.): person who habitually takes pills (esp. tranquilizers or illegal drugs) >*I want all the pill poppers and other druggies out of here.*

PILL PUSHER

— **pill pusher** (sl., pej.): medical doctor >*Some pill pusher told me I got gallstones.*

PIN

— **(it's so quiet) you can hear a pin drop** (see HEAR)

* **pin down** (vt) (colloq.): force to make a decision or commitment >*I'll see if I can pin down the contractor on a start-up date.*

— **pin [s/one's] ears back** (colloq.): thoroughly beat [s/one], decisively defeat [s/one] >*If that loudmouth doesn't watch out, somebody's going to pin his ears back.*

* **pin [s/thing] on** (colloq.): ascribe the guilt or responsibility for [s/thing] to,

blame [s/thing] on >*The police are trying to pin three robberies on him.*

PINCH

— **pinch**[1] (sl.): arrest >*I'll scare 'em out, and you make the pinch.*

— **pinch**[2] (vt) (sl.): arrest >*The cops pinched him when he came outta the store.*

— **pinch**[3] (vt) (sl.): steal >*Where'd ya pinch the tape player, Ralph?*

* **in a pinch** (colloq.): in an emergency, if need be >*This small truck doesn't hold much, but it'll do in a pinch.*

* **pinch pennies** (colloq.): be stingy, be miserly (cf. "**PENNY PINCHER**") >*Stop pinching pennies and have some fun!*

PINCH-HIT

* **pinch-hit** (vi) (colloq.): substitute (for s/one), take (s/one's) place (esp. in an emergency) >*You'll have to pinch-hit for Terry at the sales meeting today— he's out sick.*

PINHEAD

— **pinhead** (sl.): stupid person >*That pinhead couldn't figure it out if he had to.*

PINK

— **in the pink** (colloq.): in good health >*Doc says he's in the pink.*

— **tickled (pink)** (see **TICKLED**)

PINK ELEPHANTS

— **see pink elephants** (colloq.): have alcohol-induced hallucinations >*Ev was seeing pink elephants when they hauled him off to jail.*

PINKIE

* **pinkie** (ping´kē) (colloq.): little finger >*He looks kind of silly with his pinkie sticking up in the air.*

PINKO

— **pinko** (ping´kō) (sl., pej.): left-winger, communist sympathizer (also adj.) >*I say we get all the dang pinkos outta the government.* >*They're poisonin' our kids' minds with their pinko ideas.*

PINK SLIP

* **pink slip** (colloq.): notice of being dismissed or laid off >*Fifty workers got their pink slips today because sales are really down.*

PINK-SLIP

— **pink-slip** (vt) (colloq.): dismiss, lay off >*The supervisor's going to pink-slip Gray if he doesn't start working harder.*

PINKY

— **pinky** (see "**PINKIE**")

PINT-SIZE

— **pint-size(d)** (colloq.): small, smaller than normal >*I just don't feel comfortable driving those pint-size cars.*

PIPE

* **pipe** (colloq.): passage or tube (in the body) >*A piece of meat went down the wrong pipe, and I about choked to death.* >*The doctor says my heart's working too hard because my pipes are all clogged up.*

* **pipe down** (vi) (sl.): quiet down, stop speaking loudly, be quiet >*Hey, pipe down! I'm tryin' to talk on the phone.*

— **pipe up** (vi) (colloq.): speak up, raise (one's) voice >*You got Maxwell mad when you piped up at the meeting about how he'd messed up.*

— **put that in your pipe and smoke it!** (sl.): understand and accept that no matter what your objections are! >*I'll take your daughter out if I want to, and I'll marry her some day, too! Put that in your pipe and smoke it!*

PIPELINE

— **in the pipeline** (colloq.): being developed, under production >*We got a new model in the pipeline that should be out early next year.*

PIPES

— **(set of) pipes** (colloq.): vocal chords, voice (esp. seen as strong) >*Does that* *screaming kid ever have a set of pipes on her! >What that singer can do with those pipes of his!*

PIPING

* **piping hot** (pī´ping …) (colloq.): very hot (said of food or drink) >*There's nothing like a piping hot cup of coffee on a cold morning.*

PIPSQUEAK

— **pipsqueak** (pip´skwēk´) (colloq.): small and insignificant person (esp. seen as contemptible) >*I ain't afraid of that little pipsqueak.*

PISS

** **piss**[1] (pis) (sl., freq. vulg.): urine >*I hate it when there's piss on the toilet seat!*

** **piss**[2] (vi) (sl., freq. vulg.): urinate >*Some slob pissed on the floor.*

— **full of pee/piss and vinegar** (see **FULL**)

— **not have a pot to piss in** (see **POT**)

— **piss away** (vt) (sl., freq. vulg.): squander, spend foolishly >*I can't believe he pissed away the whole $3000 in just one week!*

** **piss (off)** (vt) (sl., freq. vulg.): make angry, irritate >*Man, it really pisses me off when people interrupt me like that. >Glenn got really pissed when he lost the game.*

* **piss off!** (vulg.): go away! stop annoying me! >*Piss off, will ya? You're gettin' on my nerves.*

— **piss on …!** (vulg.): I don't care at all about …! I find … contemptible! >*Well, if he don't like it, piss on him!*

** **take a piss** (sl., freq. vulg.): urinate >*Be right back—I gotta take a piss.*

— **… the piss out of [s/one]** (sl., freq. vulg.): … [s/one] to the utmost degree, … [s/one] extraordinarily (esp. in a neg. way) >*It bugged the piss outta Trudy when Lou told her he didn't like her new hairdo.*

PISSANT

— **pissant** (pis´ant´) (sl.): small and insignificant person (esp. seen as contemptible) >*Tell your little brothers and those other pissants to get outta there!*

PISSED

** **pissed** (pist) (sl., freq. vulg.): angry >*Don was really pissed when he found out what they were sayin' about him!*

PISSER

— **pisser** (pis´ər) (sl., freq. vulg.): something unpleasant, difficult or disappointing thing or situation >*That big chemistry test was a pisser.*

PISS-POOR

— **piss-poor** (pis´pŭr´) (sl., freq. vulg.): inferior, of poor quality, bad >*What a piss-poor job those idiots did!*

PITCH

* **pitch**[1] (colloq.): speech or argument (used to sell or win approval for s/thing) >*I don't want to hear this guy's sales pitch. >He made a pitch for the building project at the city council meeting.*

* **pitch**[2] (vt) (colloq.): speak or argue for (s/thing one is trying to sell or win approval for) >*The salesman's going to pitch the new land development.*

* **pitch in** (vi) (colloq.): help, contribute work or support >*If everyone pitches in, we can get this place cleaned up in a couple of hours.*

PITCHING

— **in there pitching** (colloq.): putting out a determined effort, trying hard, coping >*Paulson's slowed down some, but he's still in there pitching. >Stay in there pitching, and don't let them bother you.*

PITS

* **the pits** (sl.): very unpleasant or bothersome thing or occurrence, very irritating or boring situation, the worst >*This sleezy bar is the pits. >Workin' for that arrogant jerk is the pits.*

PIT STOP

* **make a pit stop** (sl.): stop to go to the bathroom (esp. to urinate, esp. when traveling) >*Let me make a pit stop before we go on to Hank's.*

PIX

— **pix** (see "PICS")

PIZAZZ

* **pizazz** (pə zaz´) (colloq.): liveliness, energy, zest, flair >*This move will put a little pizazz in your dancing.*

PIZZA-FACE

— **pizza-face** (voc.) (sl., pej.): pimply-faced person >*Nice bunch of pimples ya got there, pizza-face.*

PIZZAZZ

— **pizzazz** (see "PIZAZZ")

P.J.S

* **P.J.s** (pē´jāz´) (colloq.): pajamas >*Let's get Tommy's P.J.s on him and put him to bed.*

PLACE

— **wide place in the road** (see WIDE)

PLACES

* **go places** (colloq.): advance in (one's) career, gain success, have a promising future >*He's a sharp guy who's going places in this business.*

PLAGUE

— **avoid [s/one, s/thing] like the plague** (see AVOID)

PLAIN JANE

— **plain Jane** (colloq.): unattractive woman >*How did that plain Jane get such a handsome husband?*

PLANT

* **plant¹** (colloq.): person secretly placed in a group to spy on its members or influence them >*I think he's a plant the police sent to check up on us.*

— **plant²** (colloq.): thing designed to be discovered and to incriminate another >*He swears the cocaine they found in his house was a plant.*

* **plant³** (vt) (colloq.): place (s/thing) to be discovered and to incriminate another >*The killer planted the murder weapon in the other guy's car.*

* **plant⁴** (vt) (colloq.): place (s/one) secretly in a group to spy on its members or influence them >*The owners have planted a couple of guys in the union to spy on us.*

— **plant⁵** (vt) (sl.): deliver (a blow), place (a kiss) >*Greg planted a right jab on his chin.* >*She planted a big wet kiss on his cheek.*

— **plant⁶** (vt) (sl.): bury (a corpse) >*She killed her husband and planted the body in the desert.*

PLASTER

— **plaster** (vt) (colloq.): hit forcefully, beat, defeat decisively >*She plastered the guy with her purse.* >*We're going to plaster that team next week.*

PLASTERED

* **plastered** (sl.): very drunk >*When Joey's girl left him, he went to a bar and got plastered.*

PLASTIC

** **plastic¹** (colloq.): credit cards, credit afforded by credit cards >*I ain't got money, but I got plastic.* >*Don't worry about the cost—we'll get it with plastic.*

— **plastic²** (colloq.): insincere, ungenuine, artificial >*I hate her plastic smile.*

PLATINUM

— **platinum** (sl.): (a record) having sold at least two million copies as a single or one million as an album (cf. "GOLD") >*After twenty years in the business she finally got a platinum record.*

PLAY

— **play** (vi) (colloq.): gain acceptance, succeed, fare >*The proposed tax increase isn't going to play well with the middle class.*

— **make a play for** (colloq.): try to attract or obtain, flirt with >*Our competitor's* making a play for Reynolds' business. >*That hussy always makes a play for other women's husbands.*

* **play along** (vi) (colloq.): cooperate or collaborate (esp. despite doubts or reservations) >*All right, I'll play along with you—we'll say you really are the mayor's brother.*

* **play around** (vi) (colloq.): pass time idly, work halfheartedly or unproductively >*You've been playing around too much and haven't gotten anything done.*

* **play around (with)** (colloq.): be sexually involved (with) (esp. illicitly), be sexually promiscuous >*Getting married sure didn't stop him from playing around.* >*His wife suspects he's been playing around with his secretary.*

* **play (around) with** (colloq.): treat without due respect or seriousness, handle capriciously, toy with >*Don't play around with him, because he's a big shot around here.* >*Don't play with the accounts!*

— **play ball (with)** (see BALL)

* **play [one's] cards right** (colloq.): act astutely or cautiously, use correct strategies >*If you play your cards right, you can make a lot of money on this deal.*

— **play catch-up** (see CATCH-UP)

— **play chicken (with)** (see CHICKEN)

— **play doctor** (see DOCTOR)

— **play dumb** (see DUMB)

— **play fast and loose** (colloq.): deal irresponsibly or carelessly >*He loves to play fast and loose with other people's money.* >*She should dump the bum. He's been playing fast and loose with her affections.*

— **play footsie(s) (with)** (see FOOTSIE)

— **play [s/one] for a fool/sucker** (colloq.): treat [s/one] as a fool, manipulate [s/one] through deception >*Chet thinks*

Blanche is in love with him, but she's playing him for a sucker.

— **play hardball** (see HARDBALL)

— **play hard-to-get** (see HARD-TO-GET)

— **play hooky** (see HOOKY)

— **play in Peoria** (… pē ôr´ē ə) (colloq.): succeed among the American mainstream, be accepted by the common people >*The proposal seems OK to most of the Senate, but how will it play in Peoria?*

* **play it by ear** (colloq.): react to the situation as it reveals itself, improvise >*I'm not sure just what'll happen at the meeting, so we'll have to play it by ear.*

* **play it cool** (sl.): behave in a calm and controlled way, keep (one's) composure >*Ya gotta play it cool with those gang members, 'cause they don't take crap from nobody.*

* **play it safe** (colloq.): proceed cautiously, not take chances, avoid risk >*Let's play it safe and take along the flashlight just in case.*

— **play it straight** (colloq.): deal honestly, proceed conventionally >*I'd play it straight with the judge if I was you.*

— **play possum** (see POSSUM)

* **play rough** (colloq.): resort to extreme or violent measures (to ensure winning) >*Don't even think of stealing from them, because they play rough.* >*If you want to play rough, I'll take you to court!*

— **play second fiddle (to)** (see SECOND FIDDLE)

* **play the field** (colloq.): date several people during the same period (instead of having a single romantic interest) >*I told her she was too young to get married and that she should play the field for a while.*

* **play the game** (colloq.): follow the rules, behave as expected, accept how things work (in a certain situation)

>*Yeah, I don't like these company parties either, but you got to play the game.*

— **play up to** (colloq.): try to gain favor with, flatter, try to please (esp. insincerely or with ulterior motives) >*She's been playing up to the supervisor so he'll give her the easy assignments.*

* **play with [oneself]** (colloq.): masturbate >*She got all upset because she caught her son playing with himself.*

PLAYER

— **player** (colloq.): participant, involved party >*We can make this deal work if we can just get all the key players together.*

PLAYGROUND

— **playground** (colloq.): place of amusement, area used for fun >*Las Vegas is his playground.* >*Want to see the waterbed in my playground?*

PLAYING

* **not be playing with a full deck** (sl.): not be completely sane, have irrational behavior >*That guy talkin' to himself over there ain't playin' with a full deck.* >*What a weirdo! Is she playin' with a full deck?*

PLAYMATE

— **playmate** (colloq.): sexual companion >*I saw him taking another one of his playmates into his apartment last night.*

PLEA

— **cop a plea** (see COP)

PLEASE

— **pretty please (with sugar on it)!** (see PRETTY)

PLENTY

* **plenty** (colloq.): very, quite, sufficiently >*Dad was plenty mad about the broken window.* >*This rope is plenty strong to tie it down.*

PLOW

* **plow into** (colloq.): move quickly and forcefully into, crash into, attack >*He*

sat down at his desk and plowed into his work. >*The car plowed into the fence.* >*I said something he didn't like, and he just plowed right into me.*

PLUG

* **plug¹** (colloq.): recommendation, favorable mention, appeal (for s/one to buy or seek s/thing) >*He gave a plug for his new movie when he was on the talk show.*

* **plug²** (vt) (colloq.): promote, mention favorably, actively recommend >*I can't believe he went around at church plugging his product line!*

— **plug³** (vt) (sl.): shoot, hit with a bullet >*He plugged a bank guard during the robbery.*

* **plug away/along** (colloq.): work steadily >*I'm going to keep plugging away at this report till I finish it.* >*He doesn't work too fast, but he plugs along.*

* **pull the plug (on)** (colloq.): terminate support or permission (for), discontinue (s/thing) >*The poor guy's nothing but a vegetable—why don't the doctors just pull the plug?* >*The government's pulled the plug on that child-care program.*

PLUGGED

— **plugged in(to)** (colloq.): having a continual source of information (about), have connections with >*That lobbyist is really plugged into what's going on in Washington.* >*Get Sweeney to ask the front office people about it—he's plugged in there.*

PLUGGED NICKEL

— **[neg.] a plugged nickel** (colloq.): no money at all >*They didn't pay me a plugged nickel for my time.* >*This piece of junk isn't worth a plugged nickel.*

PLUM

— **plum¹** (colloq.): highly prized reward or privilege, very desirable position >*That* *vice-presidency is quite a plum for an ambitious guy.*

— **plum²** (see "PLUMB")

PLUMB

— **plumb** (colloq.): absolute, complete, exact (esp. in neg. contexts) (also adv.) >*He's a plumb fool to go there at night by himself.* >*It landed plumb in the middle.* >*Robbins is plumb crazy if he thinks we'll go along with that.*

PLUMBING

— **plumbing** (sl., freq. hum.): digestive system >*He needs a laxative to clean out his plumbing.*

PLUNGE

— **take the plunge** (colloq.): take a course of action (after a period of deliberation or hesitancy) >*Herb was a confirmed bachelor until he met Carrie—then he decided to take the plunge.*

PLUNK

— **plunk down** (plungk ...) (vt) (colloq.): pay (a sum of money) (esp. in a daring or sacrificing way) >*Abe plunked down two grand for that stereo system.*

PLUS

* **plus** (colloq.): and, also >*He's a really nice guy, plus he's rich.*

— **have ... plus** (colloq.): have ... to an impressive degree >*She's got personality plus.*

PLUSH

* **plush** (plush) (colloq.): showy and expensive, luxurious >*They're staying at some plush hotel downtown.*

PLUSHY

— **plushy** (plush´ē) (colloq.): showy and expensive, luxurious >*They spent a week at a plushy resort in Florida.*

POCKET

— **in [one's] pocket** (colloq.): under [one's] control or influence >*That land developer has three city council members in his pocket.*

POCKETS

— **line [one's] (own) pockets** (see LINE)

P.O.'D

* **P.O.'d** (pē´ōd´) (= "pissed off") (sl.): angry, irritated >*Harry's P.O.'d because we didn't invite him.*

PODUNK

— **Podunk** (pō´dungk) (colloq.): a remote and insignificant town >*She left Podunk for Chicago when she was eighteen.*

— **Podunk U.** (colloq.): a remote and insignificant college or university >*Yale? Ha! He got his degree from Podunk U.*

POINTS

* **make points (with)** (colloq.): gain favor (with), obsequiously impress, ingratiate (oneself) (to) >*Merv thinks he's making points with the boss by agreeing with everything she says.*

POINTY-HEADED

— **pointy-headed** (sl., pej.): intellectual (esp. as a neg. trait) >*He don't like them pointy-headed lawyers tellin' him what to do.*

POISON

— **poison** (sl.): hard liquor >*Give me a shot of that poison you're drinkin' there.* >*Name your poison!*

POKE

— **poke** (vt) (vulg.): have sex with (a woman) >*He said he was gonna poke her tonight.*

* **poke around** (vi) (colloq.): pry, meddle, investigate (without invitation) >*Some private detective's been poking around here asking a lot of questions.*

— **stick/poke [one's] nose in(to)** (see STICK)

POKEY

— **the pokey** (see POKY)

POKY

— **the poky** (... pō'kē) (sl.): jail, prison >*He's back in the poky for violatin' his parole.*

POL

— **pol** (pol) (colloq.): politician (esp. seen as neg.) >*The pols will meet and divide up the funds among themselves.*

POLACK

* **Polack** (pō'läk/pō'lak) (sl., pej.): Pole, Polish, Polish-American >*Grandpa always said the Polacks lived in that part of town.* >*He hates Polack jokes.*

POLI SCI

* **poli sci** (pol'ē sī') (colloq.): political science (esp. as a course of study) >*She changed her major to poli sci.*

POLISH

* **polish off** (vt) (colloq.): finish off (esp. food or drink) >*Let's polish off the casserole so we don't have leftovers.*

POLLUTED

— **polluted** (sl.): drunk, intoxicated >*He got real polluted at the wedding reception and embarrassed the bride.*

PONY

— **pony** (colloq.): racehorse >*He likes to bet on the ponies.*

POOCH

— **pooch** (pūch) (colloq.): dog (also voc.) >*What a pretty pooch! What's its name?* >*Come here, pooch!*

POOH-POOH

— **pooh-pooh** (pū'pū') (vt) (colloq.): express disdain for, make light of, belittle >*Don't pooh-pooh the idea— I'm serious.*

POONTANG

— **poontang**[1] (pūn'tang) (vulg., pej.): woman or women (seen as sex object[s]) >*He said he was goin' to a bar to pick up some poontang.*

— **poontang**[2] (vulg.): sexual intercourse (with a woman) (freq. used with *some* or *any*) >*He says he got some poontang last night.*

POOP

* **poop**[1] (pūp) (sl.): excrement, dung >*There's dog poop on the lawn.*

— **poop**[2] (sl.): pertinent information, news (esp. when confidential or little known) >*What's the poop? Is he gonna retire or not?* >*Give me the poop on the new supervisor.*

* **poop**[3] (vi) (sl.): defecate >*Mommy, Cindy just pooped in her diaper.*

** **poop (out)** (vt) (sl.): tire out, exhaust, fatigue >*That exercise class really pooped me out.* >*Let me rest awhile— I'm pooped.*

POOPER-SCOOPER

* **pooper-scooper** (pū'pər skū'pər) (colloq.): small shovel-like device for picking up dog excrement (esp. when one is walking the dog in a public place) >*Be sure to bring the pooper-scooper in case Buck poo-poos again.*

POO-POO

— **poo-poo**[1] (pū'pū') (colloq.): excrement, dung (used esp. with children) >*Clean the poo-poo off your shoe.*

— **poo-poo**[2] (vi) (colloq.): defecate (used esp. with children) >*Now, you tell me if you need to poo-poo.*

— **poo-poo**[3] (see "POOH-POOH")

POOR

— **poor bastard** (see BASTARD)

* **poor excuse (for/of a)** (colloq.): an inferior specimen or unworthy example (of) >*He's a poor excuse for a man if he doesn't stick up for his wife.*

— **poor slob** (see SLOB)

POOR WHITE TRASH

* **poor white trash** (colloq., pej.): poor white person/people with little education (esp. from a rural environment) (seen as contemptible) >*She's so afraid her darling Herbert's going to marry some poor white trash.*

POP

* **pop**[1] (colloq.): carbonated beverage, soft drink, soda *>You want a beer or a pop? >Do I have to pay a deposit on the pop bottles?*

— **pop**[2] (colloq.): father (also voc.) *>My pop works in that factory. >Can I borrow the car, Pop?*

— **Pop**[3] (voc.) (colloq.): old man *>Watch out there, Pop, or you'll get hurt.*

* **pop**[4] (vt) (sl.): take (pills) (esp. habitually) *>He's been poppin' pain pills for years.*

— **pop**[5] (vt) (colloq.): hit, strike *>He was mouthing off so I popped him one.*

— **pop**[6] (vt) (sl.): shoot *>He just pulled out a gun and popped the dude.*

** **pop**[7] (colloq.): popular, appealing to the general public *>That tune was number four on the pop music survey last week. >That snob says she hates pop culture.*

* **a pop** (sl.): apiece, each *>How many silk shirts ya think I can afford at sixty bucks a pop?*

— **pop [s/one's] cherry** (vulg.): take away [s/one's] virginity, deflower [s/one] *>He claims he's the one that popped her cherry.*

— **pop/blow [one's] cork** (see CORK)

— **pop for** (sl.): pay for, accept the expense of *>Since you bought the drinks, I'll pop for dinner.*

* **pop in/by** (colloq.): appear for a brief visit, stop by (esp. unexpectedly) *>Martha said she'd pop in some time to see how Mom's doing. >Jeff popped by this morning to say hi.*

— **pop off** (vi) (sl.): speak forcefully or inconsiderately *>I'm tired of that jerk poppin' off about what a bad job we're doin'.*

— **pop the clutch** (colloq.): engage the clutch (of a vehicle) instantaneously (esp. to cause the tires to squeal on the pavement) *>He popped the clutch and roared off.*

* **pop the question** (sl.): ask (s/one) to marry (one), propose marriage *>Wish me luck—I'm gonna pop the question to Lucy tonight.*

* **pop up** (vi) (colloq.): appear (esp. suddenly, unexpectedly, or repeatedly) *>He popped up in Wyoming after vanishing for over a year. >That kind of restaurant's been popping up all over the country.*

POPPA

— **poppa** (see "PAPA")

POP QUIZ

— **pop quiz** (colloq.): unexpected or unannounced quiz (in school) *>The teacher gave us a pop quiz today, and I know I did lousy on it.*

POPS

— **Pops** (voc.) (colloq.): old man *>Hey, Pops, come over here for a second.*

PORK

— **pork** (vt) (vulg.): have sex with *>I don't really believe he porked her.*

PORK BARREL

— **pork barrel** (colloq.): government project or funds assigned for political reasons *>The congressman worked hard on that pork barrel. He thinks it'll get him reelected.*

PORKY

— **porky** (pôr´kē/pōr´kē) (colloq.): fat, obese (also voc.) *>Why don't they put that porky kid on a diet? >You ought to lose a few pounds, porky!*

PORN

** **porn** (pôrn) (colloq.): pornography (also adj.) *>He made his money selling porn. >She was featured in some porn magazine.*

PORNO

** **porno** (pôr´nō) (colloq.): pornographic *>He rented a couple of porno videos.*

POSSUM

* **play possum** (... pos´əm) (colloq.): pretend to be asleep or dead >*He ain't asleep—he's just playing possum.* >*Did you kill it, or is it just playing possum?*

POSTOP

— **postop** (pōst´op´) (colloq.): the postoperative recuperation ward or room of a hospital (also adj.) >*He's resting comfortably in postop.* >*Postop care is real important with this kind of surgery.*

POT

** **pot**[1] (sl.): marijuana >*All her worthless son wants to do is smoke pot.*

* **pot**[2] (sl.): large and round stomach, potbelly >*Look at the pot Darrin's got on him from drinkin' so much beer!*

* **go to pot** (colloq.): deteriorate, become ruined >*The whole program's gone to pot since it lost its federal funding.*

— **not have a pot to piss in** (... pis ...) (sl., freq. vulg.): have nothing to one's name, be destitute, be very poor >*Where's he gonna get the dough? He ain't got a pot to piss in.*

* **the pot** (sl.): the toilet >*He said he was sittin' on the pot when the earthquake hit.*

POTGUT

— **potgut** (sl.): large and round stomach, potbelly >*I better cut down on the beer—I'm gettin' a potgut.*

POTHEAD

* **pothead** (sl.): habitual marijuana smoker >*That pothead's not interested in findin' a job.*

POTLUCK

— **take potluck** (colloq.): choose from what is available, accept leftovers >*By the time we get there all the good seats will be taken, so we'll have to take potluck.*

POTSHOT

* **take a potshot (at)** (colloq.): make an unfair or ill-considered critical remark (about), criticize (s/one) irresponsibly or treacherously >*That columnist loves to criticize. He takes potshots at everybody in politics.*

POTTED

— **potted** (pot´əd) (sl.): drunk >*She was pretty potted by the end of the party.*

POTTY

* **potty** (pot´ē) (colloq.): toilet, bathroom >*Can I use your potty?*

* **go potty** (colloq.): urinate or defecate (used esp. with small children) >*I think Janey's got to go potty.*

POUND

* **pound** (vt) (sl.): defeat decisively >*We pounded 'em, eleven to nothin'.*

— **pound the pavement** (colloq.): walk the streets (esp. to accomplish a task) >*Get out there and pound the pavement— you're not going to sell any subscriptions just sitting around.*

POUNDING

* **take a pounding** (colloq.): suffer a severe loss or defeat >*His business is taking a pounding during the recession.* >*The Yankees took a pounding last night.*

POUR

* **pour it on** (colloq.): proceed with greater determination, intensify (one's) efforts >*They poured it on the last five minutes and came from behind to win.*

* **pour on** (vt) (colloq.): apply with great determination, do intensely (esp. a dramatic gesture) >*When Rod pours on the charm, he can persuade anybody to do anything.* >*She really poured on the poor innocent victim act on the witness stand.*

POWDER

— **powder [one's] nose** (colloq.): use the bathroom (said of women) >*Betty'll be right back—she's just powdering her nose.*

— **take a powder** (sl.): leave quickly, escape >*When the security guard showed up, they took a powder.*

POWERFUL

— **powerful** (colloq.): very, quite >*She's a powerful good-looking woman.* >*They've got a powerful lot of money.*

POWER TRIP

* **power trip** (sl.): activity or behavior where (one) makes a display of (his/her) power or authority >*He's been on a power trip, givin' orders right and left, ever since they put him in charge.*

POWWOW

— **powwow**[1] (pou´wou´) (colloq.): conference, meeting >*The managers are having a powwow right now about how to deal with this.*

— **powwow**[2] (vi) (colloq.): confer, meet >*We powwowed about it and decided to give him another chance.*

PRAYER

* **[neg.] have a prayer** (colloq.): [neg.] have any chance at all >*That team doesn't have a prayer of winning the championship this year.* >*He never had a prayer against the champ.*

PRECIOUS

— **precious** (voc.) (colloq.): sweetheart, dear >*Anything you say, precious.*

PREEMIE

* **preemie** (prē´mē) (colloq.): prematurely born infant >*She was a preemie and weighed only three pounds at birth.*

PRELAW

* **prelaw**[1] (prē´lô´) (colloq.): study program in preparation for law school >*He's doing prelaw because his father's a lawyer.*

* **prelaw**[2] (colloq.): involved in a study program in preparation for law school >*Are you prelaw, too?*

PRELIM

* **prelim** (prē´lim) (colloq.): preliminary exam (esp. in a doctoral program) >*You got to pass the prelims before they'll let you go on with the program.*

PREMED

* **premed**[1] (prē´med´) (colloq.): premedical study program >*Organic chemistry's a requirement for premed.*

* **premed**[2] (colloq.): involved in a premedical study program >*Jason's a music major, and his sister's premed.*

PREMIE

— **premie** (see "PREEMIE")

PREP

* **prep** (prep) (vi, vt) (colloq.): prepare, get ready >*He knows how to prep for exams.* >*The patient's prepped for surgery.*

PREPPY

* **preppy** (prep´ē) (colloq.): person who dresses or behaves like a traditional preparatory school student, person who prefers a casual but high-quality clothing style (also adj.) >*He's a preppy that doesn't want anything to do with the middle-class kids.* >*Here she comes in her preppy shorts and sweater.*

PRESS

— **press the flesh** (colloq.): shake hands (esp. repeatedly, esp. for political gain) >*The candidate's out pressing the flesh at the factory today.*

PRETEND

* **pretend** (colloq.): make-believe, simulated >*Don't worry—it's just a pretend gun.*

PRETTY

** **pretty** (colloq.): in a pleasing way, beautifully >*She sure sings pretty.*

* **a pretty penny** (colloq.): a large amount of money >*Paul's going to make a pretty penny on that real estate deal.*

* **(as) pretty as a picture** (colloq.): very pretty >*Your little girl is pretty as a picture in that new dress.*

— **pretty please (with sugar on it)!** (colloq.): (intens. of "please!") >*Oh, let *me go, too, pretty please with sugar on it!*

— sitting pretty (see SITTING)

PRETTYBOY

— prettyboy (colloq.): young and handsome man (esp. seen as vain) (also voc.) >*Does that prettyboy think all the girls want him?* >*Get out of here, prettyboy! This is work for a real man.*

PREZ

— prez (prez) (colloq.): president >*If that's what the prez wants, that's what the prez' ll get.*

PRICK

* prick[1] (vulg.): contemptible or reprehensible person (esp. a man) (also voc.) >*I'm not lettin' that prick get away with it.* >*Get outta here, prick!*

* prick[2] (vulg.): penis >*He says he's got a sore on his prick.*

PRICK-TEASER

— prick-teaser (vulg.): woman who arouses a man sexually without allowing him to have sex with her, sexually flirtatious woman >*I ain't buyin' no more drinks for that prick-teaser.*

PRIMO

— primo (prē′mō) (sl.): first-class, most valued >*This place's the primo nightclub in town.* >*He's a primo player in this law firm.*

PRINCE

— prince (colloq.): admirable and likable person (esp. a man), fine man >*You'll really like Curt—he's a prince.*

PRIOR

— prior (colloq.): prior criminal conviction >*Edwards is going to do some hard time in prison because he's got three priors.*

PRIVATE EYE

* private eye (colloq.): private investigator, private detective >*She hired a private eye to follow her husband.*

PRIVATES

* [one's] privates (colloq.): [one's] genitals >*Those guys were wearing tiny bathing suits that barely covered their privates.*

PRIZE

* be no prize (colloq.): be s/thing of little value, be a person of few qualities >*The job they offered me is no prize, but it's better than nothing.* >*I tell you, that clown she married is no prize.*

PRO

** pro[1] (prō) (colloq.): professional, expert (also adj.) >*He'll do it right—he's a pro.* >*He played pro basketball for two years.*

— pro[2] (colloq.): prostitute >*That flashy blonde on the corner looks like a pro.*

PROB

— prob (prob) (colloq.): problem >*Hey, what's the prob here?*

PROBLEM

** have a problem (colloq.): not accept completely, have a doubt or reservation about >*To tell you the truth, I have a problem with your explanation of how the money disappeared.* >*The boss has problems with him being put in charge.*

** no problem (colloq.): you're welcome, that's all right >*Hey, no problem— that's what friends are for.*

PRODUCTION

* make a big production out of (colloq.): exaggerate the importance or seriousness of, give excessive attention to >*He didn't mean anything by what he said. Don't make a big production out of it.* >*They made a big production out of their daughter's sixteenth birthday party.*

PROF

* prof (prof) (colloq.): professor >*He's a psych prof at the university.*

PROGRAM

* **get with the program** (colloq.): start participating (in s/thing) seriously, start making significant contributions (to s/thing) >*If Charlie doesn't get with the program pretty soon, he's going to find hisself out of a job.*

PROMO

* **promo** (prō'mō) (colloq.): promotion (of a product), promotional >*He gave us a promo of the car.* >*They're going to show us some promo film about their company.*

PRONTO

— **pronto** (pron'tō) (colloq.): quickly, promptly, right away >*Get that report typed pronto!*

PROPER

— **proper** (colloq.): thoroughly, mercilessly >*I told her off proper.* >*He got beat up proper.*

PROPOSE

* **propose** (vi) (colloq.): propose marriage >*I think he's going to propose tonight.*

PROPOSITION

* **proposition**[1] (colloq.): invitation or proposition to have sex (esp. an indecent one) >*When he made the proposition, she slapped his face.*

* **proposition**[2] (vt) (colloq.): invite or propose to (s/one) to have sex (esp. indecently) >*He was standing on the corner propositioning practically every woman that walked by.*

PROS

** **the pros** (... prōz) (colloq.): professional sports, professional sports people >*You got to really be good to play in the pros.* >*The pros have been watching him.*

PROTECTION

— **protection** (colloq.): money paid to ensure against threatened violence or arrest >*Sam's been paying fifty bucks a week protection to make sure he can do business.*

PSYCH

* **psych** (sīk) (colloq.): psychology (esp. as a course of study) >*Ellen got an A in psych last semester.*

* **psych out**[1] (vt) (sl.): intimidate, undermine the confidence of, unnerve >*Don't let that bigmouth psych ya out— you can beat him.*

* **psych out**[2] (vt) (sl.): determine the motives of, understand how (s/one's) mind works >*I think I finally got that weird guy psyched out.*

* **psych up** (vt) (sl.): prepare mentally and emotionally for a maximum effort or performance, excite and enthuse (to do s/thing) >*I gotta get psyched up for the oral exam.* >*The fans at the rally psyched the team up for tomorrow's big game.*

PSYCHO

* **psycho** (sī'kō) (sl.): psychopath, crazy person (esp. one tending toward violence) >*She's afraid some psycho's gonna attack her.*

P.U.

* **P.U.!** (colloq.): (interj. to express disgust for a bad smell) >*P.U.! Something smells awful!*

PUCKER

— **pucker up** (vi) (colloq.): pucker the lips (for a kiss) >*She puckered up and gave him a big kiss.*

PUD

— **pud** (pud/pŭd) (vulg.): penis >*The kid was playin' with his pud.*

PUDDLE-JUMPER

— **puddle-jumper** (colloq.): aircraft or flight that makes frequent stops >*I'm going to have to take a puddle-jumper from Cheyenne to Seattle.*

PUKE

* **puke**[1] (pyūk) (sl.): vomit >*Don't step in that puke in the gutter!*

— **puke**[2] (sl.): contemptible or reprehensible person or thing >*I don't* *want nothin' to do with that puke. >He's been readin' a lot of pornographic puke.*

* **puke (up)** (vi, vt) (sl.): vomit >*I almost puked when I heard they gave that dummy a promotion. >He puked up everything he'd drunk.*

PUKEY

— **pukey** (pyū´kē) (sl.): disgusting, contemptible >*Keep your pukey hands off me!*

PULL

* **pull[1]** (colloq.): influence, support of influential associates >*They'll listen to Sanders—she's got pull down at city hall.*

— **pull[2]** (colloq.): drawing power, attractive qualities >*This movie's going to have a lot of pull among teenagers.*

* **pull[3]** (vt) (colloq.): do (s/thing deceitful or censurable) >*I didn't like that trick you pulled. >Mason always tries to pull something funny when his wife's not around.*

— **pull[4]** (vt) (colloq.): earn or receive (a grade) >*I pulled a B+ on the final.*

— **pull a/the ...** (see entry under ... noun)

— **pull a [s/one's name]** (colloq.): do (s/thing) typical of or identified with [s/one's] behavior >*He pulled a Superman and lifted the crate all by himself.*

— **pull [s/one's] chain[1]** (sl.): deceive or mislead [s/one] >*Don't go pullin' Lou's chain 'cause he knows how to play rough.*

— **pull [s/one's] chain[2]** (sl.): harass [s/one], provoke [s/one] >*Rocky's been pullin' Rob's chain just to get him mad.*

— **pull down** (vt) (colloq.): receive as salary or income >*Hart pulls down over a hundred grand a year as manager.*

— **pull in** (vt) (colloq.): take into custody, arrest >*The cops pulled her in for questioning.*

* **pull [s/one's] leg** (colloq.): trick or tease [s/one], tell [s/one] a false story for fun >*Did I really win, or are you just pulling my leg?*

* **pull off** (vt) (colloq.): do successfully, accomplish (esp. s/thing difficult) >*If we can pull this off, we'll be rich and famous. >The robbers pulled off a big bank heist.*

* **pull [one's] (own) weight** (colloq.): do [one's] fair share of work, fulfill [one's] responsibilities >*We're going have to fire you because you haven't been pulling your weight around here. >She doesn't have to work too hard as long as she pulls her own weight.*

— **[neg.] pull [one's]/any punches** (colloq.): treat (s/one) harshly, act without restraint or mercy >*When that senator questions a witness in a hearing, he doesn't pull his punches—he grills them. >She never pulls any punches when she's on the attack.*

— **pull rank (on)** (see RANK)

— **pull (some) strings** (see STRINGS)

— **pull up stakes** (see STAKES)

PULP

— **beat [s/one, s/thing] to a pulp** (see BEAT)

PULVERIZE

— **pulverize** (pul´vər īz) (vt) (sl.): defeat decisively >*They pulverized us, ninety-nine to fifty-eight.*

PUMP

— **pump[1]** (colloq.): heart >*How's the old pump sound, Doc?*

* **pump[2]** (vt) (colloq.): question unrelentlessly >*The detectives pumped him for information for over an hour before letting him go.*

* **pump iron** (colloq.): lift weights (for bodybuilding) >*Look at those biceps! I*

see her pumping iron at the gym all the time.

* **pump up** (vt) (colloq.): excite, enthuse >*They pump the customer up about the car before they talk about the price.*

PUMPKIN

— **pumpkin** (voc.) (colloq.): dear, sweetheart >*You know I love you, pumpkin.*

PUNCH

— **beat [s/one] to the punch** (see **BEAT**)

— **pack a punch/wallop** (see **PACK**)

— **punch/put [s/one's] lights out** (see **LIGHTS**)

* **punch out** (vt) (colloq.): knock unconscious, beat up >*Some guy in a bar punched him out with one blow.*

PUNCH-DRUNK

— **punch-drunk** (colloq.): dazed, very tired mentally >*I came out of my three-hour oral exam punch drunk.*

PUNCHES

— **[neg.] pull [one's]/any punches** (see **PULL**)

— **roll with the punches** (see **ROLL**)

PUNCHING BAG

— **punching bag** (colloq.): person who is habitually beaten or mistreated >*Grace got tired of being her husband's punching bag and had him arrested.*

PUNK

* **punk**[1] (pungk) (sl.): petty hoodlum, minor criminal (esp. a young one) >*You keep hangin' around with them punks and you're gonna get in trouble with the law.*

* **punk**[2] (sl.): contemptible young person (esp. seen as inexperienced or ineffectual) >*You think any of these punks could get the job done?*

* **punk**[3] (sl.): characteristic of a shockingly unconventional and aggressive style of dress and behavior or music >*Their pink punk hair and weird punk clothes make 'em look real*

strange. >How can ya stand that punk rock music? >That real weird guy's a punk rocker.

PUNKER

* **punker** (pung'kər) (sl.): person who follows a shockingly unconventional and aggressive style of dress and behavior or music >*That new band drew every punker in town to its concert.*

PUPPY LOVE

* **puppy love** (colloq.): adolescent love or romantic infatuation >*Paul's crazy about some girl at school, but it's just puppy love.*

PURPLE

— **with a purple passion** (colloq.): ardently, impassionedly >*He hates drunk drivers with a purple passion.*

PURTY

— **purty** (pûr'tē) (colloq.): pretty, attractive >*That's a purty wife you got there, Clem.*

PUSH

** **push**[1] (vt) (sl.): sell or peddle (illegal drugs) >*He pushes crack cocaine over by the school.*

* **push**[2] (vt) (colloq.): promote or sell >*Who's that actress that pushes vitamins on TV?*

— **push a pencil** (colloq.): be a low-ranking bureaucrat, work at an insignificant desk job (cf. "PENCIL-PUSHER") >*Don't you want to do something more than push a pencil the rest of your life?*

** **push around** (vt) (colloq.): boss around, bully, control through intimidation >*That gutsy old guy doesn't let anyone push him around.*

— **push [s/one's] buttons** (sl.): provoke a reaction in [s/one] (regarding s/thing of special sensitivity to him/her) (esp. a reaction of anger) >*She knows how to push his buttons by mentionin' his ex-wife.*

* **push it** (colloq.): take too great a risk (after an easier success), go too far >*Two weeks off? You should be happy I'm letting you have one, so don't push it.* >*Driving twelve hours straight is pushing it, if you ask me.*

* **push [one's] luck** (colloq.): take too great a risk (after an easier success), go too far >*You got your mom to lend you the car. Don't push your luck by asking her for money, too.* >*You'd better stop yelling at that big guy—you're pushing your luck.*

— **push off** (vi) (colloq.): leave, depart >*I got to push off. Later!*

— **push paper** (colloq.): be a low-ranking bureaucrat, work at an insignificant desk job (cf. "PAPER-PUSHER") >*He pushes paper for some insurance company.*

— **hit/push the panic button** (see PANIC BUTTON)

* **when/if push comes to shove** (colloq.): when/if the critical moment comes (to resolve a conflict), when/if (s/one's) will must be imposed >*He may think he's controlling things, but when push comes to shove I'm going to come out on top.*

PUSHER

** **pusher** (sl.): seller or peddler of illegal drugs >*They arrested every pusher and user they could find.*

PUSHING

* **pushing** (vt) (colloq.): approaching or almost (a number) >*Grandpa's pushing ninety, and he's still real sharp.* >*Boy, is it hot! It's pushing a hundred and ten degrees in the shade.*

— **pushing up daisies** (colloq.): dead and buried >*He'll be pushing up daisies if he messes with those gangsters.*

PUSHOVER

* **pushover**[1] (pŭsh´ō´vər) (colloq.): person who is easily persuaded or prevailed over >*I'll get the twenty dollars from my dad—he's a pushover.*

>*The challenger will be a pushover for the champ.*

— **pushover**[2] (colloq.): easy thing to do >*Getting the old man's OK will be a pushover.*

PUSHY

* **pushy** (pŭsh´ē) (colloq.): bossy, bully-like, intimidating >*Tell that pushy jerk that he has to wait his turn.*

PUSS

— **puss** (pŭs) (sl.): face >*The ball hit him right in the puss.*

PUSSY

* **pussy**[1] (pŭs´ē) (vulg.): vagina >*She covered her pussy with her hand.*

* **pussy**[2] (vulg., pej.): woman or women (seen as sex object[s]) >*He said he was looking over the pussy at the party.*

* **pussy**[3] (vulg.): sexual intercourse (with a woman) (freq. used with *some* or *any*) >*He said he got some pussy last night.*

— **pussy**[4] (vulg.): cowardly or timid man >*Just tell your wife you're goin' out for a few beers, and stop bein' such a pussy!*

PUSSYCAT

* **pussycat** (pŭs´ē kat´) (colloq.): gentle or harmless person (esp. despite outward appearances) >*Leo just talks tough—he's really a pussycat, especially with kids.*

PUSSYFOOT

* **pussyfoot (around)** (pŭs´ē fŭt´ …) (vi) (colloq.): act hesitant or evasive, be overly cautious or timid, not be assertive >*Stop pussyfooting around and get to the point!* >*You can't pussyfoot with someone who's threatening you.*

PUSSY-WHIPPED

— **pussy-whipped** (pŭs´ē hwipt´/wipt´) (vulg.): dominated by a woman, henpecked (said of a man) >*Morris is so pussy-whipped that when his wife says "jump," he asks "how high?"*

PUT

— **put (a/the/[one's]/[s/one's])** ... (see entry under ... noun)

— **get/put [s/thing] across** (see ACROSS)

* **put away**[1] (vt) (colloq.): eat or drink (esp. quickly or in large amounts) >*Teenagers can really put food away.* >*He can put away a couple of six-packs of beer in one night.*

* **put away**[2] (vt) (colloq.): confine to an institution >*She went crazy and they had to put her away.* >*This conviction will put Hotchkiss away for ten years.*

— **put away**[3] (vt) (colloq.): defeat, ensure victory over >*They put us away with six runs in the seventh inning.* >*We can put away the competition with this new product.*

* **put down** (vt) (colloq.): belittle, criticize, speak badly of, humiliate >*That insensitive slob is always putting people down.* >*You shouldn't have put her down in front of her friends.*

— **put in [one's] two cents (worth)** (see TWO CENTS)

— **put it there!** (colloq.): shake hands! (said while the right hand is extended) >*Congratulations! Put it there!*

— **put it to**[1] (sl.): harm through deceit or malice, badly mistreat >*The loan company really put it to 'em on that deal.*

— **put it to**[2] (vulg.): have sex with (a woman) >*He's a jealous husband, always thinkin' somebody's puttin' it to his old lady.*

** **put on** (vt) (colloq.): tease, fool, joke with, subject to a hoax >*Are you really related to the governor, or are you just putting me on?*

— **put on the dog** (see DOG)

— **put on the feedbag** (see FEEDBAG)

— **put [s/one] on to** (colloq.): make [s/one] aware of, inform [s/one] of, introduce [s/one] to >*Gerry put me on to a great Chinese restaurant downtown.* >*I'm going to put you on to a friend of mine that might be able to help you.*

— **put out** (vi) (vulg.): readily have sex, grant sexual favors (said of a woman) >*They say she puts out if you're nice to her.*

— **put out the welcome mat (for)** (see WELCOME MAT)

— **put [s/one] out to pasture** (colloq.): fire [s/one] (considered too old), force [s/one] to retire >*The company put some of the older execs out to pasture and hired a bunch of young guys.*

* **put [s/thing] over on [s/one]** (colloq.): deceive [s/one] with [s/thing], carry out [s/thing] by fooling [s/one] >*He put the deal over on us before we knew what was happening.* >*You can't put anything over on that smart kid.*

— **put that in your pipe and smoke it!** (see PIPE)

— **put two and two together** (see TWO)

* **put up or shut up** (sl.): prove (s/thing) or stop saying (it), support (one's assertions) or keep quiet (used esp. as a command) >*I'm tired of ya callin' my friends crooks, so put up or shut up!*

* **put [s/one] up to [doing s/thing]** (colloq.): persuade or incite [s/one] to [do s/thing], get [s/one] to [do s/thing] >*Who put you up to calling her those names?*

— **stay put** (see STAY)

— **tell [s/one] where to put/stick [s/thing]** (see WHERE)

* **wouldn't put it past [s/one] (to [do s/thing])** (colloq.): would not be surprised if [s/one] ([did s/thing]), believe [s/one] presumptuous or daring enough (to [do s/thing]) >*I wouldn't put it past that jerk to try and take credit for the whole thing.* >*Grover, lie to us? I wouldn't put it past him.*

PUT-DOWN

* **put-down** (colloq.): criticism, insult, humiliation >*What a put-down when she called him a six-foot wimp!*

PUT-ON

* **put-on** (colloq.): hoax, spoof, pretense >*That comedian's famous for his put-ons about politicians.* >*That bit about her being educated in Europe is nothing but a put-on.*

Q

Q.T.
— **on the Q.T.** (colloq.): secret, quiet (also adv.) >*These negotiations have to be strictly on the Q.T.* >*They got married on the Q.T.*

QUAD
* **quad** (kwod) (colloq.): college campus square or quadrangle >*There was a rock band playing on the quad.*

QUADS
— **quads** (kwodz) (colloq.): quadriceps muscles (in the thighs) >*These squat exercises are great for building up the quads.*

QUEEN
— **queen** (sl., pej.): male homosexual (esp. an effeminate one) >*Look at that queen wearing makeup.*

QUEER
— **queer**[1] (sl., pej.): male homosexual, overly effeminate male (also adj.) >*He said some queer tried to flirt with him.* >*They say she's queer.* >*Where'd ya get that queer lacy shirt?*

— **queer**[2] (sl.): counterfeit, fraudulent >*I got a queer fifty-dollar bill at the racetrack today.*

QUESTION
— **pop the question** (see **POP**)

QUICK
* **quick** (colloq.): quickly earned (esp. unscrupulously) >*He's a con artist out to make a quick buck.*

— **quick on the draw/trigger** (colloq.): fast to react, quick-witted (cf. "**SLOW on the draw**") >*He doesn't know any more than you, but he won because he's quicker on the draw.*

— **quick one** (colloq.): quick alcoholic drink >*We got time for a quick one before dinner.*

QUICK FIX
* **quick fix** (colloq.): temporary solution, hasty repair >*The economy needs more than a quick fix to get back on track.*

QUICK-FIX
— **quick-fix** (colloq.): temporary, hasty (said of a solution or repair) >*Let's do it right—no quick-fix answers.*

QUICKIE
* **quickie**[1] (kwik´ē) (sl., freq. vulg.): hurried sexual episode >*They had a quickie at lunchtime in a nearby motel.*

* **quickie**[2] (sl.): quick, quickly completed >*They got a quickie divorce in the Caribbean.*

QUIET
— **(it's so quiet) you can hear a pin drop** (see **HEAR**)

QUIT
* **a ... that (just) won't quit** (sl.): an incomparable ..., an excellent ... >*She's got a body that just won't quit!*

QUITS
* **call it quits** (colloq.): stop (an activity), quit, desist, give up >*It's almost midnight—let's call it quits.* >*They decided to call it quits after ten years of marriage.*

R

RACK

— **rack time** (sl.): time spent sleeping, sleep >*I'm dead tired. I need some rack time bad.*

* **rack up**[1] (vt) (colloq.): accumulate (points, money, etc.) >*I was really racking up points on the pinball machine till I tilted it.* >*I've racked up a lot of miles in this old truck.* >*How much money have you racked up working for commissions on sales?*

— **rack up**[2] (vt) (sl.): wreck, smash, ruin >*Joey racked up his motorcycle and darn near got killed.* >*He racked his knee up bad playin' football.*

— **the rack** (sl.): bed, place for sleeping >*It's after ten—ya gonna stay in the rack all day?*

RACKET

* **racket**[1] (colloq.): easy way to make money (esp. unscrupulously) >*They had some telephone sales racket, but the feds shut them down.* >*He's got a nice racket going, with a twenty percent profit guaranteed.*

* **racket**[2] (sl.): business or occupation >*I'm in sales—what's your racket?* >*The real estate racket is tougher than it looks.*

RAD

— **rad** (rad) (= "radical") (sl.): wonderful, extraordinary >*Their new C.D.'s rad.*

RAG

— **rag** (colloq.): contemptible or inferior newspaper or magazine >*Why do you read that gossip rag?*

— **chew the rag** (see **CHEW**)

— **on the rag** (vulg.): menstruating, having (one's) menstrual period >*She told the guy she was on the rag so he'd stop botherin' her.*

* **rag (on) [s/one]** (sl.): complain to [s/one], pressure or criticize [s/one] >*My old lady's always raggin' on me about my schoolwork.* >*Don't let 'em rag ya about how ya wear your hair.*

RAGGED

— **run [s/one] ragged** (see **RUN**)

RAGS

— **rags** (sl.): clothes >*Nice rags you're wearin'!*

RAH-RAH

— **rah-rah** (rä´rä´) (colloq., freq. sarc.): enthusiastically supportive, enthusiastic >*I can't stand their rah-rah attitude about the company.*

RAILROAD

* **railroad**[1] (vt) (colloq.): hastily and forcefully promote and gain approval of (a law or measure) (esp. despite opposition) >*The senator tried to railroad the bill through congress at the end of a long session.*

— **railroad**[2] (vt) (colloq.): convict hastily or without a fair trial >*I tell you, I didn't know they were going to rob the store—don't try to railroad me.*

* **railroad [s/one] (into)** (colloq.): force or pressure [s/one] (into) (esp. hastily) >*I won't be railroaded into signing the petition till I've read it carefully.* >*He didn't want to retire, but they railroaded him by threatening to tie up his pension.*

RAIN

— **(as) right as rain** (see **RIGHT**)

* **rain cats and dogs** (colloq.): rain heavily >*It was raining cats and dogs when the lightning struck.*

— **rain on [s/one's] parade** (sl.): spoil [s/one's] special occasion, ruin [s/one's] good situation >*I hate to rain on your parade, but you'll have to cancel your plans.*

RAIN CHECK

** **rain check** (colloq.): promise to renew an invitation (to an event that is canceled or that cannot be attended) >*We already have plans for Saturday.*

Can we take a rain check for dinner? >I've got to call off the fishing trip for this weekend, but I'll give you a rain check.

RAISE

— raise (the) ... (see entry under ... noun)

RAKE

* rake in (vt) (colloq.): take in or gain in abundance (esp. money) >*I hear Cindy's really raking in the dough with her new job.*

— rake [s/one] over the coals (colloq.): criticize or reprimand [s/one] severely >*They raked her over the coals for being such a snob. >I got raked over the coals for something that wasn't even my fault.*

RAM

— shove/ram [s/thing] down [s/one's] throat (see SHOVE)

R. AND B.

* R. and B. (colloq.): rhythm and blues music (also adj.) >*He likes R. and B. more than jazz. >He was an R. and B. legend.*

R. AND R.

* R. and R. (colloq.): rest and recuperation, short vacation, break >*We're all going to need a little R. and R. after we finish* this *huge project.*

RANG

— you rang? (sl.): did you call me? I heard you state a need that I can fill >*You rang? I'm right here. >You rang? I'm in that very business.*

RANK

* pull rank (on) (colloq.): impose (one's) greater authority (over), get (one's) way by asserting (one's) superior position (over) >*The dean finally had to pull rank on the prof and make him apologize to the student.*

RAP

* rap[1] (rap) (sl.): criminal charge or conviction >*They threw him in jail on a burglary rap.*

* rap[2] (sl.): conversation, chat, informal discussion >*We had a good rap about what we're gonna do in the future.*

— rap[3] (sl.): talk designed to promote (s/thing) or to persuade >*I don't wanna hear his conspiracy rap again. >A lot of people bought after hearin' his rap.*

** rap[4] (vi) (sl.): chant rhyming verse with a rhythmic musical accompaniment >*Hey, let's go listen to those dudes rappin' there on the corner.*

* rap[5] (vi) (sl.): converse, chat, discuss (s/thing) >*We need to rap, man, 'cause we got a big problem.*

** rap[6] (sl.): relating to music where rhyming verse is chanted with a rhythmic accompaniment >*That rap group just finished a new record. >My old lady hates rap music.*

* beat the rap (sl.): succeed in escaping conviction or punishment for an offense (esp. when one is guilty) >*With the slick lawyer he's got, I bet he beats the rap.*

* take the rap (sl.): accept the blame and punishment for an offense (esp. when one is not guilty) >*Hey, Mikey's the one that stole the radio. I'm not gonna take the rap for him.*

RAP SHEET

— rap sheet (rap ...) (sl.): record of past arrests and convictions >*They ain't gonna give him probation with the rap sheet he's got.*

RARING

— raring to (râr´ing ...) (colloq.): eager or enthusiastic to (begin doing s/thing) >*We're all psyched up and raring to play. >Denny's raring to celebrate his big sale.*

* raring to go (colloq.): eager or enthusiastic to begin (s/thing) >*Hurry*

up and deal the cards—we're raring to go.

RASPBERRY

— **raspberry** (colloq.): noise expressing contempt or disapproval (made by extending the tongue between the lips and blowing) >*He gave the school principal a raspberry, then ran like hell.*

RASSLE

— **rassle** (ras´əl) (vi, vt) (colloq.): wrestle >*He likes watching Dangerous Dan rassle on TV.* >*They rassled the thief to the ground and handcuffed him.*

RAT

* **rat**[1] (colloq.): scoundrel, contemptible person (esp. s/one untrustworthy) >*That rat dumped his wife and ran off with some nightclub singer.*

* **rat**[2] (sl.): treacherous person, traitor, informer >*Someone here's a rat that's been talkin' to the cops.*

* **rat (on)** (sl.): inform (on), denounce >*You rat and you're dead!* >*He ratted on 'em when they wouldn't give him his cut.*

— **rat out**[1] (vi) (sl.): desert (s/one), fail to come through, retreat, quit >*If things get rough, I know Duncan'll rat out on us.*

— **rat out**[2] (vt) (sl.): inform on, denounce >*They thought they could trust Betty, but she ratted 'em out.*

— **smell a rat** (see **SMELL**)

RATE

* **rate (with)** (colloq.): be held in esteem (by), get special treatment (from), have status (with) >*They're treating Brian like a king. How does he rate?* >*Romantic guys really rate with women.*

RATFINK

— **ratfink**[1] (rat´fingk´) (sl.): scoundrel, contemptible person (esp. s/one untrustworthy) >*The ratfink was lyin' the whole time.*

— **ratfink**[2] (sl.): treacherous person, traitor, informer >*That ratfink turned in three of his old gang to the cops.*

RATHOLE

* **rathole** (colloq.): small and dirty room or apartment >*I couldn't believe the three of them were living in that stinking rathole.*

RAT RACE

* **rat race** (colloq.): unceasing exhaustive routine, continuous stressful situation (esp. in a competitive, urban setting) >*I'd like to retire to a cabin in the mountains and get out of this rat race.*

RATS

* **rats!** (colloq.): (interj. to express disappointment or irritation) >*Rats! I lost again.*

RAT'S

— **give a rat's ass** (vulg.): be concerned, care, take interest (freq. used in the neg.) >*His old man was a drunk who never gave a rat's ass about him.*

— **worth a rat's ass** (see **WORTH**)

RATTLE

* **rattle** (vt) (colloq.): unnerve, undermine the confidence of, confuse >*Murray got rattled when the boss started questioning him about the report.*

— **rattle [s/one's] cage** (sl.): unnerve or anger [s/one], upset or overexcite [s/one] >*Gee, is Jake ever steamed! Who rattled his cage?*

RATTY

* **ratty** (rat´ē) (colloq.): shoddy, dilapidated, shabby >*Haven't you gotten rid of that ratty old couch yet?*

RAUNCHY

* **raunchy**[1] (rôn´chē/rän´chē) (sl.): dirty, filthy, slovenly >*I gotta get outta these raunchy clothes and take a bath.*

* **raunchy**[2] (sl.): obscene, pornographic >*He really embarrassed the gals with his raunchy jokes.*

RAVE

* **rave** (colloq.): extremely favorable or enthusiastic appraisal (also adj.) *>The new play's gotten nothing but raves. >He gave the book a rave review.*

RAW

— **in the raw** (colloq.): naked, undressed *>They were swimming in the raw when some strangers came by.*

RAW DEAL

* **raw deal** (colloq.): unfair treatment, unjust situation (for s/one) *>Brad really got a raw deal from the company he used to work for.*

RAYS

** **catch some rays** (sl.): sunbathe, get a suntan *>Today I'm gonna hit the beach and catch some rays.*

— **cop some rays** (kop …) (sl.): sunbathe, get a suntan *>Hey, cop some rays and relax, man!*

RAZZ

* **razz** (raz) (vt) (sl.): tease, make fun of *>The other kids razzed him when he asked her to dance.*

RAZZLE-DAZZLE

— **razzle-dazzle** (raz´əl daz´əl) (sl.): showiness, flashiness, dazzling display (also adj.) *>I want a salesman that will give me straight answers without a bunch of razzle-dazzle. >The fans love his razzle-dazzle moves on the court.*

RAZZMATAZZ

— **razzmatazz** (raz´mə taz´) (sl.): showiness, flashiness, dazzling display (also adj.) *>It was a great party, with live music, a champagne fountain and a lot of other razzmatazz. >Just bring her on stage without a big razzmatazz intro, OK?*

R. & B.

— **R. & B.** (see "R. AND B.")

READ

* **read** (vt) (colloq.): understand, comprehend what (s/one) expects *>I want you to get to work, do you read me?*

* **read [s/one] like a book** (colloq.): know [s/one] thoroughly, understand well [s/one's] motives and feelings *>I can read Doug like a book, and I tell you he's feeling real nervous about the meeting.*

** **read my lips!** (colloq.): listen to me carefully! be sure you understand what I'm telling you! *>Read my lips! You will not borrow my car tonight!*

REAL

** **real** (colloq.): absolute, very much a (also adv.) *>You'll like Marty—he's a real prince. >Gee, your sister's real pretty!*

* **for real**[1] (colloq.): genuine, to be taken seriously *>Is this crazy weirdo for real? >Don't laugh, Andy! Their warning's for real.*

* **for real**[2] (colloq.): actual, real, authentic (also adv.) *>Is that a for real gun, or just a starter pistol? >Did he join the Army for real, or is he just teasing?*

* **get real!** (sl.): don't be absurd! stop your ridiculous behavior or comments! *>Get real! He's not gonna change after he's married. >Me, join the church choir? Get real!*

— **the real McCoy** (see MCCOY)

REAM

— **ream** (vt) (sl., freq. vulg.): deceive, victimize, treat unfairly *>He gave twelve good years to that company, but they ended up reamin' him royally.*

— **ream out** (vt) (sl.): severely scold or reprimand *>The sergeant would really ream us out when we'd screw up.*

REAR

* **get off [one's] rear** (sl.): stop being lazy, start moving or working *>If ya don't get off your rear, you'll never get this job done.*

— **[one's] rear** (sl.): [one]self, [one] (esp. when seen as troublesome or contemptible) >*I told him to get his rear outta there.* >*Get your rear up off the couch and do it!*

REAR END
** **rear end** (colloq.): buttocks, rump >*She sat on that filthy bench, and now her rear end's all dirty.*

REAR-END
** **rear-end** (vt) (colloq.): crash into the rear of >*Some drunk rear-ended me on the freeway last week.*

RECAP
* **recap**[1] (rē´kap´) (colloq.): recapitulation, summary >*Haines will give us a recap of what was discussed.*

* **recap**[2] (vt) (colloq.): recapitulate, summarize >*They'll recap the news at eleven.*

RECKON
— **reckon** (rek´ən) (vt) (colloq.): suppose, think >*Do you reckon it's going to rain?*

RECORD
— **(like) a broken record** (see **BROKEN**)

RED
— **Red** (voc.) (colloq.): red-headed person >*Where'd you get all those freckles, Red?*

— **(as) red as a beet** (colloq.): very red (esp. a person's face, esp. due to a strong emotional reaction) >*She got embarrassed and turned red as a beet.* >*His face was as red as a beet, he was so mad.*

* **see red** (colloq.): become furious >*He saw red when they insulted his girlfriend.*

RED CENT
— **[neg.] one/a red cent** (colloq.): no money at all >*He never pays one red cent to help out around here.* >*I didn't get a red cent for that work.*

REDEYE
* **redeye** (sl.): late-night flight >*He took the redeye to Washington.*

RED-HOT
— **red-hot**: very "hot" (see "**HOT**[1-9]")

REDNECK
* **redneck** (colloq., freq. pej.): unsophisticated or bigoted white person (esp. from a rural area) (also adj.) >*I don't want to work for that dumb redneck.* >*His redneck opinions didn't go over very well at the Multicultural Council meeting.*

REDSKIN
— **redskin** (colloq., pej.): Native American, American Indian >*The redskins were attacking the wagon train in the movie.*

REEFER
— **reefer** (rē´fər) (sl.): marijuana cigarette >*The cops busted him holdin' a couple of reefers.*

REF
** **ref** (ref) (colloq.): referee (in sports) (also voc.) >*Didn't the ref see that foul?* >*Hey, ref, time out!*

REFRIDGE
— **refridge** (ri frij´) (colloq.): refrigerator >*There's some cold beer in the refridge.*

REGS
— **regs** (regz) (colloq.): regulations, rules >*It's against dormitory regs to have beer in your room.*

REGULAR
* **regular**[1] (colloq., freq. sarc.): absolute, veritable >*Sure you're smart—you're a regular genius.*

— **regular**[2] (colloq.): down-to-earth, decent, genuine >*I know Clint won't get mad—he's a regular guy.*

REHAB
* **rehab** (rē´hab´) (colloq.): rehabilitation >*How's his drug rehab going?* >*He's been going to the rehab center since his accident.*

RELIGION

— **get religion** (colloq.): become convinced to reform (oneself), commit (oneself) to proper behavior >*After being thrown in jail for three months, he got religion and really straightened his life out.*

RENT-A-COP

* **rent-a-cop** (rent´ə kop´) (sl.): private security guard >*Two rent-a-cops! They call that security?*

REP

** **rep**[1] (rep) (colloq.): representative >*You'll have to get the service rep to help you.*

* **rep**[2] (colloq.): reputation >*That kind of rumor can give a girl a bad rep.*

REPO

— **repo** (rē´pō´) (colloq.): repossessed property (for failure to make payments) (esp. an automobile) >*This Buick's a repo, but it's in real good shape.*

REPRO

— **repro** (rē´prō) (colloq.): reproduction (esp. of a piece of art), copy >*This repro is good—looks just like the original in the museum.*

REPS

* **reps** (reps) (colloq.): repetitions (esp. in weightlifting) >*Do three sets of eight reps for the biceps.*

RERUN

* **rerun** (rē´run´) (colloq.): s/thing redone or imitated, s/thing rehashed >*This looks like a rerun of her big crisis last year.* >*That gag is a rerun of something Johnny Carson used to do.*

REST

* **give [s/thing] a rest** (sl.): stop doing or saying [s/thing] (esp. s/thing annoying) >*I wish that screamin' baby would give it a rest.* >*Give the wisecracks a rest, will ya?*

RETARD

* **retard** (rē´tärd´) (sl., pej.): retarded person, stupid or dull-witted person >*He said he didn't want that retard playin' cards with us.*

RETOOL

— **retool** (vi) (colloq.): prepare (oneself) for a change in occupation, make substantial self-improvements >*It's hard for an old guy like him to retool for a new career.*

RE-UP

— **re-up** (rē´up´) (vi) (sl.): reenlist (in the military) >*He re-upped for another four years.*

REV

* **rev up**[1] (rev …) (vt) (colloq.): accelerate (a motor) >*Rev it up a little and we'll see how it sounds.*

— **rev up**[2] (vt) (colloq.): give strength or energy to, speed up, enliven, enthuse >*Lower interest rates should rev the economy up.* >*The kids are all revved up for the game.*

— **rev up**[3] (vi) (colloq.): gain strength or energy, speed up, become enlivened >*If this party doesn't rev up pretty soon, I'm getting out of here.*

RHINO

* **rhino** (rī´nō) (colloq.): rhinoceros >*They've got a white rhino at the zoo.*

RIB

* **rib** (vt) (colloq.): make fun of, tease >*They ribbed Slick about his punk haircut.*

RIBBING

* **ribbing** (rib´ing) (colloq.): instance of teasing or making fun of >*Don't get so upset—can't you take a ribbing?*

RIBS

— **stick to [s/one's] ribs** (see STICK)

RICH

— **filthy rich** (see FILTHY)

— **strike it rich** (see STRIKE)

— **that's rich!** (colloq., freq. sarc.): that's funny! that's unbelievable! >*You mean the guy Jennifer married already had a wife? That's rich! >Him, a spy? That's rich!*

— **too rich for [s/one's] blood** (colloq.): beyond [s/one's] ability to pay, unaffordable for [s/one] >*Their poker games are too rich for my blood.*

RIDE

* **ride¹** (vt) (colloq.): tease, ridicule >*The guys have been riding Randy about the pink shirt he's wearing.*

* **ride²** (vt) (colloq.): put pressure on, harass >*Rhonda's folks have been riding her to get better grades.*

— **(just) along for the ride** (see **ALONG**)

— **let [s/thing] ride** (see **LET**)

— **ride herd on** (colloq.): keep under control, watch over, manage >*The night manager really rides herd on his workers, and production's way up.*

— **ride shotgun** (colloq.): ride in the front passenger seat (of an automobile) >*Let Nicky ride shotgun—he's tall and needs the extra legroom.*

* **take [s/one] for a ride** (sl.): swindle or cheat [s/one], deceive [s/one] >*If he insisted ya pay him first, I bet he's takin' ya for a ride. >Oscar really took her for a ride—he was seein' other women the whole time.*

RIGHT

— **right** (colloq.): very, quite >*That was a right nice thing you done for us.*

— **(as) right as rain** (colloq.): very correct or appropriate >*Their marriage is as right as rain—they were made for each other.*

— **fly right** (see **FLY**)

— **Mr. Right** (see **MR.**)

— **(straight/right) from the horse's mouth** (see **HORSE'S MOUTH**)

** **right off the bat** (colloq.): at once, without hesitation >*I met this woman and right off the bat she asks me for my phone number.*

* **right on** (colloq.): correct, to the point, true >*I'm voting for Mendez—what he says is right on.*

* **right on!** (sl.): (interj. to express approval, support, or encouragement) >*Right on, brother! You tell 'em!*

— **(right) on the money** (see **MONEY**)

— **(right) up/down [s/one's] alley** (see **ALLEY**)

— **(right) up there** (see **UP**)

* **the right side of the tracks** (colloq.): wealthy neighborhood, area where the higher socioeconomic classes live (cf. "**the WRONG side of the tracks**") >*She dreamed of marrying a boy from the right side of the tracks.*

— **would give [one's] left/right nut** (see **GIVE**)

— **would give [one's] right arm** (see **GIVE**)

RIGHTEOUS

— **righteous** (sl.): wonderful, excellent, genuine >*They play some righteous jazz in that joint. >Smiley's righteous, so don't badmouth him.*

RIGHTO

— **righto!** (rī´tō´) (sl.): right! all right! correct! >*Righto! I'll be there at three on the dot.*

RIGHTS

— **dead to rights** (see **DEAD**)

RIGHT STUFF

* **the right stuff** (colloq.): the necessary qualities or abilities >*We're looking for someone with the right stuff to run our West Coast office.*

RING

* **give [s/one] a ring** (colloq.): telephone [s/one] >*I'll give you a ring next week to see how you're doing.*

** **ring a bell** (colloq.): seem somewhat familiar, evoke a partial recollection

>*That title rings a bell, but I don't think I've read it.*

* **ring off the hook** (colloq.): (for a telephone to) ring incessantly >*How can you just sit there with your phone ringing off the hook like that?*

RINGER

— **ringer** (sl.): person with great ability brought in to compete for one side and whose ability is hidden from or misrepresented to the other side >*Where'd they get that so-called amateur? The guy's a ringer!*

— **ringer for** (sl.): person who closely resembles (another) >*The old guy with the beard is a ringer for Grampa.*

RINKY-DINK

* **rinky-dink** (ring´kē dingk´) (sl.): inferior, cheap, insignificant >*He took some rinky-dink phone sales job.* >*Get rid of this rinky-dink record player and get yourself a good stereo system.*

RIOT

* **a riot** (sl.): an extremely funny or entertaining person or thing >*You should have been at the party—it was a riot.* >*Listen to this guy—he's a riot.*

RIP

— **let 'er rip!** (see **LET**)

— **rip/take/tear apart** (see **APART**)

— **rip into** (sl.): assail, attack vigorously (physically or verbally) >*He ripped into the guy, kickin' and swingin' and yellin'.* >*The judge really ripped into the defense lawyer 'cause he wasn't prepared.*

** **rip off**[1] (vt) (sl.): steal from, cheat, exploit >*Someone broke into my house and ripped me off when I was outta town.* >*They really rip ya off in that damn bar.*

** **rip off**[2] (vt) (sl.): steal >*I left my watch on the table, and somebody ripped it off.*

RIPE

— **ripe** (colloq.): rotten, stinky >*Wow! Something in the storeroom's awful ripe.* >*Take a shower! You're pretty ripe.*

RIPOFF

** **ripoff** (sl.): theft, fraud, worthless product or service >*The cop went to investigate some ripoff at the department store.* >*That real estate deal is a ripoff.* >*Don't buy one of those lousy cars—they're a ripoff.*

RIPPED

— **ripped** (sl.): very drunk or intoxicated >*He started drinkin' at eleven, and by four he was ripped.*

RIP-ROARING

— **rip-roaring** (colloq.): boisterous, wild, exciting >*That was one rip-roaring party last night!*

RIPSNORTER

— **ripsnorter** (colloq.): remarkable or impressive example (of s/thing) (esp. in strength or action) >*That was a ripsnorter of a fight last night.* >*His new adventure film's a real ripsnorter.*

RISE

* **get a rise out of** (colloq.): get a reaction of anger or irritation from (due to provocation or teasing) >*Call him a sissy—that'll get a rise out of him.*

RISK

— **risk [one's] hide** (colloq.): put [one]self at risk, chance trouble or danger >*The pilot really risked his hide setting the helicopter down in that small clearing.*

* **risk [one's] neck** (colloq.): put [one]self at risk, chance trouble or danger >*I don't want you risking your neck for that worthless bum.*

— **risk [one's] skin** (colloq.): put [one]self at risk, chance trouble or danger >*I'm not going to risk my skin by going along with that crazy scheme.*

RITZY

*   **ritzy** (rit′sē) (sl.): elegant, fancy, costly, posh >*Herman drives a ritzy car and lives in a real ritzy apartment.*

RIVER

— **sell [s/one] down the river** (see SELL)

ROACH

— **roach** (sl.): marijuana cigarette butt >*He took one last toke on the roach.*

ROACH COACH

— **roach coach** (sl., hum.): lunchwagon, catering truck >*I'll grab a sandwich from the roach coach when it comes by.*

ROAD

— **get the/this show on the road** (see SHOW)

— **hit the road** (see HIT)

— **one for the road** (see ONE)

— **wide place in the road** (see WIDE)

ROAD HOG

— **road hog** (colloq.): driver who inconsiderately uses more space for his vehicle than is needed >*That damn road hog wouldn't let me by.*

ROAR

— **roar** (vi) (colloq.): drive fast and loudly (s/where) >*He roars around town in a big old Chevy.*

ROAST

*   **roast**[1] (colloq.): ceremony honoring s/one in which acquaintances good-naturedly tease and insult him/her in turn >*The fund-raiser's going to be a celebrity roast of a big-time movie producer.*

*   **roast**[2] (vt) (colloq.): honor s/one at a ceremony in which acquaintances good-naturedly tease and insult him/her in turn >*They roasted a well-known star in honor of his seventieth birthday.*

ROB

— **steal/rob [s/one] blind** (see STEAL)

*   **rob the cradle** (colloq.): date or marry a person much younger than (oneself)

>*She can't be over sixteen! Markham's robbing the cradle, isn't he?*

ROCK

** **rock**[1] (colloq.): rock-'n'-roll music (also adj.) >*I listen to rock more than jazz.* >*I don't care for hard rock.* >*He's a big-name rock star.*

*   **rock**[2] (sl.): precious stone, gem (esp. a diamond) >*Did ya see the size of the rock on her engagement ring?*

— **rock**[3] (sl.): rock cocaine >*Some dude's been dealin' rock there.*

*   **rock**[4] (vi) (sl.): be lively and exciting, be wildly festive >*That dance hall really rocks on Saturday nights.*

— **between a rock and a hard place** (see BETWEEN)

— **rock out** (vi) (sl.): move or dance enthusiastically to rock-'n'-roll music >*The crowd really rocked out when the band played some of the rock classics.*

*   **rock the boat** (colloq.): upset the smooth operation (of s/thing), be uncooperative, cause problems >*Don't rock the boat by asking a lot of questions.*

ROCKER

— **rocker** (sl.): rock-'n'-roll music enthusiast or musician >*The rockers went wild when he played his big hit.* >*He's been a rocker in different bands for years.*

*   **off [one's] rocker** (sl.): crazy, very irrational >*You must be off your rocker to quit that cushy job.*

ROCKET SCIENTIST

— **rocket scientist** (sl., freq. sarc.): especially intelligent person (freq. used in the neg.) >*Ya don't gotta be a rocket scientist to know that story's bogus.* >*I'm no rocket scientist, but I can figure that one out.*

ROCK HOUND

— **rock hound** (colloq.): geologist, rock and mineral collector >*I met a couple* *of rock hounds looking for rose quartz out in the desert.*

ROCKS

— **get [one's] rocks off** (vulg.): have an orgasm (esp. a male) >*Honey, all that clown wants is to get his rocks off with you.*

— **get [one's] rocks off (on)** (vulg.): enthusiastically enjoy, be very excited (by) (freq. used to express contempt) >*That jerk must get his rocks off on insultin' people.* >*Racin' boats is how he get his rocks off.*

— **have rocks in [one's] head** (colloq.): behave irrationally, use poor judgment, be foolish >*He's got rocks in his head if he bet on that lousy team.*

** **on the rocks**[1] (colloq.): with ice (said esp. of an alcoholic drink) >*Give me a scotch on the rocks.*

* **on the rocks**[2] (colloq.): in a ruinous state, in a very poor or precarious condition >*Their marriage is on the rocks because of his drinking.* >*Sell your stock quick—the company's on the rocks.*

ROD

— **rod**[1] (sl.): pistol, handgun >*He ditched the rod after pullin' the robbery.*

— **rod**[2] (vulg.): penis >*Keep your rod in your pants—she's married.*

ROGER

— **roger** (roj´ər) (colloq.): all right, I understand >*Roger. I'll be there.*

ROLL

* **roll**[1] (sl.): large amount of money (esp. in bills) >*He pulled out a huge roll and paid for the car in cash.*

— **roll**[2] (vi) (sl.): leave, depart, get going >*It's late—let's roll.*

— **roll**[3] (vt) (sl.): steal from, pick the pockets of (esp. s/one drunk or unconscious) >*They rolled him when he passed out.*

— **[for] [s/one's] head/heads [to] roll** (see **HEAD**)

** **on a roll** (colloq.): enjoying a period of luck, having a series of successes >*Gary's really on a roll—he's made all of his last twelve shots.* >*I can't stop betting now. I'm on a roll.*

— **roll in the hay** (sl.): episode of sexual intercourse >*She told him they had time for a roll in the hay.*

* **roll with the punches** (colloq.): cope successfully with difficulties, deal with adversity >*You got to learn to roll with the punches to be happy.*

ROLLING

— **get/keep the ball rolling** (see **BALL**)

* **rolling in** (colloq.): having an abundance of (esp. s/thing positive) >*She's rolling in furs and diamonds, but she's not happy.*

ROMANCE

— **romance** (vt) (colloq.): woo, seek the affection or favor of >*Jim's been romancing some gal he met at his sister's.*

ROMP

— **romp** (colloq.): very easy win or victory >*We really outplayed them—it was a romp.*

ROOF

— **go through the roof** (see **GO**)

— **hit the roof** (see **HIT**)

— **raise the roof**[1] (colloq.): celebrate wildly or noisily, be loud and rowdy >*They're going to be raising the roof on graduation night.*

— **raise the roof**[2] (colloq.): complain angrily and noisily >*The tenants raised the roof when their rent went up.*

ROOK

— **rook**[1] (rŭk) (colloq.): swindle, unfair transaction (where what one buys is not worth the money spent) >*A cover charge of fifteen bucks for that dumb show? What a rook!*

— **rook²** (vt) (colloq.): cheat, swindle
>*They're trying to rook you out of ten
bucks by adding on that extra charge.*

ROOKIE

** **rookie** (rŭk´ē) (colloq.): novice, recruit,
person with little experience (in some
occupation) (also adj.) >*Gunther's only
been here for three months—he's still a
rookie.* >*The rookie officers usually
ride with veterans.*

ROOMIE

* **roomie** (rū´mē) (colloq.): roommate
>*My roomie's gone home for the
weekend.*

ROOMY

— **roomy** (see "ROOMIE")

ROOST

— **rule the roost** (see RULE)

ROOTIN'-TOOTIN'

— **rootin'-tootin'** (rū´tin tū´tin) (sl.): noisy
and exciting, boisterous >*We had a
rootin'-tootin' good time in Vegas last
week.* >*He likes to go to some rootin'-
tootin' cowboy joint on the other side of
town.*

ROOTING-TOOTING

— **rooting-tooting** (see "ROOTIN'-
TOOTIN'")

ROPE

— **at the end of [one's] rope** (see END)

* **rope [s/one] into¹** (colloq.): commit [s/
one] to (do s/thing), pressure [s/one]
into (doing s/thing) (despite his/her
reluctance or resistance) >*How'd you
get roped into planning the conference?*

— **rope [s/one] into²** (colloq.): lure [s/one]
into (s/thing deceptive), trick into (doing
s/thing) >*I don't know how that lawyer
roped Tricia into giving him control
over her money.*

ROPES

— **on the ropes** (colloq.): close to failure,
near defeat, in a desperate situation >*I
hear their business is on the ropes.*

* **the ropes** (colloq.): the details or
particulars (of how s/thing functions,
esp. a business or occupation) >*If you
got any questions, ask Kitty—she knows
the ropes.* >*When you've learned the
ropes of this business, you'll start
making some real money.*

ROSE

— **smelling like a rose** (see SMELLING)

ROSES

— **come up roses** (see COME)

ROTGUT

— **rotgut** (sl.): inferior liquor >*Don't ya
have anything better to drink than this
rotgut?*

ROTTEN

* **feel rotten** (colloq.): feel very bad, be
ill, feel sorry >*I feel rotten after eating
all that fried food.* >*She says she feels
rotten about not helping out.*

ROUGH

— **play rough** (see PLAY)

ROUGH STUFF

* **rough stuff** (colloq.): violence,
excessive aggressiveness >*Hey, cut out
the rough stuff! No need to kick.*
>*Watch out for the rough stuff under the
basket!*

ROUND

* **go round and round** (colloq.): argue at
length, quarrel constantly >*They went
round and round about where they're
going to spend their vacation.* >*I can't
believe they stay married, the way they
go round and round.*

* **round up** (vt) (colloq.): search for and
find by chance or unconventionally,
collect any way possible >*Let's round
up something to eat—I'm hungry.* >*See
if you can round up some books on
mountain climbing.*

— **square peg (in a round hole)** (see
SQUARE PEG)

ROUNDS

* **make the rounds** (colloq.): circulate, be widely reported >*Don't just chat with Mack all night at the party—make the rounds and talk to other people, too.* >*There's a rumor making the rounds that he's been in prison.*

ROUST

— **roust¹** (roust) (sl.): raid (by the police) >*The roust netted a bunch of drug dealers.*

— **roust²** (vt) (sl.): harass, raid (said of the police) >*This cop would roust me every time I went into the park.* >*The police are always roustin' that bar.*

ROUTINE

* **routine** (colloq.): routine speech or act (used to persuade or deceive s/one) >*I can't stand his helpless-old-man routine.* >*If she's that mad, give her the old "so sorry" routine.*

ROYAL

* **a royal ...** (sl.): a real ..., an extreme ..., an awful ... (used to express contempt or dismay) >*This lawsuit's gonna be a royal mess!* >*Your brother-in-law is a royal pain in the butt!*

ROYALLY

* **royally** (sl.): extremely, thoroughly, awfully (used to express contempt or dismay) >*Our team got beaten royally.* >*They messed us up royally on that development deal.*

R. & R.

— **R. & R.** (see "R. AND R.")

RUB

* **rub elbows** (colloq.): associate, have social contact (esp. with well-known or influential people) >*He loves working in Washington, rubbing elbows with lobbyists and congressmen.*

* **rub it in** (colloq.): remind (s/one) of an embarrassment or failure in order to annoy >*OK, so I messed up that play—you don't have to keep rubbing it in.*

— **rub [s/one's] nose in [s/thing]** (colloq.): tease [s/one] about [s/thing] (which causes [him/her] embarrassment or humiliation), gloat (to [s/one]) over [s/thing] >*When Mel got the job over Brenda, he really rubbed her nose in it.*

— **rub out** (vt) (sl.): kill, murder >*He was rubbed out on Spike's orders.*

* **rub [s/one] the wrong way** (colloq.): annoy or offend [s/one], be irritating to [s/one] >*The way he's always smirking rubs everyone the wrong way.* >*I just don't like her—she rubs me the wrong way.*

RUBBER

** **rubber¹** (sl., freq. vulg.): condom >*She can't take the pill, so he uses rubbers.*

— **rubber²** (colloq.): tires >*This car needs new rubber.*

— **lay/burn rubber** (sl.): accelerate a vehicle so fast that its tires turn on the pavement and leave black marks >*With this bigger engine I can really burn rubber.* >*He floored it and laid rubber for thirty feet.*

RUBBER CHECK

— **rubber check** (colloq.): check written without sufficient funds to cover it (cf. "BOUNCE¹") >*He gave me a rubber check and left town.*

RUBBERNECK

* **rubberneck** (vi) (colloq.): turn (one's) head to look or stare >*Traffic would speed up if drivers wouldn't rubberneck every time there's a fender bender.*

RUBE

— **rube** (rūb) (colloq.): unsophisticated person from the country, rustic, yokel >*Some rube came into town last night asking about "picture shows."*

RUCKUS

* **ruckus** (ruk´əs) (colloq.): commotion, noisy disturbance, fracas >*They raised a ruckus when they found out the bus would be three hours late.* >*What was that ruckus outside all about?*

RUG

— **rug** (sl.): hairpiece, toupee >*That rug he's wearin' is awful—he looks better bald.*

* **pull the rug out from under** (colloq.): undermine, unexpectedly withdraw support for >*The legislature pulled the rug out from under us when they cut our funding.*

RUG RAT

— **rug rat** (sl.): small child, infant (esp. one in the crawling stage) (esp. when seen as annoying or contemptible) >*Now she's married and stuck at home with a couple of rug rats.*

RULE

— **rule the roost** (colloq.): be in control, dominate (esp. in a domestic situation) >*She talks tough, but the old man still rules the roost.*

RUMBLE

— **rumble**[1] (sl.): street fight (esp. one between youth gangs) >*Two young punks were stabbed during the rumble last night.*

— **rumble**[2] (vi) (sl.): have a street fight (esp. one between youth gangs) >*The two gangs have rumbled a lot the last few years.*

RUMMY

— **rummy** (rum´ē) (sl.): drunkard, alcoholic >*Some old rummy was hangin' around bummin' drinks.*

RUN

* **run**[1] (vi) (colloq.): leave, hurry off >*I need to run—got to pick Jim up in ten minutes.*

— **run**[2] (vt) (colloq.): cost >*How much does the fancier model run? >That'll run you five dollars a yard.*

* **give [s/one] a run for [his/her] money** (colloq.): be a worthy competitor or contender for [s/one] >*They gave us a run for our money, but we finally won. >Vince thinks he can control any woman, but Cindy'll give him a run for his money.*

* **run [s/one, s/thing] [s/where]** (colloq.): take [s/one, s/thing] [s/where] (esp. on a short, quick trip or errand, esp. in an automobile) >*Will you run me down to the store this afternoon? >I'll be right back—I just got to run this package over to Greg's office.*

* **run around like a chicken with its head cut off** (colloq.): move quickly all over, go quickly from place to place (esp. in an unorganized way) >*I've been running around like a chicken with its head cut off trying to get everything ready for the party.*

* **run around (on)** (colloq.): be sexually unfaithful (to) (esp. repeatedly) >*If really loves her, why is he running around on her?*

* **run around (together) (with)** (colloq.): spend a great deal of time and go to many places together (with) (esp. as friends), socialize a great deal (with) >*Me and her brother ran around together in high school. >I don't like you running around with those druggies.*

* **run [s/thing] by** (colloq.): explain [s/thing] to (esp. to get s/one's opinion or reaction) >*Let me run that idea by Cheryl to see what she thinks. >I don't get it—run that by me again.*

— **run in** (vt) (sl.): arrest, take into custody >*If he gets outta line, run him in.*

— **run interference (for)** (see **INTERFERENCE**)

* **run [s/thing] into the ground** (colloq.): overdo or overuse [s/thing], tire or bore others with an excessive amount of [s/thing] >*His puns were funny at first, but now he's running them into the ground.*

— **run off at the mouth** (sl.): talk too much, speak indiscreetly >*I don't want none of ya runnin' off at the mouth about this.*

* **run out of gas** (colloq.): become tired out, become ineffective, flag >*I can't dance another step—I've run out of gas.*

* **run out (on)** (colloq.): abandon, leave (esp. at a critical time or when escaping one's responsibility) >*Lisa's husband ran out on her when she got sick.*

* **run [s/one] ragged** (colloq.): keep [s/one] working or moving a great deal, tire [s/one] out >*My kids are running me ragged—I just can't keep up with them.*

* **run the show** (colloq.): be in control, make the decisions (in a business or situation) >*Owens is the head of the department, but her assistant really runs the show.*

* **run with**[1] (sl.): spend a great deal of time with, keep company with >*I don't like them punks he runs with.*

— **run with**[2] (colloq.): proceed with, put into action >*If they OK the program, we'll run with it.*

— **run with the ball** (colloq.): take on the main responsibility, take charge and proceed aggressively >*Gorman saw how to get the project done, and he ran with the ball.*

RUNAROUND

* **the runaround** (colloq.): evasive or delaying talk or actions >*Stop giving me the runaround and tell me when you'll have my car ready.* >*I got the runaround when I tried to find out who was responsible.*

RUN-IN

* **run-in** (colloq.): argument, confrontation, conflict >*I had a run-in today at the store with some moron who tried to cut in line in front of me.*

RUNS

* **the runs** (colloq.): diarrhea >*Something I ate last night gave me the runs.*

RUNT

* **runt** (colloq., pej.): small or short person >*Tell that little runt to mind his own business.*

RUSH

* **rush** (sl.): sudden feeling of exhilaration, surge of pleasure >*He said crack cocaine gives him a rush.* >*I felt a real rush when I got the award.*

RUSSKI

— **Russki** (rus´kē/rū´skē) (sl., pej.): Russian >*He says if we hadn't supported that dictator, the Russkies would have.*

RUSSKY

— **Russky** (see "RUSSKI")

RUSTLE

— **rustle up** (vt) (colloq.): search for and find by chance or unconventionally, collect any way possible >*I'll rustle us up some breakfast.* >*Metric wrenches? I can rustle some up for you.*

R.V.

** **R.V.** (colloq.): recreational vehicle >*That big R.V. only gets five miles to the gallon.*

S

SACK

— **sack** (vt) (sl.): fire, dismiss >*They sacked him 'cause he worked too slow.*

— **get the sack** (sl.): be fired, be dismissed >*She got the sack when she yelled at the boss.*

— **give [s/one] the sack** (sl.): fire [s/one], dismiss [s/one] >*They're gonna give Muldoon the sack 'cause he just can't do the job anymore.*

— **hit the sack** (see **HIT**)

— **sack out** (vi) (sl.): sleep, go to bed >*Don't make up a bed—I'll just sack out on the couch.*

— **sack time** (sl.): time spent sleeping, sleep >*I can't concentrate anymore—I need some sack time.*

* **the sack** (sl.): bed, place for sleeping >*Only eight-thirty and he's in the sack already?*

SACKED

* **sacked out** (sl.): having gone to bed, asleep >*He was sacked out on the couch, snorin' away.*

SAD SACK

— **sad sack** (sl.): pathetic person (esp. a contemptibly ineffectual one) >*Not him! That sad sack will just mess things up.*

SAFE

— **play it safe** (see **PLAY**)

SAID

* **you said it!** (colloq.): that's exactly right! I completely agree with you! >*You said it! That's just how I feel.*

SAIL

— **sail into** (colloq.): assail, attack vigorously (physically or verbally) >*He sailed into her for criticizing his program.*

SALE

— **no sale** (sl.): (it is/was) unsuccessful or futile, (s/one) refused (it) >*I tried to talk 'em out of it, but no sale.*

SALT

— **no/any ... worth his/her salt** (see **WORTH**)

— **salt away** (vt) (colloq.): save (money) >*Horace is a real miser—he's able to salt away half his paycheck.*

SALT MINES

— **the salt mines** (colloq., hum.): workplace, work (esp. seen as drudgery) >*Vacation's almost over. On Monday I'm back to the salt mines. >Well, I'm off to the salt mines.*

SAME

— **on the same wavelength (as)** (see **WAVELENGTH**)

* **the same difference** (colloq.): the same thing, equivalent >*Give me three fives or give me a twenty and I'll give you a five—it's the same difference.*

* **(the) same here** (colloq.): the same for me, I feel the same, I agree >*She's having a banana split? Same here. >My brother's against it, and the same here.*

SAM HILL

— **what/who/[etc.] in/the Sam Hill ...?** (sl.): (intens. expressing impatience, anger, or surprise) >*What in Sam Hill are you doin' here? >Where the Sam Hill did she go?*

SANDBAG

— **sandbag** (vt) (colloq.): coerce, intimidate (into doing s/thing) >*They're trying to sandbag us by threatening to sue.*

S. AND M.

* **S. and M.** (colloq.): sadism and masochism, sadomasochism >*He may like to try different things, but he's not into S. and M.*

SAP

— **sap** (sl.): fool, gullible person >*You're a sap if ya let 'em get away with it.*

SAPPY

— **sappy** (sap´ē) (sl.): foolish, dumb >*What a sappy thing to say, you dummy!*

SARGE

* **sarge** (särj) (colloq.): sergeant (also voc.) >*Do what the sarge says.* >*Hey, sarge, let's take a rest!*

SASHAY

— **sashay** (sa shā´) (vi) (colloq.): walk, move, go (esp. in an unconcerned or impertinent way) >*He just sashayed in and sat down right in the boss's chair.*

SASS

— **sass¹** (sas) (colloq.): impudent talk, disrespectful response >*I don't want any more of your sass, young man! Just do what I tell you.*

— **sass²** (vt) (colloq.): speak impudently to, answer disrespectfully >*You sass your mother once more and you're in big trouble.*

SASSY

* **sassy** (sas´ē) (colloq.): impudent or disrespectful in speaking >*These sassy kids nowadays don't have any respect for grown-ups.*

SATURDAY-NIGHT SPECIAL

— **Saturday-night special** (colloq.): small and cheap handgun (esp. one easily obtained) >*Every gang member with a Saturday-night special is a potential killer.*

SAUCE

— **the sauce** (sl.): hard liquor >*The way Wilkins is actin', I'd say he's been hittin' the sauce.*

SAUCED

— **sauced** (sl.): drunk >*They drank a couple of bottles of gin and got pretty sauced.*

SAVE

— **save [s/one's] bacon** (sl.): save [s/one], get [s/one] out of trouble or danger >*You owe me, buddy—remember that time I saved your bacon?*

* **save [one's] breath** (colloq.): refrain from speaking or discussing (s/thing) (because it would be futile) (used esp. as a command) >*Save your breath! I'm not interested.*

— **save [one's, s/one's] hide** (colloq.): save [oneself, s/one], get [oneself, s/one] out of trouble or danger >*Ricky's in deep trouble—I don't see how he can save his hide this time.* >*He saved my hide in the war.*

— **save it** (sl.): refrain from speaking or discussing (s/thing) (because it would be futile) (used esp. as a command) >*Save it! I'm tired of your stupid excuses.* >*Arty started complainin' about the cost again, but I told him to save it.*

* **save [one's, s/one's] neck** (colloq.): save [oneself, s/one], get [oneself, s/one] out of trouble or danger >*He doesn't care who gets hurt as long as he saves his own neck.* >*Her testimony saved his neck in court.*

* **save [one's, s/one's] skin** (colloq.): save [oneself, s/one], get [oneself, s/one] out of trouble or danger >*You'd better tell the truth if you want to save your skin.* >*That new government program saved his skin.*

SAVVY

* **savvy¹** (sav´ē) (sl.): good sense, practical knowledge, shrewdness >*Ask Victor—he's got a lot of savvy about these things.*

* **savvy²** (sl.): having good sense or practical knowledge, shrewd >*I trust Gina on this—she's pretty savvy.*

SAW

— **saw logs** (colloq.): snore loudly, sleep deeply >*Vern was sawing logs thirty seconds after his head hit the pillow.*

— **saw wood** (colloq.): snore loudly, sleep deeply >*They're all in bed, sawing wood.*

SAWBONES

— **sawbones** (sl.): surgeon, physician >*Some sawbones told her she'd have to have an operation.*

SAWED-OFF

— **sawed-off** (sl.): short, small >*That tall blonde's quite a sight next to that sawed-off guy she's with.*

SAX

** **sax** (saks) (colloq.): saxophone >*That guy can really play a sax!*

SAY

— **I'll say!** (stress *I'll*) (colloq.): I agree completely! it's certainly true! >*I'll say he's rich! He's got loads of dough.* >*You're asking if I want a vacation? I'll say!*

— **(just) say/give the word** (see **WORD**)

— **not say "boo"** (see **BOO**)

— **say/cry uncle** (see **UNCLE**)

— **say what?** (sl.): what was that? what did you say? I didn't hear you >*Say what? Speak louder, will ya?*

* **say what?!** (sl.): you don't really mean that, do you?! I don't believe what I'm hearing! >*Say what?! The principal, sellin' drugs?!*

* **say when** (colloq.): say when enough has been served, indicate at what point (an amount) is sufficient >*I don't know how much you want, so just say when.*

* **you can say that again!** (colloq.): that's very true! I completely agree! >*You can say that again! Everyone really is mad about it.*

* **you don't say!** (colloq.): Really? How interesting! How surprising! >*I won the raffle? You don't say!*

— **what do you say?** (see **WHAT**)

— **what do you say …?** (see **WHAT**)

SAYS

— **… dollars/bucks says** (see **DOLLARS**)

— **says you!** (sl.): you're wrong! I refute that! >*That bunch of losers, take the trophy? Says you!*

— **says who?** (sl.): you're wrong! I refute that! >*Says who? No way ya can beat me playin' pool.*

SAY-SO

* **say-so¹** (colloq.): authorization, approval, final decision >*I got to get my boss's say-so before I go ahead.* >*On whose say-so are you to pick up the files?*

— **say-so²** (colloq.): assertion, affirmation, report, recommendation >*Don't invest your money in anything on Wally's say-so.*

* **have (the) say-so (in/about)** (colloq.): have authority (regarding), have decision-making power (regarding) >*The floor manager has the complete say-so about the refund policy.* >*You don't have any say-so in this, so stay out of it.* >*We'll do it my way because I got the say-so.*

SCADS

— **scads (of …)** (skadz …) (colloq.): much (…), many (…) >*I got scads of work to do at the office.* >*Bea doesn't need new friends—she's got scads.*

SCALES

— **tip the scales at** (see **TIP**)

SCALP

* **scalp** (vt) (colloq.): resell (event tickets) for a profit (esp. an excessive profit) >*They were scalping tickets for ten times the original price.*

SCALPER

* **scalper** (colloq.): person who resells event tickets for a profit (esp. an excessive profit) >*The scalpers were doing a good business outside the stadium.*

SCAM

** **scam¹** (skam) (colloq.): fraudulent scheme, swindle, confidence game

>*The old couple lost their life savings in the scam.*

* **scam²** (vt) (colloq.): swindle, defraud, trick in a confidence game >*That so-called sales representative has left town with everyone's money. We got scammed.*

SCARCE

* **make [oneself] scarce** (sl.): leave, get out of sight, hide >*I'm gonna make myself scarce before that jerk comes back.*

SCARE

* **scare [s/one] shitless** (… shit´lis) (vulg.): scare [s/one] very much, terrify [s/one] >*He scared me shitless when he aimed the gun at me.*

— **scare the (living) daylights out of** (see DAYLIGHTS)

— **scare the (living) shit out of** (see SHIT)

— **scare up** (vt) (colloq.): search for and find by chance or unconventionally, collect any way possible >*The police are trying to scare up some witnesses to the shooting.*

SCARED

* **scared stiff** (colloq.): extremely frightened >*He's scared stiff about talking before a group.*

SCAREDY-CAT

— **scaredy-cat** (skâr´dē kat´) (colloq.): coward, easily frightened person (used esp. among children) >*Come on, don't be a scaredy-cat—we have a flashlight.*

SCARF

— **scarf down/up** (vt) (sl.): devour, eat voraciously >*Willie scarfed two plates of spaghetti down in no time.* >*The teenagers scarfed up everything on the buffet table.*

SCAT

— **scat** (skat) (vi) (colloq.): leave quickly, get moving >*Oh, it's late! I got to scat.* >*Scat! And stay away!*

SCENE

— **make the scene** (sl.): appear (at a place), attend (an event) >*Janie made the scene about midnight, just as the party was gettin' lively.*

* **the … scene** (colloq.): sphere of activity in the … profession, area of activity involving … >*He's a big name on the country music scene.* >*I'm not into the drug scene at all.*

SCHITZO

— **schitzo** (see "SCHIZO")

SCHIZO

* **schizo** (skit´sō) (sl.): schizophrenic (also adv.) >*Do ya really want that schizo travelin' with ya?* >*That schizo lawyer hasn't been disbarred yet?* >*Why is he talkin' so schizo?*

SCHLEP

— **schlep¹** (shlep) (vt) (sl.): lug, carry (esp. heavily or awkwardly) >*She had me schleppin' furniture from one room to another all afternoon.*

— **schlep²** (vi) (sl.): move heavily or awkwardly >*There goes old Hiram schleppin' down the sidewalk.*

SCHMALTZ

— **schmaltz** (shmälts/shmôlts) (colloq.): excessive sentimentalism >*That play has too much schmaltz for my taste.*

SCHMALTZY

— **schmaltzy** (shmält´sē/shmôlt´sē) (colloq.): overly sentimental >*How can you stand to watch those schmaltzy old movies?*

SCHMEAR

— **the (whole) schmear** (… shmēr) (sl.): all of it, the whole set, everything involved >*He gave us names, dates, addresses, contacts—the whole schmear.*

SCHMO

— **schmo** (shmō) (sl.): foolish or pathetic man, easily tricked man >*Some poor schmo tried to stop Rita, and she hit*

SCHMUCK–SCORE

him. >*Who are the schmoes listenin' to that con man?*

SCHMUCK

* **schmuck** (shmuk) (sl.): foolish or ridiculous person, contemptible person (esp. because of obnoxious behavior) >*Who's that schmuck showin' everybody the scar from his operation?*

SCHNOOK

— **schnook** (shnŭk) (sl.): foolish or pathetic man, easily tricked man >*That schnook believed the whole crazy story.*

SCHNOZ

— **schnoz** (shnoz) (sl.): (person's) nose (esp. a large one) >*Did ya see the schnoz on that guy? >A fly flew right up my schnoz.*

SCHOOL OF HARD KNOCKS

* **the school of hard knocks** (colloq.): life (as a source of practical knowledge gained through contending with adversity) (esp. in contrast to formal education) >*I learned what I needed in the school of hard knocks to be successful.*

SCHTICK

— **schtick** (see "SHTICK")

SCI-FI

** **sci-fi** (sī´fī´) (colloq.): science fiction >*He reads nothing but sci-fi.*

SCOOP

* **scoop¹** (colloq.): exclusiveness (of a news organization) in divulging a news story >*The Times had a scoop on the story.*

— **scoop²** (vt) (colloq.): precede (s/one) in divulging a news story >*They scooped all the other TV stations on the bribe scandal.*

* **the scoop** (sl.): the pertinent information, news (esp. when confidential or little known) >*I got the scoop on what's goin' on in the mayor's office.*

SCOOT

* **scoot** (vi) (colloq.): move quickly, get going >*I can only stay a minute, and then I got to scoot. >Now you kids scoot, or you'll be late for school.*

SCOPE

— **scope** (vt) (sl.): look at, study, read >*Let me scope that diagram.*

— **scope out** (vt) (sl.): look over, inspect, evaluate >*Let's go scope out the chicks at the dance.*

SCORCHER

* **scorcher** (colloq.): very hot day >*Yesterday was a real scorcher—it hit a hundred and eight degrees in the shade.*

SCORE

* **score¹** (sl., freq. vulg.): achievement of having sex, sexual conquest >*He thought she'd be an easy score.*

— **score²** (sl.): successful illegal transaction (esp. of drugs) >*The dealer's plannin' a big score tonight. >Lefty made a nice score with them hot cars.*

— **score³** (sl.): successful robbery or theft >*The gunman made a good score at the liquor store. >The bank score was right at closin' time.*

* **score⁴** (vi) (sl., freq. vulg.): achieve having sex, make a sexual conquest >*Did ya score with her? >Jeff thinks he'll score tonight if he treats her nice.*

* **score⁵** (vi) (sl.): gain an advantage, make a gain, have a success (esp. a large or surprising one) >*The prosecution really scored with that witness. >If we score big on this deal, we'll make a lot of dough.*

* **score⁶** (vi, vt) (sl.): achieve buying or obtaining (an illegal drug) >*He went out lookin' to buy some coke, but he didn't score. >That junkie's gotta score some heroin soon or he's in trouble.*

— **score⁷** (vt) (sl.): acquire, achieve obtaining >*Hey, Nick, where'd ya score the new watch?*

— **even the score (with)** (see **EVEN**)

* **know the score** (colloq.): understand how things work, know what's important, have the basic facts >*You don't have to explain anything—I know the score.* >*Trust McCain with this—he knows the score.*

* **score with** (colloq.): be successful with, favorably impress >*His nice table manners really scored with her mother.* >*The play was a flop—it didn't score with the public.*

— **the score** (colloq.): the basic facts, the main points, the current information (esp. of a situation) >*Ask Jack—he's got the score on applying for a permit.* >*What's the score on the merger proposal?*

SCOUT'S
— **scout's honor!** (sl.): I swear it's the truth! >*The guy really did eat the whole watermelon by himself. Scout's honor!*

SCRAM
— **scram** (skram) (vi) (colloq.): leave quickly, go away >*We'd better scram. Looks like trouble.* >*Scram and let me sleep!*

SCRAP
— **scrap** (colloq.): fight, dispute, argument >*The boys got into a little scrap over a football game.*

SCRAPE
— **scrape¹** (colloq.): difficult situation, predicament, trouble >*I'm in a scrape over some gambling debts.*

— **scrape²** (colloq.): fight, dispute >*I hear you were in a scrape with some cowboy in a bar.*

* **scrape the bottom of the barrel** (colloq.): use the least desirable, resort to the poorest, use what's left over >*They're really scraping the bottom of the barrel if they hired that dummy.*

* **scrape up/together** (vt) (colloq.): search for and find by chance or unconventionally, collect any way possible >*Think you can scrape up enough cash for the down payment?* >*We can scrape together a team by Saturday.*

SCRAPPER
— **scrapper** (skrap´ər) (colloq.): fighter, aggressive person, person who doesn't easily give up >*He's a pretty good scrapper who knows how to use his fists.* >*You got to be a real scrapper to get ahead in this business.*

SCRATCH
— **scratch¹** (sl.): money >*Two thousand bucks? I ain't got that kinda scratch.*

— **scratch²** (vt) (colloq.): cancel, consider (s/thing) impossible or unworkable >*Scratch the picnic. It's started to rain.*

* **from scratch** (colloq.): from the very beginning, using basic resources, starting with nothing >*This won't work—let's start over from scratch.* >*She made the cake from scratch.* >*You can't buy that kind of table, so we'll have to make one from scratch.*

— **scratch around** (vi) (colloq.): search, seek (s/thing) out >*I'm going to scratch around and see what I can find.*

* **scratch [s/one's] back** (colloq.): do [s/one] a favor, cooperate with [s/one] (esp. in exchange for his/her favor or cooperation) >*I don't mind scratching his back. He's scratched mine a lot of times.* >*I'll scratch your back, and you scratch mine.*

— **scratch up** (vt) (colloq.): search for and find by chance or unconventionally, collect any way possible >*I'll see what I can scratch up for supper.*

— **up to scratch** (colloq.): of acceptable quality, fulfilling the requirements, in acceptable condition (used freq. in the neg.) >*That player's been fielding great, but his hitting hasn't been up to scratch lately.*

SCREAM

* **a scream** (sl.): a very funny or exciting entertaining person or thing >*This comic's a scream.* >*Cameron's goin'-away party was a real scream.*

* **scream bloody murder** (colloq.): scream very loudly, complain or protest strenuously >*They were punching the kid and he was screaming bloody murder.* >*The customers scream bloody murder whenever we raise prices.*

SCREW

* **screw[1]** (vulg.): copulation, episode of sexual intercourse >*He said he had a good screw with her last night.*

— **screw[2]** (vulg.): sex partner >*She doesn't really love him—she just sees him as a good screw.*

* **screw[3]** (vi, vt) (vulg.): have sex (with) >*Wanna screw?* >*He said he screwed her all night.*

** **screw[4]** (vt) (sl., freq. vulg.): harm through deceit or malice, badly mistreat, victimize >*The bastard screwed me when he took off with my money.* >*He really got screwed in the settlement.*

* **have a screw loose** (colloq.): be crazy, behave irrationally >*That guy must have a screw loose, because he's been saying pretty strange stuff.*

* **screw ...!** (sl., freq. vulg.): I don't care about ...! I want nothing to do with ...! I find ... contemptible! >*If ya don't like it, screw you!* >*Screw it! It's not all that important.*

** **screw around[1]** (vi) (vulg.): be sexually promiscuous >*He's married, but he still screws around.*

** **screw around[2]** (vi) (sl., freq. vulg.): pass time idly, work halfheartedly or unproductively >*I wish you'd stop screwin' around and get down to business.*

** **screw (around) with** (sl., freq. vulg.): treat without due respect or seriousness, handle capriciously, toy with >*You*

screw with me and you'll be sorry. >*I screwed around with the computer but couldn't get it to work.*

— **fuck/screw [s/one's] brains out** (see FUCK)

* **screw off** (vi) (sl., freq. vulg.): pass time idly, work halfheartedly or unproductively >*Stop screwin' off in school and start doin' some studyin'!*

* **screw [s/one] out of** (sl., freq. vulg.): obtain from [s/one] through deception or unfair means, trick [s/one] out of >*That company screwed Gerson outta his pension by retirin' him early.* >*That crook tried to screw me outta five bucks.*

— **screw over** (vt) (sl., freq. vulg.): harm through deceit or malice, badly mistreat, victimize >*Those lawyers'll screw ya over if ya let 'em.*

** **screw up[1]** (vi) (sl., freq. vulg.): make a mistake, botch things up >*We can't screw up this time, or we'll be out of a job.*

** **screw up[2]** (vt) (sl., freq. vulg.): botch, ruin, spoil >*Their dumb argument screwed up our chances to make a deal.*

** **screw up[3]** (vt) (sl., freq. vulg.): injure, hurt severely >*Howard hasn't been able to work since he screwed up his back.*

* **screw up[4]** (vt) (sl., freq. vulg.): traumatize, create anxiety in, make neurotic >*You're gonna screw your kids up bad if ya keep screamin' at 'em like that.*

SCREWBALL

— **screwball** (sl.): crazy or eccentric person (also adj.) >*What's that screwball mumblin' about?* >*Get outta here with your screwball ideas!*

SCREWED

— **screwed** (sl., freq. vulg.): crazy, irrational, unworkable >*His idea of sellin' guitars door-to-door is screwed.*

— **(go) get screwed!** (vulg.): (interj. to express great anger or contempt to s/one) >*So, ya don't like it? Well, get screwed!*

— **have [one's] head (screwed) on straight** (see **HEAD**)

SCREW-OFF

— **screw-off** (sl., freq. vulg.): person who passes time idly, person who works halfheartedly or unproductively >*You didn't really expect that screw-off to keep his job for long, did ya?*

SCREWS

— **put the screws to/on** (colloq.): coerce, put a lot of pressure on >*The boss has been putting the screws to us to get the plans finished.* >*If you don't pay your bills they'll start putting the screws on you.*

SCREWUP

* **screwup**[1] (sl., freq. vulg.): mistake, blunder, botch >*Your screwup's gonna cost us plenty.*

* **screwup**[2] (sl., freq. vulg.): person who habitually makes mistakes or blunders, botcher >*It's a wonder that screwup hasn't been fired yet.*

SCREWY

* **screwy** (skrū´ē) (sl.): crazy, eccentric, strange (also adv.) >*If ya ask me, it's kinda screwy to take the longer route.* >*He's been actin' screwy since his wife died.*

SCROUNGE

* **scrounge** (skrounj) (vt) (sl.): request and receive, acquire through begging (esp. s/thing trivial) >*Can I scrounge a cigarette from ya?*

* **scrounge (around)** (vi) (sl.): search, seek (s/thing) out (esp. in an unsystematic or unconventional way) >*Let me scrounge around in the garage for some longer nails.*

* **scrounge up** (vt) (sl.): search for and find by chance or unconventionally, collect any way possible >*Willis was able to scrounge up enough driftwood for a good bonfire.*

SCROUNGY

— **scroungy** (skroun´jē) (sl.): dirty, unkempt, run-down >*Why is such a classy girl goin' out with that scroungy character?*

SCRUB

— **scrub** (vt) (sl.): cancel (esp. due to the appearance of an unforeseen difficulty) >*Scrub our plans for the weekend—I found out I gotta work all day Saturday.*

SCRUMPTIOUS

— **scrumptious** (skrump´shəs) (colloq.): delicious, tasty >*Boy, this cake is scrumptious!*

SCUMBAG

* **scumbag** (skum´bag´) (sl.): contemptible or reprehensible person (also voc.) >*Tell that scumbag to get outta here!* >*Screw you, scumbag!*

SCUMMY

— **scummy** (skum´ē) (sl.): contemptible, detestable >*I hate those scummy bums hangin' around outside.*

SCUTTLEBUTT

— **scuttlebutt** (skut´l but´) (colloq.): rumors, gossip, inside information >*The scuttlebutt is that he's being forced to resign.*

SCUZZ

— **scuzz**[1] (skuz) (sl.): dirt, grime, filth >*What's all that scuzz in the sink?*

— **scuzz**[2] (sl.): filthy or repugnant person >*I don't want that scuzz in my group.*

SCUZZY

— **scuzzy** (skuz´ē) (sl.): filthy, dirty, repugnant >*Get your scuzzy feet off the couch!*

SEAMS

— **come apart at the seams** (see **APART**)

— **coming apart at the seams** (see **APART**)

SEARCH–SET

SEARCH

* **search me!** (colloq.): I don't know! I
  have no idea! >*Where Kelly went?*
  Search me!

SEAT

— **(fly) by the seat of [one's] pants**
  (colloq.): (do s/thing) by instinct or by
  relying on guesswork (without formal
  training or technique) >*Those new*
  operators don't really know their
  machines—they're just flying by the seat
  of their pants. >*Don't plan this by the*
  seat of your pants. Follow the
  guidelines!

SECOND

— **second banana** (sl.): person of
  secondary importance, second highest
  person in a hierarchy (cf. **"TOP**
  banana") >*He doesn't like being*
  second banana while his brother runs
  the show.

SECOND FIDDLE

— **play second fiddle (to)** (colloq.): have
  an inferior role (in rank or influence)
  (to) >*I don't think Burgess will be able*
  to play second fiddle in this firm after
  running his own company for so many
  years. >*I'm not going to play second*
  fiddle to that dummy!

SEE

— **long time no see** (see **LONG**)

— **see (the) ...** (see entry under ... noun)

** **see you!** (colloq.): I'll see you later!
  good-bye! >*I got to go. See you!*

SEEN

* **have seen better days** (colloq.): be in
  decline, have passed (its/one's) prime
  >*This old car's seen better days.* >*That*
  old actor's seen better days.

SELL

— **sell [s/one] down the river** (colloq.):
  betray [s/one], inform on [s/one] >*That*
  rat went to the cops and sold us down
  the river.

— **sell/go like hot cakes** (see **HOT**
  CAKES)

* **sell [s/one] (on)** (colloq.): convince [s/
  one] (in favor of), persuade [s/one] (to
  accept) >*Think you can sell Diana on*
  going to Mexico with us? >*He's sold on*
  the idea.

* **sell out** (vt) (colloq.): betray, join (s/
  one's) opposition >*Hanson's sold us*
  out—he started campaigning for the
  other side.

* **sell out (to)** (vi) (colloq.): change
  (one's) loyalty (to), betray (one's)
  principles (by joining s/one) (esp. for
  mercenary reasons) >*He used to be a*
  liberal, but he sold out to big business.
  >*They're trying to bribe you. Are you*
  going to sell out?

SELLOUT

— **sellout** (colloq.): person who has
  betrayed his/her principles or associates,
  traitor (esp. for mercenary reasons)
  >*You can't trust Phil—he's a lousy*
  sellout.

SEMI

* **semi** (sem ĩ) (colloq.): semitrailer,
  tractor-trailer (of a large truck) >*I*
  looked in my rearview mirror and saw
  this huge semi tailgating me.

SEND

— **send up** (vt) (colloq.): sentence to
  prison >*He'll get sent up for a long*
  time if he's convicted.

SERIOUS

* **serious** (sl.): impressive, consequential,
  substantive >*I hear he's been takin'*
  some serious cocaine lately. >*We're*
  gonna make serious bucks on this deal.

SET

— **set** (sl., freq. vulg.): (woman's) breasts
  (esp. large or shapely ones) >*He says*
  she's got a nice set on her.

— **be all set** (see **ALL**)

* **set [s/one] back** (colloq.): cost [s/one]
  (a sum of money) (esp. when with
  sacrifice) >*That sports car must have*
  set him back at least thirty grand.

— **(set of) pipes** (see **PIPES**)

— **(set of) wheels** (see **WHEELS**)

* **set up¹** (vt) (colloq.): falsely incriminate, rig or contrive evidence to blame unjustly >*I didn't do it, I tell you! I've been set up!*

* **set up²** (vt) (colloq.): lure into a dangerous or unfavorable position (through deceit or manipulation), manipulate to be tricked or hurt >*Don't you see they're setting you up to do all the dirty work?* >*The victims were set up with promises of free prizes.*

— **set up³** (vt) (colloq.): dishonestly prearrange the outcome of (a game or contest) >*They say he set up the game for some big-time gambler.* >*They set that up so she'd win.*

— **set up⁴** (vt) (colloq.): have (drinks) served (at one's expense) >*Set them up all around, bartender! I'm celebrating.*

* **set (up) (for life)** (colloq.): in a very good financial situation, having a secure financial future >*If I win the lottery, I'll be set up.* >*Tom's set for life—he married the owner's daughter.*

SETUP

* **setup¹** (colloq.): arrangement, plan, organization, set of features >*What's the setup for the party?* >*I wish my place was as nice as the setup you got here.* >*He's got a good setup for his accounting business in the new building.*

* **setup²** (colloq.): false incrimination (of s/one), rigging or contriving of evidence to blame (s/one) unjustly >*It was a setup, and Marv got the blame.*

* **setup³** (colloq.): hoax, dishonest prearrangement (of the outcome of a game or contest) >*That lousy player couldn't have won the match! It had to be a setup.*

— **setup⁴** (colloq.): dangerous or unfavorable position (in which one is placed through deceit or manipulation), swindle >*Your colleagues are after you,* so watch out for a setup. >*They took over $1000 from him in that setup.*

SEW

— **sew up** (vt) (colloq.): have as certain, gain assured success or favorable conclusion regarding >*We had the game sewed up early in the second half.* >*I think I can sew up the deal with him over dinner tonight.*

SEX KITTEN

— **sex kitten** (colloq.): sexy and flirtatious young woman >*He dreams of spending the night with some sex kitten.*

SEXPLOITATION

— **sexploitation** (sek´sploi tā´shən) (colloq.): exploitation of sex (through commercial media) >*I hate the sexploitation in these beer commercials.*

SEXPOT

— **sexpot** (colloq.): provocatively sexy person (esp. a woman) >*When that sexpot walked in, all the guys just stared.*

SHABBY

* **not too shabby** (sl.): quite good >*Twenty bucks an hour ain't too shabby.* >*Her singin's not too shabby.*

SHACK

— **shack up** (vi) (sl.): live together as if married, cohabitate (including having sexual relations) >*They're gonna shack up for a while before they decide to get married.* >*I hear Burt has shacked up with Grace.*

SHADE

— **have it made in the shade** (see **MADE**)

SHADES

* **shades** (sl.): sunglasses >*He thinks he looks cool wearin' his shades at the party.*

SHADOW

— **shadow** (vt) (colloq.): follow closely (esp. secretly), trail >*We had O'Conner shadowed to see where he went and who he saw.*

SHAFT

— **shaft** (vt) (sl.): victimize, mistreat, deceive >*We've been shafted! They ain't honorin' the contract.* >*Every man she gets involved with ends up shaftin' her.*

* **the shaft** (sl.): mistreatment, deceitful or victimizing treatment >*Greene gave Hubie the shaft by takin' all the credit for their work.* >*Those farm workers have been gettin' the shaft from some growers.*

SHAKE

** **shake**[1] (colloq.): milk shake >*Want a chocolate shake?*

* **shake**[2] (vt) (colloq.): elude, throw off (one's) trail >*He followed me for half an hour before I could shake him.*

— **more (...) than you can shake a stick at** (see MORE)

— **shake a leg** (colloq.): hurry up, get moving (used esp. as a command) >*Come on, shake a leg! We've got to finish by five.*

— **shake down**[1] (vt) (sl.): extort money from, blackmail >*The gangsters have been shakin' the merchants down, offerin' "protection."*

— **shake down**[2] (vt) (sl.): search thoroughly >*The cops shook him down for drugs and weapons.*

— **shake in [one's] boots/shoes** (colloq.): be very afraid >*That rattlesnake had me shaking in my boots.*

* **shake on** (colloq.): shake hands in agreement regarding >*We came to a settlement and shook on it.*

SHAKEDOWN

— **shakedown**[1] (sl.): act of extorting money or blackmailing >*The cops saw the shakedown happen and arrested 'em.*

— **shakedown**[2] (sl.): thorough search >*We gave the place a good shakedown but came up with nothin'.*

SHAKERS

— **movers and shakers** (see MOVERS)

SHAKES

— **be no great shakes** (sl.): not be especially good, be unimpressive >*They were really impressed with that new player, but he's no great shakes.* >*The concert was no great shakes.*

* **the shakes** (colloq.): bout of trembling, manifested fear >*He gets the shakes if he goes more than four hours without a drink.* >*It gave me the shakes to meet up with that grizzly bear!*

SHAKE-UP

— **shake-up** (colloq.): complete reorganization (of an organization) >*A lot of folks got laid off during the company's recent shake-up.*

SHAKING

— **what's shaking?** (see WHAT'S)

SHAPE

— **(all) bent out of shape** (see BENT)

* **shape up** (vi, vt) (colloq.): improve (s/one) in behavior or performance, meet/make meet requirements >*You'd better shape up, or you'll get fired.* >*See if you can shape this kid up—he's just not working very hard.*

* **shape up or ship out** (colloq.): either improve (one's) behavior/performance or leave/quit (used esp. as a command) >*If you can't get it right you'll be looking for another job, so shape up or ship out.*

— **whip/lick [s/thing, s/one] into shape** (see WHIP)

SHARK

— **... shark** (colloq.): expert at ... (esp. at s/thing to exploit others) >*Some pool shark took him for twenty dollars.* >*Don't play with those card sharks.*

SHARP

* **sharp** (colloq.): stylish, elegant, attractive >*That's a real sharp shirt, man.*

— **(as) sharp as a tack** (colloq.): very sharp, very smart and quick-minded >*I'm going to hire Luisa—she's as sharp as a tack.*

SHARPIE
— **sharpie** (shär´pē) (colloq.): very sharp person, shrewd and clever person >*You can't trick that sharpie.*

SHAVER
— **little shaver** (see **LITTLE**)

SHEBANG
— **the (whole) shebang** (… shə bang´) (colloq.): all of it, the whole set, everything involved >*Newton's just a figurehead. Brownstone's the one who runs the shebang.* >*I want the whole shebang—nuts, chocolate chips, whipped cream, and a cherry.*

SHEEPSKIN
— **sheepskin** (colloq.): diploma (esp. from a college or university) >*He's going to give me a great job just as soon as I get that sheepskin.*

SHEESH
— **sheesh!** (shēsh) (colloq.): (interj. to express anger, surprise, irritation, or disappointment) >*Sheesh! Leftovers again?*

SHEET
— **(as) white as a sheet** (see **WHITE**)

SHEETS
— **between the sheets** (see **BETWEEN**)
— **three sheets to/in the wind** (see **THREE**)

SHELL
* **shell out** (vi, vt) (colloq.): pay or give (money), spend (esp. at a sacrifice) >*You'd better shell out—you lost the bet.* >*I shelled out fifty bucks for this wax job on my car.*

SHELLAC
— **shellac** (shə lak´) (vt) (sl.): defeat decisively >*We shellacked 'em, eighty-nine to fifty-one.*

SHELLACKING
— **shellacking** (shə lak´ing) (sl.): decisive defeat >*They ain't gonna forget us after the shellackin' we gave 'em.* >*They took a real shellackin' in the semifinals.*

SHENANIGANS
* **shenanigans** (shə nan´i gənz) (colloq.): mischief, pranks, deceitful activity >*When you're in the Army they won't put up with your shenanigans.* >*This deal's not right—I bet there's some shenanigans going on somewhere.*

SHINDIG
— **shindig** (shin´dig´) (sl.): party or dance, festive event >*They're gonna throw a big shindig at Dave's to celebrate the Fourth of July.*

SHINE
— **shine on** (vt) (sl.): ignore, choose not to react to >*Just shine the guy on if he starts tryin' to sell ya somethin'.*
— **shine up to** (colloq.): try to please or impress, be servile with (esp. to gain favor) >*Watch George start shining up to Moss as soon as he finds out he's rich.*
— **take a shine to** (colloq.): come to like (esp. quickly or spontaneously) >*Mrs. Edwards took a shine to my boy and gave him a job for the summer.*
— **where the sun doesn't/don't shine** (see **WHERE**)

SHINER
* **shiner** (shī´nər) (sl.): black eye >*Gail says she got that shiner when she walked into a door.*

SHINGLE
— **hang out/up [one's] shingle** (see **HANG**)

SHINOLA
— **not know shit from shinola** (see **KNOW**)

SHIP
— **jump ship** (see **JUMP**)
— **shape up or ship out** (see **SHAPE**)

— **[for s/one's] ship [to] come in** (colloq.): [for s/one] finally to make [his/her] fortune >*When my ship comes in, I'm going to buy me a small ranch up in Montana.*

SHIRT

— **keep [one's] shirt on** (colloq.): not become impatient, calm down (used esp. as a command) >*Keep your shirt on! I'll be with you in a minute.*

— **lose [one's] shirt** (see LOSE)

— **would give [s/one] the shirt off [one's] back** (colloq.): be very generous to [s/one], be willing to make any financial sacrifice for [s/one] >*You can count on Duncan—he'd give his friends the shirt off his back to help them out.*

SHIT

** **shit**[1] (shit) (vulg.): bad treatment, unjust dealings >*Why does she put up with that shit from him?*

** **shit**[2] (vulg.): lie, false or exaggerated story, nonsense (also interj.) >*Don't give me that shit about your bein' too tired to help.* >*That little guy, lift three hundred pounds? Shit!*

** **shit**[3] (vulg.): annoying or tedious work or demands >*Look at all this shit I got to take care of today!*

** **shit**[4] (vulg.): excrement, dung >*Don't step in that cow shit!*

** **shit**[5] (vulg.): junk, litter, worthless things >*Why can't they just throw their shit in the trash can?*

** **shit**[6] (vulg.): (one's) belongings, things in general (that belong to s/one) >*You can put all your shit in that closet.*

* **shit**[7] (vulg.): contemptible or despicable person >*What a shit he is to treat his kids that way!*

— **shit**[8] (vulg.): illegal drugs >*I know where we can score some real good shit.*

** **shit**[9] (vi) (vulg.): defecate >*The birds'll shit on your car if ya park under that tree.*

* **shit**[10] (vi) (vulg.): become very upset or appalled, become furious >*He's gonna shit when he sees that big scratch on his new car.*

* **shit**[11] (vi, vt) (vulg.): lie (to), tell a false or exaggerated story (to) >*It's the truth—I'm not shittin'.* >*Don't go shittin' me about all the women you've had.* >*Believe me—I shit you not.*

— **(about) shit a brick** (vulg.): become very upset or appalled, become furious >*She shit a brick when she found out her daughter dropped outta school.*

— **(about) shit (in) [one's] pants**[1] (vulg.): become extremely frightened >*He about shit his pants when he saw that big dog comin' at him.* >*The burglar's gonna shit in his pants when the cops show up.*

— **(about) shit (in) [one's] pants**[2] (vulg.): become very upset or appalled, become furious >*Jay about shit in his pants when he found out his car had been stolen.*

— **(as) ... as shit** (vulg.): extraordinarily ..., very ... >*That cat's mean as shit.* >*He hit the target just as easy as shit.*

* **beat/knock/kick the (living) shit out of** (vulg.): beat severely, beat up >*I told him I'd beat the shit outta him if I ever saw him there again.* >*The big guy knocked the living shit outta Shorty.*

— **catch shit (from)** (vulg.): be severely reprimanded or scolded (by), be severely criticized (by) >*He caught shit from his supervisor for givin' a customer the wrong info.*

— **eat shit (and die)!** (see EAT)

* **[neg.] for shit** (vulg.): very badly, in a worthless way >*Why's he on the team? He can't play for shit.* >*This damn thing never did work for shit.*

— **full of shit** (see FULL)

* **get/have [one's] shit together** (vulg.): put/have [one's] affairs in order, get/have control over how [one] lives

[one's] life, get/have things functioning well >*That guy can handle anything—he's really got his shit together.*

** **give a shit** (vulg.): be concerned, care, take interest (freq. used in the neg.) >*Go do whatever ya want! I just don't give a shit!*

— **in deep shit** (see **DEEP**)

* **like shit**[1] (vulg.): bad, badly >*This tastes like shit! What is it?* >*That guy shoots like shit—pull him outta the game!* >*She treats him like shit, but he still adores her.*

— **like shit**[2] (vulg.): wholeheartedly, to the utmost degree >*They worked like shit to finish on time.* >*We've been sweatin' like shit in this heat.*

— **like shit ...!** (vulg.): certainly not ...! not really ...! in no way ...! >*She claims she's a lawyer? Like shit she is!*

** **no shit!** (vulg., freq. sarc.): really! it's not a lie! >*The fire's hot? No shit!* >*No shit! I ain't kiddin'.*

— **not know shit from shinola** (see **KNOW**)

— **piece of shit** (see **PIECE**)

* **scare the (living) shit out of** (vulg.): scare very much, terrify >*That drunk with the gun scared the livin' shit outta me!*

** **shit!** (vulg.): (interj. to express anger, surprise, irritation, or contempt) >*Shit, Terry! Why didn't ya let me know you were in town?* >*Shit! I could beat that wimp with one hand tied behind my back.*

* **([neg.]) shit** (vulg.): nothing at all >*He doesn't do shit at the office, but he gets paid more than me.* >*I pulled out 'cause I was gonna get shit outta the deal.*

— **shit around** (vi) (vulg.): pass time idly, work halfheartedly or unproductively >*Let's stop shittin' around and get this meeting started.*

— **shit (around) with** (vulg.): treat without due respect or seriousness, handle capriciously, toy with >*Hey, stop shittin' around with them fireworks!* >*Don't shit with me, Jack!*

* **shit on** (vulg.): treat badly, deal unfairly with, mistreat >*Ya try to give a guy a hand, and he turns around and shits on ya!*

— **shit on ...!** (vulg.): I don't care about ...! I want nothing to do with ...! I find ... contemptible! >*Aw, shit on what that idiot thinks!*

* **shit out of luck** (vulg.): completely out of luck >*You're shit outta luck—the last job opening was just filled.*

— **shoot the shit** (see **SHOOT**)

— **shovel the shit** (see **SHOVEL**)

** **take a shit** (vulg.): defecate >*He's in the bathroom takin' a shit.*

— **...er than shit** (vulg.): extraordinarily ..., very ... >*It's hotter than shit outside.*

— **the shit ...!** (vulg.): certainly not ...! not really ...! in no way ...! >*With my girl?! The shit he did!*

— **[for] the shit [to] hit the fan** (see **HIT**)

* **... the shit out of [s/one, s/thing]** (vulg.): ... [s/one, s/thing] to the utmost degree, ... [s/one, s/thing] extraordinarily (esp. in a neg. way) >*His home movies bored the shit out of us.* >*The dogs trampled the shit outta her flower bed.*

— **tough shit!** (see **TOUGH**)

* **up shit creek** (vulg.): in serious trouble, in a bad predicament >*You're gonna be up shit creek if ya don't pay Big Benny back on time.*

— **what the shit!** (see **WHAT**)

— **what/who/[etc.] (in) the shit ...?** (vulg.): (intens. to express impatience, anger, or surprise) >*When the shit is this show gonna start?* >*Where in the shit did he come from?*

— **worth (a) shit** (see WORTH)

SHITFACED
— **shitfaced** (shit´fāst´) (vulg.): very drunk >*He got shitfaced at the spring party.*

SHITHEAD
* **shithead** (shit´hed´) (vulg.): contemptible or reprehensible person, stupid person (also voc.) >*Some shithead messed with my keyboard and broke it.* >*Hey, shithead, don't touch that!*

SHITHOUSE
— **shithouse** (shit´hous´) (vulg.): privy, bathroom (esp. when a separate structure) >*Is there a shithouse at the beach?*

SHITKICKER
— **shitkicker** (shit´kik´ər) (vulg.): unsophisticated rural person (esp. a young man) >*Things really get wild around here when all the shitkickers come into town on Saturday night.*

SHITKICKING
— **shitkicking** (shit´kik´ing) (vulg.): rural and unsophisticated, country-and-western >*Tell your shitkickin' buddies to quiet down.* >*All Gary listens to is that shitkickin' music.*

SHITLESS
— **scare** [s/one] **shitless** (see SCARE)

SHITLIST
* **on** [s/one's] **shitlist** (... shit´list´) (vulg.): having annoyed or angered [s/one], be the object of [s/one's] dislike or anger >*Don't talk to me about Wendell—that bum's on my shitlist.*

SHITS
* **the shits**[1] (... shits) (vulg.): diarrhea >*The last time I ate that it gave me the shits.*

— **the shits**[2] (vulg.): very unpleasant or bothersome thing or occurrence, very irritating or boring situation, the worst >*Havin' to work on Sunday is the shits.* >*His gettin' hurt like that was the shits.*

SHITTER
— **shitter** (shit´ər) (vulg.): toilet, bathroom >*Where's the shitter? I gotta go.*

SHITTY
** **shitty** (shit´ē) (vulg.): very bad, unpleasant, inferior, contemptible >*This shitty camera isn't worth two cents.* >*Keep your shitty hands off my things!*

SHITWORK
— **shitwork** (shit´wûrk´) (vulg.): annoying or tedious work >*Can't the secretary do some of this shitwork?*

SHLEP
— **shlep** (see "SCHLEP")

SHMALTZ
— **shmaltz** (see "SCHMALTZ")

SHMALTZY
— **shmaltzy** (see "SCHMALTZY")

SHMEAR
— **the (whole) shmear** (see "the [whole] SCHMEAR")

SHMO
— **shmo** (see "SCHMO")

SHMUCK
— **shmuck** (see "SCHMUCK")

SHNOOK
— **shnook** (see "SCHNOOK")

SHNOZ
— **shnoz** (see "SCHNOZ")

SHOCK
** **shock** (colloq.): shock absorber (esp. for an automobile) >*This old truck needs new shocks.*

SHOES
— **shake in** [one's] **boots/shoes** (see SHAKE)

SHOO-IN
* **shoo-in** (colloq.): person considered certain to win or be selected >*Howard's a shoo-in for the job.* >*Your opponent doesn't have any real support, so you're a shoo-in.*

SHOOK

* **(all) shook up** (sl.): very upset or nervous >*These earthquake predictions have got everybody all shook up.*

SHOOT

* **shoot** (colloq.): filming or photographic session >*That was a good shoot, people.* >*The director's going to do the shoot right on the beach.*

** **shoot!**[1] (colloq.): (interj. to express anger, surprise, irritation, or disappointment) >*Shoot! I tore my blouse.* >*Shoot! I wanted a red sweater, not a blue one.*

* **shoot!**[2] (colloq.): go ahead and speak! go ahead and ask! >*I want to hear everything. Shoot!* >*You got some questions? Shoot!*

— **shoot/fire blanks** (sl.): have infertile semen, not impregnate during sex >*Brad got a vasectomy, so now he's shootin' blanks.*

* **shoot down**[1] (vt) (colloq.): prove wrong, disparage, reject >*They really shot down his hydrogen theory.*

— **shoot down**[2] (vt) (colloq.): bring about the downfall of, ruin the efforts of, turn down >*We'll shoot down the other candidate on the jobs issue.* >*He tried to get friendly with her, but she shot him down.*

* **shoot for** (colloq.): strive toward, have as a goal >*I'm shooting for an A on the exam.* >*Shoot for the gold medal!*

— **shoot for the moon** (colloq.): strive toward the greatest or best, have the ultimate as a goal >*Most of her friends are going to go to the local college, but she's shooting for the moon and applying to Harvard.*

* **shoot from the hip** (colloq.): speak bluntly, act brashly, act without due deliberation or caution >*You won't make it in politics if you keep shooting from the hip like that.*

— **shoot [oneself] in the foot** (colloq.): cause [oneself] harm (esp. by ineptitude or carelessness) >*They shot themselves in the foot by complaining about Reese to the boss—Reese is his favorite employee.*

* **shoot [one's] mouth off** (sl.): speak indiscreetly or inappropriately >*Don't go shootin' your mouth off about my gettin' fired.* >*He starts shootin' off his mouth every time he has a couple of drinks.*

— **shoot square** (colloq.): deal honestly, treat (s/one) fairly >*I need someone that shoots square to handle this because it's real important.*

— **shoot straight** (colloq.): deal honestly, treat (s/one) fairly >*You can trust Knorr—he shoots straight.*

* **shoot the breeze** (colloq.): converse idly, chat >*We spent the afternoon drinking beer and shooting the breeze.*

* **shoot the bull** (sl.): converse idly, chat >*Don't be shootin' the bull when you're supposed to be workin'!*

— **shoot the shit** (... shit) (vulg.): converse idly, chat >*They were just sittin' around shootin' the shit.*

— **shoot the works** (sl.): expend all (one's) resources, proceed without limits, put everything into (an effort) >*Let's shoot the works and have a real fancy wedding.*

* **shoot (up)** (vi, vt) (sl.): inject (an illegal drug) intravenously >*I saw him shootin' heroin.* >*The junkies were all shootin' up in the alley.*

— **shoot up** (vt) (sl.): shoot bullets wildly at or within, damage with gunfire >*They got drunk and shot up the bar.* >*Someone shot the road sign up.*

— **shoot [one's] wad**[1] (colloq.): expend all [one's] energy or resources, spend all [one's] money (esp. without fulfilling expectations) >*He can't gear up for another project—he shot his wad on the*

SHOOT-'EM-UP–SHOT

last one. >*Doris shot her wad in the first casino she went into.*

— **shoot [one's] wad**[2] (vulg.): have an ejaculation >*He shot his wad on the sheet.*

SHOOT-'EM-UP
— **shoot-'em-up** (shūt'əm up') (colloq.): film or television show with much gunplay and violence >*The only thing good on TV tonight is some shoot-'em-up.*

SHOOTER
— **shooter** (sl.): shot of hard liquor drunk in one gulp >*How about a vodka shooter?*

SHOOTING
— **sure as shooting** (see SURE)

SHOOTING MATCH
— **the whole shooting match** (colloq.): all of it, the whole set, everything involved >*He lost his house, his car, his investments—the whole shooting match.*

SHOP
— **fold up shop** (see FOLD)

** **shop around** (vi) (colloq.): take time to compare (before committing to s/one or s/thing) >*Don't marry the first girl you meet! Shop around a little.*

* **talk shop** (colloq.): discuss (one's) business or occupation >*Hey, this is a party, so stop talking shop.*

SHORT
* **short and sweet** (colloq.): brief and pertinent >*I'll make it short and sweet—get to work or you're fired.*

* **the short end of the stick** (colloq.): the worst part of a deal, unfair treatment >*Don't agree to that—you'd be getting the short end of the stick.*

SHORT FUSE
* **have a short fuse** (colloq.): have a short temper, be easily angered >*Watch what you say to him—he's got a short fuse.*

SHORT HAIRS
— **have [s/one] by the short hairs** (sl., freq. vulg.): have [s/one] at (one's) mercy, control [s/one] by threat, have [s/one] in a helpless situation under (one's) power >*If we can get some hard evidence against that jerk we'll have him by the short hairs.*

SHORTS
— **eat my shorts!** (see EAT)

— **take it in the shorts** (sl.): suffer a decisive defeat or great loss, receive very harmful treatment >*They really took it in the shorts when their company went bankrupt.* >*You're gonna take it in the shorts if their lawyers find out about this.*

SHORTY
— **shorty** (shôr'tē) (colloq., freq. pej.): short person (also voc.) >*Who's the shorty with them?* >*What you going to do about it, shorty?*

SHOT
** **shot**[1] (colloq.): chance, possibility >*We got a shot at the championship this year.*

** **shot**[2] (colloq.): opportunity to try, attempt >*He wants a shot at being manager.* >*You can do it—let's see your best shot.*

— **shot**[3] (sl.): blow, strike (esp. with the fist) >*He took a hard shot on the chin.*

* **shot**[4] (colloq.): worn-out, in useless condition >*He can't work anymore—his nerves are shot.* >*We got to get some new shocks. These are shot.*

— **a shot** (sl.): apiece, each >*These machines cost us two grand a shot.*

** **give [s/thing] a shot** (colloq.): give [s/thing] a try, make an attempt at [s/thing] >*I'm not so good at speech making, but I'll give it a shot.*

* **shot in the arm** (colloq.): s/thing that gives new energy or enthusiasm, stimulant >*Getting that new contract was a real shot in the arm for the struggling company.*

* **shot in the dark** (colloq.): guess without any basis, wild attempt >*I can't believe I guessed the answer! It was a shot in the dark.* >*I know asking his neighbors is a shot in the dark, but someone just might know where he's gone.*

* **take/have a shot at** (colloq.): make an attempt at, try >*You want to take a shot at figuring out this map?* >*You say this game is hard? Let me have a shot at it.*

SHOTGUN
— **ride shotgun** (see RIDE)

SHOTGUN WEDDING
— **shotgun wedding** (colloq.): forced wedding (due to the bride's being pregnant) >*They had a shotgun wedding, but they seem to be happy.*

SHOTS
— **call the shots** (see CALL)

SHOULDER
— **chip on [one's] shoulder** (see CHIP)

SHOUTING
— **be all over but the shouting** (see ALL)

SHOVE
* **shove** (vt) (sl., freq. vulg.): go away with, take away (s/thing contemptible or detestable) (used esp. as a command) >*I told him to take his job and shove it.* >*Shove your stupid report!*

* **shove/ram [s/thing] down [s/one's] throat** (colloq.): force [s/one] to accept or agree with [s/thing], force [s/thing] on [s/one] >*We didn't like the recruitment plan, but the boss shoved it down our throats.*

— **shove off** (vi) (colloq.): leave, go away >*It's getting late—I'd better shove off.* >*You're getting on my nerves, so just shove off!*

* **(tell [s/one] to take [his/her s/thing] and) shove/stick it** (sl., freq. vulg.): insult or rebuke [s/one] regarding [s/thing], emphatically reject [s/thing] associated with [s/one] >*Take your sob*

story and shove it, you crybaby! >*I told the salesman to take his contract and stick it.* >*I don't want your help. Shove it!*

— **(tell [s/one] to take [his/her s/thing] and) shove/stick it up [his/her] ass** (vulg.): insult or rebuke [s/one] regarding [s/thing], emphatically reject [s/thing] associated with [s/one] >*Just tell her to take her concerns and stick 'em up her ass.* >*You can shove your disciplinary action up your ass!*

— **when/if push comes to shove** (see PUSH)

SHOVEL
— **shovel the shit** (… shit) (vulg.): tell many lies, habitually tell false or exaggerated stories >*Don't believe everything Nicky tells ya—he likes to shovel the shit.*

SHOW
* **get the/this show on the road** (colloq.): begin (an enterprise or activity), start (a program), get underway >*We got a lot to do, so let's get this show on the road.*

* **it (just) goes to show you (that)** (colloq.): that is the proof or confirmation (that) >*It goes to show you that you can't trust a used car salesman.* >*I knew that would happen—it just goes to show you.*

— **run the show** (see RUN)

** **show off** (vi) (colloq.): behave ostentatiously, brag >*Brian's kind of silly today because he wants to show off for his girlfriend.* >*That bigmouth's showing off about all the important people he supposedly knows.*

** **show (up)** (vi) (colloq.): appear, arrive >*We thought he'd make it to the party, but he didn't show.* >*Guess who showed up at my house last night.*

— **show up** (vt) (colloq.): show (one's) superiority over, prove (s/one) inferior, outdo >*He's mad because his assistant showed him up at the meeting.*

SHOW BIZ

* **show biz** (… biz) (colloq.): show business, the entertainment profession(s) >*Show biz is tough to get into.* >*Sorry you weren't a hit, but that's show biz.*

SHOWBOAT

— **showboat**[1] (colloq.): person who performs in an ostentatious or sensational way (in order to impress) >*Get that showboat off the ice!* >*There's no place for showboats on this team.*

— **showboat**[2] (vi) (colloq.): perform in an ostentatious or sensational way (in order to impress) >*Stop the showboating or you're off the team.*

SHOW-OFF

** **show-off** (colloq.): person who behaves ostentatiously, braggart >*I hate show-offs that go around flashing lots of money.* >*What a show-off! He's got to make sure everyone hears about how he won.*

SHRIMP

* **shrimp** (colloq., pej.): small person (also voc.) >*Who does that shrimp think he is?* >*Watch out, shrimp!*

SHRINK

* **shrink** (sl.): psychiatrist or psychoanalyst >*My shrink says I gotta be more assertive.*

SHTICK

— **shtick** (shtik) (sl.): characteristic speaking or behavioral routine (esp. to entertain or impress) >*That shtick always gets a lot of laughs.* >*Chester came on with the Romeo shtick, hopin' some woman would fall for it.*

SHUCK

— **shuck** (shuk) (vt) (colloq.): remove, take off (esp. clothing) >*Shuck your clothes and let's go swimming in the lake.*

SHUCKS

* **shucks!** (shuks) (colloq.): (interj. to express irritation, disappointment, or embarrassment) >*Shucks! I wanted to go, too.* >*Aw, shucks! What I did was nothing special.*

SHUFFLE

— **get lost in the shuffle** (see LOST)

SHUT

— **keep [one's] mouth shut** (see MOUTH)

— **put up or shut up** (see PUT)

* **shut [one's] face** (sl.): stop talking or yelling (esp. when being offensive) (used esp. as a command) >*Hey, shut your face, man, or there's gonna be trouble!*

* **shut [one's] trap** (colloq.): stop talking (esp. when being offensive or indiscreet) (used esp. as a command) >*Tell him to shut his trap before he tells them the whole plan.*

SHUTEYE

* **shuteye** (sl.): sleep >*It's late—let's get some shuteye.*

SHUTTERBUG

— **shutterbug** (colloq.): photographer (esp. an enthusiastic amateur) >*Her husband's a shutterbug, and he got some nice pictures on their trip.*

SHYSTER

* **shyster** (shī´stər) (sl.): unethical or unscrupulous person (esp. a lawyer) >*Don't trust that shyster! He'll cheat ya.*

SICK

* **(as) sick as a dog** (colloq.): very sick, very ill >*I got sick as a dog after I ate that stew.*

— **sick and tired (of)** (colloq.): disgusted or bored (with), no longer able to tolerate (s/thing) >*I'm sick and tired of his constant whining!*

SICKIE

* **sickie** (sik´ē) (sl.): mentally unbalanced person, morbid or perverted person >*He likes to pull the wings off flies? What a sickie!*

SICKO

* sicko (sik´ō) (sl.): mentally unbalanced person, morbid or perverted person (also adj.) >Some sicko was tryin' to sell porn to those kids. >His thinking's really sicko.

SIDE

— can't hit the (broad) side of a barn (see HIT)

— get a little/some on the side (see GET)

— get up on the wrong side of the bed (see GET)

* on [s/one's] good/bad side (colloq.): in [s/one's] favor/disfavor, liked/disliked by [s/one] >You'd better get on her good side if you want her help. >I can't ask him for a favor—I've been on his bad side lately.

* on the side[1] (colloq.): in addition to the entrée or main course, as a side dish >Give me that combination plate, with a beef taco on the side.

* on the side[2] (colloq.): in addition to (one's) regular work or interest >He works for a big firm and does some consulting work on the side. >Alice is his steady girlfriend, but he sees a couple of others on the side.

— the right side of the tracks (see RIGHT)

— the wrong side of the tracks (see WRONG)

SIDEKICK

* sidekick (colloq.): friend, constant companion >Hey, where's your sidekick today?

SIGHT

— a damn(ed) sight better (see DAMN)

— a darn(ed) sight better (see DARN)

* a sight (colloq.): person(s) or thing(s) remarkable or distasteful to see >Him parachuting off the bridge was quite a sight. >They were a sight after playing in the mud all morning.

* out of sight[1] (sl.): fantastic, extraordinary, beautiful >That drummer's outta sight. >Is that your new car? Outta sight!

— out of sight[2] (colloq.): exorbitant, excessively priced >Tomatoes are just out of sight this season.

* sight for sore eyes (colloq.): welcome sight, person or thing whose appearance is reason for relief >Boy, are you guys ever a sight for sore eyes! We thought everyone had forgotten about us.

SIGNIFICANT OTHER

* significant other (colloq.): person who is (one's) special romantic interest, spouse or sweetheart >Here's two tickets—bring your significant other.

SILLY

— (silly) goose (see GOOSE)

SIMMER

* simmer down (vi) (colloq.): calm down, become less angry >Let Amy simmer down a little, and then I'll talk to her.

SIN

— (as) ugly as sin (see UGLY)

— uglier than sin (see UGLIER)

SING

— sing (vi) (sl.): inform (on s/one), denounce (s/one) >If Duane sings to the cops, we'll all get busted.

SINK

— sink in (vi) (colloq.): come to be fully grasped or realized, finally become understood >Jess looks pretty calm—I don't think it's sunk in yet just how much trouble he's in.

* sink [one's] teeth into (colloq.): begin to eat (esp. with enthusiasm) >I can hardly wait to sink my teeth into a nice, juicy steak.

SIN TAX

— sin tax (colloq.): tax on products involving vices (esp. on tobacco and liquor) >*Increase the sin tax and you can fund cancer research.*

SIRREE
— **no sirree!** (see **NO**)

— **yes sirree!** (see **YES**)

SIS
— **sis** (sis) (colloq.): sister (also voc.) >*I don't know French, but my sis does.* >*Hey, Sis, Mom wants you.*

SISTER
* **sister**[1] (colloq.): black woman (used esp. among blacks) >*Whitey there just insulted one of the sisters.*

— **sister**[2] (voc.) (colloq.): girl, lady (used esp. with a female stranger, freq. in a contentious way) >*If you want trouble, sister, you're going to get it.*

SIT
— **sit** (vt) (colloq.): take care of, watch over (for s/one, for a while) >*Who's going to sit your house while you're on vacation?*

* **not sit still for** (colloq.): not passively accept, not tolerate >*The boss won't sit still for us coming to work late.*

** **...-sit** (vi) (colloq.): take care of (a) ... (for s/one, for a while) >*Would you dog-sit for us next weekend?* >*Vivian's going to house-sit for me while I'm away.*

** **sit around** (vi) (colloq.): remain idle, take no initiative or action >*Why don't you get a job instead of sitting around the house all day?* >*We can't just sit around. What'll we do?*

* **sit on**[1] (colloq.): delay acting on, not reveal, suppress >*You've been sitting on this proposal for six weeks!* >*Sometimes that lawyer sits on evidence that the other side's supposed to know about.*

— **sit on**[2] (colloq.): subdue, squelch, restrain >*If he starts getting rowdy I'll sit on him.* >*Deedee's been mouthing*

off a lot lately—somebody better sit on her.

— **sit on [one's] hands** (colloq.): fail or refuse to take action, choose to do nothing >*The city's falling apart, and the politicians are just sitting on their hands.*

— **sit there with [one's] thumb up [one's] ass** (vulg.): not respond, fail to take action >*Don't just sit there with your thumb up your ass! Help us out!*

* **sit tight** (colloq.): wait before taking action, remain patient until it is clear what action to take >*My broker tells me to sit tight until she gets more information.*

SITCOM
** **sitcom** (sit´kom´) (colloq.): situation comedy (esp. a television program) >*I don't watch many sitcoms—they all seem the same to me.*

SIT-DOWN
— **sit-down** (colloq.): period of sitting (esp. for resting) >*I need a little sit-down before we climb this next hill.*

SITTING
— **sitting duck** (colloq.): easy target or victim, defenseless person >*That old lady's a sitting duck for thieves.* >*We'll be sitting ducks if Schultz pulls out his support.*

* **sitting on a gold mine** (colloq.): having s/thing very valuable within (one's) grasp or under (one's) control >*That farmer's sitting on a gold mine with all his land, but he won't sell it to the developers.*

* **sitting pretty** (colloq.): in a very advantageous situation, in a good position, having gained wealth or success >*They'll be sitting pretty if they get that big contract.*

SIX
* **it's six of one, (and) half-(a-)dozen of the other** (colloq.): it's all the same, it makes no difference >*That road's*

shorter, but this one's better. It's six of one, half-a-dozen of the other which road to take.

— **six feet under** (colloq.): dead and buried >*Moe'll end up six feet under if he messes with the Mafia.*

SIX-FOOTER
— **six-footer** (siks´fŭt´ər) (colloq.): person six feet (or a little more) tall >*She's a six-footer, just like her brothers.*

SIX-GUN
— **six-gun** (colloq.): revolver that holds six bullets >*He showed up with a six-gun under his belt.*

SIX-PACK
** **six-pack** (colloq.): package of six cans or bottles (esp. of beer) >*I'll pick up a couple of six-packs, and we'll have a little party.*

SIX-SHOOTER
— **six-shooter** (colloq.): revolver that holds six bullets >*That's an old six-shooter like the cowboys used to have.*

SIXTY-FOUR(THOUSAND)-DOLLAR QUESTION
— **the sixty-four(thousand)-dollar question** (colloq.): the critical or most pertinent question >*Why he is here is the sixty-four-dollar question.* >*Now just how long can they stay in the air without refueling? That's the sixty-four thousand-dollar question.*

SIXTY-NINE
— **sixty-nine** (vulg.): simultaneous oral-genital sex between two people >*He said they did sixty-nine last night.*

SIZE
— **knock/cut [s/one] down to size** (see **KNOCK**)

* **size up** (vt) (colloq.): assess, evaluate, form an estimation of >*Size up the situation before you act.* >*Susana sized him up, then told him to get lost.*

* **that's (about) the size of it** (colloq.): that's how it is, that's essentially the

situation >*She kicked Mark out and told him she never wanted to see him again, and that's about the size of it.*

SIZZLE
— **sizzle**[1] (siz´əl) (vi) (colloq.): be very hot (weather) >*It's going to sizzle again today.*

— **sizzle**[2] (vi) (sl.): be very popular or successful >*That new group is sizzlin'—their concert sold out fast.* >*Hot? This album's gonna sizzle when it hits the stores!*

SIZZLER
— **sizzler** (siz´lər) (colloq.): very hot day >*Yesterday was a real sizzler—it broke the record for the date.*

SKEDADDLE
— **skedaddle** (ski dad´l) (vi) (colloq.): leave quickly, get moving >*I don't like the looks of this—let's skedaddle.* >*Now, skedaddle or you'll be late.*

SKEETER
— **skeeter** (skē´tər) (sl.): mosquito >*The skeeters are eatin' me alive!*

SKIDDOO
— **skiddoo** (ski dū´) (vi) (colloq.): leave quickly, get moving. >*Skiddoo, now, or you'll miss the bus.*

SKID ROW
* **skid row** (colloq.): deteriorated area of cheap bars and hotels frequented by vagrants and poor alcoholics >*He's some old drunk that lives on skid row.*

SKIDS
— **hit the skids** (see **HIT**)

— **on the skids** (sl.): in the process of ruin or failure, becoming poor or deteriorated >*The old downtown area is on the skids now.*

SKIM
* **skim (off)** (vt) (sl.): remove a portion of proceeds illegally >*They fired him 'cause he was skimmin' five percent off the top for himself.* >*The casino's been*

skimmin' a third of their take before figurin' taxes.

SKIN

* **skin**[1] (sl.): showing nudity, pornographic >*He's always buyin' skin magazines.* >*Wanna see a skin flick?*

— **skin**[2] (vt) (sl.): take all the money from (esp. through gambling or deceit) >*They skinned me at poker.* >*Looks like ya got skinned by that lawyer.*

— **(about) jump out of [one's] skin** (see **JUMP**)

— **be no skin off [s/one's] ass** (vulg.): be no loss or risk to [s/one], be of little or no concern to [s/one] >*Hey, if ya wanna take drugs, go ahead—it's no skin off my ass.*

— **be no skin off [s/one's] back** (sl.): be no loss or risk to [s/one], be of little or no concern to [s/one] >*It was no skin off his back if ya didn't pay him 'cause he knew he would get it from his insurance.*

* **be no skin off [s/one's] nose** (sl.): be no loss or risk to [s/one], be of little or no concern to [s/one] >*So what if she's goin' out with someone else? It's no skin off my nose.*

* **by the skin of [one's] teeth** (colloq.): with very little margin to spare, just barely >*Lyndon passed the test by the skin of his teeth.*

* **get under [s/one's] skin** (colloq.): cause [s/one] great irritation or annoyance >*It really gets under Bart's skin when he sees his ex-wife having fun with other guys.* >*Ignore the jerk—don't let him get under your skin.*

— **risk [one's] skin** (see **RISK**)

— **save [one's, s/one's] skin** (see **SAVE**)

* **skin [s/one] alive** (colloq.): punish or scold [s/one] severely >*Dad's going to skin you alive if he catches you with his tools.*

SKINHEAD

** **skinhead** (colloq.): person with a shaved head (esp. a youth with neo-Nazi views) >*There were some damn skinheads there yelling at the blacks in the audience.*

SKINNY

— **the skinny** (sl.): the pertinent information, news (esp. when confidential or little known) >*What's the skinny on the new secretary in the front office?* >*The skinny is that the cops are gonna start crackin' down on speeders.*

SKINNY-DIP

* **skinny-dip** (vi) (colloq.): go swimming naked >*You don't need no bathing suit—let's skinny-dip.* >*We went skinny-dipping in the river.*

SKINS

— **skins** (sl.): drums >*Man, can she ever play them skins!*

SKIP

** **skip** (vt) (colloq.): forget about, exclude >*Skip it—it's not important.* >*Skip the onions on that burger, will you?*

— **a hop, skip, and a jump** (see **HOP**)

— **jump/skip bail** (see **JUMP**)

* **skip out (on)** (sl.): abandon or desert (s/one), escape (from) >*We were countin' on him, but he skipped out on us.* >*He skipped out before the cops got there.*

* **skip town** (sl.): quickly and secretly leave a city or town (to avoid a neg. situation) >*He skipped town, leavin' a bunch of unpaid bills.* >*Bud skipped town when he heard you were lookin' for him.*

SKIPPER

— **skipper** (colloq.): leader, boss (also voc.) >*Let me get the skipper's OK.* >*What's the deal, skipper?*

SKIRT

— **skirt** (sl., freq. pej.): woman >*Benny followed some skirt into that bar a few minutes ago.*

SKIRT-CHASER

— **skirt-chaser** (sl.): womanizer (cf. "CHASE skirts") >*You marry that skirt-chaser, honey, and you're just askin' for trouble.*

SKIRTS

— **chase skirts** (see **CHASE**)

SKIVVIES

* **skivvies** (skiv´ēz) (colloq.): (men's) underwear, T-shirt and undershorts >*Mrs. Perlman got all upset when he came to the door in his skivvies.*

SKULL

— **out of [one's] skull** (sl.): crazy, very irrational >*He's gotta be outta his skull to challenge the champ.* >*I'm goin' outta my skull worryin' about her.*

SKUNK

— **skunk**[1] (colloq.): scoundrel, contemptible person >*That skunk ran off with my pen!*

* **skunk**[2] (vt) (colloq.): defeat (without allowing the opposition to score), defeat overwhelmingly >*We finally scored three points, so at least they didn't skunk us.*

— **(as) drunk as a skunk** (see **DRUNK**)

SKY

— **pie in the sky** (see **PIE**)

SLACK

— **cut [s/one] some slack** (see **CUT**)

SLAM

— **slam**[1] (sl.): strong criticism, verbal attack, insult >*Her remark about Gerty's polyester pants was quite a slam.*

— **slam**[2] (vt) (sl.): strongly criticize, verbally attack, insult >*The report really slammed the proposal.*

— **the slam** (sl.): prison, jail >*He violated his parole and ended up back in the slam.*

SLAM-BANG

— **slam-bang** (colloq.): directly, squarely, straight (esp. regarding an impact) >*The boy ran slam-bang into the door.*

SLAMMER

* **the slammer** (sl.): prison, jail >*They'll throw him in the slammer for ten years for what he did.*

SLAP

— **slap down** (vt) (colloq.): severely censure or reprimand, silence >*He slapped me down before I could explain the whole thing.*

* **slap in the face** (colloq.): insult, rebuke >*Questioning his honesty like you did in front of everyone was a real slap in the face.*

* **slap on the wrist** (colloq.): light punishment (esp. unjustly so) >*One year in jail for armed robbery is a slap on the wrist.*

— **throw/slap together** (see **THROW**)

* **slap [s/one] with** (colloq.): impose (a penalty or punishment) on [s/one] >*The judge slapped him with a contempt of court citation.* >*The city's going to slap the firm with a ten-thousand dollar fine.*

* **slap [s/one's] wrist** (colloq.): punish [s/one] lightly (esp. unjustly so) >*They just slapped his wrist because his father's the mayor.*

SLAP-HAPPY

— **slap-happy** (colloq.): dazed, giddy >*Everyone walked out of the room kind of slap-happy after watching their travel slides for four hours.*

SLAUGHTER

* **slaughter**[1] (sl.): decisive defeat >*It was a slaughter—their team was lousy.*

* **slaughter**[2] (vt) (sl.): defeat decisively >*The home team got slaughtered, sixty to six.*

SLAY

— **slay¹** (vt) (sl.): make (s/one) laugh hard
>*What a funny guy! He slays me.*

— **slay²** (vt) (sl.): flabbergast, astound, vex
>*It slays me how he insults ya one minute, then asks ya for a favor the next.*

SLEAZE

* **sleaze** (slēz) (sl.): contemptible or reprehensible person >*Why do ya hang around with a sleaze like that?*

SLEAZEBAG

* **sleazebag** (slēz′bag′) (sl.): contemptible or reprehensible person (also voc.) >*Did they let that sleazebag outta jail? >Shut up, sleazebag!*

SLEAZY

** **sleazy** (slē′zē) (colloq.): sordid, dirty, contemptible >*He grew up in a real sleazy part of town. >There were some nude shots of her in some sleazy magazine.*

SLEEP

* **can [do s/thing] in [one's] sleep** (colloq.): can [do s/thing] with great ease or assured success (esp. due to routine experience with it) >*She's done that presentation so many times she could do it in her sleep.*

* **sleep around** (vi) (colloq.): be sexually promiscuous >*She sleeps around a lot and doesn't even take any precautions.*

— **sleep like a log** (colloq.): sleep very soundly >*Barry slept like a log last night after the rough day he had.*

— **sleep like a top** (colloq.): sleep very soundly >*I slept like a top in that comfy bed.*

SLEEPER

* **sleeper** (colloq.): person or thing that performs unexpectedly well (esp. after a period of not doing so) >*That movie was the year's sleeper. >The player was a sleeper—late in the season he started setting records.*

SLEEPYHEAD

* **sleepyhead** (colloq.): sleepy person (also voc.) >*Let's put this sleepyhead to bed. >Wake up, sleepyhead!*

SLEEVE

— **ace/card up [one's] sleeve** (see ACE)

* **up [one's] sleeve** (colloq.): hidden and ready to use when needed >*Joey looks real confident. I wonder what he's got up his sleeve. >They haven't won yet—I still have a few tricks up my sleeve.*

SLEW

* **a slew (of …)** (… slū ….) (colloq.): much (…), many (…) >*There was a slew of work to finish. >Another necktie! I already got a slew of them.*

SLICE

— **(how) you cut/slice it** (see CUT)

SLICK

* **slick** (sl.): excellent, attractive, clever >*Those are slick wheels ya got on your car. >She thinks he's pretty slick. >That's a slick way to do it.*

— **slick up** (vt) (colloq.): make more attractive, improve >*You better slick up your house some before you try and sell it.*

SLIDE

— **let [s/thing] slide** (see LET)

SLIM

— **slim pickings** (colloq.): very poor selection available >*It was slim pickings at the cafeteria because we got there late.*

SLIME

* **slime** (sl.): contemptible or reprehensible person >*I don't trust that slime with my daughter.*

SLIMEBAG

* **slimebag** (sl.): contemptible or reprehensible person (also voc.) >*Some slimebag threw up on the sidewalk. >Get outta my way, slimebag!*

SLIMEBALL

* **slimeball** (sl.): contemptible or reprehensible person (also voc.) >*Get that slimeball outta here.* >*Get outta here, slimeball!*

SLING

— **[for one's] ass [to be] in a sling** (see ASS)

SLIP

— **give [s/one] the slip** (colloq.): succeed in escaping or eluding [s/one] >*He gave the cops the slip in the subway.*

— **fall/slip through/between the cracks** (see FALL)

* **slip up** (vi) (colloq.): make a mistake or blunder, cause an oversight >*Someone slipped up and didn't catch this defect.*

SLIPPING

* **slipping** (vi) (colloq.): losing some of (one's) talent or ability, in decline >*You're slipping, man—women always used to love that line.* >*I must be slipping. How did that get past me?*

SLIP-UP

* **slip-up** (colloq.): mistake, blunder, oversight >*There was some slip-up on the order, and the store delivered the wrong model.*

SLOB

* **slob** (slob) (colloq.): messy or crude person (esp. an obnoxious one) >*Look at the filthy place this slob lives in!* >*Did you hear the nasty insult from that slob?*

* **poor slob** (colloq.): very unfortunate or pathetic person >*The poor slob doesn't even know why his wife left him.*

SLOSHED

— **sloshed** (slosht) (sl.): drunk >*Manny got pretty sloshed on tequila last night.*

SLOT

* **slot** (colloq.): slot machine >*When we're in Vegas, he plays blackjack and I play the slots.*

SLOW

— **slow on the draw** (colloq.): slow to react, slow-witted (cf. "QUICK on the draw/trigger") >*Better explain that to him again—he's a little slow on the draw.*

SLOW BURN

— **do a slow burn** (colloq.): become increasingly angry, fume >*She did a slow burn while he insulted her relatives.*

SLUFF

* **sluff (off)** (sluf ...) (vi) (sl.): fail to work productively, avoid (one's) work or responsibility >*He thinks he can sluff off because he's the boss's son.* >*No sluffin' on the job!*

— **sluff off** (vt) (colloq.): ignore, not become bothered by >*I can't just sluff off an insult like that.* >*His yelling didn't get to me—I just sluffed it off.*

SLUG

* **slug**[1] (colloq.): hit, blow (esp. with the fist) >*He took a slug right in the nose, but still came back swinging.*

— **slug**[2] (sl.): slow or lazy person >*Who hired that useless slug?*

— **slug**[3] (sl.): shot or drink (of liquor) >*Wanna slug of vodka?*

* **slug**[4] (vt) (colloq.): hit or strike heavily (esp. with the fist) >*She hauled off and slugged him in the mouth.*

* **slug (away)** (vi) (colloq.): strike out, try to land blows (esp. with the fists) >*They slugged away for ten minutes before somebody finally broke it up.*

* **slug it out** (colloq.): fight with the fists until s/one wins >*They went outside the bar to slug it out.*

SLUGFEST

— **slugfest** (slug´fest´) (colloq.): fight in which many blows are landed, vigorous fistfight or boxing match >*It was a real slugfest, but Johnny finally beat the big guy.*

SLUM

* **slum** (vi) (colloq.): associate with people or visit places considered below (one's) social class >*If you want to slum, I know some cheap girls you'd like to meet.* >*Going slumming on the wrong side of the tracks again?*

S. & M.

— **S. & M.** (see "S. AND M.")

SMACK

* **smack**[1] (sl.): heroin >*He scored some smack in a downtown alley.*

* **smack**[2] (colloq.): directly, squarely, straight (esp. regarding an impact) >*The skydiver landed smack on the target.*

SMACK-DAB

* **smack-dab** (smak´dab´) (sl.): directly, squarely, straight (esp. regarding an impact) >*The truck slid off the road smack-dab into a telephone pole.*

SMACKER

— **smacker** (sl.): dollar >*Josie left twenty smackers as a tip.*

SMACKEROO

— **smackeroo** (smak´ə rū´) (sl.): dollar >*I got five hundred smackeroos for that junky old car.*

SMALL POTATOES

* **small potatoes** (colloq.): person or thing considered relatively unimportant or insignificant >*Two thousand a month is small potatoes compared to what you can make selling these import cars.* >*This guy's small potatoes—we want to talk to the head man.*

SMALL-TIME

* **small-time** (colloq.): among the lowest competitive or professional level, unimportant, insignificant >*Playing at county fairs is strictly small-time.* >*He was some small-time gambler in Reno.*

SMART ALECK

* **smart aleck** (smärt´al´ik) (colloq.): obnoxiously self-assured or conceited person, insolent person >*That smart aleck thinks he knows everything about computers.*

SMART-ALECK

* **smart-aleck(y)** (smärt´al´ik [ē]) (colloq.): obnoxiously self-assured or conceited, insolent >*I don't want to hear any more of your smart-aleck remarks.* >*That smart-alecky classmate of yours is a real jerk.*

SMART ASS

** **smart ass** (vulg.): obnoxiously self-assured or conceited person, insolent person (also voc.) >*The boss is gonna fire that smart ass one of these days.* >*Keep your mouth shut, smart ass!*

SMART-ASS

* **smart-ass** (vulg.): obnoxiously self-assured or conceited, insolent >*He'd better stop the smart-ass comments on how bad we planned everything.*

SMART MOUTH

— **smart mouth** (sl.): insolent person, person who speaks disrespectfully or impudently >*That smart mouth gets on everybody's nerves.*

SMART-MOUTH

* **smart-mouth** (vt) (sl.): speak disrespectfully or insolently to >*Don't smart-mouth me, or I'll break your face!*

SMARTS

* **smarts** (smärts) (sl.): intelligence >*Ya gotta have smarts to get into that fancy school.*

SMARTY-PANTS

— **smarty-pants** (smär´tē pants´) (colloq., sarc.): obnoxiously self-assured or conceited person, insolent person (also voc.) >*You mean that the smarty-pants didn't know the answer?* >*You were wrong that time, smarty-pants!*

SMASH

* **smash** (colloq.): person or thing that becomes very popular or successful (also adj.) >*He was a smash at the jazz*

festival. >*The book was a smash hit,*
but the movie was a flop.

SMASHED

* **smashed** (sl.): drunk >*His friends and*
him sit around gettin' smashed on wine
coolers every Saturday afternoon.

SMEAR

— **smear** (vt) (sl.): defeat decisively >*We*
smeared 'em at soccer today.

SMELL

— **smell a rat** (sl.): perceive treachery,
suspect (s/one) of betrayal >*How could*
they have known what our plan was? I
smell a rat!

— **(smell) fishy** (see **FISHY**)

SMELLER

— **smeller** (colloq.): nose (esp. as an organ
for smelling) >*My smeller tells me*
there's going to be something good for
dinner.

SMELLING

* **smelling like a rose** (colloq.): being
perceived very favorably, in a favorable
position (esp. after a period of disfavor
or danger) >*Everyone hated Dawson*
when he criticized the mayor, but he
came out smelling like a rose after the
mayor was indicted. >*She was*
criticized by everybody last year, but
she's sure smelling like a rose now.

SMIDGEN

— **smidgen** (smij´ən) (colloq.): very small
amount, very little bit >*Give me just a*
smidgen of gravy.

SMILE

— **crack a smile** (see **CRACK**)

SMITHEREENS

— **to smithereens** (… smiδ´ə rēnz´)
(colloq.): into fragments, into small
broken pieces >*The explosion blew the*
car to smithereens.

SMOKE

* **smoke¹** (colloq.): cigarette >*Could I*
bum a smoke from you?

— **smoke²** (vi) (sl.): perform very fast and
well, go very fast >*The guy on the*
drums is smokin' now. >*We were really*
smokin' when the rear tire blew out.

— **smoke³** (vt) (sl.): kill with gunfire,
murder by shooting >*He went to the*
cops, so they smoked him.

— **blow smoke** (sl.): exaggerate, mislead,
put on a pretense or sham >*They're just*
blowin' smoke when they threaten to
sue—they're tryin' to scare ya off.

— **put that in your pipe and smoke it!**
(see **PIPE**)

— **smoke and mirrors** (colloq.):
technique(s) or tactic(s) of deception or
cover-up >*They're using smoke and*
mirrors to make us believe there's a
budget surplus.

— **smoke like a chimney** (colloq.): smoke
excessively (esp. cigarettes) >*It's a*
wonder she hasn't gotten sick—she
smokes like a chimney.

— **smoke out** (vt) (colloq.): force out from
hiding, bring into the open >*The*
undercover operation smoked a lot of
crooks out. >*We got to smoke out the*
reason they're against it.

SMOKEY

— **Smokey (Bear)** (sl.): a state highway
patrol officer >*Slow down! I see*
Smokey ahead.

SMOKING GUN

— **smoking gun** (colloq.): indisputable
evidence, proof (of a crime) >*The*
canceled check was the smoking gun the
investigators had been looking for.
>*How can we indict her? There's no*
smoking gun.

SMOOCH

* **smooch¹** (smŭch) (colloq.): kiss (esp. a
hard or wet one) >*She gave him a big*
smooch on the cheek.

* **smooch²** (vi) (colloq.): engage in
kissing (esp. while engaged in
caressing) >*They were smooching in*
the backseat of the car.

SMOOTH

* **smooth operator** (colloq.): person who can easily manipulate others through charm or subtle persuasion, polished and persuasive person >*Crawford's a smooth operator—he'll have the boss convinced in no time.*

SMOOTHIE

* **smoothie** (smū´ðē) (colloq.): person who can easily manipulate others through charm or subtle persuasion, polished and persuasive person >*I just can't say no to that old smoothie.*

SMOOTH-TALK

* **smooth-talk** (vt) (colloq.): persuade through charm or manipulation >*The salesman smooth-talked her into buying the most expensive model.*

SNAFU

— **snafu** (sna fū´/snaf´ū) (sl.): confused or chaotic situation, botched plan or project, blunder >*There was this big snafu on the highway because of an overturned truck.* >*This snafu's gonna cost us time and money.*

SNAG

— **snag** (vt) (colloq.): grab, obtain quickly and unexpectedly >*I'm going to try to snag that job that's opening up next week.*

SNAP

* **snap**[1] (colloq.): very easy thing to accomplish or succeed in (also adj.) >*Don't worry, the test will be a snap.* >*This is a snap course for math majors.*

— **snap**[2] (colloq.): energy, vigor, vitality >*Pauline must be feeling good—she's got some snap in her step.*

* **snap**[3] (vi) (colloq.): have a nervous breakdown, lose emotional control, go crazy >*With all the stress he was under, one day he just snapped.*

— **(about) bite/snap [s/one's] head off** (see BITE)

* **snap out of** (colloq.): overcome, recover from (a neg. state) >*It doesn't*

do any good to feel sorry for yourself, so snap out of it! >*I hope the economy snaps out of this recession pretty soon.*

— **snap to** (vi) (colloq.): improve (one's) performance, begin meeting requirements (used esp. as a command) >*Snap to or you'll be looking for another job.*

* **snap to it** (colloq.): hurry up, do it fast (used esp. as a command) >*You guys better snap to it if you want to get done on time.*

— **snap up** (vt) (colloq.): buy or acquire eagerly >*People snapped his new novel.*

SNAPPY

— **snappy**[1] (snap´ē) (colloq.): fast and energetic >*It's a real snappy tune.*

— **snappy**[2] (colloq.): elegant, stylish >*That's a snappy car you're driving.* >*He's a snappy dresser.*

* **make it snappy** (sl.): hurry up, do it fast (used esp. as a command) >*Bring me the paper, and make it snappy!*

SNATCH

— **snatch**[1] (vulg.): vagina >*She covered her snatch with her hands.*

— **snatch**[2] (vulg., pej.): woman or women (seen as sex object[s]) >*He says he always has his eye out for snatch.*

SNAZZ

— **snazz up** (snaz …) (vt) (sl.): make more attractive or flashy >*You could snazz your car up with a new paint job.*

SNAZZY

— **snazzy** (snaz´ē) (colloq.): stylish, attractive, flashy >*Did you see his snazzy new convertible?*

SNEEZE

— **nothing to sneeze at** (colloq.): s/thing to be taken seriously, s/thing not to be viewed or treated with contempt, s/thing of value or importance >*Hey, getting promoted to vice president is nothing to sneeze at.* >*A hundred dollars isn't a* *fortune, but it's nothing to sneeze at, either.*

SNIFFLES

* **the sniffles** (... snif´əlz) (colloq.): runny nose, head cold >*I've got the sniffles. I hope it doesn't go into my chest.*

SNIT

— **in a snit** (... snit) (colloq.): irritated or upset, resentful >*Aunt Josie's in a snit because I forgot to call her.*

SNITCH

* **snitch**[1] (snich) (colloq.): informer, denouncer >*Why did you have to go and tell Mom, you snitch?* >*He's a snitch for some detective downtown.*

* **snitch**[2] (vi) (colloq.): inform (on s/one), denounce (s/one) >*He's a small-time hoodlum who snitches for the cops.*

— **snitch**[3] (vt) (sl.): steal (esp. s/thing trivial) >*I snitched a cupcake from her kitchen.*

SNOOKER

— **snooker** (snŭk´ər) (vt) (sl.): deceive, trick, swindle >*If he didn't give ya a receipt, you've been snookered.*

SNOOP

— **snoop** (snūp) (colloq.): person who pries or meddles (esp. secretively) >*Some snoop was going around asking a lot of questions about our plans.*

* **snoop (around)** (vi) (colloq.): pry, meddle (esp. secretively) >*What were you doing snooping around in my room?*

SNOOPY

— **snoopy** (snū´pē) (colloq.): meddlesome, prying >*I hate snoopy people, so mind your own business!*

SNOOT

— **snoot** (snūt) (sl.): nose >*The ball hit him right in the snoot.*

SNOOTFUL

— **a snootful** (... snūt´fŭl) (sl.): a large amount of liquor (esp. enough to intoxicate) >*Jeremy got a snootful last*

night at the party, and I had to drive him home.

SNOOTY

— **snooty** (snū´tē) (colloq.): snobbish, haughty >*I can't stand her snooty country club friends.*

SNOOZE

* **snooze**[1] (snūz) (colloq.): short period of sleep, nap >*I'm going to take a little snooze after that big lunch.*

* **snooze**[2] (vi) (colloq.): sleep lightly or for a short period of time, nap >*I snoozed on the couch for about a half an hour.*

SNORT

— **snort**[1] (sl.): shot or drink (of liquor) >*I just opened a bottle of gin. Wanna snort?*

** **snort**[2] (vt) (sl.): take (a drug, esp. cocaine) by inhaling through the nose >*He started snortin' coke last year.*

SNOT

** **snot**[1] (snot) (colloq., freq. vulg.): mucus from the nose >*The kid had snot running out his nose.*

* **snot**[2] (colloq.): obnoxiously snobbish or insolent person >*Why does that little snot talk to me like that?*

SNOT-NOSED

* **snot-nosed** (snot´nōzd´) (colloq.): insolent, disrespectful (said esp. of s/one young) >*Tell that snot-nosed punk to shut up.*

SNOTTY

* **snotty**[1] (snot´ē) (colloq.): obnoxiously snobbish or insolent >*So you went yachting—you don't have to act so snotty about it.* >*They ought to spank that snotty little brat.*

* **snotty**[2] (colloq., freq. vulg.): having mucus from the nose >*Get your snotty handkerchief off the table!*

SNOW

— **snow¹** (sl.): cocaine (in powder form) >*They ended up at Larry's snortin' snow.*

* **snow²** (vt) (sl.): persuade or trick through flattery or manipulation >*The salesman snowed poor Drew, and he ended up buying the most expensive ring.* >*Don't get snowed by his sweet talk.*

SNOWBIRD

— **snowbird** (colloq.): person who goes to a warmer climate in winter (esp. a tourist) >*Phoenix is full of snowbirds from the Midwest in December and January.*

SNOWED

* **snowed under** (colloq.): overwhelmed (with work or demands) >*We're snowed under with orders—we got two week's worth.*

SNOW JOB

* **snow job** (sl.): act of persuading or tricking (s/one) through flattery or manipulation >*Mitch did a real snow job on her, and she agreed to his plan.*

SNUFF

— **snuff (out)** (vt) (sl.): kill, murder >*Someone snuffed him when the drug deal went bad.* >*He was snuffed out by the bolt of lightning.*

— **up to snuff** (colloq.): of acceptable quality, fulfilling the requirements, in satisfactory condition (freq. used in the neg.) >*If your work isn't up to snuff you'll be fired.* >*I just don't feel up to snuff today.*

SO

** **so far, so good** (colloq.): all has gone well until now, things are proceeding well >*So far, so good, this semester. Let's see how I do on my midterm exams.*

— **[neg.] so hot** (see **HOT**)

** **so long** (colloq.): until later, good-bye >*So long, Sis—see you next week.*

* **so much for ...¹** (colloq.): ... must be considered impossible or unworkable (after an initial effort or attempt), ... has failed >*Well, so much for trying pliers—give me that pipe wrench.* >*So much for diplomacy. Hit the jerk!*

* **so much for ...²** (colloq.): ... has just been used up, there's no more ... >*So much for my paycheck—that was my last five bucks.* >*So much for the beer. Somebody better make a run to the store.*

* **so much/bad I can taste it** (sl.): (want s/thing) very much >*Jessica wants to marry Roy so much she can taste it.* >*I wanted that car so bad I could taste it.*

** **so what?** (colloq.): it's of no interest or importance, I don't care >*I hurt your stupid brother-in-law's feelings? So what?* >*So what if you don't like the way I do my job?*

— **(so) what else is new?** (see **WHAT**)

SOAK

* **soak** (vt) (sl.): overcharge >*They really soak ya in that tourist trap!*

SO-AND-SO

* **so-and-so** (colloq.): contemptible or reprehensible person >*Tell that so-and-so to mind his own damned business!* >*Some so-and-so stuck their chewing gum under the table.*

SOAP

** **soap** (sl.): soap opera (esp. on television) >*She sits home all day watchin' the soaps.*

— **no soap** (sl.): (it is/was) unsuccessful or futile, (s/one) refused (it) >*He tried to get the engine runnin', but no soap.* >*He wanted to borrow my car, but I told him no soap.*

S.O.B.

** **S.O.B.** (= "son of a bitch") (sl., freq. vulg.): contemptible or reprehensible man >*That S.O.B. cheated us.*

SOB STORY

* **sob story** (colloq., freq. sarc.): touching story or excuse (used to persuade through sympathy) >*I'm tired of your sob stories about why you're always late to work.* >*This panhandler gave me some sob story about how he lost his job.*

SOC

* **soc** (sōsh) (colloq.): sociology (esp. as a course of study) >*Gwen's a soc major.*

SOCK

— **sock¹** (colloq.): hard blow, strike (esp. with the fist) >*He took quite a sock on the jaw.*

— **sock²** (vt) (colloq.): hit hard, strike (esp. with the fist) >*She socked him in the eye.* >*Somebody socked me with a stick.*

— **put a sock in it** (sl.): stop talking or yelling (esp. when being offensive) (used esp. as a command) >*Hey, put a sock in it, will ya?! You're givin' me a headache.*

— **sock away** (vt) (colloq.): save (money) >*He's been socking away five hundred a month.*

— **sock it to** (sl.): use great energy and determination to defeat or impress, overwhelm >*Let's get in that meeting and sock it to 'em.* >*We really socked it to the audience.*

— **take a sock at** (colloq.): attempt to hit with the fist >*Dave ended up in jail after he took a sock at a cop.*

SOCKS

— **beat the socks off (of)** (see **BEAT**)

— **knock [s/one's] socks off** (see **KNOCK**)

— **... the socks off (of) [s/one]** (colloq.): ... [s/one] to an extreme degree >*His lecture's boring the socks off of everyone.*

SOFT

* **soft** (colloq.): easy, undemanding >*He's got a real soft job in his uncle's company.*

— **soft on** (colloq.): romantically fond of, in love with >*Mort's soft on Erica, all the time making eyes at her.*

SOFT-PEDAL

— **soft-pedal** (vt) (colloq.): de-emphasize, play down (a neg. aspect of s/thing to make it more acceptable) >*Let's soft-pedal the penalties and emphasize the high interest rates.*

SOFT SELL

* **soft sell** (colloq.): subtle or persuasive promotion, low-pressure selling (cf. **"HARD SELL"**) >*Bruno's a master at the soft sell—he charms them into buying.*

SOFT SOAP

— **soft soap** (colloq.): flattery (used to persuade or ingratiate oneself), cajolery >*Arnie will try the old soft soap to get his way with Allison.*

SOFT-SOAP

— **soft-soap** (vt) (colloq.): attempt to persuade or ingratiate (oneself) through flattery, cajole >*Don't try to soft-soap me—I'm not going to change my mind.*

SOFT TOUCH

* **soft touch** (colloq.): person who is easily persuaded (esp. to give money) >*Snyder's a soft touch—ask him for the money.*

SOFTY

* **softy** (sof´tē/sôf´tē) (colloq.): sentimental person, person whose sympathy is easily gained >*He's an old softy—he believes every hard-luck story he hears.*

SOLID

* **solid** (colloq.): consecutive, in an unbroken sequence (also adv.) >*He finally lost after fourteen solid wins.* >*They played poker for two days solid.*

SOME

* **some**[1] (stressed) (colloq.): quite a/some, a/some remarkable >*Boy, that's* some *bruise you got there on your arm!* >*That player's got* some *moves, I tell you!*

* **some**[2] (colloq.): somewhat, to a certain degree >*I've been thinking about it* some. >*My elbow hurts* some.

— **get a little/some** (see GET)

— **get a little/some on the side** (see GET)

— **some kind of (a)** (colloq.): quite a/ some, a/some remarkable >*Man, that is* some kind of *a car he's got!* >*That town has* some kind of *gorgeous women!*

SOMEBODY

* **somebody** (colloq.): well-known or important person, person having worth or dignity (cf. "NOBODY") >*He dreams of being* somebody *some day.* >*At least he treats me like a* somebody.

* **somebody/someone up there** (colloq.): a divine force, God, luck >Somebody *up there's watching out for me—if the robber hadn't tripped, he would have smashed my head with that pipe.*

SOMEONE

— **somebody/someone up there** (see SOMEBODY)

SOMETHING

* **be something (else)** (colloq.): be extraordinary, be especially impressive or attractive >*What a play! That player is really* something *on the field!* >*Gee, Samantha is* something else!

— **have/get something going** (see GOING)

— **make something (out) of** (see MAKE)

— **...-something** (colloq.): in (one's) ...s (decade of age) (also noun) >*She's* thirty-something, *but he's over fifty.* >*Their new ad campaign targets the* twenty-somethings.

— **something awful** (see AWFUL)

— **something fierce** (see FIERCE)

* **something tells me** (colloq.): I have the impression, I have reason to believe >Something tells me *that we're not going to finish the game before it starts raining.*

— **something terrible** (see TERRIBLE)

— **start something** (see START)

SOMEWHERE

— **get somewhere** (see GET)

SONG AND DANCE

* **song and dance** (colloq.): exaggerated or complicated story (used to persuade or manipulate) >*The kid gave me some* song and dance *about how he needed money to go to radio announcer's school.*

SONNY

— **sonny** (sun´ē) (voc.) (colloq.): fellow, boy (used esp. with a young male stranger in a contentious way) >*Quiet down,* sonny!

SON OF A BITCH

** **son of a bitch**[1] (vulg.): contemptible or reprehensible man >*Keep that lousy* son of a bitch *away from us!*

* **son of a bitch**[2] (vulg.): very difficult task, troublesome thing, arduous undertaking >*Gettin' those shelves in place was a* son of a bitch.

* **son of a bitch!** (vulg.): (interj. to express anger, surprise, or irritation) >Son of a bitch! *I cut my hand.* >Son of a bitch! *They actually won the game.*

SON-OF-A-BITCHING

— **son-of-a-bitching** (vulg.): contemptible, reprehensible >*Get your son-of-a-bitchin' car off my driveway!*

SON OF A GUN

* **son of a gun**[1] (colloq.): scoundrel, rascal, extraordinary man >*Where'd that son of a gun run off to now?* >*Man, can that son of a gun sing!*

* **son of a gun**[2] (colloq.): hard task, troublesome thing, difficult undertaking

>*It's going to be a son of a gun to get this diagram figured out.*

— **son of a gun!** (colloq.): (interj. to express surprise, wonder, or irritation) >*Son of a gun! I've run out of gas.*

SOOPER-DOOPER
— **sooper-dooper** (see "SUPER-DUPER")

SORE
* **sore** (colloq.): irritated, insulted, angry >*Don't get sore about it—I didn't mean nothing by it.* >*He's sore because you called him a jerk.*

— **sight for sore eyes** (see SIGHT)

— **stick out like a sore thumb** (see STICK)

SOREHEAD
— **sorehead** (colloq.): easily irritated person, resentful or grouchy person >*Don't be such a sorehead, just because you didn't win.* >*Who cares if that sorehead complains?*

SORT
** **sort of** (colloq.): somewhat, rather, fairly >*Yeah, I sort of like her.* >*He's sort of weird, but he's a good guy.*

SORTS
— **all sorts (of ...)** (see ALL)

SOUL
* **soul** (colloq.): African-American (esp. culturally) >*I know a great soul food place.* >*He loves soul music.* >*She's an announcer on some soul station.*

SOUL BROTHER
* **soul brother** (colloq.): black man (used esp. among blacks) >*Who's the white dude there with the soul brothers?*

SOUL SISTER
* **soul sister** (colloq.): black woman (used esp. among blacks) >*There was a soul sister there singing the blues.*

SOUND
* **sound** (sl.): song, piece of music >*I like the new sounds she just came out with.*

— **sound off** (vi) (colloq.): speak out loudly and frankly (esp. to complain) >*The crew's been sounding off about the lousy food.*

SOUP
— **soup** (sl.): thick fog >*I ain't drivin' in this soup.*

— **soup up** (vt) (sl.): modify to permit more power or speed >*He souped up that old Dodge with dual carburetors.*

SOUR
* **go sour** (colloq.): become unpleasant or unacceptable, be spoiled, fail >*Their marriage went sour after he caught her with another man.* >*Forget it—it's a deal gone sour.*

SOURPUSS
— **sourpuss** (souʹər pŭsʹ/souərʹpŭsʹ) (colloq.): grouchy or irritable person (esp. one who scowls) (also voc.) >*What's the matter with that old sourpuss?* >*Why don't you ever smile, sourpuss?*

SOUSED
— **soused** (soust) (sl.): drunk >*She actually got soused on cherry brandy.*

SOUTHPAW
* **southpaw** (colloq.): left-handed person (also adj.) >*Have Drew sit on this end—he's a southpaw.* >*The team needs a good southpaw pitcher.*

SPACE CADET
— **space cadet** (sl.): odd or eccentric person (esp. one who seems dazed or out of touch with what is happening around him/her) >*Boy, is he ever out of it! What a space cadet!*

SPACED
* **spaced(-out)** (sl.): odd or eccentric (esp. when seemingly dazed or out of touch with what is happening around one) >*That guy's really spaced—he's in his own little world.* >*She was actin' real spaced-out—you could hardly talk to her.*

SPACEY

— **spacey** (spā′sē) (sl.): odd or eccentric (esp. when seemingly dazed or out of touch with what is happening around one) >*His spacey brother's just a little too weird for me.*

SPADE

— **spade** (sl., pej.): black person >*The fight started when that redneck called Jerry a spade.*

SPAGHETTI WESTERN

— **spaghetti Western** (colloq.): low-budget Western movie shot in Europe primarily using Italian actors >*He made a couple of spaghetti Westerns, but never made it big in the U.S.*

SPANKING

* **(brand) spanking new** (colloq.): absolutely new (esp. when the newness is attractively conspicuous) >*Hugh found a spanking new bike under the tree on Christmas morning.*

SPARE TIRE

* **spare tire** (colloq.): circle of fat around the waist >*When he's wearing a bathing suit, you can really see his spare tire.*

SPASTIC

— **spastic** (sl.): awkward and odd person (esp. an annoying one) (also adj.) >*Who invited that spastic along? >You should have seen his spastic brother tryin' to play golf.*

SPAZ

— **spaz** (spaz) (sl.): awkward and odd person (esp. an annoying one) >*How're we gonna pick up any girls with that spaz hangin' around with us?*

SPEAK

* **speak [s/one's] language** (colloq.): have rapport with [s/one], have similar values or attitudes as [s/one] >*Maybe you can make Mae understand—you speak her language.*

* **speak of the devil!** (colloq.): here appears the person we are talking about! >*Well, speak of the devil! I was just telling Ned here about you and your new job.*

* **speak the same language** (colloq.): have rapport (with one another), have similar values or attitudes >*Let me work with Nolan—we speak the same language.*

SPEAKING

* **not be speaking** (colloq.): refuse to speak (to one another), be feuding >*They had an argument, and now they're not speaking.*

SPECS

— **specs** (speks) (colloq.): spectacles, eyeglasses >*The print's real small. Where are my specs?*

SPEED

* **speed** (sl.): stimulant drug (esp. amphetamine) >*The guy they arrested was freaked out on speed.*

* **[one's] speed** (colloq., freq. sarc.): what is consistent with [one's] preference, what reflects [one's] character or ability >*I like water skiing, but going bowling is more his speed. >Yeah, that weird guy is Jenny's speed.*

SPEED DEMON

— **speed demon** (colloq.): person who likes to go fast >*I ain't going if that speed demon's driving.*

SPELL

* **spell out** (vt) (colloq.): explain in very simple terms or excessive detail >*You're going to have to spell the instructions out for her. She's not too bright.*

SPIC

— **spic** (spik) (sl., pej.): Hispanic, Latino >*That stupid jerk just called Miguel a spic.*

SPICK

— **spick** (see "SPIC")

SPIEL

* **spiel** (spēl/shpēl) (colloq.): energetic speech or talk (used to persuade or convince) >*Dottie gave us some spiel about why she was the best person for the job.*

SPIFF

— **spiff up** (spif ...) (vt) (sl.): make more attractive or elegant, clean and put in order >*They spiffed up the guest room with fresh paint and new curtains.*

SPIFFY

— **spiffy** (spif´ē) (sl.): elegant, attractive, stylish >*What a spiffy car!* >*Ya look real spiffy today.*

SPIKE

* **spike** (vt) (sl.): add liquor to (a non-alcoholic drink) >*Boris just spiked the fruit punch with some vodka.*

SPILL

* **spill [one's] guts** (sl.): confess, tell everything, divulge [one's] most intimate feelings or concerns >*The punk spilled his guts to the cops.* >*If ya wanna spill your guts, go see a shrink.*

— **spill the beans** (colloq.): disclose a secret >*Someone spilled the beans, and now everyone in town knows about it.*

SPIN

— **go for/take a spin** (colloq.): go for a short ride (esp. for enjoyment or to evaluate a vehicle) >*Hey, you want to go for a spin on my motorcycle?* >*Let's take a spin in your new car to see how she handles.*

— **(so fast that) it will make [s/one's] head spin** (see HEAD)

— **spin a yarn** (colloq.): tell a story (esp. a long and complicated or exaggerated one) >*Grandpa was sitting on the front porch spinning a yarn about some guy he knew before the war.*

— **turn (over)/spin in [one's] grave** (see TURN)

SPINNING

* **spinning [one's] wheels** (colloq.): putting out effort without gaining anything, failing to make progress >*Quit that dead-end job! You're just spinning your wheels there.*

— **[for one's] wheels [to be] spinning** (see WHEELS)

SPIT

— **spit and image** (see "SPITTING IMAGE")

* **spit it out!** (colloq.): say what you have to say! (command used to make s/one who is reluctant speak) >*Stop changing the subject—just spit it out!*

SPITTING IMAGE

— **spitting image** (colloq.): exact likeness, the same in appearance (a person) >*Why, she's the spitting image of her mother.*

SPLASH

— **make a splash** (colloq.): attract much attention, make a strong and favorable impression, be an immediate success >*She made quite a splash a couple of years ago when she modeled those bikinis on national TV.*

SPLIT

* **split** (vi, vt) (sl.): leave >*Hey, man, we gotta split—it's gettin' late.* >*We split the party around eleven.*

— **(about) bust/split a gut** (see BUST)

SPOILING

— **spoiling for a fight** (colloq.): eager for or seeking a fight >*He's been spoiling for a fight ever since they laughed at him.*

SPOOK

— **spook**[1] (spūk) (colloq.): ghost >*They say there are spooks in that old house.*

— **spook**[2] (sl., pej.): black person >*That racist moron called Jeremy a spook.*

* **spook**[3] (vi, vt) (colloq.): frighten, scare >*Deer spook real easy.* >*We spooked them with a couple of firecrackers.*

SPOOKY

* **spooky** (spū′kē) (colloq.): scary, frightening >*We stayed up on Halloween night telling spooky stories.*

SPORT

* **sport**[1] (colloq.): fair and congenial person >*Sam will understand—he's a sport.* >*Be a sport and help me out here.*

— **sport**[2] (vt) (colloq.): display (clothing), wear (esp. s/thing new or showy) >*He's sporting a new hat.*

— **sport**[3] (voc.) (colloq.): fellow, friend (used esp. with a male to show friendliness) >*Good to see you, sport.*

SPORTY

* **sporty** (colloq.): stylish, showy, attractive (esp. clothing) >*Where'd you get those sporty loafers?*

SPOT

— **spot** (vt) (sl.): loan (money) >*I'll spot ya a hundred till ya get paid.*

— **hit the spot** (see **HIT**)

* **on the spot**[1] (colloq.): in an embarrassing or difficult position, under pressure to act or resolve a problem >*Those accusations really put Holten on the spot.* >*The water commissioner was on the spot during the drought.*

* **on the spot**[2] (colloq.): here and now, then and there, in the immediate time and place >*The old guy expected the tow-truck driver to fix his car on the spot.* >*They say they'll shoot Hornsby on the spot if they see him.*

— **tight spot** (see **TIGHT**)

SPOUT

— **spout off** (vi) (colloq.): speak energetically (esp. indiscreetly, pompously, or conceitedly) >*What's that idiot spouting off about now?* >*I'm sick and tired of listening to Curly spout off about all the famous people he supposedly knows.*

SPREAD

* **spread** (colloq.): abundance or variety of food (esp. when set out and ready to eat) >*I'm glad I'm hungry—just look at this nice spread.*

SPRING

— **spring** (vt) (sl.): secure the release of (s/one in custody) >*Some big shot lawyer managed to spring him on a technicality.*

— **spring for** (colloq.): pay for, accept the expense of >*She's going to try to talk her old man into springing for a trip to Europe.*

SPRING CHICKEN

— **be no spring chicken** (sl.): not be very young >*He's still in good shape, but he's no spring chicken.*

SPROUT

— **sprout** (colloq.): child >*Now, who's this young sprout?*

SPUD

— **spud** (spud) (colloq.): potato >*How do you want those spuds cooked?*

SPUNK

— **spunk** (spungk) (colloq.): liveliness, spirit, self-assuredness, pluck >*I like a guy with spunk—he'll go a long way.*

SPUNKY

— **spunky** (spung′kē) (colloq.): lively, spirited, self-assured, plucky >*They can't control that spunky kid of theirs.*

SQUARE

— **square** (sl.): overly conventional or old-fashioned person, person who disregards what is in style (also adj.) >*Don't be a square! Get with the new look, man.* >*Him and his square ideas! You'd think he was born a hundred years ago.*

— **be square with** (sl.): deal honestly with, treat fairly >*No lie, buddy—I'm bein' square with ya.*

— **fair and square** (see **FAIR**)

— **shoot square** (see **SHOOT**)

* **square away** (vt) (colloq.): put in order, get ready >*We need to get everything squared away at home before we take off.*

— **square off** (vi) (colloq.): assume a fighting stance, get ready to compete >*They squared off to fight, but the bartender broke it up.* >*The Lakers square off tonight against the Suns.*

— **square [s/thing] with** (colloq.): get (s/one's) approval or acceptance regarding [s/thing], make [s/thing] in concert or satisfactory with >*They don't like us leaving work early, but I'll try to square it with the boss for today.* >*I just can't square what Troy did with what he says he believes.*

SQUARE MEAL
* **square meal** (colloq.): substantial or nourishing meal >*Bernie looks like he hasn't had a square meal in weeks.*

SQUARE ONE
* **go back to square one** (colloq.): start again at the very beginning, start all over >*If they don't accept the plan this time, we'll just have to go back to square one.*

SQUARE PEG
— **square peg (in a round hole)** (colloq.): very unconventional person, ill-suited person (for a situation), misfit >*Let's face it—in today's world Nigel's a square peg in a round hole.* >*We're going to have to fire Crenshaw. He's just a square peg around here.*

SQUARES
— **three squares** (see THREE)

SQUARE SHOOTER
— **square shooter** (colloq.): person who deals honestly or treats people fairly >*If he's a square shooter, we'll get along just fine.*

SQUAT
— **([neg.]) squat** (sl.): nothing at all >*You'd better explain it, 'cause I don't know squat about transmissions.* >*The boss's son does squat around here.*

SQUAWK
— **squawk** (vi) (colloq.): complain loudly >*What's that bellyacher squawking about now?*

SQUAWK BOX
— **squawk box** (colloq.): loudspeaker (esp. of a two-way radio or public address system) >*They just announced the flight on the squawk box.*

SQUEAK
* **squeak by** (colloq.): win or gain success (over) by the narrowest of margins >*We squeaked by them, eighty-eight to eighty-seven.*

* **squeak by/through** (colloq.): barely survive or prevail (in), barely get through >*I don't know if I got enough dough left to squeak by till payday.* >*Everyone thought he wouldn't make it, but he squeaked through the academy somehow.*

SQUEAKER
— **squeaker** (sl.): very close game or contest >*It was a squeaker—we beat 'em by just one point.*

SQUEAKY-CLEAN
* **squeaky-clean** (colloq.): absolutely clean, untarnished or above reproach >*That shampoo got my hair squeaky-clean.* >*The guy's squeaky-clean, a model citizen.*

SQUEAL
— **squeal** (vi) (sl.): inform (on s/one), denounce (s/one) >*Somebody squealed, and the cops picked 'em up.*

SQUEEZE
— **[one's] (main) squeeze** (sl.): [one's] sweetheart >*This is Maggie—she's my main squeeze.* >*Is that chick his new squeeze?*

— **put the squeeze on** (colloq.): pressure or intimidate (into doing s/thing) >*Jenkins didn't like the plan, but the* *developers put the squeeze on him and he ended up voting for it.*

** **squeeze in** (vt) (colloq.): fit (s/one, s/thing) into a tight schedule >*We're pretty busy today, but I could squeeze you in at 4:15 if that's OK.*

SQUIRM

* **squirm out of** (colloq.): renege on or back out of (an obligation) (esp. in a sneaky or cowardly way) >*I don't know how she squirmed out of being on the cleanup committee.*

SQUIRREL

— **squirrel** (sl.): very eccentric or oddly behaving person, crazy person >*All her friends are weird—real squirrels.*

— **squirrel away** (vt) (colloq.): save or hide (for future use) >*She's been squirreling away some money for a Caribbean cruise.*

SQUIRRELY

— **squirrely** (sl.): very eccentric, having odd behavior, crazy >*Remember that squirrely kid at school who'd put mashed potatoes in his pockets?*

SQUIRT

— **squirt** (colloq.): small or short person (esp. one seen as insignificant or contemptible), impudent young person (also voc.) >*Who does that little squirt think he's talking to?* >*Hey, squirt, you really want to play basketball with us big guys?*

STAB

* **stab in the back** (colloq.): treacherous act, harmful action (done to s/one who is unsuspecting or defenseless) >*His reporting his partner to the tax people was a real stab in the back.*

* **stab/knife [s/one] in the back** (colloq.): do a treacherous act against [s/one], betray or do harm to [s/one] (who is unsuspecting or defenseless) >*After all I've done for you, you stab me in the back by badmouthing me to my boss!*

>*Grayson knifed him in the back by secretly supporting his opponent.*

* **take/have a stab at** (colloq.): make an attempt at, try >*He took a stab at acting, but never got any good roles.* >*If you can't figure the puzzle out, I'll have a stab at it.*

* **take/make a stab at** (colloq.): make a guess at, estimate >*Take a stab at how old he is.* >*You want to make a stab at how much the repairs are going to cost?*

STACK

— **a stack (of …)** (colloq.): much (…), many (…) >*They got a stack of merchandise to move before they do inventory.* >*There's a stack of people outside waiting to get in.*

— **blow [one's] stack** (see **BLOW**)

* **stack the deck/cards** (colloq.): manipulate circumstances or a situation (to one's advantage) (esp. unethically) >*Her father-in-law works in personnel, and he stacked the deck so she'd get the job.* >*Don't try it—they got the cards stacked against you.*

— **stack up** (vi) (colloq.): go along, succeed, progress >*Last year was bad for sales, but this year's stacking up pretty good so far.*

— **stack up (against)** (colloq.): compare (favorably) (with), measure up (to) >*How does she stack up against Judy?* >*We can't use your design—it just doesn't stack up.*

— **swear on a stack of Bibles** (see **SWEAR**)

STACKED

— **stacked** (sl.): having a very attractive or sexy figure (a woman) (esp. having large and shapely breasts) >*She's only sixteen, but she's really stacked!*

STAG

* **stag**[1] (colloq.): intended for or restricted to men (and freq. having pornographic entertainment) >*The guys went to a*

stag party. >She starred in a bunch of stag movies.

* **stag²** (colloq.): unaccompanied by a date (said esp. of a man) >Who cares if you don't have a date? Just go stag.

STAKES
— **pull up stakes** (colloq.): leave where (one) is established, move >If Chet loses his job, we'll have to pull up stakes and go back to Iowa.

STAMPING GROUND
— **stamping ground(s)** (colloq.): (one's) habitual or favorite place of activity, place (one) frequents, haunt >I'll show you around my old stamping grounds from when I was a kid.

STAND
* **stand on [one's] (own) two feet** (colloq.): be independent, not have to rely on others >You got to learn to stand on your own two feet, because your daddy's not always going to be there to help.

* **stand up** (vt) (colloq.): fail to keep a date or appointment with >She made a date with Matt, but I bet she stands him up.

* **stand up for** (colloq.): defend, vouch for, give support to (esp. under adversity) >I can't believe nobody stood up for me when they started giving me a hard time.

** **won't stand for** (colloq.): does not permit, will not tolerate >Don't talk back to her, because she won't stand for it.

STANDING
— **can [do s/thing] standing on [one's] head** (colloq.): can [do s/thing] with great ease or assured success (esp. due to routine experience with it) >I can make that shot standing on my head.

STANDOFF
— **Mexican standoff** (see **MEXICAN**)

STAND-UP
— **stand-up** (colloq.): trustworthy, courageous and dependable >Henry's a stand-up guy—he'll be there for you if things get rough.

STARING
* **staring [s/one] (right) in the face** (colloq.): confronting [s/one], in need of [s/one's] action or attention (esp. s/thing neg.) >Let's pay them off, or we're going to have a huge lawsuit staring us in the face.

STARS
— **see stars** (colloq.): be unconscious or very dazed (by a blow to the head) >I bet he's seeing stars after getting punched in the nose.

START
* **start in** (colloq.): begin with, start, take up (esp. s/thing neg.) >When she started in insulting my brother, I left. >Just don't start in on me. >He started in drinking as a teenager.

* **start something** (colloq.): cause an argument or a fight >If you want to start something, we can step outside. >She's going to start something if she flirts with Julie's husband.

STARTERS
* **for starters** (colloq.): to begin with, in the first place >There's a lot of reasons I'm mad. For starters, you didn't call to say you'd be late. >Let's have shrimp cocktails for starters.

STASH
— **stash** (sl.): supply of illegal drugs (esp. one's personal supply) >Your pot-smokin' friends cleaned out my stash last night, man.

STATES
** **the States** (colloq.): the United States (used esp. outside the U.S.) >She headed back to the States after a year in Peru.

STATIC

* **static** (sl.): opposition, trouble, objections >*Think the committee will give us any static over this proposal?* >*I don't want no static from ya—just do it!*

STATS

** **stats** (stats) (colloq.): statistics >*Forget your hunch—we're going with the stats.*

STAY

— **hang/stay loose** (see **LOOSE**)

** **stay put** (colloq.): remain where (one) is, not move >*We'll stay put here for a few days till we can catch a train going north.* >*Stay put till I get back!*

STEADY

— **steady** (colloq.): person that (one) dates exclusively, sweetheart >*She's been his steady for over a year.*

* **go steady (with)** (colloq.): date (s/one) exclusively >*He's going steady with a girl he met at church.* >*I hear they're going steady.*

STEAL

** **steal** (colloq.): item bought for a very low price, good bargain >*I got this watch for only fifty bucks—it was a real steal.*

* **steal/rob [s/one] blind** (colloq.): rob [s/one] thoroughly, steal a great deal from [s/one] (esp. when he/she is unaware) >*That crooked accountant was stealing the company blind.*

STEAM

— **steam¹** (colloq.): energy, power >*I can't walk any farther—I just ran out of steam.*

— **steam²** (vi) (colloq.): show great anger, be furious >*Ruth was steaming after she found out he'd lied to her.*

— **steam³** (vt) (sl.): anger, make furious >*It really steams Joe to see his ex-wife drivin' his favorite car.*

* **let/blow off steam** (colloq.): let out repressed emotions (esp. with rowdy behavior), express (one's) anger (esp. by shouting) >*The students went to a nightclub to let off steam after their exams.* >*He came to my office to blow off steam after the boss yelled at him.*

STEAMED

* **steamed (up)** (sl.): angry, furious >*Don't get so steamed up over this.* >*Boy, was Harry ever steamed when they tricked him!*

STEAMY

* **steamy** (colloq.): very passionate, erotic, arousing >*That movie has some real steamy love scenes.*

STEP

** **step on it** (colloq.): hurry up (used esp. as a command) >*We'd better step on it if we're going to get there on time.*

— **step on the gas** (colloq.): hurry up (used esp. as a command) >*Hey, step on the gas! We got to get this truck unloaded by 10:30.*

* **step on [s/one's] toes** (colloq.): offend [s/one], make [s/one] feel threatened (esp. by encroachment) >*I didn't realize I was stepping on her toes by talking to her customer.*

— **step out on** (colloq.): be unfaithful to (romantically or sexually) >*She doesn't know that her boyfriend's been stepping out on her.*

STEW

— **stew** (vi) (colloq.): fret, feel annoyance or anger >*Barney's been stewing about the bad evaluation his supervisor gave him.*

STEWED

— **stewed (to the gills)** (sl.): (very) drunk >*He staggered outta the bar stewed to the gills.*

STICK

* **stick¹** (colloq.): equipped with a manual transmission >*Is your car stick or automatic?*

* **stick²** (vt) (sl., freq. vulg.): go away with, take away (s/thing contemptible or detestable) (used esp. as a command) >*If ya don't like it, you can stick it!* >*Stick your lousy job!*

— **stick³** (vt) (sl.): deceive, swindle, cause financial harm to >*They stuck him good on that refinancing deal.*

— **get on the stick** (sl.): start moving fast or energetically, start working faster or harder >*Let's get on the stick! This ain't no party.* >*If you guys don't get on the stick, we won't finish on time.*

* **make [s/thing] stick** (colloq.): prove [s/thing] (in a trial), maintain the validity of [s/thing] over time >*They arrested him on an embezzlement charge, but they can't make it stick.* >*That's a good theory, but can you make it stick?*

— **more (...) than you can shake a stick at** (see **MORE**)

— **on the stick** (sl.): alert, sharp, competent >*I need someone that's really on the stick to take care of this for me.*

** **stick around** (colloq.): remain (s/where for a while), stay nearby >*I've been on the road so much I just want to stick around the house for a few days.* >*Here comes Greg, and he's mad. Stick around and watch what happens.*

* **stick by** (colloq.): remain faithful or dedicated to (esp. under adversity) >*They stuck by each other through the whole mess.*

* **stick it in your ear!** (sl.): (interj. to express great anger or contempt to s/one) >*That's a bunch of bull! Stick it in your ear!*

* **stick it to** (sl.): deal harshly with, take unfair advantage of, mistreat >*That judge sticks it to repeat offenders.* >*They really stick it to ya when ya buy refreshments at this theater.*

* **stick [one's] neck out** (colloq.): take a risk, put [oneself] in a vulnerable position (esp. unnecessarily) >*Why should I stick my neck out just so he can get ahead?*

* **stick/poke [one's] nose in(to)** (colloq.): pry into, meddle in, investigate (without invitation) >*I don't like people sticking their nose in my affairs.* >*Don't go poking your nose into what doesn't concern you.*

* **stick out** (vt) (colloq.): endure, stay with (s/thing) until the end >*Think you can stick out the rest of the semester?* >*Her marriage is lousy, but she's determined to stick it out for the kids' sake.*

— **stick out a mile** (colloq.): be very conspicuous or obvious >*That so-called undercover cop sticks out a mile.*

* **stick out like a sore thumb** (colloq.): be very conspicuous or obvious >*The nerdy guy in the striped jacket stuck out like a sore thumb at the dance.*

* **stick to [one's] guns** (colloq.): remain firm or resolute, not retreat or compromise >*If you believe you're right, then stick to your guns and don't let them push you around.*

— **stick to [s/one's] ribs** (colloq.): be hearty, satisfy [s/one's] hunger (said of food) >*Ah, this beef stew really sticks to your ribs.*

* **stick up** (vt) (colloq.): rob, hold up (an establishment) (esp. with a gun) >*Some drug addict tried to stick up a liquor store with a toy gun.*

* **stick up for** (colloq.): defend, vouch for, give support to (esp. under adversity) >*I want you all to stick up for the program if they start attacking it.*

* **stick with** (colloq.): stay with, remain committed to (esp. through faith or loyalty) >*Stick with me, honey, and we'll hit it big.* >*How much longer are you going to stick with that job?*

* **stick [s/one] with** (colloq.): burden [s/one] with, impose (a responsibility, esp.

a neg. one) on [s/one] >*The boss is going to stick Grey with that cleanup job.* >*I got stuck with taking care of my little brother Saturday.*

— (tell [s/one] to take [his/her s/thing] and) shove/stick it (see SHOVE)

— (tell [s/one] to take [his/her s/thing] and) shove/stick it up [his/her] **ass** (see SHOVE)

— tell [s/one] where to put/stick [s/thing] (see WHERE)

— the short end of the stick (see SHORT)

STICK-IN-THE-MUD
— stick-in-the-mud (colloq.): uninteresting or unenthusiastic person, person who refuses to try new things, socially conservative person >*Don't be such an old stick-in-the-mud—come on along with us.*

STICKS
* the sticks (colloq.): rural area (esp. a remote one) >*He comes from some little town way out in the sticks.*

STICK-TO-IT-IVENESS
— stick-to-it-iveness (stik´tū´i tiv nis) (colloq.): perseverance, tenacity, resoluteness >*Does he have the stick-to-it-iveness to make it through that training?*

STICKUP
* stickup (colloq.): holdup, robbery (esp. with a gun) >*They pulled six stickups before they were caught.*

STICKY
* sticky[1] (colloq.): awkward, tricky, delicate >*It might get kind of sticky if we invite Norma's ex-husband, too.*

— sticky[2] (colloq.): hard to get out of (one's) mind, hard to keep from thinking of (esp. a song) >*That song we heard last night's real sticky—I've been humming it all day.*

STICKY-FINGERED
— sticky-fingered (sl.): having a propensity to steal >*One of your sticky-fingered buddies swiped my gold pen.*

STICKY FINGERS
— sticky fingers (sl.): propensity to steal >*Keep an eye on that guy when he's in the store—he's got sticky fingers.*

STIFF
* stiff[1] (sl.): corpse, dead body, cadaver >*They dumped the stiff in the river.* >*This stiff goes to the medical school.*

* stiff[2] (vt) (sl.): deceive, swindle, cause financial harm to >*His brother-in-law left town after stiffin' him for two hundred dollars.* >*They tried to stiff me on this bill.*

— stiff[3] (vt) (sl.): trick, victimize, treat unfairly >*That crook set us up and stiffed us!*

— scared stiff (see SCARED)

— ... stiff (sl.): ... person (esp. a man, esp. seen enviously or as pathetic) >*Why does that lucky stiff deserve a raise?* >*The workin' stiffs are gettin' the bad end of the deal.*

STIFLE
— stifle it! (stī´fəl ...) (sl.): quiet! shut up! >*Stifle it! I'm sick of your whinin'.*

STILL
— not sit still for (see SIT)

— still kicking (see KICKING)

STING
* sting[1] (sl.): fraudulent scheme, confidence game, entrapment >*Tubby was actually plannin' a sting against some big drug dealer.* >*The cops caught a lot of crooks in that sting operation.*

— sting[2] (vt) (sl.): cheat, overcharge, harm financially >*She got stung bad when he screwed up her investments.*

STINK
* stink[1] (colloq.): noisy complaint or protest, scandalous fuss >*The*

newspapers are going to raise a big stink when they find out the police shoved him around.

** stink[2] (vi) (sl.): be very bad, be deplorable, be unjust >I saw that movie—it stinks. >The way they treat her stinks.

— stink to high heaven (colloq.): have a very foul odor, smell very bad >That rotten fish stinks to high heaven!

STINKER

* stinker (colloq.): contemptible or mean person, rascal >That stinker left me to pay the bill.

STINKING

* stinking[1] (sl.): contemptible, reprehensible, cursed >Get your stinkin' hands off her! >Keep those stinkin' punk friends of yours away from here.

— stinking[2] (sl.): extremely, excessively >We all got stinkin' drunk that night. >He can afford it—he's stinkin' rich.

STIR-CRAZY

— stir-crazy (sl.): insane or very agitated due to long confinement, very restless due to being enclosed for an excessive period of time >That old convict is stir-crazy. >I'm a little stir-crazy from being cooped up in this house all week.

STITCHES

* in stitches (colloq.): laughing uncontrollably >That comedian kept us in stitches.

STOCK

* stock (colloq.): as standard equipment, not customized (esp. on automobiles) >Automatic transmission's stock on this model.

STOKED

— stoked (stōkt) (sl.): very excited or enthusiastic, exhilarated >Everyone's stoked about winnin' first place.

STOMACH

— have a cast-iron stomach (see CAST-IRON)

STOMP

* stomp (stomp) (vt) (sl.): defeat decisively, beat up >The Dodgers stomped the Giants, eleven to two. >Jimmy got stomped in some bar by two big football players.

STOMPING GROUND

* stomping ground(s) (stom'ping ...) (colloq.): (one's) habitual or favorite place of activity, place (one) frequents, haunt >He's probably with his buddies down at Ernie's Tavern—that's his stomping ground.

STONED

* stoned (sl.): very intoxicated, completely drunk >Ya don't have to smoke much of this grass to get stoned. >He was lyin' in the gutter, stoned outta his mind.

STONEWALL

— stonewall (vi, vt) (colloq.): delay or evade, stall (s/thing politically disadvantageous) >They'll never get it passed because the opposition will just stonewall it. >The President knows more than he's letting on—he's stonewalling.

STOOL PIGEON

— stool pigeon (sl.): police informer >Some stool pigeon squealed on 'em.

STOOLIE

— stoolie (see "STOOLY")

STOOLY

— stooly (stū'lē) (sl.): police informer >The gangster said he was gonna kill that stooly.

STOP

— stop/turn on a dime (see DIME)

— stop traffic (sl.): be dazzlingly beautiful (esp. a woman) >Pretty? She stops traffic!

STORE
— **mind the store** (see **MIND**)

STORM
— **... up a storm** (colloq.): ... with great energy and determination >*He's in the kitchen cooking up a storm.* >*They were singing up a storm around the campfire.*

STORY
— **a likely story** (see **LIKELY**)

STRAIGHT
** **straight**[1] (sl.): heterosexual, not homosexual >*Is Raymond gay or straight?*

* **straight**[2] (sl.): law-abiding, no longer involved in criminal activity >*He used to steal cars, but he's straight now.*

* **straight**[3] (colloq.): honestly, straightforwardly, objectively >*She's telling it to us straight.* >*It's best to just deal with him straight.*

* **straight**[4] (colloq.): conventional, traditional, conservative >*Phil's pretty straight—I don't think he'll go for a game of poker.* >*It was a real straight wedding—nothing out of the ordinary.*

— **straight**[5] (colloq.): reliable or correct (esp. regarding information) >*This is the straight stuff—I heard it from the chairman himself.* >*You sure that info's straight?*

** **get [s/thing] straight** (colloq.): understand [s/thing] correctly >*Let me get this straight. You want me to take the blame for you?* >*You'd better get your story straight before the police get here.*

* **go straight** (sl.): stop being a criminal, become an honest citizen >*I don't think Stubby will ever go straight.*

— **have [one's] head (screwed) on straight** (see **HEAD**)

— **play it straight** (see **PLAY**)

— **shoot straight** (see **SHOOT**)

— **(straight/right) from the horse's mouth** (see **HORSE'S MOUTH**)

— **(you're) damn(ed) straight ...!** (sl., freq. vulg.): ... is the truth! absolutely ...! have no doubt that ...! >*You're damn straight he'd better pay me what he owes me!*

— **(you're) darn(ed) straight ...!** (därn[d] ...) (sl.): ... is the truth! absolutely...! have no doubt that ...! >*Darned straight I'll get my money back!*

STRAIGHT ARROW
— **straight arrow** (colloq.): person who behaves in a very moral and conventional way >*Peters is a straight arrow—no way he'll go along with that scheme.*

STRAIGHTEN
** **straighten out** (vt) (colloq.): reform behaviorally, guide to proper or responsible behavior >*Joey was starting to get in trouble at school, but a new counselor there straightened him out.*

* **straighten up** (vi) (colloq.): stop behaving improperly, begin to behave responsibly >*You'd better straighten up, young man, or you'll be in trouble.*

STRAIGHT SHOOTER
— **straight shooter** (colloq.): person who deals honestly or treats people fairly >*I don't believe a straight shooter like Gibbons would do such a thing.*

STRAPPED
— **strapped** (colloq.): lacking funds, in financial need >*Can you let me have it on credit? I'm a little strapped this month.*

STREAK
* **streak** (vi) (colloq.): dash naked through a public place (esp. as a prank) >*Some guy streaked across the stage right in the middle of the ceremony.*

STREET
* **on the street(s)**[1] (colloq.): among marginalized members of society, in the domain of petty criminality or urban poverty >*That rich kid wouldn't last ten*

minutes on the street. >She ran away from home and learned to survive on the streets.

— **on the street(s)²** (colloq.): released from custody, not jailed >I hate to think what that thug will do when he's back on the street.

STREET-SMART
* **street-smart** (colloq.): shrewdly practical or clever for survival or success (esp. in a ruthlessly competitive situation) >These street-smart kids know how to fool a lot of cops.

STREET SMARTS
* **street smarts** (... smärts) (colloq.): shrewd practicality or cleverness for survival or success (esp. in a ruthlessly competitive situation) >You got to have street smarts to make it in the music business.

STREET-WISE
* **street-wise** (colloq.): shrewdly practical or clever for survival or success (esp. in a ruthlessly competitive situation) >Only a street-wise guy like him can work with gang members.

STRESS
** **stress out** (vt) (colloq.): make overly tense, fatigue from tension or demands >Everyone was stressed out by the end of final exams. >Those long meetings stress me out.

STRETCH
— **stretch** (sl.): prison term >Frankie's doin' a five-year stretch for fraud.

* **stretch [one's] legs** (colloq.): take a break from sitting, take a walk after being inactive >Let's get up and stretch our legs a while, and then we'll finish the report.

STRIKE
— **hit/strike a (raw) nerve (with)** (see NERVE)

* **strike it rich** (colloq.): gain financial success suddenly or unexpectedly

>They really struck it rich with that last marketing plan.

* **strike out** (vi) (sl.): be unsuccessful, not achieve an objective >Joey tried to get a date with Alice, but he struck out. >We struck out—they just wouldn't buy it.

— **hit/strike pay dirt** (see PAY DIRT)

STRIKES
— **(already) have two strikes against [one]** (see TWO)

STRING
— **on the string** (colloq.): subject to (one's) whim or influence, at (one's) beck and call, being led on >She really attracts men—she's got three or four on the string.

* **string along** (vt) (colloq.): continue to give false hopes to, lead on >Allen thinks Melissa loves him, but she's just stringing him along. >They strung the old guy along for a few months, then took off with his money.

— **string along (with)** (colloq.): accompany or follow (s/one) (esp. aimlessly) >You going shopping? Mind if I string along? >I strung along with them while they ran a few errands.

— **hang/string [s/one] out to dry** (see HANG)

— **string up** (vt) (sl.): hang (to death) >Don't put 'em in jail—just string 'em up!

STRING BEAN
— **string bean** (sl.): tall and thin person >Boy, can that string bean ever pitch a baseball!

STRINGS
* **pull (some) strings** (colloq.): use influence, call on the support of influential associates (esp. in an unconventional or secretive way) >Al had to pull some strings, but he got the contract with the city.

* **strings (attached)** (colloq.): hidden conditions, unfavorable limitations >*I'll make sure you get the job with no strings attached.* >*That's too good to be true—there've got to be some strings.*

STRIPPED
* **stripped down** (colloq.): having just the essentials, with no adornments or extras >*The stripped down model will run you $3000 less.*

STRIPPER
** **stripper** (sl.): striptease artist >*She worked nights as a stripper to put herself through school.*

STROKE
* **stroke** (vt) (sl.): flatter, gratify the ego of >*Don't believe him, man—the guy's just strokin' ya.*

STROKES
* **strokes** (sl.): flattery, ego gratification >*Flo's been gettin' a lot of strokes at work 'cause of the great job she's doin'.*

— **different strokes for different folks** (see DIFFERENT)

STRONG
* **(as) strong as an ox** (colloq.): very strong >*That wrestler's strong as an ox.*

— **come on strong** (see COME)

STRONG-ARM
— **strong-arm¹** (vt) (colloq.): force physically or by threat of violence, coerce by force or intimidation >*If he's reluctant to pay, they'll strong-arm him.*

— **strong-arm²** (colloq.): using physical force or threat of violence, coercing by force or intimidation >*The judge criticized the sheriff for his strong-arm tactics.*

STRUNG
* **strung out** (sl.): suffering the effects of drugs, badly addicted to drugs, weak or nervous from prolonged drug use >*How's he gonna find work if he's all strung out on crack?* >*She's in bad shape, all strung out.*

STRUT
— **strut [one's] stuff** (sl.): display [one's] talent or attractiveness >*Look at that foxy girl struttin' her stuff on the dance floor.*

STUBBORN
* **(as) stubborn as a mule** (colloq.): very stubborn >*Don't try to change Pete's mind—he's as stubborn as a mule.*

STUCK
— **stuck on** (colloq.): infatuated with, in love with >*Charlie's really stuck on that girl he's been dating lately.*

** **stuck with** (colloq.): burdened with, left with the responsibility for >*How come I always get stuck with taking out the garbage?*

STUCK-UP
* **stuck-up** (colloq.): snobbish, conceited >*Why do you want to hang around with all those stuck-up high-society types?*

STUD
* **stud** (sl.): sexually attractive man, male who is successful at making sexual conquests (also voc.) >*Wow, look at the stud Shirley's with!* >*Bart thinks he's a real stud 'cause he has three girlfriends.* >*Think you're something special with the women, don't ya, stud?*

STUFF
** **stuff¹** (colloq.): things, possessions, matter >*What's all this stuff on the table?* >*Grab your stuff and let's go.* >*I can't get the red stuff off my shirt.* >*What did you think of the stuff he said?*

* **stuff²** (colloq.): artistic production >*That author's stuff is great.* >*They do some good stuff at that theater.*

— **stuff³** (sl.): illegal drugs >*He got some good stuff from a cocaine dealer he knows.*

* **and stuff** (colloq.): etcetera, and so forth, and the like >*She's really into pop music—she's been playing and singing and stuff around town.* >*I know

he's a good skier because he's won some prizes and stuff.

* **know [one's] stuff** (colloq.): be skilled in [one's] profession or craft, be knowledgeable in [one's] specialty >*You got to know your stuff to make a living as a broker.* >*These researchers really know their stuff.*

— **strut [one's] stuff** (see **STRUT**)

* **... stuff** (colloq.): ...-type behavior >*I didn't like some of the weird stuff that gang was into.* >*Aw, Mom, taking piano lessons is kid stuff.*

* **stuff [one's] face** (sl.): eat (esp. intently or voraciously) >*While you all were stuffin' your faces, I was sweatin' in the kitchen.*

* **stuff it!** (sl., freq. vulg.): (interj. to express great anger or contempt to s/one) >*If ya don't like how I'm doin' it, stuff it!*

STUFFED

— **(go) get stuffed!** (sl. freq. vulg.): (interj. to express great anger or contempt to s/one) >*Tell that jerk to go get stuffed!*

STUFFED SHIRT

— **stuffed shirt** (colloq.): pompous and overly formal man >*Hey, relax, Evan, and stop being such a stuffed shirt!*

STUFFING

— **beat/knock the stuffing out of** (colloq.): beat severely, beat up >*I can't believe that little guy knocked the stuffing out of that big construction worker.*

STUMBLEBUM

— **stumblebum** (stum´bəl bum´) (colloq.): clumsy and inept person >*I just know that stumblebum's going to ruin it all.*

STUMP

* **stump** (vt) (colloq.): baffle, thoroughly puzzle, perplex >*I give up—I'm stumped.* >*Those trick questions can stump you.*

STUNT

* **stunt** (colloq.): instance of misbehavior, irresponsible act >*Another stunt like that, Hargrave, and you can go look for another job.*

* **pull a stunt** (colloq.): do an act of misbehavior, do an irresponsible act >*The stunt that idiot pulled could have gotten a lot of people hurt.*

STUPID

** **stupid** (colloq.): contemptible, worthless >*Get your stupid things off my desk!* >*I don't want to go to that stupid reception.*

STYLE

— **cramp [s/one's] style** (see **CRAMP**)

— **like it's going out of style** (see **GOING**)

SUB

** **sub[1]** (sub) (colloq.): substitute >*Send in a sub, coach.*

* **sub[2]** (colloq.): submarine >*Nuclear subs can stay under a long time.*

** **sub[3]** (vi) (colloq.): substitute >*She's subbing for the regular teacher.*

SUCCESS

— **howling success** (see **HOWLING**)

SUCK

** **suck** (vi) (sl.): be very bad or unpleasant, be deplorable or unjust >*The movie was a flop 'cause it sucks.* >*He thinks school sucks.* >*Your racist jokes suck.*

— **suck face** (sl.): engage in kissing (esp. French kissing) >*Her old man don't know she's out on the porch suckin' face with Bobby.*

— **suck in** (vt) (sl.): deceive, trick, hoodwink >*How'd Olson get sucked in by such a sleazy character?*

— **suck off** (vt) (vulg.): bring to orgasm by fellatio or cunnilingus >*He paid her to suck him off.*

— **suck up** (vt) (sl.): be very receptive to, thoroughly enjoy >*Tell him he's great—*

he sucks that up. >Kids nowadays really suck up that computer stuff.

* **suck up to** (sl.): be servile or obsequious to in order to gain favor, adulate, flatter to gain favor >*Suckin' up to the supervisor by offerin' to work late, huh?*

SUCKER

** **sucker**[1] (colloq.): person who is easily tricked or cheated, gullible person, dupe (also voc.) >*There's always some sucker who will fall for this trick. >You just got cheated, sucker!*

* **sucker**[2] (sl.): thing or person (esp. seen as troublesome or contemptible) (also voc.) >*I'll need some pliers to get that sucker outta there. >Tell that sleazy sucker to get lost. >Tough luck, sucker!*

* **be a sucker for** (colloq.): be easily attracted to, have a special liking for >*He's a sucker for pouty blonds.*

— **play [s/one] for a fool/sucker** (see PLAY)

* **sucker [s/one] (into)** (sl.): manipulate [s/one] (into) (through deception), fool [s/one] (into) >*They suckered me into the casino with five free plays on the slot machines. >Think we can sucker Thompson into makin' the delivery for us? >You've been suckered, dummy!*

SUDS

— **suds** (sl.): beer >*I'll bring the pretzels, and you bring the suds.*

SUE

* **(so) sue me!** (sl.): I don't care if you don't like what I do/did! I find your objections contemptible! >*Ya don't like the schedule I gave ya? So sue me!*

SUGAR

— **sugar** (voc.) (colloq.): dear, sweetheart >*Hi, sugar. Want to buy me a drink? >You know your mother doesn't like me, sugar.*

— **pretty please (with sugar on it)!** (see PRETTY)

SUGAR DADDY

— **sugar daddy** (... dad´ē) (sl.): older man who provides gifts or money to a younger woman for sex or companionship >*She's lookin' for a sugar daddy to pay her bills.*

SUIT

— **suit** (sl.): man dressed in a suit, business executive, man in charge >*Who's the suit talkin' to Teddy? >We got to take this to the suits first and get their OK.*

SUN

— **where the sun doesn't/don't shine** (see WHERE)

SUNDAY

— **[one's] Sunday best** (colloq.): [one's] best or most formal clothes >*Here comes Jake in his Sunday best. What's the occasion?*

SUNDAY DRIVER

— **Sunday driver** (colloq.): slow or overly cautious driver >*See if you can pass this Sunday driver or we'll never get there.*

SUNDAYS

— **a month of Sundays** (see MONTH)

SUNK

* **be sunk** (colloq.): be facing inevitable loss or defeat, be doomed >*If we don't get that loan, we're sunk.*

SUPER

— **super**[1] (sū´pər) (colloq.): supervisor, superintendent (on a job) >*Ask the super if you can change shifts.*

— **super**[2] (colloq.): superintendent (of an apartment building) >*I'll ask the super if it's OK to shut off the gas.*

** **super**[3] (colloq.): excellent, outstanding, wonderful >*It was a super party. >Your new boyfriend is just super.*

* **super**[4] (sl.): very, extremely >*We were super tired by the end of the trip.*

SUPER-DUPER

— **super-duper** (sū´pər dū´pər) (sl., freq. sarc.): excellent, impressive, wonderful

>*Yeah, that's really a super-duper bow tie you're wearin', Harold.*

SURE

** **sure** (colloq.): surely, certainly >*It's sure hot today.* >*She's sure looking good.*

— **sure as shooting** (colloq.): with all certainty, undoubtedly, indeed >*Stage a rally and, sure as shooting, every weirdo from miles around will show up.* >*Adam said he'd win, and sure as shooting, he did.*

* **sure enough** (colloq.): with all certainty, undoubtedly, indeed >*I get in the bathtub and, sure enough, the darn phone rings.* >*It looked like it was going to rain and, sure enough, it did.*

* **sure thing** (colloq.): of course, certainly >*Sure thing—help yourself to whatever you want.*

SURE THING

* **sure thing** (colloq.): certain winner, assured success or gain >*I tell you, this horse is a sure thing.* >*Marlene's got the inside track for the position, but it's not a sure thing yet.*

SVILLE

— **...sville** (... s/z´vil´) (sl.): a very ... thing or experience, a place of great ... (used with adjs. and nouns) (cf. "**...VILLE**") >*This so-called party is strictly dullsville.* >*Wow! The beach is babesville today.*

SWALLOW

* **swallow** (vt) (colloq.): believe credulously, accept (a lie or deception) >*You didn't swallow that story about him having a yacht, did you?*

— **swallow [s/thing] hook, line, and sinker** (colloq.): believe [s/thing] completely, accept [s/thing] unquestioningly, be duped regarding [s/thing] >*What a dummy! He swallowed that crazy story hook, line, and sinker.*

SWAP

— **swap notes** (colloq.): exchange information, compare observations or opinions >*Teachers like to swap notes on new things they try in the classroom.*

SWEAR

* **swear by** (colloq.): have total confidence in, rely on >*My mother swears by this detergent.*

* **swear off** (colloq.): pledge to give up, renounce using >*He swore off hard liquor two years ago.*

* **swear on a stack of Bibles** (colloq.): swear fervently, avow unequivocally >*He swears on a stack of Bibles that he had nothing to do with the fire.*

— **swear up and down** (colloq.): swear fervently, avow unequivocally >*He swears up and down he was nowhere near the place when it was robbed.*

SWEAT

** **sweat**[1] (vi, vt) (sl.): be anxious (about), be worried (about) (esp. for fear of loss or failure) >*They look calm, but they're sweatin'.* >*Don't sweat it! You'll get your money back.* >*I'm really sweatin' that entrance exam.*

— **sweat**[2] (vt) (sl.): put pressure on, force by intimidation, coerce >*The boss has been sweatin' us 'cause the deadline's near.* >*They're sweatin' him to pay up.* >*Sweat him a little, and he'll tell us.*

** **no sweat** (sl.): easily, (with) no problem >*We can finish the job by tomorrow noon, no sweat.* >*Ya wanna meet her? No sweat. Come on, I'll introduce ya.*

— **sweat blood** (sl.): experience great anxiety, be very worried >*He was sweatin' blood till the jury came in and acquitted him.*

* **sweat like a pig** (sl.): sweat profusely >*Everyone was sweatin' like a pig in that hot, stuffy room.*

* **sweat out** (vt) (colloq.): anxiously await the outcome of >*We had to sweat out the committee's decision for over a*

month. >*He's sweating it out till the test results come back.*

— sweat [s/thing] out of (sl.): get (information) from (s/one) by persistent questioning >*The cops finally sweated it outta Dirksen where the money was hidden.*

SWEATS
** sweats (colloq.): sweatshirt and sweatpants, sweat suit >*I usually just hang around the house in my sweats.*

SWEEP
* sweep [s/one] off [his/her] feet (colloq.): overwhelm [s/one] favorably, completely charm or enthuse [s/one] >*The realtor swept them off their feet and got them to buy the first house they looked at.* >*He swept her off her feet, and they got married within a month.*

SWEET
— short and sweet (see SHORT)
— sweet nothings (colloq.): amorous phrases, trivial romantic talk (esp. spoken softly) >*He whispered sweet nothings in her ear.*
— sweet on (colloq.): romantically fond of, in love with >*Lew acts kind of funny around Sue—I think he's sweet on her.*
— take [one's] (sweet) time (see TAKE)

SWEETEN
— sweeten (vt) (colloq.): enhance the attractiveness of by adding value to >*The salesman sweetened the deal by adding cruise control free of charge.* >*Let's sweeten the pot—I see your bet and raise you five bucks.*

SWEETHEART
* sweetheart (colloq.): generous and likable person >*You're a sweetheart for helping out.*
* a sweetheart of a (colloq.): an excellent, a wonderful >*It's a sweetheart of a deal I just can't pass up.* >*Ginger's a sweetheart of a gal.*

SWEETIE
* sweetie (swē′tē) (colloq.): sweetheart (also voc.) >*I hear you have a new sweetie.* >*Hi, sweetie, how was your day?*

SWEETIE PIE
— sweetie pie (swē′tē …) (voc.) (colloq.): dear, sweetheart >*But, sweetie pie, you know I love you.*

SWEETS
— sweets (voc.) (colloq.): dear, sweetheart >*Give me a kiss, sweets.*

SWEET TALK
* sweet talk (colloq.): seductive or persuasive talk, cajolery, flattery >*Cut out the sweet talk—it'll get you nowhere with me.*

SWEET-TALK
* sweet-talk (vt) (colloq.): seduce or persuade with words, cajole, flatter >*Watch him—he really knows how to sweet-talk a girl.* >*I sweet-talked him into driving us there and back.*

SWEET TOOTH
* sweet tooth (colloq.): liking for sweets >*Buy her some chocolates—she's got a real sweet tooth.*

SWELL
— swell (colloq.): excellent, wonderful (also adv.) >*Your brother's a swell guy.* >*Swell! Let's see that movie.* >*She sure sings swell.*

SWIFT
— swift (sl.): ingenious, clever, excellent >*That was real swift how he got 'em to do what he wanted.* >*Pretty swift paint job on your car.*
* not too swift (sl.): not smart or clever, stupid >*That wasn't too swift, callin' the dean a fathead.* >*His goofy friend ain't too swift, is he?*

SWIG
— swig[1] (swig) (colloq.): swallow of liquor >*It's a real smooth scotch. Want a swig?*

— **swig²** (vt) (colloq.): drink heartily, take a swallow of (liquor) >*He swigged some vodka and turned red.*

SWIMMING

— **swimming in** (colloq.): having an abundance of >*Those rich collectors are swimming in expensive paintings.*

SWING

* **swing¹** (vi) (sl.): be lively and exciting, be wildly festive >*This place'll be swingin' when that band plays.* >*Billy really swings when he's partyin'.*

— **swing²** (vt) (colloq.): accomplish as desired, achieve as arranged (esp. s/thing difficult) >*I'll meet you in Lisbon if I can swing it.* >*If Todson swings that deal, it'll make him rich.*

— **swing³** (vi) (sl.): be hanged (to death) >*He'd swing for what he did if I was the judge.*

* **in(to) the swing of** (colloq.): fully involved in and adjusted to >*Don't worry—you'll get into the swing of things around here in a few days.*

* **swing by** (colloq.): come by, stop by (esp. when en route elsewhere) >*I'll swing by your place on my way to work and pick you up.*

* **swing (shift)** (colloq.): afternoon and evening work shift (generally starting at four p.m.) >*My brother works the late shift, and I work swing.*

* **take a swing at** (colloq.): attempt to hit with the fist >*He took a swing at me, but I ducked.*

SWINGER

* **swinger¹** (sl.): participant in exchanging spouses for sex >*Them and all those other couples they party with are swingers.*

— **swinger²** (sl.): wildly festive person, real fun lover >*The nerdy guy that brought his chessboard to the party ain't exactly a swinger, is he?*

SWINGING

* **swinging** (sl.): lively and exciting, wildly festive >*What a swingin' party!* >*This is where all the swingin' singles hang out.*

SWIPE

* **swipe** (vt) (sl.): steal >*Somebody swiped my suitcase at the station.*

— **take a swipe at¹** (colloq.): attempt to hit with the fist >*Marv took a swipe at the cop before she could get the handcuffs on him.*

— **take a swipe at²** (colloq.): make a critical remark about >*He took a swipe at the incumbent governor during his press conference.*

SWISH

— **swish¹** (swish) (sl., pej.): effeminate homosexual (also adj.) >*Who was that swish I saw him with?* >*And don't bring your swish friends around here no more!*

— **swish²** (vi) (sl.): walk or move in an effeminate way (said of a man) >*His gay friend was swishin' around the party.*

SWISHY

— **swishy** (swish´ē) (sl.): effeminate (said of a man) >*Why do ya wear those swishy silk shirts?*

SWITCH

— **switch off** (vi) (sl.): lose interest or goodwill, become oblivious >*When he started givin' his views on morality, everyone just switched off.*

SWITCHEROO

— **switcheroo** (swich´ə rū´) (sl.): sudden reversal, unexpected switch >*Quite a switcheroo, him changin' parties in the middle of the senatorial campaign.*

SYNC

* **in/out of sync** (… singk) (sl.): in/out of harmony, compatible/incompatible >*They get along great—they're really in sync.* >*His political views were outta sync with his boss's.*

SYSTEM

SYSTEM
* **the system** (colloq.): the established
  order of government and society >*He
  wants to be part of the system and make
  a bundle of money.*

T

T. & A.
— T. & A. (see "T. AND A.")

TAB
** **tab** (colloq.): bill (esp. for food or drink) >*Who's going to pick up the bar tab?*

TABLE
— **drink [s/one] under the table** (see **DRINK**)

* **under the table** (colloq.): in secret, clandestinely (esp. regarding business deals) (cf. "**UNDER-THE-TABLE**") >*We'll have to work this under the table to keep the tax people out of our way.*

TABLE-HOP
— **table-hop** (vi) (colloq.): go from table to table socializing with different people >*She table-hopped all night and talked to almost everyone in the bar.*

TABS
* **keep tabs (on)** (colloq.): check (on), maintain a record (concerning), keep observing >*Keep tabs on Bromwell—I want to know his every move.* >*I don't know how many boxes we've moved. Aren't you keeping tabs?*

TACH
— **tach** (tak) (colloq.): tachometer >*The tach showed the engine was turning at four thousand R.P.M.*

TACK
— **(as) sharp as a tack** (see **SHARP**)

TACKY
** **tacky** (tak´ē) (colloq.): tasteless, crude, gaudy >*I think his trying to do business at a wedding reception is pretty tacky.* >*Why is he wearing that tacky tie with a picture of a naked woman on it?*

TAD
* **a tad** (.. tad) (colloq.): a small amount, a bit >*Move it a tad to the right.* >*I'll have a tad more wine.*

TAGS
* **tags** (colloq.): vehicle license plates >*This truck's got to have commercial tags.*

TAIL
* **tail**^{1} (colloq.): buttocks, rump >*She slipped on the ice and fell on her tail.*

— **tail**^{2} (sl.): person who follows and observes (s/one) >*The cops put a tail on me, but I lost him.*

— **tail**^{3} (vulg.): sexual intercourse (with a woman) (freq. used with *some* or *any*) >*That horny kid will do anything for some tail.* >*He asked me if I'd gotten any tail lately.*

— **tail**^{4} (vulg., pej.): woman or women (see as sex object[s]) >*He kept talkin' about all the nice tail he saw at the party.*

* **tail**^{5} (vt) (sl.): follow and observe >*I think that blue pickup's been tailin' us.*

— **cannot make head(s) or tail(s) (out) of** (see **HEAD**)

— **get off [one's] tail** (sl.): stop being lazy, start moving or working >*I'm gonna get off my tail and mow the lawn.*

* **off [s/one's] tail** (sl.): no longer putting pressure on [s/one], no longer being critical of [s/one] (cf. "**on [s/one's] TAIL**^{2}") >*I'd work a lot better if the boss would just get off my tail.*

* **on [s/one's] tail**^{1} (sl.): following and observing [s/one] >*Slow down! Ya got a highway patrolman on your tail.* >*She put some private detective on his tail to see if he was meetin' another woman.*

— **on [s/one's] tail**^{2} (sl.): putting pressure on [s/one], being critical of [s/one] (cf. "**off [s/one's] TAIL**") >*I got the boss on my tail to boost production.*

— **piece of tail** (see **PIECE**)

— **[one's] tail** (sl.): [one]self, [one] (esp. when seen as troublesome or contemptible) >*He got his tail outta there quick.*

* ... [one's] tail off (sl.): ... with maximum effort or sacrifice, ... to the utmost >*Rose works her tail off at that job.* >*Jimmy ran his tail off but still lost the race.*

— turn tail (see TURN)

TAILGATE

** tailgate (vt) (colloq.): follow (a vehicle) dangerously closely (in another vehicle) >*I hate it when those big trucks tailgate me.*

TAKE

* take[1] (colloq.): amount of money taken in or obtained >*This restaurant's take was almost $10,000 last night.* >*What was the take in the robbery?*

* take[2] (vt) (colloq.): defeat, conquer >*He's pretty good—think you can take him?*

* can take [s/thing] or leave [it] (colloq.): have no special liking for [s/thing], be indifferent toward [s/thing] >*Greek food? I can take it or leave it.* >*As far as horror films go, she can take them or leave them.*

— (go) take a flying leap! (see FLYING)

— on the take (sl.): taking bribes >*If the cop is on the take, you can forget about him makin' a report.*

— take (a/the/[one's]) ... (see entry under ... noun)

— rip/take/tear apart (see APART)

— take/tear apart (see APART)

— take/knock [s/one] down a peg (or two) (colloq.): reduce [s/one's] arrogance or presumptuousness, deflate [s/one] somewhat >*It took Williams down a peg when he got beat at his own game.* >*Someone ought to knock that clown down a peg or two.*

— take five (see FIVE)

* take [s/one] (for) (colloq.): swindle [s/one] (out of an amount), get (an amount) out of [s/one] >*The con artist took him*

for over a thousand bucks. >*How much did they take you for in Las Vegas?*

— take [s/one] for a ride (see RIDE)

** take it (colloq.): endure or tolerate (a stressful or unpleasant situation) >*I got to find a new job—I just can't take it here anymore.* >*What's the matter? Can't you take it?*

— take it away! (colloq.): begin! (a performance) >*OK, maestro, take it away!*

— take it easy (see EASY)

— take it easy! (see EASY)

— take it from (colloq.): accept the expert opinion of, learn from the experience of (used esp. as a command) >*Take it from me, having a tooth pulled is no fun!*

— take it in the shorts (see SHORTS)

— take it on the chin (see CHIN)

— take [s/thing] lying down (see LYING)

** take off[1] (vi) (colloq.): leave, depart, flee >*It's late—I got to take off.* >*They took off when they saw the guard.*

* take off[2] (vi) (colloq.): grow fast, increase suddenly >*My roses just took off after I fertilized them.* >*Sales really took off in May.*

* take on (vt) (colloq.): accept the challenge of, engage (a competitor) >*You ain't so tough—I'll take you on.* >*He'll take on all challengers.*

— take out (vt) (sl.): destroy, eliminate, murder >*He took out a tank with a bazooka.* >*They took out the guard and broke in.*

** take [s/thing] out on [s/one] (colloq.): make [s/one] suffer because of (one's own) suffering, vent (one's) frustration on [s/one] because of [s/thing] >*He takes out all his humiliation on his wife by yelling at her.* >*So what if you're mad at him? Don't take it out on me!*

— take some doing (see DOING)

* **take [one's] (sweet) time** (colloq., sarc.): take too much time, be unconcerned about promptness >*That project should have been finished last week. You're sure taking your sweet time on it.*

— **take things easy** (see **EASY**)

— **take [s/one] to the cleaners** (see **CLEANERS**)

* **take [s/one] up on** (colloq.): accept [s/one's] offer or proposal regarding >*If they offer you the position, take them up on it.*

— **take up with** (colloq.): start keeping company with, become friends with (esp. s/one undesirable) >*Johnny's taken up with a couple of no-good bums.* >*My son took up with some awful woman who ruined him.*

— **(tell [s/one] to take [his/her s/thing] and) shove/stick it** (see **SHOVE**)

— **(tell [s/one] to take [his/her s/thing] and) shove/stick it up [his/her] ass** (see **SHOVE**)

TAKEOFF

* **takeoff** (colloq.): humorous parody, satirical imitation >*He did a hilarious takeoff on that sports announcer.*

TAKEOUT

* **takeout** (colloq.): food ordered to be taken out >*This place has great Chinese takeout.*

TAKES

* **it takes two to tango** (colloq.): at least two are required to have a conflict >*It can't be all her fault—it takes two to tango, you know.*

— **what it takes** (see **WHAT**)

TALK

— **talk a blue streak** (see **BLUE STREAK**)

** **talk back** (vi) (colloq.): respond disrespectfully, speak impudently (cf. "**BACK TALK**") >*If he talks back to his mom she really gets mad.*

* **talk big** (colloq.): speak boastfully, exaggerate pretentiously, brag (cf. "**BIG TALK**") >*He talks big, but he's strictly a small-time operator.*

* **talk [s/one's] ear off** (colloq.): talk excessively to [s/one], bore [s/one] with excessive talk >*Make an excuse to leave, or Ted'll talk your ear off.*

— **talk shop** (see **SHOP**)

— **talk through [one's] hat** (colloq.): say nonsense, speak out of ignorance >*He's talking through his hat if he says they'll fix your car for free.*

— **talk turkey** (see **TURKEY**)

TALKING

* **be talking** (vt) (colloq.): be referring to, mean >*Don't laugh at this deal—I'm talking big bucks here.* >*If it was premeditated, we're talking first-degree murder.*

— **look who's talking!** (see **LOOK**)

— **now you're talking!** (see **NOW**)

TALKING HEAD

— **talking head** (sl.): person whose head (and shoulders) is seen on television and who is talking (esp. while discussing s/thing), television commentator >*The talkin' heads were on TV last night analyzin' the election.*

TALKING-TO

* **talking-to** (colloq.): scolding, admonishing lecture >*I'm going to give that lazy girl a good talking-to.*

TALL ORDER

* **tall order** (colloq.): request that is difficult to fulfill >*Finding somebody with all those qualifications is a tall order, but I'll see what I can do.*

TAN

— **tan [s/one's] hide** (sl.): spank [s/one], thrash [s/one] (as punishment) >*Your dad's gonna tan your hide if ya don't behave.*

T. AND A.–TEAR

T. AND A.
— **T. and A.** (= "tits and ass") (sl.):
exhibition of women's breasts and
buttocks, soft pornography (also adj.)
>*They rated the movie "R" 'cause it's
got a lot of T. and A.* >*She stars in some
T. and A. show.*

TANGLE
— **tangle¹** (colloq.): fight, conflict, quarrel
>*Zane's all depressed because him and
his wife got into a bad tangle last night.*

— **tangle²** (vi) (colloq.): fight, enter into
conflict, quarrel >*They're really mad at
each other—I think they're going to
tangle.* >*I tangled with him once over
who was responsible for those reports.*

TANGO
— **it takes two to tango** (see TAKES)

TANK
— **the tank** (sl.): large jail cell (esp. for
drunks) >*They threw him in the tank to
sober up.*

TANKED
— **tanked (up)** (sl.): drunk >*He got
tanked up in some bar and started a
fight.* >*Pete's so tanked he can't walk.*

TAP
* **tap¹** (colloq.): wiretap >*The F.B.I. has
a tap on his phone.*

* **tap²** (vt) (colloq.): wiretap >*The
detectives tapped the phone and waited
for the info they wanted.*

* **on tap** (colloq.): readily available >*We
got extra funds on tap if they're needed.*

* **tap into** (colloq.): gain a source for, get
access to >*He's a good reporter
because he knows how to tap into the
right people.*

TAPPED
— **tapped out** (sl.): broke, having spent or
lost all (one's) money >*Can you buy
the drinks? I'm all tapped out.*

TAR
— **beat/knock the tar out of** (colloq.):
beat severely, beat up >*That big dude'll
knock the tar out of Chas.*

TARNATION
— **tarnation!** (tär nā´shən) (colloq.):
(interj. to express anger, surprise, or
irritation) >*Tarnation! Where'd I put
my glasses?*

— **what/who/[etc.] in tarnation ...?**
(colloq.): (intens. to express impatience,
anger, or surprise) >*What in tarnation
are you doing here?*

TASTE
— **so much/bad I can taste it** (see SO)

TATER
— **tater** (tā´tər) (colloq.): potato >*She
served roast beef and taters.*

TEACH
— **teach** (voc.) (colloq.): teacher >*Can I
be excused, teach?*

* **that'll teach [s/one] (to [do s/thing])**
(colloq.): that will serve [s/one] as
punishment (for [doing s/thing]), that
will convince [s/one] (not to [do s/thing])
again) >*I slapped him—that'll teach
him to get fresh with me.* >*Jack broke
his arm fighting. That'll teach him.*

TEAM
— **(a team of) wild horses couldn't** (see
WILD)

TEAR
— **rip/take/tear apart** (see APART)

— **take/tear apart** (see APART)

* **tear into¹** (tär ...) (sl.): assail, attack
(physically or verbally) >*The boss tore
into Kingsley for screwin' up the
contract.* >*They tore into the guy and
beat him up bad.*

* **tear into²** (tär ...) (sl.): begin to
consume with gusto, attack
enthusiastically >*They'll really tear
into this great cherry cobbler.* >*The
kids tore into their Christmas presents.*

TEARJERKER

* **tearjerker** (tĕr´jûr´kər) (sl.): very pathetic or melodramatically sad story or situation (also adj.) >*The story of her life's a real tearjerker.* >*Greta loves those sappy tearjerker movies.*

* **tear up**[1] (târ ...) (vt) (colloq.): cause great grief or sadness in >*Their divorce just tore his mother up.*

— **tear up**[2] (târ ...) (vt) (colloq.): play very well in/on (a sport's venue) >*The half-back tore up the field that season.* >*He rallied and started tearing up the court.*

TECH

* **tech** (tek) (colloq.): technology >*Doris's taking a computer tech class.* >*This machine's real high tech.*

** **Tech** (colloq.): Technological (in institution names) >*He got his degree at Cal Tech.*

TEE

* **tee off** (vt) (sl.): make angry, irritate >*Pearl got teed off when they laughed at her.* >*It really tees Reggie off when they call him Reginald.*

TEEN

** **teen** (tēn) (colloq.): teenager, adolescent (also adj.) >*It's a dance for teens.* >*He joined a teen club.*

TEENIE-WEENIE

— **teenie-weenie** (see "TEENY-WEENY")

TEENSY-WEENSY

— **teensy-weensy** (tĕn´sē wĕn´sē) (colloq.): tiny, very small >*This teensy-weensy bug bit me and left this huge welt.*

TEENYBOPPER

— **teenybopper** (tē´nē bop´ər) (sl.): young teenager (esp. a girl who follows fads) (also adj.) >*The teenyboppers go crazy over that rock star.* >*He's a teenybopper idol.*

TEENY-WEENY

— **teeny-weeny** (tĕn´ē wĕn´ē) (colloq.): tiny, very small >*Can you see that teeny-weeny speck there?*

TEEPEE

— **teepee** (see "T.P.")

TEETH

— **(about) drop [one's] teeth** (see DROP)

— **by the skin of [one's] teeth** (see SKIN)

— **kick in the teeth** (see KICK)

— **lie through [one's] teeth** (see LIE)

— **sink [one's] teeth into** (see SINK)

TELL

— **I hope to tell you!** (see HOPE)

* **I tell you** (colloq.): I emphasize (that), I am convinced (that), I find (s/thing) obvious >*I tell you it just won't work.* >*She's one great friend, I tell you.*

* **(I'll) tell you what** (colloq.): listen to this proposal, here's an idea >*Tell you what—buy three of them, and I'll knock ten dollars off the total.*

— **not know/can't tell [one's] ass from a hole in the ground** (see KNOW)

— **not know/can't tell [s/thing] from a hole in the ground** (see KNOW)

* **tell it like it is** (colloq.): speak truthfully, be candid and forthright >*When you testify in court, you'd better tell it like it is.*

* **tell me about it!** (sl.): I know just what you mean! you don't have to explain it to me! >*Tell me about it! That happened to me just last year.*

* **tell off** (vt) (colloq.): reprimand or rebuke >*Delores was being snotty, so I told her off in front of everybody.*

** **tell on** (colloq.): tattle on, inform on >*I'll tell on you if you do it.*

— **(tell [s/one] to take [his/her s/thing] and) shove/stick it** (see SHOVE)

— **(tell [s/one] to take [his/her s/thing] and) shove/stick it up [his/her] ass** (see SHOVE)

TELLING–THAT'LL

— tell [s/one] where to get off (see WHERE)

— tell [s/one] where to put/stick [s/thing] (see WHERE)

TELLING

* I'm telling you (colloq.): I emphasize (that), I am convinced (that), I find (s/thing) obvious >*I'm telling you, that kid needs professional counseling.* >*It's not going to rain, I'm telling you.*

* you're telling me! (colloq.): I agree completely! I'm well aware (of that)! >*You're telling me it's hot! Just look at me sweat.*

TELLS

— something tells me (see SOMETHING)

TEN

* ten (colloq.): highest rating, very high evaluation >*I'd give him a ten on the neat bookshelf he built.* >*I don't agree with the ten you gave that movie.*

* a ten (colloq.): an excellent or unsurpassable thing or person >*His performance was good, but not a ten.* >*He's gorgeous, definitely a ten.*

TEN-FOOT

— wouldn't touch [s/thing, s/one] with a ten-foot pole (see TOUCH)

TENNIES

* tennies (ten´ēz) (colloq.): tennis shoes, athletic shoes >*Wear your tennies—they're better for walking.*

TEN-SPOT

— ten-spot (sl.): ten-dollar bill >*He laid two ten-spots on the bar and said, "Keep 'em comin'!"*

TERRIBLE

* something terrible (colloq.): terribly, very badly >*I don't know what I ate, but my stomach's been hurting something terrible.*

TERRIBLY

* terribly (colloq.): very, extremely >*He's terribly excited about the game.*

TERRITORY

* come/go with the territory (colloq.): be a natural neg. accompanying factor (in some endeavor) >*If you want to be a writer, you got to put up with mean critics—they come with the territory.*

TERROR

— (holy) terror (colloq.): very contentious or mischievous person, very troublesome person >*Why don't they control that brat? He's a holy terror.* >*The boss's son is a terror around the office.*

TEX-MEX

* Tex-Mex (teks´meks´) (colloq.): combining Texan and Mexican cultures >*I love Tex-Mex food.* >*Some Tex-Mex band was playing.*

T.G.I.F.

* T.G.I.F. (= "thank God it's Friday") (sl.): (expression referring to Friday celebrations of the end of the work week and the start of the weekend) >*What a week this has been! Let's have a little T.G.I.F. party this afternoon down at Sullivan's.*

THANK

* thank [one's] lucky stars (colloq.): thank God, appreciate [one's] good fortune >*I thank my lucky stars I didn't go ahead and marry that bum.*

THANKS

— thanks a million! (see MILLION)

THATAWAY

— thataway (ðat´ə wā´) (colloq.): in that direction, in that manner, that way >*He took off running thataway.* >*You can't do it thataway—let me show you how.*

THAT'LL

* that'll be the day! (colloq.): that will never happen! >*My lazy son, help with the dishes? That'll be the day!*

— that'll teach [s/one] (to [do s/thing]) (see TEACH)

THAT'S

— **that's (about) the size of it** (see SIZE)

— **that's all she wrote!** (see ALL)

* **that's ... for you** (colloq.): that's characteristic of ... >*That's Lynn for you—she waits till the last minute, but she always comes through.*

* **that's more like it** (colloq.): that's better, that's how I prefer it >*That's more like it! You're showing me some respect now.* >*Yeah, lobster for dinner instead of hamburgers! That's more like it.*

* **that's my boy!** (colloq.): I'm proud of you! congratulations! (said to a male) >*That's my boy! I knew you could do it!*

* **that's my girl!** (colloq.): I'm proud of you! congratulations! (said to a female) >*First prize? That's my girl!*

— **that's rich!** (see RICH)

* **that's that** (colloq.): there is nothing more to be said or done, that's final >*Well, that's that. He was our last hope.* >*I won't agree to it, and that's that.*

— **that's the way the ball bounces** (see BALL)

— **that's the way the cookie crumbles** (see COOKIE)

THEIRSELVES

— **theirselves** (colloq.): themselves >*They just sat down and helped theirselves to everything on the table.*

THEM

* **them** (colloq.): those >*Hey, get them kids away from there!*

— **how do you like** *them* **apples?** (*them* stressed) (sl.): look at this and be envious! notice and admire! >*I got first prize! How do you like them apples?* >*I'm datin' Miss Miami Beach. How do you like them apples?*

THERE

— **[neg.] be all there** (see ALL)

* **have been there** (colloq.): have suffered the same experience >*I know it's tough to quit smoking—I've been there.*

— **in there pitching** (see PITCHING)

— **put it there!** (see PUT)

— **(right) up there** (see UP)

— **somebody/someone up there** (see SOMEBODY)

* **there you go** (sl.): that's right, you're correct >*There you go—that's how to do it.*

* **there you go/are** (colloq.): here/there you have it, witness (what was expected) >*There you are—ham and eggs with wheat toast.* >*Well, there you go. You fooled around and broke it.*

THERE'S

— **like there's no tomorrow** (colloq.): wildly, extravagantly, without moderation >*They were drinking and partying like there was no tomorrow.* >*She's been buying clothes like there's no tomorrow.*

* **there's ... and (then) there's ...** (colloq.): there are different types of ..., not all ... is/are the same >*There's steaks and then there's steaks. You want a T-bone, a sirloin, or what?* >*There's jewelry and there's jewelry. Just what were they selling?*

THICK

— **thick** (colloq.): slow-witted, stupid >*He's kind of thick. You'd better go over it with him again.*

* **in the thick of it/things** (colloq.): in the middle or most active part of (a situation), fully involved in (an activity) >*Whenever anyone talks about politics, you'll find Jensen in the thick of it.* >*The phone always rings when I'm in the thick of things.*

— **lay it on (thick)** (see LAY)

THIN

— **one/a thin dime** (see DIME)

THING–THREADS

THING

* **thing** (sl.): special strong feeling or mental quirk (regarding) >*She's got a real thing for oak antiques.* >*What's with this thing Jones has against musicians?* >*I don't understand his thing for blondes.*

* **a thing or two** (colloq.): a substantial amount (esp. of knowledge) >*He knows a thing or two about diesel engines.* >*I want to tell you a thing or two about what's wrong with the way you run this office.*

* **do [one's] thing** (colloq.): do what [one] is talented or adept at, do what [one] enjoys, live [one's] preferred lifestyle >*OK, you're the mechanic—do your thing.* >*He couldn't take small-town life, so now he's doing his thing in Frisco.*

— **have a good thing going** (see GOOD)

— **have another thing/think coming** (see ANOTHER)

* **[one's] (own) thing** (sl.): [one's] special lifestyle or favorite activity >*Whatever ya wanna do is fine with us—just do your own thing.* >*His thing is listenin' to jazz.* >*She likes sports, but I'm into my own thing.*

— **sure thing** (see SURE)

THINGAMABOB

— **thingamabob** (thing´ə mə bob´) (colloq.): thing, gadget, object (for which one does not know the name) >*I lost that round thingamabob off my fishing reel.*

THINGAMAJIG

— **thingamajig** (thing´ə mə jig´) (colloq.): thing, gadget, object (for which one does not know the name) >*What do you call that thingamajig that's connected to the carburetor?*

THINGS

* **see/hear things** (colloq.): see/hear imaginary things, have hallucinations >*What flying saucer? You're seeing things.* >*Am I hearing things, or is someone in the house?*

— **take things easy** (see EASY)

THINGY

— **thingy** (thing´ē) (colloq.): thing, gadget, object (for which one does not know the name) >*You'd better lift up that thingy on top of the radiator cap first.*

THINK

— **have another thing/think coming** (see ANOTHER)

— **think [one] is God's gift to** (see GOD'S GIFT)

— **think [one] is hot shit** (see HOT SHIT)

— **think [s/one] is hot shit** (see HOT SHIT)

THIRD DEGREE

* **the third degree** (colloq.): intensive questioning (to get information) >*He got the third degree from the cops, but he didn't tell them anything.* >*My parents give me the third degree about every girl I meet.*

THIS

** **this** (colloq.): a certain, some, a >*Then this big guy comes out of nowhere, pulls out this knife, and starts threatening me.*

* **it's like this:** (colloq.): the situation is the following:, this is my explanation: >*Why am I late? It's like this: my wife usually sets the alarm clock, see, and last night …*

* **this is it!** (colloq.): this is the critical moment! >*This is it, Dale! It's our turn.*

THOU

— **thou** (thou) (sl.): thousand (dollars) >*That model sells for around fifty thou.*

THOUSAND

— **bat a thousand** (see BAT)

THREADS

— **threads** (sl.): clothes >*Nice threads, man! Ya look great.*

332

THREE
— **three sheets to/in the wind** (… wind) (sl.): drunk >*Hell, no, he can't drive—he's three sheets to the wind.*

— **three squares** (colloq.): three substantial or nourishing meals (per day) >*They give you a room and three squares for twelve bucks a day.*

THREE-RING CIRCUS
— **three-ring circus** (colloq.): disorderly or noisy place or event, spectacular and confused happening >*They had this huge, fancy wedding—a real three-ring circus.*

THROAT
* **at each other's throat(s)** (colloq.): (for two or more people to be) attacking or fighting each other (esp. verbally, esp. viciously) >*I don't see how they stay married—they're always at each other's throats.*

— **cut [one's] own throat** (see CUT)

— **jump down [s/one's] throat** (see JUMP)

— **shove/ram [s/thing] down [s/one's] throat** (see SHOVE)

THRONE
— **the throne** (sl., hum.): the toilet >*He was sitting on the throne when some lady walked in on him.*

THROUGH
— **through the mill** (see MILL)

— **through the wringer** (see WRINGER)

THROW
** **throw**[1] (vt) (colloq.): give (a party), host (a celebration) >*She loves to throw parties for any occasion.* >*They threw us a big bash for our anniversary.*

* **throw**[2] (vt) (colloq.): mislead, fool, confuse >*Leonard really threw me there for a minute. I thought he was serious.*

— **throw**[3] (vt) (colloq.): lose (a sports competition) on purpose >*If you ask me, that boxer threw the fight.*

— **a throw** (sl.): apiece, each >*His sessions cost a hundred bucks a throw.*

— **throw [s/one] a curve** (colloq.): do (s/thing) unexpected to [s/one], mislead [s/one], take [s/one] by surprise >*Corky really threw me a curve when he took out the girl he knew I liked.*

— **throw/have a fit** (see FIT)

— **throw a monkey wrench into** (colloq.): create an obstacle for, spoil, be an impediment to >*Ruth's visit threw a monkey wrench into our plans for the weekend.*

* **throw [oneself] at** (colloq.): openly flirt with, clearly show [oneself] to be interested in (esp. romantically) >*Just look how she's throwing herself at Linda's husband!*

— **toss/throw back** (see TOSS)

* **throw/knock [s/one] for a loop** (colloq.): greatly surprise or shock [s/one], overwhelm [s/one] >*It threw me for a loop when I read he'd been arrested.* >*That huge bill knocked me for a loop.*

* **throw in** (vt) (colloq.): add for free, give as an extra >*Buy three at the regular price and I'll throw in a fourth one at no extra cost.*

* **throw in the towel** (colloq.): surrender, concede defeat >*There's just no way to do it. I'm ready to throw in the towel.*

— **throw money at** (colloq.): attempt to solve or remedy with money only (esp. a complex situation) >*You're not going to reform education just by throwing money at it.*

— **throw [s/thing] out the window** (colloq.): waste [s/thing], fail to take advantage of [s/thing] (esp. an opportunity) >*He had a chance at a good promotion, but he threw it out the window by demanding too much.*

* **throw the book at** (sl.): bring all possible charges against, give the maximum sentence to >*He'd been* *arrested four times before, so the judge threw the book at him.*

* **throw/slap together** (vt) (colloq.): make or elaborate hurriedly or carelessly >*We can throw together a dinner party for next Saturday, can't we? >Looks like they just slapped that house together.*

** **throw up** (vi, vt) (colloq.): vomit >*I feel sick—I'm going to throw up. >He threw up all that pizza he ate.*

* **throw [one's] weight around** (colloq.): use [one's] power or influence (esp. in a showy or arrogant way) >*The mayor's wife offends a lot of people when she tries to throw her weight around at meetings.*

THROW-UP

* **throw-up** (colloq.): vomit >*I stepped in some throw-up on the bathroom floor.*

THUMB

* **thumb** (vt) (colloq.): hitchhike (one's way) >*I'll see if I can thumb a ride to town. >Our car broke down and we had to thumb it to Fargo. >She thumbed her way across the country.*

— **sit there with [one's] thumb up [one's] ass** (see SIT)

— **stick out like a sore thumb** (see STICK)

THUMBS

* **be all thumbs** (colloq.): have poor dexterity or coordination, be clumsy or awkward >*I'm all thumbs today—I just can't seem to work these pliers right.*

— **twiddle [one's] thumbs** (see TWIDDLE)

THUMBS-DOWN

* **thumbs-down** (colloq.): show of disapproval or denial, neg. response (cf. "THUMBS-UP") >*They'll get a thumbs-down on that dumb idea.*

THUMBS-UP

* **thumbs-up** (colloq.): show of approval or assent, positive response (cf. "THUMBS-DOWN") >*We're ready to go as soon as we get the thumbs-up.*

TICK

* **tick (off)** (vt) (sl.): make angry, infuriate >*That jerk really ticks me off. >Boy, was he ever ticked! His face was red as a beet. >Don't get ticked off about it.*

* **what makes [s/one] tick** (sl.): the motives behind [s/one's] behavior, an analysis of [s/one's] character >*I wanna know what makes that strange character tick.*

TICKER

— **ticker** (sl.): heart >*Doc says my ticker's just fine.*

TICKET

* **the ticket** (colloq.): exactly what is needed, the most advisable action, the best solution >*A big glass of iced tea! That's the ticket on a hot day like this.*

TICKLE

— **tickle** (vt) (colloq.): please, delight or thrill >*This news will tickle him to death.*

TICKLED

* **tickled (pink)** (colloq.): (very much) pleased, delighted or thrilled >*Betty was tickled pink with her new microwave. >We're tickled you could come.*

TICKY-TACKY

— **ticky-tacky** (tik´ē tak´ē) (colloq.): cheap and uncreative, mass-produced and conventional (esp. housing) >*The only thing they could afford was one of those ticky-tacky tract homes built in the fifties.*

TIE

— **tie one on** (sl.): get drunk >*Gracie tied one on at the party last night, so I drove her home.*

* **tie the knot** (colloq.): get married >*They tied the knot just two months after they met.*

* **tie up** (vt) (colloq.): occupy the time and energy of, make busy >*This report will tie me up all afternoon.* >*Give me a call when you're not tied up.*

TIED

— **fit to be tied** (see FIT)

— **tied to [s/one's] apron strings** (colloq.): psychologically dependent on or controlled by [s/one] (referring esp. to a man, by his mother or wife) >*Herbie's really tied to his mother's apron strings—he doesn't make a move without asking her.*

— **with one hand tied behind [one]/ [one's] back** (see HAND)

TIGHT

— **tight** (sl.): drunk >*Walt got pretty tight after downin' those six scotches.*

— **sit tight** (see SIT)

* **tight spot** (colloq.): awkward or difficult situation >*They'll be in a tight spot if their driver is late.*

* **tight (with)** (sl.): on very friendly or confidential terms (with) >*Havens says he's tight with the important people in this town.* >*Jimmy and his partner are real tight.*

— **up tight** (see "UPTIGHT")

TIGHTEN

— **tighten [one's] belt** (colloq.): become frugal, cut back on expenses, endure financial hardships (cf. "BELT-TIGHTENING") >*If business doesn't pick up soon, we're going to have to tighten our belts.*

TIGHTWAD

* **tightwad** (colloq.): very stingy person, miser >*You think that tightwad will pay fifty bucks for a ticket?*

TIMBUKTU

* **Timbuktu** (tim´buk tū´) (colloq.): a faraway or isolated place >*He lives way out in Timbuktu.*

TIME

* **time** (colloq.): term of required service or imprisonment >*She put in her time on the assembly line before getting promoted.* >*Stubby did time for holding up convenience stores.*

— **buy time** (see BUY)

— **every time [s/one] turns around** (see EVERY)

— **give [s/one] a bad time** (see BAD)

* **have a time with** (colloq.): have frequent trouble with, suffer because of >*Stan and Betty have really had a time with that lousy car they bought.* >*They're having a time with that obnoxious son of theirs.*

— **in less than no time** (see LESS)

* **in no time (flat)** (colloq.): in a very short time, very quickly >*At this speed we'll be there in no time flat.* >*I finished the lesson in no time.*

— **long time no see** (see LONG)

** **make (good) time** (colloq.): travel at a (very) satisfactory speed >*We'll make good time now that the truck's unloaded.*

— **make time with** (sl.): be sexually or romantically involved with >*He don't even know the dude's makin' time with his old lady.*

— **take [one's] (sweet) time** (see TAKE)

* **the time of [one's] life** (colloq.): great fun or a very enjoyable experience for [one] >*I had the time of my life on that Caribbean cruise.*

— **...-time loser** (see LOSER)

— **time out!** (sl.): let me interrupt that lie! correct that before continuing! >*Time out! I did not say I'd loan ya the money.*

* **won't (even) give [s/one] the time of day** (colloq.): be very snobbish toward [s/one], ignore [s/one], snub [s/one] contemptuously >*We used to be good friends, but ever since he inherited all that money he won't even give me the time of day.*

TINKLE

— **tinkle** (ting´kəl) (vi) (colloq.): urinate (used esp. with small children) >*Mommy, I got to tinkle.*

TINSELTOWN

— **Tinseltown** (tin´səl toun´) (colloq.): Hollywood, the motion-picture community in and around Hollywood >*The talk of Tinseltown this week is a certain superstar's eight million-dollar contract for an upcoming film.*

TIP

** **tip**[1] (colloq.): helpful hint, suggestion >*Old Herb gave me some tips on fly fishing.*

* **tip**[2] (colloq.): piece of secret or privileged information >*The cops got a tip on his whereabouts.*

* **on the tip of [one's] tongue** (colloq.): almost remembered, barely escaping recollection >*His name was on the tip of my tongue, but I just couldn't come up with it.*

— **tip a few** (sl.): have a few drinks (esp. beers) >*I tipped a few with the guys after work.*

— **tip [one's] hand** (colloq.): reveal [one's] intentions or plans (esp. inadvertently) >*She tipped her hand about her trip when she asked about travel insurance.*

* **tip off** (vt) (colloq.): give secret or privileged information to, reveal (information) to, warn >*They were tipped off by an anonymous caller.* >*Someone tipped them off about the police raid.*

— **tip the scales at** (colloq.): weigh >*I bet that fatso tips the scales at over three hundred pounds.*

TIP-OFF

* **tip-off** (colloq.): revealed information, warning >*The way he was acting all nervous was the tip-off that something was wrong.* >*A guy working for the government gave Brown the tip-off*

about the investigation they were going to do on him.

TIPPYTOE

— **tippytoe** (tip´ē tō´) (vi) (colloq.): tiptoe >*I tried tippytoeing to my room in the dark, but I knocked over a lamp.*

TIPSTER

— **tipster** (tip´stər) (colloq.): person who provides secret or privileged information >*He's got a tipster that feeds him inside information.*

TIPTOP

* **tiptop** (colloq.): excellent, in the highest degree, first-rate >*After four weeks of exercising, Andy's in tiptop shape.* >*You've been doing tiptop work lately.*

TIRED

— **sick and tired (of)** (see SICK)

TIT

** **tit** (tit) (vulg.): (woman's) breast >*She thinks her tits are too small.*

TITS

— **freeze [one's] tits off** (see FREEZE)

TITS AND ASS

* **tits and ass** (tits ...) (vulg.): exhibition of women's breasts and buttocks, soft pornography (also adj.) >*My grandmother gets real upset over the tits and ass ya see in a lot of movies today.* >*They went to some tits and ass show.*

TITTY

— **titty** (tit´ē) (vulg.): (woman's) breast or nipple >*Her titties are about to fall out of that low-cut dress.* >*It was cold, and her titties were hard.*

— **tough titty!** (see TOUGH)

TIZZY

— **in a tizzy** (... tiz´ē) (sl.): very nervous or excited, agitated >*Bowers was all in a tizzy because his ex-wife was threatenin' to sue him for more alimony.*

T.J.

— **T.J.** (colloq.): Tijuana, Baja California Norte, Mexico >*They bought some souvenirs in T.J.*

T.L.C.

* **T.L.C.** (sl.): tender loving care >*Billy will heal up just fine with a little T.L.C.*

TO

— **to go** (see GO)

TO-DO

* **to-do** (colloq.): commotion, fuss, stir >*There was some to-do in the manager's office this morning. You should have heard it.* >*They made a big to-do over her coming home.*

TOE

— **toe the line** (colloq.): conform to the rules, behave in an uncriticizable manner >*You guys got to toe the line because we're going to be reviewed next month.*

TOE JAM

— **toe jam** (sl., freq. vulg.): filth that collects under the toenails and/or between the toes >*You'd think he'd clean that toe jam out if he's gonna wear sandals.*

TOES

* **on [one's] toes** (colloq.): alert, prepared to act >*A good investigator's always on his toes.*

— **step on [s/one's] toes** (see STEP)

TOGETHER

* **together** (sl.): very healthy mentally and emotionally >*Travis is a real together guy.*

— **get/have [one's] act together** (see ACT)

— **get/have [one's] head together** (see HEAD)

* **get/have it together** (sl.): find/have emotional stability, get/have (one's) life in order, resolve/have resolved personal problems >*Ozzie never really got it together after his girl left him.* >*I was in bad shape before, but I have it together now.*

— **get/have [one's] shit together** (see SHIT)

* **go together** (colloq.): date regularly, be sweethearts >*My brother and her are going together.*

— **hang together** (see HANG)

— **run around (together) (with)** (see RUN)

— **throw/slap together** (see THROW)

TOILET

— **(go) in(to)/down the toilet** (sl.): (become) wasted or ruined, (be) lost or squandered >*Our vacation plans went right into the toilet when Bobby got sick.* >*Well, I'd say the dough ya invested in that scheme is down the toilet.*

TOKE

— **toke** (tōk) (sl.): puff of a marijuana cigarette >*He lit a joint and everybody took a couple of tokes.*

TOM

— **every Tom, Dick, and Harry** (see EVERY)

TOMATO

— **tomato** (sl.): attractive young woman >*Who was that tomato I saw Tommy with at the dance?*

TOMCAT

— **tomcat (around)** (vi) (sl.): pursue women to make sexual conquests >*Willy really liked to tomcat around when he was young.* >*I guess Percy's out tomcattin' again tonight.*

TOMMY GUN

— **Tommy gun** (tom´ē…) (colloq.): submachine gun >*The gangsters shot the place up with Tommy guns.*

TOMORROW

— **like there's no tomorrow** (see THERE'S)

TON

— **like a ton of bricks** (colloq.): very heavy (also adv.) >*What've you got in this suitcase? It feels like a ton of bricks.* >*He was running full speed, and he hit me like a ton of bricks.*

TONGUE

— **on the tip of [one's] tongue** (see TIP)

— **[for] the cat [to] have [s/one's] tongue** (see CAT)

TONGUE-LASHING

— **tongue-lashing** (colloq.): severe scolding, verbal reprimand >*Ivan got a good tongue-lashing from his mom for trampling her flowers.*

TONS

** **tons (of ...)** (sl.): much (...), many (...) >*I got tons of things to do today.* >*Help yourself to some more salad—there's tons left.*

TOO

— **have one too many** (see ONE)

— **... *too*!** (stressed) (colloq.): ... indeed! (used to assertively deny s/one's neg. statement) (cf. "[neg.] ... *EITHER*!" >*You liar! I did too pay my share!* >*Don't say he's not a good player! He is too!*

— **too big for [one's] britches** (see BIG)

* **too much** (colloq.): extraordinary, impressive >*That crazy friend of yours is too much.* >*You got arrested for littering? Too much!*

— **too rich for [s/one's] blood** (see RICH)

TOOL

— **tool¹** (vulg.): penis >*Ya wouldn't have believed the tool on the dude in that porno movie!*

— **tool²** (vi) (colloq.): travel in a vehicle (esp. at a fast and steady pace) >*We were tooling down the road doing about seventy when a cop pulled us over.*

TOOT

— **toot** (sl.): cocaine >*They say he always does a little toot before he performs.*

— **blow/toot [one's] own horn** (see BLOW)

TOOTING

— **you're darn tooting ...!** (... därn ...) (sl.): ... is the truth! absolutely ...! have no doubt that ...! >*You're darn tootin' I'm gonna demand a refund!*

TOO-TOO

— **too-too** (colloq.): overly affected, pretentious, excessively elaborate >*His fancy house is just too-too, if you ask me.*

TOOTS

— **toots** (tŭts) (voc.) (sl., freq. pej.): girl, lady (used esp. in a presumptuously affectionate way) >*Hey, toots, come and sit with me a minute.*

TOOTSIE

— **tootsie** (tŭt´sē) (sl., freq. pej.): young woman, (female) sweetheart (esp. an attractive one) (also voc.) >*He showed up with some tootsie he met at a bar.* >*He's got a couple of tootsies in Louisville.* >*Hey, tootsie, wanna drink?*

TOOTSY

— **tootsy¹** (see "TOOTSIE")

— **tootsy²** (tŭt´sē) (sl., freq. hum.): foot >*These wool socks should keep your little tootsies warm.* >*He's got a blister on his tootsy.*

TOP

** **top** (vt) (colloq.): surpass, provide s/thing better than >*I bet you can't top this story.* >*He offered me the whole package for six hundred bucks. If you can top that, you got a deal.*

— **blow [one's] top** (see BLOW)

* **come out on top** (colloq.): win, prevail, gain the advantage >*Simpson wasn't a favorite in the tournament, but he managed to come out on top.*

* **from the top** (colloq.): from the beginning (esp. of s/thing being rehearsed or repeated) >*OK, people, try it again, from the top.* >*Let's hear your version of what happened, from the top.*

* **off the top** (colloq.): before any is spent or distributed >*As soon as you get the dough, I want my share off the top.*

** **off the top of [one's] head** (colloq.): extemporaneously, without deliberating, impromptu >*Off the top of my head, I'd say it would cost around twenty thousand.*

* **on top of**[1] (colloq.): in addition to, besides >*Then I got a headache on top of all my other problems.* >*He makes good money in commissions on top of his base salary.*

* **on top of**[2] (colloq.): fully informed of, having the latest information about >*Sam's a real baseball fan—he's on top of everything going on in the majors.*

* **on top of**[3] (colloq.): in control of, prepared to deal effectively with >*There's a problem in the number two generator, but Kingsley's on top of it.*

* **on top of**[4] (colloq.): very close to >*The little apartment where they had the party was really crowded—people were on top of each other.* >*We were on top of the campsite before we recognized it.*

— **sleep like a top** (see **SLEEP**)

— **the (top) brass** (see **BRASS**)

* **top banana** (sl.): chief person, leader, highest person in a hierarchy (cf. "**SECOND banana**") >*A decision this big has to come from the top banana.*

— **top dog** (colloq.): person in the highest position of power or authority (esp. in a highly competitive situation) >*Whitley's been top dog around here ever since the big merger a year ago.*

* **top dollar** (colloq.): the highest possible payment >*I'll give you top dollar for those stamps if they're in prime condition.*

— **top of the heap** (sl.): superior position of power or authority (esp. in a very competitive situation) >*He ain't aggressive enough to get to the top of the heap.*

TOP-DRAWER

— **top-drawer** (colloq.): of the highest quality or prestige >*Her sculptures are top-drawer stuff.*

TOP-NOTCH

* **top-notch** (colloq.): excellent, of highest quality, first-rate >*I want only top-notch experts working on this.*

TOPS

* **(the) tops** (colloq.): the best, the most impressive or outstanding >*We've seen some good plays, but this one was the tops.* >*She's tops in her field.*

* **... tops** (colloq.): ... maximum, at the most ... >*He makes sixty thousand a year tops in that position.*

TORCH

— **torch**[1] (sl.): arsonist (esp. one who sets fires for money) >*He hired some torch to burn his store down so he could collect on the insurance.*

— **torch**[2] (vt) (sl.): set fire to, commit arson on >*The hood threatened to torch my house.*

— **carry a torch for** (see **CARRY**)

TORCH SONG

— **torch song** (colloq.): popular song that laments failed or unrequited love >*She sat around listening to nothing but torch songs for weeks after their breakup.*

TORPEDO

— **torpedo** (vt) (colloq.): destroy, undermine, sabotage >*Somebody on the review committee torpedoed my proposal.*

TOSS

* **toss**[1] (vt) (colloq.): flip a coin with (s/one) (to determine s/thing) >*I'll toss you for the last piece of pie.* >*They tossed us to see who'd go first.*

* **toss**[2] (vt) (colloq.): throw away, discard >*Why don't you toss that rusty old lamp?*

* **toss around** (vt) (colloq.): discuss, air >*We tossed around a few ideas for the event.* >*Let's toss it around awhile before we decide.*

— **toss/throw back** (vt) (sl.): drink or eat (esp. enthusiastically) >*Hey, wanna toss back a few beers over at Danny's?* >*I threw back some bacon and eggs and took off.*

— **toss [one's] cookies** (sl.): vomit >*Suzie got carsick and tossed her cookies out the window.*

— **toss [one's] lunch** (sl.): vomit >*I felt so sick I thought I was gonna toss my lunch right then and there.*

— **toss off** (vt) (colloq.): ignore (criticism or an insult), not let (s/thing) bother (one) >*He called me a liar, but I just tossed it off.* >*It's hard to just toss off an insult like that.*

TOSSUP

** **tossup** (colloq.): even chance, choice between equals >*The championship this year is pretty much a tossup between our team and theirs.* >*For me it's a tossup between cherry pie and chocolate cake for dessert.*

TOTAL

** **total** (vt) (sl.): wreck completely (esp. an automobile) >*Art totaled his new Jaguar last weekend, but he didn't get hurt.*

TOTALLY

* **totally** (sl.): very, extraordinarily >*The concert was, like, totally awesome, man.* >*She's a totally gorgeous babe.*

TOTEM POLE

— **low/bottom man on the totem pole** (see LOW)

TOUCH

— **cannot touch** (vt) (colloq.): is/are not at all competitive with, is/are not nearly of the quality of >*Our competitors can't touch us on customer service.* >*No one can touch him when it comes to convincing juries.*

— **put the touch on** (sl.): try to get or borrow money from >*Why don't ya put the touch on your old man for the fifty bucks ya need?*

* **touch all bases** (colloq.): be thorough, make every contact necessary >*The detectives touched all bases in their investigation.*

* **touch base(s) (with)** (colloq.): make contact (with), communicate (with) (esp. to confer) >*We'll touch bases again before a final decision is made.* >*You should touch base with Jean before you mention that to anyone.*

* **wouldn't touch [s/thing, s/one] with a ten-foot pole** (sl.): want nothing to do with [s/thing, s/one], be very wary of [s/thing, s/one] >*I wouldn't touch that floozy with a ten-foot pole.* >*That whole situation's a big mess—they wouldn't touch it with a ten-foot pole.*

TOUCHIE-FEELIE

— **touchie-feelie** (tuch´ē fē´lē) (sl., sarc.): overly concerned with human sensitivity >*She belongs to one of those touchie-feelie groups where everyone dumps their problems on everyone else, and then they go around huggin' each other.*

TOUGH

** **tough¹** (colloq., freq. sarc.): unfortunate, difficult >*I've had some tough breaks lately.* >*Aw, that's tough. Her Rolls Royce got a little scratch.* >*Tough luck! I win and you lose.*

— **tough²** (sl.): excellent, attractive >*Wow, what a tough new bike!* >*He's goin' out with a really tough chick.*

— **hang tough** (see HANG)

— **tough nut** (see NUT)

— **hard/tough nut to crack** (see NUT)

* **tough out** (vt) (colloq.): persevere through, endure, continue struggling against >*Some bad times are coming, and we're going to have to tough them out.* >*Hang in there, Spike! Tough it out, man.*

* **tough shit!** (... shit) (vulg., sarc.): that's (s/one's) bad luck! >*Tough shit, dummy! You're the one that screwed it up.*

— **tough titty!** (… tit´ē) (vulg., sarc.): that's (s/one's) bad luck! >*Your team lost? Tough titty, man! What do ya want me to do about it?*

TOUGHIE

— **toughie** (tuf´ē) (colloq.): strong and aggressive person, bully >*Would you believe Reverend Canton used to be the school toughie?*

TOURISTA

— **the tourista(s)** (see "the TURISTA[s]")

TOURIST TRAP

* **tourist trap** (colloq.): establishment that exploits tourists (esp. by charging high prices for low quality) >*Don't eat at the places that guide recommends— they're all tourist traps.*

TOWEL

— **throw in the towel** (see THROW)

TOWN

— **go to town (on)** (colloq.): do (s/thing) fast and well, do (s/thing) energetically or enthusiastically >*She went to town on that crossword puzzle and finished it in ten minutes.* >*Jerome's really hungry—set those ribs down in front of him and watch him go to town.*

* **on the town** (colloq.): enjoying a city's entertainment and pleasures (esp. its nightlife) >*The sailors really enjoy their first night out on the town when they come into port.*

— **paint the town (red)** (see PAINT)

— **skip town** (see SKIP)

T.P.

— **T.P.**[1] (colloq.): toilet paper >*Hey, we need a new roll of T.P. in here.*

— **T.P.**[2] (vt) (sl.): cover (a house and/or surrounding trees and shrubs) with streamers of toilet paper (as a prank) >*Some high school kids T.P.ed Suzie's house last night.*

TRACK

* **the track** (colloq.): a racetrack (esp. for horses) >*He blows all his money betting at the track.*

TRACKS

— **tracks** (sl.): needle marks from habitual injection of drugs >*Sure he's a junkie. Didn't ya see the tracks on his arm?*

* **in [one's] tracks** (colloq.): right where [one] is/was (at a given moment) >*They spotted him and shot him in his tracks.* >*I stopped in my tracks when I heard the scream.*

— **make tracks** (sl.): take off, leave quickly, go fast >*We made tracks when he pulled a knife.*

— **the right side of the tracks** (see RIGHT)

— **the wrong side of the tracks** (see WRONG)

TRADE

— **trick of the trade** (see TRICK)

TRAFFIC

— **stop traffic** (see STOP)

TRAIL

— **hit the trail** (see HIT)

TRAIPSE

— **traipse** (trāps) (vi) (colloq.): move or walk aimlessly (s/where), go around without reaching an objective >*They were traipsing through the woods, holding hands.* >*I traipsed all over trying to find the right size curtains.*

TRAMP

* **tramp** (colloq.): sexually promiscuous or unscrupulous woman >*He left his wife for some tramp that works at his office.*

TRAP

* **trap** (sl.): mouth (esp. seen as the instrument of undesirable talk) >*Now, don't open your trap about what we saw.*

— **shut [one's] trap** (see SHUT)

TRASH

* **trash[1]** (vt) (sl.): destroy, heavily damage, vandalize >*Give 'em their money back or they're gonna trash the theatre.*

— **trash[2]** (vt) (sl.): severely criticize, give a very negative review or evaluation of >*Why is that reporter trashin' the councilman? >The critics trashed his movie.*

TRASHY

* **trashy** (colloq.): obscene, vulgar >*He keeps buying those trashy girlie magazines. >What trashy language she uses!*

TRAVEL

— **travel** (vi) (colloq.): move fast >*That car was traveling! It passed me like I was standing still.*

TREAT

* **treat [s/one] like dirt** (colloq.): treat [s/one] unjustly or with contempt, mistreat [s/one] >*I don't know why Amy puts up with him—he treats her like dirt.*

TREE

— **barking up the wrong tree** (see BARKING)

— **out of [one's] tree** (sl.): crazy, very irrational >*The guy's outta his tree to flirt with his boss's wife.*

— **up a tree** (colloq.): in a difficult situation, in a predicament or dilemma >*Betsy's up a tree. She's already signed a contract, but she just got a much better offer.*

TRENCHES

— **in the trenches** (colloq.): in the basic and difficult circumstances of a job or profession >*Rollins put in eight years in the trenches before being promoted.*

TRENDY

— **trendy[1]** (tren´dē) (colloq.): person who follows the latest trends, person who always seeks to be in fashion >*All the trendies shop at that store.*

* **trendy[2]** (colloq.): following the last trends, in fashion >*She buys trendy clothes because she wants to be in style.*

TRIBE

— **tribe** (colloq.): large family or group of relatives, kinfolk >*Mom still has the whole tribe over for dinner on Sundays.*

TRICK

* **trick[1]** (sl.): prostitute's sexual transaction >*Some call girls get five hundred bucks a trick.*

— **trick[2]** (sl.): prostitute's customer >*Her trick beat her up.*

* **do the trick[1]** (colloq.): bring about the desired result >*Move the antenna a little—that should do the trick.*

— **do the trick[2]** (vulg.): readily have sex, grant sexual favors (said of a woman) >*He says she did the trick for him on their first date.*

— **every trick in the book** (see EVERY)

— **not miss a trick** (see MISS)

— **the oldest trick in the book** (see OLDEST)

* **trick of the trade** (colloq.): special skill or restricted knowledge (to help one succeed in a given profession or activity) >*Knowing how to handle reporters is an important trick of the trade. >Sawyer's an old pro—he knows all the tricks of the trade.*

— **turn a trick** (sl.): engage in an act of prostitution >*He wanted her to turn a trick right then and there. >She turns tricks in that motel.*

TRICKS

— **how's tricks?** (see HOW'S)

TRIG

* **trig** (trig) (colloq.): trigonometry (esp. as a course of study) >*She got a B in music and an A in trig.*

TRIGGER

— **quick on the draw/trigger** (see QUICK)

TRIGGER-HAPPY
— **trigger-happy** (colloq.): tending to fire a firearm with little reason or provocation >*He says the police in that town are real trigger-happy.*

TRIGGERMAN
— **triggerman** (sl.): person who shoots s/one (esp. when hired to do it) >*Who was the triggerman on the O'Reilly murder?*

TRIKE
— **trike** (trīk) (colloq.): tricycle >*Dad just backed the car over Willy's trike.*

TRIP
* **trip**[1] (sl.): drug-induced psychedelic experience, drug intoxication >*You can have a real bad trip on L.S.D., man.*

— **trip**[2] (sl.): extraordinary person or thing, exciting or emotional experience >*Your friend with all the problems is a real trip.* >*Goin' over those rapids was a trip!*

— **trip**[3] (sl.): lifestyle, absorbing interest >*His trip is makin' all the money he can.* >*The exercise trip just isn't for me, so go joggin' by yourself.*

— **trip (out)**[1] (vt) (sl.): have a drug-induced psychedelic experience, become intoxicated by drugs >*He was really trippin' after he smoked a little crack.* >*Some tripped-out kid walked right out in front of the bus.*

— **trip (out)**[2] (vi) (sl.): enjoy (s/thing) very much, experience great pleasure or excitement >*Everyone was trippin' out at the concert.*

TRIPE
— **tripe** (sl.): nonsense, worthless opinion(s) >*Do ya really believe that tripe she was givin' us?*

TRIPLE
— **double/triple whammy** (see WHAMMY)

TROMP
* **tromp** (tromp) (vt) (sl.): defeat decisively, beat up >*They thought they were the best, but they got tromped.* >*That huge guy'll tromp ya.*

TROT
— **hot to trot** (see HOT)

— **trot out** (vt) (colloq., sarc.): bring out for display, present (esp. pointlessly or routinely) >*He trotted out half the company's executives to support his case.* >*I hope Burt doesn't trot out more of his travel slides.*

TROTS
— **the trots** (sl.): diarrhea >*I got the trots after eatin' in that cheap joint.*

TROUBLE
— **in trouble** (colloq.): pregnant (when unmarried) >*I heard she left town because her boyfriend got her in trouble.*

TRUCKING
* **keep on trucking** (sl.): carry on, keep at it, not give up >*There's gonna be good times and bad—ya gotta just keep on truckin'.*

TRUST
— **trust [s/one] (about) as far as [one] can throw [him/her]** (sl.): not trust [s/one] at all >*I'd better get a receipt from that clown—I trust him about as far as I can throw him.*

TRY
** **try** (vt) (colloq.): attempt to get in touch with (esp. by telephone) >*If there's no answer at my house, try me at the office.*

TUB
— **tub of lard** (colloq., pej.): very fat person >*I'm afraid that tub of lard's going to break the chair.*

TUBBY
— **tubby** (tub´ē) (colloq.): short and fat (also voc.; pej. when voc.) >*Why doesn't she put that tubby kid of hers on a diet?* >*Don't break the scales, tubby.*

TUBE

* **(go) down the tube(s)** (sl.): (become) wasted or ruined, (be) lost or squandered >*All our plans went down the tube 'cause the boss made me work that weekend.* >*All that money's down the tubes.*

** **the tube** (sl.): television >*Anything good on the tube tonight?*

TUCK

— **tuck away** (vt) (colloq.): eat or drink >*We tucked away a few burritos and beers before we left.*

TUCKER

— **tucker out** (vt) (colloq.): tire, fatigue >*That hike tuckered her out.* >*I'm tuckered out after eight hours in that madhouse where I work.*

TUFF

— **tuff** (see "TOUGH²")

TUMMY

** **tummy** (tum´ē) (colloq.): stomach, belly (used esp. with children) >*Mommy, my tummy hurts.*

TUMMY TUCK

— **tummy tuck** (tum´ē …) (colloq.): plastic surgery to remove excess fat and skin around the stomach, abdominoplasty >*She didn't lose that on a diet—I bet she had a tummy tuck.*

TUNE

— **change [one's] tune** (see CHANGE)

* **to the tune of** (colloq.): in the amount of (esp. when considered substantial) >*He'll be making house payments to the tune of two thousand a month.*

* **tune in** (vt) (sl.): pay attention to, heed (cf. "TUNE out") >*I just can't get my teenage son to tune me in.*

* **tune out** (vt) (sl.): pay no attention to, not heed (cf. "TUNE in") >*Stephanie can't get anything across to him—he just tunes her out.*

TURD

* **turd¹** (tûrd) (vulg.): piece of excrement >*Watch out for those dog turds on the sidewalk there.*

* **turd²** (vulg.): contemptible or reprehensible person >*I don't want that turd anywhere near me.*

TURF

* **[one's] turf** (sl.): [one's] area of authority or domination, [one's] territory >*That gang don't let nobody from outside on their turf.* >*This's my turf, where I grew up.*

TURISTA

— **the turista(s)** (… tŭ´rē stə[z]) (sl.): diarrhea affecting travelers (esp. abroad) >*I got the turistas real bad in North Africa.*

TURKEY

* **turkey¹** (sl.): stupid person, foolish and contemptible person >*Willis talked some turkey into puttin' up the dough for his scheme.*

— **turkey²** (sl.): inferior and unsuccessful production or venture >*She starred in some turkey that got trashed by the critics.* >*How'd I get involved in this project? It's a turkey.*

— **talk turkey** (colloq.): speak frankly and substantively, discuss the essentials >*Enough pleasantries—let's talk turkey.*

TURN

— **every time [s/one] turns around** (see EVERY)

— **turn a trick** (see TRICK)

** **turn down** (vt) (colloq.): reject, refuse >*Grady's all depressed because he was turned down for the job.* >*He offered me a hundred dollars, but I turned it down.*

* **turn in** (vi) (colloq.): go to bed, retire for the evening >*We'd better turn in— we got to get up early in the morning.*

** **turn off¹** (vt) (sl.): disgust, make (s/one) lose interest >*He's OK, but his bad* *breath turns me off.* >*Jack gets turned off by pushy salesmen.*

— **turn off²** (vi) (sl.): stop paying attention, become uninterested >*He just turns off when ya try to talk to him about his problems.*

** **turn on** (vt) (sl.): stimulate, create desire or excitement in, arouse >*She really got turned on by that archeological dig she helped with.* >*They say kinky sex is what turns him on.*

— **stop/turn on a dime** (see **DIME**)

— **(turn on) the waterworks** (see **WATERWORKS**)

* **turn on (to)** (vt) (sl.): create desire or excitement in (for), stimulate to use or enjoy (s/thing) >*Alfie didn't take drugs till Joanna turned him on to pot.* >*He got turned on to collectin' baseball cards when he was a kid.*

* **turn out** (vi) (colloq.): attend (a gathering or event) >*I hope enough people turn out so we don't lose any money.*

* **turn (over)/spin in [one's] grave** (colloq.): be scandalized or outraged (said of the dead) >*Bach must turn over in his grave whenever they play rock versions of his music.* >*Grandma would be spinning in her grave if she heard you use such trashy language.*

— **turn tail** (colloq.): turn and run, flee, retreat >*They turned tail when he pulled out a gun.*

— **turn yellow** (see **YELLOW**)

TURNOFF

* **turnoff** (sl.): thing or person that makes (s/one) lose interest or become disgusted (cf. "TURNON") >*His bony legs are a complete turnoff.* >*The guy's a turnoff with all those gruntin' noises he makes.*

TURNON

turnon (sl.): thing or person that stimulates or arouses, thing or person that creates desire or excitement (in s/one) (cf. "TURNOFF") >*The way that dress clings to her is a turnon.* >*The waves were perfect—a real turnon for the surfers.*

TURNOUT

* **turnout** (colloq.): attendance (at a gathering or event) >*They had a good turnout at the company picnic.*

TUSH

* **tush** (tŭsh) (sl.): rump, buttocks >*She thinks he's got a cute tush.*

TUX

** **tux** (tuks) (colloq.): tuxedo >*He looks great in a tux.*

TWAT

— **twat¹** (twät) (vulg.): vagina >*He said the picture showed her twat.*

— **twat²** (vulg., pej.): woman >*That sexist jerk called her a dumb twat.*

— **twat³** (vulg., pej.): woman or women (seen as sex object[s]) >*He says there's a lot of good-lookin' twat in that town.*

TWERP

— **twerp** (twûrp) (sl.): contemptibly insignificant person (esp. an offensive young or small one) >*If that little twerp mouths off once more, I'm gonna let him have it.*

TWIDDLE

* **twiddle [one's] thumbs** (twid'l ...) (colloq.): be idle, take no action >*We can't have our staff just sitting around twiddling their thumbs.*

TWIRP

— **twirp** (see "TWERP")

TWIST

* **twist [s/one's] arm** (colloq.): coerce [s/one], force [s/one] (to do s/thing) >*I didn't have to twist his arm to take a second helping of stew.*

— **wrap/twist [s/one] around [one's] little finger** (see **WRAP**)

TWISTER

* **twister** (colloq.): tornado >*The twister took the roof right off the house.*

TWIT

— **twit** (twit) (colloq.): foolish and bothersome person >*I don't want that twit getting in my way.* >*Not that way, you twit!*

TWO

— **a thing or two** (see THING)

* **(already) have two strikes against [one]** (colloq.): be in a very disadvantageous situation, have much working against [one] >*With his prison record and lack of experience he's already got two strikes against him when he applies for a job.*

— **have two left feet** (see LEFT)

— **it takes two to tango** (see TAKES)

* **put two and two together** (colloq.): make a deduction, draw a conclusion based on the facts, finally realize (s/thing) >*I finally put two and two together—it was Jim she was talking about, not his brother.*

— **stand on [one's] (own) two feet** (see STAND)

TWO-BIT

* **two-bit** (sl.): inferior, contemptibly insignificant >*He's some two-bit actor that can't remember his lines.* >*I don't wanna play for no two-bit team like theirs.*

TWO-BY-FOUR

— **two-by-four** (colloq.): cramped, unspacious >*How can you stand to live in this crummy little two-by-four apartment?*

TWO CENTS

* **put in [one's] two cents (worth)** (colloq.): state [one's] opinion, have [one's] say (esp. when unsolicited) >*He just had to put in his two cents worth at the meeting.*

TWO-TIME

* **two-time** (vt) (sl.): be unfaithful to, betray >*Mark thinks she's an angel, but she's two-timin' him with one of his buddies.* >*I don't know why she stays married to that two-timin' husband of hers.*

TWO-WAY STREET

* **two-way street** (colloq.): situation involving responsibilities on the part of two parties (and not just one), reciprocal situation >*Being friends is a two-way street—don't expect me to give in all the time.*

TYPE

* **... type** (colloq.): individual who typifies (a) ... (situation or occupation) >*Some big criminal type threatened to beat him up.* >*She don't care for them intellectual types.*

** **[one's] type** (colloq.): type of person [one] would be romantically interested in >*Roger's nice, but he's not her type.*

TYPO

** **typo** (tī´pō) (colloq.): typographical error >*I can't send this letter out—it's full of typos.*

U

U.
— the U. (colloq.): university >*She's taking a night class at the U.*

U.F.O.
** U.F.O. (colloq.): unidentified flying object, flying saucer >*He swears a U.F.O. landed in his backyard.*

UGLIER
— uglier than sin (sl.): very ugly >*If ya ask me, his paintings are uglier than sin.*

UGLY
— (as) ugly as sin (sl.): very ugly >*Her husband's ugly as sin, but he sure is nice.*

UH
* uh oh! (u´ō´) (colloq.): (interj. to express dismay when noting a neg. occurrence) >*Uh oh! The electricity just went off.* >*Uh oh! I guess I just ruined the surprise.*

UH-HUH
** uh-huh (u hu´/ū hū´) (colloq.): yes >*Uh-huh—it's fine with me.*

UH-UH
— uh-uh (u´u/ū´ū) (see "HUH-UH")

UMP
* ump (ump) (colloq.): umpire (in sports) (also voc.) >*It was a close play, but the ump called him out.* >*You need glasses, ump!*

UMPTEEN
* umpteen (ump´tēn´) (sl.): innumerable, very many >*I can give ya umpteen reasons why ya shouldn't go there.*

UMPTEENTH
* umpteenth (ump´tēnth´) (sl.): of a large number in succession >*I'm tellin' ya for the umpteenth time to keep quiet!*

UNCLE
— say/cry uncle (sl.): surrender, concede defeat >*Say uncle or I'll twist your arm harder!*

UNCLE SAM
* Uncle Sam (colloq.): the United States, the United States government >*They get theirselves in debt, then expect Uncle Sam to help them out.*

UNCOOL
— uncool (sl.): behaviorally undesirable, unstylish, unsophisticated >*Yellin' at your date like that was definitely uncool.*

UNDER
— get under [s/one's] skin (see SKIN)

— hot under the collar (see HOT)

— keep [s/thing] under [one's] hat (see KEEP)

— out from under (see OUT)

— (just) under the wire (see WIRE)

— (right) under [s/one's] (very) nose (see NOSE)

— six feet under (see SIX)

— under (the/[one's]) ... (see entry under ... noun)

UNDER-THE-TABLE
* under-the-table (colloq.): secret, clandestine (esp. business deals) (cf. "under the TABLE") >*He acquired it in an under-the-table deal with some strange company downtown.*

UNDIES
* undies (un´dēz) (colloq.): underwear >*It was so hot I just sat in front of a fan in my undies.*

UNGLUED
* come unglued (sl.): lose emotional control, become very upset or frantic >*When Mack saw his wife smiling at another man, he came unglued.*

UNHAPPY
— happy/unhappy camper (see CAMPER)

UNLOAD
* unload (vt) (colloq.): get rid of >*I want to unload this piece of junk.* >*See if you can unload that clown and I'll show you*

a good time. >*Don't unload that report on me.*

* **unload (on)** (sl.): relieve (oneself) (of worries, tension, etc.) by talking (to) >*Whenever Brenda's feelin' anxious, she unloads on me.* >*He's stressed out—he needs to see a shrink and unload.*

UNREAL

* **unreal** (colloq.): extraordinary, fantastic >*The lush vegetation in Hawaii is unreal.* >*Unreal, man! Did you see that?*

UNWIND

** **unwind** (un wīnd) (vi) (colloq.): relax, get rid off (one's) tension or anxiety >*A glass of wine helps me unwind at the end of the day.*

UP

* **up** (colloq.): very positive, warranting optimism >*It's been an up day—lots of good things happened.*

* **be up**[1] (colloq.): be going on, be happening >*I could tell something big was up by the look on their faces.* >*What's up? Why all the commotion?*

* **be up**[2] (colloq.): be cheerful or elated >*Tricia's really up today because she found out she made the team.*

* **be up**[3] (colloq.): be in working order (esp. after a breakdown) >*I'll finish when the computer's back up.* >*The repairman finally got the second unit up.*

* **be/feel up to** (colloq.): be/feel able to engage in, be/feel disposed or inclined to >*I'm not up to a game of tennis right now.* >*Do you feel up to painting the house today?*

— **drive [s/one] up the/a wall** (see **DRIVE**)

— **have ... up the ass** (see **ASS**)

— **have ... up the ying-yang** (see **YING-YANG**)

— **[for s/one's] number [to] be up** (see **NUMBER**)

* **on the up and up** (colloq.): honest, sincere, legitimate (also adv.) >*Stop worrying! It's all on the up and up.* >*Let's do this on the up and up to keep the auditors happy.*

— **(right) up/down [s/one's] alley** (see **ALLEY**)

* **(right) up there** (colloq.): among the best, one of the leaders >*I don't know if it's the best restaurant in town, but it's right up there.*

— **somebody/someone up there** (see **SOMEBODY**)

— **swear up and down** (see **SWEAR**)

— **... up** (colloq.): (tied) ... to ..., ... each (a score) >*It's nineteen up, with two minutes left to play.*

— **... up a storm** (see **STORM**)

— **up a tree** (see **TREE**)

— **up and ...** (colloq.): ... suddenly or unexpectedly >*Uncle Jeb just up and died last year.*

* **up and at 'em!** (... əm) (colloq.): get up and get started! >*Up and at 'em, boys! It's daylight and we got work to do.*

* **up for** (colloq.): enthusiastic and ready for, excited to engage in >*The team's really up for the game today.*

— **up for grabs** (see **GRABS**)

** **up front** (colloq.): paid in advance >*We got to have twenty percent up front before we even start a job.*

— **up in the air** (see **AIR**)

** **up on** (colloq.): well-informed about, up-to-date in (one's) knowledge about >*I try to keep up on what's going on in the world.* >*Are you up on word processing software?*

— **up shit creek** (see **SHIT**)

— **up [one's] sleeve** (see **SLEEVE**)

— **up the creek (without a paddle)** (see **CREEK**)

— **up tight** (see "**UPTIGHT**")

— **up to ([one's])** ... (see entry under ... word)

— **up your ass!** (see ASS)

— **up yours!** (see YOURS)

UPBEAT
— **upbeat** (colloq.): cheerful, optimistic >*Give me an upbeat song over a sad one any day.* >*You can't get him down—he's a real upbeat guy.*

UPCHUCK
— **upchuck** (vi, vt) (sl.): vomit >*I feel like I'm gonna upchuck after that roller-coaster ride.* >*She upchucked her dinner.*

UP-FRONT
* **up-front** (colloq.): straightforward, frank >*I like an up-front guy—you always know what he thinks.* >*I've been up-front with you, so you do the same with me.*

UPPER
* **upper**[1] (up´ər) (sl.): stimulant drug (esp. an amphetamine in pill form) >*He took a couple of uppers to stay awake, but he's gonna come down anytime now.*

— **upper**[2] (sl.): experience that causes elation or cheerfulness >*George is really a great guy—bein' around him's an upper.* >*Seein' that poor kid walk again was a real upper.*

UPPER CRUST
* **upper crust** (colloq.): highest social class >*Very exclusive restaurant—only the upper crust eats there.*

UPPER-CRUST
— **upper-crust** (colloq.): of the highest social class, snobbish >*Some upper-crust dame just walked in and started ordering everyone around.*

UPPITY
— **uppity** (up´i tē) (colloq.): snobbish, haughty, presumptuous (also adv.) >*His uppity in-laws are always putting on airs.* >*Don't you talk uppity to me!*

UPROAR
— **get [one's] bowels in an uproar** (see BOWELS)

UPSCALE
— **upscale** (colloq.): high-class, elegant, posh >*This street has all the expensive, upscale shops.*

UPSIDE
— **upside** (colloq.): positive side, pros (of a situation or matter) (cf. "DOWNSIDE") >*The upside of his proposal is that it would give us the freedom to act, but the downside is that we'll have to take the blame if something goes wrong.*

UPSTAIRS
* **upstairs**[1] (sl.): mentally, in the brain >*Ya gotta understand the poor guy ain't too sharp upstairs.*

— **upstairs**[2] (sl.): at a high level of power or authority >*We'll have to let the execs upstairs see this before we act on it.*

— **the Man upstairs** (see MAN)

UPSY-DAISY
— **upsy-daisy!** (up´sē dā´zē) (colloq.): (interj. used when lifting s/one up to reassure him/her, esp. a child) >*Ready, Patty? OK, hold on. Now, upsy-daisy!*

UPTIGHT
* **uptight**[1] (sl.): tense, nervous, angry >*Don't be so uptight, man—everything's cool.* >*The teacher got real uptight when Debbie talked back to him.*

* **uptight**[2] (sl.): overly formal or concerned about conventions >*Some uptight old lady got real mad when I said "shit."*

UPTOWN
— **uptown** (colloq.): high-class, stylish, elegant >*Man, you guys got real uptown accommodations here.*

USE
* **use** (vi) (sl.): use (drugs), take (a dose of drugs) >*He denies it, but I know he uses—just look at his eyes.*

U-Y

— **pull/make a U-y** (… yū´ē) (sl.): make a
U-turn >*Just pull a U-y and head
back.*

V

VAMOOSE

— **vamoose** (va mūs´) (vi) (sl.): leave quickly, flee >*They heard sirens and decided to vamoose.*

— **vamoose!** (sl.): go away! >*Hey, you kids—vamoose!*

VARMINT

— **varmint** (vär´mənt) (colloq.): contemptible or reprehensible person >*That varmint better not show his face around here.*

V.D.

** **V.D.** (colloq.): venereal disease >*He says he got V.D. from her.*

VEEP

— **veep** (vēp) (colloq.): vice president >*He's the new administrative veep.*

VEGAS

** **Vegas** (vā´gəs) (colloq.): Las Vegas, Nevada >*He lost over $5000 in Vegas.*

VEGETABLE

* **vegetable** (colloq.): severely incapacitated person, comatose person >*Poor guy's been nothing but a vegetable since the accident.*

VEGGIE

** **veggie** (vej´ē) (sl.): vegetable >*I like fresh veggies more than meat.*

VEGGY

— **veggy** (see "VEGGIE")

VET

** **vet**[1] (vet) (colloq.): veteran (of the armed forces) >*He's a Vietnam vet.*

** **vet**[2] (colloq.): veterinarian >*The vet said Bowser's going to be OK.*

VETTE

* **Vette** (vet) (sl.): Chevrolet Corvette automobile >*He tears around town in a red Vette.*

VIBES

* **vibes** (vībz) (sl.): general feeling or emotional signals (regarding s/thing or s/one) >*I didn't like the vibes I was gettin' from that joker.* >*I got good vibes from that school, so that's where I wanna go.*

VIBRATIONS

* **vibrations** (colloq.): general feeling or emotional signals (regarding s/thing or s/one) >*Let's get out of here—I'm getting bad vibrations from this place.*

VIDEO

** **video** (colloq.): videocassette, program taped on a videocassette >*We rented a video and stayed home last night.*

VILLE

— **...ville** (... ´vil´) (sl.): a very ... thing or experience, a place of great ... (used with adjs. and nouns) (cf. "...SVILLE") >*That roller coaster is wildville!* >*Football practice was tortureville.*

VINEGAR

— **full of pee/piss and vinegar** (see FULL)

V.I.P

** **V.I.P.** (colloq.): very important person (also adj.) >*We'll seat all the V.I.P.s at the head table.* >*They were impressed with the V.I.P. treatment they got.*

VIRGIN

* **virgin** (colloq.): person with no experience (in s/thing), naive and innocent person >*He's a complete virgin—he's never even tasted beer.*

VITTLES

— **vittles** (vit´lz) (colloq.): food (esp. already prepared) >*She can sure cook up some mighty good vittles.*

W

WACKO

* **wacko** (wak´ō) (sl.): very eccentric or crazy person (also adj.) >*What's that wacko yellin' about?* >*Get outta here with your wacko ideas.*

WACKY

— **wacky** (wak´ē) (sl.): very eccentric, crazy, outrageous >*He had some wacky plan to open an Eskimo restaurant in Miami.* >*That wacky comedian had us laughin' for hours.*

WAD

* **wad** (colloq.): large amount of money (esp. in bills) >*He was carrying a wad that could choke a horse.* >*Vinny lost a wad at the racetrack yesterday.*

— **shoot [one's] wad** (see SHOOT)

WAFFLE

— **waffle** (vi) (colloq.): be evasive or equivocal (when speaking or writing) >*The candidate waffles every time they ask him about something controversial.*

WAGON

* **wagon** (colloq.): station wagon automobile >*I don't know whether to get a truck or a wagon.*

— **fix [s/one's] wagon** (see FIX)

* **off the wagon** (sl.): drinking alcohol again (after a period of abstinence) (cf. "on the WAGON") >*He was sober for over a year, but now he's off the wagon.*

* **on the wagon** (colloq.): abstaining from alcohol (esp. after a period of excessive drinking) (cf. "off the WAGON") >*The booze was killing him, so he went on the wagon.*

WAIL

— **wail** (vi) (sl.): perform vigorously and excellently >*I wailed on that test and aced it.* >*Man, can he ever wail on those drums!*

WAIT

** **wait up** (vi) (colloq.): stop and wait (for), not proceed until (another) arrives >*Hey, you guys, wait up—I'm coming, too.*

WALK

— **walk¹** (vi) (sl.): be set free without punishment >*They couldn't prove he pulled the robbery, so he walked.*

— **walk²** (vi) (sl.): leave, abandon or desert (s/one, s/thing) (esp. because of dissatisfaction) >*Meet our demands or we walk.* >*He couldn't take his job anymore, so he walked.*

— **take a walk** (sl.): leave, walk away (from s/thing unpleasant) >*She started actin' weird, so I took a walk.*

* **walk all over** (colloq.): treat contemptuously, mistreat or exploit >*Don't let that jerk walk all over you like that. Stand up for yourself!*

* **walk away/off with** (colloq.): win, be awarded >*All that training paid off— she walked away with first prize.* >*He hopes to walk off with the award.*

* **walk off with** (colloq.): steal or shoplift >*That girl walked off with my credit card!*

** **walk out on** (colloq.): abandon or desert >*Her husband walked out on her ten years ago and she's had to raise the kids alone.*

WALKING PAPERS

— **walking papers** (colloq.): notification of dismissal, order to be fired >*Vivian screwed up the contract and got her walking papers the next day.*

WALL

— **beat [one's] head against the wall** (see BEAT)

— **drive [s/one] up the/a wall** (see DRIVE)

— **nail [s/one] to the wall** (see NAIL)

— **off the wall** (see "OFF-THE-WALL")

WALLOP

— **wallop[1]** (wol´əp) (colloq.): blow, hit
>*That was quite a wallop he took on the head during the fight.*

— **wallop[2]** (vt) (colloq.): strike hard, sock
>*She walloped him a good one with a broomstick.*

— **pack a punch/wallop** (see **PACK**)

WALLOPING

— **walloping** (wol´ə ping) (colloq.): beating, decisive defeat >*His old man gave him a walloping for what he did.* >*They took a walloping from the visiting team.*

WALLS

— **bouncing off the walls** (see **BOUNCING**)

— **climb the walls** (see **CLIMB**)

WALL-TO-WALL

* **wall-to-wall** (colloq.): completely occupied with, full of >*It was crazy— wall-to-wall people, all pushing and yelling.*

WALTZ

— **waltz** (vi) (colloq.): walk, move, go (s/ where) (esp. in an unconcerned or impertinent way) >*Tina waltzed right over to him and told him to go to hell.* >*He just waltzed in like he owned the place.*

WAMPUM

— **wampum** (wom´pəm/wôm´pəm) (sl.): money >*It's gonna take a lot of wampum to fix up this old place.*

WANABE

— **... wanabe** (see **WANNABE**)

WANNA

** **wanna[1]** (won´ə/wô´nə) (colloq.): want to >*Ya wanna go to the movies tonight?*

** **wanna[2]** (colloq.): want a >*Wanna piece of melon?*

— **... wanna be** (see **WANNABE**)

WANNABE

— **... wannabe** (won´ə bē/wô´nə bē) (= "want to be") (sl.): person who wants to be ... (s/thing or s/one that he/she is not) >*All the cowboy wannabes were in their Western clothes hangin' around the rodeo.*

WAREHOUSE

— **warehouse** (vt) (colloq.): institutionalize (the handicapped, mentally ill, or aged) for long-term care (esp. to rid oneself of the obligation to provide personal care) >*You can't believe how many parents just warehouse these poor kids.* >*A bunch of forgotten old folks are warehoused in there.*

WARM

* **warm the bench** (colloq.): play rarely or serve as a substitute (on a team) (cf. "**BENCHWARMER**") >*I wasn't such a hot player—all I did was warm the bench.*

WAR PAINT

— **war paint** (sl., hum.): women's makeup, cosmetics >*You think all that war paint ya put on's gonna help ya get a husband?*

WARPATH

— **on the warpath** (colloq.): in a hostile or combative mood, on the attack >*She's been on the warpath ever since they snubbed her.*

WARTS

— **warts and all** (colloq.): even with the imperfections, including the flaws >*If you love me, you'll accept me like I am, warts and all.*

WASH

— **wash out (of)** (colloq.): leave or be eliminated (from) (an educational or training program) due to failure >*He finished the coursework but washed out during the exams.* >*McIntire washed out of flight school.*

— **wash (with)** (colloq.): be convincing or acceptable (to), pass a test for validity (for) (used esp. in the neg.) >*The professor's analysis doesn't wash with most of his colleagues.* >*That explanation just doesn't wash.*

WASHED-UP

** **(all) washed-up** (colloq.): failed and finished, no longer useful or effective, done for >*You're all washed-up in this business, Jones!* >*Why are they asking what that washed-up politician thinks?*

WASHOUT

* **washout** (colloq.): person who leaves or is eliminated from an educational or training program due to failure >*He's some law school washout who's running for office.*

WASN'T

— **wasn't born yesterday** (see **BORN**)

WASP

** **WASP** (wosp) (colloq., freq. pej.): White Anglo-Saxon Protestant, white person in the U.S. from the middle or higher class (also adj.) >*You can't succeed in this town unless you're a WASP.* >*Get out of here with your snobbish WASP attitudes.*

WASTE

* **waste** (vt) (sl.): murder, kill >*You're gonna get wasted by some punk if ya keep mouthin' off like that.*

WASTED

* **wasted** (sl.): very drunk or intoxicated >*Everyone got wasted at the party.* >*Don't give him another beer—he's already wasted.*

WATER

— **blow [s/one] out of the water** (see **BLOW**)

— **dead in the water** (see **DEAD**)

— **hold water** (see **HOLD**)

WATERING HOLE

— **watering hole** (colloq.): bar, favorite drinking establishment >*That joint's the watering hole the guys go to every Friday night.*

WATERWORKS

— **(turn on) the waterworks** (sl.): (begin) crying >*All she's gotta do is turn on the waterworks, and she gets her way.* >*Cut the waterworks, crybaby!*

WAVELENGTH

* **on the same wavelength (as)** (colloq.): with similar attitudes or values (to), in rapport or harmony (with) >*They get along so well because they're on the same wavelength.* >*I can't work with Mick—I'm just not on the same wavelength as him.*

WAVES

* **make waves** (colloq.): create a disturbance, upset (an accepted order or situation), cause problems for the status quo >*Nobody wants to make waves, so nothing's ever done about this problem.*

WAX

— **the whole ball of wax** (see **BALL**)

WAY

* **way** (colloq.): extremely, very much, to a great extent >*I feel way better today.* >*He lives way on the other side of town.*

— **every which way** (see **EVERY**)

* **from way back** (colloq.): since a long time ago, for a long time >*He's a Republican from way back.*

— **go out of [one's] way** (see **GO**)

* **go way back** (colloq.): have a longstanding relationship (with one another), be long-time friends >*Max and me go way back, since the war.*

— **in a bad way** (see **BAD**)

— **in a big way** (see **BIG**)

— **in the worst way** (see **WORST**)

** **know [one's] way around ([s/thing, s/where])** (colloq.): be experienced and knowledgeable (regarding [s/thing, s/where]), be resourceful and effective (regarding [s/thing, s/where]) >*Green knows his way around loan agreements,* so customers can't argue with him. >*We need a lobbyist that knows his way around Washington.* >*Watch Fran—she knows her way around.*

— **muscle ([one's] way) in(to)** (see MUSCLE)

** **no way (...)!** (colloq.): under no circumstance (...)! absolutely not (...)! it's impossible (...)! >*Me, wear that? No way!* >*No way Pam's going to take him back after what he did to her!*

* **no way, Jose!** (... hō zā´) (sl.): under no circumstance! absolutely not! it's impossible! >*You want me to apologize to that jerk? No way, Jose!*

— **not know which end/way is up** (see KNOW)

— **that's the way the ball bounces** (see BALL)

— **that's the way the cookie crumbles** (see COOKIE)

— **[s/one's] way** (colloq.): in [s/one's] vicinity, near [s/one's] home >*Drop by and see us when you're down our way.*

* **way back when** (colloq.): a long time ago >*He hosted one of the first television shows way back when.*

** **way to go!** (colloq., freq. sarc.): well done! >*A three-pointer! Way to go, Sammy!* >*Way to go! You just knocked over my beer.*

WAY-OUT

— **way-out** (sl.): very unconventional, avant-garde, radical >*He's got some way-out theory on reincarnation.* >*Those purple boots are way-out, man.*

WAYS

* **a ways** (colloq.): a long distance >*We got a ways to go yet till we reach Grand Junction.* >*He lives quite a ways from here.*

WEAR

— **wear the pants** (colloq.): have a man's authority, be in charge, have the dominant role (esp. in a domestic

situation) >*Walker talks big, but his wife wears the pants in the family.*

WEASEL

— **weasel ([one's] way) out of** (colloq.): succeed in avoiding or removing [oneself] from (a task or commitment), renege on or back out of (an obligation) (esp. in a sneaky or cowardly way) >*You said you'd fix my car, and I'm not going to let you weasel out of it.* >*Somehow Gerty weaseled her way out of serving on the committee this year.*

WEATHER

* **under the weather** (colloq.): not feeling well, ill (esp. with a cold or the flu during cold weather) >*The secretary's a little under the weather and won't be in today.*

WEED

* **weed** (sl.): marijuana >*He smokes weed but doesn't drink.*

— **grow like a weed** (see GROW)

WEENIE

* **weenie[1]** (wē´nē) (vulg.): penis >*Joe said he got his weenie caught in his zipper.*

— **weenie[2]** (sl.): weak and contemptible male, cowardly or insignificant male >*That weenie couldn't fight his way out of a wet paper bag.* >*Don't be a weenie, Howie—hit him back!*

— **weenie[3]** (colloq.): wiener, frankfurter >*She brought the weenies but forgot the buns.*

WEEPY

— **weepy** (wē´pē) (colloq.): melodramatically sad, sentimentally pathetic >*Take some Kleenex to that movie—it's got a lot of weepy parts.*

WEE-WEE

— **wee-wee[1]** (wē´wē´) (colloq.): urine (used esp. with small children) >*There's wee-wee on the floor where the baby was sitting.*

* **wee-wee**[2] (vi) (colloq.): urinate (used esp. with small children) >*You let Daddy know when you have to wee-wee, OK?*

WEIGHT
— **carry (a lot of) weight** (see **CARRY**)
— **pull [one's] (own) weight** (see **PULL**)
— **throw [one's] weight around** (see **THROW**)

WEIRDO
** **weirdo** (wĕr´dō) (sl.): very eccentric or strange person, person with deviant behavior (also adj.) >*She's afraid of all the weirdos that hang around the park at night.* >*Keep Joey away from those weirdo kids next door.*

WELCH
— **welch (on)** (welch …) (see "**WELSH (on)**")

WELCOME
* **welcome to the club!** (colloq.): I'm in that situation too! you're not the only one to suffer or experience that! >*He stole money from you, too? Welcome to the club!*

WELCOME MAT
* **put out the welcome mat (for)** (colloq.): give a hearty welcome (to) >*The city put out the welcome mat for its foreign visitors.*

WELL-HEELED
— **well-heeled** (colloq.): wealthy, well-to-do >*Well-heeled doctors and lawyers can afford to live in this neighborhood, but I can't.*

WELSH
— **welsh (on)** (welsh …) (sl.): cheat by not paying (a debt) >*I ain't gonna let him welsh on what he owes me.* >*You welsh and you're finished around here.*

WET
— **(as) mad as a wet hen** (see **MAD**)
— **be all wet** (sl.): be wrong, be completely mistaken >*You're all wet if ya think her old man will let her go out with you.*

— **get [one's] feet wet** (see **FEET**)
— **(still) wet behind the ears** (colloq.): inexperienced, immature >*You ain't going to put that kid in charge, are you? Why, he's still wet behind the ears.*
— **wet [one's] whistle** (colloq.): take a drink >*I got a bottle of tequila in the car—like to wet your whistle?*

WETBACK
* **wetback** (colloq., pej.): undocumented Mexican immigrant in the U.S., Mexican-American >*That bigoted jerk calls anyone who looks Latino a wetback.*

WET BLANKET
— **wet blanket** (colloq.): person who spoils others' fun, person who discourages enthusiasm, killjoy >*Don't be such a wet blanket—stop whining about everything.*

WHACK
— **whack** (hwak/wak) (vt) (sl.): murder, kill >*He got whacked with a shotgun.*
— **give [s/thing] a whack** (sl.): give [s/thing] a try, make an attempt at [s/thing] >*This game's great—wanna give it a whack?*
* **out of whack** (sl.): out of order, not functioning properly, not adjusted right >*The TV's outta whack. We only get two channels.* >*My back's a little outta whack, so I can't pick up anything heavy.*
* **take/have a whack at** (sl.): make an attempt at, give (s/thing) a try >*I can't get this thing put together right—you wanna take a whack at it?*
— **whack off** (vi, vt) (vulg.): masturbate (said of a male) >*He likes to whack off when he feels horny.* >*He said she whacked him off last night.*

WHACKED-OUT
— **whacked-out** (hwakt´out´/wakt´out´) (sl.): crazed, behaving in a bizarre or irrational way >*Some whacked-out*

drug addict was on the corner screamin'
into the night.

WHACKO
— whacko (hwak´ō) (see "WACKO")

WHACKY
— whacky (hwak´ē) (see "WACKY")

WHALE
— whale (colloq., pej.): very large and fat
person >*Your aunt must have gained a
hundred pounds. She's a whale!*

* a whale of a (colloq.): a very
impressive, an excellent (also adv.)
>*We had a whale of a time skiing.* >*The
show was a whale of a success.* >*He's
doing a whale of a good job.*

— whale into (colloq.): attack vehemently
(physically or verbally) >*He whaled
into me when I called him a bozo.* >*She
whaled into her opponent during the
debate.*

WHAMMO
— whammo! (hwam´ō/wam´ō) (colloq.):
wham! bang! >*Then all of a sudden,
whammo! They crashed right into a tree.*

WHAMMY
— double/triple whammy (… hwam´ē/
wam´ē) (colloq.): double or second/
triple or third dose of misfortune >*The
double whammy was losing his job and
then getting sued.* >*First I got lost, and
then I ran out of gas. The triple
whammy was when they stole my car.*

— put the whammy on (colloq.): give bad
luck to >*I never wear red in Las Vegas
because it puts the whammy on me.*

WHAT
— (I'll) tell you what (see TELL)

— (just) what the doctor ordered (see
DOCTOR)

* …, or what? (colloq.): …, isn't that so?
(used after a question to affirm s/thing)
>*Hey, is my wife smart, or what?*

— say what? (see SAY)

— say what?! (see SAY)

— so what? (see SO)

* (so) what else is new? (colloq., sarc.):
that's no surprise, that's well- known
>*You need a little loan till payday
again? So what else is new?*

* what do you say? (colloq.): how have
you been? how are you doing? >*Hey,
what do you say, Carlos? Long time no
see!*

* what do you say …? (colloq.): I
propose that …, what do you think of
the idea that …? >*What do you say we
grab a couple of beers down at Patty's?*

— what [s/one] is getting at (see
GETTING)

— what gives? (see GIVES)

** what if …?[1] (colloq.): what would
happen if …? suppose that … >*What if
we ask Professor Gillian to look our
project over before we hand it in?*

* what if …?[2] (colloq.): what business is
it of (s/one's) if …? >*What if I did get
drunk last night? Who cares?*

** what it takes (colloq.): the necessary
qualities or abilities >*If you've got what
it takes, you'll go far in this business.*

— what makes [s/one] tick (see TICK)

* what the fuck! (… fuk) (vulg.): why
not allow it? I'll risk it! It's not that
important! >*Sometimes ya gotta say
"what the fuck!" and try somethin' new.*

* what the heck! (… hek) (colloq.): why
not allow it? I'll risk it! It's not that
important! >*You want to go along with
your older brother? What the heck! Go
ahead.*

* what the hell! (colloq., freq. vulg.):
why not allow it? I'll risk it! It's not that
important! >*What the hell! As long as
we're here, let's buy tickets and go in.*

— what the hey! (… hā) (sl.): why not
allow it? I'll risk it! It's not that
important! >*What the hey! I guess I can
afford a couple of raffle tickets.*

— **what the shit!** (… shit) (vulg.): why not allow it? I'll risk it! It's not that important! >*I figured, what the shit! Nothin' ventured, nothin' gained.*

— **what's what** (see **WHAT'S**)

WHATCHA

** **whatcha** (hwuch´ə/wuch´ə) (colloq.): what (do/are) you >*Whatcha wanna do?* >*Whatcha gonna do?*

WHATCHAMACALLIT

* **whatchamacallit** (hwuch´ə mə kôl´it/ wuch´ə mə kôl´it) (colloq.): thing, gadget, object (for which one does not know or cannot recall the name) >*No, put the whatchamacallit on before you screw on the nut.*

WHAT-IF

— **what-if** (colloq.): possible outcome or future problem, eventuality >*You'll go crazy worrying about all the what-ifs.*

WHAT'S

— **get what's coming to [one]** (see COMING)

** **what's happening?** (sl.): how are you? how are things? >*What's happenin', dude? Whatcha up to?*

* **what's his/her face** (sl.): that person (whose name one does not remember) >*Tell what's her face—you know, that redhead in the front office—that I'll be a little late.*

* **what's his/her name** (colloq.): that person (whose name one does not remember) >*Say hi to old what's his name at the station for me.*

— **what's shaking?** (sl.): what's happening? what's going on? >*Yo, Popeye! What's shakin', man?*

* **what's the big idea?** (colloq.): explain why you're doing (s/thing presumptuous or offensive) >*Hey, what's the big idea? That's my chair!*

— **what's the good word?** (sl.): how are things? how are you doing? what's new?

>*Hey, Ron, I ain't seen ya in months— what's the good word?*

* **what's what** (colloq.): the real situation, the complete facts >*You don't need to give her advice—she knows what's what.*

* **what's with …?** (colloq.): what's the matter with …? what's the explanation for (s/one's behavior, s/thing's presence)? >*What's with Carrie? Why's she crying?* >*Hey, Al, what's with the sunglasses? It's after midnight.*

WHEEL

* **wheel and deal** (vi) (colloq.): operate or negotiate astutely and vigorously (esp. for personal gain) >*He wheeled and dealed all over town to get support for his project.* >*She'll do good in this business because she knows how to wheel and deal.*

WHEELER

— **wheeler and dealer** (see "WHEELER-DEALER")

WHEELER-DEALER

* **wheeler-dealer** (colloq.): person who operates or negotiates astutely and vigorously (esp. for personal gain) >*Some wheeler-dealer almost talked Grampa into selling his land for half its value.*

WHEELIE

* **wheelie** (hwē´lē/wē´lē) (sl.): raising of the front of a vehicle off the ground due to rapid acceleration >*Let's see if ya can do a wheelie on this bike.*

WHEELMAN

— **wheelman** (sl.): driver (esp. in the commission if a crime) >*They use him as a wheelman on bank heists.*

WHEELS

— **hell on wheels** (see HELL)

* **(set of) wheels** (sl.): (an) automobile >*How can ya get to work without wheels?* >*Nice set of wheels ya got there.*

— **spinning [one's] wheels** (see SPINNING)

— **[for one's] wheels [to be] spinning** (colloq.): [for one to be] thinking hard >*I could see that Trish's wheels were spinning, but she just couldn't come up with the answer.*

WHEN

— **say when** (see SAY)

— **way back when** (see WAY)

WHERE

— **tell [s/one] where to get off** (colloq.): reprimand or rebuke [s/one] >*When the clerk got rude with me, I told him where to get off.*

* **tell [s/one] where to put/stick [s/thing]** (sl., freq. vulg.): insult or rebuke [s/one] regarding [s/thing], emphatically reject [s/thing] associated with [s/one] >*When that clown tried to sell me some brushes, I told him where to put 'em.* >*She told her boss where to stick his job.*

* **where [s/one] comes in** (colloq.): the part [s/one] plays (in a plan), the thing [s/one] is responsible for >*Convincing the jury is where the lawyer comes in.* >*The money for my project? That's where you come in, my friend.*

* **where does [s/one] get off [doing s/thing]?** (colloq.): how does [s/one] dare [do s/thing]? what gives [s/one] the right [to do s/thing]? >*Where do you get off telling me how to run my life?*

* **where (have) you been keeping yourself?** (colloq.): I haven't seen you in a long time, where have you been lately? >*It's been a while, buddy—where you been keeping yourself?*

* **where [s/one's] head is at** (sl.): [s/one's] mental state, [s/one's] attitudes or opinions >*I know where your head's at, man—I feel the same way.*

* **where [s/one] is coming from** (sl.): what [s/one's] beliefs or attitudes are, why [s/one] thinks or feels as [he/she]

does >*Hey, I know where you're comin' from. I used to be a socialist myself.*

* **where it's at** (sl.): where the greatest excitement is, a very popular or profitable situation or activity >*The Red Dog's where it's at. Let's go!* >*Real estate is where it's at in a slow economy, if ya ask me.*

* **where the action is** (sl.): where the greatest excitement is, a very popular or profitable situation or activity >*That bar's where the action is in this town.* >*Boat leasing's where the action is around here.*

* **where the sun doesn't/don't shine** (sl., freq. vulg.): in (one's) rectum >*They checked her everywhere for drugs—even where the sun doesn't shine.* >*Tell that moron to take his contract and stick it where the sun don't shine!*

WHERE'S

— **where's the fire?** (colloq.): why are you hurrying so? >*Hey, slow down a minute! Where's the fire?*

WHICH

— **every which way** (see EVERY)

— **not know which end/way is up** (see KNOW)

WHICHAMACALLIT

— **whichamacallit** (hwich´ə mə kôl´it/ wich´ə mə kôl´it) (colloq.): thing, gadget, object (for which one does not know or cannot recall the name) >*I got to get one of those whichamacallits for my computer so I can network.*

WHILE

— **get while the getting's good** (see GET)

WHING-DING

— **whing-ding** (hwing´ding´) (see "WING-DING")

WHIP

* **whip** (vt) (colloq.): beat, defeat >*He can whip guys twice his size.* >*We whipped them five to nothing.*

— **whip/lick [s/thing, s/one] into shape** (colloq.): make [s/thing, s/one] ready, improve [s/thing, s/one] in performance or behavior (esp. through hard work or discipline) >*My book's about licked into shape.* >*The Army will whip him into shape in no time.*

— **whip off** (vt) (colloq.): write hurriedly >*I'll whip off a news release and get it out right away.*

* **whip out** (vt) (colloq.): take out quickly (esp. with assuredness or determination) >*I was low on cash, so I just whipped out a credit card to pay for it.*

* **whip up** (vt) (colloq.): prepare quickly >*I'll whip us up an omelet for breakfast.* >*I don't think that plan Bunny whipped up will work.*

WHIPPERSNAPPER
— **whippersnapper** (hwip´ər snap´ər/ wip´ər snap´ər) (colloq.): insignificant and presumptuous or insolent person (esp. a young one) >*I could do twice the work that whippersnapper does when I was his age—and I knew how to keep my mouth shut, too.*

WHIRL
— **give [s/thing] a whirl** (colloq.): give [s/thing] a try, make an attempt at [s/thing] >*You'll like skiing—give it a whirl.*

— **take/have a whirl at** (colloq.): make an attempt at, try >*I doubt I can do it, but I'll take a whirl at it.*

WHIRLYBIRD
— **whirlybird** (hwûr´lē bûrd´/wûr´lē bûrd´) (colloq.): helicopter >*He was a whirlybird pilot in the Army.*

WHISTLE
— **(as) clean as a whistle** (see CLEAN)

— **blow the whistle (on)** (see BLOW)

— **wet [one's] whistle** (see WET)

WHISTLES
— **bells and whistles** (see BELLS)

WHISTLING
— **you just ain't (a-)whistlin' Dixie!** (colloq.): that's the truth! that's for sure! >*You just ain't a-whistlin' Dixie, because that's just what's going to happen!*

WHITE
* **(as) white as a sheet** (colloq.): very pale (said of a person's skin) >*Grace turned white as a sheet when she saw the man had a knife.*

WHITE HAT
— **white hat** (colloq.): hero, virtuous character (in a story, esp. a Western) (cf. "BLACK HAT") >*Don't worry—the white hat will ride by and save her.* >*You always think you're the white hat, don't you?*

WHITE MAN'S DISEASE
— **white man's disease** (sl., hum., freq. pej.): a complete lack of rhythm, an inability to move gracefully (in dancing) >*I hope Brent doesn't ask me to dance— he's got white man's disease bad.*

WHITE MEAT
— **white meat** (vulg., pej.): white person/ people (seen as sex object[s]) (cf. "DARK MEAT") >*He said he cruised the boulevard lookin' for white meat.*

WHITEY
— **whitey** (hwī´tē/wī´tē) (sl., pej.): white person/people (also voc.) >*Whitey gets all the breaks in this racist company.* >*Hey, whitey, whatcha doin' in this neighborhood?*

WHITY
— **whity** (see "WHITEY")

WHIZ
* **whiz¹** (hwiz/wiz) (colloq.): talented or proficient person (at an activity), expert >*He's a whiz on that computer.* >*She's a whiz at science.*

— **whiz²** (vi) (sl., freq. vulg.): urinate >*He whizzed on the grass.*

— **take a whiz** (sl., freq. vulg.): urinate
>*Be right back—gotta take a whiz.*

WHIZ KID

* **whiz kid** (hwiz´/wiz´ kid´) (colloq.):
young talented or proficient person (at
an activity), young expert >*I think
those computer whiz kids could write a
program to do that.*

WHOA

* **whoa!** (hwō/wō) (colloq.): stop what
you're saying! stop talking so fast!
>*Whoa, there! I did not say that!
>Whoa! Calm down and speak slow.*

WHODUNIT

— **whodunit** (hū´dun´it) (colloq.): murder
mystery story, detective story >*She
loves reading those British whodunits.*

WHOLE

— **a (whole) bunch (of ...)** (see BUNCH)

* **a whole 'nother** (... nuð´ər) (colloq.): a
completely different, altogether another
>*I'm just telling you what he did. Why
he did it's a whole 'nother story.*

— **the (whole) ...** (see entry under ...
noun)

WHOLE HOG

— **go whole hog** (colloq.): (do s/thing)
thoroughly or without restraints, indulge
(oneself) freely >*They went whole hog
planning this party. >He didn't have
just one or two drinks—he went whole
hog and got completely drunk.*

WHOMP

— **whomp** (hwomp/womp) (vt) (sl.): beat,
defeat decisively >*You're gonna get
whomped if ya mess with that dude.
>They whomped us sixty-six to forty.*

WHOOP

— **whoop it up** (hwūp/wūp/hūp/hwŭp/wŭp/
hŭp ...) (colloq.): celebrate noisily, have
boisterous fun >*They bought some beer
and whooped it up after winning the
game.*

WHOOP-DE-DO

— **whoop-de-do** (hwŭp´/wūp´/hūp´/hwŭp´/
wŭp´/hŭp´dē dū´) (colloq.): noisy
celebration, merrymaking >*The city
planned a big whoop-de-do for the
Fourth of July.*

WHOOPEE

— **make whoopee** (... hwūp´ē/wūp´ē/
hwŭp´ē/wŭp´ē) (sl.): have sex >*Hey,
babe, let's go make whoopee.*

* **whoopee!** (hwūp´ē´/wūp´ē´/hwŭp´ē´/
wŭp´ē´) (colloq.): (interj. to express joy
or excitement) >*Whoopee! I got the
raise. >This ride's wild! Whoopee!*

WHOOPS-A-DAISY

* **whoops-a-daisy!** (hwūps´/wūps´/
hwŭps´/wŭps´ə dā´zē) (colloq.): (interj.
to reassure a child when he/she falls)
>*Whoops-a-daisy! Three whole steps
that time!*

WHOPPER

* **whopper**[1] (hwop´ər/wop´ər) (colloq.): a
very large (example of s/thing) >*That
fish Wanda caught was a whopper.*

— **whopper**[2] (colloq.): big lie >*He told
them a whopper, saying he was a state
senator.*

WHOPPING

— **whopping**[1] (hwop´ing/wop´ing)
(colloq.): very large or extraordinary
>*He was wearing this whopping
cowboy hat.*

— **whopping**[2] (colloq.): very,
extraordinarily >*That was a whopping
good meal.*

WHO'S

— **look who's talking!** (see LOOK)

* **who's who** (colloq.): group of the most
outstanding or famous persons (of a
profession or activity) >*The who's who
of electrical engineering was at the
conference.*

WICKED

— **a wicked ...** (sl.): an excellent ..., (a) ...
done skillfully or impressively >*That*

*tennis player's got a wicked serve.
>Mort plays a wicked rhythm guitar.*

WIDE

* **wide open** (sl.): at full throttle, applying full acceleration or power >*It'll go over a hundred wide open.*

— **wide place in the road** (colloq.): very small town (esp. on a highway) >*She comes from some little town in the desert that's just a wide place in the road.*

WIDOW

— **... widow** (colloq.): woman whose husband neglects her because he devotes excessive time to ... >*Sarah's a golf widow—her old man's always out playing.*

WIENER

— **wiener** (vulg.): penis >*He made a joke about his wiener being too small.*

WIENIE

— **wienie** (see "WEENIE")

WIG

— **flip [one's] wig** (see FLIP)

— **wig out**[1] (vi) (sl.): lose (one's) self-control, become mentally unstable, go crazy >*They kept teasin' him till he totally wigged out.*

— **wig out**[2] (vi) (sl.): become very excited or enthusiastic >*The fans really wig out at his concerts.*

WIGGED

— **wigged out** (wigd ...) (sl.): having lost (one's) self-control, having become mentally unstable, crazed >*They had to call the cops 'cause the dude was totally wigged out.*

WIGGLE

* **wiggle ([one's] way) out of** (colloq.): succeed in avoiding or removing [oneself] from (a task or commitment), renege on or back out of (an obligation) (esp. in a sneaky way) >*He's not going to wiggle out of doing me this favor.* >*I*

don't know how they wiggled their way out of planning the show.

WILD

** **wild** (sl.): very stimulating, excitingly good >*The Formula One race was wild!* >*I saw a really wild movie last night.*

— **(a team of) wild horses couldn't** (colloq.): nothing could (change s/one's determined course of action) >*A team of wild horses couldn't keep me away from their party.* >*Wild horses couldn't drag any information out of that closemouthed kid.*

* **wild about/over** (colloq.): very enthusiastic about, very fond or enamored of >*Everyone's wild over that song.* >*I'm wild about that cute guy.*

WILD CARD

* **wild card** (colloq.): unpredictable element, unknown determinant >*The weather's going to be the wild card in this race.*

WILDFIRE

* **like wildfire** (colloq.): quickly and vigorously (esp. how s/thing spreads) >*Cholera went like wildfire through the city's slums.*

WILLIES

— **the willies** (... wil´ēz) (sl.): nervous uneasiness or fright, nervous shaking >*Snakes give him the willies.* >*I get the willies every time I go by that old place at night.*

WIMP

** **wimp** (wimp) (sl.): contemptibly weak or cowardly person >*Don't be such a wimp—fight back!*

— **wimp out** (vi) (sl.): retreat in a cowardly way, fail to meet a challenge due to weakness or fear >*Vic's a weenie—he wimps out every time he starts to ask Doris to go out with him.*

WIMPY

* **wimpy** (wim´pē) (sl.): contemptibly weak or cowardly >*His wimpy friend won't play football with us.*

WIN

— **win/lose by a nose** (see NOSE)

WIND

— **three sheets to/in the wind** (see THREE)

* **wind down** (wīnd ...) (vi) (colloq.): relax, relieve (one's) stress >*Coleman winds down with a cocktail every day after work.*

* **wind up**[1] (wīnd ...) (vi) (colloq.): end up, find (oneself) (in a resulting place or situation) >*He drove after he drank, and he wound up in jail.* >*You're going to wind up all alone if you keep treating people that way.*

* **wind up**[2] (wīnd ...) (vt) (colloq.): complete, be finished with >*We'll wind up the job next week.*

WINDBAG

— **windbag** (wind´bag´) (colloq.): person who talks too much (esp. while saying little of substance), pretentious talker >*You didn't take anything that windbag said seriously, did you?*

WINDOW

— **throw [s/thing] out the window** (see THROW)

WING

* **wing it** (colloq.): do (s/thing) without due preparation, improvise >*I don't know what they expect me to say at the meeting, so I'll just have to wing it.*

WING-DING

— **wing-ding** (wing´ding´) (sl.): big and noisy party or celebration >*They're gonna have a big wing-ding to celebrate his new job.*

WINNER

** **winner** (sl.): charmed or successful person, person worthy of respect (cf. "LOSER") >*That's a great kid ya got*

there—*a real winner.* >*If ya wanna be a winner, ya gotta look like one.*

WINO

* **wino** (wī´nō) (sl.): impoverished alcoholic (esp. a derelict, esp. one who drinks cheap wine) >*Nobody but drug addicts and winos stay in that cheap hotel.*

WIPE

* **wipe out**[1] (vt) (sl.): exhaust, tire completely >*Diggin' that trench wiped me out.* >*We were wiped out after that long hike.*

* **wipe out**[2] (vt) (colloq.): murder, kill >*One gangster had the other wiped out.* >*The disease wiped out the whole tribe.*

* **wipe out**[3] (vt) (sl.): defeat decisively >*The Eagles wiped 'em out in the semi-finals.*

— **wipe out**[4] (vi) (sl.): crash or fall (esp. in sports) >*When he tried to turn the corner too fast, he wiped out.*

— **wipe out**[5] (vt) (sl.): intoxicate (with drugs or alcohol) >*This coke'll wipe ya out, man.* >*Three drinks and she was wiped out.*

WIPEOUT

— **wipeout**[1] (sl.): decisive defeat >*What a wipeout! We killed 'em.*

— **wipeout**[2] (sl.): crash or fall (esp. in sports) >*A bad wipeout can really hurt a surfer.* >*The wipeout bent up her bike, but she was OK.*

WIRE

— **wire** (sl.): hidden microphone and transmitter (worn on a person) >*The cops got him to wear a wire to his meeting with the smugglers.*

— **down to the wire** (see DOWN)

* **(just) under the wire** (colloq.): just by the deadline, barely in time >*He filed for candidacy just under the wire.*

WIRED

* **wired**[1] (sl.): excited, tense, edgy >*Everyone gets real wired right before*

a game. >*I'm pretty wired after drinkin' eight cups of coffee.*

— **wired²** (sl.): intoxicated (esp. on drugs) >*He went out to his car for a while and came back totally wired.*

— **have [s/thing] wired** (sl.): be assured of success with [s/thing], have [s/thing] virtually achieved >*No problem, man— I got this exam wired.* >*He thinks he's got the job wired 'cause his old man's a buddy of the owner.*

WIRES

* **get [one's] wires crossed** (colloq.): have a miscommunication, miscomprehend [one another] >*I guess we got our wires crossed, because that's not the way I understood it.*

WISE

* **wise** (sl.): impudent or presumptuous, disrespectful >*He tried to get wise with me, so I punched him.* >*I don't like them wise teenage punks.*

* **wise to** (sl.): aware or informed of, no longer deceived by or naive about >*If the feds get wise to this, we're finished.* >*I'm wise to your scheme.*

* **wise up** (vi, vt) (sl.): become/make aware, become informed/inform (esp. to end some deceit or naiveness) >*Wise up, Chuck—she's really in love with Grant.* >*When's that dummy gonna wise up and see what they're really doin' to him?* >*I'd better wise Warren up before he makes a fool of himself.*

WISEACRE

— **wiseacre** (wīz´ā´kər) (colloq.): obnoxiously self-assured or conceited person, insolent person >*I wish someone would tell that wiseacre to keep his mouth shut.*

WISE ASS

— **wise ass** (vulg.): obnoxiously self-assured or conceited person, insolent person >*Some wise ass was pissin' everyone off sayin' how he could have done it better.*

WISE-ASS

— **wise-ass** (vulg.): obnoxiously self-assured or conceited, insolent >*Get rid of that wise-ass attitude if ya wanna keep your job!*

WISECRACK

* **wisecrack** (sl.): sarcastic or flippant remark >*Jerry's always makin' wisecracks in class and gettin' on the teacher's nerves.* >*No wisecracks about my lumpy gravy.*

WISE GUY

* **wise guy** (… gī) (colloq.): obnoxiously self-assured or conceited person, insolent person (also voc.) >*Don't be a wise guy or I'll have to shut you up.* >*Watch out, wise guy!*

WISHY-WASHY

* **wishy-washy** (wish´ē wosh´ē/wô´shē) (colloq.): indecisive, lacking in purpose >*Her wishy-washy husband can't make up his mind.*

WITCH'S

— **colder than a witch's tit** (see COLDER)

WITH

* **be with** (colloq.): be in agreement with >*I'm with Bartlett—he's got the right idea.*

— **be [s/where] with bells on** (see BELLS)

* **be with it** (sl.): be up-to-date with the latest styles, be aware of and in concert with what's going on (cf. "WITH-IT") >*You ain't gotta do drugs to be with it.*

— **what's with …?** (see WHAT'S)

— **with one hand tied behind [one]/ [one's] back** (see HAND)

WITH-IT

* **with-it** (sl.): up-to-date with the latest styles, aware of and in concert with what's going on (cf. "be WITH it") >*I've been datin' this really with-it chick.*

WOLF
— **wolf** (colloq.): man who aggressively pursues women sexually >*Watch out for that wolf, or he'll be all over you before you know it.*

WOMAN
— **the little woman** (see LITTLE)

WOOD
— **saw wood** (see SAW)

WOODS
— **neck of the woods** (see NECK)

* **out of the woods** (colloq.): no longer in danger, finally safe (freq. used in the neg.) >*The patient's improved some, but he's not out of the woods yet.* >*We won't be out of the woods until we make that last payment.*

WOODWORK
— **come/crawl out of the woodwork** (see COME)

WOOL
— **pull the wool over [s/one's] eyes** (colloq.): deceive or mislead [s/one] >*The kid thinks he's pulling the wool over his mother's eyes, but she's smarter than he thinks.*

WOP
— **wop** (wop) (sl., pej.): Italian-American, Italian >*I can't believe he actually called Marco a wop.*

WORD
* **cannot get a word in (edgewise)** (colloq.): not have a chance to say anything (because another dominates the conversation) >*Morrison started talking about politics, and nobody else could get a word in edgewise.*

— **from the word "go"** (see GO)

* **(just) say/give the word** (colloq.): you need only indicate your desire or approval, just give the signal to proceed >*Give the word and I'll beat the jerk up for you.* >*If you want another helping, just say the word.*

— **the ...-word** (colloq.): (euphemism to refer to a word beginning with the letter ...) >*Don't mention the M-word around a confirmed bachelor like Larry.* >*He's so foul-mouthed! He just said the F-word in front of these ladies.*

— **what's the good word?** (see WHAT'S)

WORK
* **work** (vt) (colloq.): gain advantage over through persuasion, exploit through cajolery or manipulation >*He knows how to work the customers till he's got them eager to buy.* >*The homeless man was out working the crowd for handouts.*

* **have [one's] work/job cut out for [one]** (colloq.): be facing a great deal of work or a difficult task >*You've got your work cut out for you cleaning up this big mess.*

— **piece of work** (see PIECE)

* **work like a charm** (colloq.): work very well, be very effective >*My story worked like a charm on that gullible receptionist.*

* **work over** (vt) (sl.): beat thoroughly or severely >*If he don't wanna cooperate, work him over till he does.*

WORKAHOLIC
** **workaholic** (wûrk´ə hol´ik/wûrk´ə hô´lik) (colloq.): compulsive worker, person who is overly dedicated to his/her job >*Some of the workaholics even come into the office on Sundays.*

WORKER
— **fast worker/operator** (see FAST)

WORKS
* **in the works** (colloq.): being prepared or planned, being developed or processed >*I hear there's a big company reorganization in the works.*

— **shoot the works** (see SHOOT)

** **the works** (colloq.): all the accompaniments, everything involved >*Give me a burger with the works.*

>He got it with air conditioning, power steering, stereo cassette—the works.

WORLD

— **dead to the world** (see DEAD)

* **out of this world** (colloq.): wonderful, excellent >Their barbecued ribs are out of this world.

* **what/who/[etc.] in the world ...?** (colloq.): (intens. expressing impatience, anger, or surprise) >Where in the world did you get that awful thing? >Why in the world didn't she say something about it?

WORM

— **worm** (colloq.): contemptibly cowardly or treacherous person, reprehensible person >I don't trust that sneaky worm that works as his aide.

WORST

* **in the worst way** (colloq.): very much, very strongly (esp. referring to desire) >She wanted him to ask her out in the worst way.

WORTH

— **for all [one] is worth** (see ALL)

— **no/any ... worth his/her salt** (colloq.): no/any ... who is competent >No accountant worth his salt would have missed that. >Any carpenter worth his salt could frame that house in three days.

** **worth a damn** (colloq., freq. vulg.): the least bit valuable (freq. used in the neg.) (also adv.) >This computer's not worth a damn to me if I don't have the right software. >Who hired him? He can't sing worth a damn.

— **worth a dang** (... dang) (colloq.): the least bit valuable (freq. used in the neg.) (also adv.) >This old typewriter's not worth a dang anymore. >Bring me a sharper knife—this one doesn't cut worth a dang.

* **worth a darn** (... därn) (colloq.): the least bit valuable (freq. used in the neg.) (also adv.) >That new guy's not worth a darn on this job. >If he can keep books worth a darn, the job's his.

— **worth a fuck** (... fuk) (vulg.): the least bit valuable (freq. used in the neg.) (also adv.) >He's a nice kid, but he ain't worth a fuck on the job. >Poor Leo can't drive a car worth a fuck.

— **worth a goddamn** (colloq., freq. vulg.): the least bit valuable (freq. used in the neg.) (also adv.) >They don't have a player that's worth a goddamn. >That player can't hit worth a goddamn.

— **worth a rat's ass** (vulg.): the least bit valuable (freq. used in the neg.) (also adv.) >This cheap wrench ain't worth a rat's ass. >Me on the team? I can't bowl worth a rat's ass.

— **worth (a) shit** (... shit) (vulg.): the least bit valuable, at all worthwhile (freq. used in the neg.) (also adv.) >Any plumber that's worth a shit could fix that leak in five minutes. >This beat-up wheelbarrow don't work worth shit. >If he can play worth a shit, he's hired.

— **worth beans** (sl.): the least bit valuable (freq. used in the neg.) (also adv.) >The crummy report she wrote isn't worth beans. >That ham can't act worth beans.

WOULD

— **would give [one's] left/right nut** (see GIVE)

— **would give [one's] right arm** (see GIVE)

— **would give [s/one] the shirt off [one's] back** (see SHIRT)

— **would ... in a minute** (see MINUTE)

WOULDN'T

— **wouldn't be caught dead** (see DEAD)

— **wouldn't put it past [s/one] (to [do s/thing])** (see PUT)

— **wouldn't hurt a fly/flea** (see HURT)

— **wouldn't touch [s/thing, s/one] with a ten-foot pole** (see TOUCH)

— **wouldn't you know it!** (see KNOW)

WOUND

* **wound up** (wound ...) (colloq.): tense, nervous >*She gets real wound up right before a performance.*

WOW

— **wow**[1] (wou) (colloq.): very impressive or exciting exhibition or person >*His juggling act is a real wow.* >*That beautiful actress is a wow!*

* **wow**[2] (vt) (colloq.): greatly impress, excite >*I know you're going to wow them with that publicity idea.*

** **wow!** (colloq.): (interj. to express wonder, surprise, or excitement) >*Wow! Did you see that lightning flash?*

WRAP

* **wrap/twist [s/one] around [one's] little finger** (colloq.): easily dominate [s/one], easily influence [s/one] to do [one's] will >*She's got her boyfriend wrapped around her little finger.*

** **wrap up** (vt) (colloq.): finish, conclude, take care of the last details of >*We ought to be able to wrap this project up by tomorrow.*

WRAPPED

* **wrapped up in** (colloq.): very involved in, overly devoted to >*How'd you get so wrapped up in motorcycle racing?* >*He's really wrapped up in his work.*

WRASTLE

— **wrastle** (see "RASSLE")

WRINGER

* **through the wringer** (colloq.): undergoing a difficult or painful situation >*Jerry's been through the wringer with that lawsuit.* >*The cops put him through the wringer till he gave them the info they wanted.*

WRINKLE

* **wrinkle**[1] (colloq.): minor problem or defect >*We got to work a couple of wrinkles out of this plan before it'll work.*

— **wrinkle**[2] (colloq.): clever trick or innovation >*The public relations guy's got a new wrinkle for his next campaign.*

WRIST

— **slap on the wrist** (see SLAP)

— **slap [s/one's] wrist** (see SLAP)

WRITE

— **nothing to write home about** (see NOTHING)

WRONG

— **barking up the wrong tree** (see BARKING)

— **get up on the wrong side of the bed** (see GET)

— **rub [s/one] the wrong way** (see RUB)

* **the wrong side of the tracks** (colloq.): poor neighborhood, area where the lower socioeconomic classes live (cf. "the RIGHT side of the tracks") >*His parents got real upset when he started seeing a girl from the wrong side of the tracks.*

WROTE

— **that's all she wrote!** (see ALL)

* **wrote the book on** (colloq.): is the original or foremost expert on (a subject) >*Everyone consults Givens— he wrote the book on designing these things.*

X

— **[one's] X** (colloq.): [one's] signature
>*Put your X right there to OK the work.*

X-RATED
** **X-rated** (colloq.): obscene, lewd
>*Bert's over there entertaining the guys
with X-rated jokes.*

Y

Y.

** **the Y.** (colloq.): the Y.M.C.A. or Y.W.C.A. (Young Men's/Women's Christian Association) (facilities) >*The Y. put on a real good Christmas program.* >*He's been staying at the Y.*

YA

** **ya** (yə) (colloq.): you (when unstressed) >*Ya know I love ya.* >*Ya gotta do what's right for you.*

YACK

— **yack** (see "YAK")

— **yack it up** (see "YAK it up")

YACKETY-YACK

— **yackety-yack** (see "YAKETY-YAK")

YACKY

— **yacky** (see "YAKKY")

YAK

* **yak** (yak) (vi) (sl.): talk or converse (esp. idly or at length), chat >*He was yakkin' at us about his in-laws.* >*We yakked for about an hour, then took off.*

— **yak it up** (sl.): converse idly or at length >*They stood on the corner yakkin' it up for over two hours.*

YAKETY-YAK

— **yakety-yak** (yak´i tē yak´) (sl.): talk or conversation (esp. when idle or lengthy), chatter >*I'm tired of all this yakety-yak about the problem—now what are we gonna do about it?*

YAKKY

— **yakky** (yak´ē) (sl.): overly talkative >*Hey, tell that yakky friend of yours to cool it for a while, will ya?*

Y'ALL

* **y'all** (yôl) (colloq.): you (plural) >*Hey, guys, what've y'all been up to?* >*This here pie's for y'all.*

YANK

* **yank** (vt) (colloq.): remove suddenly or vigorously >*He started acting weird, so they yanked him from the class.* >*The network got a lot of complaints about the show, so they yanked it.*

— **yank [s/one's] chain** (sl.): harass [s/one], provoke [s/one] >*You keep yankin' his chain and he's gonna come after ya.*

YAP

— **yap**[1] (yap) (sl.): mouth (esp. as an instrument of foolish, irritating, or indiscreet talk) >*You keep your big yap shut about this!*

— **yap**[2] (vi) (sl.): speak foolishly or irritatingly, speak indiscreetly >*What's that moron yappin' about?* >*I don't wanna listen to her yap about her aches and pains.* >*Don't go yappin' about our plans.*

YARDS

— **the whole nine yards** (see NINE)

YARN

— **spin a yarn** (see SPIN)

YEA

** **yea!** (yā) (colloq.): hurrah! >*Yea! We won!* >*Yea for our team!*

— **yea ...** (colloq.): so ..., this ... (used with a gesture to indicate size) >*The trout was yea long.* >*He's about yea tall.*

YEAH

* **yeah** (ye´ə/ya´ə) (colloq.): yes >*Yeah, I'll do it.*

** **oh, yeah?** (colloq.): I don't believe it! I won't allow it! I challenge you about that! >*Oh, yeah? You were a big football star?* >*Oh, yeah? Just try it and you'll see what happens to you!*

YELLOW

— **yellow** (sl.): cowardly, afraid >*He won't fight because he's yellow.*

— **turn yellow** (sl.): become a coward, become afraid >*I bet he turns yellow at the first sign of trouble.*

YELLOW-BELLIED

— **yellow-bellied** (sl.): cowardly >*Don't expect that yellow-bellied wimp to stand up for ya.*

YELLOWBELLY

— **yellowbelly** (sl.): coward >*That yellowbelly just turned and ran.*

YEN

* **yen** (yen) (colloq.): craving, special liking, desire >*He's got a yen for tall redheads.* >*I got a yen for popcorn right now.*

— **yen for** (colloq.): yearn for, desire, crave >*I yen for a nice quiet weekend fishing in the mountains.*

YEP

** **yep** (yep) (colloq.): yes >*Yep, that's right.*

YES

* **yes sirree!** (... sə rē´) (colloq.): of course! absolutely! >*Yes sirree! I can do it.*

YES-MAN

* **yes-man** (colloq.): person who always expresses agreement with a superior, servile flatterer >*He's so damn arrogant because he's surrounded by yes-men.*

YESTERDAY

* **yesterday** (colloq., hum.): right away (regarding when s/thing is needed) >*What do you mean, when do I need your report? I need it yesterday!*

— **wasn't born yesterday** (see BORN)

YIKES

* **yikes!** (yīks) (colloq.): (interj. to express surprise or fright) >*Yikes! I almost stepped on that snake!*

YING-YANG

— **have ... up the ying-yang** (... ying´yang´) (sl., freq. vulg.): have an abundance of ..., have ... in large supply >*I don't need no more credit cards—I got credit cards up the ying-yang as it is.*

YIPES

— **yipes!** (yīps) (colloq.): (interj. to express surprise or fright) >*Yipes! This floor is real slippery!*

YIPPEE

* **yippee!** (yip´ē´) (colloq.): (interj. to express joy or triumph) >*Yippee! I won!*

YO

* **yo!** (yō) (colloq.): hey! hello! >*Yo, Billy! Come here for a second.* >*Yo! What do you want?*

YOKEL

— **local yokel** (see LOCAL)

YOO-HOO

* **yoo-hoo!** (yū´hū´) (colloq.): (interj. to attract s/one's attention) >*Yoo-hoo, Babs! I'm over here.*

YOU

** **you guys** (... gīz) (colloq.): you (plural) >*What are you guys doing?* >*Betty, Sue! You guys come with me.*

YOU-ALL

* **you-all** (colloq.): you (plural) >*You-all come back and visit us again.* >*Why was he yelling at you-all?*

YOURS

* **up yours!** (vulg.): (interj. to express great anger or contempt to s/one) >*That's bullshit! Up yours!*

YO-YO

* **yo-yo** (yō´yō´) (sl.): contemptibly foolish or stupid person >*I don't wanna work with that yo-yo again.*

YUCK

— **yuck** (see "YUK")

** **yuck!** (yuk) (sl.): (interj. to express disgust or repugnance) >*Yuck! What is that slimy stuff floatin' on top?*

YUCKY

* **yucky** (yuk´ē) (sl.): disgusting, repugnant >*Get your yucky work clothes off the bed!*

YUK

— **yuk[1]** (yuk) (sl.): loud and hearty laugh
>*I whispered the joke to him, but he let out this big yuk that everyone could hear.*

— **yuk[2]** (vi) (sl.): laugh (esp. loudly and heartily) >*That idiot sits there yukkin' at everything everybody says.*

— **yuk!** (see "YUCK!")

— **yuk it up** (sl.): laugh and joke (esp. continuously) >*He was yukkin' it up with his buddies all night.*

YUKKY

— **yukky** (see "YUCKY")

YUMMY

* **yummy** (yum´ē) (colloq.): very delicious or appetizing, very attractive >*She makes yummy chocolate chip cookies.* >*Who's that yummy brunette he's with?*

YUPPIE

** **Yuppie** (yup´ē) (colloq., freq. pej.): young urban professional (esp. one who is affluent, trend-conscious, and materialistic) (also adj.) >*Every Yuppie dreams of owning a B.M.W. and a split-level condo.* >*She orders all her Yuppie clothes from some expensive catalog.*

Z

ZAP

— **zap**[1] (zap) (sl.): jolt or shock (esp. of electricity) >*That 220 volt outlet will give ya quite a zap.*

* **zap**[2] (vt) (sl.): cook (in a microwave oven) >*Just zap it ten minutes in the microwave instead of bakin' it for an hour.*

* **zap**[3] (vt) (sl.): jolt or shock suddenly (esp. with electricity) >*You'll get zapped good if you step on that wire barefoot.* >*It really zapped her when she heard that he died.*

* **zap**[4] (vt) (sl.): kill suddenly and violently (esp. with electricity) >*The victim's parents want 'em to zap him in the electric chair.* >*The light attracts the bugs, and then it zaps 'em.*

— **zap**[5] (vt) (sl.): severely criticize, reprimand >*Wade really got zapped by his supervisor for missin' the deadline.*

ZEES

— **cop some zees** (see "cop some ZS")

— **get/catch some zees** (see "get/catch some ZS")

ZERO

— **zero** (sl.): contemptibly insignificant person, useless or worthless person >*The guy's stupid, ugly, and a jerk—a total zero.*

— **bat zero** (see BAT)

* **zero in on** (colloq.): concentrate (one's) attention on, target >*The police have been zeroing in on the big-time drug dealers.* >*He checked out all the women, then zeroed in on a tall blond.*

ZILCH

* (zilch) (sl.): nothing at all >*He ... about runnin' a business. ... stupid deal.*

ZILLION

* **zillion** (zil'yən) (colloq.): very many, a huge number (of) >*I've got a zillion things to do before leaving on my trip.*

ZING

— **zing**[1] (zing) (colloq.): energy, vigor, vitality >*If he'd just put a little more zing in his dancing, he wouldn't be bad.*

— **zing**[2] (vt) (sl.): criticize, reprimand >*They're really gonna zing ya for not reportin' that.*

ZINGER

* **zinger** (zing'ər) (sl.): critical remark, sharp and witty criticism >*She can outtalk Clarence, but he always gets in a few good zingers.*

ZIP

** **zip**[1] (colloq.): postal zip code >*Be sure to include your zip on that form.*

* **zip**[2] (sl.): nothing at all, zero >*Why should he get a percentage? He did zip for us.* >*They beat us three zip.*

* **zip**[3] (colloq.): energy, vigor, vitality >*The old guy's got a little more zip since he got him a new girlfriend.*

* **zip**[4] (vi) (colloq.): go quickly, move fast >*He was zipping along about eighty when the cop pulled him over.* >*I'll zip down to the store for a quart of milk.*

* **zip [one's] lip** (sl.): keep quiet, shut up >*He'd better zip his lip, or I'll shut him up myself.*

— **zip up** (vt) (colloq.): add energy or zest to, give more vitality or taste to >*You need to zip this party up with some faster music.* >*This stuff really zips up a salad.*

ZIT

** **zit** (zit) (sl.): pimple >*Wouldn't you know it! I get a big zit on my nose the day of my interview.*

ZOMBIE

* **zombie** (sl.): unreacting or lifeless person, torpid person (esp. when due to drugs or exhaustion) >*She's a zombie*

when she's been takin' drugs. >I was a zombie after thirty hours without sleep.

ZONK

— **zonk** (zongk/zôngk) (vt) (sl.): put to sleep or make unconscious, exhaust >*Studyin' for final exams always zonks me.*

— **zonk out** (vi) (sl.): fall asleep or become unconscious, become exhausted >*Ward planned on stayin' up all night, but he zonked out about three a.m.*

ZONKED

— **zonked** (zongkt/zôngkt) (sl.): intoxicated (by drugs or alcohol) >*Four tokes on a joint and she's zonked. >He's too zonked to drive.*

ZOO

** **zoo** (colloq.): place or situation where there is chaos or disorderly activity >*The school was a zoo the last day of class.*

ZOOM

— **zoom in on** (sl.): notice and pay special attention to, target >*Nick zoomed in on a cute redhead as soon as he walked into the party.*

* **zoom (up)** (vi) (colloq.): increase very quickly >*Housing costs have zoomed the last couple of years.*

ZS

— **cop some Zs** (kop ... zēz) (sl.): get some sleep, take a nap >*They caught him coppin' some Zs and fired him.*

* **get/catch some Zs** (sl.): get some sleep, take a nap >*I'm gonna catch some Zs now 'cause I gotta stay up late tonight.*